MW00654493

LATINO BOOM

LATINO BOOM
An Anthology
of U.S. Latino
Literature

JOHN S. CHRISTIE
Capital Community College

JOSÉ B. GONZALEZ
United States Coast Guard Academy

PEARSON
Longman

New York San Francisco Boston
London Toronto Sydney Tokyo Singapore Madrid
Mexico City Munich Paris Cape Town Hong Kong Montreal

Managing Editor: Erika Berg
Development Editor: Mikola De Roo
Executive Marketing Manager: Ann Stypuloski
Senior Supplements Editor: Donna Campion
Production Manager: Eric Jorgensen
Project Coordination, Text Design, and Electronic Page Makeup:
    Electronic Publishing Services Inc., NYC
Cover Designer/Manager: Wendy Ann Fredericks
Cover Art: Patssi Valdez, *Spanish Chair,* 2002. Acrylic on canvas, 61 x 36 in.
    Courtesy of the Patricia Correia Gallery.
Map art: Maps.com and Jessie Levine
Manufacturing Manager: Mary Fischer

For permission to use copyrighted material, grateful acknowledgment is made to the
    copyright holders on pp. 559–564, which are hereby made part of this copyright page.

Library of Congress Cataloging-in-Publication Data

Latino boom : an anthology of U.S. Latino literature / [compiled by] John S. Christie,
José B. Gonzalez.
    p. cm.
  ISBN 0-321-09383-6
  1. American literature--Hispanic American authors. 2. Hispanic Americans--Literary
collections. I. Christie, John S., 1954- II. Gonzalez, José B.
  PS508.H57L39 2005
  810.8'0868--dc22
                                          2005015977

Visit us at www.ablongman.com

ISBN 0-321-09383-6

To Mami and Papi, for sacrificing so much for the love of familia.
—JBG

"Para ti, Lucía, la más bella historia de amor que tuve y tendré."
—JSC

 CONTENTS

Chapter 5 The Working World: Sweating Under a New Sun 121

 # PREFACE

Latino Boom presents some of the best Latino literature from the past 20 years. As the first anthology of its kind to supplement its selections with contextual background materials, it also maintains a holistic approach that distinguishes it from other available Latino literature texts. Based on our own firsthand experience as teachers, this approach will help readers make connections between Latino culture and literature and mainstream U.S. culture and enable them to more perceptively analyze these literary works from multiple angles. The flexibility and simplicity of the book's thematic organization, the richness and breadth of the selections, the contextual resources in the opening three chapters, and the pedagogical apparatus have been designed to meet the particular needs and challenges of teachers of Latino literature. This work has been tested where it counts most—in the classroom. In doing so, this collection invites teachers and students to explore and gain a heightened appreciation for a rich and vital body of literary work that is an integral part of today's American literature.

A FOCUS ON CONTEMPORARY LATINO LITERATURE

By maintaining this focus on recent writings, dating from 1985 to the present, we have been able to concentrate upon works in four major genres—the short story, poetry, drama, and the essay—and include selections our students have often found most enjoyable and fascinating. Yet we want to emphasize the fact that this anthology presents only the tail end of a long tradition of writing by Latinos, one that stretches back to the European conquest of the Americas in the early 1500s, and much of it written in Spanish.

Beyond the need to limit the scope of the book, we have chosen to concentrate on the modern period because it offers some of the richest literary achievements that have substantially changed the landscape of Latino writing. After all, it was not until the late 1980s and early 1990s that the labels themselves—Hispanic American literature and Latino literature—came into common use. All over the United States, prolific young Latino writers are reinventing the literary landscape. The explosion of South American literary works in the 1970s and 1980s—a period referred to as the "Latin American Literary Boom"—is now mirrored in U.S.

Latino literature. The "mini boom" of U.S. Latino writing that began shortly after Gabriel García Márquez was awarded the 1982 Nobel Prize for literature and continued with the success of writers such as Sandra Cisneros and Oscar Hijuelos later that decade, is in full swing. This recent explosion of writing is complicated and diverse, as the range of literary and artistic creativity in the works in this text demonstrates.

Focusing on contemporary works also allows us to broaden the book's range to include Latino authors who have been underrepresented in anthologies and other collections, namely women and other less–well-known writers from a wide range of ethnic and cultural backgrounds. With an eye toward looking at works in their entirety, we have avoided excerpts from longer fiction such as novels. There are a few exceptions to this general guideline, however: Sandra Benítez's "Fulgencio Llanos: El Fotógrafo," and—it could be argued—Edgardo Vega Yunqué's "The Barbosa Express" are both stories and individual chapters in genre-bending novels composed of a series of connected short stories.

DEFINING U.S. LATINO LITERATURE

The complexity and variety in Latino literature inevitably require us to pose some interesting questions in our attempt to define what that label really means. What is Latino literature? In what language is it written? Who is a Latino writer exactly? What makes a work "Latino"? How many generations need to pass before a writer is simply an American writer? What do we mean by "American" to begin with? (The term in the mainstream excludes the other Americas—unjustifiably, one could argue.) How can we discuss any piece of writing without getting into extensive debates of nomenclature? We cannot fully answer such questions—only raise them at the onset and present thought-provoking readings that we believe will stimulate discussion. Hispanic, Latino, Latina, Latin, Chicano, Cubano, Cuban American, Tejano, Nuyorican—labels are always insufficient, and their meanings are dependent upon personal perspectives and cultural or political attitudes. We have to recognize that no label for any group of people is all-inclusive or entirely accurate and that many, in fact, can be demeaning and derogatory.

For the sake of clarity and simplicity, in this collection, we will define Latino literature as the stories, novels, poems, plays, and essays written or conceived of (primarily) in English and within the existing borders of the United States by writers with cultural connections or family ties to Spanish Latin America. To this end, we focus upon our own boom of Latino literary works originally written in English, mainly by Cuban American, Nuyorican or mainland Puerto Rican, Dominican American, and Chicano writers. It should be clear, then, that Latin American literature—works written in Spanish that might better be studied in their original language and within the context of a particular Latin American nation—lies outside the scope of this book. For example, we have intentionally excluded the works of great "Boom" writers such as Jorge Luis Borges and Julio Cortázar from Argentina or Carlos Fuentes from Mexico. Even those Latin American authors who are now closely associated with the United States, such as Isabel Allende from Chile, Rosario Ferré from Puerto Rico, or Elena Poniatowska from Mexico, are not included.

The line between a Latin American writer and a Latino writer is often a fine one. Our decision to use works written originally in English and to avoid translations from Spanish is not meant to dismiss or disregard the heritage of Latino writing composed in Spanish and inside the borders of the United States. Throughout the works, however, the Spanish language influence is forever present, and its importance is essential to understanding Latino literature. The instructional materials in the book often point toward what writers are doing with Spanish or with English and the combinations and switches of perspective made possible by interlingual game playing. We have provided glosses and translations only when we felt it was absolutely necessary. To translate (the word itself comes from the same root as the word "traitor") constitutes, in our minds, a form of betrayal to the originality of the literature we have chosen for the anthology. After all, one Spanish word can have numerous meanings within the wider Latino environment. Most importantly, there are complicated and fascinating reasons why creative Latino writers choose Spanish, English, or the hybrid combinations of Spanglish and code-switching to present their ideas.

A LITERARY APPROACH TO THE READINGS

The focus of this collection is on the creative, imaginative, and extensively sophisticated art of a group of Latino writers. Teachers should feel free to take their classes in whatever directions (and across whatever disciplines) they wish, but the criteria for our selections and the guiding principle of the anthology's design and organization is, in the end, based on the study of literature. Obviously, the stories, poems, plays, and essays in the following pages will point readers toward sociological and political discussions. We expect them to provoke in readers a need to grapple with issues of class, ethnicity, race, and gender. They will also lead to explorations into the complexities of acculturation, immigration, and the politics of cultural traditions. In fact, some of the essays we include delve directly into such considerations. One cannot fully analyze Latino literature without being aware of the numerous valuable articles and books published each year throughout the discipline of Latino Studies that examine the impact Latinos have had on the United States over the last five centuries. Although we wholeheartedly recommend such studies, our major goal is to focus the reader's attention on the artistic merit of the stories and poems, on the quality of language and the imaginative creativity of a group of writers. Works of literature, after all, should not be seen exclusively as illustrations of current social conditions. To consider any story, poem, or play as merely an example of a sociological or political situation is to run the risk of underestimating the art involved. Why read a work of fiction or a poem at all if the intention is simply to find reflections of existing problems in the Latino world? We have tried in these selections to find works that are formally innovative and artistically distinct. After all, the language of creative writing, not simply the content, provokes powerful reactions in the reader. As William Carlos Williams often said, what the poet *makes* (what he or she builds out of language) might matter more than what the poet *means*.

A FLEXIBLE THEMATIC ORGANIZATION

First and foremost, our aim was to employ an easy-to-understand organizational structure that would make the book a useful tool for teachers, readers, and scholars and would accommodate a wide range of teaching approaches. Toward this end, *Latino Boom* is divided into two parts. Part I (Chapters 1–3), "U.S. Latino Literature: An Overview," provides background materials and contextual resources we have found to be useful in a classroom setting for the study of Latino literature. Chapters 1 and 2 contain background essays on Latino narrative and Latino poetry. The third chapter is composed of a collection of useful and provocative contextual materials such as maps and a historical timeline. In Part II (Chapters 4–8), "Readings in Latino Literature," each chapter's selections have been organized by genre (fiction, poetry, drama, and essay), and each is accompanied by an author biography. Every chapter in Part II begins with an introduction to each theme to engage students and provide them with necessary background information, and each ends with a group of pedagogical materials (described under "Features").

Although there is no such thing as a "typical" Latino experience, Chapters 4–8 have been designed to reflect some of the central common themes found in modern Latino literary works. Each chapter is labeled as a certain type of "world." The works in Chapter 4, "The Lost Worlds," imply a Latin American past, the origin countries of immigrants, and the cultural heritage and traditions beyond the United States. Chapter 5, "The Working World," contains selections that focus upon working-class narratives of Latinos, migrant labor situations, immigration, political issues, and the American dream. "The Urban World" of Chapter 6 highlights the impact of urban landscapes on Latino life. "The Fringe World" of Chapter 7 brings together writings that deal with the concept of the outsider and the ambiguities and tensions that arise when people straddle the borders (both metaphorical and literal) "between worlds." The selections in this chapter suggest issues of cultural hybridity, interlingualism, and self-identity. The final chapter, "Beyond Worlds," includes works that bend the rules for Latino writing through their unique style or theme or by speaking of places and issues beyond the expected and sometimes stereotypical territory usually assigned to Latino writers.

To make it easy for readers to locate particular writers quickly, we provide a one-page quick-reference alphabetical author listing (organized by country of heritage) on the front inside cover.

FEATURES

The following features in *Latino Boom* help to encourage readers toward a fuller, multifaceted understanding of Latino literature:

- **A rich diversity of literary selections** by prominent and emerging contemporary Latino writers. From renowned works by Sandra Cisneros, Julia Alvarez, and Jimmy Santiago Baca to more recent pieces by Sergio Troncoso, Ana Menéndez, and Lorraine López, the anthology juxtaposes well-known writers with newer voices from diverse Latino communities.

- **Brief author biographies** for every selection.

- **Helpful footnotes that define or explain Spanish terms within selections.**

- **Introductory chapters on Latino narrative and Latino poetry.** Chapter 1 and Chapter 2, "Latino Narrative" and "Latino Poetry," respectively, provide students with an overview of how Latino writers have worked within each genre in creative and innovative ways. We highlight particular writers we consider essential to the field and outline critical literary trends, influences, and experimentations to help further students' critical investigations into the field.

- **Extensive resources that place works in historical and literary context.** Some students in Latino literature courses will already have some knowledge of history and culture both of Latinos in the United States and of Latin America. For those completely unfamiliar with Latin America, however, Chapter 3, "Latino Landscapes," includes a series of **maps** and a **timeline**. These elements are intended to provoke class discussion and to guide students toward study beyond the works themselves. In our selection of historical events and dates, we have been guided by the literature itself rather than let all of Latin American history dictate which items to include. In keeping with our goal of flexibility, teachers should feel free to utilize the elements of these opening chapters to whatever degree and in whatever way they want.

- **Student-centered pedagogical apparatus, including thematic introductions, essay questions, discussion topics, and innovative "Connections" sections** that direct students to related novels, films, and themes beyond the scope of the book. Each of the five readings chapters (Chapters 4–8) opens with an introduction to the chapter's theme to engage students and give them a deeper understanding of the selections they read. The readings in each chapter are followed by a section called **"Broader Horizons: Resources for Writing and Class Discussion,"** which contains:

  - **"Literary Critical Essay/Discussion Topics"** that are designed to spark student engagement, discussion, and academic writing about the selections. We have purposely varied the questions so that readers can investigate and analyze the works from numerous perspectives. To this end, the questions run the gamut from those that relate to traditional elements of character, plot, style, point of view, imagery, and symbolic language to those that suggest feminist, cultural, political, or historical approaches to the writings. To encourage a wide range of contrasts and comparisons and to elicit innovative ways of connecting these works, we have intentionally avoided designing these questions around specific selections so students and teachers can instead apply them to the particular literature they think fits best.

- **"The Novel Connection"** segment is designed to suggest to readers ways to broaden the scope of Latino literature to longer works and to writers we have not included in this book. Overall, we cite more than fifty novels, many of them recently published. We provide these suggestions fully certain that the selections in the anthology will generate a thirst within students for additional readings in Latino literature. Teachers are free to study these connections to supplement the anthology with additional readings and point out for students the thematic relationships between the shorter and longer Latino works.

- **"The Film Connection,"** like "The Novel Connection," is designed to broaden the scope of the anthology by tying the literature to film. Films have proven to be extremely effective in provoking student interest and class discussion. In these segments, we suggest ways that a specific film by and about Latinos can be tied thematically to each chapter topic and, directly or indirectly, to the literary works included or mentioned in each of the thematic chapters. In doing so, we expect to provide students with a better sense of the continuum of Latino literature. Like Latino literature, Latino film in the United States has undergone its own "boom" in the last two decades, and it deserves further study.

- **"Thematic Connections Listing"** sections offer teachers an alternative, thematically designed table of contents for each of the five chapters. We have subdivided the larger chapter theme into smaller categories that draw the selections together in more particular ways. The intention here is to suggest juxtapositions and to help readers easily trace areas of interest—something that is especially helpful in generating ideas for student research.

ACKNOWLEDGMENTS

We are grateful to the following people at Longman for their hard work and dedication to this project: Joe Terry for his early enthusiasm and encouragement; Michelle Cronin and Judith Fifer for their early help providing us with direction; Erika Berg for getting things going with practical guidance; and Mika DeRoo, especially, for her professionalism and editorial expertise. We would also like to thank Beth Keister for her permissions work and for her much appreciated sense of humor.

We are indebted to the astute reviewers whose thoughtful suggestions and feedback have guided our work on this project in its various stages: Frederick Luis Aldama, Colorado University; Vik Bahl, Green River Community College; Stacia L. Bensyl, Missouri Western State College; Ana Maria Cobos, Saddleback College; Jason Cortés, Universitry of Massachusetts—Boston; Gloria Duarte, Angelo State University; Sandra L. Dahlberg, University of Houston—Downtown; Daryl Davis, Northern Michigan University; Anne E. Goldman, Sonoma State University; Jürgen E. Grandt, University of Georgia; Kirsten Silva Gruesz, University of California—Santa Cruz; Paul Guajardo, University of Houston; Alicia Hernandez, Rio Hondo College; Marco Portales, Texas A&M University; Barbara J. Sáez and Terrance Delaney, Three Rivers Community College; Anne Strah, Yale University; and Melody M. Zajdel, Montana State University.

Without the advice and friendship of Bob Tilton, Michael Meyer, and Gina Barreca at the University of Connecticut, this book would never have been an idea, let alone a completed project. In addition, we would like to thank our friends and colleagues at the U.S. Coast Guard Academy and Capital Community College: Rob Ayer, Anna Maria Basche, Charles Darling, Evelyn Farbman, Anne Flammang, Glaisma Pérez-Silva, Faye Ringel, and Karen Wink. In the end, we are most grateful to our family members, Kristin, Cassandra, Olivia, and Sofia Gonzalez, and Lucía, Natalia, and Gabriela Christie, for all their support and, even more often, their patience.

JOHN S. CHRISTIE
JOSÉ B. GONZALEZ

ABOUT THE AUTHORS

John S. Christie, Ph.D., is the author of *Latino Fiction and the Modernist Imagination*, published in 1995. He teaches English at Capital Community College in Hartford, Connecticut. He has contributed articles and reviews to the academic journals *Latin American Literary Review* and *American Fiction Studies*, guest-edited a special issue of the journal *LIT: Literature, Interpretation, Theory* on Latino literature, and currently serves as book review editor for the journal *MELUS (Multi Ethnic Literature of the United States)*.

José B. Gonzalez, Ph.D., was born in San Salvador, El Salvador, and immigrated to New London, Connecticut, at the age of eight. His poetry has been published in such journals as *Calabash* and *Colere*, and in anthologies including *Coloring Book: An Eclectic Anthology of Fiction & Poetry by Multicultural Writers* and *Nantucket: A Collection*. He has been the recipient of such honors as Connecticut's Higher Education Multicultural Faculty of the Year Award and is currently professor of English at the U.S. Coast Guard Academy in New London, Connecticut.

A NOTE FROM THE PUBLISHER

Penguin Discount Novel Program. In cooperation with Penguin Putnam Inc., one of our sibling companies, Longman is proud to offer a variety of Penguin paperbacks at a significant discount when packaged with any Longman title. The available works include:

- Julia Alvarez's *How the García Girls Lost Their Accents*
- Helena María Viramontes' *Under the Feet of Jesus*
- Richard Rodriguez's *Days of Obligation: An Argument with My Mexican Father*

Ask your local Longman representative how to take advantage of this special offer. To review the complete list of available titles and discounted prices of individual Penguin novels, visit the Longman-Penguin-Putnam web site, http://www. ablongman.com/penguin.

Introduction

To Students Reading *Latino Boom: An Anthology of U.S. Latino Literature*

Chicana writer Sandra Cisneros once commented that when she was in school, she did not get to read stories or poems or plays about people like herself: Latina, U.S.-born, bicultural, bilingual, and always at least partially outside the mainstream of "American" life. For those of you who are Latino, we hope this anthology of contemporary Latino literature will fill this gap. For those of you from other cultures or nationalities, we hope it will provide you with the chance to sample the vitality and energy of the literature created by this talented group of writers. We have included works to capture your attention and challenge your thinking. These portrayals of Latino life—in different styles and various genres by Latinos from all over the Americas—demonstrate the multifaceted ways Latino writers bring you into their imagined worlds.

Picture the well-known optical illusion of a female figure. From one angle, you see a young woman wearing a scarf around her neck and looking away; from another angle, you see an old woman with a large crooked nose that points down to the left. At first, you see only one picture, but when you squint your eyes a bit and turn your head, the other image appears. Once you know how to look, you can mentally flip from one image to the other: young woman, old woman. This visual puzzle is an apt metaphor for the dual perspective and the double culture of Latinos in the United States. From religion to language to food to music to employment to family life to travel—Latinos often bounce back and forth between cultural perspectives. Latino literature derives much of its power from the complexities of these mixtures and oppositions between two cultures.

Now picture another image: a map of North, South, and Central America but one that seems upside down. Lima, Peru, is in the spot where you would look for New York City. California has morphed into the vastness of Brazil. Canada has narrowed northward into a slightly curving point (this map, called "Turnabout Map of the Americas," is reproduced in Chapter 3 on page 31). The globe is a sphere that can be turned any number of ways, and it is only the dictates of historical, conventional habits that cause us to rotate it in its current direction. This map puts a different spin on geography, one that overturns accepted perspectives. It forces us to picture the world from another angle.

We assume that many of the works in this collection will do the same for you as readers. Like any artistic work, Latino literature can be provocative and unsettling. Most Latino writers strive to debunk the misguided and damaging stereotypes that too often find their way into mainstream U.S. attitudes, and many of these selections will challenge common ways of thinking and test your critical ability to analyze, investigate, and appreciate what is unfamiliar. Some stories will ask you to imagine you are living on a tiny island in the Caribbean, and a huge country—90 miles to the north and packed with nuclear weapons—is deciding your fate or determining your country's leaders. Others will require you to adjust your attitudes toward and preconceptions about the famous Texas Rangers, the Alamo, or the strawberries you eat. You may have to reevaluate such familiar things as hot dogs, bologna, and Spam. You might begin to question living a monolingual life.

BALANCING OUR APPROACHES TO LATINO LITERATURE

This anthology is composed of modern literature, but we purposely did not restrict it to a specific focus or approach. We did ensure that each selection shared two factors, however. The first is that the works are written in English but often include Spanish words and phrases; they are certainly informed by the nuances and connotations of this second language. The language, of course, is a product of the second factor: these works are bicultural. Although plots and characters may—for the most part—be centered on the U.S. side of the border, Latin American cultural attitudes and traditions are present beneath the surface of characters' personalities, provoking their actions and emotions. Latino writers very rarely separate themselves entirely from the country and culture of their heritage. A Colombian novelist, though wrapped up in the complexities of life in Queens, New York, is not entirely detached from the political turmoil that surrounds her native country. Few Cuban American writers address subjects that are not connected in some way to that island's political events over the last forty-odd years. The Caribbean islands do not disappear for Dominican American writers because they create a poem about Washington Heights or set a story in Brooklyn or New Jersey. Even second- and third-generation immigrants often live with a hybrid sense of identity, and their writing filters the U.S. world through a cultural lens. Reading these works will help you understand the fact that many Latinos have to balance at least two (usually very different) cultural perspectives and sift through the connotations of languages. You will have to constantly reevaluate and juxtapose opinions and ideas presented in the stories, poems, plays, and essays.

The difficulties and complexities of understanding Latino literature always seem to intensify once we move into history, politics, cultural studies, sociology, and economics. As readers, you must do more than understand U.S. history; you have to learn to see the same events from the Latin American perspective and sometimes to invert your mainstream U.S. view—to rewrite that history.

To some extent, the works in the anthology demand that you withhold judgment, that you suspend your own convictions in order to appreciate alternative perspectives on everything from religious beliefs, foods, and traditional ceremonies to race relations, political attitudes, economic status, and the role of women. Like most of the world's ethnic literature today, Latino writing stretches the reader's horizon across cultural borders. To embark on such a literary journey, you must try to leave behind any traces of ethnocentric, biased, or xenophobic attitudes.

THE USE OF LABELS

Questions and problems concerning nomenclature and labels for people are always at issue in the field of Latino literature (and in the more general area known as Latino Studies). It is virtually impossible to use any term without risking debate. We need, therefore, to clarify from the beginning a few word choices we have made for this collection and hope that you and your teachers will openly discuss problematic terms during classes.

1. We use the term "Latino" rather than "Hispanic" because we feel "Latino" is more deeply rooted in the Spanish language. We use the term "Latina" only when referring specifically to females.
2. We recognize that using the term "America" to refer to the United States is not always justified in the eyes of those people with a perspective centered on South America, Central America, and Canada. Whenever possible, we use "United States."
3. For Puerto Ricans living within the United States (now a greater number than those living on the island of Puerto Rico itself), we use the term "Mainland Puerto Rican," and the terms "Nuyorican" or "Neorican" to refer to the New York-based Puerto Rican community.
4. The terms "Chicano" or "Chicana" (deriving from the political movements of the 1960s that began in force after 1964 with the Voting Rights Act) refer to Mexican American men or women who live within what is now the United States.

It will be clear as you go through these selections, however, that things are always more complicated than they seem, that people cannot be satisfactorily classified in simplistic ways, under particular labels. The issue of race is especially controversial; many Latinos now classify themselves as "Other" on census forms, regardless of the color of their skin, because Latin American definitions of black and white do not conform to those of the United States. Many of the writers we include express clear opinions about labels such as "Hispanic," "Hispano," "Hispanic American," "Latino," "Chicano," "Boricua," and so on.

Latino literature is packed with an extensive variety of terms and labels for people, places, and objects, the exact meanings of which are frequently hard to pin down. For words such as "tejano" or "tejana," "pachuco" or "Xicanisma," "Spanglish" and "Rican," "spik" and "pocho," the connotations may be different each time they appear, the meanings dependent upon the writer, the speaker, and the context. It will be your job as a reader to explore the nuances of such vocabulary.

WHAT TO DO WITH THE SPANISH LANGUAGE

As you move from story to story and poem to poem, you will find Spanish words and phrases. Some Latino writers will not always provide explicit translations or sufficient contextual clues. Quite the opposite is true in some cases, especially when the writer has a political point to make, a critique of some sort, a joke to tell, a pun to stress, or a linguistic game to play. How any given author manipulates the Spanish language within his or her text is a fascinating critical issue. When and how does the writer translate? What pieces of information are left without explanation? Do characters in stories communicate in different languages under certain conditions or in certain emotional states? What can you make of the sounds and nuances of Spanish words? Throughout the readings, we provide footnotes that translate Spanish terminology where we think it especially necessary and where contextual clues are at a minimum.

The use of Spanish in these selections often signals the underlying tensions running throughout the anthology. The language is the surface indication of cultural factors that most Latinos feel in one way or another. The language and its connections to Latin American traditions, beliefs, histories, and customs always have ramifications for Latino writers inside the U.S. borders. A word in Spanish, therefore, points to the hybrid state "between worlds" where people straddle two cultures and search for a comfortable position in that sometimes precarious state. Chicana poet Pat Mora uses a Mexican indigenous word "Nepantla" for this "place in the middle." Gustavo Pérez Firmat, the Cuban American scholar, poet, and novelist, called it "life on the hyphen." The field of Border Studies is centered on such a concept of life in the liminal sphere between two worlds, on people crossing borders and the forces that push and pull them back and forth. Each chapter of the book in some way focuses on these suggestive spaces.

EXPLORING LONGER WORKS BY LATINO WRITERS: AN OVERVIEW OF "THE NOVEL CONNECTION" SECTIONS IN CHAPTERS 4–8

The purpose of the five "Novel Connection" sections (located at the end of chapters 4 to 8) is to direct you toward the vast world of Latino fiction—a collection such as this can only serve as a sample. Many Latino writers have published their work exclusively in novel form, and the importance of these longer works is obvious. The novel is often the first and only contact a reader has with any given writer. We hope that you will thematically link the material we selected in each chapter to some of the longer works and that you will find the connections useful for further study.

To make these discussions and references easier to locate, the following list includes more than fifty major writers and indicates the chapter in which the relevant "Novel Connection" section appears. Many of the novelists in the list are also discussed in greater detail in Chapter 2 on Latino narrative.

Major Latino Novelists

Names in boldface are those writers whose works are included in *Latino Boom* (see the table of contents or the index to locate them). Use the chapter references to find "The Novel Connection" section in which a particular author is discussed.

Abella, Alex; Chapter 6

Alvarez, Julia; Chapter 7

Anaya, Rudolfo; Chapter 4

Ambert, Alba; Chapter 7

Arias, Ron; Chapter 4

Barrio, Raymond; Chapter 5

Benítez, Sandra; Chapter 8

Carrillo, H.G.; Chapter 8

Castedo, Elena; Chapter 4

Castillo, Ana; Chapters 4 and 8

Chacón, Daniel; Chapter 7

Cano, Daniel; Chapter 7

Chávez, Denise; Chapter 5

Cisneros, Sandra; Chapters 5 and 7

Cruz, Angie; Chapter 4

Diaz, Debra; Chapter 5

Díaz, Junot; Chapter 8

Fernández, Roberta; Chapter 7

Fernández, Roberto G.; Chapters 7 and 8

Ferré, Rosario; Chapter 8

Fontes, Montserrat; Chapter 8

Garcia, Cristina; Chapters 4 and 8

Garcia, Guy; Chapter 4

Garcia Robinson, Delfino; Chapter 8

Gilb, Dagoberto; Chapters 5 and 7

Goldman, Francisco; Chapters 5 and 8

González, Rigoberto; Chapter 5

Hijuelos, Oscar; Chapters 4 and 6

Hinojosa, Rolando

Islas, Arturo; Chapter 7

Lamazares, Ivonne; Chapter 4

Limon, Graciela; Chapter 8

López, Diana; Chapter 7

Manrique, Jaime; Chapters 6 and 7

Martínez, Demetria; Chapter 8

Martinez, Luis Manuel; Chapters 5 and 8

Medina, Pablo; Chapter 4

Menéndez, Ana; Chapters 4 and 8

Mestre-Reed, Ernesto; Chapters 4 and 8

Mohr, Nicholasa; Chapter 7

Morales, Alejandro; Chapter 5

Obejas, Achy; Chapter 4

Ortiz Cofer, Judith; Chapter 6

Novas, Himilce

Pérez, Loida Maritza; Chapter 6

Pérez Firmat, Gustavo; Chapter 8

Pineda, Cecile; Chapters 5, 7, and 8

Portillo Trambley, Estela; Chapter 7

Quiñones, Ernesto; Chapters 6 and 8

Rechy, John; Chapters 6, 7, and 8

Rivera, Tomás; Chapter 5

Rodríguez, Abraham Jr.; Chapters 6 and 8

Rosario, Nelly; Chapter 8

Sáenz, Benjamin Alire; Chapter 8

Soto, Gary; Chapter 5

Stork, Francisco X.; Chapter 7

Suarez, Virgil; Chapter 6

Thomas, Piri; Chapter 6

Tobar, Hector; Chapter 8

Trujillo, Carla; Chapter 7

Véa, Alfredo; Chapters 7 and 8

Vega Yunqé, Edgardo; Chapters 7 and 8

Viramontes, Helena María; Chapter 5

PART I

U.S. Latino Literature: An Overview

 1
Latino Narrative

CHOICES OF NARRATIVE STYLE

In the many genres of literary fiction, writers tell their stories in both straightfor-ward and narratively complicated ways. In the former style, events and characters are plausible and plots unfold in logical, chronological order. In the latter, the fan-tastic blends with the real, the language calls attention to itself, or the narrative voices reveal things in fragments. Both types of narrative—the realist and the modern/postmodern—abound in Latino works of fiction.

Although some Latino novels are linearly structured like autobiographies, some of the most popular works (for example, by Sandra Cisneros, Julia Alvarez, and Cristina Garcia) skip around in time and jump from narrator to narrator, forc-ing the reader to question the reliability of the speakers and to arrange scattered events into chronological order. This stylistic complexity challenges the reader to look beyond the literal meaning of the story itself and to recognize and interpret the symbolic and metaphorical use of language. The style itself then mirrors the effort Latinos must make as they construct their identities from the fragmented and ever-changing world around them. In such stories, the tensions readers feel reflect the tensions felt by the characters. The purpose of this chapter is to exam-ine these (sometimes interlacing) narrative traits and to recognize how Latino writ-ers employ them as they ply their craft in a variety of fictional genres: popular, autobiographical, realist, modernist, fragmented, and experimental.

POPULAR LATINO FICTION

Although most Latino narrative falls in the category of general fiction (see also the "Novel Connections" sections at the end of Chapters 4 through 8), some writers also are effectively working with other forms of popular fiction. For example, Chicano writer Rolando Hinojosa was probably the first Latino writer to veer in the direction of detective/mystery stories with his Rafe Buenrostro mystery series, published in the early 1980s. His work paved the way for works published a decade later: the detective/mystery stories by Alex Abella, Cuban American Carolina Garcia-Aguilera's Lupe Solano police mysteries and both the Brown Angel mysteries, and the Gloria Damasco detective stories by Chicana writer Lucha Corpi. Michael Nava writes a mystery series that centers around a gay Chicano lawyer named Henry Rios. These writers incorporate the traditional story formats with the energies of Latino personalities and the nuances of the issues confronting them.

Young adult fiction is a subgenre that continues to grow in popularity with Latino authors—Julia Alvarez's *Before We Were Free* (2002) is a good example—and numerous established writers, such as Nicholasa Mohr, Gary Soto, Debra Diaz, Sandra Cisneros, Judith Ortiz Cofer, and Victor Martinez, have either aimed their work at this audience or have seen their books marketed to the young Latino reader. The youth of the Latino population in general makes such an enterprise commercially viable, and many Latino writers are openly interested in the educational value of bringing engaging stories to these young readers. Although few U.S. Latino writers have yet to gain prominence in other genres such as science fiction, historical fiction, romance, or thrillers, several are writing in the style known as magical realism, described in the following section.

MAGICAL REALISM

Nobel Prize-winner and Colombian novelist Gabriel García Márquez's famous book *One Hundred Years of Solitude* (published in Spanish in 1967 and in English in 1970), and its blending of stark realism with other-worldly events, impossible exaggerations, and miraculous scenes, prompted literary critics to expand the meaning of a critical term to describe this type of narrative: "magical realism." The complex history of the term begins with early twentieth-century art critics in Germany and moves through the works of the Cuban writer Alejo Carpentier, who spoke of the "magic within the real" (*lo real maravilloso*). A debate among Latino scholars persists about how useful the term is or whether it distorts and misrepresents the works of Latin American writers by forcing them into an allegiance they may not share with the Colombian novelist and his fictional village of Macondo. Critic Frederick Luis Aldama argues that the vagueness of the term leads to misreadings of literature, culture, and the people themselves, because it emphasizes the fantastic and can distract readers from the social and economic realities of Latin America.* To this end, young, urban Latin American writers such as Alberto Fuguet from Chile and Edmundo Paz Soldán from Bolivia have made strong efforts to distance themselves from the fantastic, hyperbolic prose of magical real-

---

*See Aldama's work: *Postethnic Narrative Criticism*.

ism by producing fiction that concentrates on the very real issues of identity, internationalism, and globalization.

However, some U.S. Latino writers, such as Alfredo Véa, Ana Castillo, Ron Arias, Rudolfo Anaya, Denise Chávez, and Roberto G. Fernández, embrace this narrative technique as a way to distort and confuse the readers' understanding of what is true and what is magical and to cause them to question their sense of reality. They use magical realism as a storytelling device to shake up certain ideological beliefs, stereotypes, and misconceptions that readers might have toward the people and events depicted in their fiction. Through magical realist fiction, writers can incorporate the oral side of their cultures, the folktales, tall tales, the unorthodox histories, and the otherworldly stories of those whose voices have not been sanctioned by the powers that be, thus presenting readers with the unofficial, sometimes nonofficial, collective voices of the people. Latino writers (like their counterparts in many postcolonial societies) use this stylistic mode to describe (nonjudgmentally) certain systems of beliefs and ideas that when presented in straight realist fashion could seem like primitive superstitions.

AUTOBIOGRAPHICAL TRENDS

Many Latino writers naturally progress from writing autobiographical works toward creating fictionalized versions of events derived in part from personal experiences. Considering the centrality of such crucial themes as cultural identity and self-recognition (issues readers will revisit throughout this anthology), it is not hard to recognize the Latino storyteller's reliance on autobiographical writing. The style is particularly common in mainland Puerto Rican literature; Puerto Rican writers Bernardo Vega and Jesús Colón began the trend in the United States with their memoir/journal-like works dealing with the first half of the twentieth century. In the late 1960s, this genre became even more popular in Puerto Rican literature in the mainland with Piri Thomas's autobiographical work *Down These Mean Streets* (1967), and its success has continued with the writings of Judith Ortiz Cofer and Esmeralda Santiago.

For Chicanos, a long history of autobiographical work stretches back to sixteenth century chronicles and travelogues and continues through the 1970s (with writers such as Oscar "Zeta" Acosta, for instance) to the present day. Autobiographical writing by Cuban Americans has a less extensive history, though it has produced notable works such as Carlos Eire's *Waiting for Snow in Havana* (2003), which won the National Book Award. The art of autobiography can be as varied in style and shape as any fictional story. The list of Latino writers whose works are for the most part autobiographical is a long one and is growing rapidly as new voices are published and forgotten writers are rediscovered. Recent significant efforts include those by Ron Arias, Luis J. Rodriguez, Mona Ruiz, Edward Rivera, Richard Rodriguez, John Phillip Santos, Luisita López Torregrosa, Marie Araña, Jimmy Santiago Baca, Gustavo Pérez Firmat, Gary Soto, Mary Helen Ponce, Pablo Medina, Virgil Suárez, and Pat Mora.

NAVIGATING THE PERSONA

One step removed from the strictly autobiographical account is the work that tells a story in the first person. This creates a separation between the content and the discourse and forces the reader to read on two levels—tracing the action of the story while simultaneously considering (questioning, second guessing) the speaker's opinions, attitudes, and overall reliability. It is part of the writer's craft to create a persona, a character, and to filter the story through that fictional voice and that personality. Sometimes the narrator is obviously a separate entity from the author (the character is a murderer, for example). It is apparent that Franz Kafka is not Gregor Samsa from *The Metamorphosis*, that William Faulkner is not Benji Compson from *The Sound and the Fury*. By the same token, Sandra Cisneros is not Esperanza, the main character from *A House on Mango Street*, and Rudolfo Anaya is not Antonio Márez from *Bless Me, Ultima*. When the work seems to be semiautobiographical (as in Judith Ortiz Cofer's *The Line of the Sun* [1989], for example), readers have to be careful to distinguish the first-person narrator from the author. The reader must watch for bits of information that signal some limitation, flaw, or subjectivity in the narrator. We need to assume, therefore, that Yunior, the narrator of Junot Díaz's *Drown* (1996), is not the author—no matter how much we may believe that he is. Even the young illegal immigrant in Manuel Luis Martinez's *Crossing* (1998), despite having the same name, Luis, is not the author. They are literary personae and part of the writer's discourse. But in many Latino novels and stories by writers such as Dagoberto Gilb, Helena María Viramontes, and Cristina Garcia, the distinctions between the narrator and the writer's own story are hazy at best.

Part of the power of Latino fiction rests in requiring the reader to decipher the point of view. Many of the narrators in stories by Dagoberto Gilb and Daniel Chacón, for example, have a similar voice that echoes working-class hardship, often from a masculine, first-person perspective. Other writers tell their stories through the eyes of young children or old women, thereby suggesting the innocence or naiveté of youth or communicating a regard for the wisdom of oral traditions carried down through a generation of women.

In some Latino fiction, the authors create multiple personae to tell the tale. Helena María Viramontes's renowned short-story collection, *The Moths* (1985), is a good example. So too are the novels of Dominican American writer Julia Alvarez; her stories feature four women (sisters) who articulate different views. Writers employing this modernist technique are shifting away from traditional autobiographical-style narration toward narrative experimentation, described in the following section.

MODERNIST LATINO FICTION

In the early years of the twentieth century, a time when societies were undergoing rapid industrialization, writers were inspired to invent new ways to describe their worlds. The arrival of movies, electricity, the automobile, and mass transit transformed the simple lives of many people into a faster-paced existence that the traditional methods of nineteenth-century storytelling no longer satisfied. New-comers looking for work burst into the busy, overcrowded streets of industrial centers such as London, Paris, and New York. As people began to consider the revolutionary ideas of Darwin and Freud and to worry about the political consequences of revolution in Russia, the complexities of life multiplied. When World War I threatened the stability of Western Europe, writers and artists looked outside their traditional forms of expression and struggled to deal with the devastating sense of chaos, alienation, and tension they were feeling by telling their stories in more complicated ways, in fragmented prose, and via other innovative, stylistic modes. As they encountered the artistic expression of nonwestern civilizations, particularly Africa, they felt an even stronger need for literary experimentation. Writers experimented with narrative techniques such as allusions and images, stream of consciousness, and multiple points of view, because such stylistic complications compelled readers to confront the difficulties of understanding things in concrete, holistic ways. The stylistic prose of these works became what literary scholars called "high modernism," and it was usually linked to the fast-paced, complicated confusion dominating the urban world. The works of James Joyce and Virginia Woolf were not easy to read, nor did the authors mean them to be. Life was not understandable from a single, simplistic point of view, and consequentially, writers abandoned omniscient narration for a fragmented, broken, and unresolved perspective on fictional events and characters. Experimentation became the norm, as poet Ezra Pound proclaimed the need to "make it new." The language was symbolic and suggestive and required the reader to work to understand it.

Fast-forward a few decades to the second half of the twentieth century; the same complexities of urban tensions and the same tangled confusions have led many Latinos to tell their stories in similarly complicated ways. Wherever novelists or short story writers let a point of view slip from one character's perspective to another or jump around in time without clarification, they are using modernist techniques. A collage of images or short sketches, an unrelated series of events jumbled together, a particularly strong persona—all these modernist tricks of the trade serve to disorient readers and ultimately force them to participate in creating the work's meaning.

SHORT FICTION AND FRAGMENTED STORIES

Short fiction is a major genre in Latino literature, perhaps accounting for the bulk of it published today. The genre dates back to the fictional pieces that were written in Spanish and published in the newspapers throughout the Southwest since the middle of the nineteenth century. Longer forms of literary fiction by Latinos, such as novels, appear for the most part much later in the second half of the twentieth century, and the jump is one from short story to the dominance of the novel form. There are few works really that fall into the vague area of novella—long short stories that could be novels such as Aphra Behn's *Oroonoko* (1688); a number of Latino works, however, function as a hybrid of shorter and longer fictional works: composed of related short stories. This link between the novel and the early sketches of literary fiction is partly reflective of the Latino writers' desire to capture the oral legends and folktales of their heritage. The oral histories of Latinos are often the sources of literary fiction, even in some cases responsible for the authors' choice of narrative style.

This fictional pattern is first encountered in other North American novels such as Sherwood Anderson's *Winesburg, Ohio* (1919) or later in Alice Munro's *The Beggar Maid* (1983), or Gloria Naylor's *The Women of Brewster Place* (1982). They look like novels, but they are divided into loosely connected short stories. The same characters or group of characters slide in and out of a sequence of related stories and in the end, the book is comprehensible as a whole. Tomás Rivera in his classic *...Y no se lo tragó la tierra* (1971) used a series of story fragments to portray a group conversation, oral history, or a communal perspective on a sequence of events. A short, almost forgotten work by Gina Valdés called *There Are No Madmen Here* (1981) is another example of this structural attempt to imitate Latino oral cultural in fiction. More famously, Rolando Hinojosa—in his 1987 *Klail City Death Trip Series*—further developed this technique of disjointed scenes, Faulknerian snapshots of Chicano lives. Other examples include Denise Chávez's *The Last of the Menu Girls* (1986), Sandra Cisneros's *The House on Mango Street* (1984), Roberta Fernández's *Intaglio* (1990), Sandra Benítez's *A Place Where the Sea Remembers* (1993), Junot Díaz's *Drown* (1996), and even to some extent, Edgardo Vega Yunqué's *Mendoza's Dreams* (1987). In all these works, the modernist fragmentation of narrative suggests the Latino's struggle to piece together a coherent sense of self even as it authenticates the voices of the people and the heritages of Latino families.

BENDING NARRATIVE RULES

A few important Latino works broke the rules in narrative Latino fiction, in particular three by Chicano authors. The first is Rudolfo Anaya's *Bless Me, Ultima*. This 1972 novel won the second Quinto Sol Literary Award, and upon publication, more people read it than any other novel by a Chicano writer. The book presented a unique view of Chicano life in the Southwest. It described in colorful, symbolic detail the rural life of the desert; authenticated the mythic structures of Mexican American/mestizo existence; and legitimized the spirituality of a people unrecognized and underappreciated by the mainstream. The narrative complexity of the novel was equally new: Anaya blurred the difference between reality and fiction so that readers were forced to question their beliefs about life, death, and the supernatural.

The second book, now almost lost in the torrent of new Latino novels published today, is a short novel by Ron Arias, *The Road to Tamazunchale* (1975), in which Arias displays a combination of the artistry of Juan Rulfo, the great Mexican writer, and Gabriel García Márquez. Filled with dreamlike sequences, time-traveling protagonists, and humorous insights into the urban realities of a dying man struggling to understand his cultural world, the novel bent the rules of Latino narrative in ways that few works have since it came out nearly three decades ago.

If Rudolfo Anaya could be called a Chicano Leo Tolstoy, Ron Arias plays the role of the first Chicano Vladimir Nabokov.

The third work, also mentioned in the previous section, is Tomás Rivera's ...*Y no se lo tragó la tierra.* First published in an English translation in 1987 as ...*And the Earth Did Not Devour Him,* this work set the stage for narrative experimentation in Latino fiction. Rivera's poetic rendition of how a small boy tries to recapture the fragments of one year with his migrant worker family was a major innovation that stood in stark contrast to more traditional and chronological Latino fiction. Each short vignette encapsulates a moment—an economic injustice, a betrayal, a glimpse into one character's thoughts or emotions, a tragedy. Powerful and artistic, Rivera's snapshots and fractured narrative would influence many writers over the next thirty years; for example, Ana Castillo uses his techniques in her novel *The Mixquiahuala Letters* (1986).

RECREATING THE PAST

The events of Latino history (sometimes repressed, certainly neglected, and often rewritten by mainstream sources) are continually surfacing as scholars explore the records and oral histories of the hidden past. In the past few decades, Latinos have published works inspired by historical events. Julia Alvarez's *In the Time of the Butterflies* (1994), for instance, recounts the tragic true story of the murdered Mirabal sisters in the Dominican Republic. Cecile Pineda's *Face* (1985) and Manuel Luis Martinez's *Crossing* (1998) were both based on news reports. Francisco Goldman's latest novel, *The Divine Husband* (2004), imagines the nineteenth-century life of an illegitimate child of Cuban poet José Martí. Ana Menéndez's novel *Loving Che* (2003) reworks the love life of revolutionary Che Guevara. Julia Alvarez's novel *In the Name of Salomé* (2000) recreates the life of the nineteenth-century Dominican poet Salomé Ureña de Henríquez.

As Latinos reimagine the past, they present the issues from new angles. In the tradition of the classic Chicano text *With His Pistol in His Hand* (1958), in which writer Americo Paredes creates a heroic narrative for Gregorio Cortez, the Mexican rebel outlaw, out of a series of folk songs, or *corridos,* Latino fiction will continue to invert stereotypes by emphasizing the unwritten histories of people previously ignored or in some way marginalized. Be it through personal memoir, realist prose, magical narrative, or some transgenre form as yet unrecognized (an early stage of hypertextual fiction?) Latino writers will find surprising and dynamic new avenues for their fictional expression of Latino culture.

SCHOLARLY PUBLICATIONS ON LATINO NARRATIVE
(See also works listed in Chapters 2 and 3)

Aldama, Frederick Luis. *Postethnic Narrative Criticism: Magicorealism in Oscar "Zeta" Acosta, Ana Castillo, Julie Dash, Hanif Kureshi and Salman Rushdie.* Austin: University of Texas Press, 2003.

Borland, Isabel Alvarez. *Cuban-American Literature of Exile*. Charlottesville: University Press of Virginia, 1998.

Brady, Mary Pat. *Extinct Lands, Temporal Geographies: Chicana Literature and the Urgency of Space*. Durham: Duke University Press, 2002.

Brown, Monica. *Gang Nation: Delinquent Citizens in Puerto Rican, Chicano, and Chicana Narratives*. Minneapolis: University of Minnesota Press, 2002.

Bruce-Novoa, Juan. *Chicano Authors: Inquiry by Interview*. Austin and London: University of Texas Press, 1980.

———. *Retrospace: Collected Essays on Chicano Literature*. Houston: Arte Publico Press, 1990.

Calderón, Héctor, and José David Saldívar, eds. *Criticism in the Borderlands: Studies in Chicano Literature, Culture, and Ideology*. Durham and London: Duke University Press, 1991.

Christie, John S. *Latino Fiction and the Modernist Imagination*. New York: Garland Publishing, 1998.

Christian, Karen. *Show and Tell: Identity as Performance in U.S. Latina/o Fiction*. Albuquerque, University of New Mexico Press, 1997.

Davidson, Ned J. *The Concept of Modernism in Hispanic Criticism*. Boulder: Pruett Press, Inc., 1966.

Gutiérrez, Ramón, and Genaro Padilla, eds. *Recovering the U.S. Hispanic Literary Heritage*. Houston: Arte Publico, 1993.

Hernández, Guillermo E. *Chicano Satire: A Study in Literary Culture*. Austin: University of Texas Press, 1991.

Hererra-Sobek, María, ed. *Beyond Stereotypes: Critical Analysis of Chicana Literature*. Binghamton, NY: Bilingual Press/Editorial Bilingüe, 1985.

———, and Helena María Viramontes, eds. *Chicana Creativity and Criticism: Charting New Frontiers in American Literature*. Houston: Arte Publico Press, 1988.

Hicks, Emily. *Border Writing: The Multidimensional Text. Theory and History of Literature Series 80*. Minneapolis and Oxford: University of Minnesota Press, 1991.

Horno-Delgado, Asunción, et al., eds. *Breaking Boundaries: Latina Writings and Critical Readings*. Amherst: University of Massachusetts Press, 1989.

Ikas, Karin Rosa. *Chicana Ways: Conversations with Ten Chicana Writers*. Reno and Las Vegas: University of Nevada Press, 2002.

Lattin, Vernon E., ed. *Contemporary Chicano Fiction: A Critical Survey*. Binghamton, NY: Bilingual Press/Editorial Bilingüe, 1986.

Luis, William. *Dance Between Two Cultures: Latino Caribbean Literature Written in the United States*. Nashville: Vanderbilt University Press, 2001.

McCracken, Ellen. *New Latina Narrative: The Feminine Space of Postmodern Ethnicity*. Tucson: University of Arizona Press, 1999.

Mujčinović, Fatima. *Postmodern Cross-Culturalism and Politicization in U.S. Latina Literature: From Ana Castillo to Julia Alvarez*. New York: Peter Lang Publishing, 2004.

Quintana, Alvina E. *Home Girls: Chicana Literary Voices*. Philadelphia: Temple University Press, 1996.

Rebolledo, Tey Diana. *Women Singing in the Snow*. Tucson/London: University of Arizona Press, 1995.

Rivera, Carmen S. *Kissing the Mango Tree: Puerto Rican Women Rewriting American Literature*. Houston: Arte Publico Press, 2002.

Saldívar, José David. *Border Matters: Remapping American Cultural Studies*. Berkeley: University of California Press, 1997.

———. *Dialectics of Our America: Genealogy, Cultural Critique, and Literary History*. Durham and London: Duke University Press, 1991.

Saldívar, Ramón. *Chicano Narrative: The Dialectics of Difference*. Madison, WI: University of Wisconsin Press, 1990.

Saldívar-Hull, Sonia. *Feminism on the Border: Chicano Gender Politics and Literature*. Berkeley: University of California Press, 2000.

Sánchez González, Lisa. *Boricua Literature: A Literary History of the Puerto Rican Diaspora*. New York: New York University Press, 2001.

Villa, Raúl Homero. *Barrio-Logos: Space and Place in Urban Chicano Literature and Culture*. Austin: University of Texas Press, 2000.

Weiss, Rachel, and Alan West, eds. *Being America: Essays on Art, Literature and Identity from Latin America*. New York: White Wine Press, 1991.

Zimmerman, Marc. *U.S. Latino Literature: An Essay and Annotated Bibliography*. Chicago: MARCH/Abrazo Press, 1992.

2
Latino Poetry

Latino poetry, as one might expect, is diverse and multifaceted, with voices that boom in Spanish, English, and Spanglish, reflecting not only Latin American roots but also celebrating the Taino, the Quechua, and other native cultures. While it would be inaccurate to say that its themes reflect any single topic or issue, there is no doubt that Latino poets revisit the lost world, the working world, the urban world, the world on the fringes, the world beyond, and other worlds that are part of the U.S. landscape. Naturally, this means that Latino poets bring up the "ethnic experience" in their works, but it also means that, like Walt Whitman, Robert Frost, and Emily Dickinson, these poets too celebrate experiences that have more to do with moments frozen in time—unrelated to their ethnic experiences. The latter point has made it difficult for Latino poets to break through, for they not only write in a genre that publishers consider commercially risky (books of poetry are not big sellers) but they also have to overcome the expectations that they only have something to say when they write about "the ethnic experience." Latino fiction writers have slowly, though not entirely, been able to move away from these expectations and publish works that are less about the sense of being Latino than about Latino human beings. Latino poets have not been as fortunate. As a result, even in the twenty-first century, fame has eluded most Latino poets except for those who first succeeded in other genres.

A short story, like a novel, has elements that help define it as such. Any student in an introductory literature course can expect to be taught about setting, foreshadowing, climax, and other concepts and terms and then to locate their usage in a piece of fiction. That same student may also learn about sonnets, iambic pentameter, rhythm, and other terms that will aid his or her understanding of poetry. One final, but important, lesson will invariably follow—the overlying rule of poetry is that there are no rules. Surely, formalist poetic traditions do exist, but ultimately, a poet can defy "logical" structure and grammar, as writers such as e. e. cummings reminded us. Yet Latino poets who have used this creative license to publish art without boundaries are not seen as stylistic pioneers but as writers whose only aim is to affirm their ethnicities. A quick glimpse at the opening lines of the poem "Sugarcane" by Achy Obejas (which appears on page 373 in Chapter 7), for example, reveals her deliberate attempt to defy simple conventional rules:

> can't cut
> cut the cane
> azuca'* in chicago
> dig it down to the
> root... (1–5)

In less than twenty words, Obejas demonstrates enough of an intentional disregard for grammar conventions to warrant at least a basic, stylistic comparison with poets such as cummings. But this part of her creativity will most likely be lost in mainstream analysis and translation—for critics will be more concerned with the anthropology of her poem than with how she constructs powerful images. The stylistic integrity of poetry by Latinos is often disregarded by publishers who cannot get beyond the Spanish influence and cultural references. As a result, even in the twentieth-first century, almost all major anthologies of American literature barely provide a glimpse of Latino poetry. Such is the world of Latino poets.

LATINO POETRY AS A PROTEST

Poetry has always been a popular genre in Latin America, where poets such as Pablo Neruda, Sor Juana Inéz de La Cruz, and Octavio Paz remain legendary. Many of these poets earned their fame as the voices of the people, often tackling social issues, from revolutions to dictatorships, and some, such as Roque Daltoñ, sacrificed their lives in their attempts to communicate through their art. Likewise, Latino poets in the United States have followed in these great ones' footsteps, using their art to criticize the working and living conditions of Latinos throughout the country. For example, the *corrido,* or border ballad, is essentially a form of poetry popularized by Mexicans since the 1800s. It evolved as a response to social injustices and usually tells of Mexicans who fought against the U.S. establishment.

In the same manner, Rodolfo "Corky" Gonzáles's "I Am Joaquin" has served as a call to arms for Chicanos since its publication in 1967. Other than this epic poem, Gonzáles, whose résumé lists a Golden Gloves boxing championship and role as founder of Denver's Crusade for Justice, never published any other work that would place him among the U.S. Latino literary elite. He did write other, lesser-known poems and plays, but Gonzáles was more of an activist than a literary figure. His famous poem is significant nonetheless because it reaffirms the connection between Latino poetry and its politicization. The poem is about the Mexican renegade Joaquin

---

*Sugar.

Murieta, who lived in the 1850s during the time when the Treaty of Guadalupe Hidalgo (see Chapter 3 for more information on this treaty and its impact) led to numerous human rights violations against Mexicans, and it reminds the reader of the need for rebellion. Throughout "I Am Joaquin," Gonzáles alludes to these abuses to emphasize a pattern of oppression that has existed in the United States and Mexico against various groups, including indigenous ones. The inspirational message of the poem, especially in the final lines, "I SHALL ENDURE! / I WILL ENDURE!" is that despite the efforts of those in power, Chicanos will thrive.

The theme of "I Am Joaquin" has appeared in different forms in various poems by Latinos, but why is this the case? In part, this question can be answered by looking at the lack of progress in improving Latinos' working conditions in the United States. For too many, the sad truth of working-class Latino life resembles that of Jorge in Martín Espada's poem "Jorge the Church Janitor Finally Quits," in which a Honduran immigrant dedicates himself to backbreaking work and gets very little in return.

CODE-SWITCHING

For poets, words are the most important element in creating their art. For Latino poets, this means that they have more ammunition within their arsenal, because they can infuse their poems with words in English as well as with Spanish from different regions and with native languages. This shifting between the two or more languages or dialects (code-switching) could be perceived as an indicator of a Latino poet's aim to reach a specific, bilingual audience, but it also demonstrates their attempts to represent a true facet of Latino life in the United States. After all, code-switching was not invented by poets; it has been a part of the lives of Latinos since they began interacting with peoples of other cultures.

The extent to which Latinos use code-switching in their poems varies, depending on their stylistic intent. They may want to magnify a single word or emphasize a whole stanza. Monolingual readers may be able to translate the literal meanings of the words using a Spanish-English dictionary, but they may miss the connotative messages that are pivotal to a true understanding of the poem. This does not mean that an audience unfamiliar with the nuances of Latino languages will be unable to appreciate poetry by Latinos. If people could only appreciate poetry in the language they were accustomed to, there would be no point in studying Shakespeare, with its archaic terminology that is unfamiliar to modern students. Instead, it illustrates two of the basic tenets of poetry—it is for everyone, as the Salvadoran poet Roque Dalton said—and poetry is not a picture in black and white but a collage in shades of gray. As the people in the United States become more accepting of other cultures, overcoming the paranoia against other languages that resulted in the English-only movements common in the latter part of the twentieth century, more readers will have the knowledge to appreciate fully the beauty of poetry by Latinos. There are some encouraging signs. For example, as Spanish is being introduced in schools as early as kindergarten, poetry that shifts between English and

Spanish is used as a learning tool. Soon, perhaps, codes in Latino poetry that are now considered obscure will be recognized by more readers.

Latino poets incorporate more than just the standard forms of British English and Castilian Spanish in their work. As a teenager might refer to a new skateboard as "rad" in front of her peers but use another term with her parents, Latino groups within the United States use the full scope of vocabulary in their poetry. In effect, code-switching is used to show what the poets are as well as what they are not: Latinos are not a monolithic group with only one code and one experience.

THE NUYORICAN MOVEMENT

Often viewed as the equivalent of the Harlem Renaissance, the explosion of art and literature created by African Americans in New York City during the 1920s, the Nuyorican movement is one of the great periods of literature. The term "Nuyorican," a combination of "New York" and "Puerto Rican," pays homage to the millions of Puerto Ricans who have made the Big Apple their home. The late 1960s movement was both a celebration and a protest, documenting the lives of Puerto Ricans who were neither accepted on the mainland nor on the island of Puerto Rico. Although in the first half of the twentieth century, people such as Jesús Colón and Bernardo Vega had written about the plight of Puerto Ricans in New York, as had the great poet Julia de Burgos, it was nothing like the 1960s mini-boom of literature by Puerto Ricans in the United States. The country, it seemed, was more than ready to embrace the work of writers of color. Amidst the civil rights and Chicano movements, in 1967, Piri Thomas published the best-selling autobiographical work *Down These Mean Streets* chronicling his life in the inner city as a black Puerto Rican. And against this backdrop, Nuyorican poets began to make their mark on a national level.

The life of the Nuyorican movement, which is still thriving, can be credited in large part to Miguel Algarín. Algarín founded the Nuyorican Poets Café circa 1973, providing rising and established poets with an arena in which they could showcase their talents. To this day, the Café still sponsors weekly poetry slams and open-mic competitions for poets.

Among the poets who have flourished from the exposure they got at the Nuyorican Poets Café are Algarín, Miguel Piñero, Pedro Pietri, and Tato Laviera. Their poems identify the realities of life in Spanish Harlem and the lower East Side in New York City—in short, the urban world. More than that, though, their poems identify their willingness to call New York home, for better or worse. Piñero's "A Lower East Side Poem" urges the reader to bury him in the lower East Side upon his death. Pietri's "Puerto Rican Obituary" pays homage to people named Juan, Miguel, Milagros, Olga, and Manuel, who lived in the inner city and "All died yesterday today / and will die again tomorrow" (28–29). Laviera's "AmeRícan" celebrates the birth of a new generation of Puerto Ricans in America who are "european, indian, black, Spanish" (11), and who define themselves in their own way.

Arguably, the poetry of the Nuyorican movement helped establish Latino poetry as a genre to be heard, not just read. In this respect, Nuyorican poetry was influenced by the *plena*, which like the *corrido*, is a musical form of storytelling. Consequently, the poetry often sounds like a song, with meter used like instruments to add beats. The oral tradition of Latino poetry has resulted in the establishment of numerous groups such as the Taco Shop Poets, who perform in taco shops. It has also produced various notable poetry slam-like competitions, such as in the Southwest, where Victor Hernández Cruz and Jimmy Santiago Baca have had the distinction of being named World Heavyweight Champion Poets by the World Poetry Bout Association.

CHICANA VOICES

On the West Coast, the political voice of Latino poetry rose full blast from various Chicano forums, from demonstrations and community events to playwright Luis Valdez's El Teatro Campesino (the Farmworkers Theater) to the establishment of Quinto Sol, the first Chicano press. As Chicana literary scholars such as Marta Ester Sanchez and Tey Diana Rebolledo have pointed out, by the early 1970s, a growing number of Latinas began to publish poetry, including Lorna Dee Cervantes, Pat Mora, Gina Valdés, and Bernice Zamora. These women and many others, such as Cherrie Moraga and Alma Luz Villanueva, fought to combat the sexist stereotypes confronting them from both Anglo and Chicano sides of the fence. The result today is a vast amount of lasting poetic expression by Latinas, whose work is the focus of many anthologies and the subject of scholarly work throughout the United States. Just as the spoken voice plays a huge part in Nuyorican poetry, so too does the oral narrative invigorate many Latina poems, especially those in which writers attempt to capture the essence and memory of a mother's or grandmother's tone, style, and manner. Combining the musical aspects of *dichos* (proverbs), songs, and rhymes with abundant images of the legends of Mexican mythic figures such as the powerful pre-Columbian Tonantzín/Coatlicue, La Malinche, La Llorona, and La Virgen de Guadalupe, Chicana poets speak of present-day conditions for women in the languages of their female ancestors. The poetry is often about sexuality, the search for self-identity and self-reliance, and the constant struggle to be Latina in ways that existing societal roles for women may not completely allow.

THE POWER OF THE SMALLER PRESSES

Without smaller, independent presses, some of which exclusively publish works by Latinos, Latino poetry would be an entirely different genre. Because the poetic tradition in Latin America has been alive and well for centuries, poets would have found ways to continue that tradition in the United States even without the help of these presses. Fortunately, however, small houses such as Curbstone Press in

Willimantic, Connecticut, did publish the works of such poets as Tino Villanueva, Naomi Ayala, and Martín Espada. The Latino poetic landscape would be very different without Arte Público in Houston, Texas, and Bilingual Review Press/Editorial Bilingüe based at Arizona State University. One can safely say that access to Latino poets would be much more limited without these publishers. In fact, many female writers (including feminist poets such as Lorna Dee Cervantes, who went on to found her own press) can credit much of their success to these specialized presses.

Major publishers started demonstrating interest in Latino poets as recently as the last quarter century; however, most of them published established names such as Sandra Cisneros and Julia Alvarez only after they had successfully published their prose. Lesser-known poets have had their works published by major presses only when their poems appear in anthologies such as this one that have a particular focus on Latino literature.

The conservative propensities of major publishers toward Latino poetry should not come as a surprise and has much to do with the genre of poetry in general. Major publishers do not view poetry as profitable and consider the market for Latino poetry too small to venture into. Smaller presses take that risk, however, and Latino poetry is alive and well.

ECHOES OF POETS

Just as the novelist William Faulkner influenced Gabriel García Márquez, who in turn influenced a generation of writers in the United States and all over the world, so too has there been a cycle of Latino poets who have had predecessors across all nationalities. Poetry, often referred to as an art of imitation, easily lends itself to this ongoing process. Upon reading the work of any of the poets in this anthology, it is possible to hear the echoes of Gabriela Mistral, Jose Martí, or Cesar Vallejo. Nobel Prize–winning poets have also given due credit to these pioneers. Likewise, Latino poets have been influenced by prominent U.S. literary figures as well. For instance, Walt Whitman's style and his emphasis on U.S. urban life have inspired numerous Latino poets.

The ongoing influence of these predecessors speaks to Latino poets as writers and artists rather than as chroniclers of "their" ethnic group's experiences. Whether using free verse without rhyme or a tightly structured sonnet, these poets make creative choices that cannot be ignored. Mainstream critics have tended to review their work, focus on the message, and overlook the way these poems come together as artistic pieces. Ironically, William Carlos Williams, whose poetry was first published in the early 1900s, has begun to garner more attention as a Latino poet but was largely disregarded as such because of the opposite reasons. Studies of his work centered around the innovative form of his poetry while avoiding mention of its ethnic subjects. If the aesthetic value of poetry by Latinos today could be studied in a way that would permit both an understanding of the role of ethnicity and the recognition of its creativity, we would have a much deeper appreciation for its place in the U.S. literary tradition. Maybe then more Latino poets such as the ones in this anthology will be praised for some of the same reasons as Williams and other widely recognized American poets.

SCHOLARLY PUBLICATIONS ON LATINO POETRY
(See also works listed in Chapters 1 and 3)

Arteaga, Alfred. *Chicano Poetics: Heterotexts and Hybridities.* Cambridge: Cambridge University Press, 1997.

Bruce-Novoa, Juan. *Chicano Poetry: A Response to Chaos.* Austin: University of Texas Press, 1982.

Candelaria, Cordelia. *Chicano Poetry: A Critical Introduction.* Westport, CT: Greenwood Press, 1986.

Dick, Bruce. *A Poet's Truth: Conversations with Latino/Latina Poets.* Tucson: University of Arizona Press, 2003.

Foster, David William. *Chicano/Latino Homoerotic Identities (Latin American Studies).* New York: Garland Publishing, 1999.

Pérez Firmat, Gustavo. *Tongue Ties: Logo-Eroticism in Anglo-Hispanic Literature.* New York: Palgrave, 2003.

Pérez-Torres, Rafael, et al., eds. *Movements in Chicano Poetry: Against Myths, against Margins (Cambridge Studies in American Literature and Culture).* New York: Cambridge University Press, 1995.

Sánchez, Marta Ester. *Contemporary Chicana Poetry.* Berkeley: University of California Press, 1985.

3
Latino Landscapes

THE MAPS

The Mexican-American War

Between 1783 and 1853, through a series of annexations, purchases, and wars, the territory of the United States changed dramatically. In 1848, the Treaty of Guadalupe Hidalgo was signed at the end of the Mexican-American War and California, Texas, and what is now the Southwest became part of the United States. Mexico had achieved independence from Spain in 1821, but just 27 years later, it lost much of its northern territory. The eighteenth-century Spanish missions set up by the powers in Spain to control and "civilize" indigenous peoples lost their backing and influence when Spain granted independence to Mexico. After 1848, the independent Spanish Mexican settlers, known as Californios, lost their lands as the United States expanded westward. The map below not only depicts the various victories and movements by each side, but it also highlights the disputed territories that were part of Mexico prior to 1848.

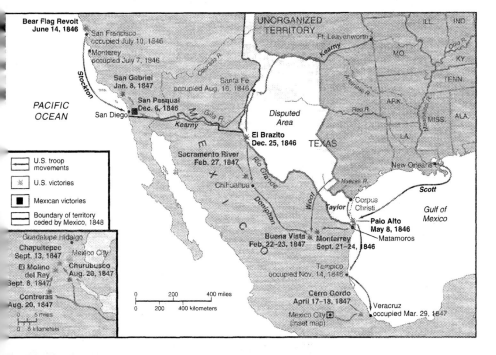

Cuba

Cuba gained independence from Spain after the Spanish-American War in 1898 and soon thereafter began a tense political relationship with the United States, 90 miles to the north. The 1959 Cuban Revolution, which brought Fidel Castro to power and led to the dissolving of diplomatic relations between the two countries, continues to have a profound impact on Cubans and Cuban Americans in the United States. As a result, two distinct Cuban communities have emerged, one in Cuba, the largest island of the Caribbean with a population of 10 million people, and the other in Miami, Florida. Forty years after the revolution, the political divisions are still vividly felt by both Cuban and Cuban American families.

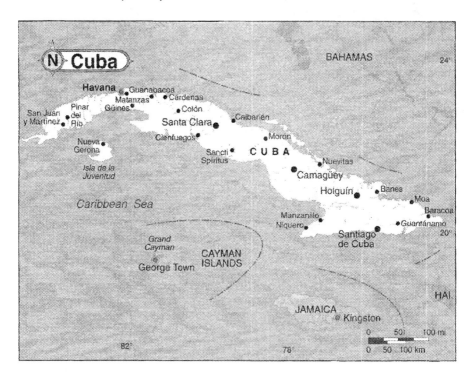

Puerto Rico

Unlike Cuba, the island of Puerto Rico was not granted independence after the Spanish-American War. Instead, it became a sort of colony of the United States, an "associated state," or commonwealth. Today, more Puerto Ricans live stateside than on the island of Puerto Rico itself. This complicated political and economic relationship between the two countries often divides allegiances among Puerto Ricans. Especially within the United States, some Puerto Ricans consider themselves intensely transnational, moving back and forth between the United States and the island, many finding themselves culturally, economically, and linguistically "between worlds."

The Dominican Republic

The colonial history of the Dominican Republic is linked to that of its island neighbor, Haiti, and the two countries share a complicated and sometimes violent heritage. The eastern half (about two-thirds) of the island has about eight and a half million people. Political repression during Rafael Trujillo's 30-year dictatorship, military interventions by the United States during the twentieth century, and ongoing general economic hardships have led an ever-increasing number of Dominicans to migrate to Puerto Rico and from there to the eastern urban centers of the United States.

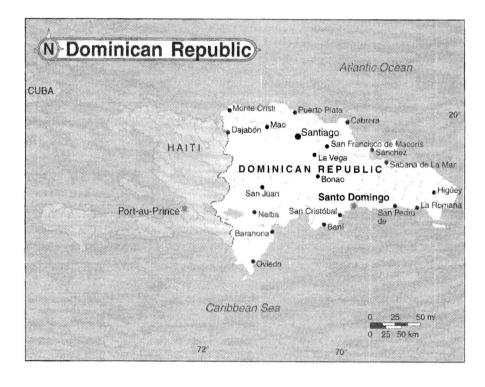

Mexico and the Modern U.S.-Mexico Border

With a rich history that includes Spanish rule and strong Indian traditions, Mexico has had a significant role in shaping political and economic policies in the United States. Beyond influencing border and immigration laws, Mexico has contributed greatly to many initiatives in the United States. The Bracero Program, for example, brought more than four million migrant workers to the United States in the middle of the twentieth century, and in 1994, the controversial North American Free Trade Agreement (NAFTA) aimed to improve opportunities for trade and investment among Mexico, the United States, and Canada.

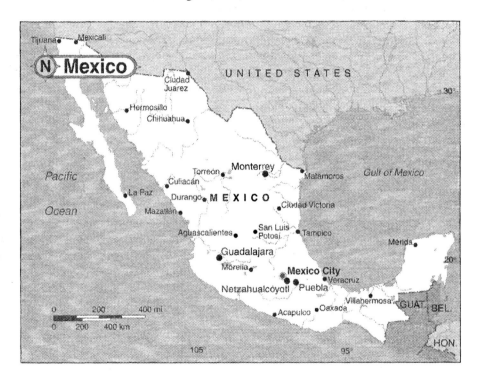

Central America

Despite their relatively small size, the seven nations that comprise Central America have a plethora of diverse cultures and traditions. English, for example, is the official language of Belize, but Spanish and Indian languages can be heard throughout all seven Central American countries, Belize included. The United States has had mixed and often charged relationships with each of these countries.

The Turnabout Map of the Americas

Jesse Levine was a graphic designer who created the Turnabout Map of the Americas in 1982 to challenge our usual way of seeing the world. Most world maps that people in the United States see—in classrooms, newspapers, magazines, books, and atlases—emphasize the northwestern continents, North America and Europe. As you examine this map, consider your reaction and what the map's "distortion" might imply. Does the map strike you as wrong? Why or why not?

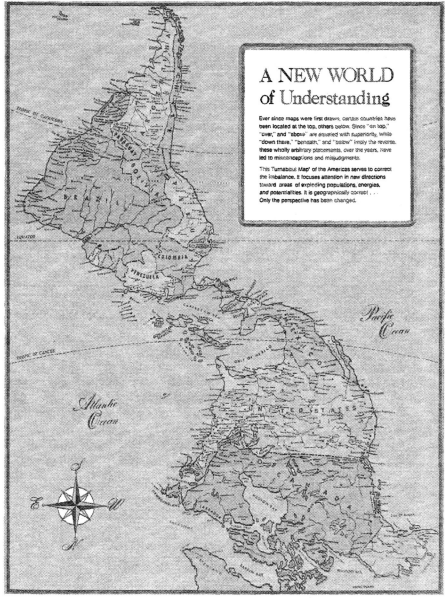

TIMELINE OF LATINO HISTORICAL AND CULTURAL EVENTS, 1492–2005

Many of the works in this anthology will refer to hundreds of places, events, issues, and people connected to the history of Latin America. We offer the following annotated timeline as an introduction to readers unfamiliar with this history and as a useful tool for teachers and students interested in placing the individual literary works in this anthology within their historical and political contexts. Obviously, this information is general, and we have no doubt omitted many dates and names that scholars of Latino and Latin American studies (historians, sociologists, ethnographers, etc.) may consider important. We recognize that each country—not to mention every region within each country—has been the subject of extensive scholarship on the events and people mentioned below. We provide a basic historical overview, keeping in mind that the emphasis of this anthology is on modern Latino literature, but we encourage readers to explore further the past of the vast, complex, and multifaceted countries to which the writers in this book often align themselves.

For convenience, we have bold-faced the names of significant people as well as major historical events and the names of countries or regions in which they occur. This should help readers follow a specific trail of dates and political events for any particular Latino population. After the timeline is a reference list of works on the subjects mentioned in the timeline.

TIMELINE OF LATINO HISTORICAL AND CULTURAL EVENTS 1492–2005

1492	**Spain** and **Portugal** begin colonization process of **Latin America**. Contact between European and Indigenous populations of what is now considered the Americas begins.
	Christopher Columbus reaches an island in the **Bahamas**, calling it **San Salvador**.
1502	Christopher Columbus takes his final voyage.
	The "encomienda" labor system in **Latin America** begins, which results in **Indians** being virtually enslaved (and Christianized) by colonists in search of gold and silver.
1510	**Spain** colonizes **Puerto Rico**.
1515	**Spain** colonizes **Cuba**.
1519	Spanish emissary **Hernán Cortés** begins conquest of **Mexico**.
	La Malinche (Doña Marina or Malinal), who was sold into slavery as a child, translates the language of the indigenous peoples of **Mexico** into Spanish for the conqueror. She was his mistress and bore him a son, the mythical "first" Chicano, or *mestizo*. Thus, she is a powerful figure in

	Chicano literature, simultaneously "betrayer" to her people and the first independently powerful, female role model. She is also a figure who blends into the myths of the weeping women, La Llorona and La Gritona.
1531	Indian **Juan Diego** sees the Virgin of Guadalupe at Tepeyac, **Mexico**.
1533	**Francisco Pizarro, another Spanish conquistador**, conquers the Incas, whose empire along the western coast of **South America** included present-day **Peru** and parts of **Ecuador, Bolivia, northern Chile, and northwest Argentina**.
1542	**Spanish** explorer **Alvar Nuñez Cabeza de Vaca** begins his famous journey from Florida to Texas.
April 1695	**Sor Juana Inés de la Cruz**—poet, writer, and important figure for **Mexican/Chicana** scholars—dies.
January 1804	**Haitian revolutionaries** are victorious in achieving independence from **Europe**.
1808–1925	**Latin American Wars of Independence** take place and are led by such men as **General Simón Bolívar (Venezuela and Colombia)** and **General José de San Martin (Argentina)** and dissenting priests such as **Miguel Hidalgo y Costilla** and **José Maria Morelos y Pavon (Mexico)**.
1822	**Brazil** becomes independent.
1823	The **United States** establishes the **Monroe Doctrine**. This declaration states that the **United States** would "protect" the **Americas** from **Europe** with the expectation that the new nations would join the **United States** in creating a democratic hemisphere. Instead, the rise of the Latin American *caudillo*, or strongman, led to numerous U.S. military interventions. Thus begins nearly two centuries of "legitimate" interventions by the U.S. military into the affairs of Latin America.
1832–1836	**Texans** revolt against **Mexico**.
1836	**Mexican leader and general Antonio Lopez de Santa Ana** wins the battle of **the Alamo**. Nevertheless, **Texas** becomes independent.
1844	The **Dominican Republic** is formed and separated from **Haiti**. **Texas** is annexed by the **United States**.
1846–1848	The **United States-Mexican War** takes place. Weakened by the Wars for Independence and **General Santa Ana's** ineptitude, Mexico cannot hold the northern territories from the invading U.S. military and to some extent the thousands of colonists moving west. The war is unpopular

Timeline *(continued from previous page)*

	with many U.S. citizens, including Ulysses S. Grant, Abraham Lincoln, and Henry David Thoreau.
1848	The **Treaty of Guadalupe Hidalgo** is approved, and 80,000 "Hispanos" in New Mexico become U.S. citizens as the **United States** takes control of **Mexican** territory from **California** to **Texas**. Half of **Mexico's** territory now belongs to the **United States**.
1849	The **U.S.** gold rush begins.
1850s	Mexican legendary figure **Joaquin Murieta** purportedly is forced off his gold mine claim by tax collectors and begins his revolt. (He serves as a model and inspiration for the figure of Zorro and for the epic poem by **Chicano Rodolfo "Corky" Gonzales**.)
1855	**U.S.**-born adventurer **William Walker** becomes ruler of **Nicaragua**.
September 1860	**William Walker** is executed in **Honduras**.
1868	"El Grito de Lares"—**Puerto Rico's** first and only battle for independence from **Spain**—takes place.
1868–1878	**Cuba** fights Ten Years' War for independence from **Spain**.
1871	**Brazil's** Rio Branco law begins the process of abolition.
1873	Slavery is abolished in **Puerto Rico**.
1880s	United Fruit Company begins its "relationship" with **Latin America**, especially **Guatemala, Honduras, Panama, Costa Rica, Ecuador**, and the northern coast of **Colombia**.
1882–1892	**Cuban** poet and leader **José Martí** lives in exile in New York organizing the independence movement with **Puerto Rican leaders** such as **Eugenio María De Hostos** and **Dr. Ramón E. Betances**.
1886	Slavery is abolished in **Cuba**.
1898	The battleship "Maine" is blown up in a **Cuban** harbor, leading to the **United States** entering the **Spanish-American War**. Cubans (along with **Puerto Ricans**) had been fighting for years for their independence. **Puerto Rico** becomes a U.S. property. **Cuban poet José Martí** dies in the early days of the war.
1901	**Mexican Gregorio Cortez** becomes an outlaw and legendary folk hero of *corridos*. The **Platt Amendment** is passed and gives the **United States** the right to intervene in **Cuba's** economic affairs and domestic politics as well as a veto over international commitments. The **United States** establishes **Guantanamo Bay** as a U.S. military base in **Cuba**.

	The **United States** invades **Cuba**.
1904	The Roosevelt Corollary to the Monroe Doctrine grants the **United States** the right to act as the international police in the Americas. This corollary signals a major shift in United States attitude and activity in **Latin America** and the **Caribbean**. At this point, the United States is economically involved in many places, and governmental and military policy is quickly arranged to allow companies to act at will.
1900	The **Foraker Act** establishes **Puerto Rico** as a U.S. territory.
1902	**Cuba** becomes independent.
1903	"The War of a Thousand Days" in **Colombia** between liberals and conservatives ends with Colombian central government in disarray. Theodore Roosevelt's "big stick" diplomacy leads to an independent **Panama** and the establishment of the **Panama Canal Treaty**, which allows the United States to build and operate a canal linking the Pacific Ocean with the Caribbean via the Isthmus of Panama.
1910–1924	The Mexican Revolution takes place, and populist figures **Emiliano Zapata** and **Pancho Villa** participate.
1912	The **United States** invades **Nicaragua** and occupies the country until 1925.
1914	The **Panama Canal** opens.
1916	The **United States** invades the **Dominican Republic** and occupies the country until 1924.
1917	U.S. President Woodrow Wilson signs the **Jones Act**, which forces U.S. citizenship upon the people of **Puerto Rico**. The Puerto Rican people were not in favor of this "half citizenship"; to this day, they do not have representation in the U.S. government and cannot vote in U.S. presidential elections. The **United States** invades **Cuba**. The **United States** enters World War I.
January 1917	The Zimmerman telegram, in which **Germany** proposes a German-Mexican alliance against the **United States**, incites the Texas Rangers (*los rinches*) to murder **Mexicans**.
1919	**Mexican** rebel **Emiliano Zapata** is betrayed and shot in an ambush by **Mexican** government soldiers.
1926	The **United States** invades **Nicaragua** and occupies the country until 1933.
1928	Workers' strike against United Fruit in **Colombia** leads to the Ciénaga massacre (see Gabriel García Márquez).
1930	**Rafael Leónidas Trujillo** comes to power in the **Dominican Republic** and rules for 31 years in a brutal dictatorship supported by the **U.S.** government until his assassination in 1961.

Timeline *(continued from previous page)*

1931	**Jorge Ubica** begins 14-year dictatorship of **Guatemala**.
December 1931	**General Maximiliano Hernández Martínez** overthrows elected popular candidate, **Arturo Araujo**, and remains dictator in **El Salvador** for 12 years.
1932	**El Salvador's** Matanza takes place: Indians and mestizos rebel against dictator **Hernández Martínez** and are repressed; 30,000 people are killed. The fledging communist movement led by **Agustin Farabundo Martí** is destroyed.
1933	**Anastacio "Tacho" Somoza** takes control of **Nicaragua**. More than 20,000 workers and peasants die during the Somoza family reign.
	Franklin Roosevelt's "Good Neighbor Program" attempts to counter the Roosevelt Corollary and influence **Latin American** countries more subtly through financial and economic aid.
February 1934	**Augusto César Sandino**, Nicaraguan peasant leader, is betrayed and murdered by **Anastacio Somoza's** soldiers. Sandino will become the inspirational leader for the Sandanistas in the years following the ousting of Somoza's ruling son "Tachito" in the 1980s.
1937	Dominican dictator **Rafael Trujillo** sanctions the murder of 30,000 **Haitian** cane workers along the Dajabon river on the border between Haiti and the **Dominican Republic**.
March 1937	The **Ponce Massacre** takes place: 22 people die and more than 100 are wounded when the military fires upon a protesting crowd of nationalists in the city of **Ponce, Puerto Rico.**
1942	The "**Sleepy Lagoon Case**" takes place in **Los Angeles,** in which the body of **José Diaz** is found at a reservoir. Although there is no evidence of foul play, hundreds of young Mexican Americans are arrested. In the end, 12 are convicted of murder and 5 are convicted of assault.
	The **Bracero Program** makes official the existing practice of allowing **Mexicans** to travel into the **United States** for temporary work in **California** and the **Southwest**.
1943	After months of tensions between military servicemen and civilians, especially **Mexican Americans,** the **Zoot Suit riots** in **Los Angeles** erupt, sparked by street fights between sailors and Mexican American young men. The riots last more than a week.
1945	**Gabriela Mistral** becomes the first **Latin American** writer to win the **Nobel Prize** for literature.
1948	The assassination of **Jorge Eliecer Gaitán** in **Bogotá, Colombia,** sets off a ten-year period of violence (known as "La Violencia") between liberals and conservatives.
1947	**Luis Muñoz Murín** becomes the first elected governor of the island of **Puerto Rico.**

	Operation Bootstrap begins, a program that its advocates say is designed to develop better economic opportunities for Puerto Ricans by improving health care, education, and farming, and by creating new industries. The arrangement gives tax breaks to large U.S. corporations on the island of **Puerto Rico,** and the resulting industrialization pushes workers to journey north to support themselves.
November 1950	Two **Puerto Rican** nationalists try to assassinate **President Harry Truman** at Blair House in Washington, DC.
1952	**Puerto Rico** becomes a **Commonwealth** (on the island, called **Estado Libre Asociado**). **Evita Perón**, an actress who married **Juan Perón**, helped him win the Argentinian presidency, and became a controversial political figure herself, dies of cancer in **Argentina** at the age of 33.
July 1953	Influential **Puerto Rican poet Julia De Burgos** dies. **Fidel Castro** and a small group of rebels attack the Moncada military barracks in a failed attempt to oust the dictator of **Cuba, Fulgencio Batista**.
1954	**Puerto Rican** nationalists **Rafael Candel Miranda, Andrés Cordero,** and **Lolita Lebron** attack the U.S. House of Representatives, wounding five congressmen. A CIA-backed military coup in **Guatemala** takes place, partly as a result of the **U.S.** government's willingness to back the **United Fruit Co.'s** interest in the face of Guatemalan efforts at land reform and nationalization of resources. Dictator **Alfredo Stroessner** takes power in a military coup in **Paraguay** and remains in power until February 1989.
September 1956	**Anastacio Somoza**, president of **Nicaragua,** is shot and killed by worker/poet **Rigoberto López**, who is, in turn, immediately killed. Somoza's sons take over the presidency and military of **Nicaragua**.
1958	Massive anti-**United States** demonstrations take place in **Caracas, Venezuela,** during Vice President Richard Nixon's visit. **Chicano Américo Paredes's** influential work *With His Pistol in His Hand* is published.
1959	**José Antonio Villarreal's** *Pocho*, considered by some to be the first **Chicano** novel, is published. The **Cuban Revolution** takes place. Perhaps no single event has impacted **United States** and **Latin American** political, economic, and cultural relationships as profoundly as **Fidel Castro's** taking power from the ousted dictator **Fulgencio Batista**. The revolution was so pivotal in the lives of **Cubans** and **Cuban Americans** that few of their works written today do not deal with its impact in some way. Cuba's example of breaking free from United States control became pivotal to U.S. government policy from this point forward.

Timeline *(continued from previous page)*

November 1960	Three women working underground for the resistance, the **Mirabal sisters** (known as the "Butterflies"), are murdered by Trujillo's military in the Dominican Republic.
1960	**Operation Pedro Pan (Peter Pan)**, in which **Cuban** families send their children (around 14,000 in all) to the United States during the early years of the Cuban Revolution, begins.
1961	**The Bay of Pigs**: The **United States** invades **Cuba** and is soundly defeated by Cuban soldiers. President Kennedy admits his mistake and refuses to send air cover to troops. Dominican dictator **Trujillo** is assassinated by the **Dominican** resistance.
1962	The **Cuban Missile Crisis** emerges, and the threat of nuclear war between the **United States** and the **Soviet Union** in **Cuba** looms large but is narrowly averted. In the **United States**, **César Chávez** forms the **National Farm Workers Association**, also known as the **Farm Workers Association (FWA)**.
November 1963	**John F. Kennedy** is assassinated in **Dallas, Texas**.
1964	The military takes control of **Brazil**, marking the beginning of a series of repressive South American regimes that lead so-called dirty wars against those opposed to military control. How these types of dictatorships functioned and how many people "disappeared" over the next two decades will always be a matter of debate, as is the role of the **U.S.** CIA in tracking the military's political opponents who fled to **Europe** in exile, or escaped across the borders of **Brazil, Argentina, Paraguay, Uruguay, Chile, and Bolivia**.
1965	**U.S.** Marines enter Santo Domingo in the **Dominican Republic**. In **California**, **César Chávez** and **Delores Huerta** begin the grape boycotts, marking the beginning of the **Chicano** movement. **Puerto Rican** nationalist leader **Pedro Albizu Campos** dies. Radical political movements, such as **"The Young Lords"** in **New York**, **"La Raza"** in **California**, and **"The Brown Berets"** in the **Southwest** and **California**, begin to develop and emerge. **Chicano playwright Luis Valdez** joins **César Chávez's** grape boycott and establishes **"El Teatro Campesino"** (the Farmworkers Theater) in Delano, **California**. **Puerto Rican memoirist and political activist Bernardo Vega** dies in New York.
1966	The military rules **Argentina** for the next seven years, foreshadowing the later dictatorship from 1976 to 1983.

October 1967	Mythic revolutionary hero **Ernesto Ché Guevara**, who has inspired numerous literary works, is captured and executed by the **Bolivian** military. His hands are chopped off for identification.
1967	**Luis Somoza Debayle** dies suddenly and his brother **Anastacio "Tachito" Somoza Debayle** takes full command of presidency and military of **Nicaragua**. **Puerto Rican** writer **Piri Thomas's** *Down These Mean Streets* is published in the **United States**. **Guatemala's Miguel Angel Asturias** wins the Nobel Prize for literature. *Cien Años de Soledad (One Hundred Years of Solitude)* by **Colombian writer Gabriel García Márquez** is published in **Argentina**.
1968	Worldwide student activism is on the rise in places such as **Chicago** and **Tlatelolco, Mexico**, where 300 students are killed by the military. **Martin Luther King, Jr.**, and **Robert F. Kennedy** are murdered.
1969	Chicano organizations vote on **"El Plan de Aztlán"**—the symbolic declaration of **Mexican American/Chicano** cultural identity.
1970	Socialist candidate **Salvador Allende** is elected president in a democratic election in **Chile**. **Chicano** political party **La Raza Unida** (Mexican-Americans United) is established. **Rubén Salazar, Chicano journalist**, is killed in East Los Angeles riots.
1971	**Chilean writer Pablo Neruda** wins the Nobel Prize for literature. **Chicano writer Rudolfo Anaya** wins the second annual Premio Quinto Sol literary award for his novel *Bless Me, Ultima*.
September 1973	The CIA backs a military coup in **Chile**, and President **Salvador Allende** is murdered. **Augusto Pinochet** takes dictatorial control with support from the **Bolivian** and **Brazilian** military governments.
June 1974	**Oscar "Zeta" Acosta**, Chicano writer, mysteriously disappears in Mexico.
March 1976	A military coup begins in **Argentina** as does its six-year "dirty war" of torturing, kidnapping, and executing anyone opposed to military law, who is therefore considered a terrorist.
1977	The grandmothers and mothers of the Plaza de Mayo of **Buenos Aires, Argentina**, begin their daily protests against the military government. Carrying pictures of dead relatives, they march for the victims of the "dirty war."
1979	Revolutionary **Sandanistas** take power in **Nicaragua** from dictator **Anastacio "Tachito" Somoza**.

Timeline *(continued from previous page)*

October 1979	A military coup starts in **El Salvador**: A series of military juntas come to power, leading to an exodus of Salvadorans, many of them seeking refugee status in the United States.
1980	The **Mariel Boatlift**: Marielitos defect from Cuba from the port of Mariel. U.S. President Ronald Reagan, fearful of too many "feet people," denies refugee status for refugees from Central America and keeps them in detention camps.
	Ex-dictator **Tachito Somoza** is blown up by a car bomb in **Paraguay**.
	The **Peruvian Maoist group**, the **Sendero Luminoso**, begins to terrorize rural Peru.
March 1980	**Archbishop Oscar Arnulfo Romero** is assassinated in **El Salvador**.
May 1980	**Salvadoran** troops massacre 600 campesinos at the Sumpul River.
May 1981	A plane crash kills the president of **Ecuador, Jaime Roldós**.
July 1981	A plane crash kills the president of **Panama, Omar Torrijos**.
December 1980	Three Connecticut Maryknoll nuns and a fellow volunteer are murdered in **El Salvador**.
December 1981	At the **Salvadoran** village of El Mezote, 900 campesinos are massacred by the military using U.S.-made M-16s.
1982	Ruling **Argentinean** generals invade "Las Malvinas" (the **Falkland Islands**), owned by Great Britain.
	Colombian writer Gabriel García Márquez wins the Nobel Prize for literature.
1983	The **United States** invades the island of **Grenada**.
	Victor Gerena (connected to the **Puerto Rican Nationalist group** known as "The Macheteros") robs Wells Fargo of $7 million in **Hartford, Connecticut**, and is never heard from again.
1984	*The House on Mango Street* by **Chicana writer Sandra Cisneros** is published.
	Chicano writer Ernesto Galarza, author of *Barrio Boy*, dies.
	Chicano writer Tomás Rivera, author of *...Y no se lo tragó la tierra*, dies.
September 1985	Major earthquakes in **Mexico City** kill thousands and subsequently lead to increased immigration to the United States.
1988	The **United States** invades **Panama**. Thousands of urban poor are killed in Panama City.
June 1988	**Nuyorican writer Miguel Piñero** dies in New York City.
August 1989	**Louis Carlos Galán**, popular presidential candidate in **Colombia**, is assassinated by drug cartel mafia in Bogotá.

1990	**Mexican writer Octavio Paz** wins Nobel Prize for literature. **Cuban American Oscar Hijuelos** becomes the first Latino writer to win a Pulitzer Prize for his novel *The Mambo Kings Play Songs of Love*.
February 1991	**Chicano novelist Arturo Islas** dies.
April 1992	**Peruvian** President **Alberto Fujimori** takes control of the government in an *autogolpe*, or self-coup. Leader of the Peruvian revolutionary group **"The Shining Path" (or *Sendero Luminoso*), Abimael Guzman**, is captured and imprisoned. **Guatemalan Mayan activist Rigoberta Menchú** wins the Nobel Peace prize.
April 1993	**César Chávez, Chicano leader**, dies.
1994	The **North American Free Trade Agreement (NAFTA)** is passed and goes into effect. Simultaneously, the **Zapatista National Liberation Army**, named after the murdered leader **Emiliano Zapata**, becomes active in southern **Mexico**. The **Balseros** (raft people) leave **Cuba** for the **United States**, becoming the third major wave of refugees from that island. **Nuyorican playwright Reinaldo Povod** dies in New York.
November 1995	**California**'s Proposition 187 is passed in a government attempt to remove state support for education and social services for illegal immigrants.
1999	**President Bill Clinton** grants amnesty to 16 **Puerto Rican** nationalists including **Juan E. Segarra Palmer**. **Americo Paredes, Chicano writer and folklorist**, dies.
November 1999	**Cuban** refugee **Elián González** is rescued.
April 2002	Miami **Cuban Americans** protest the U.S. government's position regarding the legal status of **Elián González**.
2003	The **U.S.** Census Bureau reports that Latinos are the largest minority group in the nation.
March 2004	**Nuyorican poet Pedro Pietri** dies.
2004	The U.S. Navy leaves **Vieques, Puerto Rico**, after extended protests over use of the island for military exercises.
May 2004	**Chicana feminist scholar Gloria Anzaldúa** dies.
2005	**Alberto Gonzales** becomes the first Latino to serve as **U.S.** Attorney General.

SELECTED PUBLICATIONS IN LATINO STUDIES

Acuña, Rodolfo. *Occupied America: A History of Chicanos, 3rd ed.* New York: Harper Collins, 1988.

Anzaldúa, Gloria. *Borderlands/La Frontera: The New Mestiza.* San Francisco: Spinsters Aunt Lute Book Company, 1987.

Brown, David H. *Santería Enthroned.* Chicago: University of Chicago Press, 2003.

Broyles-González, Yolanda. *El Teatro Campesino: Theater in the Chicano Movement.* Austin: University of Texas Press, 1994.

Cypess, Sandra Messinger. *La Malinche in Mexican Literature: From History to Myth. Texas Pan American Series.* Austin: University of Texas Press, 1991.

Davis, Mike. *Magical Urbanism.* London, New York: Verso, 2000.

De la Torre, Aldela, and Beatríz M. Pesquera, eds. *Building with Our Hands: New Directions in Chicana Studies.* Berkeley: University of California Press, 1993.

Díaz-Quiñones, Arcadio. *La memoria rota.* Rio Piedras, Puerto Rico: Ediciones Huracán, Inc., 1993.

Flores, Juan. *Divided Borders: Essays on Puerto Rican Identity.* Houston: Arte Publico Press, 1993.

———. *From Bomba to Hip-Hop: Puerto Rican Culture and Latino Identity.* New York: Columbia University Press, 2000.

Fregoso, Rosa Linda. *The Bronze Screen: Chicana and Chicano Film Culture.* Minneapolis: University of Minnesota Press, 1993.

Fusco, Coco. *English Is Broken Here: Notes on Cultural Fusion in the Americas.* New York: New Press, 1995.

Gonzalez, Juan. *Harvest of Empire: A History of Latinos in America.* New York: Viking, 2000.

Mariscal, George, ed. *Aztlán and Vietnam: Chicano and Chicana Experiences of the War.* San Diego: University of California Press, 1999.

Meier, Matt S., and Feliciano Ribera. *Mexican Americans/American Mexicans: From Conquistadors to Chicanos.* New York: Hill and Wang, 1993.

Morales, Ed. *Living in Spanglish.* New York: St. Martins, 2002.

Moraga, Cherríe, and Gloria Anzaldúa, eds. *This Bridge Called My Back: Writings By Radical Women of Color.* New York: Kitchen Table: Women of Color Press, 1981.

Oboler, Suzanne. *Ethnic Labels, Latino Lives: Identity and the Politics of Re(Presentation) in the United States.* Minneapolis: University of Minnesota Press, 1995.

Ornelas, Michael P. *Beyond 1848: Readings in Modern Chicano Historical Experience.* Dubuque: Kendall Hunt Publishing, 1999.

Rodríguez, Clara E., ed. *Latin Looks: Images of Latinas and Latinos in the U.S. Media.* Boulder: Westview Press, 1997.

———. *Heroes, Lovers and Others: The Story of Latinos in Hollywood.* Washington, DC: Smithsonian Press, 2004.

Sánchez, Rosaura. *Chicano Discourse: Socio-historic Perspectives.* Rowley, MA: Newbury House Publishers, 1983.

———. *Telling Identities: The Californio Testimonios.* Minneapolis: University of Minnesota Press, 1995.

Sandoval-Sanchez, Alberto. *José Can You See?: Latinos On and Off Broadway.* Madison: University of Wisconsin Press, 1999.

Shorris, Earl. *Latinos: A Biography of the People.* New York: Norton, 1992.

Stavans, Ilan. *The Hispanic Condition: Reflections on Culture & Identity in America*. New York: Harper Collins, 1995.

Suárez-Orozco, Marcelo M., and Mariela M. Páez, eds. *Latinos Remaking America*. Berkeley: University of California Press, 2002.

Suro, Roberto. *Strangers Among Us: How Latino Immigration Is Transforming America*. New York: Knopf, 1998.

Tobar, Héctor. *Translation Nation: Defining a New American Identitiy in the Spanish Speaking United States*. New York: Riverhead Books, 2005.

Trujillo, Carla, ed. *Living Chicana Theory*. Berkeley, CA: Third Woman Press, 1997.

SELECTED PUBLICATIONS IN LATIN AMERICAN HISTORY

Cockcroft, James D. *Latin America: History, Politics, and U.S. Policy, 2nd ed.*. Boston: Houghton Mifflin, 1996.

Chasteen, John Charles. *Born in the Blood of Fire: A Concise History of Latin America*. New York: Norton, 2001.

Galeano, Eduardo. *Memory of Fire: Part One: Genesis*. New York: Pantheon, 1985.

———. *Memory of Fire: Part Two: Faces and Masks*. New York: Pantheon, 1987.

———. *Memory of Fire: Part Three: Century of the Wind*. New York: Pantheon, 1988.

———. *Open Veins of Latin America: Five Centuries of the Pillage of a Continent*. New York: Monthly Review Press, 1973.

Keen, Benjamin. *A History of Latin America, 5th ed*. Boston: Houghton Mifflin, 1996.

LaFeber, Walter. *Inevitable Revolutions: The United States in Central America*. New York: Norton, 1983.

PART II

Readings in Latino Literature

4
The Lost Worlds

Once Upon a Latin Moon

INTRODUCTION

The works in Chapter 4 focus on the process of acculturation and the psychological challenges associated with exile, assimilation, and memory. Although in some cases the themes are explicitly related to geographical change—traveling, moving, migrating—the overall connections here are those of cultural loyalty, spiritual and emotional identity, and the ways in which a "past" culture—often different from the mainstream U.S. culture—lingers beneath the surface and influences the lives of Latinos in the United States. Be they solid or distant, Latinos' ties to their Latin American heritage take center stage.

The metaphor of the United States as a "melting pot" in which immigrants supposedly dissolve into some vague, homogenized substance known as "American" has long been considered inadequate. For Latinos, currently the largest minority group in the United States, nothing close to melting has or ever will occur. Sociologists now see the United States as resembling a salad, or as the poet Gustavo Perez Firmat describes it, an "*ajiaco*"—a sort of international stew. In spite of which demographic food metaphor is used, Latinos will remain Latino; it is the United States that will become "Latinized." People across the country, regardless of nationality, may exchange the so-called traditional American foods—processed cheese, hot dogs, hamburgers, and Spam—in favor of Latin American chiles and salsas.

Beyond Immigration

Latino literature is not exclusively about immigration for the simple reason that not all Latinos are immigrants. This fact may be obvious to some (and should be to all), but there is a common misunderstanding that Latinos always write about "coming" to the United States as foreigners, that they are aliens (legal or not) and therefore second-class citizens who need to adjust in some way. As will be made clear in the selections of the chapters that follow, Latino literature delves into more than the theme of cultural assimilation and the ordeals of coping with the prejudices and obstacles that confront new arrivals. For example, Puerto Ricans are American citizens by birth (and have been since 1917), and many Chicanos can point to ancestors who have lived within the present U.S. borders since the sixteenth century.* The bumper-sticker racist mentality exemplified by the phrase "Welcome to America—Now Speak English" is often, at least subliminally, directed toward Spanish-speaking Latinos regardless of their cultural claim to U.S. roots. In fact, English-speaking European immigrants arrived on the East Coast after the Spanish arrived in California and Florida, making Spanish, in a sense, the first language of the United States.

These works, therefore, derive, in some way or another, from immigrant or ethnic communities and are not necessarily dependent on the story of traveling from a home country to a new world—what might be called the literature of immigration. Such journeys may energize the plot lines in a few selections, but they serve more often as backgrounds, foundations, or structures on which writers work out the issues of biculturalism, bilingualism, and hybridity. Because this is a collection of recent literature, many of the poems, plays, and stories were written by second- or third-generation Latinos, and thus the experiences of their parents or grandparents that they are describing have been filtered through a different cultural criteria and perspective. There will be less of boats, documents, planes, and the Statue of Liberty and more of memory, nostalgia, family heritage, and assorted ghosts of the past. Latino literature will always include variations of the "American Dream," but common themes of these selections center more on how people feel about the lost Latin worlds and in what ways traditional aspects of the old days relate to modern life.

The Mythic Past World

It is an accepted premise that we all yearn for a return to some original homeland, a place of safety and peace, where life was ordered and understood and where we were once innocent and free of sin, death, and time. The cultural ingredients that make up Latino life are connected to places distinctly distant from the United States, so Latino writers frequently weave this universal longing into their works, creating fictional characters (or poetic voices) looking longingly toward a world that no longer exists and using patterns of imagery or narrative structure to bring that world into their writing.

---

*See the maps in Chapter 3.

Cuban American writers probably most clearly address the myth of a lost paradise simply because of the political disconnections between that island and the United States. Their physical inability to return to their homeland makes them especially nostalgic for it. Those Cubans who left in the early days of the revolution (between 1959 and 1964) have a particularly potent sense of attachment to the life they abandoned, either voluntarily or not. Later generations of Cuban immigrants—those arriving around the period of the Mariel Boat Lift (1984) or the *balseros* who came in the 1990s—have a different bond with the island that is important to understanding their experience. Cuba is almost always a part of Cuban American literature, even for Cuban writers born several generations from living there.

The literary connections to the lost island of Puerto Rico are different. Some works by Puerto Ricans are nostalgic visions of a rural paradise (the life of the *jíbaro*), but this focus has become less common in more contemporary literature. The urban existence of the Nuyorican is central now, and the dominant issues concern the split between loyalty to the island and life in the United States. More Puerto Ricans live stateside than on the island itself, and the presence of U.S. companies; the pervasive influence of television, movies, and other media; and other aspects of U.S. consumer culture in Puerto Rico have blurred the differences between the two locales. Most Puerto Ricans go back and forth regularly across the so-called *charco*, or puddle. Still, the issue of identity and one's relationship to the past is a central element for mainland Puerto Rican writers. Many are inspired to tackle the dualities and hybrid cultural factors of their world, and they see the lost island through a particularly complex lens. The island itself is always relevant in some way.

For the Chicano, there is first of all the country and the idea of Mexico. Some Chicano works depict the journey to *el Norte* (literally, "the North") in all its complexity and variation, and others redirect the journey back southward as protagonists search for their cultural past and spiritual affiliations. The same sort of nostalgic cultural ties that are in Cuban American and mainland Puerto Rican literature are in the Latino stories, poems, and plays coming out of places such as Texas, California, and other southwestern states. Yet the situation is different, because the mythic country to which Chicanos point as their homeland is not always geographically Mexico; this place of spiritual origin *was once* Mexico but after 1848, it was wrenched away into another, inaccessible country—it became the United States. Hundreds of years ago, Aztec tribes lived in what is now the southwestern United States before moving south, eventually establishing what is now Mexico City. During the 1960s, Chicano activists called this area *Aztlán* to refer to a Mexican mythic homeland. Aztlán has come to be recognized as the origin of the indigenous peoples who became Mexicans after the arrival of Columbus. In Chicano writings, there are references to both the lost world of the home country, Mexico, with all its cultural attachments, and the mythic land beyond the literal reality of Chicano life, with its connections to the *mestizo*, Native American, and noneurocentric spiritual practices and beliefs. Chicanos may be connected to a foreign past world but equally dedicated to regaining some part of these United States as their original homeland.

Descending Toward Self-Discovery

As Homer's Odysseus ventured into the underworld in search of knowledge and direction, journeying into the land of the dead, the past, the unconscious, has been a trip characters take in story after story. In stories by Latino writers, this journey can be a literal one, in which the Latino character actually travels south, or a metaphorical one, in which the character looks introspectively at a Latin American country of origin. In both cases, however, descending into a Latino underground has to do with the character's need for rebirth through the initiation process of understanding the connection between the past, the traditions he or she has grown up with, and the cultural values associated with that lost place. A character, seeking to belong to two worlds at once, journeys south in an attempt to retrieve a part of the self that has been displaced or lost in the turmoil of a usually fast-paced, materialistic U.S. way of life. The character dives into the past to redirect his or her future, just as Odysseus had to learn about the deaths of his mother and Agamemnon before he could find his way home.

The Indigenous Past

The Latinos' "quest" motif frequently points them toward a non-Western tradition. These connections to Africa and to the numerous indigenous populations of the Americas play a role in the search for a cultural heritage. The Latino literary journey south sometimes becomes an attempt to understand the way the world is seen by people who live or have lived with an alternative, yet coherent, system of beliefs. Understanding one's *latinidad* can mean connecting to things beyond the realm of practical, modern life, just as it can also mean understanding the flip side of recent U.S. political history in places such as Grenada, Panama, Guatemala, Nicaragua, Chile, Cuba, and El Salvador.

In concrete terms, this accounts for Latino writers wanting to explore the African religious systems in the Caribbean or the shaman practices of the pre-Columbian Southwest. They seem increasingly interested in examining and referencing the Tainos, Mayans, Incas, Aztecs, Yaquis, and the many other Indian tribes who inhabited the Americas before the Spanish arrived. Consequently, in many Chicano stories and poems, writers refer to *curandero/as*, midwives, herbalists, healers, and *brujo/as*. Fiction and poetry by Chicanas frequently reinvigorates the traditional Mexican folktales of feminine legends such as La Llorona (or La Gritona), La Malinche (or Doña Marina), and the Virgin of Guadalupe; themes of these stories also play essential roles in Chicana feminist literary criticism.

The African Presence

Writers with ties to the Caribbean islands of Puerto Rico, the Dominican Republic, and Cuba also probe beyond their non-European ancestors to find connections with their past. However, these connections are less powerful because the indigenous peoples (Arawaks, Caribs, and Tainos) of these islands were for the most part wiped out by Europeans. What is more essential to Caribbean-based Latino literature is the relationship between writers (or their characters) and the ancestral religious influences stemming from the African Diaspora. The slave populations brought to the "new world" managed to continue their African religious traditions, which flourished with varying levels of success in the different Caribbean islands and the eastern coast lands of South and Central America. From the *quilombos* of Brazil (entire enduring cities built and controlled by escaped slaves) to the communities of maroons in the mountains of Jamaica and especially in Haiti, Africans maintained their cultural ties despite obvious obstacles. In the Spanish-speaking Caribbean, African religious beliefs survived below the surface of the dominating practices of the Spanish Catholic church. The result is a series of syncretic religious systems throughout the Caribbean: *Santería* in Cuba, Puerto Rico, and the Dominican Republic; *Obeah* in Jamaica; *Vodou* in Haiti; and *Candomblé* in Brazil. In the Spanish colonies, Africans (the majority of whom were Yoruba from western Nigeria) continued to worship their own complex pantheon of *orishas*, or spirits, disguising their rituals and practices in the new world by associating each individual African god with a specific Catholic saint: Changó/Saint Barbara, Oggún/Saint Peter, and so on. It is from this blending of religious traditions that the name *Santería*, or "the Worship of the Saints," derives. The rituals and practices (particularly those involving music and dance) eventually meshed with the European cultural traditions in increasingly complicated ways.

In the last few years, as issues of racial attitudes have become more important in the overall search for cultural identity, Latino writers have been progressively exploring these Afro-Latino ancestral heritages in their literary works. Since the early decades of the twentieth century, Latin American writers such as Alejo Carpentier, from Cuba, and Miguel Asturias, from Guatemala, have written of African and indigenous connections, respectively, just as painters such as Wilfredo Lam dealt with the Afro-Cuban world in art. Contemporary Latino writers seem especially devoted to legitimizing and authenticating these sorts of non-European aspects of their family roots. The evidence is in the sheer numbers of references writers are including in their work to *Babalaos*, *santero/as*, offerings, alters, *botanicas*, and the *orishas* themselves: Changó, Oggún, Yemayá, and Eleugguá. Beyond the historical and anthropological significance of these names and ritualistic practices, Latino writers often explore the way such ideas and belief systems influence the question of identity Latinos have today. They frequently juxtapose everyday Latino life in a modern society with the dramatic cultural ties to an African spiritual heritage. Given the extensive mixing of the Spanish conquerors with both indigenous and African populations, it is not hard to explain the present-day Latino writer's interest in both directions of genealogical investigation.

Mining the Harvest

In Latino writing (and perhaps in all writing), the questions "Who am I?" and "Where do I belong?" lead directly into explorations of the family and family heritage. As anyone who has pursued genealogy studies knows, it does not take long for a family tree to become entwined in a chaos of complications. When the roots and branches cover large families in which ancestors traveled back and forth between countries and there were frequent relationships between indigenous and African slave populations, the lines are particularly complex. Latino writers cannot easily avoid the connections that result from tracing back to their ancestors, and once they embark on such examinations, all sorts of questions and problematic issues arise. Which pieces of a family history and which government systems deserve allegiance? What form of spiritual belief is legitimate? What separates superstition from truth? Which cultural rituals, customs, and traditions are antiquated or sexist? Which merit protection? What is the Latino's relationship with ghosts and the dead? Are music and dance somehow inherently tied to the orishas of Africa? What links the *abuela* with the *curandera*, the herbalist with the midwife? What remnants of the conquistador's brutality resurface in family members? What foods are bridges into the Latin American world families are striving to preserve? The answers are the subjects of countless works as Latino writers struggle to juxtapose the flavors of the past with the practical reality of North American mainstream life. These artists journey south to gather the fruits of their cultural past to make sense of the present, to deal with the dualities of living as Latinos within U.S. borders.

FICTION

Rudolfo A. Anaya

Rudolfo Anaya is seen by many as the godfather of Chicano literature. He was born into a large family on October 30, 1937, in Pasturas, New Mexico, and later moved to Albuquerque. His first novel, *Bless Me, Ultima* (1972), is his most famous. Critic Ramón Saldívar has called the book a "New Mexican portrait of the artist as a young boy." Until the recent success of several Latina writers in the 1980s, no Latino work of literature was more highly praised. Besides teaching at the University of Mexico, he has written an extensive number of novels, short stories, essays, and stories for children. Anaya was one of the first Chicano writers to veer away from straight realist, urban portraits of Latinos and structure his work on literary and mythic patterns.

In Search of Epifano

She drove into the desert of Sonora in search of Epifano. For years, when summer came and she finished her classes, she had loaded her old Jeep with supplies and gone south into Mexico.

Now she was almost eighty and, she thought, ready for death but not afraid of death. It was the pain of the bone-jarring journey which was her reality, not thoughts of death. But that did not diminish the urgency she felt as she drove south, across the desert. She was following the north rim of El Cañon de Cobre towards the land of the Tarahumaras. In the Indian villages there was always a welcome and fresh water.

The battered Jeep kicked up a cloud of chalky dust which rose into the empty and searing sky of summer. Around her, nothing moved in the heat. Dry mirages rose and shimmered, without content, without form. Her bright, clear eyes remained fixed on the rocky, rutted road in front. Around her there was only the vast and empty space of the desert. The dry heat.

The Jeep wrenched sideways, the low gear groaning and complaining. It had broken down once, and had cost her many days' delay in Mexicali. The mechanic at the garage told her not to worry. In one day the parts would be in Calexico and she would be on her way.

5   But she knew the way of the Mexican, so she rented a room in a hotel nearby. Yes, she knew the Mexican. Part of her blood was Mexican, wasn't it? Her great-grandfather, Epifano, had come north to Chihuahua to ranch and mine. She knew the stories whispered about the man, how he had built a great ranch in the desert. His picture was preserved in the family album, at his side his wife, a dark-haired woman. Around them, their sons.

The dry desert air burned her nostrils. A scent of the green ocotillo reached her, reminded her of other times, other years. She knew how to live in the sun, how to travel and how to survive, and she knew how to be alone under the stars. Night was her time in the desert. She liked to lie in her bedroll and look up at the swirling dance of the stars. In the cool of evening, her pulse would quicken. The sure path of the stars was her map, drawing her south.

Sweat streaked her wrinkled skin. Sweat and dust, the scent commingling. She felt alive. "At least I'm not dry and dead," she said aloud. Sweat and pleasure, it came together.

The Jeep worried her now. A sound somewhere in the gearbox was not right. "It has trouble," the mechanic had said, wiping his oily hands on a dirty rag. What he meant was that he did not trust his work. It was best to return home, he suggested with a shrug. He had seen her musing over the old and tattered map, and he was concerned about the old woman going south. Alone. It was not good.

"We all have trouble," she mumbled. We live too long and the bones get brittle and the blood dries up. Why can't I taste the desert in my mouth? Have I grown so old? Epifano? How does it feel to become a spirit of the desert?

10   Her back and arms ached from driving; she was covered with the dust of the desert. Deep inside, in her liver or in her spleen, in one of those organs that the ancients called the seat of life, there was an ache, a dull, persistent pain. In her heart there was a tightness. Would she die and never reach the land of Epifano?

She slept while she waited for the Jeep to be repaired. Slept and dreamed under the shade of the laurel in the patio of the small hotel. Around her, Mexican sounds and colors permeated her dream. What did she dream? That it was too late in her life to go once again into the desert? That she was an old woman and her life was lived, and the only evidence she would leave of her existence would be her sketches and paintings? Even now, as weariness filled her, the dreams came, and she slipped in and out of past and present. In her dreams she heard the voice of the old man, Epifano.

She saw his eyes, blue and bright like hers, piercing but soft. The eyes of a kind man. He had died. Of course, he had died. He belonged to the past. But she had not forgotten him. In the family album, which she carried with her, his gaze was the one that looked out at her and drew her into the desert. She was the artist of the family. She had taken up painting. She heard voices. The voice of her great-grandfather. The rest of her family had forgotten the past, forgotten Mexico and the old man, Epifano.

The groaning of the Jeep shattered the silence of the desert. She tasted dust in her mouth, she yearned for a drink of water. She smiled. A thirst to be satisfied. Always there was one more desire to be satisfied. Her paintings were like that, a desire from within to be satisfied, a call to do one more sketch of the desert in the molten light before night came. And always the voice of Epifano drawing her to the trek into the past.

The immense solitude of the desert swallowed her. She was only a moving shadow in the burning day. Overhead, vultures circled in the sky, the heat grew intense. She was alone on a dirt road she barely remembered, taking her bearings only by instinct, roughly following the north rim of the Cañon de Cobre, drawn by the thin line of the horizon, where the dull peaks of las montañas met the dull blue of the sky. Whirlwinds danced in her eyes, memories flooded at her soul.

15 She had married young. She thought she was in love; he was a man of ambition. It took her years to learn that he had little desire or passion. He could not, or would not, fulfill her. What was the fulfillment she sought? It had to do with something that lay even beneath the moments of love or children carried in the womb. Of that she was sure.

She turned to painting, she took classes, she traveled alone. She came to understand that she and the man were not meant for each other.

She remembered a strange thing had happened in the chapel where the family gathered to attend her marriage. An Indian had entered and stood at the back of the room. She had turned and looked at him. Then he was gone, and later she was not sure if the appearance was real or imagined.

But she did not forget. She had looked into his eyes. He had the features of a Tarahumara. Was he Epifano's messenger? Had he brought a warning? For a moment she hesitated, then she had turned and said yes to the preacher's question. Yes to the man who could never understand the depth of her passion. She did what was expected of her there in the land of ocean and sun. She bore him a daughter and a son. But in all those years, the man never understood the desire in her, he never explored her depth of passion. She turned to

her dreams, and there she heard the voice of Epifano, a resonant voice impart-
ing seductive images of the past.

Years later she left her husband, left everything, left the dream of southern
California where there was no love in the arms of the man, no sweet juices in
the nights of love pretended. She left the circle of pretend. She needed a meaning, she needed desperately to understand the voices which spoke in her soul.
She drove south, alone, in search of Epifano. The desert dried her by day, but
replenished her at night. She learned that the mystery of the stars at night was
like the mystery in her soul.

20   She sketched, she painted, and each year in springtime she drove farther
south. On her map she marked her goal, the place where once stood Epifano's
hacienda.

In the desert the voices were clear. She followed the road into Tarahumara
country, she dreamed of the old man, Epifano. She was his blood, the only one
who remembered him.

At the end of day she stood at the side of a pool of water, a small, desert spring
surrounded by desert trees. The smell of the air was cool, wet. At her feet, tracks
of deer, a desert cat. Ocelot. She stooped to drink, like a cautious animal.

"Thank the gods for this water which quenches our thirst," she said, splash-
ing the precious water on her face, knowing there is no life in the desert without the water which flows from deep within the earth. Around her, the first
stars of dusk began to appear.

She had come at last to the ranch of Epifano. There, below the spring where
she stood, on the flat ground, was the hacienda. Now could be seen only the
outlines of the foundation and the shape of the old corrals. From here his family had spread, northwest, up into Mexicali and finally into southern California. Seeds. Desert seeds seeking precious water. The water of desire. And only
she had returned.

25   She sat and gazed at the desert, the peaceful, quiet mauve of the setting sun.
She felt a deep sadness within. An old woman, sitting alone in the wide desert,
her dream done.

A noise caused her to turn. Perhaps an animal come to drink at the spring,
the same spring where Epifano had once wet his lips. She waited, and in the
shadows of the palo verde and the desert willows she saw the Indian appear.
She smiled.

She was dressed in white, the color of desire not consummated. Shadows
moved around her. She had come home, home to the arms of Epifano. The
Indian was a tall, splendid man. Silent. He wore paint, as they did in the old
days when they ran the game of the pelota up and down las montañas of the
Cañon de Cobre.

"Epifano," she said, "I came in search of Epifano." He understood
the name. Epifano. He held his hand to his chest. His eyes were bright and
blue, not Tarahumara eyes, but the eyes of Epifano. He had known she would
come. Around her, other shadows moved, the women. Indian women of the
desert. They moved silently around her, a circle of women, an old ceremony
about to begin.

The sadness left her. She struggled to rise, and in the dying light of the sun a blinding flash filled her being. Like desire, or like an arrow from the bow of the Indian, the light filled her and she quivered.

30 The moan of love is like the moan of life. She was dressed in white.

Daniel Chacón

Daniel Chacón was born in California and graduated from the University of Oregon. He has published a single collection of short fiction, *Chicano Chicanery* (2002). His stories concentrate on the quirky male characters of the Latino working class in a wide variety of situations. He has also written a novel entitled *and the shadows took him: A Novel* (2004). Like Dagoberto Gilb, and to some extent, Oscar Hijuelos, Chacón is unafraid to sound sexist or politically incorrect, and his biting, sometimes sarcastic humor is uncommon to Latino fiction.

The Biggest City in the World

Harvey Gomez stepped off the plane in Mexico City and couldn't believe what he saw: Among the multitudes of *mestizos* walking through the airport was Professor David P. Rogstart, followed by a little Mexican boy carrying his luggage. Gomez quickly showed his papers to the Mexican official and ran through the crowd to catch the professor. When he got close enough to where he could see the familiar red-orange shine of Rogstart's bald head, he yelled, "Professor Rogstart! Professor Rogstart!"

The professor, at least a foot taller than almost everyone else in the airport, turned around, not as if surprised to hear his name, but with impatience, as if to say, "What do you want now?"

Gomez jumped on his toes as he walked, trying to show himself above the heads of the Mexicans. He raised his hands and yelled, "Here, Professor, here!"

Gomez tried to move faster, but the crowd was too dense. Then a little Indian woman, even shorter than him, stood right in front of him with sad eyes, a wrinkled face, and an empty palm extended for alms. "*Por favor, joven, regálame un taco.*"[1]

5 "Yeah, right," he said to himself as he twisted around her like a matador. Finally, he reached the professor.

"Professor, it's me!"

Rogstart stopped and looked around, but his gaze was high, so Gomez, feeling a little silly, had to raise his arm, as if to say, "I'm down here."

"Oh, hello, Harvey," the professor said, as if running into him were something ordinary.

But Gomez didn't think it was ordinary, so he spilled out his words like a child: "Imagine you and I seeing each other in the world's biggest city! How weird! Isn't that the weirdest thing in the world?"

---

[1]"Please, young one, let me have a taco."

10   "Actually, no," said the professor, quite calmly. "In fact, it makes a lot of sense that we would run into each other."

"How's that?"

The professor, removing the specs from his pale blue eyes, spoke with a hint of impatience, like professors sound when asked questions that have already been answered. "You're a graduate student," he said, "who studies Mexico. I'm a professor and scholar of Mexican history. It's winter vacation, so we have a month off. This is an historically important city. In fact, the only thing that might surprise me is that we weren't on the same flight."

"But Mexico City's the biggest city in the world!"

"It makes complete sense," Rogstart said, the subject closed.

15   A Mexican man in rags came up and asked something of the professor, but he spoke so fast that Gomez could hardly catch it. The professor pulled some change from his pocket and gave it to the man, who bowed "thank you" and then looked at Gomez with begging eyes. The man's teeth were rotten and he smelled like mildew and motor oil. Gomez felt in his pocket for his roll of bills. After having saved money for years and having won the Hispanic Scholarship Award from the Grape Growers of America Association, this was the first time that he was able to travel. His father, a postal worker, never had enough money to help him with school, and, in fact, spent most of his life in debt. This beggar must have seen a rich man when he saw Gomez. Although the student was simply dressed in black canvas slacks, a pullover shirt with the Polo emblem at the breast, and comfortable black shoes, each item of clothing, Gomez figured, probably cost more money than the man earned in a year. Still, he wasn't rich, and it seemed a crime to just give money away to this stranger. He felt the roll of bills in his front pocket.

"I don't have any change," he said.

"Anything will be fine," the man said, his eyelids collapsing with sadness and fatigue.

Gomez looked up at Rogstart, who turned away.

"Just go," Gomez said softly.

20   The man made a show of thanking Rogstart again, looked at Gomez one last time through the thick hair that hung over his face, and then walked off with as much dignity as he could muster.

"Well, Harvey, I hope you have a fine vacation," said the professor.

"Oh, thank you, thank you, sir," Gomez said, as the professor walked off.

At baggage claim, he found the worn, vinyl suitcase that had belonged to his grandparents and dragged it through the airport which seemed to grow bigger and wider with every step, like a coliseum flooded with lights. A boy came up and asked him something, but Gomez didn't understand because he spoke too fast, so the boy asked in English, "Carry your bag, *joven?*" [2]

"Oh, I speak Spanish," Gomez said in English. "I just didn't hear what you said. And no thank you. I'll carry my own bag."

---

[2] young one

25   Outside, the heavy, gray air smelled of gasoline and exhaust fumes, and the wide streets were wild with cars and noise. With both hands grasping the handle, he held his suitcase in front of him. Hundreds of taxicabs swarmed around like sharks or were triple parked at the curbs. He looked for a bald red-orange head in the back of the cabs, hoping it wasn't too late to share a ride, but he saw only Mexicans, sometimes entire families squeezed into the back seats. He thought about going back inside the airport to call his father in California and let him know that he had arrived safely, but he wasn't sure how the phone system worked and was too afraid to ask. So he stood, his suitcase getting heavier.

Out the window of his high-rise hotel, he watched the golden angel. She stood on an ivory-colored base in the center of the traffic circle where Avenida de la Reforma meets Insurgentes, her arms raised to the heavens. These were large, wide avenues, the likes of which he had never seen except on postcards or in movies set in Paris. A stream of cars flowed around the circle from all directions, many of them green and white VW Bugs, taxis, which from his window looked like toys. He could see, too, the rooftops of La Zona Rosa, the rich shopping district, and he could see the glass towers of the most expensive hotels sparkling over the dull-colored city. The sun, trying to burst through the blanket of smog, appeared like a vague circle in the gray sky.

He had never been on a plane before, so for the first time he suffered jet lag. Every time he paced the room, it felt as if the floor were moving. He was content to stay in his bed until it passed, like a patient determined to enjoy the rest that sickness brought.

After two days, he rose from his bed, left the room, rode down the elevator, and stepped onto the street. The tunnel of brownstone buildings, crumbling yet dignified, looked like a scene in Europe. Small trees and old street lamps shaped like giant candles rose from the cracked sidewalks. He sighed contentedly. "A beautiful city," he said. Then he went back inside. The next day he was bored enough to leave his room and walk onto the wide, busy avenue toward the golden angel and into the heart of La Zona Rosa. The expensive shops, Gucci, Polo, Yves St. Laurent, relaxed him because they reminded him of Beverly Hills, a place he had once driven through.

He chose an outdoor Italian cafe for lunch and for planning his itinerary, minus the three days he had spent in his room. The weather was sunny and breezy, and the overhanging trees surrounding the buildings kept out the gasoline smell of the city. He was happy.

30   Then something happened.

The busboy tapped him on the shoulder and said, "*¿Qué 'stas haciendo aquí, primo?*" [3]

In his head, Gomez tried to understand what the guy had said, but he had spoken so fast. "Kay Deesay?" he asked.

The boy looked surprised at Gomez, as if he had expected smooth easy Spanish to flow from his mouth, not slow deliberate words which fell like

---

[3]"What are you doing here, cousin?"

chunks. "Oh, nothing," the boy said in accented English. "I thought you were…" and left on the table a glass of water and a basket of bread.

The waiter took his order in English. As Gomez started eating, he was surprised again when he saw Professor Rogstart, this time coming into the same restaurant. He carried a newspaper under his arm and sat a few tables away. Gomez was sure the professor would be surprised now. What were the chances of seeing each other twice in the world's biggest city? Gomez sat silently, hoping the professor would see him, but he was so preoccupied with his newspaper that he didn't look up.

35   Leaning back in his chair, Gomez said, like a movie villain who has finally trapped the desperate hero, "Well professor, what do you think now?"

The professor looked up. "Oh, hello, Harvey. How are you today?" he said, calmly. Gomez took a drink of his water—nervously hoping it was safe to sip—and said, "Don't tell me that you're not surprised to see me again. This is pretty weird that we see each other, not once, but twice in the world's biggest city. Wouldn't you say?"

"Actually, I wouldn't," the professor said, patiently folding his newspaper. "Indeed I find your surprise at this to be the only strange thing. We're in La Zona Rosa, which is only a four or five block area, full of people from the U.S. My hotel is here, your hotel is probably here. It makes complete sense that I would see you, especially at this restaurant. It's very popular with *gringos*."

Gomez felt like reminding the professor that he wasn't a *gringo*.

"The food is good," the professor continued, "the service is excellent, and the prices reasonable. Completely logical." Then, as if to further his point, the professor spoke the history of La Zona Rosa, why it had always been a place for Europeans and Americans to gather.

40   As Gomez listened, he realized something: Rogstart was enjoying this conversation, as if they were colleagues talking about some fine historical point. He wanted to turn the conversation into Spanish so the waiter and busboys would know what high things they spoke of, scholars both, but he didn't try because he wasn't sure he could be as articulate. Still, he listened, nodded his head, and to satisfy that need to speak Spanish, he said, "*sí, sí*" nodding, nodding. "*Sí, sí*," with different inflections, and when the professor said something he had already known, "Ooooh, *síí, sí*." He had always wanted to have a deep discussion with Rogstart, one of the world's leading historians on Mexico. He wanted to get up, join him at his table, and they could spend all day together drinking strong Italian coffee and talking about history. But after the professor was done lecturing, he looked down at his newspaper and continued reading. He never invited Gomez to the table. He didn't look up again except for when he left, telling Gomez to have a good day.

When he got his bill, he couldn't believe it was so expensive, a hundred dollars. He wanted to complain but didn't want to seem too cheap. He was going to pay, touching the roll of bills in his front pocket, when he realized, feeling a bit *silly, that it was in pesos*, not dollars. He left a fifty-peso tip and went back to his hotel room.

The next time the student saw the professor, he suppressed the feeling of surprise. He spotted him at the Aztec ruins which stubbornly stuck from the ground in the downtown plaza, the *zócalo*, between the ancient cathedral and the palace of the government. Rogstart was looking with reverence at a stone slab carved with the faces of Aztec gods. Gomez approached and stood next to him, putting his hands on the rail, and he, too, looked at the faces. One of them had an open mouth and wide eyes as if frightened. Gomez wondered how many Aztecs were scared into believing in their gods, like his father tried to make him believe in Jesus and the Virgin Mary, using stories of Hell and fire, religious baggage he was glad to toss in the closet when he went away to college. Now he was a scholar first and foremost.

As he continued to stare at the masks, he calmly said. "This time I'm not surprised, Professor. You're right, it makes complete sense. You're a scholar of Mexican history, I'm a sch—... a student of Mexican history. So it makes a whole lot of sense that we're both here at this Aztec ruin. I mean, doesn't it?"

Rogstart looked at him, surprised. "No, actually, this time I'm surprised."

45 "Really?"

"I think this qualifies as quite a coincidence," Rogstart said.

"Yeah, I guess so. So, uh, is this the first time you've been here? It is for me."

"I've been here more times than I can count," Rogstart said. "I used to live a few blocks away from here." His eyes suddenly looked dreamy, as if he were about to share some intimate memory with Gomez, but he shook it off and went back to examining the faces. As the silence grew between them, Gomez felt the pressure to say something profound about history, so with a voice that pretended at religious awe, he said. "Think of it: Here was the great city of Tenochtitlan. And the Spaniards destroyed it all. This is all that remains."

Immediately he knew what he had said didn't sound as scholarly as he had hoped, but rather like something a tourist would say. He knew he had to say something else so the words didn't hang in the air like a sign advertising his simplicity.

50 "How did you get here from La Zona Rosa?" he asked.

"I rode the metro," said the professor.

"Oh. I took a cab."

And it was expensive and the driver, impatient with Gomez' Spanish, wouldn't answer his questions and probably took advantage of him. He suspected that tourists didn't have to pay one hundred pesos more than what the meter read, which was, the cab driver had said, the price for Mexican citizens. He would have asked Professor Rogstart how much he should have paid, but didn't want to appear naive. In fact, as a man with Mexican blood, he should be more knowledgeable than Rogstart, but he had only been to Tijuana one Friday night with a bunch of drunk friends when he was an undergraduate. What he knew about Mexico that was not from a book or from Rogstart was what his grandparents had told him. They had described their tiny ranch in Michoacán, a place he had never seen but often dreamed of, sometimes imagining himself returning to reclaim their land. He pictured the townsfolk, men dressed in white cotton pants and *huaraches*, women in long dresses and flowers in their hair.

The Mexicans are gathered around a gazebo in the town plaza, whispering to each other, wondering who he is, this tall, dark stranger who walks with such authority.

55   But, of course, he wasn't tall, just dark, very dark.

Now he wanted to take the bus or the metro back to his hotel because it would be cheaper, but he didn't know how and wasn't even sure whom to ask for such directions. It was less intimidating to take a cab, but expensive. He hadn't that much money. He put his hand in his pant pocket to feel the roll. It was still there, but thinner than before.

He watched as Rogstart stared at the masks.

He asked the professor, "When are you going back?"

"To California?" the professor asked.

60   "No, to La Zona Rosa," Gomez said.

"Later."

Gomez said, "Do you mind if I tag along with you? I mean, maybe you can show me some things."

Rogstart didn't say anything. He sighed discontentedly, and, as if he hadn't heard him, he said, "I'm off, Harvey. Have a good day."

"Can I come with you? I mean, for a little while?"

65   Rogstart put his hands on his hips and looked around the sky. "Sure, I guess. Come on."

For the first time Gomez was able to enjoy Mexico City. They went to the palace of the government and saw the Diego Rivera murals that depicted the Spanish conquest of Mexico. Rogstart, feeling a professorial obligation, explained to Gomez the meaning of each panel, each symbol, giving such fine details that other tourists stopped and listened, too; and some, as if students in his class, asked questions. Gomez felt a sense of pride as Rogstart spoke and the people listened, like a boy proud of his father. When one of the tourists asked a question about an historical fact, Rogstart turned to Gomez and said, "I think Professor Gomez can answer that one."

Gomez was high. "Yes, I uh, think the best way to answer that is to consider the lifestyle of the *mayaque*, which was, essentially, the Aztec *peon...*"

People listened.

On the way out, as they descended the wide stairs to the bottom floor, Rogstart pulled from his pant pocket a box of mints, shook a few of the green pellets into his palm, threw them in his mouth, and sucked, his jaw moving back and forth. Then he held the tiny box to Gomez, who gladly opened his palm.

70   They walked through the *zócalo*.[4] He wanted to invite Rogstart to a nice place for lunch. He felt in his pocket for the roll of bills, wondering where Rogstart would choose and how much it would cost.

---

[4]main square

They walked past the booths where Indians and mestizos sold T-shirts, jewelry, and handmade dolls dressed like the New Zapatistas in Chiapas. The professor stopped at a booth where an Indian woman sold what looked to Gomez like thick blue tortillas smothered with some sort of grey-green paste. It looked sickening to him, but the professor was apparently excited as he waited for the lady to prepare his. He turned around and asked Gomez if he wanted one, too. "No, no, thank you," he said. "In fact, I was going take you to lunch, sir. If you want."

"This is enough for me," Rogstart said, turning around to watch the lady prepare his food.

Gomez noticed a booth where someone was selling used books. He walked over and looked at the titles and saw an old copy of *México Viejo*, a history book. The vendor, a young man with long hair and beard, watched. When he asked how much he wanted for the book, the vendor looked him up and down, as if it were Gomez that was being sold. "Fifty pesos," he said.

Gomez, wondering if it was worth it, turned to ask Rogstart.

75 The professor was happily eating his fat blue tortilla. Gomez stepped toward him, but between them came a stream of Aztec dancers, young people with plumed head dresses. One of the dancers waved and said something to the young bookseller.

When the stream of dancers passed, Rogstart wasn't in the same spot.

Gomez walked over to the food booth and looked around, but he couldn't see the familiar head in the crowd.

Then the *zócalo* exploded with voices, car horns, and thumping of feet of thousands of people. The Aztec dancers began their dance by blowing a horn and ritually facing the four directions, the leader holding a vase of burning sage to the heavens. They wore colorful, feathered costumes and had bare feet, with ankle bracelets of clanking nuts. The twirling of feathers and bodies made the sound of wind through trees.

He turned toward the lady selling the food, who held out a plate and asked if he wanted one. Unconsciously, he held his stomach, as if he might vomit, and said, in broken Spanish, no thank you, but did she see what happened to the tall white guy who was standing here eating? The lady laughed, her broken teeth showing through the flabby, wrinkled mouth.

80 He turned around, and a man and a woman stood in front of him, their palms open, faces twisted with hunger. They said, *Un peso por favor.*[5]

"Get away from me," he said.

He spun around and walked through the *zócalo* searching for his professor. Other beggars, ladies, children, old men were determined to get something from him, anything. They practically surrounded him. *Un peso por favor.*

"No!" he screamed, breaking through and running deeper into the plaza, looking for that red-orange bald head. The young man at the book booth yelled, "*¿Y México Viejo? ¿No quieres México Viejo?*"[6]

---

[5]"A peso, please."
[6]"And Old Mexico? Don't you want *Old Mexico?*"

He went into the cathedral hoping the professor might be there, because it was the first cathedral in Mexico and of great historical significance.

85   Inside he felt a spirit of peace in the air, but every time it tried to enter him, he resisted and went on walking deeper into the darkness, the ancient walls rising around him like canyons of a desert. All the voices of the tourists and worshipers were as one, the sound of wind whispering off walls. The interior was held up by crisscrossing metal scaffolds. The further he went into the belly of the cathedral, the darker it got and the more things glowed: statues of saints, Jesus, and La Virgen, gold crosses, communion goblets.

He sat at a wooden pew before one of the altars and caught his breath. He knew Rogstart would be in here, and this time, when he saw him, he wouldn't let him go. He would beg, plead if he had to, *please, let me follow you around,* for the rest of the trip, not as his equal, but as a student, a servant if Rogstart wanted. He'd even carry his luggage. The city scared him.

But Rogstart was nowhere in the cathedral.

Gomez ran, still determined to find him, into sunlight and smog. At the cathedral gate, a lady with one foot, her wound white with pus and slimy red, her eyes brimming with pain, sat holding up an empty hand. She said to Gomez, looking into his eyes, *por favor, por favor,* but he ran around her, through the *zócalo.* He remembered that the museum of Bellas Artes was nearby, so he asked what looked like a white tourist for directions. He ran out of the *zócalo,* through a narrow downtown street whose tall, old buildings rose up around him like the walls of a dark, cold dungeon. He passed little ladies sitting on blankets selling *chicle,*[7] skinny children with their open palms raised, lone men sitting on curbs, mangy dogs sniffing for food. He ran all the way to the museum, a grand structure shining like a white mosque in the middle of the gray city. He paid the twenty pesos to get in and looked around, not at art, but for Rogstart.

He never found him, and an hour later he sat on the wide steps of the museum.

90   He didn't care how much it would cost. He didn't care that the driver might make fun of his Spanish or roll his eyes when he spoke English; he didn't care that he had come so far from home and had not seen or would not see anything he had come to see. Chapúltepec Park, the Museum of Anthropology, the pyramids. All he cared about was getting a taxi back to his hotel, where he would close the curtains in his room and lay on the bed—for the rest of the vacation. He hated Mexico. He'd order room service and watch TV. Might even change his graduate school emphasis to European History.

Across the street, several taxis were lined up at the curb, so he stood up and walked toward them. He slipped his hand into his pocket for his roll of bills. When he didn't feel the money there, he felt, for a flash, a sense of panic, but he chuckled at his foolishness when he figured he had put it in his other pocket.

He put his hand in the other pocket.

Empty.

---

[7]gum

"Oh shit," he said as he patted his back pockets. "Oh, shit, no."

95   His shirt pockets.

"Oh, God no," he whispered. "Please, God, don't do this to me." He felt his ankles just in case he forgot that he had put it in his socks, but all he felt was bone.

"Oh shit. Oh shit. Oh shit," he chanted as he walked around in circles, trying not to panic, trying to believe there was some explanation.

But all that came to him was that he had lost it.

"No. No."

100 He walked quickly up the wide stairs of the museum, but a security guard pulled him by the arm and told him something in Spanish.

"I paid already," Gomez said, but the man, wearing a blue suit and tie with a wire to his ear like a Secret Service agent, calmly shrugged his shoulders to show he didn't understand English. He pointed to the ticket window downstairs.

"Please," said Gomez, about to cry, as if saying it made it more true: "I just lost all my money. Please, I have to look!"

The guard began to lead Gomez down the stairs, but the student twisted from his grip and ran up. "Sorry," he yelled. "I have to find it."

It was all he had, the whole roll. And because he had feared that the hotel maid would go through his things and find it, he hadn't left any of it in his room. He ran, chanting, "Oh, no, oh no, no no no no."

105 People stepped out of the way and watched him and the two security guards chasing him. He ran up another flight of stairs. And then he saw it. On the ground, the cash wad reflecting on the shiny floor. "Oh, thank you," he whispered as he shifted into a higher gear, running as fast as he could. Before he got to it, he slid to a stop as if he were on ice. He bent down and grabbed a crumpled up, empty pack of cigarettes. The security guards grabbed him by both arms.

"I lost my money," he cried, as they dragged him outdoors, all the way across the museum plaza, and discarded him on the sidewalk.

He ran back to the *zócalo*, searched the floors of the cathedral, the government palace, and then found, standing side by side watching the dancers, the young book vendor and the lady with the blue tortillas. He asked them if they had seen a roll of money, at which they looked at each other and laughed.

After he didn't know where to look anymore, he walked back and forth from the museum to the *zócalo*, his arms out, as if grabbing for something in the air, a gesture of which he wasn't conscious. Dirt and dust had gotten on his clothes and his hair was disheveled. He had no credit cards, no ATM card. He couldn't call his father, who had no money and would just call him an idiot. If he didn't find Rogstart, then he had no hope. He mumbled *No no no no no*.

A white couple, walking hand and hand in his direction, saw him and averted their gaze. One young American girl, a hippie in her twenties, dressed in a peasant skirt and with her hair in braids, watched him with compassionate blue eyes, and when he passed, she said, "*¿Señor?*" and put a coin in his extended hand. He kept walking, without panic because shock had set in. At an outdoor cafe, he approached a blue-eyed man eating his lunch. "I lost all my money. All my money."

110   The man wore an expensive suit and tie. He shrugged his shoulders and said, "*No hablo inglés,*"[8] and gave Gomez some coins. Gomez turned around and, without looking to see if it were safe, crossed a narrow side street. A taxi braked to avoid hitting him and the driver honked the horn, angrily raising his fist in the air, but when Gomez—with a wave of his hand—indicated that he needed a cab, the driver smiled and nodded and pulled over.

    "I don't speak Spanish," he said, as he entered. "Take me to the Zona Rosa."

    "I thought you were Mexican," said the cab driver.

    "No, no I'm not. The Zona Rosa please."

    "Yes, sir," the driver said. He was a chubby-faced man with large, gold eyes and a balding head.

115   The cab pulled onto the street. A picture dangled from the rear view mirror, the sacred, bloody heart of Jesus. Gomez leaned back, and for some reason he felt relaxed. He knew that he would have to find a way to run from the cab before it got to his hotel, but he would bother with the details later, because it was a long drive.

    He hoped.

    "I don't have a meter," said the driver, looking over his shoulder at Gomez.

    "That's okay."

    "It cost one hundred pesos."

120   "That's fine," said Gomez. And it felt good saying it. Charge me two hundred, he might have told the driver.

    "You are visiting Mexico for pleasure?"

    "Pure pleasure," Gomez said, and that made him feel even better, more relaxed.

    "Have you go to the Basilica? *Muy* beautiful."

    "No, not yet."

125   "I take you there. I can show you many beautiful places."

    Gomez nodded, acknowledging his offer. At an intersection they waited at a red light, where a dark, dirty young man stood facing the line of waiting cars, as if he were on stage and they were the audience. With a flourish he held up a flaming stick in one hand and an old plastic milk container in the other. He drank from the container and put the flame into his mouth and blew out fire like a dragon. He did this several times and then bowed for applause. He went to the car windows with an open hand. Most people ignored him through their closed windows, but a few gave. When he got to Gomez, he said, "*Por favor.*" Gomez handed him the coins the people had given him. The cab driver, watching through the rear view mirror, smiled.

    When they got close to La Zona Rosa, Gomez began to worry. How could he escape? The cab was a VW Bug and he would have to flee from the

---

[8]"I don't speak English."

passenger's side, somehow lifting the front seat, grabbing the door handle and jumping out. He looked down the side streets to see where he might run.

That's when he saw him walking into a fancy hotel made of glass: Professor David P. Rogstart.

Then the cab pulled over. "Here we are," said the driver.

130   He was going to yell out the window, "Professor, Help!" but something stopped him, some nagging deep in his heart. He looked in the rear view mirror at the cab driver's gaze, those large eyes, and he thought of his father. When Gomez had told him about the trip, his father, who hardly ever had something good to say, was actually proud. Gomez could tell.

"I never been there," he told his son, unbuttoning his postal worker's jacket.

"It's the biggest city in the world," Gomez said.

"Yeah, that's good," said the father. "Maybe you're not such a big dummy after all."

"I changed my mind," Gomez said to the cab driver.

135   "What is that?" asked the driver.

"I don't want the Zona Rosa."

"No?"

He looked out the window. "Take me to Chapúltepec Park."

"Oh, yes," said the driver, seeming very happy. "It's beautiful there. You must see the castle where jumped *los niños herores*.[9] You know this story?" he asked.

140   "Yeah, yeah, take me there. And after that let's go to Garibaldi Square."

"You like the music of mariachis, eh?"

"I love it," said Gomez. "Love it."

"*Ay*, see?" said the driver, pointing his finger at Gomez, "You *are* a Mexican!"

They laughed as the taxi pulled into traffic.

Sandra Cisneros

Probably the most well-known Latina writer today, Cisneros was born in Chicago in 1954. She has written books of poetry, including *My Wicked Wicked Ways* (1987) and *Loose Woman* (1994), children's books, and three major contributions to Latino fiction: *The House on Mango Street* (1984), *Woman Hollering Creek* (1991), and *Caramelo* (2002). Cisneros's heroine Esperanza, the narrator of *The House on Mango Street*, is probably the most famous Latina protagonist in Latino literature. In Esperanza, Cisneros gave voice to a feisty Latina spirit and a strength of female character that had not been heard from before. Cisneros's activist commitment to working-class Latinos and Latinas is always conveyed in stylistically inventive and lyrical writing, with an emphasis on detail and a poet's acute sensibility to the sounds of prose.

---

[9]the heroic children

One Holy Night

About the truth, if you give it to a person, then he has power over you. And if someone gives it to you, then they have made themselves your slave. It is a strong magic. You can never take it back.

—*Chaq Uxmal Paloquin*

He said his name was Chaq. Chaq Uxmal Paloquin. That's what he told me. He was of an ancient line of Mayan kings. Here, he said, making a map with the heel of his boot, this is where I come from, the Yucatán, the ancient cities. This is what Boy Baby said.

It's been eighteen weeks since Abuelita chased him away with the broom, and what I'm telling you I never told nobody, except Rachel and Lourdes, who know everything. He said he would love me like a revolution, like a religion. Abuelita burned the pushcart and sent me here, miles from home, in this town of dust, with one wrinkled witch woman who rubs my belly with jade, and sixteen nosy cousins.

I don't know how many girls have gone bad from selling cucumbers. I know I'm not the first. My mother took the crooked walk too, I'm told, and I'm sure my Abuelita has her own story, but it's not my place to ask.

Abuelita says it's Uncle Lalo's fault because he's the man of the family and if he had come home on time like he was supposed to and worked the pushcart on the days he was told to and watched over his goddaughter, who is too foolish to look after herself, nothing would've happened, and I wouldn't have to be sent to Mexico. But Uncle Lalo says if they had never left Mexico in the first place, shame enough would have kept a girl from doing devil things.

5   I'm not saying I'm not bad. I'm not saying I'm special. But I'm not like the Allport Street girls, who stand in doorways and go with men into alleys.

All I know is I didn't want it like that. Not against the bricks or hunkering in somebody's car. I wanted it come undone like gold thread, like a tent full of birds. The way it's supposed to be, the way I knew it would be when I met Boy Baby.

But you must know, I was no girl back then. And Boy Baby was no boy. Chaq Uxmal Paloquin. Boy Baby was a man. When I asked him how old he was he said he didn't know. The past and the future are the same thing. So he seemed boy and baby and man all at once, and the way he looked at me, how do I explain?

I'd park the pushcart in front of the Jewel food store Saturdays. He bought a mango on a stick the first time. Paid for it with a new twenty. Next Saturday he was back. Two mangoes, lime juice, and chili powder, keep the change. The third Saturday he asked for a cucumber spear and ate it slow. I didn't see him after that till the day he brought me Kool-Aid in a plastic cup. Then I knew what I felt for him.

Maybe you wouldn't like him. To you he might be a bum. Maybe he looked it. Maybe. He had broken thumbs and burnt fingers. He had thick greasy fingernails he never cut and dusty hair. And all his bones were strong ones like a man's. I waited every Saturday in my same blue dress. I sold all the mango and cucumber, and then Boy Baby would come finally.

10   What I knew of Chaq was only what he told me, because nobody seemed to know where he came from. Only that he could speak a strange language that no one could understand, said his name translated into boy, or boy-child, and so it was the street people nick-named him Boy Baby.

I never asked about his past. He said it was all the same and didn't matter, past and the future all the same to his people. But the truth has a strange way of following you, of coming up to you and making you listen to what it has to say.

Night time. Boy Baby brushes my hair and talks to me in his strange language because I like to hear it. What I like to hear him tell is how he is Chaq, Chaq of the people of the sun, Chaq of the temples, and what he says sounds sometimes like broken clay, and at other times like hollow sticks, or like the swish of old feathers crumbling into dust.

He lived behind Esparza & Sons Auto Repair in a little room that used to be a closet—pink plastic curtains on a narrow window, a dirty cot covered with newspapers, and a cardboard box filled with socks and rusty tools. It was there, under one bald bulb, in the back room of the Esparza garage, in the single room with pink curtains, that he showed me the guns—twenty-four in all. Rifles and pistols, one rusty musket, a machine gun, and several tiny weapons with mother-of-pearl handles that looked like toys. So you'll see who I am, he said, laying them all out on the bed of newspapers. So you'll understand. But I didn't want to know.

The stars foretell everything, he said, My birth, My son's. The boy-child who will bring back the grandeur of my people from those who have broken the arrows, from those who have pushed the ancient stones off their pedestals.

15   Then he told how he had prayed in the Temple of the Magician years ago as a child when his father had made him promise to bring back the ancient ways. Boy Baby had cried in the temple dark that only the bats made holy. Boy Baby who was man and child among the great and dusty guns lay down on the newspaper bed and wept for a thousand years. When I touched him, he looked at me with the sadness of stone.

You must not tell anyone what I am going to do, he said. And what I remember next is how the moon, the pale moon with its one yellow eye, the moon of Tikal, and Tulum, and Chichén, stared through the pink plastic curtains. Then something inside bit me, and I gave out a cry as if the other, the one I wouldn't be anymore, leapt out.

So I was initiated beneath an ancient sky by a great and mighty heir—Chaq Uxmal Paloquín. I, Ixchel, his queen.

The truth is, it wasn't a big deal. It wasn't any deal at all. I put my bloody panties inside my T-shirt and ran home hugging myself. I thought about a lot of things on the way home. I thought about all the world and how suddenly I became a part of history and wondered if everyone on the street, the sewing machine lady and the *panadería* saleswomen and the woman with two kids sitting on the bus bench didn't all know. *Did I look any different? Could they tell?* We were all the same somehow, laughing behind our hands, waiting the way all women wait, and when we find out, we wonder why the world and a million years made such a big deal over nothing.

I know I was supposed to feel ashamed, but I wasn't ashamed. I wanted to stand on top of the highest building, the top-top floor, and yell, *I know.*

20   Then I understood why Abuelita didn't let me sleep over at Lourdes's house full of too many brothers, and why the Roman girl in the movies always runs away from the soldier, and what happens when the scenes in love stories begin to fade, and why brides blush, and how it is that sex isn't simply a box you check *M* or *F* on in the test we get at school.

I was wise. The corner girls were still jumping into their stupid little hopscotch squares. I laughed inside and climbed the wooden stairs two by two to the second floor rear where me and Abuelita and Uncle Lalo live. I was still laughing when I opened the door and Abuelita asked, Where's the pushcart?

And then I didn't know what to do.

It's a good thing we live in a bad neighborhood. There are always plenty of bums to blame for your sins. If it didn't happen the way I told it, it really could've. We looked and looked all over for the kids who stole my pushcart. The story wasn't the best, but since I had to make it up right then and there with Abuelita staring a hole through my heart, it wasn't too bad.

For two weeks I had to stay home. Abuelita was afraid the street kids who had stolen the cart would be after me again. Then I thought I might go over to the Esparza garage and take the pushcart out and leave it in some alley for the police to find, but I was never allowed to leave the house alone. Bit by bit the truth started to seep out like a dangerous gasoline.

25   First the nosy woman who lives upstairs from the laundromat told my Abuelita she thought something was fishy, the pushcart wheeled into Esparza & Sons every Saturday after dark, how a man, the same dark Indian one, the one who never talks to anybody, walked with me when the sun went down and pushed the cart into the garage, that one there, and yes we went inside, there where the fat lady named Concha, whose hair is dyed a hard black, pointed a fat finger.

I prayed that we would not meet Boy Baby, and since the gods listen and are mostly good, Esparza said yes, a man like that had lived there but was gone, had packed a few things and left the pushcart in a corner to pay for his last week's rent.

We had to pay $20 before he would give us our pushcart back. Then Abuelita made me tell the real story of how the cart had disappeared, all of which I told this time, except for that one night, which I would have to tell anyway, weeks later, when I prayed for the moon of my cycle to come back, but it would not. PREGNANT

When Abuelita found out I was going to *dar a luz,* she cried until her eyes were little, and blamed Uncle Lalo, and Uncle Lalo blamed this country, and

Abuelita blamed the infamy of men. That is when she burned the cucumber pushcart and called me a *sinvergüenza* because I *am* without shame.

Then I cried too—Boy Baby was lost from me—until my head was hot with headaches and I fell asleep. When I woke up, the cucumber pushcart was dust and Abuelita was sprinkling holy water on my head.

30   Abuelita woke up early every day and went to the Esparza garage to see if news about that *demonio* had been found, had Chaq Uxmal Paloquín sent any letters, any, and when the other mechanics heard that name they laughed, and asked if we had made it up, that we could have some letters that had come for Boy Baby, no forwarding address, since he had gone in such a hurry.

There were three. The first, addressed "Occupant," demanded immediate payment for a four-month-old electric bill. The second was one I recognized right away—a brown envelope fat with cake-mix coupons and fabric-softener samples—because we'd gotten one just like it. The third was addressed in a spidery Spanish to a Señor C. Cruz, on paper so thin you could read it unopened by the light of the sky. The return address a convent in Tampico.

This was to whom my Abuelita wrote in hopes of finding the man who could correct my ruined life, to ask if the good nuns might know the where-abouts of a certain Boy Baby—and if they were hiding him it would be of no use because God's eyes see through all souls.

We heard nothing for a long time. Abuelita took me out of school when my uniform got tight around the belly and said it was a shame I wouldn't be able to graduate with the other eighth graders.

Except for Lourdes and Rachel, my grandma and Uncle Lalo, nobody knew about my past. I would sleep in the big bed I share with Abuelita same as always. I could hear Abuelita and Uncle Lalo talking in low voices in the kitchen as if they were praying the rosary, how they were going to send me to Mexico, to San Dionisio de Tlaltepango, where I have cousins and where I was conceived and would've been born had my grandma not thought it wise to send my mother here to the United States so that neighbors in San Dionisio de Tlaltepango wouldn't ask why her belly was suddenly big.

35   I was happy. I liked staying home. Abuelita was teaching me to crochet the way she had learned in Mexico. And just when I had mastered the tricky rosette stitch, the letter came from the convent which gave the truth about Boy Baby—however much we didn't want to hear.

He was born on a street with no name in a town called Miseria. His father, Eusebio, is a knife sharpener. His mother, Refugia, stacks apricots into pyra-mids and sells them on a cloth in the market. There are brothers. Sisters too of which I know little. The youngest, a Carmelite, writes me all this and prays for my soul, which is why I know it's all true.

Boy Baby is thirty-seven years old. His name is Chato which means fat-face. There is no Mayan blood.

I don't think they understand how it is to be a girl. I don't think they know how it is to have to wait your whole life. I count the months for the baby to be born, and it's like a ring of water inside me reaching out and out until one day it will tear from me with its own teeth.

Already I can feel the animal inside me stirring in his own uneven sleep. The witch woman says it's the dreams of weasels that make my child sleep the way he sleeps. She makes me eat white bread blessed by the priest, but I know it's the ghost of him inside me that circles and circles, and will not let me rest.

40   Abuelita said they sent me here just in time, because a little later Boy Baby came back to our house looking for me, and she had to chase him away with the broom. The next thing we hear, he's in the newspaper clippings his sister sends. A picture of him looking very much like stone, police hooked on either arm...*on the road to* Las Grutas de Xtacumbilxuna, *the Caves of the Hidden Girl...eleven female bodies...the last seven years...*
Then I couldn't read but only stare at the little black-and-white dots that make up the face I am in love with.

All my girl cousins here either don't talk to me, or those who do, ask questions they're too young to know *not* to ask. What they want to know really is how it is to have a man, because they're too ashamed to ask their married sisters.
They don't know what it is to lay so still until his sleep breathing is heavy, for the eyes in the dim dark to look and look without worry at the man-bones and the neck, the man-wrist and man-jaw thick and strong, all the salty dips and hollows, the stiff hair of the brow and sour swirl of sideburns, to lick the fat earlobes that taste of smoke, and stare at how perfect is a man.
I tell them, "It's a bad joke. When you find out you'll be sorry."

45   I'm going to have five children. Five. Two girls. Two boys. And one baby.
The girls will be called Lisette and Maritza. The boys I'll name Pablo and Sandro.
And my baby. My baby will be named Alegre, because life will always be hard.

Rachel says that love is like a big black piano being pushed off the top of a three-story building and you're waiting on the bottom to catch it. But Lourdes says it's not that way at all. It's like a top, like all the colors in the world are spinning so fast they're not colors anymore and all that's left is a white hum.
There was a man, a crazy who lived upstairs from us when we lived on South Loomis. He couldn't talk, just walked around all day with this harmonica in his mouth. Didn't play it. Just sort of breathed through it, all day long, wheezing, in and out, in and out.
50   This is how it is with me. Love I mean.

Antonio Farias

Antonio Farias is a freelance writer and diversity consultant of Ecuadorian background. His work, including a collaborative photo-essay, "My Own Private Ecuador," has appeared in regional magazines such as *Urban Latino*. He is currently working on his first novel, *An Incan Fisherman in the Lower East Side*, and has a collection of short stories forthcoming. Farias has worked as a jet mechanic, infantryman, college lecturer, and most recently as an academic advisor, championing student-of-color recruitment and retention at small liberal arts colleges. He holds a master's degree in ethnic studies and a bachelor's degree in comparative literature/creative writing from the University of California, Berkeley.

Red Serpent Ceviche[1]

He searches their faces trying to find his own. More different than alike, he thinks, as he continues to scan their features, letting the steady rumble of the 7 train mesh with his thoughts. He spies his father sitting at the other end of the train, his thoughts off somewhere, inhabiting a place Simon can no longer afford to follow.

We eat different cheeses, drink different liquor, speak different tongues—I crave ceviche while you cherish cuy,[2] pero somos una gente?[3] My people were fishermen, we harvested an ocean before it was sold to gringos—did you know that gringos are now Japanese? Diversity isn't all it's cracked up to be, tu sabes.

Mi gente son galleros, mi gente macheteros, brujos[4] healing an ancient wound? I travel 3000 miles south as my mind navigates through ancient stories to find you. I write countless words to make you mine; take your photographs hoping they'll solve the riddle that tumbles in my head—quien somos?[5]

In the end, the nostalgia that haunts my dreams belongs to my father. Mi gente[6] are here among me now, en el corazon.[7] Un pueblo salpicado[8] with salsa, burritos, mofongo[9] and barrio dreams—un pueblo waiting for its sons and daughters to embrace it, even as they leave behind a broken heart.

5   *There, mornings grew thick with comfortable smells. The kitchen upstairs, with its firestone oven, was where I learned to eat. Still, I smell the moist yucca bread, and the hypnotizing smell of coffee.*

La Cabuya[10] exists on no map, yet its people are firmly rooted in the land. They have cemeteries to prove it. It exists in the hearts of those that call it home, those that left thinking they could forget. Those like me, who claim it, pull it out of the past and dust it off. We need cuentos[11] and images of our own if we're ever going to feel secure enough to let go and make the future ours.

Simon catches the brief stare of a fellow passenger, who quickly looks away.

---

[1] a Latin American coastal dish consisting of mixed seafood that is "cooked" in lemon juice
[2] The *cuy* resembles a guinea pig and is considered a delicacy in the Sierra Mountain region of Ecuador.
[3] But are we the same kind of people?
[4] My people raise roosters, my people use machetes, my people are shamans
[5] Who are we?
[6] my people
[7] in my heart
[8] a village flavored
[9] a dish consisting of mashed plantains
[10] a rural area in Ecuador located north of Bahia de Caraquez
[11] stories

You see longing in my eyes as we ride the #7, red serpent carrying us from one millennium to the next—acknowledge me, your brother, hermano, father, Mámak[12] to those yet to come.

The train pulls into Queensboro Plaza, where the mass of crayon people line the platform.

In this city, signs abound, overloading the senses and making it impossible to read them accurately. Sometimes there are strong warnings, signs whose meanings people have forgotten, leaving behind a tremor that can be felt but not explained. There are still a few who can read the pig's liver, interpret the movement of the waters, and look into the souls of broken men.

10   *The brujo was my compadre, my friend, he rescued himself from a life in a Guayaquil[13] sweatshop in order to arrive just in time to help a dying child, mi hermano. If you call him Pacha,[14] he'll smile and take you for someone who knew him in a past life. He once cured a traficante of a common cold and was proclaimed a miracle worker.*

"You see, mijo," Pacha once said, "the local priest believed that liberation for los pobres[15] could be found in this world, so now he sleeps with a bullet in his head."

In Brooklyn basements, Florida swamps, California deserts, they fight roosters and go to jail, their families going hungry, as animal rights advocates hurry back behind their suburban walls. Here and there they are men entering the ring with roosters who have none of their ego problems. Majestic animals, they live and die so their masters can release their frustrations, messengers to the ancient guardians that still inhabit the hills, the jungle, the erupting Cordillera[16] of the condor. They leave this world carrying the poison of rage so that the workers' machetes can sleep another night.

Simon looks over and traces out his father's features, letting his hand absently follow along the contours of his own face, as he wonders what made it possible for that man, whose blood beats through his veins, to have let go of a past long enough to let the future take root. He wonders if he can ever put an end to his perpetual wandering, in order to live here, in the urban heart of a new people.

Mi nueva gente,[17] he thinks, letting the words tumble as the train veers around a corner, about to go underground.

15   Memories well up and gently crawl into a comfortable position next to him, his father, the last remnant of a world without bridges.

Simon gets up, offering his seat to a pregnant woman who could pass for the sister he never had. He walks over toward his father, sure to surprise him, thinking there will be fewer and fewer opportunities to meet up with him like this, two men riding the red serpent into an unknown future, inextricably bound by the haunting of a place they can never return to.

---

[12]Quechua word meaning "mother, originator of life"
[13]major coastal city in Ecuador
[14]Quechua word meaning "place-time, Earth"
[15]the poor
[16]a mountain range that spans from Colombia to Bolivia, its peaks in places extending above 20,000 feet
[17]My new people [or community]

Guy Garcia

Guy Garcia is the author of two novels, *Skin Deep* (1988), which draws on the famous Laguna Beach episode in Chicano history, and *Obsidian Sky* (1994). Both works concern young Chicanos coming to terms with their Mexican American heritage and identity. He was born in Los Angeles in 1955 and has written for various magazines including *Rolling Stone* and *Time*.

La Promesa

Tom Cardona had been in Mexico for exactly forty minutes when the old woman approached his rental car and pressed her face against the window. Flattened by the glass, her cheeks were like weathered mahogany, cracked and pitted by the elements, and framed by a curtain of stringy hair. She opened her mouth to speak, but her voice was drowned out by the roar of a landing jet. Assuming she wanted money, Tom leaned across the seat, rolled down the window and placed a five thousand peso bill in her hand. The claw-like fingers retracted, then returned, groping for the door handle. It took Tom a second to realize that she was trying to get into the car. Panicking, he grabbed her withered paw and pushed it away as his foot hit the gas pedal. The car bolted forward, but when Tom looked in the rearview mirror the toll plaza was empty.

He joined the torrent of traffic and consulted his map, Guanajuato was roughly 200 miles from Mexico City, a trip that he calculated would take at least three to four hours. Even if he started now and skipped lunch, he would be lucky to get there before dark. Which meant there was no way he could avoid spending the night, which meant that his return reservation was useless.

"Terrific," Tom muttered to himself, suddenly annoyed at the traffic, the smog, the absurdly heavy Mexican coins that tugged on his trouser pockets. The whole God-forsaken country. The tangled freeways and flat skyline—so eerily similar yet different from Los Angeles—only heightened his sense of dislocation. He was a stranger in a strange land, except that the natives looked just like him. He felt uneasy in his own skin. This is what he had feared, this was why he had procrastinated for years, telling himself that he couldn't afford the airfare, couldn't spare the time. No one could blame him for putting his job and family first, for taking care of the home front instead of Estella's pointless goose chase.

Two hours out of Mexico City the terrain became Alpine, a vertical landscape of sheer gigantic peaks and evergreen pines. Sunlight blinked through the treetops, casting helioscopic patterns on the rock cliffs. Eventually the mountains gave way to rolling hills and the road opened up, giving Tom a view of the broad sloping valley that led to the flatlands around Queretaro. Off to the west he could see a thunderhead moving swiftly across the plain, a dark funnel of rain dragging behind it like a widow's veil. A stubble of young corn grew over freshly-tilled fields and if it weren't for the pitiful shacks lining the road Tom could have been back in the Golden State.

5   He missed it already. His wife and kids and friends were all back there, waiting for him while he wandered unmarked roads in a foreign country in a rented
car. And all for what? The futility of it had struck him from the moment his
grandmother had pulled the box of pictures down from the closet and showed
him the faded photograph of a light-skinned Mexican girl with wide oval eyes
and arching eyebrows. "That was my nanny, Blanca Morrell, who raised me
when I was a little girl. We told each other everything, even the deepest secrets."
        Estella had paused, searching Tom's face for a reaction, but he only
shrugged, trying to stifle his impatience. He was just home from college and
anxious to unpack and call his girlfriend.
        "That's great, grandma. But I've really got to go."
        But Estella had held him there, clasping his hands in her own. "I told her
that no matter what happened I would never forget her," she said, her voice
thick with emotion. "But for years my letters have been returned unopened. I
will not rest in peace until I know what has happened. I would go myself, but
I'm too old. You are young and strong. You can go to Mexico and make sure
she doesn't need anything. Not now; don't worry. Later. I'll give you the
money. There's no hurry. Promise me, mi'jito. Promise you'll put your grandmother's soul to rest."
        It came up a few more times in the ensuing years, always when Tom and
Estella were alone, always with the same conclusion. By the time Tom was married and his visits to Estella's house limited to holidays and funerals, her references to Blanca became less frequent. And after the birth of his first child, to
his great relief, she had dropped the subject altogether.
10   The day Estella died—they found her in her garden, her arms spread as if
in mid-flight to heaven—he had assumed the whole matter was moot. There
was no one left to care, least of all himself, who regarded the fate of his grandmother's nanny about as relevant as the courting habits of the Aztecs. After
all, he was an American, the son of an American, born and raised in the elevated suburb of Fullerton Hills. His house had a swimming pool and two cars
in the garage—three if you counted the tri-wheel off-roader he'd bought for
laughs the summer before. He listened to classic rock and roll, cheered for the
Lakers and had voted Republican in the last two elections. He'd gone to night
school for his engineering degree and had worked hard to become regional
sales manager for the world's largest tire manufacturer. You wouldn't see him
with his hand out for welfare. He cringed whenever a robbery suspect on the
local news was identified as a "Hispanic male."
        It was just that he considered his ethnic origins a footnote, a given part of
the social equation. As a second-generation Chicano he had moved from point
A to point B, just as his children would go on to point C. And on and on until
it didn't matter where you came from or who your grandparents were. That
was progress, the American way. Point A, the past, the world of Estella's youth,
was dead and buried under the parched hills of central Mexico, deep in the sil-
ver-plated heart of the country. Or so he had thought. Then the lawyer called
about the money and Estella's posthumous request.

His grandmother's instructions were unsentimental and succinct: "I hereby leave $30,000 to my grandson, Tomas Cardona, on the condition that he travel to my birthplace of Guanajuato, Mexico, and ascertain the fate of my childhood nanny, Blanca Morrell."

Tom told himself that he wasn't doing it for the money, that he was doing it for Estella. But who was he trying to kid? Thirty grand was thirty grand. Within minutes he was resigned to the journey, mentally booking a plane, packing light. He had to hand it to the old girl. Unable to persuade him while she was alive, Estella, in death, had finally bent him to her will.

Making good time, he pulled abreast of a young Mexican family in a silver Mercedes sedan. A little girl, her neatly-braided hair gathered in ribbons, waved to him from the side window as he passed. Tom waved back. It was hard for him to believe that the girl and the wizened crone at the toll booth were from the same century, let alone the same country. The thought of rich Mexicans stirred something in him, a twinge of pride that said brown-skinned people could drive German cars. Tom mentally applauded. *Drive fast, don't look back.*

15   The sun was slouching over the horizon when Tom reached the turn-off to Guanajuato. The land had become hilly again and he traveled past small towns perched on steep inclines, their stucco church belltowers anointed by the day's dying rays. The road dipped into a narrow canyon bounded by oak and flowering cactus and the car was soon shuddering over the cobblestone streets in the center of town. Even in the murky twilight Tom could tell that Guanajuato was an unusually beautiful city. It was just as Estella had described it: ornate colonial buildings painted in orange and lime pastels, narrow, winding streets and tree-lined plazas with gurgling fountains. And there, off to the right, was the famous Alhóndiga de Granaditas, the grain warehouse where the Spaniards made their last stand during the War of Independence.

Tom followed Estella's written directions, driving back to the main square and into the descending ramp that became Calle Miguel Hidalgo. He had read about Guanajuato's mummy museum and underground streets, but was still amazed to find himself driving through a subterranean cause-way, its jagged rock walls illuminated by an occasional lightbulb. The road snaked under the city, twisting and looping like a giant's entrails. Then the mouth of the tunnel suddenly yawned and Tom was back on the surface. He followed the street into a well-to-do neighborhood of proud mansions and serene villas draped with clusters of bloody bougainvilla. He found the house, a faded pink manor decorated with stone statues and urns, on a quiet avenue that limned a placid lake. The lights inside were on, and through the slightly parted curtains Tom spied the seated profile of a young woman, her hands fluttering like doves as she spoke to an invisible listener.

Tom lifted the heavy brass knocker and dropped it against the door. A resounding thud echoed through the house and a few seconds later he heard the scrape of a chair being pushed back on the wooden floor. Footsteps approached and the door swung open. The girl was in her early twenties, her hair and clothes fashionably up to date.

"May I help you, please?" she asked in Spanish.

"Hablas Ingles?" [1]

20   "Yes. Can I help you?"

"I hope so," he said. "My name is Tom Cardona. I'm here because my grandmother used to live in this house. Her name was Estella Cardona, and I'm trying to find out what happened to her nanny."

The girl let out a high giggle of disbelief.

"Are you serious?" she inquired in English.

"Yes, I am. I know it sounds crazy, but it was my grandmother's last wish. She died two weeks ago. I flew here today from Los Angeles."

25   The girl opened the door a notch wider.

"I'm not from around here either," she confessed. "I'm studying at the University. But Mrs. Velasquez—she's the lady who lives here—might know something. The house has been in her family for ages. Please, come in."

She ushered him into the paneled foyer and asked him to wait. He could smell the inviting aromas of dinner, and Tom's stomach noisily reminded him that he hadn't eaten since breakfast.

The mansion, which he guessed was at least two hundred years old, had not aged gracefully. There were watermarks on the plaster ceiling and the floor-boards creaked from a million human footsteps. But the furniture had been freshly dusted and the cut-crystal chandelier sparkled. A servant slipped into one of the rooms carrying a silver coffee service. The place reeked of old money—the miserly, slightly tarnished lucre of wealth no longer interested in appearances or the effort required to keep them up.

Tom could hear the girl speaking to someone in the dining room. When she returned she was smiling. "You should feel lucky," she said as she escorted him in. "Mrs. Velasquez doesn't usually receive visitors without an appointment. But when I told her you were visiting from America, she agreed to make an exception."

30   Mrs. Velasquez was a paraplegic woman of some 65 years, with long braided hair and an imperious manner. A pair of half-moon reading glasses dangled from a silver chain around her fleshy neck. The girl introduced him and Mrs. Velasquez nodded impatiently.

"I think I can assume that you've already met Celia," she said in slightly nasal English. "She comes twice a week to read to me and keep me company in my old age."

"You are not old, Señora," Celia protested.

"Oh, hush, you young thing. What do you know about age? Your life is still ahead of you. The world is your oyster, and I am just a shriveled up old clam."

Her tirade over, Mrs. Velasquez turned her attention back to her guest. "Mr. Cardona," she said pleasantly, "would you like some coffee?"

35   *"Muchas gracias."*

"Hablas Español?"

---

[1] "Do you speak English?"

"Only a little."

"*Qué lástima*. It's a pity when we lose the tongue of our ancestors."

A servant appeared with a cup and saucer. The service was of delicate china decorated with a coat of arms that Tom assumed was the family crest.

40   "Are you by any chance familiar with the name Morrell?"

Mrs. Velasquez regarded him over the top of her glasses.

"My dear, the Morrell family built this house. My father bought it from them in the 1940s, long before you were even born. Sugar?"

"Are you sure?" Tom said.

Mrs. Velasquez made a sour face. "Of course, I'm sure. I may be a crippled old woman but I'm not senile yet."

45   Tom groped for the words. "I'm sorry... It's just that... You see I'm here at my grandmother's request. Her name was Estella Cardona and her nanny was named Blanca Morrell."

Mrs. Velasquez's face became a mask of scorn.

"I don't know what you think you're doing young, man, but your joke is not the least bit amusing."

"So you knew Blanca Morrell?"

Mrs. Velasquez rattled her cup in her saucer and leaned forward. "I didn't have to meet her to know that she was a disgrace to her family. They tried to save her by sending her to live in the United States but she had to come back and humiliate her relatives. It's because of her that the Morrells sold this house and left, so maybe I should be grateful."

50   The cup suspended in Tom's hand became impossibly light, as if it would float away if he didn't hold on tight.

"Do you know where the Morrells went after they left Guanajuato?"

Mrs. Velasquez placed her hand on her sequined breast.

"My dear boy," she intoned. "I had expected you to tell *me*. If they had any sense at all, they went back to France. That's where I would have gone." Her voice acquired the tinny echo of a vintage gramaphone. "They say that the French are cold, but I disagree. I'd take Paris any day over Rome, or even my beloved Madrid. How I miss the charms of the Champs Elysées, the Louvre, the Eiffel Tower. Ah, now there is a city made for summer dreams." Her gaze focused again. "I must say that I fail to understand why on earth anyone would want to know anything about Blanca Morrell."

"It's just that I'd assumed she'd be poor."

55   "Ha!" Mrs. Velasquez grimaced through layers of rouge and lipstick. "She was a rich woman with common characteristics."

"What do you mean?"

"She lived a whore's life and died a whore's death before she reached thirty."

Tom leaned back in his chair.

"But it doesn't make any sense."

60   "What sense can there be in self-destruction, the final sin of a damned spirit?"

"She committed suicide?"

"Yes." Mrs. Velasquez reached for her cup with a trembling hand.

"Can you tell me how?"

She shuddered, as if shaking off a bad memory. "I'm sorry, I can't help you. I'm too old to consort with the devil's darlings. If you are smart, you'll go back to America, Señor. Those who wake the dead pay the demon's due. Goodnight!"

65   Before Tom could respond, she closed her eyes and started to moan. "Celia!" she called. "I'm getting another attack!"

Mrs. Velasquez's hands were still over her face as Celia wheeled her through the door and disappeared down the receding hall of mirrors.

Tom was famished. Even his disturbing audience with Mrs. Velasquez had failed to blunt his appetite. He retraced his path into the center of town and checked into a small hotel on the edge of the central square. The evening was cool, but not unpleasantly so, and the sidewalks were alive with children's voices and lovers strolling hand in hand down the bustling avenues. Tom took a lungful of the fragrant mountain air, so unlike the smog that smothered Mexico City, and felt the muscles in his neck unwind. A person could live well here, a long and happy life, unless something intervened and cut it short. Something that caused old women to cover their eyes and grow faint.

Determined to get himself a proper dinner, he followed the aroma of grilled meat and cilantro to a crowded café decorated with pottery and Indian blankets. Taking a seat near the kitchen, he ordered enchiladas suizas and pork carnitas and two Dos Equis to wash it all down. The food was rich and intoxicating—nothing like the fast-food burritos he was accustomed to—with a pleasant chile afterburn that left his whole mouth tingling. His hunger finally sated, the implications of what he had just been told began to sink in. According to Mrs. Velasquez, his grandmother's nanny was a rich woman, a suicide, and a whore. Impossible. But why would the old woman lie?

Tom paid the check and ventured out into the square. Most of the restaurants and stores had closed, but the bars were still full and he could hear the distant strain of mariachi music coming from a saloon at the end of the block. Unaccountably, he had a momentary sensation that he'd been here before. When Tom was a baby, his parents had traveled with him in Mexico, but that was such a long time ago. Had they come to Guanajuato? He couldn't possibly remember. And yet....

70   He was about to turn back toward the garage when he noticed a storefront with the lights still burning. A sign over the door identified it as a venue for the construction and sale of funeral caskets. Succumbing to curiosity, Tom approached the threshold and poked his head inside.

"Come in, come in," urged a mellifluous voice. "Don't be timid. Take a look around. If you don't see your size we can have one custom-made to fit your dimensions."

Tom did as the voice asked. The room was long and narrow and filled from floor to ceiling with rows of polished coffins. There were ornate coffins with gleaming lacquer patinas and brass handles, simple coffins made of unfinished pine, coffins in basic black and others in powder blue, purple and cream. There were long skinny coffins, extra-wide coffins and coffins that looked small enough to bury a doll.

An overstuffed man in an overstuffed chair beckoned from the end of the room. He had jovial eyes and a wide, licentious mouth. His body was a series of convex forms culminating in a spherical belly that tortured the buttons of his starched guayabera. When he spoke his ample stomach jiggled in agreement. His plump fingers held a similarly-shaped cigar.

The fat man smiled and shifted his bulk in the chair. "It's obvious you are not from Guanajuato. Texas?"

75 "California," Tom said.

"Ah, California," the fat man pronounced the word like something delicious. "The Golden Gate. Hollywood, Mickey Mouse. *El raton Miguelito*, we call him. I lived in Texas for a while, many years ago. But it is not the same. I think."

"No. It's not the same."

"You are too young to be shopping for yourself. A relative perhaps? I have many customers there. Shipping is no problem. If you do not see what you like, I can build it for you. Very fine workmanship. You cannot find quality like this in the U.S.A., not even for double the price."

The fat man pointed to a casket with an open lid. "Take a look," he urged. "We use only the best woods, the finest silks, the most luxurious quilting. All the stitching is done by hand."

80 "It's very nice," Tom said.

Having made his pitch, the fat man settled back in his chair, struck a match, and started to relight his cigar stub. "So, if it is not Molina's quality coffins that bring you to Guanajuato, then what does? You have come to see the mummies, perhaps? They are hideous but very interesting—preserved by the special minerals in the soil. I can arrange for a personal tour if you wish."

Tom shook his head. "I'm looking for somebody, a person who was born here."

Molina nodded through a cloud of blue smoke.

"Then you've come to the right place, my friend. I know everyone in Guanajuato—alive or dead."

85 "I'm glad to hear that, because this person is deceased. At least, I think so." Molina exuded empathy.

"Do you have a name?"

"Yes, her name is...."

"No," Molina interrupted, "I mean your name."

90 "Tom Cardona."

"Tom. Like the actor Tom Cruise?"

"Yeah, like Tom Cruise."

Molina's belly jiggled with amusement. "I know a Cardona family—a very respectable family—that lives near the University. Professor Cardona was buried in one of my coffins. It was silver, with brass handles and a dark blue lining...."

"The person I'm looking for had the surname Morrell. She was my grand-mother's nanny. I think she was known as La Blanca."

95 Molina's belly inflated. "Ah, naturally. *La Blanca.*"

"So you knew her?"

"Everybody knows La Blanca."

"What do you mean?"

"Please," Molina waved Tom to a chair. "Sit down. Would you like some tea? A cigar perhaps?"

100 "No thanks."

Molina produced a fresh Havana, snipped off the tip, and torched it with a Bic lighter, sending smoke rings floating toward the ceiling. As he inhaled, his throat made the raspy whistle of air being forced through a narrow aperture.

"Everyone knows the legend of La Blanca. A Mexican ghost story. They say it's true." Molina hunched his bulky shoulders. "After all, the Morrell family certainly existed and the house still stands out by La Olla, the pot—that's what we call the municipal reservoir."

"Out by the Velasquez place."

Molina's mouth stretched into a leer.

105 "You know Doña Sara?"

"We've met."

"There are stories about her, too," he said with a wink. "But that is not what you came to hear."

"No."

Molina sucked on his cigar.

110 "According to the story," he began, "Blanca was the only daughter of Alain Morrell, a retired French soldier who owned several bakeries, and Rosa Vega, a Creole girl whose parents owned a silver mine north of town. Blanca was viva-cious, reckless and blessed with almost unbearable beauty. She was the flower whose perfume made the bees dizzy. The suitors came and went. Blanca would meet them, let them do their best to woo her, then reject them. She broke many hearts and made enemies that would one day contribute to her ruination.

"In any case, news of this unapproachable beauty spread through the moun-tains and reached the ears of Eugenio Sanchez, the dashing heir of a wealthy cattle family from San Miguel de Allende. Eugenio's father, Don Arturo, had served as ambassador to France and the family traced its lineage to the Bour-bon court of Spain. The Morrells were prominent, but the Sanchez clan was both rich and aristocratic. For Blanca's parents, it was an ideal match. With her looks and his money, the offspring of their union would be like royalty. An introduction was arranged, and Eugenio was instantly smitten. An expert horseman, he invited her to go riding with him and they were seen galloping together on the vast lands of the Sanchez estate. Two months later, Eugenio asked Blanca's father for her hand in marriage. Blanca's father accepted, and the town braced itself for the wedding of the century.

"The ceremony was to take place at the Cathedral with the Bishop presid-ing, the reception in the lobby of the grand Teatro Juárez. The guest list numbered more than one thousand, including many of Mexico's most distinguished families. To feed the hordes, Don Morrell had ordered five hundred chickens, fifty sides of beef and twenty barrels of beer, not counting brandy and champagne. An orchestra of thirty-six mariachis from Guadalajara had been hired to entertain, along with an assortment of dancers, mimes and strolling magicians. The wedding cake alone weighed twenty kilos, and Blanca's dress, a rippling river of white brocade, lace and silk, was on its way by steamship from one of the most exclusive salons of Paris.

"In the final weeks before the wedding, Blanca stopped going to the Sanchez hacienda and locked herself in her rooms, refusing to come out. For three whole days a terrible sobbing shook the house. Finally, when her parents threatened to break the door down, she emerged and told them that she could not marry Eugenio because she loved someone else. 'If you force me to go through with it,' she told them, 'I'll kill myself. I would rather be dead than married to that man.'

"Two weeks before Eugenio and Blanca were due to march to the altar, the wedding was called off. The fiasco cost the Morrells hundreds of thousands of pesos and brought great shame to the family. Don Morrell became a laughingstock and his business suffered. Partly as an act of retribution and partly to shield her from the outpouring of scorn, Blanca was sent with her nanny to live in America. It is said that she had a child out of wedlock. *A pocho bastard.* A few months later, the Morrells liquidated their holdings, sold the house and left Guanajuato forever."

115   "The nanny," Tom interrupted, "Do you remember her name?"

Molina's brow furrowed in concentration. "I believe it was Estella," he said.

The slurred Spanish of two passing drunks intruded through the open door. "Is something the matter?" Molina asked.

"No. I was just wondering, would you happen to remember the nanny's surname?"

120   Molina's brow creased in concentration.

Tom said, "Could it have been Cardona?"

Molina's head bobbed in confirmation.

"Yes, I believe that's it! What a strange coincidence! Are you sure you're all right, my friend?"

"I'm fine. Please go on."

125   "Perhaps it is the altitude."

"Yes, the altitude. Tell me the rest of the story."

"Well, several months passed. Then the most extraordinary thing happened. At first, no one could believe it was her, that she had the audacity to come back to the scene of her dishonor. It was like seeing a ghost. Not only that, but she had taken a cheap room at the edge of town, not far from where we sit, a blue house with two balconies on Calle Ramona. It was unheard of for a lady of her breeding to be living alone in such a place. As you might imagine, the gossips were in paradise. Some said that she had gone nuts and had been sent away to the United States to be put in an asylum, from which she had escaped. Others held that she had murdered her nanny and child. The more pious observers contended that the gringos had made her into a prostitute and that she had returned to ply her wares. In any case, polite society treated her like a leper, which seemed to suit Blanca just fine. The truth is, with her emerald eyes and long brown hair, she never looked more beautiful.

"Soon afterward Blanca was spotted riding with a handsome dark man. The following Sunday the couple was seen again, this time drifting in a rowboat on La Olla. Spies soon identified the man as Juan Fuerza, a mestizo laborer who worked in the silver mines. Then someone remembered that Fuerza's previous job was as a stable boy at the Sanchez hacienda. Yes, he had worked there when Blanca used to go riding and even served as her guide on more than one occasion. Well, you didn't have to be a genius to figure out that Fuerza was the mystery love who had foiled Blanca's marriage to Eugenio Sanchez. Had Blanca and Fuerza tasted forbidden fruit in the trees of the Sanchez property, as some claimed? Or had they merely planted the seeds of a romance that would blossom much later. Who can say? Blanca took the answer to her grave. What is certain is that within a few weeks of Blanca's return, the outcast couple was living together in sin at the flat on Calle Ramona."

Molina paused and used a match to revive his cigar.

130 "Are you sure you are enjoying this story, señor? Would you like a glass of water?"

"Thank you, no. Please go on."

"Anyway, as you might have guessed, we are near the end. As soon as Eugenio Sanchez learned the identity of Blanca's new lover, he began to plot his revenge. Fuerza was a soulful boy with a firm jaw, straight black hair and eyes like coal. His body was lean and hard from working in the mines all day, but he also had an artistic temperament and liked to play his guitar and sing romantic ballads. On Saturday nights he would leave Blanca's house and join his friends for a song and a drink at the bar right here on the corner, which at the time was called El Espejo Oscuro. It was a warm, moonless night, and when Fuerza left the bar with two buddies he was in high spirits. At the intersection, Fuerza bade his friends goodnight and started alone down the sidestreet, the one over there with the light, on his way home to Blanca's house. The neighbors could hear him singing, as young drunks, and even old drunks, will do. Then the singing turned to shouts of terror. A band of assassins had been waiting for Fuerza, and when he turned the corner they attacked him with their machetes. It was over in a minute. Blanca ran out of her house and found her lover's butchered body in the street, his blood draining into the gutter.

"It was at that point, I believe, that she did actually go insane. When Blanca saw that Fuerza was dead, she let out a horrible scream, a guttural wail that gathered force until every dog in town was barking and people were quaking in their beds. Mad with grief, Blanca went to the police station, but the police had been bribed by the Sanchez family and they told her to go home and forget about it. There would be no protest, no outcry, no official investigation of any kind. It was as if the killing had never happened, and who could prove otherwise? The body, or what was left of it, was disposed of in secret, probably at the bottom of a mine. Even Fuerza's birth certificate vanished."

"What about Blanca?"

135   "A terrible end for such a beautiful girl," Molina lamented. "My father, who was a boy at the time, never stopped having nightmares about it. All through the night, Blanca walked through the town like a zombie, her hands and dress soaked with Fuerza's blood, screaming for a doctor, for the police, for anyone who would help her. But people only locked their doors and drew their curtains. By now she had become an almost supernatural figure. To touch her would be to touch the devil, to look into her eyes would be to glimpse into a living hell. It is not an opportunity that the God-fearing strive for, I assure you. In any case, she wandered through the city for hours, scaring the daylights out of people as she pounded on their doors and beseeched them to let her in, like a succubus, then moving on to the next street, the next house. She came at last to her childhood home, which was now owned by the Velasquez family. Doña Sara, who had hated Blanca ever since she stole Eugenio Sanchez away from her, opened one of the windows on the second floor and threw cold water on her, causing Fuerza's blood to stain the cement in front of their door. The next morning, they found Blanca's body floating in La Olla. The authorities reported it as an open and shut case of accidental drowning. For months, no one would go boating there, and for a time people tried to avoid drinking water, fearing that Blanca's deranged spirit would somehow enter their body. There were those who also believed that the blood on the Velasquez steps was a curse of some sort."

"A curse?"

"Well, my professional efforts notwithstanding, we Mexicans are not very good at burying our dead. They live with us, behind doors, under creaking beds, in the cobwebs that cling to the walls, watching, judging…. Ah, but of course you don't believe me. It is fashionable in this day of computers and moon landings to pretend that what I just told you is merely a myth, that none of it ever happened. And, who knows, maybe it never did. But this much is certain: the stain on the Velasquez steps is still there, and parents still invoke the ghost of La Blanca to keep their children from playing near La Olla at night."

"Where was she buried?"

Molina seemed annoyed by the question. "In the municipal cemetery," he said. "No one claimed the body and she was interred in a pine box that my grandfather donated. There is no marker on her grave. There is nothing to see. Trust me, going there would be a waste of time."

140   The municipal cemetery was on the outskirts of town, at the end of a dusty road that coiled up into a dry gully. Several of the tombs were built above ground in the shape of small buildings with tiny windows and doors. Others were marked with a simple wooden or iron crucifix. All the graves, from the richest to the poorest, were adorned with bouquets of plastic flowers—yellow,

blue, red and pink. Wildflowers had grown up around the ersatz blooms so that the two appeared to be growing from the same roots. In the hammering sunlight the colors were almost unbearably bright, and they stabbed at Tom's eyes as he wandered through the rows of strangely festive graves, his ears ringing with the drone of flying insects. Most of the plots were unidentified and Tom quickly realized that he would never find what he was looking for without some help. A few yards away a shirtless young man was raking dead leaves and rocks into a neat pile. Tom approached him and smiled.

"*Buenos días.*"

"*Buenos días,*" the man uttered without looking up. Tom strained his memory for the Spanish word for grave.

"*Por favor, dónde está la tumba de la Señora Blanca Morrell?*"[2]

"*El entierro?*"[3]

145 "*Sí,*" Tom said, "*el entierro de Blanca Morrell.*"[4]

The man looked at Tom as if he were mad. "*Aquí no está,*"[5] he said. Then the man put down his rake and fled.

"What did you ask him?" The question was posed by an elderly bearded man in a plain black suit. His starched collar was tattered but clean and he held a bunch of fresh carnations in his hands.

"I asked him to show me the grave of Blanca Morrell."

"Oh my," the man remarked. "No wonder he ran away. The Indians are very superstitious, especially when strangers ask to see the graves of ghosts."

150 "She's not a ghost," Tom replied acidly. "She was a woman who lived here and died here and was buried somewhere in this cemetery."

"Yes, I've heard that story too. It could very well be true. But I've been coming here every Sunday to leave flowers for my wife, and I've never seen a tombstone for Blanca Morrell."

"I don't think there ever was a marker."

"So the family never claimed the body?"

"I don't think so."

155 "When did she die?"

"I'm not sure. A long time ago."

The man removed his hat and wiped the sweat from his brow. "You know, it's just possible...." The man left the sentence unfinished.

"What's possible?"

"Well, you've heard about the museum of the mummies, haven't you?"

160 "It was mentioned in my guidebook," Tom replied. "Something about bodies that were preserved by the minerals in the soil."

"That's what I'm saying. You see, the city's policy has always been that unclaimed bodies would be buried for five years. After that, if the family failed

---

[2]"Please, where is the tomb of Mrs. Blanca Morrell?"
[3]"The grave?"
[4]"Yes, Blanca Morrell's grave."
[5]"It's not here."

to claim them, they could be exhumed and cremated. But some of the bodies never decomposed. They are on display in the museum. I'll tell you, it's really something to see."

The midday sun pressed down with a vengeance, sapping the blood from Tom's arms and legs. "You're telling me that my grandmother's body might be on display as a tourist attraction?"

The man blanched. "Your grandmother? Good God. Forgive me, I had no idea."

"Neither did I."

165   It took him a few minutes to muster the courage, but once he decided to go, it wasn't hard to find. Halfway back into town a small sign announced *Momias*[6] with a hand-painted arrow pointing to the right. Tom had to back up to make the hair-pin turn, then he was climbing a one-lane road carved into the side of a hill. As he neared the entrance, a gaggle of children ran alongside the car shouting, "*Las momias! Las momias!*" the museum was situated in a dirt plaza ringed by souvenir shops selling mummy T-shirts and plastic goblins. As Tom climbed out of the car, another gang of youngsters surrounded him. "*Momias de dulce*," they yelled, hawking ghoulish candy skeletons mounted on a stick and packaged in clear plastic wrappers that looked like body bags. Tom waved the children away and tipped the parking lot guard to watch the car.

After standing in line to pay for his admission ticket for the English tour, Tom was ushered into a windowless waiting room with about thirty other visitors. An American boy wearing a Yankees baseball cap asked his mother if there was really a restaurant where you could look at the mummies while you ate. "I hope not," his mother said with revulsion. Tom wasn't feeling so well himself. His head throbbed and the huevos rancheros he'd had for breakfast were churning in his gut, undigested. He told himself it was the stuffy room or nerves or the altitude—anything but the real reason. The night before, he had hardly slept. He had driven back to the hotel in a daze, refusing to believe that his father was the bastard offspring of La Blanca Morrell, the raving witch of Guanajuato. On the road, he'd narrowly missed hitting a goat. It sprang into the headlights out of nowhere, its eyes lit with panic.

A stern-looking woman entered the waiting room and introduced herself as their guide. She addressed the group in Spanish first, then English, both spoken with supercilious precision. "For some reason," she explained, "perhaps because of the high mineral content of the soil or the dryness of the air, the bodies left in the crypt of the Pantheon, or municipal cemetery, did not decompose. Instead, they mummified."

"Excellent," the boy with the cap exclaimed.

"Until recently, any corpses that remained unclaimed in the municipal cemetery were taken to an underground crypt, where they became preserved in a most unusual state. The museum exhibit includes nearly one hundred bodies, some of which date back to the turn of the century. No flash is allowed. Now please stay together and follow me."

---

[6]Mummies

170   Tom followed last, lingering at the edge of the group.

The museum seemed to be made up of a series of interconnecting rooms, each one of which contained a dozen or so cadavers displayed in glass cases. Tom steeled himself and crossed the threshold into the first chamber. Most of the corpses were naked, their withered and dusty private parts plainly visible. Others sported the moth-eaten remains of their burial suits and dresses. One woman still had her stockings on, her emaciated legs disappearing into a pair of once-fashionable boots. Only a thin sheet of glass separated Tom from the countenance of death. The eyeless sockets stared into space, the lipless mouths yawned open. The poor lighting and horizontal arrangement of the display cases only added to Tom's claustrophobia.

The group seemed to be moving in slow motion. As he waited for the crowd to file through the narrow doorway, a young woman asked him to take a picture of her and a friend in front of one of the bodies. The pair mugged as if the carcass were some sort of decomposing celebrity. Tom clicked the shutter and felt another wave of nausea.

As the tour group meandered through the adjoining chambers, Tom tried to imagine what Blanca might look like after time and death had sucked the sweetness from her features. Could she be that one over there with the sunken cheekbones and startled expression, as if mortality had come as an unpleasant surprise? Or maybe that one in the corner, with the faded ribbon still knotted to the wiry strands bristling from her cranium? It was hopeless. Blanca could never be any of the ghastly fossils around him; she had gone to a place where no one could see her.

The guide beckoned the group into the next room. "This is a particularly interesting mummy," she noted, "for as you can see she was buried alive. By mistake, of course."

175   There were gasps from the group and Tom felt something nudging toward his esophagus.

"We believe that the woman probably suffered a stroke or heart attack and went into a coma," the guide explained in a slightly jaded monotone. "She was mistaken for dead and buried. But, of course, she was still alive. If you look closely at the hands you can see that the nails were damaged when she tried to scratch open the lid."

Tom felt his blood congeal. The curdled face, its black lizard lips stretched into a silent scream, was the very same that had pressed against his car window at the airport parking lot. The beseeching black sockets, more accusing than eyes, bore into him, drew him closer. Her expression tore at his intestines, gnawed at his bones, until something lurched in Tom's belly.

Across the room, the guide was eyeing him suspiciously.

"*Por favor, señor.*[7] Please don't touch the glass."

180   "Where is the exit?" Tom gasped.

"We are almost to the end of the tour, sir. If you could just wait one moment."

---

[7]"Please, sir."

Instead of answering, he pushed his way through the crowd and staggered out the exit into the garden, where he doubled over and heaved his breakfast into a bed of blooming marigolds. His vomit was volcanic, an eruption of rich food and denial that had taken decades to reach the surface. Blinded by the Aztec sun, Tom bowed like a believer as the violent spasms emptied him, cleansing him of pride and worldly pretense. He gagged and heaved until there was nothing left, nothing but an aching void and the fragrant embrace of the sweet, forgiving earth.

Ana Menéndez

Ana Menéndez was born in the United States, the daughter of Cuban exiles, and has worked as a journalist for the *Miami Herald* and the *Orange County Register*. Her collection of stories, *In Cuba I Was a German Shepherd* (2001), and her recent novel, *Loving Ché* (2003), have received positive reviews.

Confusing the Saints

Long ago, before this story began, the orishas took a look at the warm new world forming at their feet, the green hills and the sky filling with blue, and decided it should be theirs alone. The thin new trees, the boiling new sea—why share it with the All-Powerful, who was too far away to enjoy it anyway? And so they entered into a quarrel with Him. Night meetings, cells, plots, the diagram of a coup written on a grain of sand.

And that grain of sand flew to heaven. Or an informant sold the plans for a single blade of grass. And the All-Powerful shook the back of the clouds with his anger and cursed the orishas. He ordered the rain to stop. He held back the water. In Miami, the palm trees shriveled and the ocean receded to Havana.

Felipe at the restaurant says to make an offering to Santa Barbara. He says Santa Barbara protects travelers and sailors. But I think Felipe has it wrong. It's someone else who protects men lost in dark waters. Santa Barbara you only think about when it thunders. And who's thinking about thunder when it hasn't rained for weeks and every day we get a new group of rafters, red and dry from the sun, and not one of them is Orlandito.

By the calendar, it's been almost a week since I talked to his parents. It was well after midnight and I was dreaming of tiny fingers that held me fast to the sheets, a distant bell that warned me of never waking again. When the phone finally tore me from sleep, I picked it up with sweating hands. I heard the crackle of a terrible connection and knew. And then there I was, screaming into the phone the way we all end up talking to Cuba. His mother cried so much that I couldn't understand and I screamed louder for her to calm down. Then there was a crash and I thought I had lost the call and I began to scream, OYE OYE.[1] That's when his father came on. He was trying to be calm even though

---

[1] Listen, listen.

he was yelling too. Listen, he said, and there was more static. And then I heard him say Orlandito. And I screamed QUE PASA.[2] "Orlandito," he said raising his voice again, "left this morning."

I dropped the phone. Dropped it with a clack on the floor and I could still hear his father's faraway voice calling Clarita. Clarita. And all that static cutting in like metal in his throat.

I begged him not to do it. Begged him. I sent him more than a dozen letters. I don't even know if he can swim. And this makes me want to pull down the sky. I don't even know if my own husband can swim.

The next morning, I called Máximo at the restaurant and said I couldn't go in and when he started asking questions, I hung up. When the phone rang again, I didn't answer. Then I worried that it had been Orlandito and I called the restaurant and asked for Máximo. "Did you just try to call?" "Yes," he said, and I hung up again. I lay in bed and looked out the window at the wide blue of the sky. A flock of white birds flew by around noon and then they were gone and the sky was blue and hot again. I put the phone next to my pillow and waited. I thought of calling my mother, but I worried that I would miss his call. So I lay very still, my fingers dead, my arms dead, a weakness so complete that I imagined my breath turning to stone. I thought of Orlandito breathing, his lungs alive beneath his chest. And I was filled then with a certainty that he lived. That it was his voice I heard inside my thoughts. I got up and walked around the room. I felt the blood back in my fingers. I leaned out the window. The sky was bare and dry, its blue happiness drowning every memory of rain. Below, a paper cup floated on a small wind. I followed it with my eyes as it slid along the gutter and lifted into the street. It turned in circles and then rolled beneath a car, falling under its own shadow.

5   When I was a child and something was lost, my grandmother prayed to Santa Gema. Money, jewelry, papers. If she could, Santa Gema returned them. When my mother lost a pair of emerald earrings she had smuggled out of Cuba, the whole family held hands around the lemon tree in the backyard while my grandmother prayed to Santa Gema. Weeks went by. At the beginning of the summer, my father went out to trim the lemon tree and as he climbed up into the branches, he saw something reflecting the sunlight. My mother's earrings sat in a crook, a tiptoe beyond arm's reach. They were as shiny as the day she had reached up and set them there before gardening or as the day Santa Gema plucked them from oblivion and saw fit to return them.

"Santa Gema, blessed Santa Gema," I whisper. But then I am tired and want to dream a long dream of lightning and rain.

I sit at the counter telling Felipe the same story over and over. Felipe bends his long fingers around a rag and listens, quiet, his face long and gray.

Orlandito's parents woke to find his note—"Mami, Papi: Los quiero, pero este lugar no sirve pa' nada." That's it. He didn't sign it, but his parents burned

---

[2]What's happening?

it in the ashtray, afraid of where such papers can travel on their own. I tell Felipe that it doesn't bother me that Orlandito didn't mention me. I know he was tired sore of his country and of course that's what would be on his mind when he got the courage to leave. Still, I think he could have said something about me, about being reunited with his wife.

He doesn't regret marrying me, does he?

10   Felipe shakes his head and smooths the rag on his lap. He reaches out to touch my hair.

"Don't say those things," he says. "The saints punish that kind of talk."

But one month has gone without rain. Almost two weeks without my husband. And my fears pursue me. I abandon them for sleep and in the morning they return, bald-headed and rested as if night had restored them instead of me. They whisper that maybe Orlandito just wanted to disappear, erase the idea of knowing me. They look me up and down and snicker at one another. Poor thing, they say, he married her just to get out and she can't even see it.

I met him in Havana, in my grandmother's house where photographs of serious people covered the pits in the concrete walls. All night, the old women had been holding their hands to my face, telling me stories about myself that I couldn't remember. I saw him walk in with a small bag that he handed to my grandmother. And then I watched him greet the others, each with a hug, the tiny old women disappearing for a moment in his arms. My grandmother walked to where I stood watching and whispered, "The eyes don't age."

I thought, What a hard thing to have to wait until old age to receive a hug from a man like Orlandito. To have to wait until the years have chastened me, deemed me safe. I wondered who he loved. I'd lived as myself long enough to know that men like Orlandito don't love women like me. Sometimes I'll go days without looking in a mirror for longer than it takes to brush my teeth. And then I'll pass a long shiny window and wonder about the plump girl with frizzy brown hair looking back. And then it's impossible not to believe that Orlandito didn't marry me just to get out of Cuba.

15   He had that easy way that beautiful people have around the rest of us. Trying hard to pretend they don't notice how conversation slows around them. When, after the cake and wine, he finally walked up to me, the first thing he said was that my hands were cold. I thought he would take them in his and warm them. So what if that is what I wished? But he didn't. Instead, Orlandito patted me on the back. He smiled and bowed. He said that he was pleased to meet me and he shook my hand. At the end of the evening, he gave me a kiss on the cheek, no more tender than the one he gave my grandmother. That night I lay in bed listening to the drip of a faucet and willed myself to forget him.

Today, Wednesday, the Coast Guard rescued twenty-three Cuban refugees, two made it to South Beach on their own, attracting a crowd of beachgoers, and one died on the way to the hospital. Fifty-five Haitian refugees were res-

cued near the Bahamas and returned before evening. On television, the weath-
erman said it hadn't rained for thirty-five days straight because of a high-pres-
sure system over the Atlantic. It's one of the worst droughts in Miami's history
and we've been told to not waste water. The earth has started to crack.

The day after the party, Orlandito returned during the noon-time meal. My
grandmother rolled her eyes. This boy has perfect timing, she said so only I
could hear. Then she turned to him. "Clarita ate the last of the picadillo, so
you'll have to content yourself with plain rice today."

Orlandito put his hands in his pockets and shrugged. "Gracias, Señora," he
said. "But I've already eaten."

He'd come by, he said, to show me something. First I thought he was playing a game, working out an old joke between them. But my grandmother
stood in the kitchen with one plate aloft and looked at him. Finally she gave
out a breath halfway between a sigh and a laugh. She walked back to the sink
without saying a word. And then I didn't think of why he came. I stood and
followed him out the door.

20   We walked through the narrow streets of Old Havana, all the city in the
streets, old men with their skinny dogs, beautiful mulatas in tight red pants,
young men in shirtsleeves, their feet bare on the cobblestone. A woman sang
a song I didn't recognize and Orlandito stopped, listened, and then sang it
back. It was late afternoon, the streets washed in shadow, when we arrived at
a narrow door, painted yellow. It was like a happy secret in the middle of that
gray block, I saw how different it was, how hopeful, and it made me sad, looking up at him, because I had been dreaming this whole time, pretending we
had known each other all along. I was the woman he loved, walking through
the streets with him. And now standing at the yellow door, I knew that he was
an entire world I knew nothing about.

He pushed the door open. The light fell in dusty ribbons from the top windows, resting like a caress on the figures below. Small wooden birds stood next
to gigantic apples. Carved shoes dwarfed tiny houses, rendered to the last blind
in the window. I walked over sawdust to the desk where his tools lay. In a corner, a carving sat apart, light and speckled, its skin translucent. I picked it up.

"That one," he said, "is real."

I looked at him and then at the pear in my hands. I held it up and took a
bite. It was dry and gritty like sand in my mouth.

A week before I was to leave for Miami, he came by my grandmother's
house with a bunch of white gardenias. We walked along the Malecón. He held
my face as the old women had done. I tasted the salt on his lips. It was December, a tropical winter, dry and cool. The water was coming fast on the seawall,
crashing in white sprays. He whispered something and I bent in closer, straining to hear above the waves.

25   The rafter crisis—that's what the newspapers call it—is almost a month old.
Three hundred Cubans have already arrived. Today I saw a picture of a man

wearing a new white T-shirt that said Coca-Cola. He wasn't Orlandito and I couldn't even be happy for his family.

I light a candle and sit in my room. Where are you? Where are you? Damn you, Orlandito. I said I would get you over. I begged you to wait. How hard was that, idiot fool? I hate you! You deserve whatever happens to you now.

Oh Lord Jesus and the blessed saints forgive me.

I'm behind the counter thinking about the gray rag that I'm using to wipe up rings of coffee and thinking someone needs to wash it and how hopeless the whole thing is, how the rag will just get grayer and grayer. And then I hear my name being called. I stop and listen again. A boy's voice saying he wants to speak to Clarita Fuentes. My lungs become small cold marbles in my chest. Messengers in the middle of the day are like vultures. I tell Felipe to tell the boy no such person exists and then I back into the kitchen, not feeling my feet on the linoleum. I push pots into the sink. I grab a sponge and start scouring. Felipe comes into the kitchen and shuts off the water.

"It's okay," he says and takes my elbow. "Come."

30   The man is about Orlandito's age. Or even younger, so thin and brown. He fidgets in place.

"Señorita Clarita," he says, looking into my eyes. He shakes his head. "Señora, pardon me. I recognized you from the photo he had."

I cannot speak, only nod by closing my eyes from his gaze. I think, Had, had? Just like that, the past tense? I feel someone take my hands.

"I left before Orlandito," he says. "From Cojimar. Orlandito said he was coming a day after me, maybe two."

I open my eyes and he looks away.

35   "He asked me to find you here. He had a letter for you and a gift."

I look at the boy's empty hands, his thin T-shirt. Had? Had? The boy opens his arms.

"I'm so sorry," he says. "I tried to put it in my shoes, but my shoes. Something happened to them."

The restaurant is hot and moist like an animal breathing close to me. What kind of summer is this, the traffic going on as if nothing, the absurd desert sky?

"Ha muerto," I say suddenly, screaming and backing into the kitchen. "You're using the past tense. You're not looking me in the eye. He's dead! You used my maiden name! He's dead! I know he's dead!"

40   The boy takes a small step forward. His eyes open large in his thin face. Small drops of sweat hang on his forehead like a fever.

"Oh no, no." He looks to Felipe. "Please, you can't believe that. I wouldn't be the one to come. You must believe me. He just promised me to come and find you and give you the letter and the—the other thing. I'm sorry I lost it. A sculpture. I don't know what happened. We were seven on the raft. I was thirsty."

The boy looks to Felipe.

"Oh my God, what am I thinking," Felipe says. "You poor boy."

He screams back into the kitchen, "Raúl, get me an order of picadillo and some Pepsi for this boy."

45 Felipe puts his hand on my shoulder and disappears into the kitchen.
The boy turns to me. "He made me promise." He looks to the floor.
"Stop it, stop it!" I shout. "I'm the one who's supposed to cry!"
What kind of thing was happening? Time had a quality I barely recognized, a way of running over itself. The questions balled in my throat. Was he afraid? Why did he come? How many times did he say my name?
"What kind of sculpture?" I finally ask.
50 The boy shakes his head. His eyes and nose are red and they seem the only living things in his dry face.
"Don't cry, please."
The boy makes a small sound and nods. When Raúl puts the plate of food down before him, he bursts into tears.

Now I know that he was thinking about me when he left. I thought this would make me happy—to know he was thinking about me. But that doesn't matter anymore. I only want him to be here, I want him to be dry and warm. That's all. I tell myself he couldn't have the bad luck to marry an ugly woman and drown in the middle of nowhere, alone under the stars. I say it as a joke to myself, but even then it comes out wrong. Maybe the sculpture was of a pear. Maybe the boy on the raft tried to eat it.

I light a candle and hold out the ring Orlandito carved for me: its surface crisscrossed in a diamond pattern, the inside engraved with an O and a C laced together. I try to pray. But I can't look at this ring without feeling so tired sad I can't move my lips. And I lie in bed looking out at the blue, blue sky, the sun that is drying me from the inside out, and think: watersharkswatersharks-raftssunburnsharksdehydrationwaterwatersunsharksraftswater drowndrowndrown.

55 Today, Felipe passed me the number of a woman who works with herbs. I haven't decided whether I should go. I keep thinking the phone's going to ring. The Coast Guard, saying "Mrs. Alarcon?" I've imagined it so many times, down to the timbre of the voice on the other line. "Mrs. Alarcon, we have good news." And I seize on the Mrs. Because that's what I am. "Mrs. Alar-con, we have your husband." And I imagine how I let go of the phone, and the sound of it dropping. I imagine it so well that when I woke this morning, I thought it had already happened. And then how terrible to wake when sleep is the thin blanket you wrap yourself in against your thoughts.

Felipe asks me every day if I pray. He says to pray to Santa Barbara of the lost sailors. I correct him, tell him he's confusing the saints again.

He opens his hands. I think of calling him an old fool, but stop when I see the calluses and scratches like lines in a book.

"Some of those rafts come in empty and others don't," I say instead. "I wonder what saint can explain that."

Everyone is saying how if it doesn't rain soon, the government is going to have to seed the clouds. They do that in some kind of special plane. I wonder why can't they send the plane to look for my husband?

60   Oh Orlandito, where are you right this moment, this second that I stare at
the cloudless sky?

The herb woman Felipe told me about lives in a house hidden by trees at
the end of a street of big, quiet houses in Coral Gables. She opens the door in
a red suit, a white handkerchief at her neck, and I tell her she doesn't look like
a Santera.

She leads me to a room, empty except for a white rug and a circle of red
chairs around a table piled with fresh leaves.

"I'm not a Santera," she says. "But I used to be a saint."

She smiles and motions me to sit. I wonder if I am meant to laugh.

65   "Your husband is lost," she says, and I don't like the way her voice refuses
to rise into a question.

I shake my head to show that she is mistaken. "I'm here to see you about
the rain."

"Then your husband has been found?"

I close my eyes. "All I want is for the drought to end."

The woman looks at me and then takes a small bunch of leaves in front of
her and begins to weave them together.

70   "Yes," she says finally. "It hasn't rained for a very long time."

She stops and turns toward the door. A man carries a tray of tea. He is so
pale that his eyes are rimmed in red as if he's been weeping since the beginning of the world.

"Please drink," the woman says.

"I don't need anything to calm me," I say.

She shakes her head.

75   "No," she says. "It will give you strength."

"I don't want potions."

The woman motions to the man. With one hand, he pushes back the pile
of leaves from the table and with the other, he sets the tray down. He bows
and leaves the room.

She pours a cup for me and one for herself. I wait for her and then hold the
cup to my lips, but I don't drink.

"I don't know what I'm doing here," I say. I want to stand, but I cannot
move; sitting is much easier. I am so tired.

80   "You are trying to find the lost rain," she says. "Please stay. I will tell you
how."

She takes another sip of her tea and looks up at me. Her eyes are clear and
big, like the sea.

"Droughts are very old," she says. "Even though we always think we are
the first to suffer."

After a while she says she will tell me a story so that I understand the songs
in the grass, the structure of leaves.

She begins in her low voice.

85   "In the beginning the orishas, the gods of the lesser world, rebelled against
Olodumare and plotted to divide his powers among themselves. But nothing

can be hidden from Olodumare. He sees even to the liquid center of the world and pulls back the dark cover on the thoughts of man. One night without moon, Olodumare discovered the plot. He took his pain and rage and molded them into revenge and that same night he held his hands out and stopped the rain.

"On the earth, the clouds evaporated before day. The morning arrived dry and blue and at first the orishas celebrated the new light. For seven weeks they danced under the sun. But as they danced, the rivers slowly disappeared back into the earth. The green crops dried to brown. Until the whole world rose in lament, hungry and dry and mournful of all the rain they had forsaken."

The woman puts her cup down and closes her eyes, as if a great fatigue had overtaken her. After a while she begins again.

"The empty sky now seemed sinister, an eye into the wide possibilities of a world they didn't really know. Both the mortal and the immortal felt alone and exposed. They hid in the light of day. And then the orishas began to fight among themselves, each assigning blame to the other."

The woman stops and opens her eyes. She leans back in her chair. Her face is pale above the dark hollows.

90   "You see," she says. "It has always been the same."

She drinks from her cup and sits for a long while before continuing.

"Only one orisha, the beautiful Oshun who had taken the form of a peacock, rose to offer a solution. She would fly to heaven herself and plead with the All-Mighty for mercy. The others laughed at her, a vain and worthless bird. But Oshun didn't listen. Oshun flew to heaven, the sun burning her feathers, she flew to heaven."

She stops and waits for me to answer.

"Suffering is very old," the herb woman says when I stand to go. "Older than man."

95   I walk out of the herb woman's house and curse the blue, tell it to explode in flames, go black with smoke, collapse onto the world. I shout to the sky, He's not dead! He's not dead! All you unbelievers will see.

I lie in bed and try to sleep. All suffering is not the same. Mine is the first suffering. Orlandito is the only man like himself, the first with three freckles on his back and long arms and big hands for sculpting.

I pray to Santa Gema to find my lost husband, I pray to Santa Barbara of the lost thunder, and I pray to the Virgin of Charity, reminding her of the fishermen she saved once, reminding her of her duty to Cuba.

And then I pray to the All-Mighty for rain that darkens the sky and brings night and with it the sweet sleep that suspends memory.

We drove to Cojimar on a Tuesday. I remember passing through the countryside as through water, the car heavy, the air heavy, the slow ramble past liquid landscapes. And in me, the weightlessness of happiness. Feeling that this was the reason people continued to live past disappointments and tragedies, for moments when the body floats on its own joy.

100   Images return to me now in fragments. Orlandito's thick hands on the wheel, his fingers tapping out a tune he carries in his head. His hair tumbling in the wind. Orlandito turning to me, putting out his arm and drawing me closer so that I could inhale the warm scent of him, like the earth after a rain.

The fisherman had been a priest before the revolution and now lived in a wood house he'd built for himself and the woman who had called him into his new life. They were both old and thin, slow to gesture with their hands. They stood in the open door together without speaking, just looking at us. And then the old fisherman clapped Orlandito on the back and said, "Well, congratulations, young man."

He married us on the sand, with the sea to our backs. His wife stood by his side, holding open a book of poetry that the fisherman read through half-closed lips. The wind batted the sand on my bare legs and, behind me, the ocean told story after story.

We spent the night in a room with bare windows open to the black sky. We lay close and listened to the wind in the stars. He warmed my hands in his. After a while I felt him move and then he sat and I asked him what he thought.

"You leave in two days," he said.

105   I told him we had agreed not to say it.

"But you do and then I'll be alone again."

I told him I would bring him back with me. He was my husband. I was Mrs. Alarcon. He shook his head and turned his face away from me. Not an official ceremony, no papers. Don't worry about the papers, I said. I was a real wedding. I would talk with a lawyer. I would bring him back.

He lay down and looked up at me. His face was dark in the shadow and I could see just his hands in the starlight.

"You are beautiful," he said after a moment. "You don't know this. But you are so beautiful and you will forget about me one day."

110   I made promises as the night shivered through the open window.

A wet wind has come up. I call in sick and hear Felipe's tired voice like bubbles on the line. I feel nothing. I'm thinking this wind that's come up, the ocean, the ocean and drowning.

I start to think it's going to be fine because these things don't happen to women like me. What was I? A waitress in Little Havana. I cared that I had frizzy hair and what a lifetime of platanitos had done to my figure.

To be that woman again! To worry about those things. Not the ocean that gets into my dreams now, the waves dampening the sheets. How can I say that I still have heard nothing. That I pray every night into a black space that waits to strangle me in the dark.

The sun today, bright in a deep sky. Orlandito, did you see it?

115   And then, like waking, comes the herb woman with the story of Oshun. Who turned to me and said, "Already you know your husband is dead."

Today, I prayed only for rain, rain that falls in blue drops, that restores the ocean, that blocks the sun. If it would rain, we could breathe again. But there is too much light and a month has gone by without word.

I am learning again to fly. The silence is like the open sky I carry on my back. And there is so much I've forgotten. How quiet it is up here and clear. The sun is hot through my feathers, and at first I am afraid that my colors will bleed. Below, a white basin where the ocean used to be, its ribs glistening in the light.

Even if I tire, I will fly. Climb the air like a bridge. The sun that grows bigger will burn my beautiful feathers black. I will arrive in heaven bald and hunchbacked, my face a shriveled countenance for the Lord. And he will take pity on me.

And the rain fell in heavy sheets that touched the earth again with green, a blue restoring rain. It washed out the dust of summer, crowded the sky with clouds. The green hills rose again like the first time, the world warmed at their feet, the thin new trees straightened in the moist wind.

And the rain fell over mountains where yellow flowers grew and over plains of tall grass. It taught the young crops to breathe again and filled the white basin of the sea. The rain restored the blue oceans. And everything was as it should be and the new waters rippled gently away from Cuba as if the island itself were a stone dropped by God above.

POETRY

Jimmy Santiago Baca

A self-taught poet and essayist, Jimmy Santiago Baca was born in Santa Fe, New Mexico, in 1952. When he was five years old, his alcoholic father died, and Baca was placed in an orphanage. Like Miguel Piñero, his early adult years involved drugs, crime, and prison, where he began to write. He recently earned a doctorate in literature at the University of Mexico and has won numerous prizes, including the Pushcart Prize in 1988, the National Hispanic Heritage Award in 1989, and the American Book Award, also in 1989. His publications include several works of poetry: *What's Happening* (1982), *Martin and Meditations on the South Valley* (1987), *Black Mesa Poems* (1989), *Immigrants in Our Own Land* (1991), and *Healing Earthquakes* (2001); a memoir, *A Place to Stand* (2001); and a collection of poetic vignettes based on the lure of addiction to cocaine, *C-Train and 13 Mexicans* (2002).

Roots

Ten feet beyond the back door
the cottonwood tree
is a steaming stone of beginning time.
A battle-scarred warrior
5   whose great branches knock
telephone poles aside, mangle trailers
to meager tin-foil in its grasp,
clip chunks of stucco off my house

10 so sparrows can nest in gaps,
wreck my car hood, splinter
sections of my rail fence,
   all,
    with uncompromising nostalgia
    for warring storms.

15 I am like this tree
Spanish saddle-makers copied
dressing from.
The dense gray wrath of its bark
is the trackway
20 shipwrecked captains, shepherds, shepherdesses,
barn-burners, fence cutters followed.
Camped here at the foot of Black Mesa,
beneath this cottonwood,
leaned muskets on this trunk,
25 stuck knife blades into its canyon valley bark,
red-beaded tasseled arm sleeves clashing
with each throw, as the knife
pierced cattail or bamboo
pinched in bark.

30 I come back to myself
near this tree, and think of my roots
in this land—
Papa and me working in the field.
I tell Papa, "Look, here comes someone."
35 He rises, pulls red handkerchief from back pocket,
takes sombrero off, wipes sweat from brow.
You drive up to our field. Unclip briefcase
on the hood of your new government blue car.
Spread official papers out, point with manicured fingers,
40 telling Papa what he must do.
He lifts a handful of earth by your polished shoe,
and tells you in Spanish, it carries the way of his life.
Before history books were written,
family blood ran through this land,
45 thrashed against mountain walls and in streams,
fed seeds, and swords, and flowers.
"My heart is a root in this earth!" he said in Spanish, angrily.
You didn't understand Spanish, you told him,
you were not to blame for the way things must be.
50 The government must have his land.
The Land Grant Deed was no good.
You left a trail of dust in our faces.

I asked Papa how a skinny man like you
could take our land away.
55 He wept that night, wept a strong cry,
as if blood were pouring from his eyes,
instead of tears. I remember hearing his voice
coming through the walls into my bedroom,
"They twist my arms back and tear the joints,
60 and they crush my spine with their boots…"

In my mind's eye I looked into the man's face
for a long time. I stared at his car for a long time,
and knew as a child I would carry the image
of the enemy in my heart forever.

65   Henceforth,
          I will call this cottonwood
          Father.

Dust-Bowl Memory

for Abaskin

My ancient neighbor, Mr. Abaskin,
was born in Russia, roamed Europe,
and when the call came from America,
he boarded ship and came.
5 Seventy years farming this land.
Every morning he walks the dirt road
with his aging wife, reminding me
of two solitary mesquite trees
rooted high at the edge of a rocky cliff,
10 overlooking a vast canyon gorge.
Hands hardened, yellow claws
from farming tenderly pocket candy
in my son's pants.
He scolds his shepherd Kiki
15 for exciting grazing sheep or scaring
Rhode Island Reds. We meet every noon
by the fence where our feed is
and small talk
conditions of fields,
20 how he and his wife could buck
three hundred bales an afternoon
when they were my age.
His memory an old dust-bowl town,
he remembers who lived where
25 before we came, who was born to whom,

when Williams' Packing Company started
stealing people's cattle, when people
started locking their screen doors,
and a time when only Spanish was spoken in this valley.
30   "Didn't have to go to town. These Mexican folk
had the finest gardens in the world,
why tomatoes and chile you wouldn't believe...."

Victor Hernández Cruz

Victor Hernández Cruz was born in Puerto Rico in 1949 and moved to East Harlem when he was five years old. He is the author of several collections of poetry including *Snaps* (1969), *Mainland* (1973), *Tropicalization* (1976), *By Lingual Wholes* (1982), *Rhythm, Content and Flavor* (1989), *Red Beans* (1991), *Panaramas* (1997), and *Maraca: New and Selected Poems 1965–2000* (2001). He is known for incorporating musical rhythms (in this case, salsa) into his lyrics. Considered an important contributor to the Nuyorican poet group, Cruz has also reached deep into mainstream audiences and won praise from academic scholars for his linguistic, code-switching style.

African Things

o the wonder man   rides his space ship/
        brings his power through
many moons
        carries in soft blood   african spirits
5   dance & sing in my mother's house. in my cousin's house.
black as night can be/   what was Puerto Rican all about.
        all about the
indios & you better believe it the african things
        black & shiny
10   grandmother speak to me & tell me of african things
            how do latin
boo-ga-loo   sound like you
        conga drums in the islands   you know
the traveling through many moons
15   dance & tell me black african things
i know you know.

Diane de Anda

Diane de Anda was born in Los Angeles and teaches in the Department of Social Welfare at the University of California, Los Angeles. Her poetry has been published in the Chicano journal *El Grito*. Besides poetry, de Anda has written a children's book, *Dancing Miranda/Baila Miranda baila* (2001), and two collections of short stories for young readers, *The Ice Dove and Other Stories* (1997) and *Immortal Rooster and Other Stories* (1999). De Anda has also written nonfiction related to her field of social work.

Abuelas[1]

Into the whirlwind of their history
we strode in soldiers' boots and *bandoleras,* [2]
wrestling the wailing grasp of girlhood ghosts
caught on the horse hooves of *la Revolución.*

5   They spun their life songs in trilling chords,
spilling dark memories in secret whispers,
weaving *dichos*[3] across my childhood,
chanting magic to quell my children's cries.

Alone with the remnants of their memories,
10   the spirits they conjured lie still and fading.
The fire that forged breath into shadows past,
branding their phantoms into my senses—
APAGADO[4]

Written on the death of my grandmother,
Nacha, and the passing of a generation.

Carolina Hospital

Poet, translator, and essayist Carolina Hospital was born in Havana, Cuba, in 1957 and moved with her family to Miami in 1961. She is the author of a novel, *A Little Love* (2000, under the pen name C.C. Medina), and has published stories and poems in numerous anthologies, journals, and magazines. In 1996, she coedited a collection, *A Century of Cuban Writers in Florida: Selected Prose and Poetry.* Her book *A Child of Exile: A Poetry Memoir* was published in 2004. Hospital teaches English at Miami Dade Community College.

Finding Home

I have travelled north again,
to these gray skies
and empty doorways,

---

[1]Grandmothers
[2]bandoleers
[3]proverbs
[4]extinguished

Fall, and I recognize
5   the rusted leaves descending
near the silence of your home.
You, a part of this strange
American landscape with its
cold dry winds,
10   the honks of geese and
the hardwood floors. It's more
familiar now than
the fluorescent rainbow on the overpass,
or the clatter of politicos in the corners,
15   or the palm fronds falling by the highway.
I must travel again, soon.

Magdalena Gómez

Magdalena Gómez is a poet, playwright, journalist, and performance artist. She has written numerous works for the theater, including the plays *No Greater Love*, *The Paschal Mystery*, *Lobster Face (or the shame of Amanda Cockshutt)*, and *In Loving Memory*. Currently she is a teaching artist in the Arts and Literacy Project of Brown University. Gómez has received acclaim for her solo performance pieces such as *Chopping*, and *Cha-Cha in Love with Antonio Banderas*. She is working on a CD of poetry entitled *AmaXonica: Howls from the Left Side of My Body*.

Mami

Mami, your hand reaches across the island
pushing palm trees aside
clutching birds in mid-flight
spin the sun on the finger
5   that pointed to all my faults
clouds slip through the spaces of your grasp
you immigrate into my dreams
I blame restlessness on too much
café y cigarillos
10   too many carros
y las windows slapping up and down
letting in the day
keeping out the night
y la T.V. y las pepsicocasevenupandown
15   y el screeching del subway through
my empty stomach
y las garbage can congas
y las manos that beg me for what I don't have
and visions of the World Trade Center
20   crumbling from an earthquake of greed
and a lingering spell from the witch who

raised you hauling buckets of blood and water
to and from the river
where you drowned before you died

25 you spin my head on the finger
that pointed to all my faults
my eyes cannot find me
only rage stops the spinning
when the courage for anger comes

30 drawing a spear of light from my womb
I seek the look that mutilates
    cripples
    but does not kill

the potion of your suffering brews and spills
35 burning my hand
spear turns to glass

I see your face in mine
child in chains
beats child with chains
40 one by one the shadows fall
two by two they multiply
rage melts into pity

as it was done to you
let it be done to me

45 the slaying can wait one more day

Pat Mora

Pat Mora was born in El Paso, Texas. Her collections of poetry *Chants* (1984), *Borders* (1986), *Communion* (1991), and *Agua Santa: Holy Water* (1997) have garnered her considerable praise—she has twice received the Southwest Book Award—and her poems are widely anthologized. She has also written a memoir, *House of Houses* (1997), and a book of essays, *Nepantla: Essays from the Land in the Middle* (1993). In addition to these works, Mora is the author of a long list of literature for children.

Curandera[1]

They think she lives alone
on the edge of town in a two-room house
where she moved when her husband died
at thirty-five of a gunshot wound
5 in the bed of another woman. The *curandera*

---

[1] a female healer

and house have aged together to the rhythm
of the desert.

She wakes early, lights candles before
her sacred statues, brews tea of *yerbabuena.* [2]
10 She moves down her porch steps, rubs
cool morning sand into her hands, into her arms.
Like a large black bird, she feeds on
the desert, gathering herbs for her basket.

Her days are slow, days of grinding
15 dried snake into powder, of crushing
wild bees to mix with white wine.
And the townspeople come, hoping
to be touched by her ointments
her hands, her prayers, her eyes.
20 She listens to their stories, and she listens
to the desert, always, to the desert.

By sunset she is tired. The wind
strokes the strands of long gray hair,
the smell of drying plants drifts
25 into her blood, the sun seeps
into her bones. She dozes
on her back porch. Rocking, rocking.

At night she cooks chopped cactus
and brews more tea. She brushes a layer
30 of sand from her bed, sand which covers
the table, stove, floor. She blows
the statues clean, the candles out.
Before sleeping, she listens to the message
of the owl and the coyote. She closes her eyes
35 and breathes with the mice and snakes
and wind.

Judith Ortiz Cofer

Judith Ortiz Cofer was born in 1952, in Hormigueros, Puerto Rico, and moved to Patterson, New Jersey, as a child. She is probably best known as the author of *Silent Dancing* (1990) but has also published a partly autobiographical novel, *The Line of the Sun* (1989); a collection of stories for young readers, *An Island Like You* (1995); and several works that interweave poetry with prose, *The Latin Deli* (1993) and *The Year of Our Revolution* (1998). She has also written a collection of essays and three books of poetry, *Peregrina* (1986), *Terms of Survival* (1987), and *Reaching for the Mainland* (1987). Often cited by younger writers as an

---

[2]herb

inspiring force, Ortiz Cofer is considered one of the most important mainland
Puerto Rican writers in Latino literature.

The Latin Deli: An Ars Poetica

Presiding over a formica counter,
plastic Mother and Child magnetized   *Virgin Mary / Virgin of Guadalupe*
to the top of an ancient register,
the heady mix of smells from the open bins
5   of dried codfish, the green plantains
hanging in stalks like votive offerings,
she is the Patroness of Exiles,
a woman of no-age who was never pretty,
who spends her days selling canned memories
10   while listening to the Puerto Ricans complain
that it would be cheaper to fly to San Juan
than to buy a pound of Bustelo coffee here,
and to Cubans perfecting their speech
of a "glorious return" to Havana—where no one
15   has been allowed to die and nothing to change until then;
to Mexicans who pass through, talking lyrically
of *dólares* to be made in El Norte—
    all wanting the comfort
of spoken Spanish, to gaze upon the family portrait
20   of her plain wide face, her ample bosom
resting on her plump arms, her look of maternal interest
as they speak to her and each other
of their dreams and their disillusions—
how she smiles understanding,
25   when they walk down the narrow aisles of her store
reading the labels of packages aloud, as if
they were the names of lost lovers: *Suspiros*,
Merengues, the stale candy of everyone's childhood.
        She spends her days
30   slicing *jamón y queso*[1] and wrapping it in wax paper
tied with string: plain ham and cheese
that would cost less at the A&P, but it would not satisfy
the hunger of the fragile old man lost in the folds
of his winter coat, who brings her lists of items
35   that he reads to her like poetry, or the others,
whose needs she must divine, conjuring up products
from places that now exist only in their hearts—
closed ports she must trade with.

---

[1]ham and cheese

Ricardo Pau-Llosa

Ricardo Pau-Llosa was born in Cuba in 1954 and moved to the United States six years later. He is a poet, short story writer, teacher (at Miami Dade Community College), and art critic. Pau-Llosa has published several collections of poetry, including *Sorting Metaphors* (1983), which won the first Anhinga Poetry Prize; *Bread of the Imagined* (1992); *Cuba* (1993); *Vereda Tropical* (1999); and *The Mastery Impulse* (2002). He has also written extensively on Latin American art and Cuban artists.

Frutas

Growing up in Miami any tropical fruit I ate
could only be a bad copy of the Real Fruit of Cuba.
Exile meant having to consume false food,
and knowing it in advance. With joy

5   my parents and grandmother would encounter
Florida-grown mameyes and caimitos at the market.
At home they would take them out of the American bag
and describe the taste that I and my older sister
would, in a few seconds, be privileged to experience

10   for the first time. We all sat around the table
to welcome into our lives this football-shaped,
brown fruit with the salmon-colored flesh
encircling an ebony seed. "Mamey,"
my grandmother would say with a confirming nod,

15   as if repatriating a lost and ruined name.
Then she bent over the plate,
slipped a large slice of mamey into her mouth,
then straightened in her chair and, eyes shut,
lost herself in comparison and memory.

20   I waited for her face to return with a judgment.
"No, not even the shadow of the ones back home."
She kept eating more calmly,
and I began tasting the sweet and creamy pulp
trying to raise the volume of its flavor

25   so that it might become a Cuban mamey. "The good
Cuban mameyes didn't have primaveras," she said
after the second large gulp, knocking her spoon
against a lump in the fruit and winking.
So at once I erased the lumps in my mental mamey.

30   I asked her how the word for "spring"
came to signify "lump" in a mamey. She shrugged.
"Next you'll want to know how we lost a country."

Aleida Rodríguez

Aleida Rodríguez was born in Güines, Cuba, in 1953, and in the early 1960s, she was one of approximately 15,000 Cuban children sent to the U.S. via Operation Peter Pan, a collaboration between the Catholic Church and the CIA. She was relocated to a foster home in Illinois, where she awaited the arrival of her parents, who were still in Cuba and who reunited with her two years later. Her poetry has been published in more than 75 publications over more than three decades. She has received numerous grants, fellowships (including one from the National Endowment for the Arts), and awards, among them the PEN USA 2000 Literary Award in Poetry for her collection *Garden of Exile* (1999). She lives in Los Angeles.

The First Woman

She was my Sunday school teacher
when I was just seven and eight.
He was the newly hired pastor,

5   an albino, alarming sight
with his transparent eyelashes
and mouse-pink skin that looked like it

might hurt whenever she caressed
his arm. Since Eva was her name,
to my child's mind it made great sense

10   that she should fall in love with him.
He was Adán. Before the Fall
and afterward, her invert twin.

And she, Eva, was blonde as well,
though more robust, like Liv Ullmann.
15   I loved her honey hair, her full

lips; her green eyes a nameless sin.
(Not that I worried all that much—
the church was Presbyterian.)

In Sunday school, her way to teach
20   us kids to pray was to comment
on all the beauty we could touch

or see in our environment.
My hand was always in the air
to volunteer my sentiment.

25   Since other kids considered prayer
a chore, the floor was usually mine.
My list of joys left out her hair

but blessed the red hibiscus seen
through the windows while others bowed
30   their heads. Her heart I schemed to win

with purple prose on meringue clouds.
—For who was Adán, anyway,
I thought, but *nada* spelled backward?

While hers, reversed, called out, *Ave!*
35   *Ave!* The lyric of a bird
born and airborne on the same day.

But it was night when I saw her
outside the church for the last time:
yellow light, mosquitoes, and summer.

40   I shaped a barking dog, a fine
but disembodied pair of wings
with my hands. She spoke in hushed tones

to my parents. The next day I would find
myself up north, in a strange house,
45   without my tongue and almost blind,

there was so much to see. This caused
Cuba, my past, to be eclipsed
in time, but Eva stayed, a loss.

Ave, I learned, meant also this:
50   *Farewell!* I haven't seen her since.

Gary Soto

Gary Soto was born to a family of migrant workers in Fresno, California, in 1952. His father died when Soto was five years old, and his family moved to an Anglo part of Fresno where he grew up somewhat distanced from the 1960s *movimiento*. One of the most published Latino authors, his memoir, *Living Up the Street* (1985), earned the National Book Award. In addition to his seven books of poetry, he has published several novels and numerous works for children and young adults.

History

Grandma lit the stove.
Morning sunlight
Lengthened in spears
Across the linoleum floor,
5   Wrapped in a shawl,
Her eyes small
With sleep,

She sliced *papas*,
Pounded chiles
10   With a stone
Brought from Guadalajara.

                    After
Grandpa left for work,
She hosed down
15   The walk her sons paved
And in the shade
Of a chinaberry,
Unearthed her
Secret cigar box
20   Of bright coins
And bills, counted them
In English,
Then in Spanish,
And buried them elsewhere.
25   Later, back
From the market,
Where no one saw her,
She pulled out
Pepper and beet, spines
30   Of asparagus
From her blouse,
Tiny chocolates
From under a paisley bandana,
And smiled.

35   That was the fifties
And Grandma in her fifties,
A face streaked
From cutting grapes
And boxing plums.
40   I remember her insides
Were washed of tapeworm,
Her arms swelled into knobs
Of small growths—
Her second son
45   Dropped from a ladder
And was dust.
And yet I do not know
The sorrows
That sent her praying
50   In the dark of a closet,
The tear that fell

At night
When she touched loose skin
Of belly and breasts.
55   I do not know why
Her face shines
Or what goes beyond this shine,
Only the stories
That pulled her
60   From Taxco to San Joaquin,
Delano to Westside,
The places
In which we all begin.

ESSAY

Richard Rodriguez

A prize-winning nonfiction writer, Richard Rodriguez is the author of the controversial memoir, *Hunger of Memory: The Education of Richard Rodriguez* (1983), in which he suggests the need for Chicanos to abandon their cultural Spanish past to succeed in the English-speaking United States. The book continues to draw fire from supporters of bilingual education and affirmative action. His second work, *Days of Obligation* (1993), and his latest book, *Brown: The Last Discovery of America* (2003), have established his reputation as a major essayist. He is a contributing editor to *Harper's Magazine*, Pacific News Service, and *U.S. News and World Report*. Over the last 20 years, he has provided essays and commentaries to National Public Broadcasting and to most of the major newspapers and magazines in the United States.

Go North, Young Man

Traditionally, America has been an east-west country. We have read our history, right to left across the page. We were oblivious of Canada. We barely noticed Mexico, except when Mexico got in the way of our westward migration, which we interpreted as the will of God, "manifest destiny."

In a Protestant country that believed in rebirth (the Easter promise), land became our metaphor for possibility. As long as there was land ahead of us—Ohio, Illinois, Nebraska—we could believe in change; we could abandon our in-laws, leave disappointments behind, to start anew further west. California symbolized ultimate possibility, future-time, the end of the line, where loonies and prophets lived, where America's fads necessarily began.

Nineteenth-century real estate developers and 20th-century Hollywood moguls may have advertised the futuristic myth of California to the rest of America. But the myth was one Americans were predisposed to believe. The idea of California was invented by Americans many miles away. Only a few early voices from California ever warned against optimism. Two decades after California became American territory, the conservationist John Muir stood at the edge of California and realized that America is a finite idea: We need to preserve the land, if the dream of America is to survive. Word of Muir's discovery slowly traveled backward in time, from the barely populated West (the future) to the crowded brick cities of the East Coast (the past).

I grew up in California of the 1950s, when the state was filling with people from New York and Oklahoma. Everyone was busy losing weight and changing hair color and becoming someone new. There was, then, still plenty of cheap land for tract houses, under the cloudless sky.

5   The 1950s, the 1960s—those years were our golden age. Edmund G. "Pat" Brown was governor of optimism. He created the University of California system, a decade before the children of the suburbs rebelled, portraying themselves as the "counterculture." Brown constructed free-ways that permitted Californians to move farther and farther away from anything resembling an urban center. He even made the water run up the side of a mountain.

By the 1970s, optimism was running out of space. Los Angeles needed to reinvent itself as Orange County. Then Orange County got too crowded and had to reinvent itself as North County San Diego. Then Californians started moving into the foothills or out to the desert, complaining all the while of the traffic and of the soiled air. And the immigrants!

Suddenly, foreign immigrants were everywhere—Iranians were buying into Beverly Hills; the Vietnamese were moving into San Jose; the Chinese were taking all the spaces in the biochemistry courses at UCLA. And Mexicans, poor Mexicans, were making hotel beds, picking peaches in the Central Valley, changing diapers, even impersonating Italian chefs at Santa Monica restaurants.

The Mexicans and the Chinese had long inhabited California. But they never resided within the golden myth of the state. Nineteenth-century California restricted the Chinese to Chinatowns or to a city's outskirts. Mexicans were neither here nor there. They were imported by California to perform cheap labor, then deported in bad economic times.

The East Coast had incorporated Ellis Island in its myth. The West Coast regarded the non-European immigrant as doubly foreign. Though Spaniards may have colonized the place and though Mexico briefly claimed it, California took its meaning from "internal immigrants"—Americans from Minnesota or Brooklyn who came West to remake their parents' version of America.

10   But sometime in the 1970s, it became clear to many Californians that the famous blond myth of the state was in jeopardy. ("We are sorry to intrude, señor, we are only looking for work.") Was L. A. "becoming" Mexican?

Latin Americans arrived, describing California as "el norte." The "West Coast" was a finite idea; *el norte* in the Latin American lexicon means wide-open. Whose compass was right?

Meanwhile, with the lifting of anti-Asian immigration restrictions, jumbo jets were arriving at LAX from Bangkok and Seoul. People getting off the planes said about California, "This is where the United States begins." California objected, "No, no. California is where the United States comes to an end—we don't have enough room for you." Whose compass was truer?

It has taken two more decades for the East Coast to get the point. Magazines and television stories from New York today describe the golden state as "tarnished." The more interesting possibility is that California has become the intersection between comedy and tragedy. Foreign immigrants are replanting optimism on California soil; the native-born know the wisdom of finitude. Each side has a knowledge to give the other.

Already, everywhere in California, there is evidence of miscegenation—Keanu Reeves, sushi tacos, blond Buddhists, Salvadoran Pentecostals. But the forces that could lead to marriage also create gridlock on the Santa Monica freeway. The native-born Californian sits disgruntled in traffic going nowhere. The flatbed truck in front of him is filled with Mexicans; in the Mercedes next to him is a Japanese businessman using a car phone.

15   There are signs of backlash. Pete Wilson has become the last east-west governor of California. In a state founded by people seeking a softer winter and famous internationally for being "laid back," Californians vote for Proposition 187, hoping that illegal immigrants will stay away if there are no welfare dollars.

But immigrants are most disconcerting to California because they are everywhere working, transforming the ethos of the state from leisure to labor. Los Angeles is becoming a vast working city, on the order of Hong Kong or Mexico City. Chinese kids are raising the admission standards to the University of California. Mexican immigrant kids are undercutting union wages, raising rents in once-black neighborhoods.

Californians used to resist any metaphor drawn from their state's perennial earthquakes and floods and fires. Now Californians take their meaning from natural calamity. People turn away from the sea, imagine the future as existing backward in time.

"I'm leaving California, I'm going to Colorado."

"I'm headed for Arizona."

20   After hitting the coastline like flies against glass, we look in new directions. Did Southern California's urban sprawl invent NAFTA? For the first time, Californians now talk of the North and the South—new points on our national compass.

"I've just bought a condo in Baja."

"I'm leaving California for Seattle."

"I'm moving to Vancouver. I want someplace cleaner."

"Go North, young man."

25   Puerto Ricans, Mexicans: early in this century we were immigrants. Or not immigrants exactly. Puerto Ricans had awakened one day to discover that they suddenly lived on U.S. territory. Mexicans had seen Mexico's northern territory annexed and renamed the southwestern United States.

We were people from the South in an east-west country. We were people of mixed blood in a black and white nation. We were Catholics in a Protestant land. Many millions of us were Indians in an east-west country that imagined the Indian to be dead.

Today, Los Angeles is the largest Indian city in the United States, though Hollywood filmmakers persist in making movies about the dead Indian. (For seven bucks, you can see cowboys slaughter Indians in the Kevin Costner movie—and regret it from your comfortable chair.) On any day along Sunset Boulevard you can see Toltecs and Aztecs and Mayans.

Puerto Ricans, Mexicans—we are the earliest Latin American immigrants to the United States. We have turned into fools. We argue among ourselves, criticize one another for becoming too much the gringo or maybe not gringo enough. We criticize each other for speaking too much Spanish or not enough Spanish. We demand that politicians provide us with bilingual voting ballots, but we do not trouble to vote.

Octavio Paz, the Mexican writer, has observed that the Mexican-American is caught between cultures, thus a victim of history—unwilling to become a Mexican again, unable to belong to the United States. Michael Novak, the United States writer, has observed that what unites people throughout the Americas is that we all have said goodbye to our motherland. To Europe. To Africa. To Asia. Farewell!

30   The only trouble is: *Adios* was never part of the Mexican-American or Puerto Rican vocabulary. There was no need to turn one's back on the past. Many have traveled back and forth, between rivals, between past and future, commuters between the Third World and First. After a few months in New York or Los Angeles, it would be time to head "home." After a few months back in Mexico or Puerto Rico, it would be time to head "home" to the United States.

We were nothing like the famous Ellis Island immigrants who arrived in America with no expectation of return to the "old country." In a nation that believed in the future, we were a puzzle.

We were also a scandal to Puerto Rico and Mexico. Our Spanish turned bad. Our values were changing—though no one could say why or how exactly. *Abuelita* (grandmother) complained that we were growing more guarded. Alone.

There is a name that Mexico uses for children who have forgotten their true address: *pocho*. The *pocho* is the child who wanders away, ends up in the United States, among the gringos, where he forgets his true home.

The Americas began with a confusion about maps and a joke about our father's mistake. Columbus imagined himself in a part of the world where there were Indians.

35   We smile because our 15th-century *papi* thought he was in India. I'm not certain, however, that even today we know where in the world we live. We are only beginning to look at the map. We are only beginning to wonder what the map of the hemisphere might mean.

Latin Americans have long complained that the gringo, with characteristic arrogance, hijacked the word *American* and gave it all to himself—"the way he stole the land." I remember, years ago, my aunt in Mexico City scolding me when I told her I came from "America." *Pocho!* Didn't I realize that the entire hemisphere is America? "Listen," my Mexican aunt told me, "people who live in the United States are *norteamericanos.*"

Well, I think to myself—my aunt is now dead, God rest her soul—I wonder what she would have thought a couple of years ago when the great leaders—the president of Mexico, the president of the United States, the Canadian prime minister—gathered to sign the North American Free Trade Agreement. Mexico signed a document acknowledging that she is a North American.

I predict that Mexico will suffer a nervous breakdown in the next 10 years. She will have to check into the Betty Ford Clinic for a long rest. She will need to determine just what exactly it means that she is, with the dread gringo, a *norteamericana.*

Canada, meanwhile, worries about the impact of the Nashville music channel on its cable TV; Pat Buchanan imagines a vast wall along our southern flank; and Mexican nationalists fear a Clinton bailout of the lowly peso.

40   We all speak of North America. But has anyone ever actually met a North American? Oh, there are Mexicans. And there are Canadians. And there are so-called Americans. But a North American?

I know one.

Let me tell you about him—this North American. He is a Mixteco Indian who comes from the Mexican state of Oaxaca. He is trilingual. His primary language is the language of his tribe. His second language is Spanish, the language of Cortes. Also, he has a working knowledge of U.S. English, because, for several months of the year, he works near Stockton, Calif.

He commutes over thousands of miles of dirt roads and freeways, knows several centuries, two currencies, two sets of hypocrisy. He is a criminal in one country and an embarrassment to the other. He is pursued as an "illegal" by the U.S. border patrol. He is preyed upon by Mexican officers who want to shake him down because he has hidden U.S. dollars in his shoes.

In Oaxaca, he lives in a 16th-century village, where his wife watches blond Venezuelan soap operas. A picture of la Virgen de Guadalupe rests over his bed. In Stockton, there is no Virgin Mary, only the other Madonna—the material girl.

45   He is the first North American.

A journalist once asked Chou En-lai, the Chinese premier under Mao Zedong, what he thought of the French Revolution. Chou En-lai gave a wonderful Chinese reply: "It's too early to tell."

I think it may even be too early to tell what the story of Columbus means. The latest chapter of the Columbus saga may be taking place right now, as Latin American teenagers with Indian faces violate the U.S. border. The Mexican kids standing on the line tonight between Tijuana and San Diego—if you ask them why they are coming to the United States of America, they will not say anything about Thomas Jefferson or The Federalist Papers. They have only heard that there is a job in a Glendale dry cleaner's or that some farmer is hiring near Fresno.

They insist: They will be returning to Mexico in a few months. They are only going to the United States for the dollars. They certainly don't intend to become gringos. They don't want anything to do with the United States, except the dollars.

But the months will pass, and the teenagers will be changed in the United States. When they go back to their Mexican village, they will no longer be easy. They will expect an independence and an authority that the village cannot give them. Much to their surprise, they will have been Americanized by the job in Glendale.

50   For work in the United States is our primary source of identity. There is no more telling question we Americans ask one another than "What do you do?" We do not ask about family or village or religion. We ask about work.

The Mexican teenagers will return to Glendale.

Mexicans, Puerto Ricans—most of us end up in the United States, living in the city. Peasants end up in the middle of a vast modern metropolis, having known only the village, with its three blocks of familiar facades.

The arriving generation is always the bravest. New immigrants often change religion with their move to the city. They need to make their peace with isolation, so far from relatives. They learn subway and bus routes that take them far from [home] every day. Long before they can read English, they learn how to recognize danger and opportunity. Their lives are defined by change.

Their children or their grandchildren become, often, very different. The best and the brightest, perhaps, will go off to college—become the first in their family—but they talk about "keeping" their culture. They start speaking Spanish, as a way of not changing: they eat in the cafeteria only with others who look like themselves. They talk incessantly about "culture" as though it were some little thing that can be preserved and kept in a box.

55   The unluckiest children of immigrants drop out of high school. They speak neither good English nor Spanish. Some end up in gangs—family, man— "blood." They shoot other kids who look exactly like themselves. If they try to leave their gang, the gang will come after them for their act of betrayal. If they venture to some other part of the city, they might get shot or they might merely be unable to decipher the freeway exits that speed by.

They retreat to their "turf"—three blocks, just like in their grandmother's village, where the journey began.

One of the things that Mexico had never acknowledged about my father— I insist that you at least entertain this idea—is the possibility that my father and others like him were the great revolutionaries of Mexico. *Pocho* pioneers. They, not Pancho Villa, not Zapata, were heralds of the modern age in Mexico. They left for the United States and then they came back to Mexico. And they changed Mexico forever.

A childhood friend of my father's—he worked in Chicago in the 1920s, then returned one night to his village in Michoacan with appliances for *mamasita* and crisp dollars. The village gathered round him—this is a true story—and asked, "What is it like up there in Chicago?"

The man said, "It's OK."

60   That rumor of "OK" spread across Michoacan, down to Jalisco, all the way down to Oaxaca, from village to village to village.

Futurists and diplomats talk about a "new moment in the Americas." The Latin American elite have condos in Miami and send their children to Ivy League schools. U.S. and Canadian businessmen project the future on a north-south graph. But for many decades before any of this, Latin American peasants have been traveling back and forth, north and south.

Today, there are remote villages in Latin America that are among the most international places on earth. Tiny Peruvian villages know when farmers are picking pears in the Yakima valley in Washington state.

I am the son of a prophet. I am a fool. I am a victim of history. I am confused. I do not know whether I am coming or going. I speak bad Spanish. And yet I tell Latin America this: Because I grew up Hispanic in California, I know more Guatemalans than I would if I had grown up in Mexico, more Brazilians than if I lived in Peru. Because I live in California, it is routine for me to know Nicaraguans and Salvadorans and Cubans. As routine as knowing Chinese or Vietnamese.

My fellow Californians complain loudly about the uncouth southern invasion. I say this to California: Immigration is always illegal. It is a rude act, the leaving of home. Immigration begins as a violation of custom, a youthful act of defiance, an insult to the village. I know a man from El Salvador who has not spoken to his father since the day he left his father's village. Immigrants horrify the grandmothers they leave behind.

65   Illegal immigrants trouble U.S. environmentalists and Mexican nationalists. Illegal immigrants must trouble anyone, on either side of the line, who imagines that the poor are under control.

But they have also been our civilization's prophets. They, long before the rest of us, saw the hemisphere whole.

BROADER HORIZONS: RESOURCES FOR WRITING AND CLASS DISCUSSION

Literary Critical Essay / Discussion Topics

1. Focus on one or two characters from any of the selections in this chapter and trace his or her mythic journey into the underworld. Clues to such a "descent" will lie in journeys south, dreams of the past, and in various "otherworldly" characters seen along the way. Analyze the effects of such a trip, real or imaginary, on the character.

2. For many writers, the lost island paradise is something especially nurturing and peaceful. For others, the very idea of a perfect place of sanctuary and peace is a destructive illusion, a pipe dream and an obstacle to survival in present day reality. Discuss how

these conflicting ideas are presented in one or two stories or poems and which side each writer seems to support.

3. Consider the notion of characters struggling to understand their cultural heritage by traveling, literally or through pictures, books, or conversations, into the lost worlds of their own ancestors. What is it that these characters get from looking back at beliefs, customs, and traditions that are related to the past? How might this process help them understand people in the present?

4. Pick a family in any of the works in this selection (or in other parts of the anthology) and discuss each family member's relationship to the lost world of his or her heritage. Consider age and gender and try to determine if such factors influence the way a person feels about the past world. Which sorts of characters are more apt to need this type of self-discovery through the old world, and which ignore it?

5. Identify the indigenous or the African elements that some of the works present. How does the writer or protagonist relate to "things" connected to African or indigenous cultures, and why are these elements important in the modern U.S. world?

6. Discuss the beliefs in the supernatural in any of the selections in this section. In what ways would you consider these beliefs to be somehow magical, fanciful, or superstitious?

The Novel Connection

To quote the famous short story by the Cuban writer Alejo Carpentier, the "journey to the source"—the quest for one's personal cultural heritage—is somehow connected to nearly every Latino novel, but this theme stands out as particularly important in several works. We have already discussed in Chapter 1 two of the most important Chicano novels, *Bless Me, Ultima* (1972) by Rudolfo A. Anaya and *The Road to Tamazunchale* (1978) by Ron Arias, and shown how both depict the Latino's psychological, emotional, and spiritual connections to a Latin American and indigenous heritage. Both novels are filled with archetypal symbolism and magical dreams, and the narratives focus on characters who wrestle with the practical U.S. "real" world and the other world of non-Western traditions and beliefs. Two novels by Chicano writer Guy Garcia, *Skin Deep* (1989) and *Obsidian Sky* (1994), expand on the theme of his story "La Promesa," included in this chapter on p. 74: that of a search for self-identity in the obscurity of a Mexican past. More recently, two novels by Rick Rivera, *A Fabricated Mexican* (1995) and *Stars Always Shine* (2001), similarly explore the importance of a Chicano's ties to a Mexican heritage. Elena Castedo's hard-to-find novel *Paradise* (1990) plays with the idea of a shifting sense of paradise as each character comes to his or her own understanding of what paradise means. It could be the past perfection of a small town in Spain or the comfort of a wealthy estate in Chile, or it may not really exist at all. The first novel by Chicana writer Ana Castillo, *The Mixquiahuala Letters* (1986), is an epistolary novel (told in letter format) about two friends encountering their Mexican heritage. It is a story of a Latina's need for an authentic connection to a valued heritage and the frustrations of dealing with traditional societal rules imposed upon Mexican women. At issue is whether one can really belong completely to the past world any more than one can be entirely happy within the modern U.S. mainstream.

The descent into the underworld theme described in the chapter's introduction is in many novels, but two particularly apt examples deserve mention. Cristina Garcia's 1992 *Dreaming in Cuban* is one of the most important Latino novels of the 1990s. The central heroine, Pilar, journeys "South" to encounter her Cuban heritage, which has been somewhat misrepresented by her American-flag waving, ultrapatriotic, exiled Cuban mother. As the bridge (her last name is Puente) between her mother and her grandmother, between Cuba and the United States, and between practical reality and the artistic world, Pilar serves to connect the various facets inherent to being a Cuban American in a contemporary, political, and spiritual world. Though not the only novel to deal with these issues, it ranks as one of the most balanced versions of life within the Cuban exile community. The voice of Pilar Puente—sarcastic, rebellious, and youthful—has generated a host of similar-sounding first-person narrators such as Soledad in Angie Cruz's recent novel of that name. Garcia's second novel, *The Agüero Sisters* (1997), centers on two sisters piecing together the mystery of their parents' past and examines how understanding that past as it has been retold and revised over the years will eventually lead the sisters to reunite. Her most recent novel, *Monkey Hunting* (2003), again about Cuba, traces the historical migration of a Chinese family to Cuba and elsewhere over the last two centuries. Told in Garcia's usual fragmented manner, with shifting narrative points of view, the three works constitute a major voice in Cuban American literature.

Nearly all Cuban American novels have something do with the notion of exile and the idea of a lost paradise. The range of specific subject matter, however, stretches across a large and diverse terrain. There are, for example, the detective/police novels of Alex Abella's West Coast Cubans and Carolina Garcia-Aguilera's mysteries set in Miami. Perhaps more important from a literary standpoint, however, are the works of Roberto G. Fernández (discussed in Chapters 7 and 8) and the writings of Virgil Suárez, particularly his novel *Latin Jazz* (1989), which deals directly with the immigration to Miami of Cubans after the 1959 revolution. Suárez is especially interested in the psychological intricacies of those in the Cuban exile community and how they come to terms with shifts and changes in social traditions in Florida.

The most famous Cuban American novelist is Oscar Hijuelos, best known for his Pulitzer Prize-winning work, *The Mambo Kings Play Songs of Love* (1989). His first novel, however, *Our House in the Last World* (1983), best conforms to this section's thematic issues. In many ways, this novel is a story of people relating to their pasts, sometimes capable of succeeding in a different new world and at other times succumbing to defeat, somehow emotionally and spiritually incapable of surviving the cultural uprooting, remaining, as Cristina Garcia has put it, "untransplantable."

Also of note are a few recent works that point the way toward new versions of the Cuban American story. Pablo Medina's *The Return of Felix Nogara* (2000) begins with the fall of a dictator from a small island (called Barata in the novel, but it is obviously a stand-in for Cuba) and involves a journey of rediscovery and reacquaintance. It is a novel about exile and the emotional power of cultural ties to a past world. One of the most innovative literary works to come from a Cuban American is Ernesto Mestre-Reed's *The Lazarus Rumba* (1999). Lengthy, detailed, imaginative, humorous, and playful, the book covers a variety of characters and plots over the last fifty or so years of Cuban history. Mestre-Reed's second novel, *The Second Death of Única Aveyano* (2004) traces the sorrowful nostalgia of an elderly Cuban. Humor is also a huge part of Achy Obejas's *Memory Mambo* (1996), in which a young gay woman tries to figure out the truth of her past amid the memories and recollections of a host of Cubans in exile in Miami and on the island itself. Ana Menéndez's first novel, *Loving Ché* (2003), is a curiously apolitical novel about the affair between a married Cuban woman and the famous revolutionary as seen through the eyes of a daughter researching her family heritage. Ivonne Lamazares's well-written *The Sugar Island* (2000) is an interesting and engrossing short book about a mother and daughter and their journey from Cuba to Miami. Lamazares is particularly good at avoiding stereotypical attitudes toward each country and manages to show both political sides in an enlightened, balanced way.

The Film Connection

In-depth Film Connection
El Norte (1983)
Directed by Gregory Nava

To appreciate fully the modern world of Latinos, readers new to Latino literature and Latin American history will need to get a sense of "the Lost Worlds" of the Latino immigrant experience, which plays such a strong role in the Latino literary imagination. Gregory Nava's *El Norte* (1983) provides that introduction through the lives of a Guatemalan Mayan brother and sister who leave their native homeland to escape from an oppressive, perilous environment and come to the United States in the hopes of establishing a better, safer life.

In Spanish with English subtitles, *El Norte* mostly centers on the siblings' struggles as they make their way to and live in the United States—the North. In 1995, the Library of Congress placed this masterpiece in the National Film Registry, which is designed to "reflect the full breadth and diversity of America's film heritage," making it at the time 1 of only 175 films to earn that distinction. A classic, it presents the physical act of crossing borders in possibly the most disturbing, yet most real, way ever shown on the big screen.

At the film's outset, Enrique and Rosa are living in a village in which fear and intimidation rule. Their father has joined a clandestine group formed to rebel against the government, which, along with the wealthy landowners, sees the peasants as "just a pair of arms." Eventually, the military regime murders their father, cutting off his head and hanging it from a tree as a symbol of dominance. Enrique discovers the head and winds up killing one of the soldiers in an act that is more representative of his fear than his rage. Knowing that they must escape or face the same deadly fate experienced by many people in the village, Enrique and his sister decide to depart for the Promised Land—the United States—crossing the border illegally, risking their lives, and even crawling through a rat-infested sewer tunnel.

The image of his father's head haunts Enrique and the audience, for it serves as a reminder of a past that cannot be left behind quite so easily. As Enrique and Rosa escape turmoil, they also abandon a native beauty, and Nava's cinematography purposefully highlights Guatemala's aesthetic landscape. In similar ways, the authors of the works in this chapter stress their connection to the past, sometimes nostalgically, but mostly as a contrast to what they have encountered in the new world. Like the husband in Ana Menéndez's "Confusing the Saints" (see p. 88), Enrique and Rosa immigrate because they are left with no choice. Yet, as these stories and the film illustrate, although each Latino group shares some experiences, there is no such thing as a common Latino immigrant experience. Enrique and Rosa are indigenous Mayans and face prejudices even from Mexicans on their trek up North.

In the United States, the two siblings undeniably face a better life, but the film asks the question: At what cost? The ending shows this, but so too do their hardships as they scrape by on jobs that offer menial pay and little reward, reminding the audience of the siblings' father's ominous words: the poor are seen as nothing more than a "pair of arms." In many ways, it is as if Enrique and Rosa have exchanged one desperate situation for another, and in this respect, the film makes the point that escaping oppression is not a simple matter of crossing borders.

Although not a tremendous commercial success, *El Norte* received great reviews and helped pioneer a boom in films that incorporated Latino characters. Nava has since become a celebrity of sorts, going on to make such box-office hits as *Selena* (1997), *My Family: Mi Familia* (1995), and *Frida* (2002). Earlier films in the United States had touched upon the plight of Latinos in this country. The movie *Giant* (1956), based on the Edna Ferber novel by the same title, for example, was one of the first in the United States to depict discrimination of Latinos without being overly sentimental, yet the focus of the film was on the lives of the main characters, played by superstars Elizabeth Taylor, James Dean, Rock Hudson, and Dennis Hopper. *El Norte* is just the opposite, a film featuring relative unknowns and independently produced in conjunction with PBS's *American Playhouse*, yet it earned an Academy Award nomination for Best Original Screenplay and a Writer's Guild of America Award nomination.

Other Recommended Films:

> *The Ballad of Gregorio Cortez* (1982)
> *Bitter Sugar* (1996)
> *El Super* (1979)
> *Fidel* (2002)
> *I Am Cuba* (1995)
> *The Maldonado Miracle* (2003)
> *Nueba Yol* (1996)
> *The Mambo Kings Play Songs of Love* (1992)
> *The Motorcycle Diaries* (2004)

Thematic Connection Listing

1. The Descent into Cultural Self: Reconnections with the Past

Fiction
> Guy Garcia: "La Promesa"
> Daniel Chacón: "Biggest City in the World"
> Rudolfo Anaya: "In Search of Epifano"

Essay
> Richard Rodriguez: "Go North, Young Man"

2. The Spiritual Heritage and Syncretic Ghosts

Fiction
> Antonio Farias: "Red Serpent Ceviche"
> Ana Menéndez: "Confusing the Saints"

Poetry
> Victor Hernandez Cruz: "African Things"
> Ricardo Pau-Llosa: "Frutas"
> Carolina Hospital: "Finding Home"

3. Paradises Lost

Fiction
> Sandra Cisneros: "One Holy Night"

Poetry
> Jimmy Santiago Baca: "Roots" and "Dust-Bowl Memory"
> Judith Ortiz Cofer: "The Latin Deli"

4. The Abuelita and the Maternal Voices

Poetry
> Diane de Anda: "Abuelas"
> Pat Mora: "Curandera"
> Magdalena Gómez: "Mami"
> Gary Soto: "History"
> Aleida Rodríguez: "The First Woman"

5
The Working World

Sweating Under a New Sun

INTRODUCTION

Work, in a world so dependent upon financial and commercial systems, is such a huge and amorphous concept that all Latino literature might be said to fall into this category. Many Latino writers address working-class issues and the anxieties relevant to the disempowered, the marginalized, and those who live within and close to the so-called underground economic structures of the United States. In this chapter, the focus is mostly on working-class people, with pieces that are directly concerned with issues of labor, wages, unions, the lack of work, stigmas, and prejudices that swamp people into dead-end jobs.

The Latino Worker: A Brief Overview

A vast number of historical, political, and sociological works provide a full and detailed history of the Latino as worker in the United States, particularly the famous study by Rodolfo Acuña, *Occupied America: A History of Chicanos* (1999; now in its fourth edition) or Ronald Takaki's *A Different Mirror: A History of Multicultural America* (1993). Many books also center on the issue of work and the U.S. border, including those by Luis Alberto Urrea and Rubén Martínez. This introductory section provides a general historical framework to the chapter's selections.

The types of jobs in which Latinos are employed go beyond migrant farm work, as important as that work might be. Obviously, migrant laborers are not unique to the United States, nor are they all of Mexican heritage. In the early 1800s, Chinese workers helped build the transcontinental railroad to the western states. Later, Japanese laborers came in to work in the fields of the fertile, newly accessible California farming valleys. By 1920, the same Euro-American racism that made life difficult for Chinese workers (and prompted many to establish private enterprises and small businesses, particularly in San Francisco) also drove out many of the Japanese work-ers. Mexican Americans then arrived in the United States to fill the shortages. Dur-ing the Mexican Revolution, between 1910 and 1920, thousands of immigrants moved across the U.S.-Mexican border to pick crops in the large tracts of land con-trolled by a few wealthy land owners always in need of field workers. As the effects of the Great Depression of the 1930s worsened, small Mexican American-owned businesses faltered and failed, and the unemployed, along with a multitude of bank-rupt farmers, traveled from the dustbowl lands of Oklahoma, Texas, and the South-west to join the ranks of California's migrant field workers.

As is always the case, U.S. immigration laws go hand in hand with the need for labor. In good times, the workers come in unrestricted; in bad times, the U.S. government sends them back. When the Depression came to an end with the United States' entry into World War II and men, including thousands of Latinos, left their homes to fight overseas, the need for labor increased and Mexicans immi-grated north in greater numbers once again. With the forced relocation of the Japanese on the West Coast to internment camps, there emerged a desperate need for labor. This led the U.S. government to establish the Bracero Agreement with Mexico, which officially allowed certain numbers of Mexican immigrants into the United States to work in fields even as far north as Idaho and Wyoming. This con-troversial arrangement endured in various forms from 1942 until the early 1960s. When the need for labor shifted after the war, many Mexicans were deported. The tensions caused by too many workers and not enough jobs contributed to the famous Los Angeles "Zoot Suit," or "Sailor" riots of the late 1940s when U.S. soldiers returned to find that Mexicans and Mexican Americans had taken their places within the job market.

On the East Coast, Puerto Ricans arrived to work after the Spanish American War in 1898 (which led to the independence of Cuba and the "colonization" of Puerto Rico by the United States). Writings by Bernardo Vega and Jesús Colón provide an insider's perspective of this period in the first half of the 1900s, with intriguing descriptions of the *Tabaqueros* in Manhattan, who rolled the tobacco leaves into cigars for the U.S. market. Jesús Colón's "sketches" trace the building of a Puerto Rican social and political consciousness as the *lectores* read novels and newspapers to these cigar makers while they worked.*

World War I provided the impetus for the U.S. government to grant citizen-ship to Puerto Ricans (in essence to enlist more soldiers) in 1917. In 1947, there followed another government program called Operation Bootstrap, intended to improve Puerto Rican economic opportunities. In practice, among other effects, the arrangement gave tax breaks to large U.S. corporations on the island of Puerto Rico. The resulting industrialization encouraged workers to move to the urban centers of the island and then to migrate north, mainly to work in the tobacco, fruit, and vegetable fields of Connecticut, New Jersey, eastern Pennsylvania, and Ohio. The migrants came as well to work in low-paying manufacturing jobs, build-ing every conceivable type of product in the mills and factories situated in small

---

*The theme has recently been taken up by the Cuban American dramatist Nilo Cruz in his Pulitzer Prize-winning play, *Anna in the Tropics* (2003).

towns across the East Coast. Puerto Ricans filled the needs for unskilled labor in hospitals, hotels, and restaurants across the East Coast, particularly in New York City. Seamstresses worked under grueling conditions in the Manhattan garment shops, and industrious merchants opened *bodegas* (small shops) in East Harlem.

It Is All About Jobs

Immigration continues to swell the number of Latinos in the United States today as people venture toward *el Norte* to work as domestics, landscapers, meat packers, and field hands. They mostly move north into California, Texas, and the Southwest through the large "double" cities that line the border with Mexico and mirror each other (e.g., Tijuana and San Diego in California and Matamoros and Brownsville in Texas). The cultural dynamic of these borderlands is a subject now extensively explored by sociologists and other scholars. Some workers cross the *frontera*, or border, daily, and the economies of the double cities depend on each other. Many workers who settle in the United States remain closely tied to the small villages in their homelands, and their labor in the United States finances those towns in the form of remittances, or cash sent home for family and friends. In fact, the total amount of remittances paid back to the small Caribbean and Latin American nations often exceeds the amount the United States supplies those countries in foreign aid. In Mexico and Central America, in some cases, the young depart to the United States for work at such a rate that the villages left behind are entirely dependent on the cash sent home.

The 1960s and *La Causa, La Raza,* and the Movement

In some cases in the 1960s, Latinos fought along with African Americans in the struggle for civil rights. The lessons learned and taught by Martin Luther King, Jr., and Malcolm X were not lost on the politically minded leaders of Mexican American workers in the fields of California or elsewhere. The beginning efforts to establish the United Farm Workers (UFW) labor union in 1962, led by César Chávez and Delores Huerta, in some ways signaled the birth of the Chicano movement. The grape boycotts and Chávez's hunger strikes galvanized working Latinos in the name of *La Causa* (the Cause). By 1967, groups of young Mexican Americans calling themselves Brown Berets—following the Black Panthers—organized protests and celebrated the now classic epic poem "I am Joaquín" by Rodolfo "Corky" Gonzales. On the streets of New York City, the Young Lords party led urban Puerto Rican youth in community organizing on behalf of working Puerto Ricans. During this time, the signs of Chicano cultural awareness and ethnic pride in all things Latino increased. Young people of Mexican descent seized the slang word "Chicano" and made it their own. The same name appropriation by young people of Puerto Rican descent would soon work for "Nuyoricans."

Latino literary output went hand in hand with Latino political movements. The plays of Luis Valdez performed in his San Bautista, California-based Teatro Campesino (Farmworkers Theater); the journal *El Grito* out of Berkeley, California; and other artistic outlets fed the Chicano movement. In the East, Nuyorican poets of the Lower East Side of Manhattan and the writers in Spanish Harlem constantly created works that addressed the daily struggles of working-class Latinos.

Latino professionals have lived and worked for years in the United States. Unfortunately, the media has tended to stereotype them by equating the average working Latino with the image of a would-be landscaper waiting on some city street corner for a suburban job handout. Such a picture is all too often considered the truth. Likewise, in some sense, Latino literature has yet to reflect the true diversity of Latino working life in the United States. Undoubtedly this will change as Latino writers begin to publish stories, plays, and poems about the working worlds of successful Latinos: corporate and political leaders, owners of companies, and successful businesspeople such as the highly regarded farmer of Mexican herbs in New York's Hudson River Valley. For now, except for the occasional educator or small businessowner—the bodega or restaurant owner, for example—the central literary focus of most Latino literature remains firmly based on the lives of such blue-collar workers as bus drivers, maids, field hands, fruit pickers, factory workers, gardeners, maintenance workers, and sales clerks. This can be expected to change as the Latino professional class grows and publishers and writers turn their attention to the likes of nurses, social workers, and scholars.

The working life of the Cuban American stands in stark contrast to that of other Latino workers. In part, as a result of the U.S. government's unique arrangement with exiled Cubans after the revolution in 1959, Miami Cubans entered a different sort of job environment that was often subsidized and supported by official programs such as the Cuban Relief Program. These and other initiatives provided new arrivals with job training, housing arrangements, and loans, particularly in the 1960s. The political situation between Cuba and the United States created unique opportunities for middle-class professional Cubans arriving in the early 1960s. Their professional skills and education were welcomed by the U.S. government, and they were supported by the relaxation of standard immigration rules and regulations. The results of these programs are clear when comparing the high-income levels of Cuban Americans with those of other Latino groups. As is reflected in the literature, however, this dynamic is changing as Cubans who arrived in more recent waves of immigration have often been less educated than the doctors and landowners who fled the island just after 1959.

FICTION

Norma Cantú

Norma Cantú is the author of a memoir, *Canicula: Snapshots of a Girlhood En La Frontera* (1995), as well as the editor of *Chicana Traditions: Continuity and Change* (2002), an anthology of writings dealing with Chicana expressive culture. She is a professor of English at the University of Texas at San Antonio.

Se me enchina el cuerpo al oír tu cuento...[1]

how the day after graduating as valedictorian from the high school in the Rio Grande Valley you helped your family board up the door and windows of the frame house and pack the old pick-up truck to make your annual trek north. After three days on the road arriving at the turkey farm and being led to your quarters. The family, tired, looks to you. "What's this?" you ask, for you, the favored son, speak English; you can communicate with the bosses.

"This is where you're gonna live."

Perplexed you say, "But it looks like a chicken coop."

"It is, but it's not good enough for the chickens," the Anglo responds with a sneer.

5   And you take it, and you suffer as your mother and your sisters make the best with the chicken coop. They hang curtains and sweep the floor and burn candles to the Vírgen.

Then the work, arduous and demeaning, begins. Working night shifts after long days...plucking feathers, forcibly breeding the toms and the hens, and your Dad ages from day to day before your very eyes.

Until one day you've been working hard, and you look for your Dad, and barely see his head in one of the buried barrels full of feathers, working away. Suddenly he's gone, and you think you're imagining things; how could he disappear? and you remove your gloves and risk the foreman's wrath. You run to your father; jump in; he is almost smothered by feathers, and you say, "Enough!"

You take control and pack the family off. "No pay for all your work if you leave."

And you say, "We're leaving." The favored son, who speaks to the bosses, has spoken. And driving the Midwest farm road almost crossing the state line you spy a sign "Labor Relations," and you stop. And, yes, you are owed your wages, and the bosses pay reluctantly. No one had ever done that before. But you read the language of the bosses. You move on with your family, and your father is pleased; your mother beams but is afraid in her heart for her son who speaks the language of the bosses.

10   Years later a lover will wonder why you refuse to sleep on feather-filled pillows, and you want to tell, to spill your guts, but you can't, you refuse. You hold your words like caged birds.

Memory's wound is too fresh.

And more years later when you tell the story, I cringe and get goosebumps: you tell your story and are healed, but there's still a scar and like an old war wound or surgical scar it hurts when the weather changes or the memory intersects with this time and place.

---

[1] I cringe and get goose bumps when I hear your story. . . .

Cristina Garcia

The popularity and critical acclaim for Cristina Garcia's three novels have garnered her a unique place in Latino literature written by Cuban Americans, and she is certainly the most prominent Cuban American woman writing today. She was born on July 4, 1958, in Havana and grew up in New York when her parents left Cuba in 1960 after the revolution. During the 1980s, she worked as a reporter for the *Boston Globe* and later wrote for *Time* magazine. Her *Dreaming in Cuban* (1992), arguably one of the most influential Latino novels of recent years, was nominated for a National Book Award. She has also written the novels *The Agüero Sisters* (1997) and *Monkey Hunting* (2003). Her novels are told from multiple points of view, and her elegant prose captures the fragmented lives of Cuban exiles with humor and poetic description. Perhaps more importantly, Garcia refuses to allow stereotypical versions of the Cuban American to enter her books.

Tito's Goodbye

Agustin "Tito" Ureña thought at first that the massive heart attack that would kill him in a matter of seconds was just a bad case of indigestion. He had eaten spareribs with pork fried rice, black beans, and a double side order of sweet plantains at a new Cuban-Chinese cafeteria on Amsterdam Avenue the night before and he hadn't felt quite right all day. "Okay, okay, I hear you!" he lamented aloud, rubbing his solar plexus and dropping his fourth pair of antacid tablets in the dirty glass of water on his desk. He remembered with longing the great spits of suckling pigs dripping with fragrant juices back in Cuba, the two inches of molten fat beneath their crispy skins.

"*Coño!*"[1] Tito Ureña protested as a violent spasm seized his heart then squeezed it beyond endurance. He stood up, suddenly afraid, and with a terrible groan he slumped forward, his arms swimming furiously, and swept from his oversized metal desk a half-eaten bag of candy corn, the citizenship papers of a dozen Central American refugees, his Timex travel clock in its scuffed plastic case, and the stout black rotary telephone he tried in vain to reach.

It was late Friday afternoon and Tito told his secretary to leave after lunch because it had started to snow and she lived in Hoboken, but mostly because he could deduct the eighteen dollars from her weekly pay. His law office, a squalid room over a vegetable market in Little Italy, was convenient to the federal courts downtown, his prime hunting grounds for the illegal immigrants who made up the bulk of his clients. Tito's specialities were self-styled—forging employment records, doctoring birth certificates, securing sponsors, thwarting deportation, applying for political asylum. Only rarely did he achieve the ultimate, the most elusive victory: procuring a legitimate green card.

Tito worked with the poorest of New York City's immigrants, uneducated men and women from the Dominican Republic, Mexico, El Salvador, Peru, Guatemala, Panama. He impressed them with his deliberate, florid Spanish, with

[1]"Damn!"

the meaningful pauses and throat clearing they had come to expect from important men. In reality Tito Ureña's qualifications, elaborately set out and framed on the wall behind his secondhand executive chair, came from a correspondence school in Muncie, Indiana. This did not deter him, however, from charging many thousands of dollars, payable in monthly installments ("I'm not an unreasonable man," he protested again and again, his arms outstretched, palms heavenward, when his clients balked or appeared uncertain), for his dubious efforts.

5   Occasionally Tito Ureña would come by small-time jobs for the mob, defending lowlifes fingered to take the rap for their bosses. These cases paid handsomely and required virtually no work. Tito only had to be careful that his "defense" went off without a hitch and the saps went directly to jail. It helped take the pressure off the mob's local operations. Last year, flush with cash from two such cases, Tito bought sixty seconds of air time on late-night Spanish television to advertise his legal services. With his thick mustache and broad reassuring smile, he received over four hundred calls on the toll-free hotline in less than a week. The only trouble was that his wife, who was something of a night owl, also saw him on TV. Haydée called his office, posing as a rich widow from Venezuela, and made an appointment with her husband the following day. It took Tito months to cover his tracks again.

Tito Ureña had been separated from Haydée for nearly sixteen years and in all that time she had steadfastly refused to divorce him. Whenever she located her husband, Haydée managed to wring from him considerable sums of money to maintain, she said, the lifestyle to which she had grown accustomed as a descendant of the Alarcón family, the greatest sugarcane dynasty in Trinidad, Cuba. Tito insisted that Haydée could smell his cash three miles away in her tiny apartment on Roosevelt Island, even on the hottest days of summer when the stench from the East River and all that was buried there would have stopped a bloodhound dead in its tracks with confusion.

For a while Tito skittered from place to place in the vast water-front complexes of apartment buildings near Wall Street which, during a downturn in the economy, were offering three months' free rent with every two-year lease. Tito rented beige furniture, always beige (he preferred its soothing neutrality), and lived high above the river, face-to-face with the lights of the city in his glass box suites in the sky.

It snowed hard the night Tito Ureña died of a heart attack in his office in Little Italy. Nine inches fell in the space of twelve hours. It continued to snow the next day, blanketing the city's rooftops and fire escapes, its parks and delivery trucks, awnings and oak trees with a deceptive peacefulness, and it snowed the day after that. It snowed on the black veiled hat Haydée had stolen from Bloomingdale's that very afternoon and which she would later come to interpret as a premonition of her husband's death. It snowed on the sliver of concrete she called a balcony, decorated with a life-sized plastic statue of Cinderella. It snowed on Tito's daughter's brick Colonial house in western Connecticut, across from the country club with its own riding stable. Inés

Ureña had married a Yale-trained cardiologist the year before and devoted her days to mastering the baroque recipes in *Gourmet* magazine. It snowed especially hard in Prospect Park, near where her older brother, Jaime, had rented a room and plastered his walls with posters of Gandhi, Beethoven, and Malcolm X.

Tito lay dead in his office all weekend as it snowed, well preserved by the freezing temperatures. His mistress, Beatrice Hunt, called him Saturday night from Antigua, where she had returned to visit her family for an extended holiday. She cut her trip short when a policeman, who had found her number in Tito's wallet, called her in St. Johns. Beatrice, dressed in her Sunday finery, went to claim her lover's body at the Manhattan city morgue. After four days, nobody else had come.

10   If Tito Ureña had had the chance, if he had known that only a few moments remained of his life and that it was neither indigestion nor an incipient ulcer that was causing his gastric discomfort, he might have permitted himself the brief luxury of nostalgia. He would have remembered the warmth of his mother's cheek, smelling faintly of milk, and her face the last time he saw her (Tito was only nine when she died), or the sight of his father's hands—enormous hands with stiff hairs sprouting near the knuckles—stroking the doves that roosted in his study. He would have remembered the girl he loved madly when he was seven years old and in a moment of melancholy would profess to love still.

And since these would be the very last moments of his life, Tito might even have permitted himself the memory of his first glimpse of Haydée at sixteen, riding her thoroughbred, English style, along the road which marked the southern boundary of her father's vast plantation. She was a magnificent sight—so small, so white, a china doll. How afraid he was of breaking her on their wedding night! He would have remembered, too, her belly, swelling with his child, and the pride he felt strolling with her through the Plaza Mayor. This was long before the problems began, long before they'd sent their son to the orphanage in Colorado to save him from the Communists, who, it was rumored, were planning to ship Cuba's children to boarding schools in the Ukraine. Jaime was still healthy and without rancor then, and Tito's daughter, Inés, danced to please him, clapping her dimpled hands.

It was that life that Tito Ureña would have remembered if he had had the opportunity, a life richly marred by ignorance.

But he had no time to reminisce when his heart attack came. No time to save the Salvadorans from deportation or to pick up the dry cleaning Beatrice Hunt had forgotten on Broadway and 74th Street. No time to call his brothers, whom he hadn't seen in five years, or his sister, Aurora, in New Jersey, who'd announced her determination to save his soul. No time to have dinner with his daughter, Inés, estranged from him in her brick Colonial house in western Connecticut (Tito had missed her fancy wedding and she never forgave him). No time to apologize to his son, if he could have even worked up the courage, or to earn enough money to finally keep Haydée happy. No time to visit his father in Cuba or to plant jonquils on his mother's sad grave. No, Tito no longer had time even to hope. When his hour came on that snowy winter afternoon in Little Italy, all Tito had time to do was say *coño.*

Dagoberto Gilb

Dagoberto Gilb was born in 1950 in Los Angeles and worked at various construction-type jobs over a period of years, experiences from which he draws powerful and realistic accounts of working-class Latinos laboring at their trades throughout the United States. In 1993, when Gilb's first collection of short fiction was published, few Latino writers were so immediately hailed as major figures in the field—he was commonly compared with Ernest Hemingway and Raymond Carver. The book, *The Magic of Blood,* won the PEN/Hemingway Award and was a PEN/Faulkner Award finalist. His work has appeared in numerous magazines, journals, and anthologies since then and won praise from many of the most popular names in Latino literature. His novel *The Last Known Residence of Mickey Acuña* (1994) and a second collection of stories, *Woodcuts of Women* (2001), were also well received. His most recent book is a collection of essays called *Gritos* (2003).

Al, in Phoenix

My car needed a new wheel bearing. I knew it because I'd been hearing it in there for over a year, but also because of that, for it so long always sounding the same, no better no worse, I wasn't so worried. I didn't want it to freeze up and ruin the axle too, so I knew I should do something, at least have something done since I hate to work on my own car now, on anybody's car, though sometimes I'll do this or that on somebody else's, you know how that goes. Most of the time it's easy enough really and I almost always know what's wrong, what to fix, because I did it so much when I was a kid. I was concerned enough anyway to see what might be done, what this mechanic in Blythe would say about it. I knew the guy, I knew the place, because I almost always stop for gas on my way through, one time to change a tire, another to take a look at some loose tappets I heard. Blythe's the last real stop before Phoenix, and it's a long, sandy desert between, and not a great place to break down. I'd have thought the guy'd remember me and my car, since one like this can't come through that often I'm sure, and that time he snugged-up my tappets I had him go ahead and tune it up too, and I went out and bought us some beers. He didn't act like it though, or if he did he wasn't giving me any deals. I'd asked about a new tire first and he wanted twice as much as I'd ever paid anywhere, looked at me like I was from a different planet when I asked suggestively if he couldn't do just a touch better than that, or if not, give me some idea of a place in town that might. I needed the tire too, it was in bad shape, closing in on the first layer of ply. So then I asked about the wheel bearing, how much he thought it'd cost me if I let him have at it. He had no idea, he'd have to tear it down first and see. That didn't sound too reasonable to me, as you can imagine, since once it was apart I'd have already lost time and money if his price was gonna be high. So that was it for Blythe. Like I told him, I was feeling lucky, so I decided I'd get it to Phoenix, maybe get the tire there at a discount place I knew, I had a good spare anyway, and I'd have the other work done there where prices wouldn't be so last-chance high.

My luck held too. The wheel bearing wore out within the Phoenix city limits. I drove it slow, on the shoulder of the freeway to be exact, until I got it to an off-ramp, and then I coasted, the wheel smoking and stinking until I'm over to the side of the road in front of a business establishment, which lets me use its phone to call Triple-A, which I consider one of the really great American services, which everyone always welcomes you to use the phone to call. In no time at all I have a tow-truck pulling up and hooking me on.

"So where d'ya wanna take it?" the tow-truck driver asks. He's a young guy, with long straight blond hair that's neat, cut well, and clean.

"You know a good mechanic? You know, not too much, not so cheap you worry the guy's stupid?"

5   "Not really. My station's good though. We got this mechanic named Al there. He's maybe the best I've ever seen."

I think this guy's an innocent, a true-believer type, hasn't been around long enough to know. Has a first kid, a young wife, thinks he's got a good job. "I don't trust Triple-A stations, if you know what I mean. They know they've got ya."

"I don't know any other place," he says. "I do know that my station'll get you in and out, and that Al'll do it right. I don't get any money for saying that, or taking you there either."

An innocent. It probably never occurred to him that if he didn't take the breakdowns to his station he wouldn't have the job. On the other hand, what'd be the difference? How much could a wheel bearing be if the guy charged too much? More than in Blythe? Probably not. And if the guy is fast I could get back on the highway and save spending the night in Phoenix. So far everything'd been going smooth and on schedule. "Take me to your leader," I tell him. "I wanna get it done."

"You'll get it done," he says, "and Al'll do it right. He'll find whatever's wrong and tell you what's about to go wrong too."

10   "Sounds heroic enough to me."

The tow-truck driver laughs. He drives straight and confidently, his dispatch radio blaring, then pulls into a station at the crossroads of two freeways. He's gone almost the moment he gets there, barely exchanging a word with the station mechanic whose oval name patch has "Al" stitched in it.

Al is either prematurely gray or a very healthy old guy in his sixties. He's working on a Cadillac, jumping a battery. He revs the engine, listens, and shuts it down. He adjusts some dials on the battery charger and lowers the hood about half-way. I'd swear he's humming a song to himself, one of those mellow classics everybody even my age knows for better or worse, but not a sound is parting Al's lips.

"So," I say to him to start up a conversation.

"Sir," he says, almost closing his eyes at me, "why don't you have a seat in the waiting room and I'll be with you."

15   "No problem," I say. I walk away nervously, because I'm always nervous, thinking I should be more patient, the guy must have tons of work to do and thousands of people to deal with. I wait, pacing around the station and not in the waiting room listening to the ting-ting of cars stopping for gas. A short, muscular guy takes care of them. Finally Al comes out from the back of the garage, as excited as ever, and goes over to my car, and starts up the engine.

"It's a wheel bearing," I tell him.

He doesn't respond. He rolls the car forward, into one of the stalls, then positions the steel arms of the hydraulic lift under the chassis. He stands up, goes over to the controls, moves the lever and brings the car up.

"Great invention," I say. "I remember when I was a kid this neighbor had a pit with stairs in it. He always had to carry around a light. It was always dark down there anyway, and greasy." Al is spinning the wheels of my car. "And he'd have to block the car up to work on the wheels, stoop over." I get close to my tire, the one that Al's near and about to take off to get at the wheel bearing.

"Sir," he says, "please wait in the waiting room. The sign says only employees are allowed in this work area." He stops what he's doing to say that to me directly, irritated.

20   "No problem," I say. "I understand." I do. It is hard to work all day with distractions, people under your feet. I'd be the same way if I had to work on these cars all day, everyday. So I go into the waiting room, this grease-coated room where they have two worn-out couches and a table between them. In the corner nearest the door leading into the work area is an up-to-date cash register, the plastic on it still polished, and above that a sign: ABSOLUTELY NO CHECKS! This all used to be the gas station office, now it's the waiting room, quote unquote. On the table there's a pile of newspapers and a stack of car magazines. The newspaper is today's, so I read it until Al comes in.

"It's only the wheel bearing, so you were lucky. I checked the one on the other side and you've had that one done recently. I'll have to have it pressed on. This is the cost." He has it itemized on a form. The price is good, average at best, not above anyway.

"Do it," I say. I sign the form. "How long you think it'll take?"

"Can't say."

"I mean estimate. More or less how long, that's what I mean."

25   "Can't say."

I don't like that much. That being his attitude. Like he doesn't give a shit about me, me sitting here, waiting. I almost say something to him. Then I say this anyway. "I only wanna know so I can make some plans if I have to. Like get a motel room if I have to spend the night." It wasn't late, it was afternoon in fact, but I can see the possibility, it wouldn't be his fault or attitude that would make a part hard to get, and I understood that he was having the bearing pressed on somewhere else.

"I can't say, sir," he enunciates. "Everything takes time."

A real philosopher. I don't argue. The car is still up there on the lift, tires and axles off. I'd made good time today, and I figure I can afford to relax. I know a good motel, cheap, with a cable television. So I go on reading the paper, then I look at those magazines, shut my eyes a little, walk around this Phoenix gas station.

I talk to the short, husky-armed guy, name tag Nick, who works the full-serve and takes the money for the self-serve. "Your partner isn't the friendliest in the world."

30   "Al? Al and me get along pretty good. I understand him cuz we're both from Detroit."

That made sense. I don't try talking to him much after that. He's too busy anyway. I do listen to Al talk to this other couple from Georgia, Georgia plates anyway, who came in with an almost new car. Al has the hood open, staring and fiddling with all the tubes and wires it has. The couple stands by uncomfortably, wordless. Did I say listen? I mean I watch. There are no memorable words traded. Just about an ignition key and gas, what the car sounded like when the trouble started. Al disappears and the couple whisper. Maybe ten, fifteen minutes go by. He comes back, tells them what's wrong, a timing chain, how these cars are famous for this, and for all the work it's gonna cost them this big figure. He doesn't say it, but it's obvious that he's telling them he disapproves of their car, that it's the proverbial hunk of, but it's also clear he's not gouging them on account of his dislike of the car, it's not a willful price, and he gives them the figures on paper like he did me. He waits a moment or two, I can't hear what they say to him, but he walks away and they whisper some more and go to a phone booth. Al doesn't look under that hood again. They get into a taxi and drive away as quietly as they came.

I'm patient, I'm prepared for the long wait, but then I see a small foreign pickup squeal in and a delivery boy carrying my old axle with a new wheel bearing. In no time at all. Al gets right to it. In his way that is. Like I said, humming one of those old songs. I know better now though. But he does get right to it. I watch him without so much as putting my toe in the forbidden work zone, leaning into the door opening of the wait room. He greases the axles, slips them in, tightens a couple of bolts, then comes the drums, the tires. He checks the rear-end grease. He adjusts the brakes while it's up in the air. Methodically, unrushed. He lowers my car, disappears, returns with the bill. All this as disinterested as the rest.

I'd bought myself a soda, and I put in a couple extra quarters for him. "I'd have bought you a beer but the machine man must of forgot to put them in. Didn't know what kind you liked, so I guessed." I set the cold soda next to where he puts the paperwork.

"It's not necessary, sir. No thank you."

35   Okay. I pay cash. Not a dime more than what he'd said. I say thanks, leave the soda, and drive off. I couldn't believe how early it still was, how little it cost, I mean I really expected to pay much more, being on the road and all, and so I decide to take it easy and spend the night. First I buy a new tire. Then I check into that motel I mentioned. I take myself to a restaurant where there's a bar, drink a couple beers, and call it a night. I was happy between those crackly motel sheets, a cable movie on. I nodded out.

    I was up early and felt great. I stopped for a big breakfast. Everything was going so well. I like to hit the road just as the dawn breaks, and I did. I gotta say I like driving through Phoenix in the morning. I like the light, that pink-ish-blue, mixed with black. Pretty. I also like leaving Phoenix. So I was rounding this on-ramp and I hear what I thought was like pieces of gravel under my floorboard. Then again. Then a bad sound, not like gravel, but like engine, like pieces of rod all of the sudden coming apart. I pull over. The oil-light had gone on. The sun was on the rise. The engine won't turn over. I walk over to the restaurant where I'd just eaten and use the phone to call Triple-A. I wait maybe half-an-hour, maybe forty-five minutes for a tow-truck. It wasn't the same driver or the same truck, but it's the same people.

    "Take me to Al's station," I tell the driver, another young guy with long hair, only his more scraggly, like he isn't married, doesn't have a first kid.

    "We got another station right over here, closer, if you want."

    "No, I think this guy Al's a good mechanic, and I want a good mechanic." I am not feeling too happy.

40   "We got Hank over at the other station. He's a good mechanic too."

    "As good as Al?"

    "Maybe. About the same. Al's real good though."

    "Take me to Al. I guess I trust him."

    "Yeah, Al don't want anybody in his way, but he's good. One of the best. Maybe *the* best."

45   I feel like I haven't gotten enough sleep. "I'll bet you get tired of having to come for us breakdowns. All depressed and worried. I don't even wanna know what's wrong with this car. I don't even wanna hear it. It's bad news, I'm sure already."

    "Nah, we make lotsa folks happy. Starting up a car that won't, fixing a flat. Al'll probably get you going too."

    Naive, don't you think? The point isn't whether or not he can get me going, but whether he'll do it for a price I can pay. I've lost cars this way, two to be exact, two because I couldn't pay for the repairs. In both those cases it wasn't whether a mechanic was able, anybody can bolt-in a new engine, hook the wires back up. The question is, is it worth it? The question is, how many options do I have so far away from home, from friends, from tools?

    When we get to the station, the truth is I'm embarrassed to be back, and I don't even want to talk to Al about what's wrong. Early as it is, he's already there, not humming any melodies I know, leaning under the hood of some other car. A simple tune-up, it looks like. This time I'm even nervous for me.

Not just from the breakfast coffee. When he finally talks to the towtruck driver about my troubles, I don't know, it just seems to me he's irritated, you know, the way someone says *What this time?* Like that, you know? And he doesn't go over to my car. He doesn't look over at me. He goes back to what he was doing, with the same sort of attitude toward it, no more, no less. I can barely take it.

Did I say I don't like Phoenix? I don't like Phoenix. There's something about the place. You wonder what draws people here at all. It's the weather, the climate. I do know this, I know that that's why all these easterners come out, why the city gets all the business it gets. I can see why someone'd want to live in Arizona, it's pretty, the country is, all desolate, rugged, but not Phoenix. Phoenix always seems about as interesting as that TV show that was set here, about the diner, if you know what I mean. I do like Goldwater, by that I mean only the man, but I'll bet he doesn't live in Phoenix. Like here at this gas station. What's unique? It's like every gas station anywhere. And beyond, in the neighborhood? Faceless buildings, an American flag, not even that big of one really, palm trees. Palm trees? Phoenix is not Hawaii, not even L.A. And then all these guys who work here. Uniforms with their names on them. And everyone of them has a beard. Not even interesting ones. They're all cut and cared for. Not like strong statements. Just uninteresting beards and bellies and blue uniforms.

50   So when Al's done playing with that tune-up, he goes over to a car he has up on the rack. A brake job, it looks like. Okay, so there's some cars ahead of me and I gotta wait my turn. I can understand that. Though he could take a look at what's with mine and give me an estimate so I can make some plans if I have to, make some decisions. That's what I think, that would seem like the courteous thing to do if you were to ask me. Then another tow-truck pulls in with another car. Al goes over to it, he talks to the owner, he pops the hood, he goes around, starts the engine, turns it over anyway, then has the driver do that while he looks under the hood. Then he talks some more. It's nothing at all like how I was treated, and, I don't know, maybe this other guy does look better than me, a suit and everything, a newer car on the expensive side, but so what? My money's the same as his, my money was good enough yesterday, my clothes were no fancier then either.

When he gets done with talking to that man, getting a phone number, and the man leaves in the tow-truck, Al goes back to the brake job. Now I'm upset, which I can be from time to time. I'm worried about my car you see, worried about my money, my life, and I'm worried that it's Friday, and the next day's the weekend, and maybe even if it can be it might not be done until the weekend's over, I mean I can understand how that could happen. I mean it's probably going to be a big job if I have them do it, and there's gonna be parts to find, all these things I can understand, so it's reasonable of me to be thinking the things I am, worrying about making plans.

So I go over to Al. "So whadaya think? When do you think you'll get at mine?"

"I can't say, sir." He doesn't even look at me.

"All I mean is when do you think you'll be able to tell me what you think is wrong?"

55   "Sir, I can't say. Everything takes time."

"Look," I say, biting my angry tongue, "all I wanna know is if you're gonna look at my car when you're done with this one, in an hour, in two. I have to make plans."

"Sir. Please. I cannot say. I'll get to it." He stares at me.

I can't believe it either, but what can I do? Have it towed somewhere else? Where? At what expense? I can do nothing now and I know it. I can do nothing but hate Phoenix, hate waiting.

I try the room for this, for waiting. I listen to the boys with the bellies. The only one without a beard, name tag Nick, the stocky guy with the arms, who's from Detroit too, like Al, tells how the guard at his prison wouldn't let him out this morning until he went back and shaved closer. He'd thought he'd shaved close enough, but the guard doesn't like him for racial reasons. Then he asks if he could have an extra hour at lunch, to get his horns clipped. A normal request, and the other guy with the blue shirt, name tag Rick, doesn't lose a moment from the newspaper to say why not. I spy what looks like a boss. A grayer beard, a bigger belly. He talks to Al once or twice, interrupts him, doesn't go to the pumps or collect money. I get his attention.

60   "I realize your man over there is busy, by himself, all that, but can you do me a favor? He's very hard to talk to. I need to know when my car's going to be looked at so I can make plans. I don't know if I'm going to have to reserve a motel room, get more money, nothing. All I'm asking for is the estimate, not the actual work, I wanna know when I'm probably gonna get that."

"Sure," this man, name tag Bill, says easily. "I'll find out for you." He comes right back, not thirty seconds. "Within the hour."

I don't know why Al couldn't tell me the same thing. I'm not happy about that, that being his attitude, and I'm still not happy about how long it all has been taking. But I try hard to have patience. I try to make contingency plans. I go to a phone booth and look up a bank where I can get some money. I find an address.

"Where's 2400 Van Buren?" I ask Rick, who's still reading the newspaper and now eating a pop-tart or whatever they're called that he bought off the roach coach that just came by. It's getting close to lunch.

"It depends," he tells me wisely.

65   I'm feeling like I'm working I'm so tired by now. "It depends?"

"Yeah. It depends."

I wait, but I figure out that I have to ask. "It depends on what?"

"Whether it's east or west. Whether it's 2400 East Van Buren or 2400 West Van Buren." To him, it's a dumb question, an obvious distinction.

"I'll go look it up again. Can you give me directions for both?"

70   He does that well, and quickly, I'm afraid to ask for a repeat, so I think to call the bank, ask for directions over the phone, but then I see that Al is pushing my

car into the garage. I won't help or even think to. The guy with the arms does though.

I watch now. He gets it started, which makes me very pleased, excited even, because that means I didn't blow up the engine after all. That means it's the transmission, or something else. Al listens. I position myself at the doorway of the waiting room once again, and I listen too. Finally he takes the car up in the air. He takes out the drive shaft, gets the transmission out, works on the bell housing, takes that off, leaving the pressure plate. He disappears. Fifteen minutes later he steps into the waiting room with his paper and figures.

"The clutch was put in backwards. You need a new one. There were rocks in the bell housing too. Some bolts sheared off, probably because whoever did the clutch—it wasn't too old, but it's ruined—put in the saddle, which holds up the transmission, wrong and it's been twisted because of the angle."

He gives me the estimate. I can't believe how little it is, at least how reasonable. I mean it'd cost me that at home, at places I know to go, and his labor charge, well, it's only for two hours, and he's already spent one messing around with it. I sign the document willingly. "How about a beer? I'm so happy! I'll walk over to some store and buy a six-pack. Whadaya like?"

"That won't be necessary."

75   It's more than that. He doesn't want me to, I can sense that. Maybe he doesn't like me, like my type, my skin, my clothes, my eyes, my nose, my out-of-state plates, my talk. But who cares? I don't care! Fix my car and I'm on the road, I'm gone.

All I gotta do is wait again. It's lunch time, there's no reason I shouldn't go have a beer or two just because Al from Detroit doesn't want any, and maybe by the time I get back he'll be closing in on it. So I go across the street to this bar and slide over a stool. It's not much of a place, a hangout for real unattractive people who wouldn't think that about themselves, a crowd big on Levi jackets and earrings, on both sexes. Beer's beer though, and I have two of them. I ignore the activity I could stare at in the mirror, all the making-out in the back.

That's my lunch. Hours pass, my car's still up in the air, and I'm wondering. "So, uh, when do you think you'll be through with mine?" I ask Al.

"I can't say, sir."

80   I can't understand what it could be. Other than this guy's attitude, I like him. I can't understand what it is he doesn't like about me. Or maybe my car. Maybe because the work on it is too shabby? Okay, so me and a friend didn't do it so right. That was years ago, we'd been drinking beers, and, after all, it's an older car, almost rare—who'd expect this thing to keep on going like it has? Or maybe it's the whole picture: me, my car, my looks. Maybe he thinks I don't live right. Maybe he thinks I should have a newer car, car payments, house payments, an office job, a white shirt and tie, at least some uniform with a name tag like him. Maybe he envies me, thinks I'm living loose, drinking beer, driving around with out-of-state plates in all these other states, playing with girls. Maybe he's not married and wants to be. Maybe he is married and

miserable. Maybe he's got a daughter, or two, or more, and he thinks it's guys like me. Maybe he's just a jerk who never learned not to be one.

"Look it, it's only that I need to know so I can make some plans. You can understand that, can't you?"

He almost scowls at me this time. "Sir, everything takes time. How can I say?"

So now I'm mad. It doesn't seem right to me. It seems discourteous, nasty, thoughtless, unbusinesslike. Which makes me think of Triple-A.

So I dial their number. The woman on the other end understands what I'm telling her, she agrees.

85   "I think he's a good mechanic, but I don't think there's any excuse for him treating customers the way he does, and I think if you send someone out here, like as an experiment, you'd see what I mean. I had my car towed here because it's a membership station, and I've come to expect, well, courtesy, and professionalism."

"I agree with you, sir."

"I am glad of that. Do me a favor though. Don't make the complaint today, however it works. I have my car here now, I can't take it anywhere else, and I don't want the work on my car to be stalled on account of this. I just think you people should reprimand this station, so that other people, in similar situations, won't have this, this aggravation."

"Thank you for telling me about this, sir."

"No problem. Thank you."

90   It's late now, mid-afternoon, but Al's back on my car, a new clutch has been delivered, he's putting it in. I can still do some driving, I can get out of here. Then he throws down a part, cussing, and disappears the usual amount, then returns, holding the metal fork that takes the throw-out bearing.

"Whoever replaced your clutch should have replaced this too. It was a sloppy job. I have to buy another now. It'll cost this much more."

He shows me the numbers on the paper. No more labor, just that part. I nod my head. I want to ask him about finding it because I know it won't be easy, the car being unique and all. I do. "You can get it?"

"I can't say, sir."

I don't bother to ask about the time. I know the answer. I wait. Two more hours in that room. In Phoenix. Which I hate. I'm afraid even to turn on the radio since I hadn't heard it either of these days I've been waiting waiting. Then Al's working on my car again. Slipping parts back in, bolting. It's 4:30 p.m. when he's got the drive shaft back in and he can lower it down. He starts it up. There's this horrible sound. Like grinding rocks. The same sound that brought me in here by tow-truck. Al listens to this several times. It's ugly and causes him to cuss behind the wheel. Me, I'm thinking of money again, where I'll stay, the value of fixing versus the savings of walking away, my life. I'm tired. My legs hurt so much I feel like I've been holding that car up in the air all day.

95   Al doesn't talk to me. He brings the car back up and starts disassembling again, down to the pressure plate. I don't even bother to ask him, I know I'm

in Phoenix for another day at the very least now, and I'm very worried about how much time it's taking him, the new expenses. I'm worried he's gonna say forget it, I'm done for the day and for the weekend and with this car, good luck, goodbye, and I'll still owe them money, which I don't have a tree full of.

Everybody else has gone home except Al and his Detroit friend with the arms and the prison sentence, name tag Nick.

"I can't believe it," I tell him. "I thought he had it. Now he's at the beginning again."

"It happens," Nick says.

"The guy's been on my car since this morning. I bet he can't stand working on it anymore."

100   "It goes that way sometimes."

"I'm afraid it's something else, and he's gotta figure out what it could be all over again."

"I know Al. He'll find it."

Nick doesn't appear to be the least worried about the hour, about his friend Al's will to work, and he shrugs off my concern like it's so much small change.

What can I do? I stick around. But I watch from a distance, because I feel bad about Al, who's still in there working, on the wrong thing I'm convinced, not that he wasn't right, but that there's more and he can't face it. The light in Phoenix is changing. It's as pretty as in the morning, pink and blue, the palm trees black silhouettes against that sky, the flag put away in the comfortable night air. The brightest light around is in the garage where Al is still working on the underside of my car, and the light gets brighter and brighter as the darkness gets darker and darker. Al keeps at it, methodically, unrushed, an even pace. Nick is closing one of the gas pump islands. I decide to go ahead and rent a room, I'm not gonna try to drive tonight, even if he does get it tonight, which he won't, but I'm not going to tell him to stop, I'm not going to say anything to him, go near that forbidden work area. I go over to this one motel. It's cheap enough, cheaper than that to be honest, but the best room, the room that doesn't have one broken window—it's the only one like it, this is what the owner or motel manager or clerk or whoever she is tells me—well, it's hard to describe, but the smell alone, and the stains on the rug, the bad ones I'm talking about, not all the others, and then the ones on the mattress and box springs and I'm talking about them because that's what I was shown, all these things reminded me of worse places than where those people in the bar hang their jackets, so I go across the street. The room is more money, more than the place I stayed last night, but it's got cable too, and I figure I'll get used to the smell—some kind of rug cleaner, or insect bomb—and otherwise it's not too bad. I take it, pay the money, turn on the tube, walk back to the station a half-hour later, and though from a distance I can see, without walking the two blocks, I can see Al still in there, still working, the car in the air, I walk over.

105   "I'm afraid to talk to him," I tell Nick. "I can't believe he's still at it."

"He won't give up. That's how he is."

"Here's the number of the motel where I'm staying. Give him it if he needs me."

"Sure thing."

I go back. I buy some donuts and milk from one of those establishments across the street. I watch half of an hour television program. I have to go back. I go the two blocks. I really can see him in there without going all the way to the station, I can see just by standing on the street in front of the motel. But I go, into the waiting room, not too close to the door that leads into the garage area. I don't think he sees me, and I don't go there so he does, but I go there. Every half-hour I do this, out of a need. After four of them I see he's putting things back together. I get further away to watch. He lowers the car. More sounds, not as serious, but the same kind, and he grinds the gears as he shifts. He takes the car up again, takes out the drive shaft, the transmission, and I can't watch, I walk back to the motel, tortured by the scene, miserable, guilt-ridden, exhausted. Several more half-hours. Each time Nick is doing something else that he does at the station, checking gas levels, cleaning an area, washing something, and he's as indifferent to Al's working as Al himself appears to be.

110 It's ten o'clock, a little bit after. A local news show has started. I go over to the station. Al's bolting down the drive shaft. Then he lowers the car. Goes around to the door. Turns the ignition. It starts. No ugly sounds. No grinding gears. He revs the engine, shifts the gears several more times, then stops. He pops the hood. He checks things. He checks the battery, puts in water, greases the clamps, then closes the hood. He disappears for his usual time, then comes to me with his paper.

It's the price he quoted, not a nickel more. I notice he's washed his hands, but I'm sure he hasn't touched another part of his body, and there's not a gray hair on his head or in his beard that is out of place, smudged, or damp. His friend from Detroit, with the arms, from the prison, Nick, is sweeping the waiting room where I'm counting cash. They don't say a word to each other.

"I can't believe you wouldn't give up on it," I tell him. "You gotta be starving."

"I won't let it beat me," he says directly.

"I guess not." I thank him and back out of the garage. I pull onto the street, but drive past the motel room I've rented to get the feel of the car. It's never felt better, never shifted smoother in all the time I've driven it.

Ray Gonzalez

Born in El Paso, Texas, Ray Gonzalez is best known in Latino Studies as the editor of several distinguished anthologies of Latino and Chicano literature. He has also written half a dozen books of poetry; two collections of short stories, *The Ghost of John Wayne* (2001) and *Circling the Tortilla Dragon* (2002); and a memoir, *Memory Fever* (1999). His book of poems, *Turtle Pictures* (2000), received the Minnesota Book Award for Poetry. Gonzalez teaches creative writing at the University of Minnesota in Minneapolis and has received a long list of honors and fellowships.

Invisible Country

Mario rose from his crouching position behind the pile of tumbleweeds to get a better view of the two Border Patrol officers pulling the body from the Rio Grande. He knelt down again when he thought one of them spotted him across the swollen river. They struggled up the bank, the heavy, bloated body between them. When they disappeared in the tall cattails, he let out his breath. He didn't think they would return to the water's edge. He had seen the drowned man trying to cross the river an hour before the Border Patrol van had pulled into the cottonwoods beside his grocery store, whose back faced the water, which was twenty feet from his fence. Mario saw many things from there—high school kids partying naked, and trucks from the cement plant dumping strange-colored chemicals in the water. Most of all, Mario observed the people who hurried through the thick vegetation across the river. The majority were illegal aliens from Mexico. Mario had gathered tumbleweeds, tree trunks, pieces of wood, and the rusting frame of a 1953 pickup truck against the fence, a mass of junk and wild growth like any other spot along the river. It was the ideal place to hide and watch whatever came by.

He liked to get out of the store each day after the evening rush. As the owner of the only grocery store in town, he talked to many people every day. Dealing with so many people made him nervous. Therefore, each evening he left Neto, the boy he hired to help him, in charge, unlocked the back gate to his property, closed it behind him, and found a comfortable spot in the camouflaged area. There, he sat on one of the logs and gazed across the rapidly flowing water. Most nights, there was nothing to see. Across the river, rolling hills led west into the desert. Sometimes, things happened to change the deceptively peaceful atmosphere. Each day, Border Patrol vehicles drove along the opposite bank but rarely stopped. A Border Patrol van was the last thing he usually saw before returning to his store. A half hour of gazing was all he needed. Then he was calm enough to help Neto clean up for the nine p.m. closing. He rarely missed his nightly escape to the river.

That evening, he had not seen the man drown, but witnessing the Border Patrol agents pulling him out was the most disturbing thing he'd seen in all of his years of watching the river. Where did they take dead illegal aliens? He was about to return to his store when he saw one of the officers through a gap in the cattails on the opposite bank. The man drew his gun from his holster and looked down at the ground. The gunshot echoed across the water. A cloud of blue smoke rose around the officer, who holstered his gun and disappeared.

Mario had seen them dump the body into the back of the van, so what was the officer shooting at? He rose ten minutes later and went to help Neto close. Rounding the corner of the building, he heard car motors in the distance.

5   Several days passed. Mario thought about the incident constantly. He was fifty-four years old, and things like this troubled him deeply. He had a hard time sleeping. He wanted to tell someone what he had seen. Who or what had the officer shot? He searched the newspaper for a story about a drowning but found nothing. Several days after it happened, he almost called Roberto, the local sheriff, but replaced the receiver on the telephone without out dialing. He had known Roberto for a long time, but something kept Mario from calling him. He knew that Border Patrol agents did wrong things from time to time. Friends of his had been harassed, questioned by aggressive officers about their nationality. Some had been accused of being wetbacks. A few had been falsely arrested as illegals, then released without apology when they proved they were U.S. citizens. These things happened along the border all the time.

One week after the incident, a Border Patrol agent walked into Mario's store. It was early in the afternoon. The place was empty. Neto was cleaning the small freezers in the back of the store. Mario was doing the bookkeeping in the ledgers he kept behind the counter that served as his desk.

The officer strolled slowly toward him. He looked at Mario, his eyes hidden behind sunglasses.

"Do you work here?" the officer asked him in a quiet, even tone.

"I am the owner of this store," Mario answered. He closed the ledger and set it aside.

10   "How long have you been in business?" the officer asked. His hidden eyes roamed the shelves of canned goods, bread, and soda cans.

"I have been here twenty-five years," Mario answered. He felt his chest tightening, but he was surprising himself with his ability to talk to this man.

"That's a long time," the officer said as he turned back to look at him directly. He removed his sunglasses and set them gently on the glass counter. "You must see many things going on in this town."

"What do you mean?" Mario asked. The doorbell rang, and Leo, one of the many unemployed men in town and one of Mario's closest friends, strolled in. Leo came in to chat around this time every afternoon. Mario gave him credit against his unemployment checks and sometimes a free Coke or coffee.

The officer placed both hands level on the counter and leaned forward. Mario shifted his feet and moved a rack of beef jerky closer to the counter. He had not broken out in a sweat as he thought he would.

15   "You know lots of things that happen in this area," the officer went on. "That's what people tell me around here."

Leo took a newspaper off the stack by the door. Mario could tell that he was listening closely.

"Like what?" Mario asked the officer. His anger was starting to emerge. He was surprised the conversation was going this well.

The officer sighed and pulled a bag of beef jerky off the rack. He spoke as he tried to open the stiff plastic. "I'm investigating a murder that took place near here a few days ago. I know a lot of wet—Excuse me. I know many illegal Mexicans cross near here, and I'm wondering if you've seen anything unusual lately." He stared at Mario with clear green eyes.

Mario wasn't nervous. "We've had vandalism around here, but that's been going on for years. I see people cross the river sometimes, but they just pass through on their way to somewhere else." Leo shuffled the pages of his newspaper. Mario wondered where Neto was.

20   "The people we suspect of this murder may not be illegals." The officer took his first bite from the string of meat, made a face, then chewed slowly.

"Have you talked with the sheriff?" Mario asked. He was breathing a little harder and wanted to be friendly to this man. He knew he was not one of the agents who had pulled the body out of the water.

The officer seemed annoyed by Mario's question. He stepped back from the counter. "I wanted to check with some of the people around here first. Have you ever seen people with drugs across the river? Be easy for somebody like that to cross behind your store."

"No." Mario swallowed.

As if on signal, Leo walked to the counter. "Hello, Mario. Just the paper today." He did not look at the officer.

25   "Hello, Leo." Mario breathed. "I'm sorry, officer. I can't help you." He rang up the quarter for the paper.

The officer looked at Neto as the boy appeared from the back room. "Thanks anyway," he said and quickly walked out without paying for the jerky.

Mario let him go.

The green patrol car churned up a cloud of dust as it left the dirt lot.

"What was that all about?" Leo asked.

30   "I don't know," Mario said. He couldn't tell Leo about what he had witnessed.

"I've never seen *la Migra*[1] in here before," Neto said in his squeaky voice. "Man, something must be happening for them to come around here."

"Yeah," muttered Mario as he pulled out the ledgers. Leo was watching him closely.

That evening, Mario took his usual break, leaving Neto in the store and strolling around the building, feeling self-conscious as he made his way through the junkyard. He looked around several times, half-expecting the officer who had visited him to pop from behind a tree. He stepped over an old car tire, then sat in a crooked folding chair he'd placed behind the stack of wood after the incident with the agents. He wanted to be able to watch for a long time.

As the evening grew darker, there was nothing to see except the familiar change of color in the sky. The clouds in the west brushed into layers of red as the sun went down. The river ran straight and fast, the late sky shimmering on the water in long ribbons of gray light. Sometimes, the dance of evening colors brought Mario a memory of his recurring dream of a desperate attempt to cross the river. In the dreams, Mario rose from the muddy water. His head and clothes dripped with slime and mud. His arms flailed in the air. He couldn't see anything for a few smothering moments. His cries for air went unnoticed.

---

[1] Immigration officials

No one was there to help him out of the water, to keep him from drowning. As he gasped and crawled up the bank, his clothes transformed themselves into a clean white. By the time he had stumbled back to his store, he was no longer covered in mud. He leaned against his front door, absolutely dry, fumbled for his keys, then unlocked the door to find his long dead father and mother, covered in the same river mud, cleaning the store. The sight of his parents woke him up.

35   Sometimes Mario would gasp awake, caught in the rush of the dream. Other times, he would awaken in a peaceful daze despite the dream's last few moments. Sometimes he thought about the dream when he came to his hiding place. He had no idea what it meant because he had never fallen or gone swimming in the river. He was born in El Paso, was not an illegal from Mexico who'd attempted to cross. The dreams had started three years ago. There had been no dreams since the drowning he'd witnessed.

Now, as it grew darker, Mario thought that if it weren't for business, he would come here earlier in the day to see what went on in broad daylight. He looked across the river, anticipating the first patrol vehicle. Why had the officer questioned him? Had the others spotted him and sent today's agent to check him out? The sound of an approaching car broke into his thoughts. He could tell the direction and distance of motors after hearing so many patrol cars go by. Mario looked to his right and saw an old pickup on the opposite bank. He had never seen this one before. It moved slowly through the trees.

The pickup stopped fifty yards upriver. Mario couldn't see what the two men in the truck looked like. He recalled the agent's question about drugs. He got up from the chair and moved closer to the fence. He pushed a couple of logs aside to get a better look. One man climbed out of the passenger side and went to the back of the truck. He leaned into the bed and shuffled boxes around. Mario looked at his watch. The man climbed back into the truck. It started moving. It was directly across from Mario when it stopped again. The truck idled for a few moments. Then the driver turned on his headlights. The truck went another hundred yards along the bank before turning onto the levee road that led into town. Mario sighed. As he grew curious about a truck he had never seen before, he told himself to do something about what he had seen, days ago. Who would listen to him? Most complaints against Border Patrol agents were never investigated by the authorities. Could he tell a convincing story?

He walked back to the store to find that Neto had finished cleaning and was waiting for him to lock up so he could go home. Neto never asked where Mario went on his breaks. Mario assumed the boy knew he was always in the back.

"I was worried," Neto said as he stepped inside. "I didn't know where you were."

40   "Just out back," Mario answered. "Sorry I took so long."

He went to the cash register to close it out. Neto stood across the counter with a worried look on his face.

"Was it that Migra guy? Did he come around again?"

Mario shook his head. Since the officer's visit, the boy had been quieter than usual. In a way, it made Mario feel good that someone was worried about him. He knew Leo was also watching him closely.

Neto shrugged. "When I went to lunch after he left, I saw two Migra cars parked at Roberto's office."

45 Mario counted the bills in the register. "Why don't you go home, Neto. I'll close up. Everything looks fine for tomorrow. Take off."

"Are you sure?" Neto had never hesitated about leaving before.

"Go on. I'll see you tomorrow."

He watched the boy go. The dim ceiling lights cast a blue glow over the neat rows of cans and boxes. Mario finished in half an hour, checked the windows and back door, then stepped out the front door and locked up.

He was unlocking the door of his old yellow Mustang when headlights came on across the street. The patrol van came out of the night and pulled in behind his car. Mario placed his keys in his shirt pocket as the van lights went off. Two officers stepped out.

50 "Hold it right there," one of them said in a loud voice.

They were the two officers who'd pulled the body out of the river.

The second one held a clipboard casually at his side. The first man rested his right hand on his holstered gun.

Mario stifled a deep urge to run. "What's the problem?"

The two men stood on either side of him. "We've had reports that you've been hiding wetbacks in your store," the one with the clipboard told him.

55 Mario smelled the sweat and the lotion on the men. One of them sported a crewcut and was very tall. The agent with the clipboard was older, with graying hair. He acted like he was in charge.

"I don't know what you mean," Mario answered, his heart pounding. "I would never do anything like that."

"We know who you are," the officer continued. "You've had this place for a long time, but it looks like all of a sudden you've decided to be a local hero for these wetbacks. We could arrest you right now." His partner glared at Mario. He was the one who'd fired the gun. No one moved.

Mario felt dizzy. "Why are you doing this?" he managed to ask, even though he had the answer. "Another officer came to talk to me."

He leaned against his car to try to get rid of his dizziness. He breathed evenly as he waited for something to happen. The silence was broken by the van's squawking radio. The tall man went to answer the call. Mario couldn't make out the quick radio exchange, but it made both men climb back into the van. Thinking they were going to leave, he breathed a sigh of relief. But they sat in the van for several more excruciating minutes, blocking his car. He was afraid to get into the car or make a wrong move. The cool night chilled the sweat that ran down his back. Would they shoot him to get rid of their witness? There was no one else around.

60   The van's engine started with a roar that startled Mario. He was suddenly afraid that they would ram his car as a warning. But the van backed up slowly and pulled out of the lot, picked up speed and turned down a street that led to the nearest bridge. Mario brushed his slick black hair back from his sweating forehead and climbed into his car.

    That night, he hardly slept. At five in the morning he rose and ate breakfast. He usually got to the store by seven for the nine a.m. opening. This day, he dressed early and left his house in the morning darkness. A mid-September fog hung over the valley. It floated over the river in long stretches of heavy whiteness. Mario drove past his store and turned down the street toward the bridge. Scattered houselights from early risers cut through the fog that hung between the small houses. The high street lamps and the lights on the railroad crossing burned in the mist, their globes illuminating the coming dawn. He looked both ways and drove carefully over the tracks. The final minutes of night blanketed everything. It looked like the fog had taken the whole town away, leaving only the white gleam of the river.

    He crossed the bridge to the west side of the river, turned right on the levee road, and followed the narrow dirt strip along the water. The cottonwood trees and rows of mesquite bushes protruded through the mist, Mario's low headlights illuminating their thick black branches. Twisted shapes hung over the road, limbs scratching against Mario's car as he weaved through them. He stopped directly across from his store. The fog was too thick to see clearly to the other side, but he knew where he was. He turned off the engine and the headlights, surprised at how brightly the fog floated in the night air. As he got out, he heard a barking dog across the river—Rudy's dog, down the street from his store.

    He walked carefully toward the bank, pushing green limbs aside, stumbling a couple of times in the wet reeds and sticky cattails, unafraid as he heard the low sound of the rushing water. He stood near the spot where the officer had fired his gun. Somehow, in the eerie morning darkness, he felt that this was the exact spot. Without a flashlight, he couldn't see anything on the ground. Anyway, he didn't know what he was looking for.

    Rudy's dog barked again at the same instant the vehicles broke the eerie calmness of the river. Two sets of headlights moved slowly through the fog. They came from opposite directions, a hundred yards apart and heading for Mario's car. He crawled several yards away and crouched under a mesquite bush. He heard the idling engines, then car doors slamming. He got down on all fours and felt the cold, wet mud penetrate his clothes. He heard men crashing through the trees. Twigs snapped as they pushed through the mass of mesquite. When they reached the river, the footsteps stopped. Mario trembled in the dampness and chill. It would be daylight soon. The fog would not hide him much longer.

65   He heard three different voices. He got down flat on his belly as they drew nearer. He scratched his face in the dark but managed to roll farther under the

mesquite. The men trampled around him, not speaking. He couldn't tell if they were agents. He was afraid they would use flashlights. As he waited, water oozed through his pant legs, its cold movement pressing him harder into the ground. He closed his eyes. The men moved away from him. Car doors closed. The vehicles drove away.

Mario's back hurt as he crawled out. The early morning light clarified the vegetation around him. His car sat undisturbed. Whoever they were, the men could identify his yellow Mustang. If they were waiting out there in the fog, they could get him when he drove off. He couldn't stay there any longer. He did not turn on his lights as he drove quickly toward the bridge. The fog started to lift as the first aura of sunrise formed to the east. As he entered his store's dirt lot, he saw Roberto and Leo standing by the sheriff's car.

"Good morning, Mario," Roberto said, a worried look on his face as Mario climbed from his car. "How are you?" His eyes went to Mario's mud-stained pants and shirt.

"Hey, Roberto, Leo. What's going on so early?"

"We need to talk," Roberto told him and patted him on the back.

70   Mario avoided looking at either of the men as they entered the cold building. Roberto motioned to them to sit at the tiny folding table Mario kept near the front for coffee drinkers. Mario finally looked at Roberto. He should have told him everything that first day.

"A Border Patrol officer came by to tell me about an investigation they are doing. I don't know if you heard about the drug bust across the river a couple of weeks ago. One of the men they arrested was Lalo Acosta. I don't know if you knew him. He'd lived in town for about six months."

Roberto paused as Leo motioned that he was going to make coffee in the brewer Mario kept on the counter. "Anyway," Roberto continued, "they found Acosta murdered across the river from here. I'm not sure why the Border Patrol is involved. They usually leave this kind of stuff to us and the FBI in El Paso. I thought it was just another drug thing until Leo came by early this morning to tell me a Border Patrol officer came in here to ask you questions. Mario, what does this Acosta thing have to do with you?" Roberto shifted in his seat and set his cowboy hat on the table.

He brushed the mud and grass from his knees. "I don't know this Acosta, but I think they killed him."

"What?"

75   "I think the Border Patrol shot someone across the river, over a week ago. I was out behind the store taking a break and saw two of them pull a body out of the water. Then, a few minutes later one of them fired his gun at something on the ground. I don't know what it was because I think they'd already dumped the body in their van."

Mario blurted it out so fast that the two other men just stared at him. Leo placed his arm on Mario's shoulder. Mario hung his head and wept quietly. "I didn't think they saw me watching them, but the same two agents threatened me yesterday." He told them about the encounter beside his car.

Roberto scratched his chin and frowned. Leo had not said a word.

"Why didn't you come talk to me?" Roberto asked.

"I couldn't."

80 "Why not?" Roberto raised his voice impatiently.

"I don't know."

"Why were you hiding back there, Mario?" Leo asked. They were the first words he'd spoken.

Mario shrugged. "Not really hiding. I go behind the store to look at the river. I just happened to be out there when it happened."

Roberto stared out the windows. "The officer who spoke to me said they found Acosta shot in the head. He didn't say anything about a drowning. Why would two Border Patrol agents shoot a drug suspect, and if he was already dead when they pulled him out, why would they shoot him?"

85 Leo brought cups of coffee to Mario and Roberto.

Roberto rose without touching his coffee. He put his hat on and started to leave. "I'm going to have Teddy and Juan patrol around here more often. If anything comes up, call me right away. I just wish you had told me sooner, Mario." He didn't wait for a response but closed the door quietly behind him.

Neto would be in soon, thought Mario, to get things going for the day.

"What are we going to do, Mario?" Leo asked in a low voice.

"I don't think you have to worry, Leo." Mario sighed. "Perhaps, all this is nothing. I don't really know what I saw."

90 Nothing happened for the next four days. Mario was grateful for Roberto's deputies patrolling by the store. He didn't go behind the store during those days. He saw no green vans during those four days.

The following Saturday brought heavy rains to the valley, and the river rose. By Sunday morning part of the town was flooded. Hardly anyone came into Mario's store. Neto didn't work on Sunday, so Mario spent the day mostly alone. The parking lot was a lake. Mario spotted an occasional sheriff's car on the street. A couple of hours before closing time, Leo came in and invited Mario to eat dinner with him at Sylvia's Cafe. He'd just cashed his unemployment check. Mario said he didn't feel like it. Leo said he'd come back at closing time to see if Mario had changed his mind.

Mario found his plastic raincoat in the storeroom and an old pair of boots he hadn't worn in years. He pulled them on and went out into the rain. The water in the lot hadn't quite reached porch level, but another day of heavy rain would threaten the store. He pulled the coat's yellow hood over his head and splashed through the mud to the back. He opened the gate to find that the rain had washed much of the junk away. Tree trunks and wood hung over the bank above the roaring water. As he kicked soaked weeds and pieces of cardboard aside, part of his wooden fence fell into the river.

He reached to save some of the fence and slipped and almost fell into the river. He scooted back on his rear, pushing himself with his hands. More of the fence dropped into the water. Mario rolled onto his knees and stood up. He wiped the rainwater off his face as the two agents entered the gate. The men's faces were hooded in olive green raincoats. Mario stared through the pellets of rain. The men kept their hands hidden under the plastic. As Mario moved away from the bank, one of them showed him the revolver under the coat. Mario tried to move to his left, slipped in the mud, and dove into the remaining pile of tree trunks and car tires. As he rolled, one green raincoat surged toward the disintegrating edge of the bank.

Mario's eyes stung with water as someone pushed the agent into the river. Flat on his stomach, Mario tried to reach for a long stick wedged under a tire. The first gunshot tore above his head. He pushed his body deeper into the logs. They fell on top of him. He watched Leo wrestle with the second agent. The logs were crushing him. He pushed against them, and the ground beneath him gave way. As he tumbled amid the logs rolling toward the river, his hand shot out and clutched the broken fence. Leo and one of the agents fell past him into the river and were swept away. Mario heard sirens. He hung on, inches from the roaring water. Roberto and four deputies appeared, guns drawn. Hands reached for him, pulled.

95   When he awoke in the Las Cruces hospital the next morning, Roberto was standing by his bed, the bright sunlight of a clear day sparkling off the shiny badge on his chest. Mario tried to turn his head, but the tubes in his nostrils wouldn't let him.

"Leo?" he managed.

Roberto pinched his hat in his fists. "I'm sorry, Mario. Leo drowned."

Mario's tears blended into patterns of light he was used to seeing in his dreams of the river. "And the two agents?"

"One drowned. The other has been arrested. The FBI thinks Acosta was a drug runner for a group of agents."

100   "Leo was coming to take me to eat at Sylvia's."

"I know," said Roberto. "He called me yesterday when he saw one of the green vans waiting across from Sylvia's. I wish he'd waited for us. When you feel better, I have to get a statement from you."

"Leo saved my life."

Roberto nodded. "I'll talk to you tomorrow."

After Roberto left, Mario tried to stay awake, but he was exhausted and fell into the dream he had been waiting for. The river flowed slowly as he stood on the bank. His barrier of solitude had been rebuilt, the tires and trees piled higher than before. He stood there peacefully and watched the grove of cottonwoods across the water. Their thick green branches swayed above the greener mesquite. He was still the boy who built his first raft with his brother, Francisco, but he was not going to be the boy whose father tore the small platform apart and threw it into the river. His father screamed at him never to build a raft again because he did not want his sons to be mistaken for "mojados." He said only "mojados" would think of building such a thing to get across, especially when the river was deep and they couldn't wade into America. Mario stood behind his wall of junk, crouched lower in the evening light of a peaceful and passable river and dreamed he came out from behind the barrier to wave to his father on the other side. He dreamed his father stopped hating the river, turning from the opposite bank instead. He pointed to let Mario know which direction to go to find the nearest bridge to his side. When he found the bridge, Mario joined his father in a dry crossing over water that did not need to be disturbed.

Alberto Ríos

Alberto Ríos was born to a Guatemalan father and an English mother in Arizona in 1952. His first book of poems, *Whispering to Fool the Wind* (1981), won the Academy of American Poets Walt Whitman Award. Among other works, he has published *Elk Heads on the Wall* (1979), the short-story collection *The Iguana Killer: Twelve Stories of the Heart* (1984), and *Nogales Memoir* (1999). A recipient of such as honors as the Pushcart Prize for fiction, Ríos is Regents Professor of English at Arizona State University.

The Child

The bus station in Guaymas was crowded with friends and relatives of the few people coming or going. The wordless singing of tears, *abrazos*,[1] laughter, and hand-shaking was common on Sundays and Wednesdays. These were the two days that the bus from Mexico City stopped here on its way to Nogales. It was for this Wednesday's trip that the widows Sandoval and García had purchased tickets and had come several hours early to make sure they would not miss the bus.

The two ladies shared a single face, held together by an invisible net, made evident by the marks it left on their skins. They wore black, more out of habit than out of mourning for their husbands, both of whom had been dead for more than ten years. Ten or eleven, it was difficult to say. Time was different now. Each of the ladies carried roughly woven bags with deep purple and yellow stripes. Aside from more black clothing, particularly black shawls, the bags both contained food—lemons, tortillas, sweet breads, cheese, sugar, all gifts. In their free hands, the women carried rosaries made of hard wood and their tickets. On their heads they wore black veils and on their legs black stockings with lines up the back and through which the leg hair showed. These stockings were rolled up just past their knees, worn in the manner of most of the other ladies their age who were at the bus station just then.

The bus arrived at about eleven-thirty and was not yet running too far off schedule. Some of the people coming from Mexico City got off to stretch, but the majority remained. The widows Sandoval and García said goodbyes to those who had come with them, crossed themselves, and got on the bus, which

---

[1]hugs

was not crowded this Wednesday, not as crowded as on Sundays, when people had to stand in the aisle. The two ladies found a pair of seats near the back.
It took them some time to get the seats because bags and suitcases cluttered
the aisle. Their own bags were stretched beyond their original intentions and
knocked into people, especially the men who wore straw cowboy hats with
wide brims for traveling. After many *excuse me's* and *con permiso's*, the ladies
got to their places. Although they had gotten on first, they were the last to get
settled. Both were shaped like large eggs, formless and mostly bottom-halved,
so bus seats never seemed to be quite big enough.

   The bus driver with green-tinted glasses and a thin-thin moustache watched
and waited with much patience until they were accommodated to start the bus.
As it pulled away, relatives and friends waved and shouted last minute messages, very long, but the two ladies even after considerable effort could not get
their window open. The embarrassment was short-lived as smoke from the bus
soon covered their view.

5   The two women were uncommonly quiet as the bus hurtled along. Mrs.
Sandoval looked out the window and fanned herself with a magazine she had
already read many times, the kind with brown pictures on newsprint that never
gets thrown away. Mrs. García, the more talkative and gossipy of the two, held
her brown bead rosary and looked around at the other people. In front of her
she could see only the backs of heads and cowboy hats. One little girl, her lips
white from candy, was standing up on a seat and looking back at her. Across
the aisle a man sat pulling a blanket around the head of a little boy. The boy
was asleep, and Mrs. García was envious because she had always found sleeping on a bus impossible. Behind her sat another man with a cowboy hat who
was reading a magazine. Brown pictures on newsprint. The other few seats
were empty.

   It was almost noon now, and the bus was getting very hot. The black clothes
of the two ladies did not help matters, but they had grown quite used to sweating. Each agreed, this was their lot. They complained to each other now,
after many years of friendship and funerals, only with large sighs. No words.
Sometimes they would shake their heads, and this said all the words. Everyone on the bus today seemed uncommonly quiet, not just the ladies, as if
these people all knew why the two were making the trip. The man across the
aisle began to smoke. Mrs. García sighed, and Mrs. Sandoval understood. The
other words.

   "Excuse me. Is the child all right?" asked Mrs. García. The man next to her
was thin and moved like an ostrich, not smooth but in jerks, so that he almost
could not light the newest in a line of cigarettes he had kept in his hand. He
had green-tinted glasses on, too.

   "Well, no, he is sick," answered the man. He did not seem very talkative
either, like Mrs. Sandoval, thought Mrs. García. One would think the Republic was at war again, or somesuch. Mrs. García waited for more but the man
said nothing.

After a few minutes, Mrs. García, as was her habit, asked him, "What is wrong with the child?" Her custom was not necessarily to ask about the health of children, but rather, simply to *ask*.

10   "I don't know exactly. We are going to see a doctor, a specialist in Nogales, maybe Tucson."

"Weren't there any specialists in Mexico City? I have heard of some very good doctors. Dr. Olvera. Do you..."

"Well, yes, but they have advised me to go to Nogales and see an American doctor. You know."

"Oh, I see, of course," said Mrs. García. She nodded her head to say yes in the other language. He understood clearly, with his head, also.

Mrs. Sandoval nudged her. "You should stop talking so much, you are going to wake the child," she whispered.

15   "Yes, yes, you are right. Poor thing." More words to the man, "I'm sorry" with her eyes.

"Poor Agustín," said Mrs. Sandoval.

"What?" said Mrs. García. Spoken words were not always understandable.

"Agustín, poor Agustín," repeated Mrs. Sandoval. She raised her eyes to the roof of the bus. Quickly, and back down.

"He has gone to fine things. All we can do is pray for him," said Mrs. García. Both woman gripped their rosaries and immediately began praying. They prayed the rosary several times together. It did not take them long because they had become very fast at it from many dragging years of practice. When they finished, Mrs. Sandoval went back to looking out the window and Mrs. García looked around at the people again.

20   She decided to talk to the man once more because there was no one else within speaking range. In any language. This time she was careful to whisper.

"Have you been to this doctor before?"

"What? Oh, no. This is the first time."

"I thought you had because I could not help noticing your American cigarettes. They smell different."

"Oh, uh, yes. No I've never been. A friend..." He offered the cigarettes. Mrs. García shook her head. It said no.

25   "Did you try giving him some *yerba buena* tea?"

"Pardon me?" said the man. He was surprised at her whispering and showed effort in turning his head to hear her again.

"Oh, I am whispering because I don't want to wake, you know, the boy."

"Oh," he said. And yes with his head.

"What I asked was, did you try giving him some *yerba buena* tea?" Eyebrows up.

30   "Oh, uh, yes, we did." Eyebrows down, clearly.

"Did you try honey and lemon? Maybe with little bit of tequila? That always helps." Still up.

"Yes, we gave him everything, but nothing helps. Really." Brows, if possible, even lower.

"That is very strange. He must be very sick. Does he have a fever?" Still.

"No, no, he gets chills. That's why I wrapped him in this blanket. I think it helps him to sleep better, too, and the doctor said that he needs lots of sleep." The ostrich in his body was uncomfortable.

35 "Yes, then that is the thing to do, of course. Keep him well wrapped. Chills can be very terrible, especially if you have arthritis. I have this bracelet for arthritis and it helps a little. Copper. It is the only thing the doctor has given me that helps. Dr. Valenzuela. Do you know him? Sometimes it helps the pain I get in my left shoulder, too. And a lot of liquids. Don't they always say that."

"Pardon me?" He almost was not turning his head to listen.

"And you should give him a lot of liquids, no doubt." Lips pressed.

"Yes, yes, that's right. Excuse me, I am going to try and sleep." He smiled a smile faster than the moment he had taken previously to light a match.

"Oh, of course, go right ahead. I hope you can," said Mrs. García. She let go of him with her eyes. She wished that she could get to sleep. Bus rides always seemed to be endless and her neck always ached, as it did now, a great deal. They would be at *El Sopilote* soon and she could get out and stretch. She sighed, but Mrs. Sandoval was asleep, and did not hear.

40 The bus stopped at *El Sopilote*, and some of the people got off. Some were to stay here while the others just got off to stretch themselves. Mrs. García got off, the man next to her, the bus driver, and several of the men with cowboy hats, Mrs. Sandoval, the child, and most of the women stayed in the bus. It was too hot outside, and the women preferred to stay out of the sun in their black clothes. Mrs. García's neck was more painful than the heat, and needed to be walked.

Some rearranging when everyone got back on the bus accommodated the new people who had been waiting. The two widows and the man with his child kept their seats. The man who had been behind the two ladies had gotten off and now no one sat back there.

The bus started up again, and the driving was soon a blur that felt like the times one counts and counts for no particular reason, to a hundred, a thousand. More. Like counting stars, but not giving up, not being able to give up. Mrs. Sandoval was able to half fall asleep. Mrs. García, tired of looking at the desert scrub and occasional mesquite trees, read the magazine that Mrs. Sandoval had fanned herself with earlier. Read it, really, for the third time. The man next to them stared out of his window and from time to time fixed the blanket around the still sleeping child.

Mrs. García finished rereading the magazine and began fanning herself with it. She sighed to no one in particular, to herself, maybe, if only to tell herself how uncomfortable things were. She looked around and wondered with her eyebrows down if all the smoking the man next to her was doing might not be bothering the child. It was starting to bother her, certainly.

"We are going to a funeral."

45 "Pardon me?" said the man. Mrs. García was whispering again. His neck almost would not let his head turn around, this time more than ever.

"I said we are going to a funeral."

"Oh, I'm sorry." His head said yes, up and down, but he listened actually with the side of his face, since his neck was strong.

"It was this lady's poor brother." She motioned in the direction of Mrs. Sandoval.

He saw, like people sometimes can, without turning his face. "I'm very sorry to hear that. Uh, how far are you going?"

50 Her eyebrows went up. Good. At last, "Oh, we're going as far as you are, to Nogales." She forgot the smoke. Forgot in the sense of excused.

"I see," said the man. He fussed with the boy's blanket again.

"How old is the child?" asked Mrs. García. She could only see his short hair from her angle.

"Oh, he is five years old." His head nodded yes.

"He will be starting school soon." Her eyebrows made this a question.

55 With the side of his face he heard the eyebrows rise. "Yes, I suppose he will." He almost shrugged his shoulders. His body was moving so much, just a little but all over, that perhaps it just seemed like he shrugged, or almost shrugged.

"He died of cancers is what the doctor said." Mrs. García turned her head to look straight forward, and sighed.

As if his face were tied by an invisible string, it turned now toward her at the same moment she looked forward. "Pardon me?"

"This lady's brother. He died of the cancer somewhere in his bones." No motions.

"I'm sorry to hear that." Flat.

60 Mrs. Sandoval had heard the last parts of the conversation. She spoke to Mrs. García, "The man has got enough troubles without you telling him ours."

"Oh, of course, you are right. I'm sorry," she said to the man. She turned to him.

And in the same moment, he faced forward. The string had turned slack, and released him. "That's all right, really," he said, more to the seat in front of him. "Excuse me, I think I will move the child to the back. He will be more comfortable if he lies across two seats, I think."

"Of course," said Mrs. García. She moved her bag with the purple and yellow stripes out of the way to say yes as the man picked up the child and spread him out across the two seats directly in back of the two women. The boy did not wake up. The man sat in the closest of the adjoining two seats so that he was still opposite the two ladies, but one row back.

"The child has slept for a long time," said Mrs. Sandoval to Mrs. García.

65 Mrs. García sighed. She wished she could sleep like that. "Yes, and isn't his face pale though? A little honey and lemon would surely help some. He must be very sick."

"Agustín was such a good man," said Mrs. Sandoval.

"Yes, yes he was." They both nodded up, and down. Yes.

The traveling was like an hour hand's and several more people got on the bus. They had been waiting along the road and had probably come from one of the ranches because the men wore cowboy hats and the women were not used to shoes. The hats were a cheaper quality of straw. The two widows had prayed the rosary again after mentioning Mrs. Sandoval's brother. They would soon be in Hermosillo. That would surely be like a drink of water. It had been a long time since she had eaten *quesadillas* at the *El Yaqui*, remarked Mrs. García. She put her hand on her stomach. Mrs. Sandoval said that she was not hungry. She put her hand flat on the top part of her chest.

The bus stopped in Hermosillo and almost everyone got out this time. One man was too fat, and did not find rising worth the trouble. He was so used to sitting now, he said, to Mrs. García, who asked, that standing felt unnatural, really. He slept sitting, too, because his stomach felt like a horse stepping on his chest when he stretched out on his back. Mrs. García's head said no, God, from side to side, it's too much to bear. But we're like that, aren't we, said her head. She decided she would not offer to bring him anything from the restaurant. She certainly would not eat if she were like that. The two ladies went out and were followed, patiently because he had no choice, by the man who was sitting now behind them.

70   "Are you going to bring the child?" asked Mrs. García, in all the ways she was capable. They were already outside the bus, and he did not have the boy with him.

"No, I don't want to wake him. He needs all the sleep he can get." The man crushed his cigarette on the ground.

"Yes, of course. By the way, I recommend very highly the *quesadillas* here. No place has *quesadillas* like *El Yaqui*." She smiled.

"So I have heard," said the man. Yes, nodding.

The ladies went into the restaurant. The man said that he would be right in, but that he had to stretch first, that he felt like crumpled paper. He pulled out one of his American cigarettes. Everyone in the restaurant ordered the *quesadillas* without exception. Rumor had made them larger than any of the other choices, had put more letters in their name. Mrs. García felt that it was the quality of the cream in the white cheese. The man came in a little later and ordered the same. Of course, nodded Mrs. García. He sat by himself at a table near the turquoise painted door.

75   Mrs. Sandoval ordered an orange soda, preferably a Mission if they had any. Mrs. García ordered an *agua de manzana*[2] and a glass of water. The ladies finished quickly and commented on the tastiness of the food. Yes, yes. Mrs. Sandoval had ordered only one *quesadilla* and Mrs. García had ordered three. They finished eating at the same time.

"I think the *agua de manzana* will given you heartburn," said Mrs. Sandoval. "You ate too fast."

"It's very good for the stomach." She was sure.

"It has always given me heartburn. Why did you order the water when you haven't even tasted it?"

"I am going to take it to the boy. He should have lots of liquids." Certainly, on her face. The doctor, after all, had said so.

---

[2]apple juice

80   "Shouldn't you leave that to his father?"

"The poor man is dazed," said Mrs. García. "I don't think he knows what to do for the child. Anyway, a little water won't hurt, and the poor thing hasn't had any since we got on the bus. His throat must be like the road."

"Yes, yes, that is true," said Mrs. Sandoval. "But shouldn't you tell the man?"

"I told him the child needs lots of liquids but, like I said, he is in a daze. Let the poor man eat. Come on, a little water will be a big help for the boy." The two ladies paid their bill and took the water out. They told the *señora* of the restaurant that they would bring the glass back in a couple of minutes. Yes would have been the word in the *señora's* mouth, opened like a question, yes, of course.

The two widows got back on the bus. It was much easier for them since the bus was almost empty. They made their way past the few people, the fat man, yes, hello, he was eating *quesadillas* someone had brought, and got to the back where the child was. Mrs. García saw that he was still sleeping.

85   "Do you think that you should wake him?" asked Mrs. Sandoval.

"It won't hurt him. He needs the water, especially in this heat." She reached for the covers and moved them from his face.

"Ah, this child is cold. His chills must be like ice," said Mrs. García. Her eyebrows.

"Here, let me see." Mrs. Sandoval's hands.

"Wait," said Mrs. García. She moved the blanket so as to rearrange it and stared at the white child. Vanilla ice cream. "Oh, oh my God!" she screamed, and moved like she had put her hands into the flames of a stove, like when she first learned to make tortillas. She was a young girl then. She moved back with the same kind of strength. Mrs. Sandoval caught her as she fell, fainted.

90   "*¡Dios mío!*[3] Jesus? Help, ah, this child is dead, he is dead!" screamed Mrs. Sandoval in much the same voice as Mrs. García had screamed. Very high. All the people jumped to get over them. Everyone started screaming, and crying. The fat man came. Mrs. García was laid down in the adjoining chairs and Mrs. Sandoval sat with her, crying and clasping her rosary, squeezing it so that if it had been plastic.... A man with a cowboy hat—one of them, they were all mixed up—covered the child again with the blanket.

"Get the police, get the police, the Red Cross," yelled the man, too loudly. "Who is this, whose child is this?"

Mrs. Sandoval gasped. There was a loud implication not only in the question, but in the way he grabbed the seat to push himself, once he was aimed. "He's the man's, the man who ate alone." Mrs. Sandoval half stood. Her eyes went through the bus with sharp edges and fast.

By this time the bus driver was calling for the police. The man was nowhere to be found although everyone looked for him. Every person was asking what happened and the bus was an elevator full of voices. Too many, and they bounced into each other. Mrs. García was brought out and lay resting in a bedroom behind the restaurant. Mrs. Sandoval sat with her, praying out loud. The child was left where it was. Nothing moved it.

[3]My God!

When the police arrived, the bus stop was much quieter. Too quiet, like it had been too loud. Everyone was sitting in the restaurant. No one could believe it, and where was the father? The Red Cross ambulance arrived just after the police and took the child away. Just picked him up.

95 The head policeman was trying to get everyone's attention. "All right, all right, who can tell me what happened here? I am the Sergeant."

Mrs. García's name was mentioned by Mrs. Sandoval. The policeman asked where she was and Mrs. Sandoval led him to the bedroom in back where she was resting. The *señora* was fanning her. Mrs. Sandoval pointed with her eyes.

"Mrs. García?"

"Yes, yes, at your service." She would talk. Of course, if it would help.

"I understand that you can tell me something about what has happened here." It all came from his mouth, like a sergeant.

100 "Well, only that the man said that the child was sick, and when I tried to give it some water I saw that it was dead. The boy, I mean."

"Can you describe the man?"

"Oh, yes, of course." Her eyebrows went up, one a little more than the other. "He was..."

"Well, I would rather you tell me this at the station house. Is that all right with you?" Like a sergeant still.

"Well, we are going to a funeral." Her eyes looked at the floor.

105 "I'm sorry. It won't take too long, and there are a number of other busses. Where are you going?" Less like a sergeant. Funerals do that.

"To Nogales," replied Mrs. García.

"Ah, yes, certainly there are other busses going to Nogales today." Head up and down. He was a man after all. She felt better.

"Would I be able to telephone from the station in case something happens to keep me?" She kept her head down.

"Of course, yes of course." Not impatiently.

110 Mrs. García looked at Mrs. Sandoval. "You go on ahead. I should stay and help. All right?" She asked with all her body.

Mrs. Sandoval nodded her head. "Yes, if you'll be okay." She glanced at the Sergeant. "Try and get to Nogales in time. We will all be waiting for you. It's not too far, anyway."

"I will, I promise." Yes.

The policeman told the passengers that they could get back on the bus. After some hesitation—they wanted to know more, they were still hungry—everyone was ready to go.

"Please call if anything comes up. Be careful," said Mrs. Sandoval, as she hugged Mrs. García.

115 "I will, I will, Go on now." With the tips of her fingers.

Mrs. Sandoval got back on the bus but this time she sat in front. Mrs. García got into the police car. They waved at each other. Both, in the hands they could not see, held their rosaries. If they had been plastic....

Once the bus got going, Mrs. Sandoval could not help thinking about the child. She prayed the rosary almost all the way to Nogales. What tragedies, her brother and then this child, this innocent child. She would wear black for the rest of her life, she decided. Her life would not last so long. This was the least she could do.

At the bus station in Nogales, relatives looking smaller than she remembered were waiting for her. The funeral was to go on as planned. She told them the story of the child and they were all moving their faces in a thousand ways, each in a manner no one else could. They made words, and half-words. And the idea of the father running away, that was unbearable. She gave them the food she had brought.

Mrs. García was still not there by the time the wake was almost over. Mrs. Sandoval could only frown, could not draw her face into comfort. Her face became smaller as it forced itself together, crowding in the lines, making her almost too young. She wondered whether or not she should call the police station in Hermosillo. Mrs. García called before she could make up her mind.

120   Somewhere out there she was crying. Mrs. Sandoval listened but almost did not, her head moving too fast from side to side, so that some of the words could not find her. *Dios mío, Dios mío* was all that her mouth could say. Relatives came too close around her. What happened to the boy? Doña Carolina, what's the matter? What is she saying? Is she still going to come? Did they find the father? And?

Mrs. Sandoval spoke. She spoke the words of Mrs. García, who had spoken the words of the Sergeant, who had spoken the words of the doctor. More truthfully, she carried the words.

The child was dead. It had been dead for a long time. That is true. But it had also been operated on. The boy's insides had been cleaned out and replaced with bags of opium. They had tested to be certain. Then the boy was sewn up again, put into clothes. Sometimes this happens. This was not the first.

Oh my God, *Dios mío, Dios mío* was all Mrs. Sandoval kept saying, maybe with words, saying just like Mrs. García. Their heads moved from side to side, but not fast enough.

Helena María Viramontes

Helena María Viramontes was born in East Los Angeles on February 26, 1954, the daughter of Mexican immigrants. Her works include *The Moths and Other Stories* (1985) and *Under the Feet of Jesus* (1995). Her short stories are some of the most anthologized in Latino literature and are systematically praised for their modernist style and powerful portrayals of disempowered Latinos in various working-class environments. Viramontes has been a recipient of a National Endowment for the Arts fellowship grant and the John Dos Passos Prize for Literature. She is currently associate professor of English at Cornell University.

The Cariboo Cafe

I.

They arrived in the secrecy of night, as displaced people often do, stopping over for a week, a month, eventually staying a lifetime. The plan was simple. Mother would work too until they saved enough to move into a finer future where the toilet was one's own and the children needn't be frightened. In the meantime, they played in the back allies, among the broken glass, wise to the ways of the streets. Rule one: never talk to strangers, not even the neighbor who paced up and down the hallways talking to himself. Rule two: the police, or "polie" as Sonya's popi pronounced the word, was La Migra in disguise and thus should always be avoided. Rule three: keep your key with you at all times—the four walls of the apartment were the only protection against the streets until Popi returned home.

Sonya considered her key a guardian saint and she wore it around her neck as such until this afternoon. Gone was the string with the big knot. Gone was the key. She hadn't noticed its disappearance until she picked up Macky from Mrs. Avila's house and walked home. She remembered playing with it as Amá walked her to school. But lunch break came, and Lalo wrestled her down so that he could see her underwear, and it probably fell somewhere between the iron rings and sandbox. Sitting on the front steps of the apartment building, she considered how to explain the missing key without having to reveal what Lalo had seen, for she wasn't quite sure which offense carried the worse penalty.

She watched people piling in and spilling out of the buses, watched an old man asleep on the bus bench across the street. He resembled a crumbled ball of paper, huddled up in the security of a tattered coat. She became aware of their mutual loneliness and she rested her head against her knees blackened by the soot of the playground asphalt.

The old man eventually awoke, yawned like a lion's roar, unfolded his limbs and staggered to the alley where he urinated between two trash bins. (She wanted to peek, but it was Macky who turned to look.) He zipped up, drank from a paper bag and she watched him until he disappeared around the corner. As time passed, buses came less frequently, and every other person seemed to resemble Popi. Macky became bored. He picked through the trash barrel; later, and to Sonya's fright, he ran into the street after a pigeon. She understood his restlessness for waiting was as relentless as long lines to the bathroom. When a small boy walked by, licking away at a scoop of vanilla ice cream, Macky ran after him. In his haste to outrun Sonya's grasp, he fell and tore the knee of his denim jeans. He began to cry, wiping snot against his sweater sleeve.

5   "See?" She asked, dragging him back to the porch steps by his wrist. "See? God punished you!" It was a thing she always said because it seemed to work. Terrified by the scrawny tortured man on the cross, Macky wanted to avoid his wrath as much as possible. She sat him on the steps in one gruff jerk. Seeing his torn jeans, and her own scraped knees, she wanted to join in his sor-

row, and cry. Instead she snuggled so close to him, she could hear his stomach growling.

"Coke," he asked, Mrs. Avila gave him an afternoon snack which usually held him over until dinner. But sometimes Macky got lost in the midst of her own six children and...

Mrs. Avila! It took Sonya a few moments to realize the depth of her idea. They could wait there, at Mrs. Avila's. And she'd probably have a stack of flour tortillas, fresh off the comal, ready to eat with butter and salt. She grabbed his hand. "Mrs. Avila has Coke."

"Coke!" He jumped up to follow his sister. "Coke," he cooed.

At the major intersection, Sonya quietly calculated their next move while the scores of adults hurried to their own destinations. She scratched one knee as she tried retracing her journey home in the labyrinth of her memory. Things never looked the same when backwards and she searched for familiar scenes. She looked for the newspaperman who sat in a little house with a little T.V. on and selling magazines with naked girls holding beach balls. But he was gone. What remained was a little closet-like shed with chains and locks, and she wondered what happened to him, for she thought he lived there with the naked ladies.

10   They finally crossed the street at a cautious pace, the colors of the street lights brighter as darkness descended, a stereo store blaring music from two huge, blasting speakers. She thought it was the disco store she passed, but she didn't remember if the sign was green or red. And she didn't remember it flashing like it was now. Studying the neon light, she bumped into a tall, lanky dark man. Maybe it was Raoul's Popi. Raoul was a dark boy in her class that she felt sorry for because everyone called him sponge head. Maybe she could ask Raoul's Popi where Mrs. Avila lived, but before she could think it all out, red sirens flashed in their faces and she shielded her eyes to see the polie.

The polie is men in black who get kids and send them to Tijuana, says Popi. Whenever you see them, run, because they hate you, says Popi. She grabs Macky by his sleeve and they crawl under a table of bargain cassettes. Macky's nose is running, and when he sniffles, she puts her finger to her lips. She peeks from behind the poster of Vincente Fernandez to see Raoul's father putting keys and stuff from his pockets onto the hood of the polie car. And it's true, they're putting him in the car and taking him to Tijuana. Popi, she murmured to herself. Mamá.

"Coke," Macky whispered, as if she had failed to remember.

"Ssssh. Mi'jo, when I say run, you run, okay?" She waited for the tires to turn out, and as the black and white drove off, she whispered "Now," and they scurried out from under the table and ran across the street, oblivious to the horns.

They entered a maze of allies and dead ends, the long, abandoned warehouses shadowing any light. Macky stumbled and she continued to drag him until his crying, his untied sneakers, and his raspy breathing finally forced her to stop. She scanned the boarded up boxcars, the rows of rusted rails to make sure the polie wasn't following them. Tired, her heart bursting, she leaned him against a tall, chainlink fence. Except for the rambling of some railcars, silence prevailed, and she could hear Macky sniffling in the darkness. Her mouth was parched and she swallowed to rid herself of the metallic taste of fear. The shadows stalked them, hovering like nightmares. Across the tracks, in the distance, was a room with a yellow glow, like a beacon light at the end of a dark sea. She pinched Macky's nose with the corner of her dress, took hold of his sleeve. At least the shadows will be gone, she concluded, at the zero zero place.

II.

15   Don't look at me. I didn't give it the name. It was passed on. Didn't even know what it meant until I looked it up in some library dictionary. But I kinda liked the name. It's, well, romantic, almost like the name of a song, you know, so I kept it. That was before JoJo turned fourteen even. But now if you take a look at the sign, the paint's peeled off 'cept for the two O's. The double zero cafe. Story of my life. But who cares, right? As long as everyone 'round the factories know I run an honest business.

The place is clean. That's more than I can say for some people who walk through that door. And I offer the best prices on double burger deluxes this side of Main Street. Okay, so its not pure beef. Big deal, most meat markets do the same. But I make no bones 'bout it. I tell them up front, 'yeah, it ain't dogmeat, but it ain't sirloin either.' Cause that's the sort of guy I am. Honest.

That's the trouble. It never pays to be honest. I tried scrubbing the stains off the floor, so that my customers won't be reminded of what happened. But they keep walking as if my cafe ain't fit for lepers. And that's the thanks I get for being a fair guy.

Not once did I hang up all those stupid signs. You know, like 'We reserve the right to refuse service to anyone,' or 'No shirt, no shoes, no service.' To tell you the truth—which is what I always do though it don't pay—I wouldn't have nobody walking through that door. The streets are full of scum, but scum gotta eat too is the way I see it. Now, listen. I ain't talkin 'bout out-of-luckers, weirdos, whores, you know. I'm talking 'bout five-to-lifers out of some tech. I'm talking Paulie.

I swear Paulie is thirty-five, or six. JoJo's age if he were still alive, but he don't look a day over ninety. Maybe why I let him hang out 'cause he's JoJo's age. Shit, he's okay as long as he don't bring his wigged out friends whose voices sound like a record at low speed. Paulie's got too many stories and they all get jammed up in his mouth so I can't make out what he's saying. He scares the other customers too, acting like he is shadow boxing, or like a monkey hopping on a frying pan. You know, nervous, jumpy, his jaw all falling and his eyes bulgy and dirt yellow. I give him the last booth, coffee and yesterday's donut holes to keep him quiet. After a few minutes, out he goes, before lunch. I'm too old, you know, too busy making ends meet to be nursing the kid. And so is Delia.

20   That Delia's got these unique titties. One is bigger than another. Like an orange and grapefruit. I kid you not. They're like that on account of when she

was real young she had some babies, and they all sucked only one favorite tit-tie. So one is bigger than the other, and when she used to walk in with Paulie, huggy huggy and wearing those tight leotard blouses that show the nipple dots, you could see the difference. You could tell right off that Paulie was proud of them, the way he'd hang his arm over her shoulder and squeeze the grapefruit. They kill me, her knockers. She'd come in real queen-like, smack-ing gum and chewing the fat with the illegals who work in that garment ware-house. They come in real queen-like too, sitting in the best booth near the window, and order cokes. That's all. Cokes. Hey, but I'm a nice guy, so what if they mess up my table, bring their own lunches and only order small cokes, leaving a dime as tip? So sometimes the place ain't crawling with people, you comprende buddy? A dime's a dime as long as its in my pocket.

Like I gotta pay my bills too, I gotta eat. So like I serve anybody whose got the greens, including that crazy lady and the two kids that started all the trou-ble. If only I had closed early. But I had to wash the dinner dishes on account of I can't afford a dishwasher. I was scraping off some birdshit glue stuck to this plate, see, when I hear the bells jingle against the door. I hate those fuck-ing bells. That was Nell's idea. Nell's my wife; my ex-wife. So people won't sneak up on you, says my ex. Anyway, I'm standing behind the counter star-ing at this short woman. Already I know that she's bad news because she looks street to me. Round face, burnt toast color, black hair that hangs like straight ropes. Weirdo, I've had enough to last me a lifetime. She's wearing a shawl and a dirty slip is hanging out. Shit if I have to dish out a free meal. Funny thing, but I didn't see the two kids 'til I got to the booth. All of a sudden I see these big eyes looking over the table's edge at me. It shook me up, the way they kinda appeared. Aw, maybe they were there all the time.

The boy's a sweetheart. Short Order don't look nothing like his mom. He's got dried snot all over his dirty cheeks and his hair ain't seen a comb for years. She can't take care of herself, much less him or the doggie of a sister. But he's a tough one, and I pinch his nose 'cause he's a real sweetheart like JoJo. You know, my boy.

It's his sister I don't like. She's got these poking eyes that follow you 'round 'cause she don't trust no one. Like when I reach for Short Order, she flinches like I'm 'bout to tear his nose off, gives me a nasty, squinty look. She's maybe five, maybe six, I don't know, and she acts like she owns him. Even when I bring the burgers, she doesn't let go of his hand. Finally, the fellow bites it and I wink at him. A real sweetheart.

In the next booth, I'm twisting the black crud off the top of the ketchup bottle when I hear the lady saying something in Spanish. Right off I know she's illegal, which explains why she looks like a weirdo. Anyway, she says something nice to them 'cause it's in the same tone that Nell used when I'd rest my head on her lap. I'm surprised the illegal's got a fiver to pay, but she and her tail leave no tip. I see Short Order's small bites on the bun.

25   You know, a cafe's the kinda business that moves. You get some regulars but most of them are on the move, so I don't pay much attention to them.

But this lady's face sticks like egg yolk on a plate. It ain't 'til I open a beer and sit in front of the B & W to check out the wrestling matches that I see this news bulletin 'bout two missing kids. I recognize the mugs right away. Short Order and his doggie sister. And all of a sudden her face is out of my mind. Aw fuck, I say, and put my beer down so hard that the foam spills onto last months Hustler. Aw fuck.

See, if Nell was here, she'd know what to do: call the cops. But I don't know. Cops ain't exactly my friends, and all I need is for bacon to be crawling all over my place. And seeing how her face is vague now, I decide to wait 'til the late news. Short Order don't look right neither. I'll have another beer and wait for the late news.

The alarm rings at four and I have this headache, see, from the sixpak, and I gotta get up. I was supposed to do something, but I got all suck-faced and forgot. Turn off the T.V., take a shower, but that don't help my memory any.

Hear sirens near the railroad tracks. Cops. I'm supposed to call the cops. I'll do it after I make the coffee, put away the eggs, get the donuts out. But Paulie strolls in looking partied out. We actually talk 'bout last night's wrestling match between BoBo Brazil and the Crusher. I slept through it, you see, Paulie orders an O.J. on account of he's catching a cold. I open up my big mouth and ask about De. Drinks the rest of his O.J., says real calm like, that he caught her eaglespread with the Vegetable fatso down the block. Then, very polite like, Paulie excuses himself. That's one thing I gotta say about Paulie. He may be one big Fuck-up, but he's got manners. Juice gave him shit cramps, he says.

Well, leave it to Paulie. Good ole Mr. Fuck-Up himself to help me with the cops. The prick O.D.'s in my crapper; vomits and shits are all over—I mean all over the fuckin' walls. That's the thanks I get for being Mr. Nice Guy. I had the cops looking up my ass for the stash; says one, the one wearing a mortician's suit, We'll be back, we'll be back when you ain't looking. If I was pushing, would I be burning my goddamn balls off with spitting grease? So fuck 'em, I think, I ain't gonna tell you nothing 'bout the lady. Fuck you, I say to them as they drive away. Fuck your mother.

30   That's why Nell was good to have 'round. She could be a pain in the ass, you know, like making me hang those stupid bells, but mostly she knew what to do. See, I go bananas. Like my mind fries with the potatoes and by the end of the day, I'm deader than dogshit. Let me tell you what I mean. A few hours later, after I swore I wouldn't give the fuckin' pigs the time of day, the green vans roll up across the street. While I'm stirring the chili con carne I see all these illegals running out of the factory to hide, like roaches when the lightswitch goes on. I taste the chile, but I really can't taste nothing on account of I've lost my appetite after cleaning out the crapper, when three of them run into the Cariboo. They look at me as if I'm gonna stop them, but when I go on stirring the chile, they run to the bathroom.

Now look, I'm a nice guy, but I don't like to be used, you know? Just 'cause they're regulars don't mean jackshit. I run an honest business. And that's what I told them Agents. See, by that time, my stomach being all dizzy, and the cops all over the place, and the three illegals running in here, I was all confused, you know. That's how it was, and well, I haven't seen Nell for years, and I guess that's why I pointed to the bathroom.

I don't know. I didn't expect handcuffs and them agents putting their hands up and down their thighs. When they walked passed me, they didn't look at me. That is the two young ones. The older one, the one that looked silly in the handcuffs on account of she's old enough to be my grandma's grandma, looks straight at my face with the same eyes Short Order's sister gave me yesterday. What a day. Then, to top off the potatoes with the gravy, the bells jingle against the door and in enters the lady again with the two kids.

III.

He's got lice. Probably from living in the detainers. Those are the rooms where they round up the children and make them work for their food. I saw them from the window. Their eyes are cut glass, and no one looks for sympathy. They take turns, sorting out the arms from the legs, heads from the torsos. Is that one your mother? one guard asks, holding a mummified head with eyes shut tighter than coffins. But the children no longer cry. They just continue sorting as if they were salvaging cans from a heap of trash. They do this until time is up and they drift into a tunnel, back to the womb of sleep, while a new group comes in. It is all very organized. I bite my fist to keep from retching. Please God, please don't let Geraldo be there.

For you see, they took Geraldo. By mistake, of course. It was my fault. I shouldn't have sent him out to fetch me a mango. But it was just to the corner. I didn't even bother to put his sweater on. I hear his sandals flapping against the gravel. I follow him with my eyes, see him scratching his buttocks when the wind picks up swiftly, as it often does at such unstable times, and I have to close the door.

35   The darkness becomes a serpent's tongue, swallowing us whole. It is the night of La Llorona. The women come up from the depths of sorrow to search for their children. I join them, frantic, desperate, and our eyes become scrutinizers, our bodies opiated with the scent of their smiles. Descending from door to door, the wind whips our faces. I hear the wailing of the women and know it to be my own. Geraldo is nowhere to be found.

Dawn is not welcomed. It is a drunkard wavering between consciousness and sleep. My life is fleeing, moving south towards the sea. My tears are now hushed and faint.

The boy, barely a few years older than Geraldo, lights a cigarette, rests it on the edge of his desk, next to all the other cigarette burns. The blinds are down to keep the room cool. Above him hangs a single bulb that shades and shadows his face in such a way as to mask his expressions. He is not to be trusted. He fills in the information, for I cannot write. Statements delivered, we discuss motives.

"Spies," says he, flicking a long burning ash from the cigarette onto the floor, then wolfing the smoke in as if his lungs had an unquenchable thirst for nicotine. "We arrest spies. Criminals." He says this with cigarette smoke spurting out from his nostrils like a nose bleed.

"Spies? Criminal?" My shawl falls to the ground. "He is only five and a half years old." I plead for logic with my hands. "What kind of crimes could a five year old commit?"

40   "Anyone who so willfully supports the contras in any form must be arrested and punished without delay." He knows the line by heart.

I think about moths and their stupidity. Always attracted by light, they fly into fires, or singe their wings with the heat of the single bulb and fall on his desk, writhing in pain. I don't understand why nature has been so cruel as to prevent them from feeling warmth. He dismisses them with a sweep of a hand. "This," he continues, "is what we plan to do with the contras, and those who aid them." He inhales again.

"But, Señor, he's just a baby."

"Contras are tricksters. They exploit the ignorance of people like you. Perhaps they convinced your son to circulate pamphlets. You should be talking to them, not us." The cigarette is down to his yellow finger tips, to where he can no longer continue to hold it without burning himself. He throws the stub on the floor, crushes it under his boot. "This," he says, screwing his boot into the ground, "is what the contras do to people like you."

"Señor. I am a washer woman. You yourself see I cannot read or write. There is my X. Do you think my son can read?" How can I explain to this man that we are poor, that we live as best we can? "If such a thing has happened, perhaps he wanted to make a few centavos for his mamá. He's just a baby."

45   "So you are admitting his guilt?"

"So you are admitting he is here?" I promise, once I see him, hold him in my arms again, I will never, never scold him for wanting more than I can give. "You see, he needs his sweater..." The sweater lies limp on my lap.

"Your assumption is incorrect."

"May I check the detainers for myself?"

"In time."

50   "And what about my Geraldo?"

"In time." He dismisses me, placing the forms in a big envelope crinkled by the day's humidity.

"When?" I am wringing the sweater with my hands.

"Don't be foolish, woman. Now off with your nonsense. We will try to locate your Pedro."

"Geraldo."

55   Maria came by today with a bowl of hot soup. She reports in her usual excited way, that the soldiers are now eating the brains of their victims. It is unlike her to be so scandalous. So insane. Geraldo must be cold without his sweater.

"Why?" I ask as the soup gets cold. I will write Tavo tonight.

At the plaza a group of people are whispering. They are quiet when I pass, turn to one another and put their finger to their lips to cage their voices. They continue as I reach the church steps. To be associated with me is condemnation.

Today I felt like killing myself, Lord. But I am too much of a coward. I am a washer woman, Lord. My mother was one, and hers too. We have lived as best we can, washing other people's laundry, rinsing off other people's dirt until our hands crust and chap. When my son wanted to hold my hand, I held soap instead. When he wanted to play, my feet were in pools of water. It takes such little courage, being a washer woman. Give me strength, Lord.

What have I done to deserve this, Lord? Raising a child is like building a kite. You must bend the twigs enough, but not too much, for you might break them. You must find paper that is delicate and light enough to wave on the breath of the wind, yet must withstand the ravages of a storm. You must tie the strings gently but firmly so that it may not fall apart. You must let the string go, eventually, so that the kite will stretch its ambition. It is such delicate work, Lord, being a mother. This I understand, Lord, because I am, but you have snapped the cord, Lord. It was only a matter of minutes and my life is lost somewhere in the clouds. I don't know, I don't know what games you play, Lord.

These four walls are no longer my house, the earth beneath it, no longer my home. Weeds have replaced all good crops. The irrigation ditches are clodded with bodies. No matter where we turn, there are rumors facing us and we try to live as best we can, under the rule of men who rape women, then rip their fetuses from their bellies. Is this our home? Is this our country? I ask Maria. Don't these men have mothers, lovers, babies, sisters? Don't they see what they are doing? Later, Maria says, these men are babes farted out from the Devil's ass. We check to make sure no one has heard her say this.

Without Geraldo, this is not my home, the earth beneath it, not my country. This is why I have to leave. Maria begins to cry. Not because I am going, but because she is staying.

Tavo. Sweet Tavo. He has sold his car to send me the money. He has just married and he sold his car for me. Thank you, Tavo. Not just for the money. But also for making me believe in the goodness of people again... The money is enough to buy off the border soldiers. The rest will come from the can. I have saved for Geraldo's schooling and it is enough for a bus ticket to Juarez. I am to wait for Tavo there.

I spit. I do not turn back.

Perhaps I am wrong in coming. I worry that Geraldo will not have a home to return to, no mother to cradle his nightmares away, soothe the scars, stop the hemorrhaging of his heart. Tavo is happy I am here, but it is crowded, the three of us, and I hear them arguing behind their closed door. There is only so much a nephew can provide. I must find work. I have two hands willing to work. But the heart. The heart wills only to watch the children playing in the street.

65   The machines, their speed and dust, make me ill. But I can clean. I clean toilets, dump trash cans, sweep. Disinfect the sinks. I will gladly do whatever is necessary to repay Tavo. The baby is due any time and money is tight. I volunteer for odd hours, weekends, since I really have very little to do. When the baby comes I know Tavo's wife will not let me hold it, for she thinks I am a bad omen. I know it.

Why would God play such a cruel joke, if he isn't my son? I jumped the curb, dashed out into the street, but the street is becoming wider and wider. I've lost him once and can't lose him again and to hell with the screeching tires and the horns and the headlights barely touching my hips. I can't take my eyes off him because, you see, they are swift and cunning and can take your life with a snap of a finger. But God is a just man and His mistakes can be undone.

My heart pounds in my head like a sledge hammer against the asphalt. What if it isn't Geraldo? What if he is still in the detainer waiting for me? A million questions, one answer: Yes. Geraldo, yes. I want to touch his hand first, have it disappear in my own because it is so small. His eyes look at me in total bewilderment. I grab him because the earth is crumbling beneath us and I must save him. We both fall to the ground.

A hot meal is in store. A festival. The cook, a man with shrunken cheeks and the hands of a car mechanic, takes a liking to Geraldo. It's like birthing you again, mi'jo. My baby.

I bathe him. He flutters in excitement, the water grey around him. I scrub his head with lye to kill off the lice, comb his hair out with a fine tooth comb. I wash his rubbery penis, wrap him in a towel and he stands in front of the window, shriveling and sucking milk from a carton, his hair shiny from the dampness.

70   He finally sleeps. So easily, she thinks. On her bed next to the open window he coos in the night. Below the sounds of the city become as monotonous as the ocean waves. She rubs his back with warm oil, each stroke making up for the days of his absence. She hums to him softly so that her breath brushes against his face, tunes that are rusted and crack in her throat. The hotel neon shines on his back and she covers him.

All the while the young girl watches her brother sleeping. She removes her sneakers, climbs into the bed, snuggles up to her brother, and soon her breathing is raspy, her arms under her stomach.

The couch is her bed tonight. Before switching the light off, she checks once more to make sure this is not a joke. Tomorrow she will make arrangements to go home. Maria will be the same, the mango stand on the corner next to the church plaza will be the same. It will all be the way it was before. But enough excitement. For the first time in years, her mind is quiet of all noise and she has the desire to sleep.

The bells jingle when the screen door slaps shut behind them. The cook wrings his hands in his apron, looking at them. Geraldo is in the middle, and they sit in the booth farthest away from the window, near the hall where the toilets are, and right away the small boy, his hair now neatly combed and split to the side like an adult, wrinkles his nose at the peculiar smell. The cook wipes perspiration off his forehead with the corner of his apron, finally comes over to the table.

She looks so different, so young. Her hair is combed slick back into one thick braid and her earrings hang like baskets of golden pears on her finely sculptured ears. He can't believe how different she looks. Almost beautiful. She points to what she wants on the menu with a white, clean fingernail. Although confused, the cook is sure of one thing—it's Short Order all right, pointing to him with a commanding finger, saying his only English word; coke.

75   His hands tremble as he slaps the meat on the grill; the patties hiss instantly. He feels like vomiting. The chile overboils and singes the fires, deep red trail of chile crawling to the floor and puddling there. He grabs the handles, burns himself, drops the pot on the wooden racks of the floor. He sucks his fingers, the patties blackening and sputtering grease. He flips them, and the burgers hiss anew. In some strange way he hopes they have disappeared, and he takes a quick look only to see Short Order's sister, still in the same dress, still holding her brother's hand. She is craning her neck to peek at what is going on in the kitchen.

Aw, fuck, he says, in a fog of smoke his eyes burning tears. He can't believe it, but he's crying. For the first time since JoJo's death, he's crying. He becomes angry at the lady for returning. At JoJo. At Nell for leaving him. He wishes Nell here, but doesn't know where she's at or what part of Vietnam JoJo is all crumbled up in. Children gotta be with their parents, family gotta be together, he thinks. It's only right. The emergency line is ringing.

Two black and whites roll up and skid the front tires against the curb. The flashing lights carousel inside the cafe. She sees them opening the screen door, their guns taut and cold like steel erections. Something is wrong, and she looks to the cowering cook. She has been betrayed, and her heart is pounding like footsteps running, faster, louder, faster and she can't hear what they are saying to her. She jumps up from the table, grabs Geraldo by the wrist, his sister dragged along because, like her, she refuses to release his hand. Their lips are mouthing words she can't hear, can't comprehend. Run, Run is all she can think of to do, Run through the hallway, out to the alley. Run because they will never take him away again.

But her legs are heavy and she crushes Geraldo against her, so tight, as if she wants to conceal him in her body again, return him to her belly so that they will not castrate him and hang his small, blue penis on her door, not crush his face so that he is unrecognizable, not bury him among the heaps of bones, and ears, and teeth, and jaws, because no one, but she, cared to know that he cried. For years he cried and she could hear him day and night. Screaming, howling, sobbing, shriveling and crying because he is only five years old, and all she wanted was a mango.

But the crying begins all over again. In the distance, she hears crying.

80   She refuses to let go. For they will have to cut her arms off to take him, rip her mouth off to keep her from screaming for help. Without thinking, she reaches over to where two pots of coffee are brewing and throws the streaming

coffee into their faces. Outside, people begin to gather, pressing their faces against the window glass to get a good view. The cook huddles behind the counter, frightened, trembling. Their faces become distorted and she doesn't see the huge hand that takes hold of Geraldo and she begins screaming all over again, screaming so that the walls shake, screaming enough for all the women of murdered children, screaming, pleading for help from the people outside, and she pushes an open hand against an officer's nose, because no one will stop them and he pushes the gun barrel to her face.

And I laugh at his ignorance. How stupid of him to think that I will let them take my Geraldo away, just because he waves that gun like a flag. Well, to hell with you, you pieces of shit, do you hear me? Stupid, cruel pigs. To hell with you all, because you can no longer frighten me. I will fight you for my son until I have no hands left to hold a knife. I will fight you all because you're all farted out of the Devil's ass, and you'll not take us with you. I am laughing, howling at their stupidity. Because they should know by now that I will never let my son go and then I hear something crunching like broken glass against my forehead and I am blinded by the liquid darkness. But I hold onto his hand. That I can feel, you see, I'll never let go. Because we are going home. My son and I.

POETRY

Julia Alvarez

Julia Alvarez was born in 1950 in New York City but spent her childhood in the Dominican Republic. Her family moved to the United States in 1960, a year before the infamous Dominican dictator, Rafael Leonides Trujillo, was assassinated. Her novel *How the Garcia Girls Lost Their Accents* (1992) placed her among the literary elite in the United States. She teaches creative writing at Middlebury College in Vermont and has published an extensive list of works that includes stories, novels, poems, children's stories, and young adult fiction. She is recognized today as a major Latina writer, and her work is extremely popular.

Woman's Work

Who says a woman's work isn't high art?
She'd challenge as she scrubbed the bathroom tiles.
Keep house as if the address were your heart.

We'd clean the whole upstairs before we'd start
5   downstairs. I'd sigh, hearing my friends outside.
Doing her woman's work was a hard art

to practice when the summer sun would bar
the floor I swept till she was satisfied.
She kept me prisoner in her housebound heart.

10 She'd shine the tines of forks, the wheels of carts,
cut lacy lattices for all her pies.
Her woman's work was nothing less than art.

And, I, her masterpiece since I was smart,
was primed, praised, polished, scolded and advised
15 to keep a house much better than my heart.

I did not want to be her counterpart!
I struck out... but became my mother's child:
a woman working at home on her art,
housekeeping paper as if it were her heart.

Jimmy Santiago Baca

See the biographical note about Baca on page 97.

Work We Hate and Dreams We Love

Every morning
Meiyo revs his truck up
and lets it idle. Inside the small adobe house,
he sips coffee
5   while his Isleta girlfriend
Cristi
brownbags his lunch.
Life is filled with work
Meiyo hates,
10 and while he saws, 2 × 4's,
rims lengths of 2 × 10's on table saw,
inside his veins another world
in full color etches
a blue sky on his bones,
15 a man following a bison herd,
and suddenly his hammer becomes a spear
he tosses to the ground
uttering a sound we do not understand.

Martín Espada

Martín Espada was born in Brooklyn, New York, in 1957. He has written several important collections of poetry, including *Imagine the Angels of Bread* (1996), which won an American Book Award. He has also cotranslated the poems of Clemente Soto Vélez; written a book of essays, *Zapata's Disciple* (1998); and edited two collections of Latino and Latin American poetry, *Poetry Like Bread: Poets of the Political Imagination* (1994) and *El Coro: A Chorus of Latino and Latina Poetry* (1997). Espada's most recent collection, *Alabanza: New and Selected Poems 1982-2002* (2003), recaps his prolific career. Espada teaches at the University of Massachusetts at Amherst.

Who Burns for the Perfection of Paper

At sixteen, I worked after high school hours
at a printing plant
that manufactured legal pads:
Yellow paper
5   stacked seven feet high
and leaning
as I slipped cardboard
between the pages.
then brushed red glue
10   up and down the stack.
No gloves: fingertips required
for the perfection of paper,
smoothing the exact rectangle.
Sluggish by 9 PM, the hands
15   would slide along suddenly sharp paper,
and gather slits thinner than the crevices
of the skin, hidden.
Then the glue would sting,
hands oozing
20   till both palms burned
at the punchclock.

Ten years later, in law school,
I knew that every legal pad
was glued with the sting of hidden cuts,
25   that every open lawbook
was a pair of hands
upturned and burning.

Jorge the Church Janitor Finally Quits

Cambridge, Massachusetts, 1989

No one asks
where I am from,
I must be
from the country of janitors,
5   I have always mopped this floor.

Honduras, you are a squatter's camp
outside the city
of their understanding.

No one can speak
my name,
I host the fiesta
of the bathroom,
stirring the toilet
like a punchbowl.
The Spanish music of my name
is lost
when the guests complain
about toilet paper.

What they say
must be true:
I am smart,
but I have a bad attitude.

No one knows
that I quit tonight,
maybe the mop
will push on without me.

Federico's Ghost

The story is
that whole families of fruitpickers
still crept between the furrows
of the field at dusk,
when for reasons of whiskey or whatever
the cropduster plane sprayed anyway,
floating a pesticide drizzle
over the pickers
who thrashed like dark birds
in a glistening white net,
except for Federico,
a skinny boy who stood apart
in his own green row,
and, knowing the pilot
would not understand in Spanish
that he was the son of a whore,
instead jerked his arm
and thrust an obscene finger.

The pilot understood.
He circled the plane and sprayed again,

watching a fine gauze of poison
drift over the brown bodies
that cowered and scurried on the ground,
and aiming for Federico,
25 leaving the skin beneath his shirt
wet and blistered,
but still pumping his finger at the sky.

After Federico died,
rumors at the labor camp
30 told of tomatoes picked and smashed at night,
growers muttering of vandal children
or communists in camp,
first threatening to call Immigration,
then promising every Sunday off
35 if only the smashing of tomatoes would stop.

Still tomatoes were picked and squashed
in the dark,
and the old women in camp
said it was Federico,
40 laboring after sundown
to cool the burns on his arms,
flinging tomatoes
at the cropduster
that hummed like a mosquito
45 lost in his ear,
and kept his soul awake.

Diana García

Diana García was born in 1950 and raised in Merced, California, which is in
the San Joaquin Valley. She received an MFA from San Diego State University,
where she now teaches. Her poems have been published in various journals
and anthologies, and her debut collection of poems about migrant workers in
California, *When Living Was a Labor Camp* (2000), won an American Book
Award in 2001.

When Living Was a Labor Camp Called Montgomery

Back in the forties, you joined the family each summer to sort
dried figs. From Santa Maria to Gilroy, Brawley to Stockton,
you settled in rows of red cabins hidden behind the orchards.

You recall how the red cabin stain came off on your fingers,
5 a stain you pressed to your cheeks so you looked like
Dolores del Rio, the famous Mexican actress.

Her high-sculpted glow stunned the guys who dogged you
to the theater, the coolest building in town, where you escaped
the San Joaquin heat and fruit flies.

10 You wiggled in velvet-backed chairs, split popcorn with your
cousins. When the film's hero, the rancher's son, rode horseback
to the river and spied Dolores washing her hair, you'd swoon.

Just for a moment, a small eternity, the hero's hacienda, its dark
wood beams and low-slung chandelier, were yours. You were tall
15 and thin and everything looked good on you.

To tell the truth, though, you preferred Lauren Bacall's whistle.
So at the packing shed you eyed your brothers' friends, not
the pickers, the carpenters, those who wanted

out of the fields. You picked one with a full-mouthed smile, not
20 your mother's choice, but a tall man with papers who wanted
to join the army and live in L.A.

And perhaps, in the end, everything didn't look good on you:
maybe your hair didn't look good auburn; maybe
pillow-breasted women weren't meant to wear sheaths.

25 You visit the camp each summer reunion. Your sisters snatch
peeks at your husband. His teeth still look good. A cousin
glides you through a *cumbia*;[1] you dreamt he kissed you once.

You catch the stench of rotting figs, of too-full outhouses. The
nose closes off. You feel how hot it was to sleep two to a
30 mattress, the only other room a kitchen.

You thought your arms thickened long ago lugging trays of figs.
You thought you had peasant ankles. You thought you could die in
the camp and no one would know your smell.

José B. Gonzalez

See the biographical note about Gonzalez on page xii.

Because No One Should Say "Chávez Who?"

Just as the banana knows its own republic
Remembers the fingerprints of a migrant
Whose sweat watered its mother tree
Gave its family rise, cradled it in its fall,
5 So too does the strawberry tells of its
Origins as it bleeds sweetly, paying

---

[1] a type of dance

Homage to *campesinos*[1] who don't care
Whether it is used to balm ruby lips or
Garnish a dessert, for like the lean coffee
10   Bean, these fruits have tasted
And coughed chemicals, inhaled
The sprays from overhead planes, been
Plucked at young ages, survived Prospero's
Tempests, cheered for the table grape
15   And awaited the birth of another
César Chávez.

Carolina Hospital

See the biographical note about Hospital on page 101.

Blake in the Tropics

We leave the Jaragua Hotel
in our stocking feet and shaven faces
to stumble over these bodies
yet to reach puberty.

5   They have turned dust into blankets
and newspapers into pillows
on a street edged in refuse.
Warm waves break against the sea wall,

never touching their bodies.
10   We are not in Blake's London and
the black on these boys
will not wash off with the dawn.

Luis J. Rodríguez

Luis J. Rodríguez was born on the U.S./Mexico border in 1954. His most widely acclaimed book, *Always Running: La Vida Loca, Gang Days in L.A.* (1993), about his life as a gangster, was an international bestseller, earning the Carl Sandberg Literary Award and a designation as a *New York Times* Notable Book. Rodríguez has also published collections of poetry including *The Concrete River* (1991), and *Trochemoche* (1998); children's books, such as *America Is Her Name* (1998); and a collection of short stories, *The Republic of East L.A.* (2002).

---

[1]farm workers

Hungry

My wife left me, taking the two kids
and everything
but the stereo, TV and a few dishes.
Later in this squalid hour,
5   I began an affair
with my wife's best friend.
But she already had three kids and no man
and talked about love and marriage
and I didn't know how to get out of it,
10   being also an alcoholic.
Soon I couldn't pay the rent
so I kept getting notices in death tones,
insinuating broken bones or whatever.
My friend Franco helped me sneak
15   out of the place.
Franco and me arrived in the middle of the night,
and loaded what I had left onto a pickup truck.
I would come back
on other late nights to get the mail.
20   And the woman, who was alone with three kids
and looking for a husband,
kept leaving notes,
and I kept throwing them away.
But the hunger had just begun.
25   My only property of value was a 1954
red Chevy in mint condition.
It had the original skirts, whitewalls
and chrome hood ornament.
What a prize!
30   I never wanted to part with it,
even as layoff slips and parking tickets
accumulated on the dashboard,
even when I found myself living with Mom and Dad
and the '54 Chevy got stashed out in back.
35   But the hunger and the drinking
and looking for love in all the wrong races
blurred into a sort of blindness.
I stared out the back window,
at that red Chevy,
40   and thought how it resembled a large steak
with egg yolks for headlights.
No, no, I couldn't do it;

I couldn't turn my back on it now.
The days withered away
45 and again I looked out that window,
with Mom yelling behind me
about getting a job,
and I could taste that last scotch,
that last carnitas burrito,
50 and perhaps take in the stale scent
of a one-room apartment somewhere.
Then the hunger became a fever.
The fever a pain in my head.
And as soon as some dude with 200 bucks came along.
55 I sold it. God almighty,
I sold my red Chevy!
For 200 bucks!
For nothing, man.
Oh, I thought it would help
60 stop my wife's face
in every reflection;
her friend's staring out of my coffee cup.
That it would help hold me
for more than a week,
65 and end the curses
ringing in my ear.
I sold it! My red Chevy.
Prized possession.
200 bucks.
70 Gone forever.
Days later, the 200 bucks spent,
I was still hungry.

Gary Soto

The following poem comes from Soto's first poetry collection of the same title, published in 1977 to critical acclaim. For more information on Soto, see the previous biographical note on page 108.

The Elements of San Joaquin

for César Chávez

Field

The wind sprays pale dirt into my mouth
The small, almost invisible scars
On my hands.

The pores in my throat and elbows
5   Have taken in a seed of dirt of their own.

After a day in the grape fields near Rolinda
A fine silt, washed by sweat,
Has settled into the lines
On my wrists and palms.

10   Already I am becoming the valley,
A soil that sprouts nothing.
For any of us.

Wind

A dry wind over the valley
Peeled mountains, grain by grain,
15   To small slopes, loose dirt
Where red ants tunnel.

The wind strokes
The skulls and spines of cattle
To white dust, to nothing,

20   Covers the spiked tracks of beetles,
Of tumbleweed, of sparrows
That pecked the ground for insects.

Evenings, when I am in the yard weeding,
The wind picks up the breath of my armpits
25   Like dust, swirls it
Miles away

And drops it
On the ear of a rabid dog,
And I take on another life.

Wind

30   When you got up this morning the sun
Blazed an hour in the sky,

A lizard hid
Under the curled leaves of manzanita
And winked its dark lids.

35   Later, the sky grayed,
And the cold wind you breathed
Was moving under your skin and already far
From the small hives of your lungs.

Stars

At dusk the first stars appear
40   Not one eager finger points toward them.

A little later the stars spread with the night
And an orange moon rises
To lead them, like a shepherd, toward dawn.

Sun

In June the sun is a bonnet of light
45 Coming up,
Little by little,
From behind a skyline of pine.

The pastures sway with fiddle-neck,
Tassels of foxtail.

50 At Piedra
A couple fish on the river's edge,
Their shadows deep against the water,
Above, in the stubbled slopes,
Cows climb down
55 As the heat rises
In a mist of blond locusts,
Returning to the valley.

Rain

When autumn rains flatten sycamore leaves,
The tiny volcanos of dirt
60 Ants raised around their holes,
I should be out of work.

My silverware and stack of plates will go unused
Like the old, my two good slacks
Will smother under a growth of lint
65 And smell of the old dust
That rises
When the closet door opens or closes.

The skin of my belly will tighten like a belt
And there will be no reason for pockets.

Harvest

70 East of the sun's slant, in the vineyard that never failed,
A wind crossed my face, moving the dust
And a portion of my voice a step closer to a new year.

The sky went black in the ninth hour of rolling trays,
And in the distance ropes of rain dropped to pull me
75 From the thick harvest that was not mine.

Fog

If you go to your window
You will notice a fog drifting in.

The sun is no stronger than a flashlight.
Not all the sweaters
80   Hung in closets all summer

Could soak up this mist. The fog:
A mouth nibbling everything to its origin,
Pomegranate trees, stolen bicycles,

The string of lights at a used-car lot,
85   A Pontiac with scorched valves.

In Fresno the fog is passing
The young thief prying a window screen,
Graying my hair that falls
And goes unfound, my fingerprints
90   Slowly growing a fur of dust—

One hundred years from now
There should be no reason to believe
I lived.

Daybreak

In this moment when the light starts up
95   In the east and rubs
The horizon until it catches fire,

We enter the fields to hoe,
Row after row, among the small flags of onion,
Waving off the dragonflies
100   That ladder the air.

And tears the onions raise
Do not begin in your eyes but in ours,
In the salt blown
From one blister into another;

105   They begin in knowing
You will never waken to bear
The hour timed to a heart beat,
The wind pressing us closer to the ground.

When the season ends,
110   And the onions are unplugged from their sleep,
We won't forget what you failed to see,
And nothing will heal
Under the rain's broken fingers.

SUMMER

Once again, tell me, what was it like?
115 There was a windowsill of flies,
It meant the moon pulled its own weight
And the black sky cleared itself
Like a sneeze.

What about the farm worker?
120 He had no bedroom. He had a warehouse
Of heat, a swamp cooler
That turned no faster than a raffle cage.

And the farms?
There were groves
125 Of fig trees that went unpicked.
The fruit wrinkled and flattened
Like the elbows
Of an old woman.

What about the Projects in the Eastside?
130 I can't really say. Maybe a child
Burned his first book of matches.
Maybe the burn is disappearing
Under the first layer
Of skin.

135 And next summer?
It will be the same. Boredom,
In early June, will settle
On the eyelash shading your pupil from dust,
On the shoulder you look over
140 To find the sun rising
From the Sierras.

FIELD POEM

When the foreman whistled
My brother and I
145 Shouldered our hoes,
Leaving the field.
We returned to the bus
Speaking
In broken English, in broken Spanish
150 The restaurant food,
The tickets to a dance
We wouldn't buy with our pay.

From the smashed bus window,
I saw the leaves of cotton plants
155 Like small hands waving good-bye.

Mexicans Begin Jogging

At the factory I worked
In the fleck of rubber, under the press
Of an oven yellow with flame,
Until the border patrol opened
5   Their vans and my boss waved for us to run.
"Over the fence, Soto," he shouted,
And I shouted that I was American.
"No time for lies," he said, and pressed
A dollar in my palm, hurrying me
10 Through the back door.

Since I was on his time, I ran
And became the wag to a short tail of Mexicans—
Ran past the amazed crowds that lined
The street and blurred like photographs, in rain.
15 I ran from that industrial road to the soft
Houses where people paled at the turn of an autumn sky.
What could I do but yell *vivas*
To baseball, milkshakes, and those sociologists
Who would clock me
20 As I jog into the next century
On the power of a great, silly grin.

ESSAY

José Antonio Burciaga

The author of two enlightening and humorous books on Chicano culture, *Drink Cultura: Chicanismo* (1992) and *Spilling the Beans: Loteria Chicana* (1995), Burciaga was also a muralist, activist, community leader, and founding member of the theatrical comedy company Culture Clash. His book of poems, *Undocumented Love*, won the Before Columbus American Book Award in 1981. Raised in El Paso, Texas, Burciaga died of cancer on October 7, 1996.

Pachucos and the Taxicab Brigade

Thursday, June 3, 1943, was a warm inviting night for over 50,000 military servicemen stationed around the Los Angeles area. Weekends began on Thursdays and this particular Thursday was soon after payday.

That evening, a group of eleven sailors walked into the middle of a barrio along the 1700 block of North Main Street. According to their documented statement, they were attacked by a gang of young Mexicans. The sailors, who claimed they were outnumbered three to one, suffered minor cuts and bruises.

The incident was reported to a police station. There, some of the policemen formed a "vengeance squad" and set out to arrest the gang that had attacked the sailors. By the time they got to the scene there were no Mexicans or Mexican Americans. The police raid was a fiasco, and the only solution left was to report it to the newspapers, which in turn whipped up the community and the military against the Mexican population.

The next night, approximately two hundred sailors decided to take the law into their own hands hiring a fleet of twenty taxicabs and cruising down the center of town toward East L.A. The first victim of the "Taxicab Brigade" was a young Mexican "zoot suiter" who was left badly beaten and bleeding. The total tally for that night: two 17-year-olds, one 19-year-old and one 23-year-old, all left on pavements or sidewalks for the ambulances to pick up. The police were unable or refused to intercept the Taxicab Brigade. It was just another punitive military expedition.

5   On June 4, the L.A. newspapers took a rest from the war news to play up the "Zoot Suit War," named after the zoot suits worn by Mexican-American youths. The local press adopted a just and righteous attitude on the part of the servicemen. On the following day, hundreds of soldiers and sailors paraded through downtown L.A., warning zoot suiters to closet their drapes or suffer the consequences. L.A. police, shore patrol and military police did nothing, apparently because of the number of frenzied servicemen involved.

On June 7, civilians joined their military counterparts and mobbed restaurants, bars and theaters in search of not only Mexicans but also "Negroes," and Filipinos.

The following is one eye-witness account by Al Waxman, editor of the *Eastside Journal:* "Four boys came out of a pool hall wearing the zoot suits. Police ordered them into arrest cars. One refused...The police officer answered with three swift blows of the night-stick across the boy's head and he went down. As he lay sprawled, he was kicked in the face. Police had difficulty loading his body into the vehicle because he was one-legged and wore a wooden limb...

"At the next corner, a Mexican mother cried out, 'Don't take my boy, he did nothing. He's only fifteen years old...' She was struck across the jaw with a night-stick and almost dropped the two and a half year old baby that was clinging in her arms..."

Waxman witnessed several other incidents and pleaded with the local police station but they answered, "It is a matter for the military police." The Mexican community was in turmoil. Mothers, fathers, sisters, aunts, and uncles swarmed police stations looking for their lost children.

10   By June 8, the L.A. district attorney declared "the situation is getting entirely out of hand." The mayor, however, thought matters would eventually blow over and after a count of the Mexicans in jail, the chief of police thought the situation had cleared up.

But it was not over for the press. The *Los Angeles Times* stated the riots were having a "cleansing effect." A *Herald-Express* editorial said the riots "promise to rid the community of...those zoot suited miscreants." Meanwhile, the "miscreant" military operations spread to the suburbs. The Los Angeles City Council adopted a resolution making the wearing of zoot suits a misdemeanor.

Finally, on the heels of a Navy declaration that downtown L.A. was "out of bounds," and following the Mexican ambassador's formal inquiry to the U.S. secretary of state, and other expressions of international concern, the *Los Angeles Times* took a conciliatory and pious tone, disassociating any possibility of bigotry from the riots. At the same time, the *Times* went on the offensive, attacking defenders Carey McWilliams and Eleanor Roosevelt for stirring up racial discord.

Similar "zoot suit" disturbances were reported in San Diego on June 9; in Philadelphia on June 10; in Chicago on June 15; and in Evansville, Indiana, on June 27. Bigotry-based riots also occurred in Detroit, Harlem and Beaumont, Texas.

Relations with Mexicans and Mexican Americans had seemed warm and friendly up to that point. But those were only diplomatic relations. In 1941, a bracero program had been agreed upon and signed by the two countries allowing Mexican farm workers to work on this side, thus freeing U.S. fieldhands to work in defense industries or in the military. A month before the June 3 riots, Mexican soldiers had paraded through downtown Los Angeles in a Cinco de Mayo celebration. At the same time, Mexican and U.S. navys exchanged information on Japanese activities off the coast of Baja California.

15 The riots lasted for ten days, ending on June 13, 1943. Unlike modern riots, these were sporadic and scattered fights. No one was killed or sustained massive injuries. Property damages and convictions were minimal. And it was not the Mexican American youths who rioted but the military. Carey McWilliams, author of *North From Mexico*, called them "Government Riots."

In *The Zoot Suit Riots*, Mauricio Mazón, a history professor at the University of Southern California, wrote, "at least for ten days in Southern California...the military lost control of several thousand servicemen." Several archived military memos confirm the image of an impotent military brass. The frenzy was fed by the press, which predicted massive retaliations by Mexican zoot suiters.

There were no political manifestos or heroes originating from the riots— except for the "pachucos," the first Mexican American youths to rebel and strike their own self-identity through the zoot suit. To this day they live in literature, films, murals, dance and historical accounts. They live, too, through their social and cultural descendants, the *cholos*.

The pachuco has enjoyed a cultural aura, complete with stylistic pathos. He was both a tragic and heroic figure—a mythical creation. El Pachuco is the preeminent Don Quixote of Aztlán (the mythical southwest where the Aztecs began their journey to found Tenochtítlan, today's Mexico City).

This powerful figure has captured the imagination of artists, writers, poets and philosophers including Nobel prize winner Octavio Paz who in 1950 devoted the first chapter of *Labyrinth of Solitude*, his classic study of the Mexicano character, to "El Pachuco and Other Extremes." Although Paz maligned the Pachuco, he now recants and regrets that early analysis. His chapter offered a derisive condemnation of not only an adolescent caught between adulthood and youth but also caught between two countries, two vastly different cultures. The carefree adolescent years enjoyed by Anglo-American youths of the '40s were nonexistent in Mexican culture. For Mexican youth, the age of fifteen became a rite of passage into adulthood, while young Mexican Americans chose to affirm a new identity.

20   A few years ago, Octavio Paz came to Stanford. At a dinner party my wife and I politely asked him for his views about Chicanos. *¡No sé!* he answered, refusing to touch the topic but attentive to our views.

Even before Paz's essay, Chilean author and Stanford University Emeritus Professor Fernando Alegría wrote the first known short story on El Pachuco in 1945, "Al Otro Lado De La Cortina."

José Montoya, a Chicano multidisciplinary artist, poet, muralist, musician, founder and general of Sacramento's RCAF (Royal Chicano Air Force, earlier known as the Rebel Chicano Art Front), has concentrated many of his poetic, musical and artistic works on El Pachuco. He lived the pachuco era, and his poem "El Louie" is a classic Chicano poem.

Luis Valdez's award-winning play and film *Zoot Suit* was the national debut for Edward James Olmos, who played the character of El Pachuco and whose black, zoot-suited image on posters elevated the zoot suit to the realm of an icon. Olmos then wrote, directed and starred in the film *American Me*, which captures the Zoot Suit riots of 1943 and follows the pachuco's descendants right down to the present day cholos. The tragedy of urban Mexican-American youth has also been explored in *Stand and Deliver*, and most recently *Bound by Honor*.

Within this cultural aura, lies an important linguistic mystery: the origin of the term "pachuco." McWilliams suggests that the term came from Mexico and denoted resemblance to the gaily costumed people living in the town of Pachuca. He further suggests that it was first applied to border bandits in the vicinity of El Paso. Although McWilliams believes that the pachuco stereotype was born in L.A., it was El Paso, Texas, better known as EPT or El Chuco that had the reputation for the "meanest" pachucos.

25   Another little known theory is offered by 79-year-old San José State University Emeritus Professor Jorge Acevedo. As a conscientious objector, Acevedo resisted induction into WWII. For this action, he was sentenced to San Quentin but soon released to do community work as a counselor for braceros and homosexuals. Acevedo's theory is that the pachucos grew out of the repatriation program when more than 350,000 Mexicanos and Mexican Americans (the unofficial count among some historians is double that number) were deported to Mexico by the government during the Depression.

Acevedo recalls working through churches and social organizations to smuggle U.S. citizens of Mexican descent back to their homes in this country. He remembers *el barrio* Belvedere in East Los Angeles being emptied overnight. "They came at five in the morning with trucks and buses to drive them to Tijuana. Through a desire for vengeance and revenge, pachucos came from this experience." Pachucas were equals with their male peers because of equal victimization and codependency.

Most history books in this country are silent on this subject. To combat this vacuum of history, Stanford University Chicano students at Casa Zapata, the Chicano Theme residence, annually celebrate Zoot Suit Month. For one month each year, talks, lectures, films, discussions and workshops on the zoot suit, dress styles, hairdos, dancing and music of that era are presented.

In a recent panel discussion entitled "El Pachuco: the Myth, the Legend and the Reality," Fernando Soriano, a visiting psychology professor at Stanford, presented a study on contemporary Chicano gangs. He noted the lack of real role models for Chicano youth and how the figure of the pachuco fills the gap by offering a role model and a sense of rebellion against society, an opportunity to gain respect even if negative.

Professor Soriano noted the significant increases in gang activities and the growing number of female Chicanas in gangs. From 452 gang-related homicides in 1988, the number jumped to 700 homicides in 1992 in L.A. He questioned what gangs and homicides have to do with pachucos.

30   Fast to respond, José Montoya declared, "Gangs and homicides have nothing to do with pachucos. The drug lords dumped this shit on our barrios and we are stuck with it. The cartel brought in the drugs, firepower and finances to move kids away from the fast food franchises." He went on to advise, "We need to lay down our fears about glamorizing the pachuco and showcase the important and viable aspects of the Chicano experience. As offspring of Mexican and Mexican-American parents we need to see what it was like growing up…

"Working-class servicemen from other parts of the country came thinking the L.A. barrios were exotic ports of entry. Seeing Chicanos for the first time freaked them out. Industrialists, such as newspaper mogul William Randolph Hearst were already angry with Mexican President Cárdenas's nationalization of the oil industry. This wartime hysteria was translated for the Spanish lanzguage media, such as *La Opinión*. This didn't help Mexican and Mexican-American parents understand their children's rebellion."

Montoya calls the historical silence on these roundups shameful for this country, "…but they shouldn't be for us. This is something that was put upon us at the same time Chicano soldiers were disproportionately winning more Congressional Medals of Honor than any other group. Pachucos were not all gangsters or *batos locos*. Some came from the fields and dressed up on weekends."

The third panel member, Renato Rosaldo, Professor of Social Anthropology at Stanford and author of *Culture and Truth* agreed with Montoya.

Rosaldo noted the pachuco's exaggeration of the social norm, "putting it in your face…The pachuco exaggeration is a way of producing cultural resistance, a cultural style to modify the existing norm with little or no Mexican symbolism. There is a kind of reversal resistance," he added, "the slow and low of a lowrider when the opposite American ethic is fast and efficient. Nothing is so infuriating as a car that's going very slow and low. Worse than speeding."

35   Rosaldo noted the dress styles and how the body goes beyond the clothes to become part of the style. Instead of leaning slightly forward, slouch shouldered like business men, the Pachucos leaned back, shoulders thrown back and with long hand gestures. There is a Mexicaness in the formality along with self dramatization and theatricality. Whereas the Anglo-American norm tends to be spontaneous, "be yourself," and informal, without spelling it out or being conscious.

In *American Me* Rosaldo saw very little heroism left in the heroic figure, finding instead a devastating criticism of a version of masculinity where there is no alternative. Olmos seemed to be crying out, "Stop the war! Wherever this stuff is coming from it's destroying us!"

Rosaldo also believes it is demeaning to us to believe that a style of dress is responsible for the present day tragedies. A good example is the zoot suit style of dress. The origin of the zoot suit has been traced to New York and Detroit, but it goes further back to Europe. In an interview with Chuy Varela of Berkeley, California, renowned musician Cab Calloway traced the Zoot Suit to England. In the thirties, according to Calloway, the British clothing industry manufactured thousands of zoot suits as the latest style which would take hold. It didn't catch on and so they were dumped on the U.S. Market. When they reached New York, and Harlem in particular, African Americans took to them with pleasure and satisfaction. From New York's Harlem they were passed on to Detroit and Chicago. Those were the direct lines of migration for African Americans. For the Mexican-American urban migrants it was El Paso, Chicago, Detroit and Los Angeles. African-American ghettoes, jobs, modest modes of transportation, music and styles of dress greatly attracted Mexican Americans.

The comparisons between yesterday's pachucos and today's cholos are fascinating. Psychohistorian and USC Professor Mauricio Mazón authored the book *The Zoot-Suit Riots: The Psychology of Symbolic Annihilation*. During and after the riots, Mexican-American youth were known to have shaved their heads, "a kind of scarification that indicated their victimization by servicemen." Fifty years later, some cholos tattoo a black tear below one of their eyes as a mark of incarceration.

Cholos are cultural descendants of the pachucos. A *cholo* is defined as a *mestizo* of Indian and European blood, in most Spanish dictionaries. A secondary definition is tinged with old world bigotry as it defines a cholo as a "civilized Indian." The term came to this country through the many Peruvians who arrived here during the California Gold Rush. It was used to describe Indians living along the Peruvian Coast. In California the Peruvians called poor mestizos *cholos*.

40   Closely related to the word cholo is the term *bato*. Pancho Villa's revolutionary army was made of *batos vagos*, vagrant friends. *Batos vagos* has further evolved into the caló slang as *bato locos*, crazy dudes. The slang, called caló but better known as Spanglish or Mex-Tex, has been utilized by the pachuco and the cholo both. Caló was originally *zincaló*, the idiom of Spanish gypsies. Interestingly enough, *calcos* is the same word pachucos, cholos and gypsies use for shoes.

In Mexico, the pachuco was seen as the Anglo-Americanization of a Mexicano or, according to Paz, an extremity of what a Mexicano can become. In Mexico pachucos were called Tarzanes, perhaps because pachucos had long hair like Tarzan in the popular movies. Through Mexican comedian and film actor Germán Valdés, popularly known as "Tin Tan," the pachuco became a novelty in Mexico.

Tin Tan has to be credited with taking Mexican-American influences to Mexico in the form of dress styles, music, caló and english words. Germán Valdés was the son of a mexican consul who took his family to live in Laredo, El Paso and Los Angeles. When Tin Tan was young he befriended Mexican-American pachucos, took their music and style, introducing it with humor on Mexico City stages and theater. He made over one hundred films and became a legend. In Juarez, Mexico, a zoot-suited Tin Tan sculpture looks over the old *Mercado*.

The pachuco was also called a *tirilongo* and though the word's origin is vague pachucologist José Montoya believes it might have been related to pachucos declaring their citizenship at the bridge. Instead of declaring U.S. Citizen, they blurted, "tirilongo." *Tirilón* also meant long threads, thus Tirilongo was a blend of the english and spanish. But a *tirilona* was not a pachuca, she was an informant.

Social anthropologist José Cuellar, alias musician Doctor Loco, further sees the pachuco as one of the first precursors to multiculturalism, without the pachuco knowing what the word meant. In style, language, dress but especially in music, the pachuco borrowed from the Anglo-American, the African American, the Mexicano and the Caribbean to create a new and different kind of music. We now call it transculturalism.

45   In the end, the pachuco was the precursor of the Chicanos and the Chicano Movement. The pachucos were the first Mexican Americans to rebel against this country and their mother country, the first to stake their own universal identity and independence from both oppressive cultures, to mold their own, a renaissance-hybrid of both.

Beyond the zoot suit riots are the unmistakable spiritual cries of aesthetic expression through pachucos, cholos, zoot suiters, low riders, murals, language, cholos. Through Chicano theater, film, literature and art, there is an assertion, a cultural and aesthetic identity that today takes its place as part of the American experience.

BROADER HORIZONS: RESOURCES FOR WRITING AND CLASS DISCUSSION

Literary Critical Essay/Discussion Topics

1. Make a list of the images that come to mind of migrant workers, be they from film or news reports. With the list in hand, choose characters from any of these selections that depict migrant workers, and write an essay confirming or invalidating the items from your list. Does the literature undermine stereotypes or not? In what ways?

2. From the selections, pinpoint three different types of jobs presented, and analyze the rewards that each employee gets from working. How do they feel about the work, and what does it do for them? Are they working to live or living to work? Why?

3. The dustbowl years of the early 1930s have lived on in the creative works of John Steinbeck's novels and Woody Guthrie's songs. Investigate either of these artists, and write an essay discussing whether themes in their works are relevant in today's society. What issues or conditions found in the selections by Latino writers parallel those found in *The Grapes of Wrath* or in the songs of Woody Guthrie? You might also listen to the *Ghost of Tom Joad* or *Devils and Dust* CDs by Bruce Springsteen and analyze how the selections relate to these songs. Do any other contemporary artists look at these issues? Why or why not?

4. Find depictions of Latino workers in pictures by one or both of the famous Depression-era photographers Dorothea Lange and Walker Evans or refer to the "Workers" photography of Brazilian photographer Sebastián Salgado. Write an essay discussing how the workers are pictured. What sorts of images in the works you have read bring out feelings similar to those conveyed in photos?

5. Compare and contrast the obstacles faced by Latino characters in cities and rural areas. Which environment offers more promise? Why? Which requires more sacrifice? Which of the obstacles are particular to Latino populations?

6. Many workers come into this country illegally to work, and they send money back to their families in the form of remittances. Sometimes entire towns or villages and small Caribbean islands are supported by this cash. Discuss the portrayal of such a character in one of these selections. What are the major obstacles he or she faces? How do other characters feel about these types of arrangements? How is the worker affected by the financial commitment to those left behind?

7. "The American Dream" is part of every working person's thinking. Consider whether this notion is tantalizing or inspirational for the characters in these works.

The Novel Connection

Perhaps the most famous Latino migrant worker novel is the classic Chicano work *...Y no se lo tragó la tierra* (*...And the Earth Did Not Devour Him* [1971]), written in Spanish by Tomás Rivera. This narratively sophisticated series of poetic sketches, or prose pieces—a stylistic innovation that Sandra Cisneros would later use for her *The House on Mango Street* (1984)—tells the multiple tales of migrant workers as they travel the country during a particular one-year period of a young boy's life. Thus far, no other Chicano book better captures the hardships and betrayals of this sort of working life. In the tradition of John Steinbeck's *The Grapes of Wrath*, Rivera's classic brilliantly portrays the migrant life of a family and its disjointed community.

Other Latino works have also focused on this theme. Raymond Barrio's *The Plum Plum Pickers* (1969) was often cited by leaders of the Chicano movement for political reasons as a way of pointing out the hardships and entrapment of the farm laborers. Debra Diaz's short novel *The Red Camp* (1996) takes place in an early twentieth-century labor camp (El Campo Colorado) in southern California in which Latinos worked the citrus trees. The more recent *Crossing Vines* (2003) by Rigoberto González deals with the same region for a present-day story of the hardships suffered by the grape pickers. *The Brick People* (1982) by Alejandro Morales is a historical novel that is based on the Mexican American workers who labored in the brickyards of nineteenth-century Pasadena, California. Cecile Pineda's *Frieze* (1986) takes readers even further back in time and tells a tale of tenth-century stonecutters and the building of the Borobudur temple in Java. The book poetically depicts the same issues of labor and worker exploitation that take place to this day.

It is interesting to compare how two other writers treat the story of the young migrant laborer in a pair of relatively recent novels. Helena María Viramontes's short novel *Under the Feet of Jesus* (1995) lyrically describes the thoughts and feelings of a young girl coming to terms with her transitory migrant life and the "family" around her. Manuel Luis Martínez's *Crossing* (1998) describes a young boy's struggle to understand his past and to survive the ordeal of border crossing while trapped in a boxcar with a group of illegal immigrants and a viciously evil *coyote* (one who profits from transporting illegal immigrants across the border). In both novels, the young protagonist goes on an initiative journey toward self-understanding and spiritual fulfillment.

In contrast, two other novels send characters in essentially the opposite direction. Dagoberto Gilb's first novel, *The Last Known Residence of Mickey Acuña* (1994), describes the downward spiral of a group of vagabonds in a YMCA, hopelessly pipe-dreaming of miracles that never arrive. Francisco Goldman's *The Ordinary Seaman* (1997) traces a Central American refugee's struggles in a ship docked on a pier in New York City. In the Gilb novel, the traps are psychological; in Goldman's, they are literal. For a slightly less destitute picture of working-class unemployed, Gary Soto's *Nickel and Dime* (2000) tells three related stories about three men down on their luck in the 1990s, each trying to salvage his dysfunctional life.

The Latino blue-collar world is reflected in a wide range of novels, including *The Wedding* (1989) by Mary Helen Ponce, *Sofia's Saints* (2002) by Diana Lopez, and the writings of Dagoberto Gilb and Daniel Chacón. Denise Chávez's first major fictional work, *The Last of the Menu Girls* (1986), is a complicated narrative of "ordinary" working-class characters, and her later novel, *Face of an Angel* (1994), traces the adventures of a "wise waitress" in a fictional Southwestern town.

Nonfiction writers such as Studs Terkel, Barbara Carson, Eric Schlosser, and Barbara Ehrenreich have chronicled the perils of the working world, and Latino essayists are participating in this discussion. Novelists such as Theodore Dreiser, Upton Sinclair, John Steinbeck, and William Kennedy have built their fiction around work or the lack of it. Given the number of Latino workers in the United States today—beneath and within the economic system—it is hardly surprising that Latino fiction provides the perfect forum for writers to continue this rich tradition in American literature and explore the experiences of Latinos at work.

The Film Connection

In-depth Film Connection
My Family/Mi Familia (1995)
Directed by Gregory Nava

My Family/Mi Familia (1995), starring a dream team cast that includes Edward James Olmos, Esai Morales, Jimmy Smits, Lupe Ontiveros, and even Jennifer Lopez, is a touching epic saga that portrays the life of a Mexican American family in East Los Angeles. Directed by Gregory Nava, one of the most widely acclaimed Latino directors of the twentieth century, the film effectively depicts the intricacies of the attempts to achieve the American Dream. Like so many immigrants who sacrifice all their possessions and risk their lives to make a better living, the characters in this movie demonstrate that there is no easy formula for becoming socioeconomically successful in the United States. To watch this film is to get a true sense of the paths that workers at many levels take, whether by choice or necessity, to improve their lives.

Much has been published about the plight of the migrant worker in the United States, yet this movie puts a face on the struggles undergone by so many families. Like the film *El Norte* (1984), a masterpiece that Nava also directed, this movie highlights the fact that achieving the opportunity to work is at times more challenging than the work itself. The patriarch of the film, José Sanchez, arrives in the United States during the 1920s, a time when anti-immigration policies resulted in many Latinos being corralled like wild animals and sent back to their homelands. He works as a gardener and eventually marries a woman named Maria, who one day falls victim to the government's inhumane actions and is sent back to Mexico. With her baby, she miraculously returns to the United States, risking her life along the way.

Each of the family members sacrifices something to become financially independent. The mother and father, of course, perform backbreaking labor so that they can provide for all their children, who in turn find different ways to make money. Paco, their oldest and the narrator, portrayed by Olmos, joins the military—an act that symbolizes, historically, the path that so many young Chicanos have taken in defense of their adopted country. Toni devotes her life to the convent and then to social causes, working as an activist. Irene opens her own restaurant. Memo becomes an attorney; and the two most intriguing characters in the film, Chucho and the youngest child, Jimmy, rebel against a society that has not rewarded their family for their hard labor.

Attracted to the promise of fast money, Chucho sells drugs as part of a gang, much to the dismay of his father, who is disappointed that his son would sacrifice the ideals of a strong work ethic that have characterized so many immigrants. To José, Chucho's drug dealing indicates a rejection of everything for which he and his wife have fought so hard. To Chucho, dealing represents a way to scale quickly up the social ladder without having to experience the exploitation that gardeners, migrant workers, and maids—the people he knows best—have experienced. The gangster lifestyle eventually catches up to Chucho. He gets into a fight with a rival gang member and winds up killing him. In a thrilling scene that relives the kind of police abuse that was so rampant against Chicanos in Los Angeles during the Sleepy Lagoon era, officers from the Los Angeles police department hunt Chucho down and shoot him dead—in front of his younger brother, Jimmy. This, of course, becomes a turning point for Jimmy, who like his brother perceives society as an antagonistic barrier that is not there to serve him.

Scarred for life, Jimmy spends much time in and out of jails, and in many respects, he is the antithesis of his brother Memo. While the former refuses to sacrifice his beliefs to achieve any ends, the latter sacrifices virtually anything to be successful, including his Mexican nickname, preferring to be called Bill in front of his wife's family. In one scene, Memo's flawless English and his denial of any remnant of Mexican history/influence in his family's house serves as a sad but sobering reminder of how assimilation plays such a tremendous role in shaping the socioeconomic vitality of Latinos. Of all the family members, he is the one closest to achieving the American Dream, yet he is also the one who pays the highest cultural price.

Like the colorful family in the film, the characters and voices in the works included in this chapter make obvious sacrifices in the jobs they hold. Each literary piece from "Blake in the Tropics" to "Al, in Phoenix" explores the working lives of Latinos toiling in jobs with little internal or financial reward; *My Family* also shows an array of such characters and provides a perspective on why so many of them sing the working-class blues.

Other Recommended Films:

...And The Earth Did Not Swallow Him (1994)

Manito (2002)

El Otro Lado (1979)

The Milagro Beanfield War (1988)

Salt of the Earth (1954)

Selena (1997)

Tortilla Soup (2001)

Zoot Suit (1981)

La Ciudad (1998)

Thematic Connection Listing

1. Working Class Blues

Fiction

Ray Gonzalez: "Invisible Country"

Alberto Ríos: "The Child"

Poetry

Carolina Hospital: "Blake in the Tropics"

Gary Soto: "The Elements of San Joaquin"

"Mexicans Begin Jogging"

Essay

José Antonio Burciaga: "Pachucos and the Taxi Cab Brigade"

2. The Modern Dustbowls: Migrant Workers

Fiction

Norma Cantú: "Se me enchina el cuerpo al oír tu cuento..."

Poetry

José B. Gonzalez: "Because No One Should Say 'Chávez Who?'"

Diana Garcia: "When Living Was a Labor Camp Called Montgomery"

Martín Espada: "Federico's Ghost"

Luis J. Rodríguez: "Hungry"

3. Stories from the Trades: Narratives on the Job

Fiction

Cristina Garcia: "Tito's Goodbye"

Dagoberto Gilb: "Al, in Phoenix"

Poetry

Martín Espada: "Who Burns for the Perfection of Paper"

"Jorge the Church Janitor Finally Quits"

Julia Alvarez: "Woman's Work"

Jimmy Santiago Baca: "Work We Hate and Dreams We Love"

4. Crossing the Border

Fiction

Helena María Viramontes: "The Cariboo Café"

6
The Urban World

Weaving Through City Streets

INTRODUCTION

In his important work with the semi-literary title *Magical Urbanism*, sociologist Mike Davis talks about how Latinos are "reinventing" and "tropicalizing" certain urban spaces of the United States. Cities are always in a state of flux as populations shift within them, and it is usually the negative aspects of these changes that draw attention and not how Latinos might be, as Davis says, "bringing redemptive energies to the neglected, worn out cores and inner suburbs of many metropolitan areas." Associating Latino literature with the urban streets and the negative stereotypes of all they imply is as common now as it was 40 years ago when the famous musical *West Side Story* misrepresented Puerto Rican youth to mainstream "America." New York, Miami, San Diego, East Los Angeles, South Chicago, El Paso, and the barrios and smaller cities that feed off these huge centers of Latino homelands provide the settings for the majority of Latino literature. The city landscape continues to dominate Latino writing, and understanding what writers do with that landscape is important if we are to avoid stereotypical associations and narrow, debilitating attitudes toward the urban Latino. In the mainstream English vocabulary for cities, words like "sprawl" and "congested" carry connotations of disease and contamination. Newspapers speak of "aliens" and "foreigners" spreading themselves outward in a haphazard, uncontainable way. We want to militarize our borders, guard the airports against intruders, and seal the entrances off from the urban blight. Many Latino writers struggle to combat such attitudes as they portray characters living within the contact zones of urban worlds.

Latinos and the Cities

A quick look at any recent demographic report will tell you that most Latinos (more than half) live in California and Texas and the rest primarily in New York and Florida. Over 90% live in urban areas, so it should come as no surprise that Latino creative imagination is tied to the city landscape, that urban images filter through nearly all the writing in one way or another. What *is* surprising is the extent and facility with which Latino writers control and manage their creative use of the urban world. Each writer seems to find a new way to maneuver within the same sorts of streets and to adjust the corners and alleys and parks for their own imaginative purposes. These writers explore the way Latinos cope with urban spaces and how they find valued homes and communities within them. Readers need to go beyond the urban hardship story—cockroaches and rats and drugs and crime—in order to understand the interaction between Latino life and the culture of the city.

Symbolism of the City

In Chapter 7, "The Fringe World," we will look at Latinos on the outside of mainstream society, and some of the works in that section will overlap with the thematic subject of this chapter. Hundreds of thousands of urban people, Latino or not, live on the fringes of the city, beneath the pulse and dynamic of the metropolitan commerce and industry. The focus in this portion of the book is on how the writers portray the city and how their creative imaginations use the elements of urban life to communicate, symbolically, metaphorically, or literally, what the urban experience means to Latinos. It will be obvious that Latino writers regard the city with ambivalent attitudes. On the one hand, the city is *la comunidad*, the sanctuary for like-minded populations, and on the other, it is filled with dangers and obstacles. This creates in the works of art (not just in the literature) another element of tension, another oppositional thematic issue—like that of biculturalism and bilingualism—that feeds the works and adds to their intensity.

El Barrio

Whether in Los Angeles or New York, the space known as the barrio grows out of a need for the urban poor to associate with each other, to establish some sort of meaningful community, and to find a way to survive within the often oppressive restrictions of a society where power and influence are regulated and controlled by attitudes toward race, class, and gender. The migratory trends in all countries lead from rural to urban as people search for jobs, seek independence, flee poverty, escape repression, etc. The extreme examples are the world's largest urban hubs, Mexico City, São Paulo, and Bombay, but all cities draw people toward them, and Latino literature nearly always reflects some aspect of a city's influence.

The most obvious portrayal is the ghetto world and the dangers of the streets. From Piri Thomas's *Down These Mean Streets* (1967) to Luis Valdez's *Zoot Suit* (1978), the depicted Latino environment is often one of poverty, crime, and the varied ways the city streets become a labyrinth and a trap from which the Latino heroes and heroines must escape if they are to succeed. The oppressive buildings, projects, the unnatural "concrete jungles" of the city are laid out as obstacles the urban Latino must overcome. As suburban growth continues, the inner cities become increasingly fragmented and the centers cannot hold. By the early 1980s, according to historian Juan Gonzalez, the inner cities were "verging on chaos." During the second half of the twentieth century, the government-subsidized, centrifugal expansion outward (through the construction and expansion of highways, to cite one example) and away from the city tended to leave the inner world poorer, weaker, and open to division and conflict. Often, in fact, the highways themselves became barriers separating the haves and the have-nots.

The Urban Schools

Given that study after study has documented the youth of the overall Latino population (nearly half under the age of 25), it is easy to see why so many writers delve into the importance of education (or lack of it) and the role it plays in Latino lives. We see the issues confronting the school-age Latino portrayed on the big screen as early as the 1950s—in films like *Black Board Jungle* and *Rebel Without a Cause*—and as recently as in *Stand and Deliver* (1988) and *Real Women Have Curves* (2002). Many Latino writers also look back on their own childhoods and socializing experiences spent in the urban public schools, where they had to learn how to brace themselves against prejudice and racism, where they came up against teachers who rejected them, guidance counselors who argued they would never be able to go to college, peers who led them in the direction of street life, or school officials who prohibited their use of Spanish. Conversely, when schools encourage young Latinos to further their education, these students are still often caught between the family's traditional demands and their own desire for independence and a professional status. The combination of poverty rates and the lack of state and federal funding for the urban educational systems throughout the United States is a subject that finds its way into Latino literary works in all genres.

Sanctuary Within the Streets

From the alleys and back lots of Spanish Harlem, the South Bronx, or Brooklyn Heights to the apartment complexes in Paterson, New Jersey, to East L.A. and Miami—hundreds of images in Latino writing convey the urban world. Autobiographical experiences of urban life fill the books of most New York–based Puerto Rican writers from Piri Thomas to Ernesto Quiñonez. Luis J. Rodríguez charts the California streets in his poetry and fiction. It is always interesting to see how characters interact with these archetypal spaces. The relationship between character and space, between writers' ideas about culture and their sense of place, is immensely important in Latino works. For example, a bodega* on the corner might relate to nostalgic dreamers and their pasts. It could just as easily signal the dead-end future for a young student. What does a young Latina wife see as she

---

*The word is sometimes translated as "warehouse," but for Puerto Ricans literally refers to a small store selling a variety of items. For Nuyorican writers, the word carries a wealth of metaphorical connotations.

gazes out a third-story window and looks down on the kids playing with the open fire hydrant? How is the city seen differently by the Latinos within it and by those who cruise through it? The small places of sanctuary within the urban world—churches and gardens and libraries—serve all sorts of needs for all sorts of people. As noted earlier, the highway construction systems create barriers or challenges—physical borders or obstacles.

Bridges speak of connections. Communities survive beneath the freeways, on the edges of parks, in tiny "casitas" between the underpasses, and in the tunnels underground. Murals communicate in underground urban languages, and gardens crop up in front yards. The subways and buses, trains and taxis: These are the landscapes that frequent the writings where movement and change take place. The classic journey/quest motif is filtered through the system of mass transportation that preoccupies Latino literature.

Everything Conceals Something Else

In his novel *Invisible Cities*, Italian writer Italo Calvino says that "cities, like dreams, are made of desires and fears, even if the thread of their discourse is secret, their rules are absurd, their perspectives deceitful, and everything conceals something else." The city, he claims "does not tell its past, but contains it like the lines of a hand, written in the corners of the streets, the gratings of the windows, the banisters of the steps...every segment marked in turn with scratches, indentations, scrolls." If we read the works in this section, paying attention to the scratches and indentations, the images that convey some Latino writer's sense of the past, we might find something concealed, some underground current of meaning. What can the worn front steps, a darkened stairwell, or a busy intersection reveal to us as readers? How is the Latino journey mirrored in the cities' street pattern? What surrealistic quality of the urban world speaks to us of dreams and fears and desires? Beyond the literal and physical urban environment, we have to remember that there can also be a city of the mind, where actions and desires and attitudes are influenced by the city, its history, its design, and its past.

FICTION

Sandra Cisneros

See the biographical headnote of Cisneros on page 66.

Bread

We were hungry. We went into a bakery on Grand Avenue and bought bread. Filled the backseat. The whole car smelled of bread. Big sourdough loaves shaped like a fat ass. Fat-ass bread. I said in Spanish, *Nalgona* bread. Fat-ass bread, he said in Italian, but I forget how he said it.

We ripped big chunks with our hands and ate. The car a pearl blue like my heart that afternoon. Smell of warm bread, bread in both fists, a tango on the tape player loud, loud, loud, because me and him, we're the only ones who can stand it like that, like if the bandoneón, violin, piano, guitar, bass, were inside us, like when he wasn't married, like before his kids, like if all the pain hadn't passed between us.

Driving down streets with buildings that remind him, he says, how charming this city is. And me remembering when I was little, a cousin's baby who died from swallowing rat poison in a building like these.

That's just how it is. And that's how we drove. With all his new city memories and all my old. Him kissing me between big bites of bread.

Junot Díaz

Junot Díaz was born in Santo Domingo, Dominican Republic, and has a BA degree from Rutgers University and an MFA from Cornell University. He has edited collections of fiction and published several short stories in anthologies and various magazines such as *The New Yorker*, but his work *Drown* (1996), a collection of interconnected short stories, won exceptional acclaim. His work represents the sole major contribution to Dominican American literature written from a male perspective.

Edison, New Jersey

The first time we try to deliver the Gold Crown the lights are on in the house but no one lets us in. I bang on the front door and Wayne hits the back and I can hear our double drum shaking the windows. Right then I have this feeling that someone is inside, laughing at us.

This guy better have a good excuse, Wayne says, lumbering around the newly planted rosebushes. This is bullshit.

You're telling me, I say but Wayne's the one who takes this job too seriously. He pounds some more on the door, his face jiggling. A couple of times he raps on the windows, tries squinting through the curtains. I take a more philosophical approach; I walk over to the ditch that has been cut next to the road, a drainage pipe half filled with water, and sit down. I smoke and watch a mama duck and her three ducklings scavenge the grassy bank and then float downstream like they're on the same string. Beautiful, I say but Wayne doesn't hear. He's banging on the door with the staple gun.

At nine Wayne picks me up at the showroom and by then I have our route planned out. The order forms tell me everything I need to know about the customers we'll be dealing with that day. If someone is just getting a fifty-two-inch card table delivered then you know they aren't going to give you too much of a hassle but they also aren't going to tip. Those are your Spotswood, Sayreville and Perth Amboy deliveries. The pool tables go north to the rich suburbs—Livingston, Ridgewood, Bedminster.

You should see our customers. Doctors, diplomats, surgeons, presidents of universities, ladies in slacks and silk tops who sport thin watches you could trade in for a car, who wear comfortable leather shoes. Most of them prepare for us by laying down a path of yesterday's *Washington Post* from the front door to the game room. I make them pick it all up. I say: Carajo, what if we slip? Do you know what two hundred pounds of slate could do to a floor? The threat of property damage puts the chop-chop in their step. The best customers leave us alone until the bill has to be signed. Every now and then we'll be given water in paper cups. Few have offered us more, though a dentist from Ghana once gave us a six-pack of Heineken while we worked.

5   Sometimes the customer has to jet to the store for cat food or a newspaper while we're in the middle of a job. I'm sure you'll be all right, they say. They never sound too sure. Of course, I say. Just show us where the silver's at. The customers ha-ha and we ha-ha and then they agonize over leaving, linger by the front door, trying to memorize everything they own, as if they don't know where to find us, who we work for.

Once they're gone, I don't have to worry about anyone bothering me. I put down the ratchet, crack my knuckles and explore, usually while Wayne is smoothing out the felt and doesn't need help. I take cookies from the kitchen, razors from the bathroom cabinets. Some of these houses have twenty, thirty rooms. On the ride back I figure out how much loot it would take to fill up all that space. I've been caught roaming around plenty of times but you'd be surprised how quickly someone believes you're looking for the bathroom if you don't jump when you're discovered, if you just say, Hi.

After the paperwork's been signed, I have a decision to make. If the customer has been good and tipped well, we call it even and leave. If the customer has been an ass—maybe they yelled, maybe they let their kids throw golf balls at us—I ask for the bathroom. Wayne will pretend that he hasn't seen this before; he'll count the drill bits while the customer (or their maid) guides the vacuum over the floor. Excuse me, I say. I let them show me the way to the bathroom (usually I already know) and once the door is shut I cram bubble bath drops into my pockets and throw fist-sized wads of toilet paper into the toilet. I take a dump if I can and leave that for them.

Most of the time Wayne and I work well together. He's the driver and the money man and I do the lifting and handle the assholes. Tonight we're on our way to Lawrenceville and he wants to talk to me about Charlene, one of the showroom girls, the one with the blowjob lips. I haven't wanted to talk about women in months, not since the girlfriend.

I really want to pile her, he tells me. Maybe on one of the Madisons.

Man, I say, cutting my eyes towards him. Don't you have a wife or something?

10   He gets quiet. I'd still like to pile her, he says defensively.
    And what will that do?
    Why does it have to *do* anything?
    Twice this year Wayne's cheated on his wife and I've heard it all, the before
and the after. The last time his wife nearly tossed his ass out to the dogs. Neither of the women seemed worth it to me. One of them was even younger
than Charlene. Wayne can be a moody guy and this is one of those nights; he
slouches in the driver's seat and swerves through traffic, riding other people's
bumpers like I've told him not to do. I don't need a collision or a four-hour
silent treatment so I try to forget that I think his wife is good people and ask
him if Charlene's given him any signals.
    He slows the truck down. Signals like you wouldn't believe, he says.
15   On the days we have no deliveries the boss has us working at the showroom,
selling cards and poker chips and mankala boards. Wayne spends his time
skeezing the salesgirls and dusting shelves. He's a big goofy guy—I don't
understand why the girls dig his shit. One of those mysteries of the universe.
The boss keeps me in the front of the store, away from the pool tables. He
knows I'll talk to the customers, tell them not to buy the cheap models. I'll
say shit like, Stay away from those Bristols. Wait until you can get something
real. Only when he needs my Spanish will he let me help on a sale. Since I'm
no good at cleaning or selling slot machines I slouch behind the front register
and steal. I don't ring anything up, and pocket what comes in. I don't tell
Wayne. He's too busy running his fingers through his beard, keeping the waves
on his nappy head in order. A hundred-buck haul's not unusual for me and
back in the day, when the girlfriend used to pick me up, I'd buy her anything
she wanted, dresses, silver rings, lingerie. Sometimes I blew it all on her. She
didn't like the stealing but hell, we weren't made out of loot and I liked going
into a place and saying, Jeva, pick out anything, it's yours. This is the closest
I've come to feeling rich.
    Nowadays I take the bus home and the cash stays with me. I sit next to this
three-hundred-pound rock-and-roll chick who washes dishes at the Friendly's.
She tells me about the roaches she kills with her water nozzle. Boils the wings
right off them. On Thursday I buy myself lottery tickets—ten Quick Picks and
a couple of Pick 4s. I don't bother with the little stuff.

    The second time we bring the Gold Crown the heavy curtain next to the
door swings up like a Spanish fan. A woman stares at me and Wayne's too busy
knocking to see. Muneca, I say. She's black and unsmiling and then the curtain drops between us, a whisper on the glass. She had on a t-shirt that said
No Problem and didn't look like she owned the place. She looked more like
the help and couldn't have been older than twenty and from the thinness of
her face I pictured the rest of her skinny. We stared at each other for a second
at the most, not enough for me to notice the shape of her ears or if her lips
were chapped. I've fallen in love on less.
    Later in the truck, on the way back to the showroom Wayne mutters, This
guy is dead. I mean it.

The girlfriend calls sometimes but not often. She has found herself a new boyfriend, some zángano who works at a record store. *Dan* is his name and the way she says it, so painfully gringo, makes the corners of my eyes narrow. The clothes I'm sure this guy tears from her when they both get home from work—the chokers, the rayon skirts from the Warehouse, the lingerie—I bought with stolen money and I'm glad that none of it was earned straining my back against hundreds of pounds of raw rock. I'm glad for that.

20   The last time I saw her in person was in Hoboken. She was with *Dan* and hadn't yet told me about him and hurried across the street in her high clogs to avoid me and my boys, who even then could sense me turning, turning into the motherfucker who'll put a fist through anything. She flung one hand in the air but didn't stop. A month before the zángano, I went to her house, a friend visiting a friend, and her parents asked me how business was, as if I balanced the books or something. Business is outstanding, I said.

That's really wonderful to hear, the father said.

You betcha.

He asked me to help him mow his lawn and while we were dribbling gas into the tank he offered me a job. A real one that you can build on. Utilities, he said, is nothing to be ashamed of.

Later the parents went into the den to watch the Giants lose and she took me into her bathroom. She put on her makeup because we were going to a movie. If I had your eyelashes, I'd be famous, she told me. The Giants started losing real bad. I still love you, she said and I was embarrassed for the two of us, the way I'm embarrassed at those afternoon talk shows where broken couples and unhappy families let their hearts hang out.

25   We're friends, I said and Yes, she said, yes we are.

There wasn't much space so I had to put my heels on the edge of the bathtub. The cross I'd given her dangled down on its silver chain so I put it in my mouth to keep it from poking me in the eye. By the time we finished my legs were bloodless, broomsticks inside my rolled-down baggies and as her breathing got smaller and smaller against my neck, she said, I do, I still do.

Each payday I take out the old calculator and figure how long it'd take me to buy a pool table honestly. A top-of-the-line, three-piece slate affair doesn't come cheap. You have to buy sticks and balls and chalk and a score keeper and triangles and French tips if you're a fancy shooter. Two and a half years if I give up buying underwear and eat only pasta but even this figure's bogus. Money's never stuck to me, ever.

Most people don't realize how sophisticated pool tables are. Yes, tables have bolts and staples on the rails but these suckers hold together mostly by gravity and by the precision of their construction. If you treat a good table right it will outlast you. Believe me. Cathedrals are built like that. There are Incan roads in the Andes that even today you couldn't work a knife between two of the cobblestones. The sewers that the Romans built in Bath were so good that they weren't replaced until the 1950s. That's the sort of thing I can believe in.

These days I can build a table with my eyes closed. Depending on how rushed we are I might build the table alone, let Wayne watch until I need help putting on the slate. It's better when the customers stay out of our faces, how they react when we're done, how they run fingers on the lacquered rails and suck in their breath, the felt so tight you couldn't pluck it if you tried. Beautiful, is what they say and we always nod, talc on our fingers, nod again, beautiful.

The boss nearly kicked our asses over the Gold Crown. The customer, an asshole named Pruitt, called up crazy, said we were *delinquent*. That's how the boss put it. Delinquent. We knew that's what the customer called us because the boss doesn't use words like that. Look boss, I said, we knocked like crazy. I mean, we knocked like federal marshals. Like Paul Bunyan. The boss wasn't having it. You fuckos, he said. You butthogs. He tore us for a good two minutes and then *dismissed* us. For most of that night I didn't think I had a job so I hit the bars, fantasizing that I would bump into this cabrón out with that black woman while me and my boys were cranked but the next morning Wayne came by with that Gold Crown again. Both of us had hangovers. One more time, he said. An extra delivery, no overtime. We hammered on the door for ten minutes but no one answered. I jimmied with the windows and the back door and I could have sworn I heard her behind the patio door, I knocked hard and heard footsteps.

30 We called the boss and told him what was what and the boss called the house but no one answered. OK, the boss said. Get those card tables done. That night, as we lined up the next day's paperwork, we got a call from Pruitt and he didn't use the word delinquent. He wanted us to come late at night but we were booked. Two-month waiting list, the boss reminded him. I looked over at Wayne and wondered how much money this guy was pouring into the boss's ear. Pruitt said he was *contrite* and *determined* and asked us to come again. His maid was sure to let us in.

What the hell kind of name is Pruitt anyway? Wayne asks me when we swing onto the parkway.
Pato name, I say. Anglo or some other bog people.
Probably a fucking banker. What's the first name?
Just an initial, C. Clarence Pruitt sounds about right.
35 Yeah, Clarence, Wayne yuks.
Pruitt. Most of our customers have names like this, court case names: Wooley, Maynard, Gass, Binder, but the people from my town, our names, you see on convicts or coupled together on boxing cards.
We take our time. Go to the Rio Diner, blow an hour and all the dough we have in our pockets. Wayne is talking about Charlene and I'm leaning my head against a thick pane of glass.

Pruitt's neighborhood has recently gone up and only his court is complete. Gravel roams off this way and that, shaky. You can see inside the other houses, their newly formed guts, nailheads bright and sharp on the fresh timber. Wrinkled blue tarps protect wiring and fresh plaster. The driveways are mud and on each lawn stand huge stacks of sod. We park in front of Pruitt's house and bang on the door. I give Wayne a hard look when I see no car in the garage.

Yes? I hear a voice inside say.

40 We're the delivery guys, I yell.

A bolt slides, a lock turns, the door opens. She stands in our way, wearing black shorts and a gloss of red on her lips and I'm sweating.

Come in, yes? She stands back from the door, holding it open.

Sounds like Spanish, Wayne says.

No shit, I say, switching over. Do you remember me?

45 No, she says.

I look over at Wayne. Can you believe this?

I can believe anything, kid.

You heard us didn't you? The other day, that was you.

She shrugs and opens the door wider.

50 You better tell her to prop that with a chair. Wayne heads back to unlock the truck.

You hold that door, I say.

We've had our share of delivery trouble. Trucks break down. Customers move and leave us with an empty house. Handguns get pointed. Slate gets dropped, a rail goes missing. The felt is the wrong color, the Dufferins get left in the warehouse. Back in the day, the girlfriend and I made a game of this. A prediction game. In the mornings I rolled onto my pillow and said, What's today going to be like?

Let me check. She put her fingers up to her widow's peak and that motion would shift her breasts, her hair. We never slept under any covers, not in spring, fall or summer and our bodies were dark and thin the whole year.

I see an asshole customer, she murmured. Unbearable traffic. Wayne's going to work slow. And then you'll come home to me.

55 Will I get rich?

You'll come home to me. That's the best I can do. And then we'd kiss hungrily because this was how we loved each other.

The game was part of our mornings, the way our showers and our sex and our breakfasts were. We stopped playing only when it started to go wrong for us, when I'd wake up and listen to the traffic outside without waking her, when everything was a fight.

She stays in the kitchen while we work. I can hear her humming. Wayne's shaking his right hand like he's scalded his fingertips. Yes, she's fine. She has her back to me, her hands stirring around in a full sink, when I walk in.

I try to sound conciliatory. You're from the city?

60 A nod.

Where about?

Washington Heights.

Dominicana, I say. Quisqueyana. She nods. What street?

I don't know the address, she says. I have it written down. My mother and my brothers live there.

65 I'm Dominican, I say.
You don't look it.
I get a glass of water. We're both staring out at the muddy lawn.
She says, I didn't answer the door because I wanted to piss him off.
Piss who off?
70 I want to get out of here, she says.
Out of here?
I'll pay you for a ride.
I don't think so, I say.
Aren't you from Nueva York?
75 No.
Then why did you ask the address?
Why? I have family near there.
Would it be that big of a problem?
I say in English that she should have her boss bring her but she stares at me
blankly. I switch over.
80 He's a pendejo, she says, suddenly angry. I put down the glass, move next
to her to wash it. She's exactly my height and smells of liquid detergent and
has tiny beautiful moles on her neck, an archipelago leading down into her
clothes.
Here, she says, putting out her hand but I finish it and go back to the den.
Do you know what she wants us to do? I say to Wayne.

Her room is upstairs, a bed, a closer, a dresser, yellow wallpaper. Spanish
Cosmo and *El Diario* thrown on the floor. Four hangers' worth of clothes in
the closet and only the top dresser drawer is full. I put my hand on the bed
and the cotton sheets are cool.

Pruitt has pictures of himself in his room. He's tan and probably has been
to more countries than I know capitals for. Photos of him on vacations, on
beaches, standing beside a wide-mouth Pacific salmon he's hooked. The size
of his dome would have made Broca proud. The bed is made and his
wardrobe spills out onto chairs and a line of dress shoes follows the far wall.
A bachelor. I find an open box of Trojans in his dresser beneath a stack of
boxer shorts. I put one of the condoms in my pocket and stick the rest under
his bed.

85 I find her in her room. He likes clothes, she says.
A habit of money, I say but I can't translate it right; I end up agreeing with
her. Are you going to pack?
She holds up her purse. I have everything I need. He can keep the rest of it.
You should take some of your things.
I don't care about that vaina.[1] I just want to go.
90 Don't be stupid, I say. I open her dresser and pull out the shorts on top and
a handful of soft bright panties fall out and roll down the front of my jeans.
There are more in the drawer. I try to catch them but as soon as I touch their
fabric I let everything go.

---

[1]stuff (or thing)

Leave it. Go on, she says and begins to put them back in the dresser, her square back to me, the movement of her hands smooth and easy.

Look, I say.

Don't worry. She doesn't look up.

I go downstairs. Wayne is sinking the bolts into the slate with the Makita. You can't do it, he says.

95 Why not?

Kid. We have to finish this.

I'll be back before you know it. A quick trip, in out.

Kid. He stands up slowly; he's nearly twice as old as me.

I go to the window and look out. New gingkoes stand in rows beside the driveway. A thousand years ago when I was still in college I learned something about them. Living fossils. Unchanged since their inception millions of years ago. You tagged Charlene, didn't you?

100 Sure did, he answers easily.

I take the truck keys out of the toolbox. I'll be right back, I promise.

My mother still has pictures of the girlfriend in her apartment. The girl-friend's the sort of person who never looks bad. There's a picture of us as the bar where I taught her to play pool. She's leaning on the Schmelke I stole for her, nearly a grand worth of cue, frowning at the shot I left her, a shot she'd go on to miss.

The picture of us in Florida is the biggest—shiny, framed, nearly a foot tall. We're in our bathing suits and the legs of some stranger frame the right. She has her butt in the sand, knees folded up in front of her because she knew I was sending the picture home to my moms; she didn't want my mother to see her bikini, didn't want my mother to think her a whore. I'm crouching next to her, smiling, one hand on her thin shoulder, one of her moles showing between my fingers.

My mother won't look at the pictures or talk about her when I'm around but my sister says she still cries over the breakup. Around me my mother's polite, sits quietly on the couch while I tell her about what I'm reading and how work has been. Do you have anyone? she asks me sometimes.

105 Yes, I say.

She talks to my sister on the side, says, In my dreams they're still together.

We reach the Washington Bridge without saying a word. She's emptied his cupboards and refrigerator; the bags are at her feet. She's eating corn chips but I'm too nervous to join in.

Is this the best way? she asks. The bridge doesn't seem to impress her.

It's the shortest way.

110 She folds the bag shut. That's what he said when I arrived last year. I wanted to see the countryside. There was too much rain to see anything anyway.

I want to ask her if she loves her boss, but I ask instead, How do you like the States?

She swings her head across at the billboards. I'm not surprised by any of it, she says.

Traffic on the bridge is bad and she has to give me an oily fiver for the toll. Are you from the Capital? I ask.

No.

115   I was born there. In Villa Juana. Moved here when I was a little boy.

She nods, staring out at the traffic. As we cross over the bridge I drop my hand into her lap. I leave it there, palm up, fingers slightly curled. Sometimes you just have to try, even if you know it won't work. She turns her head away slowly, facing out beyond the bridge cables, out to Manhattan and the Hudson.

Everything in Washington Heights is Dominican. You can't go a block without passing a Quisqueya Bakery or a Quisqueya Supermercado or a Hotel Quisqueya. If I were to park the truck and get out nobody would take me for a deliveryman; I could be the guy who's on the street corner selling Dominican flags. I could be on my way home to my girl. Everybody's on the streets and the merengue's falling out of windows like TVs. When we reach her block I ask a kid with the sag for the building and he points out the stoop with his pinkie. She gets out of the truck and straightens the front of her sweatshirt before following the line that the kid's finger has cut across the street. Cuídate, I say.

Wayne works on the boss and a week later I'm back, on probation, painting the warehouse. Wayne brings me meatball sandwiches from out on the road, skinny things with a seam of cheese gumming the bread.

Was it worth it? he asks me.

120   He's watching me close. I tell him it wasn't.

Did you at least get some?

Hell yeah, I say.

Are you sure?

Why would I lie about something like that? Home-girl was an animal. I still have the teeth marks.

125   Damn, he says.

I punch him in the arm. And how's it going with you and Charlene?

I don't know, man. He shakes his head and in that motion I see him out on his lawn with all his things. I just don't know about this one.

We're back on the road a week later. Buckinghams, Imperials, Gold Crowns and dozens of card tables. I keep a copy of Pruitt's paperwork and when the curiosity finally gets to me I call. The first time I get the machine. We're delivering at a house in Long Island with a view of the Sound that would break you. Wayne and I smoke a joint on the beach and I pick up a dead horseshoe crab by the tail and heave it in the customer's garage. The next two times I'm in the Bedminster area Pruitt picks up and says, Yes? But on the fourth time she answers and the sink is running on her side of the phone and she shuts it off when I don't say anything.

Was she there? Wayne asks in the truck.

130   Of course she was.

He runs a thumb over the front of his teeth. Pretty predictable. She's probably in love with the guy. You know how it is.

I sure do.

Don't get angry.

I'm tired, that's all.

135   Tired's the best way to be, he says. It really is.

He hands me the map and my fingers trace our deliveries, stitching city to city. Looks like we've gotten everything, I say.

Finally. He yawns. What's first tomorrow?

We won't really know until the morning, when I've gotten the paperwork in order but I take guesses anyway. One of our games. It passes the time, gives us something to look forward to. I close my eyes and put my hand on the map. So many towns, so many cities to choose from. Some places are sure bets but more than once I've gone with the long shot and been right.

You can't imagine how many times I've been right.

140   Usually the name will come to me fast, the way the numbered balls pop out during the lottery drawings, but this time nothing comes: no magic, no nothing. It could be anywhere. I open my eyes and see that Wayne is still waiting. Edison, I say, pressing my thumb down. Edison, New Jersey.

Dagoberto Gilb

See the biographical headnote of Gilb on page 129.

Love in L.A.

Jake slouched in a clot of near motionless traffic, in the peculiar gray of concrete, smog, and early morning beneath the overpass of the Hollywood Freeway on Alvarado Street. He didn't really mind because he knew how much worse it could be trying to make a left onto the onramp. He certainly didn't do that everyday of his life, and he'd assure anyone who'd ask that he never would either. A steady occupation had its advantages and he couldn't deny thinking about that too. He needed an FM radio in something better than this '58 Buick he drove. It would have crushed velvet interior with electric controls for the LA summer, a nice warm heater and defroster for the winter drives at the beach, a cruise control for those longer trips, mellow speakers front and rear of course, windows that hum closed, snuffing out that nasty exterior noise of freeways. The fact was that he'd probably have to change his whole style. Exotic colognes, plush, dark nightclubs, maitais and daquiris, necklaced ladies in satin gowns, misty and sexy like in a tequila ad. Jake could imagine lots of possibilities when he let himself, but none that ended up with him pressed onto a stalled freeway.

Jake was thinking about this freedom of his so much that when he glimpsed its green light he just went ahead and stared bye bye to the steadily employed. When he turned his head the same direction his windshield faced, it was maybe one second too late. He pounced the brake pedal and steered the front wheels away from the tiny brakelights but the smack was unavoidable. Just one second sooner and it would only have been close. One second more and he'd be crawling up the Toyota's trunk. As it was, it seemed like only a harmless smack, much less solid than the one against his back bumper.

Jake considered driving past the Toyota but was afraid the traffic ahead would make it too difficult. As he pulled up against the curb a few carlengths ahead, it occurred to him that the traffic might have helped him get away too. He slammed the car door twice to make sure it was closed fully and to give himself another second more, then toured front and rear of his Buick for damage on or near the bumpers. Not an impressionable scratch even in the chrome. He perked up. Though the car's beauty was secondary to its ability to start and move, the body and paint were clean except for a few minor dings. This stood out as one of his few clearcut accomplishments over the years.

Before he spoke to the driver of the Toyota, whose looks he could see might present him with an added complication, he signaled to the driver of the car that hit him, still in his car and stopped behind the Toyota, and waved his hands and shook his head to let the man know there was no problem as far as he was concerned. The driver waved back and started his engine.

5   "It didn't even scratch my paint," Jake told her in that way of his. "So how you doin? Any damage to the car? I'm kinda hoping so, just so it takes a little more time and we can talk some. Or else you can give me your phone number now and I won't have to lay my regular b.s. on you to get it later."

He took her smile as a good sign and relaxed. He inhaled her scent like it was clean air and straighted out his less than new but not unhip clothes.

"You've got Florida plates. You look like you must be Cuban."

"My parents are from Venezuela."

"My name's Jake." He held out his hand.

10   "Mariana."

They shook hands like she'd never done it before in her life.

"I really am sorry about hitting you like that." He sounded genuine. He fondled the wide dimple near the cracked taillight. "It's amazing how easy it is to put a dent in these new cars. They're so soft they might replace waterbeds soon." Jake was confused about how to proceed with this. So much seemed so unlikely, but there was always possibility. "So maybe we should go out to breakfast somewhere and talk it over."

"I don't eat breakfast."

"Some coffee then."

15   "Thanks, but I really can't."

"You're not married, are you? Not that that would matter that much to me. I'm an openminded kinda guy."

She was smiling. "I have to get to work."

"That sounds boring."

"I better get your driver's license," she said.

20 Jake nodded, disappointed. "One little problem," he said. "I didn't bring it. I just forgot it this morning. I'm a musician," he exaggerated greatly, "and, well, I dunno, I left my wallet in the pants I was wearing last night. If you have some paper and a pen I'll give you my address and all that."

He followed her to the glove compartment side of her car.

"What if we don't report it to the insurance companies? I'll just get it fixed for you."

"I don't think my dad would let me do that."

"Your dad? It's not your car?"

25 "He bought it for me. And I live at home."

"Right." She was slipping away from him. He went back around to the back of her new Toyota and looked over the damage again. There was the trunk lid, the bumper, a rear panel, a taillight.

"You do have insurance?" she asked, suspicious, as she came around the back of the car.

"Oh yeah," he lied.

"I guess you better write the name of that down too."

30 He made up a last name and address and wrote down the name of an insurance company an old girlfriend once belonged to. He considered giving a real phone number but went against that idea and made one up.

"I act too," he lied to enhance the effect more. "Been in a couple of movies."

She smiled like a fan.

"So how about your phone number?" He was rebounding maturely.

She gave it to him.

35 "Mariana, you are beautiful," he said in his most sincere voice.

"Call me," she said timidly.

Jake beamed. "We'll see you, Mariana," he said holding out his hand. Her hand felt so warm and soft he felt like he'd been kissed.

Back in his car he took a moment or two to feel both proud and sad about his performance. Then he watched the rear view mirror as Mariana pulled up behind him. She was writing down the license plate numbers on his Buick, ones that he'd taken off a junk because the ones that belonged to his had expired so long ago. He turned the ignition key and revved the big engine and clicked into drive. His sense of freedom swelled as he drove into the now moving street traffic, though he couldn't stop the thought about that FM stereo radio and crushed velvet interior and the new car smell that would even make it better.

Sergio Troncoso

The son of poor Mexican immigrants, Sergio Troncoso was born and grew up on the East Side of El Paso, Texas. He graduated from Harvard University, was a Fulbright Scholar to Mexico, and studied international relations and philosophy at Yale University where he now teaches creative writing during the summer. His collection of short stories, *The Last Tortilla & Other Stories,* won both the Premio Aztlán prize for best book of Chicano fiction in 1999 and the Southwest Book Award. He has also published various articles and *The Nature of Truth* (2003), a novel about a young researcher exploring philosophical issues raised by the Nazi Holocaust. He lives in New York City.

My Life in the City

I almost left the City because I could not find myself there anymore. I found many desires in the City. My gaze would never settle on one thing. It would jump from face to face to face. I enjoyed watching the many beautiful women in the City. Yes, I would study their faces and bodies. I would imagine making love to them. I would imagine their touch on my own body. Sometimes they would smile in return. Sometimes I would talk to them, and their eyes would sparkle. Often they would turn away. A few seemed angry at my open look. But I never meant any harm. I simply wanted to find myself there, to find someone, and I wanted to reach out. But there was nothing there. Or else, it was simply too far away. They were too far away. I was not there. I did not know where I was.

Cars always sped a few inches past me whenever I crossed the street to buy groceries. It was this near danger that one day prompted me to think about the lack of God here. One wrong moment, a misstep, and you die a chance death. A beautiful woman with dark brown curly hair, deep brown eyes, and a friendly, casual air about her stopped a few inches from me on the curb. We waited for the light to change to cross the street. There were others too, in heavy coats, with briefcases or shopping bags, all waiting. She stepped off the curb, ready to jump into the road as soon as the danger was gone. Her face turned toward me as she drifted farther into the street, almost swaying with readiness. Behind her, I saw first the bright lights, then heard the roar of the engine, and before I could say anything—would I have said anything or would I simply have watched the spectacle if given another moment?—a speeding blue and white bus brushed against her hair just as she turned to face it. She fell back as if into an abyss, her face white and blank. Her knees buckled. She smiled nervously, took a deep breath, and watched the bus zoom across the intersection. She seemed stunned, and I wanted to hold her, at least to say something, but I didn't. I was afraid too. I felt lost.

I took my groceries up to my apartment on 86th Street and Broadway. I shop when I don't want to be alone in my apartment, when the silence seems too loud. I also shop when I don't have food. Often, these two things coincide. Shopping is about walking in the street. Walking on Broadway is about getting away from yourself and apparently going somewhere. Apparently. But now, as I put away my orange juice and seltzer, I thought about the dark-haired woman who had almost died a few minutes before, and about the lack of God in the City. It was something palpable here. There was a certain meaninglessness to what happened on these streets. A wrong step and you might be crushed. And then your family would spend days, and then years, adding meaning to what happened to you, adding religion, adding morality.

But really, there was nothing there to begin with, just that wrong step, just her slight smile before the headlights flashed against her face, just *us*. Some of you might think that this meaninglessness I sense on the streets of the City, like a thick cloud, is reason for despair. I don't think so. Or you might think that this lack of meaning is the reason for my thinking about leaving the City. But again you would be wrong. I just find the lack of meaning on Broadway to be the present state of things. The way things are. There is only the urgency to do something about this present, to create what might be a passing fancy into, well, an idea. I feel the need to take out my hammer and *work*, but not the swoon of not finding a grand blueprint in front of me. As for leaving the City, I will tell you about that later.

5   I needed butter and bagels, so I went out again, toward H & H Bagels. I mean, I didn't *need* them, what I needed was to think, and I did my best thinking on the move. Walking is almost synonymous with thinking in the City, with an added numbness that prevents you from going too far. Walking almost teases you to think, and yet it's just a tease. You have to enjoy it for what it is, or you'll be disappointed once you stop. There will be no grand revelation at the end of it, just your body warm and sweaty, maybe your mind at ease. I wanted to think about the dark-haired woman again. Maybe I'd run into her again. Maybe I just wanted to immerse myself in that meaningless present on the street again. I wasn't sure what I wanted.

I didn't meet her, but I did meet someone else. Maybe I exuded the scent of wanting to meet someone. Maybe I had a certain kind of look, I don't know. I bought a poppy, a sesame, and two sourdough bagels, and then I walked across the street for the ninety-nine-cent toilet paper. Might as well, I thought, I'm already here.

In the drug store I was looking at sport bandages. My left ankle was still tender from veering off the pathway to the boardwalk on 79th Street to avoid a pit bull off its leash. I had twisted my foot on a rock, but I had escaped the savage animal, which hadn't been very savage then, just savage looking. I also dropped a box of Equal into my red basket. A woman next to me, with blond, slightly disheveled, shoulder-length hair, said, "That stuff will kill ya." She smiled at me, and I liked the way she looked—slim, not deformed in any observable way, possibly intelligent, big blue-gray eyes—so I asked her how, exactly, I was poisoning myself with this sugar substitute.

She said it contained "chemicals" and that something like honey would probably be better. I said I'd try honey in my coffee, but that I also thought the caffeine would kill me first—or at least scramble up my neurons to leave me permanently damaged—before anything I added to make it sweet. "Going herbal" was best, she said, which made me immediately suspicious of her. Maybe she was a radical tree-hugger type, in which case I wasn't sure why she was talking to me except to save my body and tell me what to do. I asked her if she was a vegetarian too. Vegetables had chemicals sprayed on them, didn't they? She said she occasionally ate meat, which made me like her again. At least she wasn't a wild-eyed fanatic. I said I would buy the Equal and take my chances. Live free or die, I thought. She smiled at me and asked me what I did for a living.

I told her I was independently rich, which was a lie, and which she knew was a lie because I was grinning too much. We walked to the checkout counter of the drug store. Really, I said, I was an architect. I especially liked doing bridges I told her, which wasn't a lie. She was in front of me in line, and I noticed again that she was pretty, a little funky in dress—jeans, boots, sweater, a big loose jacket, a red scarf around her neck, like the pit bull, and big triangular earrings—and about my age. Young, but not stupidly young. She was a "performance artist," which I thought meant she was unemployed. But I was wrong. She had had shows at Dia and a few other places I recognized, although she said things were kind of slow now. She was working on music for a new show, and writing. Maybe she was making it in the City, I thought, which was good. Or maybe she was independently wealthy and talented, which was even better for her. In any case, I still liked her, and she was still being friendly. On Broadway she gave me her phone number, and I gave her my e-mail address, and we agreed to have lunch or something someday. We said goodbye, and just as she walked toward Zabar's, she turned her blond head and smiled again. I was feeling pretty good myself. I bought a bar of chocolate on the way home.

10   As soon as I walked into my apartment, I washed my dishes from last night and picked up the few things that shouldn't be on the floor but were. It was Sunday, and I almost called my parents in Texas—it was cheaper on Sundays—but then I decided to wait until night. I'd have that little something to end my weekend, and calling them usually made me happy because they were in love with each other and never really bothered me about my life in the City. I did some push-ups because I sensed the atrophy in my arms. Sometimes my brain felt like that too, and having a good conversation with a friend usually remedied that terrible encroaching weakness. I suited up for running, which meant black shorts and a thick, oversized navy blue sweatshirt that I loved because it was comfortable. I was ready to kick some pit bull ass.

As I worked up to my pace on Riverside Drive, I first thought about the dark-haired woman who had almost died. Well, not about her exactly, but about what she had taught me about living in the City. I saved performance-artist Becky for the end of my run. It was okay not to have God here. In fact, it was better than okay. It was liberating. I didn't mean it in a drunken sort of way. It was pleasantly free. I could understand that some people needed the Godhead, needed the structure provided by knowing what would happen to them once they died, or needed reasons for the evil acts or accidents that befell them. God was reason and order for many, even though God was often inscrutable. That heavenly world, that world in the beyond, gave meaning to that Ford Explorer's crushing you at the 96th entrance to the Henry Hudson.

But what if you didn't need God anymore? What if you could deal with your attempts to make the world a secure and happy place for you, alongside the unpredictability and chaos and vulnerability of life? I guess if you were hooked on the ultimate meaning of the holy world, this rip-roaring view of life would mean everything you do is okay. Let's start slashing each other with knives, raping your neighbor if you can get away with it, and stealing whatever your arms can carry home. But we have this extreme reaction to the lack of God simply because our minds are accustomed to giving so much power to God in the first place. Without Him, we're lost, but only because we expect so little from us in this world. Get used to a godless world and you depend on yourself more, and you expect more of yourself, and you still know that shit can happen. That way of looking at things seemed to me like a great and dormant freedom coming from my bones, but also like a call to get to work. Time's a wastin'!

I didn't see any pit bulls on the way up to Columbia, and the air seemed suddenly cleaner and crisp. I was having a damn good run. My head seemed clearer too. Okay, so God was outta' here. Where did that leave me? I wasn't panicking, and I wasn't feeling high. I was excited, and yet I was also a little mad at myself. I felt like I had suddenly found myself in the middle of a construction site with my people asleep on the job and the deadline looming. Okay, so I wasn't going to be a great poet or a legendary writer. I wouldn't lead revolutions, and I wouldn't compose extraordinary music. I was only a guy who had just found the world as it was, after throwing our thousands of years of dreams and nightmares to secure my fragile existence. Maybe I was just playing catch-up, and everybody else was already there. Nobody had mentioned it to me. Still, the fresh air stung my cheeks. It was good to feel the pain a bit. It was good to want to turn the page to the next part of your story. Let's pick up the pace and get a move on. That girl who whizzed by me in black spandex had such a nice ass.

Immediately I started thinking about Becky the blond. Enough of this God-business. I'd sort it out one burst at a time. Sure, I wanted to sleep with her. If it didn't happen, it didn't happen. But I would give it a shot. I wasn't looking for a one-night stand, but I was lonely. I was open to a sexual friendship, and maybe more. We would just have to see what happened. Maybe she had just been friendly for its own sake, and yet she had flirted too. It was tough to tell this early in the thing, and I'd call her tomorrow to push it further along. It was never good to wait. She'd become another unfulfilled dream, perfect because it's far away. She'd get mad at you and move on. She, or you, might disappear into thin air, just like that. Anything could happen in the City.

15 After playing phone tag for a few days, we agreed to have dinner on Friday. Dinner and maybe a movie. Becky sounded happy to have heard from me so soon, and our conversation gave me the impression that she was pretty busy for not being busy at all. I liked that. She was negotiating a contract for something or other, she had a rehearsal, and she was also traveling upstate to participate in a workshop and seminar. More than anything else, I got the

impression that she was smart and active. I really liked that. I thought that maybe my initial suspicion of her being a fruitcake was way off, and probably a defensive maneuver on my part. There *were* plenty of fruities in the City, committed souls hell-bent on ideas and causes rather than on just living a life, making a few good friends, tasting that perfectly toasted sesame bagel. An obsession with ideas had often fucked us up, and the God-idea was only the first among many such disasters. It was better to keep an idea at bay, to use it as a tool, to criticize it and laugh at it once in a while. What was the point of substituting your mind for the real world? So Becky seemed scrappy and practical, and had already taught me a lesson about not jumping to conclusions. I had my own idea prejudices to fight against after all.

The other thing I liked about our phone conversation was her voice. She really had a sexy voice. I hadn't noticed it in the drug-store, probably because my eyes had taken over my mind's focus then. But on the phone I had just her voice in front of me, as it were. It was first an absolutely clear voice. I'm a little hard of hearing, especially the lower tones, so it's kind of important to me. I had already had a girlfriend in college who mumbled just the slightest bit, and in a low voice. I'd spend half the day asking her to repeat herself and feeling like a stupid invalid. Even when I asked her to speak up because of my hearing problem, she wouldn't really. She always thought I was admonishing her or something. We lasted just short of three semesters, and then she flew off to San Francisco to become a mumbling oncologist.

Not only was Becky's voice clear, but it was also the slightest bit squeaky, in a singsong way. I knew some girls created this affected, come-hither squeak to sound pretty for the guys. That sorority squeak. But Becky's squeak was nothing like that at all. It was sort of a natural squeak, if that makes any sense. It was a soft squeak at the end of a sentence, a squeak and a pause and a rhythm that seemed unique to her and also perfect. We could've easily gone for another hour about her rehearsal or my latest project in Philadelphia, but it was already ten o'clock. I hadn't eaten dinner yet. And yet her words and cadence had mesmerized me after a long day at work. It was a good feeling.

I was feeling a little lonely again Thursday night, so I took another walk around the Upper Westside. Walking at night is nothing like walking during the day. I feel excited when I see all the life on the street at night. During the day, the crowd in front of me just walks too slowly. At night, there is time to kill, time to think, a possibly adventurous and even dangerous time. In the morning or when I come home from work, my mind focuses on tasks-to-be-done. Nighttimes and weekends—there really should be more of them.

I've been in the City for years, and I still love seeing the lights at night. They don't even have to be lights from a skyscraper or anything. Brownstone lights are just as good, or even better. The lights of grocery stores or cafés. The lights in pre-war buildings that seem more yellowish and soft. In fact, one of my favorite lights is from an old block-long apartment building on Broadway. The apartment's on the first floor, and all the windows are covered with old newspapers and magazines. Real newsprint light. It's been that way for years, ever since I first saw it. Someone does live there. I have occasionally seen a shadow gently walk across the yellowish light and sit down—maybe an old New Yorker who knows she can do whatever the hell she wants with her windows. I don't know if I'll be here that long.

20   On Amsterdam, I started thinking about God again. Or the lack of God. What kind of life was left here on the street, in my home, without the mean-ingfulness of the Holy, or its counterparts like Linear Progress, Eternal Life, and Ultimate Victory? I had my life here, with its fragility up front, its occa-sional power, random possibilities around it like flies circling shit, and this ves-sel of desires and thoughts that was my self. A sort of self, who's here and not here, who stood apart from this beautiful woman strolling with her little white dog, who was made by her when she offered me the slightest of smiles. I felt like dancing, but I didn't know why. Maybe Fred Astaire was left, or the *desire* to be Fred Astaire. But I really wasn't that good of a dancer.

No, I thought, what was left after God was something else. At least for me. It could, and probably would, be different for each person. You'd have to take that road and understand yourself in the way that you would, that certain cold-ness in the air that was beyond the work of winter. What was left for me was first a little fear that I was walking without any protection anymore, that I was walk-ing without a net under me. I really did feel like a reckless trapeze artist. I still *hoped* I wouldn't be hit by lightning or run over by those god-awful cabbies. But I knew this hope was my doing, and only my own. It was like a beer for my mind to make me brave about walking naked outside. I really was naked in a way now.

But the next thing that occurred to me, as I crossed over to Broadway on 79th Street, was that nothing terrible had yet happened. I mean, I did stop at the stoplights, even though the goddamn cabbies didn't. I had some time here. Sure, anything *could* happen now. I might feel pain at any moment, and it'd just be what happened to me. I wouldn't moralize my suffering anymore. But if I watched my back and looked where the hell I was going, probably noth-ing painful would happen. It could, but it probably wouldn't. With just a bit of luck, there was this time to do something. My brief, or not-so-brief, life. No heaven afterward. No becoming a giant panda later. No starship to take me away. My life, period.

So I thought, what was left after God were the days of my life. A few days, many days, let's keep our fingers crossed and say many years. My life would end, and that would be that. And yet I still had my days, and nights. I'd be remembered, or not, by what I did during my days. I might be remembered for what I did, my work. Maybe my family would remember me, my kids. Maybe my friends. If I had been a shit during most of my days, that's proba-bly what I would pass on: life is shit, and some people crack quickly and give out as much shit as they get. Look, I didn't resolve then and there to be a saint. Why create another stupid ideal that's unnatural, unattainable, and self-destructive? But I knew I could be much better. That's when I started think-ing that maybe I shouldn't be in the City.

You see, I have a temper. Everybody's different and responds to different environments differently. I'm the type who gets a little too worked up when the delivery guy on a bike, swinging a monstrous chain around his neck, just misses my liver by a few inches as he weaves up the sidewalk with his dumplings. Actually, that kind of stuff used to bother me much more, and now I just get out of his way and wish the marauder a slow and painful death. In New York, you yell at someone, and you're liable to be shot. *Everybody* here will call your bluff. So it's better to move along and live for another day.

25   So I thought that maybe I shouldn't be in the City. This environment aggravated a character like mine, or at least it forced me to use a lot of energy to counteract myself in the desire to function well in the battle zone. But change the environment, and maybe I could do something more fulfilling than getting by during my days. Yes, these days. Now, in my mind, they were all I had. Really, I don't blame New York at all. It is what it is. Too many rats in too small a box. Some of these rats really liked it that way. Maybe this rat wanted to try something else.

Becky. Becky. Becky. It was Friday, and I was meeting her at Isabella's. It was a little fancy for a first date, but what the hell. I was feeling pretty good about my days. I hadn't done anything about my future yet, but I did feel good. Becky was right on time, and we got a small table by the windows. I could see the castle-like red stone facade of the American Natural History Museum and decided then and there to check out the dinosaur exhibit that weekend. I had really liked Pteranodon and Deinonychus in Texas, as a kid. Becky was being super-nice, and she was wearing a long wool skirt that was sexy because it tugged at her hips in just the right way. Under her black leather jacket, she had on this vest and crisp white shirt that kind of lured me in by showing enough, but not too much. Where the hell did I ever get the impression she was a fruitcake? I can be an idiot sometimes.

She told me she lived a few blocks away. Actually, she lived in that big apartment building with the newspapers on the first-floor windows. She was a born New Yorker and had lived her entire life on the Upper Westside, except of course during college, when she had lived in Boston. She had inherited her rent-controlled two-bedroom (with twelve-foot ceilings and a marble fireplace!) from her mother, who had moved to Sanibel, Florida, years ago. Becky wasn't rich or anything, but I got the sense that she had a modest income from a trust fund or the like. I told her about growing up in the desert of West Texas, around cotton fields and combines and cattle guards. I told her about going to school in Austin and swimming naked in the Brazos River. I didn't mention my obsessive love of genuine pit barbecue because I didn't want to provoke her if she didn't like meat that much. Hey, if I had been born and raised in New York City, I probably wouldn't like barbecue either. It was generous to call the stuff they served here "meat." I also told her how a chance glance at a recruitment letter on a bulletin board had metamorphosed into the better part of a decade in the City.

Becky really had a sweet laugh. When she laughed, her blond hair would dance around her head. It was very festive looking. When I told her some of the stupid things I'd done as a kid, and the more recent stupid things I'd done as an adult, her laugh would tumble out, and she would smile this tight little smile, as if catching herself from going too far. Yet her eyes would shine mischievously, as if the laughter continued inside her head, rolling and rolling. The room started to get quiet even though it was packed, she started to tease me just a bit and one-up me with horror tales from her past and time slipped away into the cold night outside like the steam heat from the street gutters. We had both stumbled onto a really good time.

We were nearing the end of our main course, and I was imagining dessert, when I did something a little rash. We had been thinking of a movie, but the night had only gotten colder outside. I could feel the chilly breeze whip around my ankles as it slipped through the cracks of the white window doors next to us. Really, I thought, I'd rather spend more time with her than simply looking at a movie screen in adjacent seats in the dark. I really wanted to hold her, that's all. Strangely enough, it wasn't a horny feeling. I was cold, and I wanted to hold her, and I thought she might share the thought. It wasn't yet love, I knew that. It was more like wanting warmth and a little attention, and finding someone across the table who got along with you and who was pretty good-looking. I thought about my days too. So I reached across the table, and told her I really appreciated her company, and kissed her hand.

30   At first, for a second or two, Becky seemed stunned, and she blushed just the slightest bit. Then, immediately, her blue-gray eyes searched my own like lasers seeking the truth, whatever this obscure thing was. I was trying to look harmless, just trying to communicate that I simply liked being with her, which was exactly what I meant—nothing more, nothing less. Then, after what seemed centuries gone by, she squeezed my hand and said she enjoyed being with me too. I really didn't know where we were anymore. It seemed as if we had suddenly gotten lost together.

She asked me if I was cold too. I said that I was. I said I liked holding her hands because they were so warm, and they were. It was as if she had a little heater inside her body. Dessert came, and we were drinking hot coffee. She asked if I still wanted to see a movie. "Still" was exactly the word she used too. She wasn't exactly smiling, and yet her eyes gleamed. I was really lost now, and for some reason I felt a fluttering in my chest, as if a sparrow had gotten stuck in my chest cavity. Maybe I was having a heart attack, I thought. It was cold and also suddenly hot in that restaurant. I told her I'd be open to her suggestions. I really couldn't think of anything else to say, and I thought I stammered. How about renting a video and going back to her place and starting up her fireplace? That sounded like a really good idea, I said. The sparrow seemed stuck in my throat now, but I did manage a smile. My mind was blank, and I at once thought I was a passenger on a boat mysteriously guiding itself through a dense and dark jungle.

We rented the video, but I don't really remember what it was anymore. Most movies are not that memorable. They're meant to waste your time, and that's not a bad thing to do once in a while. But it'd be better if you had just a few movies every year that would really challenge the culture instead of just reciting acceptable platitudes under the guise of being serious. I guess they have to sell whatever they make, and therein lies the problem. The other reason I didn't focus on the video was that I was listening to a really good story Becky was telling me about her most recent performance. It was a piece that included her own music, a poem by Li-Young Lee, and some "interpretive movement" about the destruction and creation of life between men and women. To tell you the truth, I didn't understand everything she said. I don't think she was making it up. I think she knew what she was talking about, and was earnest about it. It just wasn't my language yet. I'd have to read the poem and see her performance and think about it, and then I might understand what she was trying to do. Anyway, her talk about her work was better than any goddamn movie, and it almost prompted me to ask her what she thought about a godless world, and your days in it, but I didn't. We were soon at her apartment.

The tiny black elevator with the accordion door creaked and groaned as it jiggled upward to the sixth floor. The hallways were long and spooky even though bright brass lamps glowed every few feet. This building was old and, I guess, had once been luxurious. My own building really had a completely different feel. Modern, yuppie, clean. I sometimes found it charmless. No dead souls behind its walls. Becky's building, however, teemed with ghosts, it seemed. I immediately thought of "The Cask of Amontillado," and the body or bodies I might find behind this white plaster. Poe had actually lived not far from here, on 84th Street. Maybe if I hung around the hallway for a while, I might spot an old woman, one eye askew, clutching a butcher knife, a trowel, and half-smiling at me.

Inside Becky's apartment, I was surprised again. My bit of excitement at the hallway gloom transformed into a feeling of comfort at the quiet inside. It was quiet and warm. I hardly felt like I was in the City anymore. On one wall of her living room were these old wooden shelves with glass doors and shiny brass locks. Behind the glass were dozens of books, odd figurines, the foot-long jaw of an animal, ornate metal and wooden boxes, and a squar, bejeweled vase that probably housed an evil genie. I felt like quizzing her about the origin of each of these items, like an anthropologist, but left that for another day. I sat on one side of an L-shaped sofa, a beige brocade from another time and place too, and tried to take in more of this musty, odd labyrinth I had stepped into. Amid this museum were things like a digital answering machine and a monstrous color TV buffered by minispeakers. Becky said she'd make popcorn and hot chocolate. In the kitchen, too, I noticed this old-new coexistence. An old-fashioned milk pail sprouting tiny purple flowers. Shiny copper vats hanging from a grid in the ceiling. A pristine white microwave, its clock glowing a soft neon green. I helped her bring the hot chocolate to the living room, and we settled into her couch, next to each other, in front of the humongous tube.

35   It was right at the beginning of the movie, when we stopped chatting about the actors in it, when Becky gave me another mischievous smile. Her mind was rolling again, but we hadn't been talking about anything funny. I reached out

and held her hand. She put her hand around my waist and kissed me. And I kissed her. It was really the most delicious of kisses. Wet, but not slimy. Our lips playing off each other so easily. A sort of rhythm building up, like a crescendo, and dropping off to stoke our desire. Becky became much more beautiful to me when I kissed her. What she could do and what I felt seemed to flash over me like a new kind of light that transformed what I saw in front of me. I touched her face and stroked her shoulders and gently rubbed her legs as if to confirm this strange and wonderful metamorphosis. This was the same face, and yet it wasn't. Her body had been pretty, but now when I touched it, when she let me touch it, it seemed I was touching a star exploding alone in the abyss of the universe. I was short of breath, and it wasn't simply because I was excited to be with her. The hard reality of this City, this black pavement, seemed suddenly alive like skin. I was crashing through this surface into—what?—the vibration of life. It was better than walking down Broadway at night, the cold on your checks. It was like walking, and then levitating into the lights.

Helena María Viramontes

See the biographical headnote of Viramontes on page 157.

Neighbors

I

Aura Rodriguez always stayed within her perimeters, both personal and otherwise, and expected the same of her neighbors. She was quite aware that the neighborhood had slowly metamorphosed into a graveyard. People of her age died off only to leave their grandchildren with little knowledge of struggle. As a result, the children gathered near her home in small groups to drink, to lose themselves in the abyss of defeat, to find temporary solace among each other. She shared the same streets and corner stores and midnights with these tough-minded young men who threw empty beer cans into her yard; but once within her own solitude, surrounded by a tall wrought-iron fence, she belonged to a different time. Like those who barricaded themselves against an incomprehensible generation, Aura had resigned herself to live with the caution and silence of an apparition, as she had lived for the past seventy-three years, asking no questions, assured of no want, no deep-hearted yearning other than to live out the remainder of her years without hurting anyone, including herself.

And so it came as no surprise that when a woman appeared on a day much like every day, Aura continued sweeping her porch, oblivious to what her neighbors had stopped in mid-motion to watch.

The massive woman with a vacuous hole of a mouth entered Bixby Street, a distinct scent accompanying her. She was barefooted and her feet, which were cracked, dirty, and encrusted with dry blood, were impossible to imagine once babysmall and soft. The woman carried her belongings in two soiled brown bags. Her mouth caved into a smile as the neighbors watched her black, cotton wig flop to one side. They stared at her huge breasts sagging like sacks of sand and wobbling with every limp. Mrs. García pinched her nose as the woman passed, and Toastie, washing his candied-apple red Impala, threatened to hose her down. Aura stopped sweeping her porch and leaned on her broomstick, not to stare at the woman's badly mended dress or her wig that glistened with caked hairspray, but to watch the confident direction she took, unmoved by the taunts and stares. Aura did something she had not done in a while: she smiled. However, when the woman stopped at her gate, Aura's smile evaporated. Haphazardly, the woman placed one bag down in order to scratch beneath her wig.

"Doña Aura Rodríguez," she said finally, her toothless mouth collapsing with each word, making it difficult for Aura to understand. "Where is Señor Macario Fierro de Ortega? Where is he?"

5   Macario Fierro de Ortega? Aura repeated the name as she stepped down her porch steps hesitantly, dragging the broom behind her. Fierro had lived behind her house for nearly thirty years, but she had never known his full name. Perhaps she was not referring to *her* Fierro.

"Señor Macario Fierro de Ortega?" she asked, eyeing the woman suspiciously. Aura knew of at least four ways of describing the smell of neglected flesh, but none seemed adequate to describe what stood in front of her. The woman became nervous under Aura's scrutiny. She began rummaging through her bags like one looking for proof of birth at a border crossing, and found what she had been looking for. Pinching the corner of the matchbook cover, Aura read the barely visible scribbling: 1306 Bixby Street. It was Fierro's address, all right. She returned the matchbook and eyed the woman, all the while debating what to do. The woman was indeed a massive presence, but although she overshadowed Aura's small, delicate frame, the whites of her eyes were as vague as old memories. Hard years had etched her chapped and sunburnt face. It was because of this that Aura finally said:

"In the back," and she pointed to a small weather-worn house. "But he's not home. On Tuesday's they give ten cent lunches at the center." The woman's scent made it unbearable to stand near her for long, and Aura politely stepped back.

"Who cares?" The woman laughed, crumbling the matchbook and tossing it behind her shoulder. "Waiting I know how to do!" She unhinged the gate and limped into Aura's yard, her scent following like a cloud of dust.

Aura was confused as she returned to her house. Her memory swelled with old stories which began with similar circumstances, and she began to worry about being duped. As she opened the door to a cluttered room, one thing struck her as strange, so she drew the Venetian blinds and locked the door behind her: how did the woman know her name?

II

10   Dressed in his Saturday sharpest, Chuy finished the last of his beer behind the Paramount Theater before meeting Laura in the balcony, "the dark side."

When he threw the *tall dog* into a huge trash bin, three men jumped the alley wall and attacked him. As they struck at him, he managed to grab a 2 by 4 which was holding the trash lid open, but it was no match for the switchblade which ripped through his chest. Chuy was nineteen when Fierro identified the body. He slowly pried the 2 by 4 from his son's almost womanly slender fingers and carried the blood-stained plank of wood home with him. Years and years later, as his legs grew as feeble as his mind, he took the 2 by 4 from his closet and sat on Aura's porch, whittling a cane for himself and murmuring to his son as she watered her beloved rose bushes, chinaberry tree, and gardenias.

The neighbors, of course, thought him crazy. Pabla from across the street insisted that talking to a dead son was an indication of senility. But others swore on their grandmother's grave that he or she saw Chuy sitting on Aura's porch, combing his hair "the way they used to comb it then." Although each aired their opinion of Fierro's son while waiting in the checkout line at the First Street Store, everyone agreed on one thing: Fierro was strangely touched. The fact that no one, not even the elderly Castillos could remember his first name, added to the mystery of the man. The butcher with the gold tooth, the priest at the Virgen de Guadalupe Church, and the clerk who collected the money for his Tuesday ten cent lunch addressed him as Don Fierro, but behind his back everyone shook their head with pity.

All the neighbors that is, except Aura. Throughout the years of sharing the same front gate, a silent bond between the two sprouted and grew firmer and deeper with time. As a result, he alone was allowed to sit on her porch swing as he whittled. With sad sagging eyes and whiskey breath he described for hours his mother's face and the scent of wine grapes just before harvest. He often cried afterwards and returned home in quiet shame, closing his door discreetly. Aura would continue her watering into the evening, until she saw the light in his kitchen flick on. Then she was sure that he was now sober enough to fix himself something to eat. Not until he had finished whittling the cane did he stop sitting on Aura's porch.

With the help of his cane, Fierro walked home from the Senior Citizen Center Luncheon. He coughed up some phlegm, then spit it out in disgust. Eating was no longer a pleasure for him; it was as distasteful as age. The pale, saltless vegetables, the crumbling beef and the warm milk were enough to make any man vomit. Whatever happened to the real food, the beans with cheese and onions and chile, the flour tortillas? Once again he did what he had done every Tuesday for the last five years: he cursed himself for having thrown away priceless time.

He walked with great difficulty and when he reached the freeway on-ramp crossing, he paused to catch his breath. The cars and trucks and motorcycles, in their madness to reach an unknown destination, flung past him onto the freeway causing his green unbuttoned vest to flap open. With his free hand he held the rim of his grey fedora. Fierro slowly began his trek across the on-ramp while the truckers honked impatiently.

15   "Cabrones!" he yelled, waving his cane indignantly, "I hope you live to be my age!" And he continued his walk, turning off his hearing aid so that the

sounds in his head were not the sirens or motors or horns, but the sounds of a seashell pressed tightly against his ear. When he finally reached the freeway overpass, he stood there, listening to the absence of sound.

"Fierro, Don Fierro!" A young woman and her daughter stood in front of him. He saw the young child retreat behind her mother's skirt, frightened by the ancient face. "Don Fierro, are you all right?" The woman shouted over her grocery bag and into his ear. He remembered to turn on his hearing aid, and when he did, he heard her ask, "Are you all right?!"

"Heartaches," he said finally, shaking his head. "Incurable. It's a cancer that lays dormant only to surprise you when you least expect it."

"What could it be?" the young woman asked as she went into her bag and busted a chip of chicharrón. Loosening her grip on her mother's apron, the child took the chicharrón and chewed loudly, sucking the fat.

"Memories," Fierro said.

20   He heard the sirens again, the swift traffic whirling by beneath him. He was suddenly amazed how things had changed and how easy it would be to forget that there were once quiet hills here, hills that he roamed in until they were flattened into vacant lots where dirt paths became streets and houses became homes. Then the government letter arrived and everyone was forced to uproot, one by one, leaving behind rows and rows of wooden houses that creaked with swollen age. He remembered realizing, as he watched the carelessness with which the company men tore into the shabby homes with clawing efficiency, that it was easy for them to demolish some twenty, thirty, forty years of memories within a matter of months. As if that weren't enough, huge pits were dug up to make sure that no roots were left. The endless freeway paved over his sacred ruins, his secrets, his graves, his fertile soil in which all memories were seeded and waiting for the right time to flower, and he could do nothing.

He could stand right where he was standing now and say to himself, here was where the Paramount Theater stood, and over there I bought snow cones for the kids, here was where Chuy was stabbed, over there the citrus orchards grew. He knew it would never be the same again, never, and his greatest fear in life, greater than his fear of death or of not receiving his social security check, was that he would forget so much that he would not know whether it was like that in the first place, or whether he had made it up, or whether he had made it up so well that he began to believe it was true. He looked down at the child munching on the last of the chicharrón. I remember when you were that age, he wanted to say to the woman, but he was not sure anymore, he was not sure if he did. With his swollen, blotched hands, he tipped his grey fedora, then patted her hands softly.

"I'll be just fine," he reassured her, taking a last look at the child. "It's Tuesday," he said finally, and turning off his hearing aid once again, he prepared himself for the long walk across the ruins that still danced with Chuy's ghost.

III

When she heard the gate open, Aura's first impulse was to warn Fierro of the woman who had been sitting on his porch for the last two hours. But since she respected him too much to meddle in his affairs, she went to the back room of her house and did something else she hadn't done in a long time: she peaked through her washroom window.

Contrary to her expectations, Fierro was not at all bewildered or surprised. He stood there, leaning on his cane while the woman rose from the porch with difficulty. They exchanged a few words. When Aura saw Fierro dig into his pocket, it infuriated her to think that the woman had come for money. But instead of producing his wallet, he brought out his keys and opened the door. The woman entered majestically while a pigeon on his porch awning cooed at her arrival.

IV

25   There was a group of pigeons on Fierro's awning by morning, and it was the cooing and not the knock that awoke her. Aura finally sat up, the familiar ache of her swollen feet pulsating, and with one twisted finger guided a Ben Gay-scented house slipper onto each foot. She leaned against the wall as she walked to the door, her bones, joints, and muscles of her legs and feet throbbing under the weight of her body. By the time she got to the door, no one was there. Aura retreated to her room, leaning from chair to table, from couch to wall. Her legs folded under her as she collapsed on the bed.

By the evening, she had tried almost everything to rid herself of the pain and her lips were parched with bitterness. Miserable and cornered, she began cursing her body, herself for such weakness. She slept little, rocking her head helplessly against the pillow as the pain continued to crawl up and down her body. She began to hate. She hated her body, the ticking of the hen-shaped clock which hung above the stove or the way the dogs howled at the police sirens. She hated the way her fingers distorted her hand so that she could not even grasp a glass of water. But most of all she hated the *laughter and the loud music* which came from the boys who stood around the candied-apple red Impala with the tape deck on full blast. They laughed and drank and threw beer cans in her yard while she burned with fever. The pain finally made her so desperate with intolerance, that she struggled to her porch steps, tears moistening her eyes, and pleaded with the boys.

"Por favor," she said, her feeble plea easily swallowed up by the blast of an oldie. "Don't you have homes?"

"What?" Toastie asked, not moving from where he stood.

"Go home," she pleaded, leaning against a porch pillar, her legs folding under her. "Go home. Go home."

30   "We *are* home!" Rubén said while opening another malt liquor. The others began to laugh. She held herself up because the laughter echoed in her head and she refused to be mocked by these little men who knew nothing of life and respect. But she slipped and fell and they continued to laugh. It was their laughter at her inability to even stand on her own two feet that made her call the police.

She raged with fever and revenge, waiting for the police to arrive. She tipped the slats of the Venetian blinds to watch the boys standing in a circle passing a joint, each savoring the sweet taste of the marihuana cigarette as they inhaled. She remembered Toastie as a child. She had even witnessed his baptism, but now he stood tall and she wondered where he had learned to laugh so cruelly. She lowered her head. The world was getting too confusing now, so that you even had to call the police in order to get some kindness from your neighbors.

Her feeling of revenge had overcome her pain momentarily, but when the police arrived, she fully realized her mistake. The five cars zeroed in on their target, halting like tanks in a cartoon. The police jumped out in military formation, ready for combat. The neighbors began emerging from behind their doors and fences to watch the red lights flashing against the policemen's batons. When the boys were lined up, spreadeagled for the search, Toastie made a run for it, leaping over Aura's wroughtiron fence and falling hard on a rose bush. His face scratched and bleeding, he ran towards her door, and for a moment Aura was sure he wanted to kill her. It was not until he lunged for the door that she was able to see the desperation and confusion, the fear in his eyes, and he screamed at the top of his lungs while pounding on her door, the *vowels* of the one word melting into a howl, he screamed to her, "Pleeeeeeease."

He pounded on the door, please. She pressed her hands against her ears until his howl was abruptly silenced by a dull thud. When the two policemen dragged him down the porch steps, she could hear the creak of their thick leather belts rubbing against their bullets. She began to cry.

It was not until way into the night, after she locked each window, each door, after her neighbors had retreated behind their T.V.s leaving her alone once again, that she remembered the last thing Rubén yelled as the patrol cars drove off, the last words he said as he struggled with the handcuffs.

35   "We'll get you," he said. "You'll see."

V

For several days the brooding clouds began to form into animal and plant shapes until they finally burst, pelting her windows with rain. Fearful of her light bulbs attracting lightning, she turned them off and was content to sit in the dark next to the stove while the gas burners flickered blue and yellow fire upon the wall. She sat there quietly with a quilt over her shoulders, her shadow a wavering outline of a woman intimidated by natural forces. Aura sat and listened to the monotony of seconds, the thunderclaps, the pelting against her windows. It was only after the rain had subsided that a faint nasal melody playing against a rusty needle penetrated her darkness and she cocked her head to listen. Aura carried her chair to the washroom window. She seated herself, pulled up the Venetian blind slats and sought the source of the music.

The music was faint, barely an audible tune, but she recognized it just the same. She pressed her face against the coldness of the window glass and tried to remember why the song seemed so familiar. The Hallmark dance floor. She remembered the Hallmark dance floor and smiled. The toilet tank had been broken, and for a few dollars, plus tips, she was hired to fill buckets of water and pour them in the tank after every flush. She was 13 years old and the manager, a round stout man who wore a bulky gold diamond ring on his small finger, warned her against peeking out the door. She remembered sitting next to the sinks with her buckets full, tapping her feet to the rhythm of the music, as she did now, listening intently. And she imagined, as she imagined then, the prism ball encircling the couples with pieces of diamond specks. She recalled the glitter, the laughter, conversations, the thick level of cigarette smoke which hovered over the dancers so that it seemed they were dancing in clouds. It was nice to hear the laughter again, and mist collected on the window from her slow breathing. As night filtered in, Aura made out a silhouette against the shade of Fierro's room, and she recognized the massive shape immediately. The woman was dancing, slow lazy movements like those of a Sunday summer breeze teasing a field of tall grass. She held a scarf and slowly manipulated it as though it were a serpent. Fierro was laughing. The laugh was an unfamiliar sound to Aura's ears, as if a screw had loosened somewhere inside his body and began to rattle. But he continued to laugh a laugh that came from deep within and surfaced to express a genuine enjoyment of living.

Aura felt like an intruder, peering into their bedroom window and witnessing their intimacy. Although she hated herself for spying, she could not pry herself away from the window, away from the intimacies, away from the tune she had buried so far down that she had forgotten its existence. She listened way into the night, keeping the rhythm of the music with her foot, until the record finished with a scratch and Aura went to bed, cold under the bleached, white sheets.

VI

Aura was in the mood to dance, to loosen her inhibitions from the tight confines of shoes and explore a barefoot freedom she had never experienced in her wakeful hours. But she awoke to stare at her feet, to inspect the swelling, to let reality slowly sink in, and she was thankful and quite satisfied simply to be able to walk.

She dressed slowly because she felt weak and uneasy, and at first attributed the hollowness of her stomach to the medication she had taken throughout those endless nights. But when she lifted the blinds to the washroom window and saw the woman standing barefoot on the porch, tossing bread crumbs to the pigeons while her bracelets clinked with every toss, Aura knew it was not the medication. She watched the woman scratch beneath her huge breasts while she yawned, then turn towards the door, closing it with a loud slam. Aura's heart sank like an anchor into an ocean of silence. She drew the blinds quietly.

In the kitchen Aura flipped up the lid of the coffee can, spooned the grinds into the percolator, dropped in a stick of cinnamon and put the pot to boil. When the coffee was done, she poured herself a cup. It was bitter, and the more she thought about the woman, the more bitter the coffee became. She heard the children of Bixby Street, who were especially happy to see the storm pass. Having been imprisoned by the rains, they were now freed from behind their doors and allowed to run the streets under the bright sun. Aura heard their shouts, their laughter, and she yearned to feel right again.

She collected a sunbonnet, gloves and garden tools. Since the rainfall had soaked the soil, she could not pass up the opportunity to weed out her garden, and even though her movements were sluggish, she prepared herself for a day's work.

Once outside and under the bright sun, Aura was blinded for a moment. She bit her fist in disbelief. Most of the graffiti was sprayed on her front porch with black paint, but some of it was written with excrement. As she slowly stepped down, she inspected the windows, steps, walkway, pillars, all defaced with placas, symbols, vulgarities. She rushed over the chayote vine and made a feeble attempt to replant it, but everything, her flowers, chayotes, gardenias, rose bushes, were uprooted and cast aside. Some of her bushes were twenty years old, having begun as cuttings from her mother's garden. She had spent years guiding and pruning and nurturing them until they blossomed their gratitude. She tried unsuccessfully to restore them, the thorns scratching her face, her bare hands bleeding. When she fell to her knees and began clawing away at the mud in hopes of saving some of her bushes, she failed to notice that the children had stopped their play and stood in front of her yard, their red, puffy faces peering from between her wrought-iron bars. It was their look of bewilderment and pity that made her realize the hopelessness of her actions.

"Leave me alone!" Aura screamed at the children, raising her arms like a menacing bird. "Leave me alone or I'll...," she shouted, and the children scattered in all directions like cockroaches. She stood up, her knees trembling, and took one last look at her plants. All that remained intact was her chinaberry tree. Aura slowly returned to the house, her hands dangling uselessly at her side. "I'm so glad," she thought, fighting back the tears as the mutilated bushes began shriveling under the morning sun, "I'm so glad I'm going to die soon."

45   She closed the door behind her, made sure all the locks were locked, unrolled the Venetian blinds, closed the drapes. She heard Rubén's voice: "We'll get you." Picking up the phone, she decided against calling the police and making another mistake. Fierro? She was totally alone. "We'll get you, you'll see." She would have to take care of herself. She was marked, proof to other neighbors that indeed the "BIXBY BOYS RULE," as they had sprayed the neighborhood in huge bold letters. NO. She refused to be their sacrificial lamb. She shook her head as she got a candlestick out of the linen closet. She pushed the kitchen table aside, grunting under its weight, then rolled up the carpet. She lit the candlestick and opened the cellar door because she refused to be helpless.

Cupping the faint flicker of the candle, she slowly descended into the gut of the cellar, grasping at the spider webs which blocked the way to her destination. She ignored the distorted shadows of the undisturbed furniture, ignored the scent of moistened, decayed years, and moved towards the pile of boxes stacked in the corner. She opened the first box with little difficulty, the motes of dust dancing around her until they settled once again to begin a new accumulation of years. She dug her hands into the box, groping, feeling beneath the objects, kitchen utensils, books, photographs, but found nothing. She threw the box aside and opened another. And another. With each box her anger and desperation rose so that the search became frantic, almost obsessive. Finally, in the last of the boxes, her fingers froze to the cool touch. She blew the dust away and examined it like the foreign object that it was. It felt cold and clumsy in her small hand. Nonetheless, she triumphantly placed the gun in her apron pocket and blew out the last of the candlestick.

VII

As the days passed, Fierro knew little of what went on in the neighborhood. When he heard the sirens and screams and CB radios spitting out messages, he refused to go outside for fear of finding Chuy's body limp and bloody once again. Then, this morning as he turned from his side of the bed to examine the woman's slow breathing, he couldn't imagine what had caused Aura to scream so loudly that it startled him out of a sleepy daze, though he wore no hearing aid. All that Fierro knew was that he awoke one morning to find the warm mass of a woman sleeping beside him and this was enough to silence any curiosity. He also knew never to ask a question if he wasn't prepared for the answer, and so he was content to let her stay for as long as she wanted without even asking he name.

Fierro sat up in bed, rubbed his eyes, palmed his hair back, yawned the last of his sleep away. As though in thoughtful meditation, he allowed his body to slowly return to consciousness, allowed the circulation to drive away the numbness from his limbs. Only then was he ready to make the walk across the room to the bathroom. He winced as he walked on the cold floor, and he took one last look at the woman before he closed the door.

Inside the bathroom, Fierro urinated, washed his hands and face in cool water, inspected the day's growth of beard in the mirror. He rinsed his dentures under running water, then slipped them into his mouth, clacking his jaws twice to make sure they fell securely in place. Not until he had almost finished his shave, did it occur to him that he had been humming. While he stood in front of the mirror, his raspy voice vibrated a tune. A ballroom dancing, nice-smelling women tune. He hummed louder as he shook some Wildroot into his hands and palmed his hair a second time. He combed it into a glossy duck-tail, smoothed his mustache, smiled. He was about to slap on some cologne when Chuy stopped him.

50   "Can I do it," his young son asked eagerly. As he had done every morning, the boy stood on the toilet seat to watch his father's daily shave. He was small and thin, and the crotch of his underwear hung to his knees. "Can I?" Chuy repeated.

The boy had great respect for the daily shave. He would watch his father maneuver the single blade across his cheek with the same admiration he felt watching a performer swallow a sword. But Chuy knew that, unlike sword swallowing, shaving would be accessible if only he studied it with the watchful eye of an apprentice. So it was a ritual each morning to spend the time necessary to stare at the blade, apply the cologne, and touch his own cheek for hair growth.

"Ay, qué M'ijo. ¿Por qué no?" Fierro poked his son's belly with the bottle. He handed it to Chuy, and tugged up his calzones. While the boy shook a few drops onto his palm, Fierro noticed how dirty his son's fingernails were. He would bathe him when he returned home.

"Ready?" Chuy asked. He kept his eyes on the palm of his hand, then when Fierro was close enough, he slapped his father's face as hard as he could. Fierro's exaggerated wince made the boy laugh.

"Now your turn." The boy enjoyed this part of the ritual because his father's scent would be with him all day. Fierro shock the scented rose water onto his cement-burned hand: But time had a way of passing so that the few seconds it took to shake out some of his son's favorite cologne turned into years, and the admiration in the boy's eyes had disappeared.

55   "I'm 19. I think I can do it myself." Fierro felt the rose water dripping through his fingers. It seemed like only yesterday... The bathroom seemed too small now, and they both elbowed one another. Fierro finally won over the mirror, but the defeat did not keep Chuy from trying to catch a glimpse of himself from behind his father's shoulders.

"Where do you think you're going?" Fierro asked, looking at Chuy's reflection, his face threatening a mustache. The answer was automatic:

"Out."

"Don't get smart, Chuy." Fierro was becoming increasingly disturbed that Chuy was running the streets. "Hijo, you're not a dog. You have a home to live, to sleep, to eat in."

"Listen, Jefe," Chuy replied, tired of the same Saturday night dialogue. "I'm old enough to know what I'm doing."

60   "Then why don't you act like it?"

"Shit, Jefe. Lay off for once."

"Qué lay off, ni qué ojo de hacha," Fierro replied angrily. "And don't be using that language with me, you understand?"

There was an icy silence. Chuy combed his hair back. He waited patiently for the right time to break the silence and still save face. Finally:

"Listen, Apá. I'm not going cruising, if that's what you want to know."

65   Fierro thought for a moment. Finally: "Good, mijito. Good. It's just that those chavalos are a bunch of good for nothings. Thieves. Murderers and thieves."

"You forgot tecatos."

"That too."

"They're my friends."

"Bah! Qué friends! Look what they did to the Reyes boy."

70   Chuy bent over to smooth out the creases of his khaki pants, unconcerned by the accusation. When he looked up, he was face to face with his father. Barely whispering he said, "He had it coming to him."

"Do you really, really believe that?" In disbelief he looked into his son's eyes and realized how little he really knew him. How could anyone deserve to be murdered? It grieved him to think that Chuy was no different than the rest. But he was; Chuy, his son, his boy, had a good heart, and that made him different. Bad ways, but a good heart. Chuy defiantly returned his father's stare, until his face broke into a smile.

"Apá," he said, slapping his father on the shoulder, "are you gonna lend me the cologne or what?" He rubbed each shoe against his pant leg. His shoulders were now stooped so that he was no longer taller than his father. "Laura and me, we're gonna go to a movie."

"Ay, qué mi'jo!" Fierro was relieved. Get him out of the neighborhood. That much he knew if he wanted to save his son's good heart. He slapped the cologne on both sides of Chuy's face. "Ay, qué mi'jo. Laura and you!"

The woman pounded on the door.

75   "Got your key, mi'jo? And don't forget to lock the door after…"

"Ay te watcho, Jefito," Chuy interrupted. Taking a last look at his reflection, he winked at his father and was gone.

The woman pounded on the door again and Fierro opened it. She handed him the hearing aid, and after a few adjustments, he was able to hear. As he followed her into the kitchen, he wanted to tell her about Chuy, but once he caught the aroma of the beans, he immediately forgot what he had wanted to say.

The woman grated some cheese, then sprinkled it on the boiling beans. After the cheese had melted, she spooned the beans onto the flour tortillas. Fierro ate the burritos as greedily as the pigeons pecked their crumbs of bread outside. As he licked his fingers, she poured some instant coffee into his tin cup, added some milk and honey. His hands trembled whenever he lifted the cup to his lips, sipping loudly.

"Good," he finally said. "It's all so good," and he reached over the table to touch her hand. As he had done for the past several days, Fierro studied her face, the crevices and creases, the moles and marks, studied those things which distinguish one person from another, in hopes of finding something which would deliver immediate recognition. But in the end, as always, his mind became exhausted, and once again he failed. Beads of perspiration formed on the temples of his forehead, and the room began to circle and circle around him.

80   "Macario!?" the woman asked, but before he could answer, he fainted. Kneeling beside him, she looked around the room in confusion and fear hoping to find something that would revive him and make him well; but all she could do, all she could think of, was to get the dishcloth and place it on his forehead. He began to squirm. Finally, when he was semi-conscious, he whispered to her, his lips feeling heavy and swollen, "Heartaches."

She helped him to the bed, pulling the blankets aside, and he slipped into sleep, smelling her scent in the sheets. He slept for a while, dreaming of watermelons so cool and refreshing to his lips, until the first abdominal cramp hit and he groped around for her hand. He wanted to ask for water, but his lips were swollen and dried and he couldn't speak. He was extremely thirsty and craved melons: crenshaw melons, honeydew melons, cantaloupe melons, watermelons. The woman bathed him in cool water, but the water could not extinguish the burning in his mouth and stomach and a second spasm hit without warning, his whole body cramping into a fetal position. With the onset of the third spasm, the retching began.

The woman became frantic and she paced around and around his bed like a caged lioness. He was dying and she couldn't do anything because he had already made up his mind, and she wrung and wrung her hands in helplessness. When she finally picked up the phone, Fierro, barely able to move, motioned with his finger NO, then pointed to a chair. The hours passed as she sat next to him, rocking herself back and forth, mesmerized in deep prayer.

His lips were parched but his craving for coolness suddenly disappeared. He turned to look at the woman and finally, after some time, finally, recognized her. Before he could say her name again, he felt an avalanche crush his chest and he could no longer breathe. Fierro desperately inhaled in hopes of catching some air, but the more desperate he became, the less he could breathe. In short fits of spasms, his life snapped.

The pillow fell to her feet and she gently lifted his head to replace it. She tried to arouse him, but he lay still, his eyes yellow and dull. She pressed her ear against his chest. There was no breathing, no heart beat, just a faint buzzing sound. The woman shook her head sadly as she slowly reached into his shirt pocket and turned off the hearing aid. She began moaning. At first light and hardly audible, her moaning began to crescendo into high wails of sorrow and disbelief. Shrieking angrily at the God who convinced Fierro to die, the barefooted woman ran out, the screen door slamming behind her.

VIII

85   With her heart beating in a maddening race, Aura sat facing the front door, the gun on her lap. Her sunbonnet still hung limply by the side of her head, and her hands and face were smeared with dry blood and mud. The hours came and went with the ticking of the clock and she waited, cocking the gun whenever she heard car brakes, her fear swelling to her throat, then releasing the trigger and relaxing once the car had spun away.

The summer of the rattlers. The Vizcano desert was far away, yet she could almost feel the rattlers coiled up under the brittle bushes waiting for her. As a child she was frightened by their domination of the desert. If they were disturbed, they struck with such force that it was always too late to do anything. Her grandfather had taught her how to look for them, how to avoid them, and if necessary, how to kill them, but the sight of one always made her immobile because she had no protection against their menacing appearance, their slickness as they slowly slithered to a cooler location, their instinct to survive. And so she never left the house without grandfather; but he was dead and she would be soon if she didn't protect herself. Her eyes grew heavy with sleep but she refused to close them, for the rattlers were out there. Somewhere.

Aura finally dozed, her head falling forward until the loud door slam startled her into wakefulness and she groped around for the gun. She could not keep her body from trembling as she stood up from her chair to listen to the sounds coming from outside. She heard running footsteps, panting, and she felt the sweat dripping between her breasts. Someone was on her porch and she prayed to be left alone. She held the gun high with both hands, squeezing, tightly squeezing it as she aimed at the door.

POETRY

Jack Agüeros

Jack Agüeros was born in East Harlem in New York City in 1934. His collection of short stories, *Dominos and Other Stories from the Puerto Rican* (1993), is considered a classic. He has written several collections of poetry, including *Correspondence Between the Stonehaulers* (1991), *Lord, Is This a Psalm?* (2002, from which the following poem comes), and *Sonnets from the Puerto Rican* (1996) and translated *Song of the Simple Truth: The Complete Poems of Julia De Burgos* (1996). Agüeros has also written for television and served as director of the famous El Museo Del Barrio in East Harlem for nearly ten years.

Psalm for *Coquito*

Lord, it was Christmas time,
and I was drinking homemade
Coquito,
a nog with coconut milk and rum,
5   condensed and evaporated milk and rum,
cloves, eggs, more rum, nutmeg, cinnamon
and a little more rum,
and I was reading the daily newspapers.

I read Exxon and Mobil had merged
10   proudly firing thousands of people
and expunging the word "oligarchy"
from the dictionary.
I thought Olivetti made typewriters
but I read it was really in optical fibers,
15   and a German bank was buying an

American bank, even though the
American bank was being sued
sor stealing money from Jews
during the Holocaust.
20 The old Philadelphia Car Battery Company
and Campbell's Soup and Heinz Ketchup
had reorganized and were now making
hostile intercontinental ballistic missiles.

Lord, my mistake was not in drinking the rum,
25 my mistake was reading the newspapers,
because that night, Lord, I had a dream
that our national motto was now
"Where's Mine?"
and that a dark-skinned family was evicted
30 from a manger in the South Bronx
and the brilliantly named
Department of Wealth Acquisition
sent them to the only Municipal Shelter
where there were no beds or blankets
35 but José got Prozac,
María got Methadone,
and Baby Jesus got scolded for not having a job yet.

Lorna Dee Cervantes

Frequently seen as a leading voice in Chicana poetry, Lorna Dee Cervantes has
written several collections of poetry, including the major work *Emplumada*
(1981), winner of the 1982 American Book Award, and *From the Cables of Geno-
cide: Poems on Love and Hunger* (1991). Cervantes's work has been extensively
anthologized, and her poems are the subject of academic scholarship in numerous forums. She was born on August 6, 1954, in San Francisco, California, of
Mexican and Chumash Indian ancestry. She now teaches creative writing at the
University of Colorado, Boulder. Her activist background during the 1960s and
early 1970s informs her powerful and lyrical poetry.

Freeway 280

Las casitas[1] near the gray cannery,
nestled amid wild abrazos of climbing roses
and man-high red geraniums
are gone now. The freeway conceals it
5 all beneath a raised scar.

But under the fake windsounds of the open lanes,
in the abandoned lots below, new grasses sprout,

---

[1]little houses

wild mustard remembers, old gardens
come back stronger than they were,
10   trees have been left standing in their yards.
Albaricoqueros, cerezos, nogales…
Viejitas[2] come here with paper bags to gather greens.
Espinaca, verdolagas, yerbabuena…

I scramble over the wire fence
15   that would have kept me out.
Once, I wanted out, wanted the rigid lanes
to take me to a place without sun,
without the smell of tomatoes burning
on swing shift in the greasy summer air.

20   Maybe it's here
en los campos extraños de esta ciudad[3]
where I'll find it, that part of me
mown under
like a corpse
25   or a loose seed.

Beneath the Shadow of the Freeway

1
Across the street—the freeway,
blind worm, wrapping the valley up
from Los Altos to Sal Si Puedes.
I watched it from my porch
5   unwinding. Every day at dusk
as Grandma watered geraniums
the shadow of the freeway lengthened.

2
We were a woman family:
Grandma, our innocent Queen;
10   Mama, the Swift Knight, Fearless Warrior.
Mama wanted to be Princess instead.
I know that. Even now she dreams of taffeta
and foot-high tiaras.

Myself: I could never decide.
15   So I turned to books, those staunch, upright men.
I became Scribe: Translator of Foreign Mail,
interpreting letters from the government, notices
of dissolved marriages and Welfare stipulations.
I paid the bills, did light man-work, fixed faucets,

---

[2]old ladies
[3]in the strange foreign fields of this city

20   insured everything
      against all leaks.

      3
      Before rain I notice seagulls.   *Organized*
      They walk in flocks,   *chaos*
      cautious across lawns: splayed toes,
25   indecisive beaks. Grandma says
      seagulls mean storm.

      In California in the summer,
      mockingbirds sing all night.   *Loyalty*
      Grandma says they are singing for their nesting wives.
30   "They don't leave their families
      borrachando."
          "Drunkard"
      She likes the ways of birds,
      respects how they show themselves
      for toast and a whistle.

35   She believes in myths and birds.
      She trusts only what she builds
      with her own hands.   *self-accountability*

      4
      She built her house,
      cocky, disheveled carpentry,
40   after living twenty-five years
      with a man who tried to kill her.

      Grandma, from the hills of Santa Barbara,
      I would open my eyes to see her stir mush
      in the morning, her hair in loose braids,
45   tucked close around her head
      with a yellow scarf.

      Mama said, "It's her own fault,   *Blaming*
      getting screwed by a man for that long.   *weakness/*
      Sure as shit wasn't hard."   *ignorance*
50   soft she was soft

      5
      in the night I would hear it
      glass bottles shattering the street
      words cracked into shrill screams
      inside my throat a cold fear
55   as it entered the house in hard
      unsteady steps stopping at my door
      my name bathrobe slippers
      outside a 3 A.M. mist heavy

60 as a breath full of whiskey
stop it go home|come inside
mama if he comes here again
I'll call the police

inside
a gray kitten a touchstone
65 purring beneath the quilts
grandma stitched
from his suits
the patchwork singing
of mockingbirds

6
70 "You're too soft...always were.
You'll get nothing but shit.
Baby, don't count on nobody."
—a mother's wisdom.
Soft. I haven't changed,
75 maybe grown more silent, cynical
on the outside.

"O Mama, with what's inside of me
I could wash that all away. I could."

"But Mama, if you're good to them
80 they'll be good to you back."

Back. The freeway is across the street.
It's summer now. Every night I sleep with a gentle man
to the hymn of mockingbirds,

and in time, I plant geraniums.
85 I tie up my hair into loose braids,
and trust only what I have built
with my own hands.

Victor Hernández Cruz

See the biographical headnote of Cruz on page 100.

Their Poem

Pat
China
& Rosa
all walking
5 down the street
with carriages

the babies
hanging out
they belong
10   to my friends
who say:

someday we will get married.

their poem continued
what are you looking in that store window for what are you
15   looking
     to die with jingle bells by whores i know from
     lexington ave. who now make it with politicians
     to die by a christmas tree all the lights
     on you
20   with $110 in the bank a ring on your fingers
     a shelf with two books…dictionary
     to die with this
you don't want this
Instead look how you dance talk & scream how you shine
25   the lipstick it's ugly let me tell you take it off
It's bad for the hallway leaning against the mailboxes
how much better it could be the wind falling on your face
drag your ass this way when your mother would come
& not see us when you almost giggled
30   it just ain't right, she said
they broke the windows & put holes in the building
& Elba's son Ray wanted to be a doctor
he deals medicine to get high on now

WE TOOK WILLY HOME WITH HIS EYES DRAGGING ON THE
    STAIRS
35   he gave Barbara a baby & she left him & married
now has a house in Brooklyn & Perry Como records
she plays for her guests she won't come around
because it's too dirty her husband is stupid
bought a big car he didn't know them white folks
40   like little ones to put liberal magazines on the back seats
they even have pancakes for breakfast

Judy got a secretary job
           with a lawyer
                pays good
45   she likes it
                    because she carries
                    a brief case & newspaper

when she goes dancing saturday her bottle of Wilson
sticks out of her pocketbook
50   maybe i should tell her

Tito standing with me as we listened to my uncle's
stupid advice he thought he was smart & really
believed what he said

Rosa is not married her son is now in school
55   she keeps it up her mother's house when she parties
that big house on the corner where i got lost
chasing her friends one time in the dark
room to room my hands in the air
hoping for better things to touch

60   she had a fake brother we never saw him
but they say he was in jail

Julio wears forty-two-dollar knits with 'gators
& shining slacks that were handmade
because he works overtime & deals cocaine
65   his girl loves him they want to get married in the fall
they will wear rings & walk together on third avenue
her stomach falling in front of her he will offer soda
& run down:
                    do we need milk or something

70   Carlos with cons & new blue shades goes to college
plays pool at the bar on the corner of 109th Street

either i'm stupid or i don't know what you're talking about,
he said
turning to look in the mirror
75   middle-class stupidity staring
                                    at him

Chino came back with an army suit on i guess this was
suppose to be hip
when he walked with his old girl & took pictures
80   by the park
he kissed his mother hard & caught a train back

Carmen
there was three Carmens this one from the projects
we went to the East River when it rain & stored
85   at the water but not for long
Norma came & stay with Harold in the shadow of a tree

Carmen stares at my clothes & wonders
why I don't wear knits like all the people
she talks to me now when I visit though
90   she thinks I'm a little crazy

Helen is a jewish neighbor so I told her what the names
meant
we lived on the same block I explained to her
we went upstate together
95   we came out together
went dancing together
gave our girls babies together
went on junk together
& didn't get off together

100   Helen did not understand

(O funny, it used to be babycakes, but not no more funny)

Mildred was big
somehow she got small & skinny she visits me
sat on me half a day once telling me lies
105   & kissing me showing me the things her boyfriend
buys her a good leather jacket & beatnik earrings
a new book by Dracula or somebody she smiles
on the train going uptown I'm sweating bricks

Benny writes to me from jail
110   he robbed a drugstore & beat a policeman up on
broadway then he stole a car & was caught
kissing the tires in Florida

JADE TURNED INTO JIVE DUST WONDERED IF IT WAS
VOODOO
I told him it was panamanian red when he recovered
115   he lowered his head & continued to ask what happened
Candy was the girl I was to marry
but we ran into storms & I had to bust her lip
one time
& she didn't speak to me & winter came
120   I saw her shadow going past me the last time

Little Man always comes around with his scars
& his son that runs & walks
Little Man would understand even now when I see him

he wonders
125   why I still carry a knife
them days are over, he tells me & I stare at him
& he understands

maybe that last one was too close to me
she got upset when I put my hand in her blouse
130 she made coffee for me
&
all these years how old I must be getting
but no
    I turn to the mirror & stare at my youth
135   & wonder at my intelligence.

Julio Marzán

Poet, translator, and scholar Julio Marzán has been an influential force in mainland Puerto Rican literary circles. He edited the collection *Inventing a Word: An Anthology of 20th Century Puerto Rican Poetry* (1980), published a book of poems, *Translations Without Originals* (1986), and in 2001 translated the work of Puerto Rican poet Luis Pales Matos. He is perhaps best known for his scholarly work *The Spanish American Roots of William Carlos Williams* (1994). He teaches English at Nassau Community College on Long Island and is the author of the pedagogical work *Luna Luna: Creative Writing Ideas from Spanish and Latino Literature* (2000). Marzán's most recent book is the novel *The Bonjour Gene* (2005).

Grand Central Station

The baby-faced Rican,
duffel bag bursting,
just down from Upstate,
pedals in fidget,
5 unicycle his pause,
asking for direction
to the Bronx subway.

Cuts notch pale ears,
nicks fleck his nose,
10 a shaved patch spotlights
a fresh scalp wound.
Pedaling he delivers,
packed in shy glance,
a hair-trigger anger.

15 Double-barrels aim
along my stretched arm
and beyond my finger
to screeching tracks
of his Bronx subway,
20 its long lighted tunnel
to his stop with no light.

Willie Perdomo

Willie Perdomo was born in Harlem and has published two books of poems, *Where a Nickel Costs a Dime* (1996) and *Smoking Lovely* (2003), as well as a CD/book edition of his spoken word poetry called *Smoking Lovely* (2003), which reflects his musical style and highlights the vibrancy of his performances at the famous Nuyorican Poet's Café. *Where a Nickel Costs a Dime* was selected by the American Library Association as a Popular Paperback for Young Adults. He is also the author of a children's book about Langston Hughes, *Visiting Langston* (2002).

Reflections on the Metro-North, Winter 1990

Saturday night
I'm on the 8:40
to New Rochelle
and points North
5   I'm running away
with my woman
running away from
El Barrio, New York City
Fast playing games
10   symbolic names
Slick Rick
Big Money D.
Hey you!
Who me?
15   Yeah, you.
Red light, green light, 1, 2, 3
Red light, green light, 1, 2, 3,
On the green—WALK
On the red—DON'T WALK
20   Stop! Freeze! Don't run.
Cuz you might get shot
for looking like
the wrong Black man
And whatever you do
25   please
please
don't sniff dope
three days in a row

Train is ready
30   steam whispers
a slow drag
out of Grand Central
through dark tunnels
where foot-long rats

35   swim in puddles
of leftover rain
Tanisa
my woman
lays her head
40   on my shoulder
I'm suppose
to be here
I'm doing the
right thing

45   Like a bullet
the iron horse
will shoot out of
the hole
on 98th Street and Park Avenue
50   We never see
how the rich really live
with gardens
in the middle of
the street
55   Doormen hailing taxis
in the rain
for poodles in
custom-made shearlings

Soon we'll see
60   where I'm from
I can never forget this panorama
of the other Park Avenue
Papo's Park Avenue
sounds like
a million hands
clapping in guaguanco[1] time
Elevator in my stomach
where I stash
my dark secrets
70   starts to rise
I'm ready to get off
on 125th Street
so I could dive
into those hands

75   The streets
can kill you—
it's true

---

[1] a style of rumba dance

Clanging cuchifrito pots
compassionate curses ricochet off ho' row
80   my muses are calling, baby
I got to go
Forget our weekend in New Rochelle
Sunday paper
bagel brunch
85   sleeping in
after loving all night
Home is where I like to
find myself
when it's cold

90   110th Street
History of El Barrio, Spanish Harlem
salsa street legends
manteca[2] bombs
many a bad muthafucka
95   done laughed and cried
ran and died
in the swollen arms
of this street
life and death
100   Boricuas in Nueva York
celebrate with this song
forever
para siempre,[3] mami
para siempre

105   116th Street
LA MARQUETA is glittering
I don't need books
My culture
My history
110   is in the aisles
of bacalaito salt codfish fritters
"ajecito chiles"
tomato   sofrito ← in this
based   pulpo octopus
sauce
115   mi pana my boy
I stretch my neck
to see
if I see
mi panas

---

[2]heroin
[3]forever

120 Carlito y Marc
walking toward Madison Avenue
to buy a bag
half-n-half
for the rest of the night
125 awwwright!
a dripping leak-leaky bag
of Purple Rain
so that we can tranquilize
our souls
130 time
confusion
heartbreak
and get blind
Is that me
135 I see?
looking for a familiar dance
to a warm hip-hop boogie
writing a mad poem
to a sad beat
140 because the guns we play with
don't squirt water
or make that simulated machine gun rattle

Tanisa is sleeping now
she might be dreaming
145 about happy we gonna be
If it wasn't for her
my girl
my woman
my wifey
150 my main flame
my baby
always and forever
with a kiss
from Harlem
155 moreno[4] Harlem
same beat
like my Barrio
soul y salsa
if it wasn't for her
160 I would be standing on the corner
thinking about the world
drinking blackberry brandy

---

[4]dark-skinned

keeping a cold hustler company
with stories from back in the days

165   "Damn, Papo. Things ain't like they use to be. . ."

125th Street
Harlem, USA
I'm ready to jump off
before the doors close
170   have a nice day
and if this poem is too long
I really don't give a fuck
Because my heart is beating
and I'm alive
175   You know what I'm sayin'?
Can you hear my muses, Tanisa?
Shhhh…
I could tell her that I got some business to take care of
but she'll look at me with those sleepy eyes and that
180   soft voice and she'll say:
        "I am your business, Will."
And that's it—
Apollo Theater to the West
Willis Avenue Bridge to the East
185   A river waiting at each end of the boulevard
Poets and dead gangsters
chillin' at the bottoms
Nothing for me to do but jump
or turn back
190   cuz it ain't my time yet

I close my eyes and clench my teeth
I ask my grandmother's spirit for the strength to say no
I kiss Tanisa
careful not to shake her awake from her dreams

195   Doors close
steam whispers
a slow drag
away
I'm running away
200   with my woman
and I can't turn back
the El Barrio
Harlem night
Is no longer mine

Pedro Pietri

Pedro Pietri was born in Ponce, Puerto Rico, in 1944. He and his family moved to Harlem, New York, when he was three years old, and he continued to live there until his death in 2004. His work has appeared in many anthologies. He has the distinction of having had his work translated into numerous languages. Although best known for his poetry, which he performed in such places as the Nuyorican Poets Café, he also published such dramatic works as *Illusions of a Revolving Door: Plays* (1992). His collection of poetry, *Puerto Rican Obituary* (1973), is considered a classic. His humorous, parodic, one-act political play, *The Masses are Asses*, was published in 2003.

Puerto Rican Obituary

They worked
They were always on time
They were never late
They never spoke back
5   when they were insulted
They worked
They never took days off
that were not on the calendar
They never went on strike
10   without permission
They worked
ten days a week
and were only paid for five
They worked
15   They worked
They worked
and they died
They died broke
They died owing
20   They died never knowing
what the front entrance
of the first national city bank looks like

Juan
Miguel
25   Milagros
Olga
Manuel
All died yesterday today
and will die again tomorrow

30   passing their bill collectors
    on to the next of kin
    All died
    waiting for the garden of eden
    to open up again
35   under a new management
    All died
    dreaming about america
    waking them up in the middle of the night
    screaming: Mira Mira[1]
40   your name is on the winning lottery ticket
    for one hundred thousand dollars
    All died
    hating the grocery stores
    that sold them make-believe steak
45   and bullet-proof rice and beans
    All died waiting dreaming and hating

    Dead Puerto Ricans
    Who never knew they were Puerto Ricans
    Who never took a coffee break
50   from the ten commandments
    to KILL KILL KILL
    the landlords of their cracked skulls
    and communicate with their latino souls

55   Juan
    Miguel
    Milagros
    Olga
    Manuel
    From the nervous breakdown streets
60   where the mice live like millionaires
    and the people do not live at all
    are dead and were never alive

    Juan
    died waiting for his number to hit
65   Miguel
    died waiting for the welfare check
    to come and go and come again
    Milagros
    died waiting for her ten children
70   to grow up and work
    so she could quit working

---

[1]Look Look

Olga
died waiting for a five dollar raise
Manuel
75 died waiting for his supervisor to drop dead
so he could get a promotion

Is a long ride
from Spanish Harlem
to long island cemetery
80 where they were buried
First the train
and then the bus
and the cold cuts for lunch
and the flowers
85 that will be stolen
when visiting hours are over
Is very expensive
Is very expensive
But they understand
90 Their parents understood
Is a long non-profit ride
from Spanish Harlem
to long island cemetery

Juan
95 Miguel
Milagros
Olga
Manuel
All died yesterday today
100 and will die again tomorrow
Dreaming
Dreaming about queens
Clean-cut lily-white neighborhood
Puerto Ricanless scene
105 Thirty-thousand-dollar home
The first spics on the block
Proud to belong to a community
of gringos who want them lynched
Proud to be a long distance away
110 from the sacred phrase: Que Pasa[2]

These dreams
These empty dreams
from the make-believe bedrooms

[2]What's happening

their parents left them
115 are the after-effects
of television programs
about the ideal
white american family
with black maids
120 and latino janitors
who are well train—
to make everyone
and their bill collectors
laugh at them
125 and the people they represent

Juan
died dreaming about a new car
Miguel
died dreaming about new anti-poverty programs
130 Milagros
died dreaming about a trip to Puerto Rico
Olga
died dreaming about real jewelry
Manuel
135 died dreaming about the irish sweepstakes

They all died
like a hero sandwich dies
in the garment district
at twelve o'clock in the afternoon
140 social security number to ashes
union dues to dust

They knew
they were born to weep
and keep the morticians employed
145 as long as they pledge allegiance
to the flag that wants them destroyed
They saw their names listed
in the telephone directory of destruction
They were train to turn
150 the other cheek by newspapers
that mispelled mispronounced
and misunderstood their names
and celebrated when death came
and stole their final laundry ticket

155 They were born dead
and they died dead

Is time
to visit sister lopez again
the number one healer
160   and fortune card dealer
in Spanish Harlem
She can communicate
with your late relatives
for a reasonable fee
165   Good news is guaranteed
Rise Table Rise Table
death is not dumb and disable—
Those who love you want to know
the correct number to play
170   Let them know this right away
Rise Table Rise Table
death is not dumb and disable
Now that your problems are over
and the world is off your shoulders
175   help those who you left behind
find financial peace of mind
Rise Table Rise Table
death is not dumb and disable
If the right number we hit
180   all our problems will split
and we will visit your grave
on every legal holiday
Those who love you want to know
the correct number to play
185   Let them know this right away
We know your spirit is able
Death is not dumb and disable
RISE TABLE RISE TABLE

Juan
190   Miguel
Milagros
Olga
Manuel
All died yesterday today
195   and will die again tomorrow
Hating fighting and stealing
broken windows from each other
Practicing a religion without a roof
The old testament
200   The new testament

according to the gospel
of the internal revenue
the judge and jury and executioner
protector and eternal bill collector

205 Secondhand shit for sale
Learn how to say Como Esta Usted[3]
and you will make a fortune
They are dead
They are dead
210 and will not return from the dead
until they stop neglecting
the art of their dialogue—
for broken english lessons
to impress the mister goldsteins—
215 who keep them employed
as lavaplatos[4] porters messenger boys
factory workers maids stock clerks
shipping clerks assistant mailroom
assistant, assistant assistant
220 to the assistant's assistant
assistant lavaplatos and automatic
artificial smiling doormen
for the lowest wages of the ages
and rages when you demand a raise
225 because *is* against the company policy
to promote SPICS SPICS SPICS

Juan
died hating Miguel because Miguel's
used car was in better running condition
230 than his used car
Miguel
died hating Milagros because Milagros
had a color television set
and he could not afford one yet
235 Milagros
died hating Olga because Olga
made five dollars more on the same job
Olga
died hating Manuel because Manuel
240 had hit the numbers more times
than she had hit the numbers

---

[3]How Are You?
[4]dishwashers

Manuel
died hating all of them
Juan
245   Miguel
Milagros
and Olga
because they all spoke broken english
more fluently than he did

250   And now they are together
in the main lobby of the void
Addicted to silence
Off limits to the wind
Confined to worm supremacy
255   in long island cemetery
This is the groovy hereafter
the protestant collection box
was talking so loud and proud about

Here lies Juan
260   Here lies Miguel
Here lies Milagros
Here lies Olga
Here lies Manuel
who died yesterday today
265   and will die again tomorrow
Always broke
Always owing
Never knowing
that they are beautiful people
270   Never knowing
the geography of their complexion

PUERTO RICO IS A BEAUTIFUL PLACE
PUERTORRIQUENOS ARE A BEAUTIFUL RACE
If only they
275   had turned off the television
and tune into their own imaginations
If only they
had used the white supremacy bibles
for toilet paper purpose
280   and make their latino souls
the only religion of their race
If only they
had return to the definition of the sun
after the first mental snowstorm

285 on the summer of their senses
     If only they
     had kept their eyes open
     at the funeral of their fellow employees
     who came to this country to make a fortune
290 and were buried without underwears

     Juan
     Miguel
     Milagros
     Olga
295 Manuel
     will right now be doing their own thing
     where beautiful people sing
     and dance and work together
     where the wind is a stranger
300 to miserable weather conditions
     where you do not need a dictionary
     to communicate with your people
     Aqui[5] Se Habla Espanol[6] all the time
     Aqui you salute your flag first
305 Aqui there are no dial soap commercials
     Aqui everybody smells good
     Aqui tv dinners do not have a future
     Aqui the men and women admire desire
     and never get tired of each other
310 Aqui Que Pasa Power is what's happening
     Aqui to be called negrito
     means to be called LOVE

Miguel Piñero

Miguel Piñero's life has been well documented countless times, most graphically
in the recent film *Piñero* (2001) discussed in this anthology. Born in 1947, he was
an actor, playwright, poet, and co-founder of the Nuyorican Poets Café. The fame
that resulted from his powerful autobiographical play, *Short Eyes* (New York
Drama Critics Circle Award for Best American Play, 1973–1974), landed him jobs
writing for and starring in movies, television, and theater. He wrote many other
plays collected in the publications, *The Sun Always Shines for the Cool* (1984),
Outrageous One Act Plays (1986), and a collection of poetry entitled *La Bodega
Sold Dreams* (1980). He died in 1998, leaving a lasting influence on spoken word
poets and Nuyorican Latino literature.

---

[5]Here
[6]Spanish Is Spoken

La Bodega Sold Dreams

dreamt I was a poet
&
writin' silver sailin' songs
words
5   strong & powerful crashin' thru
walls of steel & concrete
erected in minds weak
&
those asleep
10   replacin' a hobby of paper candy
wrappin', collectin'
potent to 'pregnate sterile young
thoughts

I dreamt I was this poeta
15   words glitterin' brite & bold
strikin' a new rush for gold
in las bodegas

A Lower East Side Poem

Just once before I die
I want to climb up on a
tenement sky
to dream my lungs out till
5   I cry
then scatter my ashes thru
the Lower East Side.

So let me sing my song tonight
let me feel out of sight
10   and let all eyes be dry
when they scatter my ashes thru
the Lower East Side.

From Houston to 14th Street
from Second Avenue to the mighty D
15   here the hustlers & suckers meet
the faggots & freaks will all get
high
on the ashes that have been scattered
thru the Lower East Side.

20   There's no other place for me to be
there's no other place that I can see

there's no other town around that
brings you up or keeps you down
no food little heat sweeps by
25   fancy cars & pimps' bars & juke saloons
& greasy spoons make my spirits fly
with my ashes scattered thru the
Lower East Side…

A thief, a junkie I've been
30   committed every known sin
Jews and Gentiles…Bums and Men
of style…run away child
police shooting wild…
mother's futile wails…pushers
35   making sales…dope wheelers
& cocaine dealers…smoking pot
streets are hot & feed off those who bleed to death…
all that's true
all that's true
40   all that is true
but this ain't no lie
when I ask that my ashes be scattered thru
the Lower East Side.

So here I am, look at me
45   I stand proud as you can see
pleased to be from the Lower East
a street fighting man
a problem of this land
I am the Philosopher of the Criminal Mind
50   a dweller of prison time
a cancer of Rockefeller's ghettocide
this concrete tomb is my home
to belong to survive you gotta be strong
you can't be shy less without request
55   someone will scatter your ashes thru
the Lower East Side.

I don't wanna be buried in Puerto Rico
I don't wanna rest in long island cemetery
I wanna be near the stabbing shooting
60   gambling fighting & unnatural dying
& new birth crying
so please when I die…
don't take me far away
keep me near by
65   take my ashes and scatter them thru out
the Lower East Side…

Gloria Vando

Gloria Vando, who is of Puerto Rican descent, was born in 1934 and raised in New York City. Her publications include *Promesas: Geography of the Impossible* (1993) and *Shadows and Supposes* (2001), which won the Latino Literary Award for Best Poetry Book. Her work has appeared in numerous journals and magazines including *Kenyon Review* and *Seattle Review*. She is the founder of Helicon Nine Editions, an independent non-profit literary press, and co-founded, with her husband, The Writers Place in Kansas City. She has won numerous awards for her poetry as well as for her work editing and publishing feminist writing.

In the Dark Backward

for Nina

How is it I was not raised
on the riverfront block
with the tall trees and a tall woman
calling my name, the sweetness
5   of warm peaches on her breath,
her arms like soft vowels
cushioning me from death? Why
is it I was confined to night,
forced to travel the shaft tunnel
10   below Manhattan before alighting
blonde and blue-eyed in Washington
Heights, where your mother
would add another plate for supper
and, long after the sun
15   had painted the Palisades across
the Hudson a deep bronze, wonder
aloud whether I'd be going soon?
I would pretend I had not heard
so I could stay until the moon
20   rose over the cliffs, when we'd
slip out and walk across the bridge
to the Jersey side where we'd sit
on the rocks and talk and watch
the early morning light patch up
25   the city's wounds. Was it Godly spite
that bore me to the wrong block
far from your haven on Haven Avenue—
or was it luck that locked
me in that dry-dock, where nothing but
30   my mind could billow in the breeze
and only the cries of kindred
children, like windswept echoes from
a ghost ship, could free my grief?

DRAMA

Josefina López

Having had over 80 professional productions of her plays throughout the United States, Josefina López is one of today's preeminent Chicana writers. She has written such plays as *Simply Maria, Or the American Dream, Confessions of Women from East L.A., Boyle Heights, Lola Goes to Roma, Food for the Dead, Unconquered Spirits,* and *Real Women Have Curves.** She is the co-screenwriter of the movie version of *Real Women Have Curves,* which garnered much acclaim, including at the 2002 Sundance Film Festival where the film won the Audience Award and a Special Jury Award for Acting.

López has a screenplay at HBO titled *Loteria for Juarez* about the mysterious murders of women in Juarez. She has written several other screenplays, including *ADD Me to the Party,* an original comedic screenplay about three Latinas addicted to adrenaline who drive around in an Impala looking for the next distraction; *Lola Goes to Roma,* a mother-daughter comedy that takes place in Europe; a bio-pic titled *Queen of the Rumba*; and a family comedy titled *No Place Like Home.*

López has won several awards, including a Gabriel García Márquez award from the L.A. Mayor in 2003. She was also recognized by the Writers Guild of America (WGA) with the cover story for the December 2002/January 2003 issue of the prestigious WGA magazine *Written By,* entitled "Real Writers Have Courage." Lopez and co-writer George LaVoo won the Humanitas Award for Screenwriting. She was awarded a Screenwriting Fellowship by the California Arts Council for 2001, and in 1988, she was recognized by California Senator Barbara Boxer as a "woman who has made history in the entertainment industry."

She has an MFA in screenwriting from the prestigious UCLA Film and Television school. López was born in San Luis Potosi, Mexico, is happily married with one son, and lives in Paris.

Playwright's Notes

When I was very young my best friend and I were walking to the corner store. My parents had warned me not to tell anyone I didn't have "papers" and to be careful walking the streets. On the way to the store we saw "la migra" (INS/immigration/Border Patrol). I quickly turned to my friend and tried to "act white," I spoke in English and talked about Jordache jeans and Barbie dolls hoping no one would suspect us. When I finally got my legal residence card, I remembered this incident knowing that I would never have to hide and be afraid again. I also laughed at my *naivete* and fear because what I had thought was la migra was only the L.A. Police Meter Maid.

In 1987 the Simpson-Rodino Amnesty Law, designed to stop the influx of undocumented people entering the country, granted thousands of undocumented people living in the U.S. since 1982 legal residency. This was an oppor-

*Note: The published version of *Real Women Have Curves* included a glossary translating the Spanish used throughout the play. We have reprinted it, and it appears after the play here; for this reason, we have not included footnote glosses as we have elsewhere in this anthology.

tunity of a life-time. However, thousands, not trusting the government, hesitated to apply, fearing this was a scheme to deport them. They, like me, couldn't believe that after hiding and being persecuted for so long they were finally going to have the freedom to live and work in this country.

I got my residence card soon after I graduated from high school and was then able to apply to college. I had been accepted to New York University, but I had to wait a year to be eligible for financial aid. During this year I worked at McDonald's, but I hated it. Then, desperate for a new job, I asked my sister to let me work at her tiny sewing factory. I worked there for five months and my experiences at the factory served as inspiration for REAL WOMEN HAVE CURVES. At the factory there were a few Latina women, all older than me. They liked working for my sister because she wasn't stingy. We spent so much time together working, sweating and laughing, that we bonded. I remember feeling blessed that I was a woman because male bonding could never compare with what happens when women work together. We had something special and I wanted to show the world.

In the U.S. undocumented people are referred to as "illegal aliens" which conjures up in our minds the image of extraterrestrial beings who are not human, who do not bleed when they're cut, who do not cry when they feel pain, who do not have fears, dreams and hopes…Undocumented people have been used as scapegoats for so many of the problems in the U.S., from drugs and violence, to the economy. I hope that someday this country recognizes the very important contributions of undocumented people and remembers that they too came to this country in search of a better life.

Josefina López
Los Angeles
March 1992

Real Women Have Curves

A Full-length Play For Five Women

Characters

ANA 18, plump and pretty, sister of Estela, daughter of Carmen. She is a recent high school graduate and a young feminist

ESTELA 24, plump, plain-looking, owner of the "Garcia Sewing Factory"

CARMEN 48, a short, large woman, mother of Ana and Estela. She has a talent for storytelling

PANCHA 32, a huge woman who is very mellow in her ways, but quick with her tongue

ROSALI 29, only a bit plump in comparison to the rest of the women. She is sweet and easygoing

Setting:

A tiny sewing factory in East Los Angeles.

Time:

The first week of September 1987.

Note: Words in Spanish are in bold print. You will find a glossary and Spanish terms in the back of the play.

Synopsis of Scenes

Act One

Scene 1: Monday morning, September 7, 1987, about 7:00 a.m.
Scene 2: A few hours later, about 11:30 a.m.
Scene 3: A few hours later, about 3:45 p.m.
Scene 4: The following day, about 7:10 a.m.
Scene 5: Later the same day. Late afternoon.

Act Two

Scene 1: Wednesday, September 9th, about 8:15 a.m.
Scene 2: Thursday, September 10th, about 2:00 a.m.
Scene 3: Same day, about 2:00 p.m.
Scene 4: Friday, September 11th, about 2:25 p.m.

Act One

Scene One

> *AT RISE: The stage becomes visible. The clock on the wall shows it is 6:59 a.m. Keys are heard outside the door. The door opens. ANA and CARMEN enter. ANA drags herself in, goes directly to the electricity box and switches it on. Automatically all the machines "hummmm" loudly. The lights turn on at different times. The radio also blasts on with a song in Spanish. CARMEN quickly turns off the radio. She puts her lunch on the table. ANA slumps on a machine. CARMEN then gets a broom and uses it to get a mousetrap from underneath the table. She prays that today will be the day she caught the mouse. She sees the mousetrap empty and is very disappointed.*

CARMEN. **¡Pinche rata!** I'll get you. (*CARMEN returns the broom. She takes two dollars from her purse, approaches ANA and presents them to her.*) Ten. Go to the bakery.

ANA. No. I want to go back to sleep!

CARMEN. **¡Huevona!** If we don't help your sister who else is going to? She already works all hours of the night trying to finish the dresses. **Por fin** she's doing something productive with her life.

ANA. I know I'm trying to be supportive, **ayy!** I don't want to go to the bakery. I don't want any bread.

CARMEN. That's good, at least you won't get fatter.

ANA. **¡Amá!**

CARMEN. I only tell you for your own good. **Bueno,** I'll go get the bread myself, but you better not get any when I bring it. *(CARMEN walks to the door.)* Ana, don't forget to close the doors. This street is full of winos and drug addicts. And don't you open the door to any strangers!

ANA. Yeah, yeah, I know! I'm not a kid. *(ANA locks both doors with a key. She goes toward the toilet and turns on the water in the sink. ANA splashes water on her face to awaken. She sticks her hand behind the toilet seat and gets out a notebook and a pen. Spotlight on ANA. She sits and writes the following:)* Monday, September 7, 1987...I don't want to be here! I only come because my mother practically drags me out of bed and into the car and into the factory. She pounds on the...No... *(Scratches "pounds.")* She knocks on...No...*(She scratches "knocks.")* She pounds on the garage wall, and since I think it's an earthquake, I run out. Then she catches me and I become her prisoner...Is it selfish of me not to want to wake up every morning at 6:30 a.m., Saturdays included, to come work here for 67 dollars a week? Oh, but such is the life of a Chicana in the garment industry. Cheap labor...I've been trying to hint to my sister for a raise, but she says I don't work fast enough for her to pay me minimum wage...The weeks get longer and I can't believe I've ended up here. I just graduated from high school...Most of my friends are in college...It's as if I'm going backwards. I'm doing the work that mostly illegal aliens do...*(Scratches "illegal aliens.")* No, "undocumented workers"...or else it sounds like these people come from Mars...Soon I will have my "Temporary Residence Card," then after two years, my green card...I'm happy to finally be legal, but I thought things would be different...What I really want to do is write...

CARMEN. *(off, interrupting).* Ana, open the door! *(CARMEN pounds on the door outside. ANA quickly puts her writing away and goes to open the door.)* Hurry up! There's a wino following me! *(ANA gets the keys and unlocks both doors.)* Hurry! He's been following me from the bakery.

> *(ANA opens the first door. CARMEN is behind the bar door and is impatiently waiting for ANA to open it. ANA opens the door. CARMEN hurries in nervously. ANA quickly shuts the doors. ANA looks out the window.)*

ANA. **Amá,** that's not a wino, it's an "Alelullah"!

CARMEN. But he was following me!

ANA. I know, those witnesses don't give up. *(CARMEN puts the bag of bread on the table. She fills a small pot with water and puts it on the little hot plate to boil the water for coffee.)*

CARMEN. **Pos yo ya no veo.** I can't see a thing. *(CARMEN goes to her purse and takes out her glasses. She puts them on. She looks out the window and sees no one.)* I should retire and be an **abuelita** by now, taking care of grandchildren... I don't know why I work, I have arthritis in my hands, I'm losing my sight from all this sewing, and this arm, I can hardly move it anymore... *(ANA does not pay attention as usual.)*

ANA. *(unsympathetically)*. Yeah, **Amá.**

CARMEN. I wonder where's Estela. She should have been here by now.

ANA. I thought she left the house early.

(PANCHA appears behind the bar door.)

PANCHA. **Buenos días, Doña** Carmen. Can you open the door?

CARMEN. **Buenos días,** Pancha. **¿Cómo está?**

PANCHA. Not too bad.

CARMEN. **Que bien.** I brought my **mole** today for all of us.

PANCHA. You're so generous, **Doña** Carmen.

CARMEN. It was in the 'frigerator for three days, and I thought it was turning green, so I brought it. Why let it go to waste?

PANCHA. Is it still good?

CARMEN. Of course, I make great mole.

(ROSALI appears behind the bar door.)

ROSALI. **Doña** Carmen, the door.

   Carmen. It's open, Rosali. **Buenos días.** How are you?

ROSALI. *(entering)*. Okay, like always, Doña Carmen.

CARMEN. I brought my **mole** for all of us.

ROSALI. Did you? **Ayy, gracias,** but remember I'm on a diet.

CARMEN. Just try a small taco, **no te va hacer daño.** Try it.

ROSALI. I'm sure it's delicious, but I'm this close to being a size seven.

CARMEN. **Si.** You're looking thinner now. How are you doing it?

ROSALI. I'm on a secret diet… It's from the Orient.

CARMEN. A-ha… It's true, those Japanese women are always skinny. **Pues,** give me your secret, Rosalí. Maybe this way I can lose this ball of fat! *(She squeezes her stomach.)* **No mas mira que paresco.** You can't even see my waist anymore. But you know what it really is. It's just water. After having so many babies I just stopped getting rid of the water. It's as if I'm clogged.
   (ROSALI and ANA laugh.)

ROSALI. **Sí, Doña** Carmen.

ANA. Yeah, sure, **Amá!**

CARMEN. **¿Y tu?** Why do you laugh? You're getting there yourself. When I was your age I wasn't as fat as you. And look at your **chichis.**

ANA. **¡Amá!**

CARMEN. *(grabs ANA's breasts as if weighing them)*. They must weigh five pounds each.

ANA. **Amá,** don't touch me like that!

ROSALI. Where's Estela?

CARMEN. We don't know. Ana, I think you better call home now and check if she's there.

ROSALI. Because her torment is outside washing his car.

ALL. He is?

(From under a large blanket on the floor ESTELA jumps out. The WOMEN are startled and scream, but they quickly join her as she runs to the window to spy on her Tormento.)

ESTELA. **¡Ayy que buenote!** He's so cute.

ANA. Don't exaggerate.

ESTELA. **¡Mi Tormento! ¡O mi Tormento!**

CARMEN. We thought you left home early.

ESTELA. No, I worked so late last night I decided to sleep here.

CARMEN. Then why didn't you tell us when—

ESTELA. I heard you come in, but I wanted to listen in on your chisme about me, **Amá.**

CARMEN. Me? I don't gossip!

ESTELA. Sure, **Amá**…I'm going to the store. *(ESTELA runs to the mirror.)*

PANCHA. I don't know why you bother, all he cares about is his car.

CARMEN. **Véngans,** I think the water is ready. *(The WOMEN gather around the table for coffee. PANCHA and CARMEN grab bread. ESTELA goes to the bathroom and brushes her hair, puts on lipstick, then she puts on a girdle under her skirt, which she has great trouble getting on, but she is determined. She grabs a deodorant stick and applies it. She also gets a bottle of perfume and sprays it accordingly.)*

ESTELA. **Aquí por si me abraza.** *(She sprays her wrist.)*

ANA. *(mocks ESTELA in front of the WOMEN).* Here in case he hugs me.

ESTELA. **Aquí por si me besa.** *(She sprays her neck.)*

ANA. Here in case he kisses me.

ESTELA. **Y aquí por si se pasa.** *(She sprays under her skirt.)*

ANA. And here in case he…you know what. *(The WOMEN are by the door and windows looking out. ESTELA comes out of the bathroom.)*

ROSALI. He's gone.

CARMEN. **Sí, ya se fue.**

ESTELA. No! Are you sure? *(ESTELA goes toward the door, before she reaches it CARMEN shuts the door.)*

CARMEN. *(scared),* **¡Dios mio!** *(CARMEN quickly takes a drink of her coffee and can hardly breathe afterwards.)*

ESTELA. **¿Qué? ¿Amá, qué pasa?**

CARMEN. I saw a van!

ROSALI. What van?

CARMEN. **¡La migra!** *(All the WOMEN scatter and hide waiting to be discovered. Then after a few seconds PANCHA makes a realization.)*

PANCHA. Pero, why are we hiding? We're all legal now.

CARMEN. **¡Ayy, de veras!** I forget! All those years of being an ilegal, I still can't get used to it.

PANCHA. Me too! *(She picks up a piece of bread.)* I think I just lost my appetite.

ROSALI. I'm not scared of it! I used to work in factories and whenever they did a raid, I'd always sneak out through the bathroom window, **y ya.**

ANA. Last night I heard on the news that la migra patrol is planning to raid a lot of places.

PANCHA. They're going to get mean trying to enforce that Amnesty law.

ANA. Thank God, I'm legal. I will never have to lie on applications anymore, except maybe about my weight...

ROSALI. **¿Saben qué?** Yesterday I got my first credit card.

CARMEN. **¿Pos cómo le hiciste?** How?

ROSALI. I lied on the application and I got an **Americana** Express.

ANA. And now you have two green cards and you never leave home without them. (*ANA laughs her head off, but none of the WOMEN get the joke. ANA slowly shuts up.*)

PANCHA. **Doña** Carmen, let those men in their van come! Who cares? We're all legal now! (*PANCHA goes to the door and opens it all the way. They all smile in relief and pride, then ESTELA, who has been stuffing her face, finally speaks up.*)

ESTELA. I'm not. (*PANCHA slams the door shut.*)

EVERYONE. You're not?!!!

ANA. But you went with me to get the fingerprints and the medical examination.

ESTELA. I didn't send them in.

ROSALI. But you qualify.

ESTELA. I have a criminal record.

EVERYONE. No!

ESTELA. So I won't apply until I clear it.

CARMEN. Estela, what did you do?

PANCHA. **¿Qué hiciste?**

ESTELA. Well, actually, I did two things.

CARMEN. Two?! **¿Y por qué no me habias dicho?** Why is the mother always the last one to know?

ESTELA. Because one is very embarrassing—

CARMEN. **¡Aver dime, condenada!** What have you done?

ESTELA. I was arrested for illegal possession of—

ROSALI. Marijuana?!

PANCHA. A gun?!

ESTELA. A lobster.

EVERYONE. No!

ESTELA. Out of season!

CARMEN. **¡Mentirosa!**

WOMEN. You're kidding:

ESTELA. A-ha! I'm not lying! I almost got handcuffed and taken to jail. Trying to "abduct" a lobster is taken very seriously in Santa Monica Beach. They wanted me to appear in court and I never did.

PANCHA. That's not a serious crime; **¿de qué te apuras?** Why worry?

CARMEN. (*not amused*). That was the first crime? You mentioned two.

ESTELA. I'm being sued for not keeping up with my payments on the machines.

ANA. **Y los** eight thousand dollars you got from your accident settlement weren't enough?

CARMEN. But I thought that everything was paid for.

ESTELA. I used most of it for a down-payment, but I still needed a new steam iron, the over-lock...I thought I could make the monthly payments if everything went as planned.

CARMEN. ¿**Pos qué paso?**

PANCHA. What happened?

ESTELA. You know that we never finish on time. So the Glitz company doesn't pay me until we do.

ROSALI. Pero the orders are too big. We need at least two more seamstresses.

ESTELA. **Pues sí.** But the money they pay me is not enough to hire any more help. So because we get behind, they don't pay, I can't pay you, and I can't pay those pigs that sold me those machines.

CARMEN. **Ayyy,** Estela, how much do you owe?

ESTELA. Two thousand dollars...

CARMEN. **¡Hora si que estamos bien jodidas!** (*The WOMEN sigh hopelessly.*)

ESTELA. ...I tried. I sent some money and explained the situation to them two weeks ago, but I got a letter from their lawyer. They're taking me to court...

PANCHA. So you had money two weeks ago? Hey, hey, you told us you couldn't pay us because you didn't have any money. You had money! Here we are **bien pobres,** I can't even pay for the bus sometimes, and you care more about your machines than us.

ESTELA. They're going to take everything!

ROSALI. **¡¿Qué?!**

ESTELA. They're going to repossess everything if I don't pay them. And if I appear in court they'll find out that I don't have any papers.

ANA. Then why don't you apply for Amnesty?

ESTELA. Because I won't get it if they find out about my lawsuit.

ANA. You don't know that, Estela, you should talk to this lawyer I know.

ESTELA. Ana, you know I can't afford a lawyer!

CARMEN. **Ayy,** Estela, **¡ya ni la friegas!** (*ESTELA fights the urge to cry.*)

ROSALI. If I had money I'd lend it to you.

PANCHA. (*aside*). I wouldn't.

ROSALI. (*kindly*). But I don't have any money because you haven't paid me.

ESTELA. Miren, the Glitz company has promised to pay me for the last two weeks and this week if we get the order in by Friday.

ANA. How much of the order is left?

ESTELA. About 100 dresses.

PANCHA. **N'ombre.** By this Friday? What do they think we are? Machines?

ESTELA. But they're not that difficult! Amá, you're so fast. This would be a cinch for you. All you have to do are the blusas on the dresses. Rosali, the over-lock work is simple. It's a lot, but you're the best at it. And, Pancha, all you have to do is sew the skirts. The skirts are the easiest to sew. Now, Ana,

with you doing all the ironing, we'll get it done by Friday. You see if we do little by little at what we do best…**¡Andenle!** We can do it. **¿Verá que sí Ana?**

ANA. *(uncertain).* Sure we can.

ESTELA. **¿Vera que sí, Amá?**

CARMEN. **Pos** we can try.

ROSALI. Estela, we can do it. *(ESTELA looks to PANCHA. PANCHA remains
quiet. CARMEN breaks their stare.)*

CARMEN. Wouldn't it be funny if the **migra** came and instead of taking the
employees like they usually do, they take the **patrona.** *(The WOMEN laugh
at the thought.)*

ESTELA. Don't laugh! It could happen. *(The WOMEN become silent.)*

CARMEN. **Ayy,** Estela, I'm just kidding. I'm just trying to make you feel better.
(Beat.)

ROSALI. **Bueno,** let's try to be serious…I'll do the zippers.

ESTELA. Yes, **por favor.** And, Pancha, please do the hems on the skirts.

PANCHA. The machine is not working.

ESTELA. Not again! *(ESTELA goes to the machine. She fusses around with it trying to make it work. With confidence.)* There. It should be ready. Try it.
*(PANCHA sits down on a chair and tries the machine. She steps on the pedal
and the machine makes on awful noise. Then it shoots off electric sparks and
explodes. PANCHA quickly gets away from the machine. The WOMEN hide
under the machines.)*

WOMEN. **¡Ay, ay, ay!**

ESTELA. Augghh! All this equipment is junk! *(ESTELA throws a thread spool
at the machine and it explodes again.)* I was so stupid to buy this factory!
*(ESTELA fights the urge to cry in frustration. The WOMEN stare at her
helplessly.)*

CARMEN. **Pos no nos queda otra.** Pancha, can you do the hems by hand?

PANCHA. **Bueno,** I guess I have to.

ESTELA. **Gracias**…Ana, turn on the iron, I'm going to need you to do the
ironing all this week…Tell me when the iron gets hot and I'll show you what
you have to do.

CARMEN. I'll help Rosalí with the zippers.

ESTELA. No…I need you to do the blusas on size 7/8.

CARMEN. Didn't I already do them?

ESTELA. No.

CARMEN. I guess it was size 13/14 then.

ESTELA. You couldn't have, because there is no size 13/14 for this dress style,
Amá.

CARMEN. No?…**Hoye** did you get any more pink thread from the Glitz?

ESTELA. Oh, no. I forgot…Go ahead and use the over-lock machine. That is
already set up with thread.

ANA. What does the over-lock do?

ROSALI. It's what keeps the material from coming apart. *(ROSALI shows
ANA.)*

CARMEN. Why don't you give me the pink thread from the over-lock machine, then when you get the thread you can set it up again?

ESTELA. No. I don't know how to set it up on that new machine.

CARMEN. Rosali can do that later. She knows how to do it; **qué no,** Rosalí?

ROSALI. **Sí, Doña** Carmen.

ESTELA. Why don't you just do what I'm asking you to do?

CARMEN. Estela, **no seas terca.** I know what I'm telling you.

ESTELA. So do I. I want to do things differently. I want us to work like an assembly line.

CARMEN. Leave that to the big factories. I've been working long enough to know—

ESTELA. I haven't been working long enough, but I'm intelligent enough to—

CARMEN. Estela, my way is better!

ESTELA. Why do you think your way is better? All my life your way has been better. Maybe that's why my life is so screwed up!

CARMEN. **¡Desgraciada!** I'm only doing it to help you!

ESTELA. Because you know I won't be getting married any time soon so you want to make sure I'm doing something productive with my life so I can support myself. I don't need your help! *(Beat.)*

CARMEN. Where did all that come from? I thought we were arguing about the thread.

ESTELA. You know what I mean. You know I'm right!

CARMEN. All right. If you want me to do the over-lock work I'll do it…I have to remember I work for you now.

ESTELA. **Amá,** don't give me that!

CARMEN. What?

ESTELA. Guilt!

CARMEN. Well, it's true! It's not usual that a mother works for her daughter. So I have to stop being your mother and just be a regular employee that you can boss around and tell what to do.

ESTELA. **¡Ayy, Amá, parele!** You are my mother, but sometimes you get out of line. How can I tell Rosalí and Pancha to stop gossiping when it's you who initiates the **chisme?** You're a bad example!

CARMEN. **Ay, sí.** Blame me! **¡Echame la culpa!** You gossip too when it's convenient.

ESTELA. Look, **Amá,** I don't want to argue with you anymore. I'm frustrated enough by the thought that I might get deported, at the sight of that machine, and at the thought that I am the biggest fool for buying all this junk. So I don't need my mother to make my life any worse! *(Beat.)*

CARMEN. So what are we going to do about the thread?

ESTELA. **¡Oiiiii!** And we're back to the same thing! *(She goes to the over-lock machine and angrily tears a thread spool from the machine and throws it at CARMEN.)* Here! **¡Tenga!** *(The thread spool misses CARMEN by a hair.)*

CARMEN. *(dramatically).* **¡Pegame, Pegame!** Go ahead! Hit me! God's gonna punish you for **enojona!**

ANA. Estela, the iron is ready.

ESTELA. **Amá,** give me a finished dress from the box.

CARMEN. Where are they?

ESTELA. Right next to you by the pile.

CARMEN. **Qué** size?

ESTELA. For the mannequin.

CARMEN. What size is it?

ROSALI. It's a size seven, **Doña** Carmen.

CARMEN *(sarcastically)*. Thank you, Rosali. *(CARMEN digs into the box and gets a dress. She gives it to ESTELA who begins to iron the dress carefully.)*

ESTELA. *(to ANA)*. Pay close attention to how I'm ironing this dress. Always, always use the steam. And don't burn the **tul, por favor.** On the skirt just a couple of strokes to make it look decent. It's real easy, just don't burn the **tul,** okay?

ANA. Okay.

ESTELA. Check the water, and when it gets low…Tell me so I can send you to buy some more water for it.

ANA. Why do you have to buy the water?

ESTELA. Because regular water is too dirty, it needs distilled water for clean steam. *(ESTELA finishes ironing the dress. She shakes it a bit then puts it on the mannequin. All the WOMEN stare at the dress.)*

ROSALI. **Que bonito.** How I would like to wear a dress like that.

PANCHA. But first you have to turn into a stick to wear something like that.

ROSALI. Yeah, but they're worth it.

ANA. How much do they pay us for making these dresses?

ROSALI. Estela, we get thirteen dollars for these, no?

ANA. Oh, yeah? How much do they sell them for at the stores?

ESTELA. They tell me they sell them at Bloomingdale's for about two hundred dollars.

WOMEN. ¡¡¿Qué?!!

ANA. Dang!! *(Lights fade.)*

Scene Two

> AT RISE: *Lights come on. The* WOMEN *are busy working. The* **"Cucaracha"** *is played on the horn by the lunch mobile outside announcing its arrival.*

ANA. Okay, there's the **lonchera.** Anybody want anything for lunch?

CARMEN. The **lonchera** is here already?

ESTELA. Ana, just hurry back.

ROSALI. Can you get me something to drink? How much are those tomato juices?

ANA. A V-8?

ROSALI. **Si, eso.**

ANA. I think they're 80 cents. You want anything else?

ROSALI. No, no, I'm not hungry.

ESTELA. Ana, lend me a dollar.

ANA. What do you think I am? A bank? This is the third time. One can only go so far on 67 dollars a week.

ESTELA. Ana, if you are not happy here go back to working at McDonald's.

ANA. I would… (*CARMEN stares at ANA.*)…But…You still want to borrow the dollar?

ESTELA. Are you going to charge me interest?

ANA. Of course. What do you want me to buy you?

ESTELA. A burrito **de chicharrón.**

ANA. Pancha, do you want anything?

PANCHA. **Si.** Bring me four tacos.

CARMEN. Pancha, aren't you going to want some of my mole?

PANCHA. Ana, bring me three tacos, **no más.** (*PANCHA gives ANA money.*)

ESTELA. Ana, if you have money left, could you buy some distilled water at the corner store?

ANA. Anything else, boss? (*ANA leaves to buy the food. CARMEN waits until ESTELA shuts the door.*)

CARMEN. **Bueno,** if we are already going to hell for being a bunch of **chismosas,** there's no use in hiding it any longer. (*CARMEN digs into a pile of dresses and takes out a book. She shows it to PANCHA and ROSALI. CARMEN whispers.*) **¡Miren!** (*ROSALI quickly sees the illustrations on the front cover and is shocked.*)

ROSALI. **Doña** Carmen!

CARMEN. I was cleaning the garage and I found a whole pile of dirty books. I think they belong to my oldest son.

PANCHA. What's the book called?

ROSALI. (*reading title*). Two Hundred Sexual Positions Illustrated.

PANCHA. I didn't know there were so many. (*ROSALI and PANCHA gather around CARMEN to look at the book. ESTELA has not noticed them. Instead she notices a letter being dropped in the mail slot. ESTELA reads the letter.*)

ROSALI. (*shocked*). **Ay, Dios,** how can these women do this?

PANCHA. They're probably gymnasts.

CARMEN. The photographer must have used a special lens on this picture.

PANCHA. Which picture?

CARMEN. The one on page 69.

ROSALI. I didn't know people could do that.

PANCHA. **¡Hijole!** Imagine if you had married this man, and you had never seen him until your wedding night.

CARMEN. **¡N'ombre, ni lo mande dios!** How it hurt with a regular one.

PANCHA. **Mire, Doña** Carmen. This woman looks like you, but that doesn't stop her.

CARMEN. Ahh. She's so big. **No le da verguenza.**

ROSALI. I didn't know they had large women in porno books.

PANCHA. I guess some men enjoy watching big women.

ESTELA. (*sees them looking at the book*). What are you looking at? You're suppose to be working! The food has not gotten here yet.

PANCHA. Estela, come look. It's a dirty book.

ESTELA. Why are you looking at that?

CARMEN. Estela, **no mas ven a ver.** *(ESTELA hesitates, but is curious and gives in. She sees the pictures of the large women and is shocked.)*

ESTELA. People this fat shouldn't be having sex! Ichhh!

ROSALI. Look, Estela, there's a guy in here that looks like your "Tormento."

ESTELA. Where?!! *(ROSALI shows her, then suddenly the door is kicked open.)* Aughhhhhh!!!!!

> *(ANA enters with her hands full of food.)*

PANCHA. Estela, calm down.

ESTELA. I thought it was **la migra!**

ANA. Sorry! I kicked the door open because my hands are full...

ESTELA. From now on these doors are to remain closed and locked at all times, okay? If you go outside, you knock on the door like this... *(She knocks in code rhythm.)*...so we know it's just one of us. Don't ever kick the door again.

ANA. Isn't that going a bit to extremes?

PANCHA. **Vamos a estar como gallinas enjauladas.**

ESTELA. No. We just have to be careful.

ROSALI. So how do you do the knock?

ESTELA *(exemplifies)*. Knock once. Pause. Then knock twice. Then repeat.

ANA. Well, if it makes you feel better...

ESTELA. Yes. it would.

ANA. All right. Here's the food. *(ANA places the food on the table.)*

ESTELA. Did you remember the water?

ANA. Yeah, I brought the water! *(ANA gives the bottle of water to ESTELA and distributes the food. To the WOMEN:)* What were you doing?

ALL. *(hiding the book)*. Nothin'.

ANA. What are you hiding?

ALL. Nothin'. *(Pause.)*

PANCHA. We don't want to pervert you.

ANA. You don't want to pervert me more than I've already perverted you?

ROSALI. It's a dirty book.

ANA. Let me see it.

CARMEN. No! You're too young to be looking at these things.

ANA. Fine. You've seen them once, you've seen it all.

PANCHA. Ana!

CARMEN. ¿Qué? Repeat what you just said. Don't tell me you've been "messing around."

ANA. No. It's just that I probably know more than most of you and you're thinking that you can pervert me. Stuuuuupiiid!!

CARMEN. And how is it that you know so much if you haven't done it?

ANA. ...I read a lot.

PANCHA. But not because you read a lot means you know what's what.

ANA. Go ahead. Ask me anything you always wanted to know about sex but were afraid to ask. I'll tell you. *(All the WOMEN are tempted.)*

ROSALI. How do you masturbate...? *(PANCHA, CARMEN, and ESTELA stare at ROSALI in shock.)*

ANA. What?

CARMEN. **¡Híjole!** If your **Apá** were to hear you...**¡Híjole!**

ANA. I wouldn't be talking like this in front of my father.

CARMEN. Can you believe her? Girls nowadays think they know so much that's why they end up **panzonas.**

ANA. No. They end up pregnant because they don't use contraceptives.

PANCHA. Are you sure all you do is read a lot?

CARMEN. Your husband's not going to like you knowing so much.

PANCHA. A girl shouldn't know so much.

ANA. I'm not a girl, I'm a woman.

PANCHA. **Uuy, uy, la** Miss Know-it-all.

CARMEN. In my day, a girl became a woman when she lost her virginity.

ANA. That was then. I read somewhere that calling someone a "girl" is just as bad as when white men used to call black men—

CARMEN. *(starts to laugh uncontrollably).* I...I...remember...

ESTELA. **Amá,** it's 12:20, no more stories. If we gossip people are gonna hear everything outside and even if we close the doors they'll know it's a sewing factory because only women talking chisme can sound like chickens cackling.

CARMEN. But it's what I know how to do best, my reason for living.

ESTELA. I'm begging you. *(CARMEN remains quiet for a few seconds then she begins to laugh uncontrollably again.)*

PANCHA. Why are you laughing? *(CARMEN continues laughing, unable to speak.)*

ANA. **¿Amá, qué le píco?** *(The laughter is contagious.)*

CARMEN. I just got a back flash of when I lost my virginity.

ANA. That bad, huh?

CARMEN. The night I eloped with your father on the bike...

ESTELA. **Bueno,** if the **migra** deports me we know whose fault it is. **Amá,** no work, no money, no factory! Is that clear enough?!

CARMEN. **Pero,** don't get upset. Estela, it's lunch time.

PANCHA. **Pues sí.**

ESTELA. It gets me so annoyed to hear her talk and talk... And with all the work we have! Just promise me that you'll finish, all right? I'll stop bothering you if you can do that.

WOMEN. *(look to each other).* **Pues bueno.** We promise.

ESTELA. If not you'll go to hell?!

WOMEN. *(look to each other again and think about it).* **Pues bueno.**

CARMEN. **Sí, sí, sí,** we'll go to hell. Can I continue? Okay, **pues** after riding on his bike for so long, I had to pee so bad! So we stopped in the mountains somewhere. I ran behind a tree, squatted, and just peed. That night, after we got settled, I didn't know what was going to happen. After we did it, I started itching and scratching down there 'til my **cuchupeta** got so red. I thought something was wrong, but I asked him and he said it was suppose to hurt and bleed. Then I found out it wasn't him. I had peed on poison ivy. And how it hurt! *(The WOMEN laugh sympathetically and slowly gather around the table to eat.)* **Panchita,** try some of my **mole.**

PANCHA. *(looking at mole).* But, **Doña** Carmen, it's green.

CARMEN. It's green **mole**...Ana, you didn't try some **mole.** It's real good.

ANA. No way! It looks like...yukkkk!

CARMEN. **Aver,** Rosalí, come try some. There's plenty.

ROSALI. Thank you, **pero,** I'm not hungry.

CARMEN. But you haven't eaten anything.

ROSALI. I drink eight glasses of water a day and I don't feel hungry. Water gets rid of the fat.

CARMEN. Ana, you should be drinking eight waters.

ANA. And you should too...Oh no, you get clogged.

ESTELA. **Amá** just be very careful with the **mole.** I don't want any of the dresses getting stained. *(PANCHA scoops some mole with a piece of tortilla. She eats the scoop.)*

CARMEN. You like it, Pancha?

PANCHA. *(lying).* Yeah, it's real good, **Doña** Carmen... *(ROSALI carefully strays away from the table and drinks her V-8. ROSALI swallows a pill. She goes to the window and peeks out through the curtain. She spots **el Tormento** outside.)*

ROSALI. **¡Miralo!** There's Andrés! Estela, come to the window! Your Tormento is outside! *(PANCHA, CARMEN, and ANA run to the window, beating ESTELA.)*

ESTELA. No, don't go to the window! Get away from the window!

ANA. No one can see us!

ESTELA. Get down! Make some room for me!

CARMEN. I don't see what you could possibly see in him.

ESTELA. He's cute and he likes me.

CARMEN. He doesn't even have good **nalgas.** They're this small. *(She exemplifies with her hands.)*

ANA. **Amá,** why are you so preoccupied with the size of a man's butt?

ROSALI. That's not what counts.

CARMEN. Because your father doesn't have any. *(ESTELA goes to the door and opens it. She fixes herself a bit and stands in front of the door.)*

PANCHA. Estela, I thought you said that door was going to remain closed.

ROSALI. Estela, get away from the door, because if the van passes they'll just see the **nopal** on your forehead and take you away.

ESTELA. But he wants to talk to me. He sent me a letter. *(ESTELA leaves, closing the door. CARMEN and PANCHA are still eating their tacos. They stick to the window like flies.)*

CARMEN. What could he be telling her? She's laughing her head off.

ROSALI. **¡Miren cómo coquetea!** What a flirt. You never suspected she had it in her.

PANCHA. She's worse than Ana.

ANA. What's that suppose to mean? *(CARMEN holds her taco carelessly and the mole spills out onto some dresses.)*

PANCHA. ¡**Mire, Doña** Carmen! You're spilling the mole!

ANA. **Amá,** Estela is going to kill you!

CARMEN. ¡**Ayy, no!** *(CARMEN quickly puts the taco on the table. She grabs a cloth and tries to clean the dresses.)*

PANCHA. ¡**Aguas!** Here she comes!

CARMEN. What am I going to do?

ANA. *(runs to the door and locks it).* Quick, **Amá.** Hide the dresses! We'll clean them later.

CARMEN. ¿**Dónde los escondo?**

ROSALI. Anywhere! *(ESTELA tries to open the door. While the women run around hysterically trying to find the best place to hide the dresses.)*

ESTELA. Let me in.

ANA. Who is it?

ESTELA. You know who it is!

ANA. I don't know who. *(She gestures to the women to hurry.)* You think we should open the door? What if it's **la migra?**

ESTELA. Ana, open the door! *(She pounds on the door.)*

ANA. How do we know it's you?

(ESTELA finally knocks the secret code and ANA lets her in.)

ESTELA. When the cat is away the mice come out to play. What were you doing?

WOMEN. Nothing!

CARMEN. **Ahora si.** Show us the letter first, and tell us what you talked about.

ESTELA. It's private.

ROSALI. Come on, Estela, **no te hagas de rogar,** you know you want to show it to us.

ESTELA. ¡**Que metiches!** This letter is for me. He only intended for me to read it…All right, I'll read it out loud. *(The WOMEN pull out their chairs and get comfortable. ESTELA clears her throat and reads the letter dramatically.)* "Dear Estela…" *(The WOMEN get excited after the first "Dear.")* "Dear Estela…How I dig you. Let me count the waves."

ROSALI. Ahhh, it's a poem.

ESTELA. "Wave one: 'cause you look real nice when you pass by me and say, 'Hi.' Wave two: 'cause you seem real smart, Wave three: 'cause your eyes are like fresas. And your lips are like mangos, juicy and delicious, **listos para chupar."**

PANCHA. Maybe he works at the supermarket in the fruit section.

ESTELA. *(continues).* "So how about it? You wanna go cruising down Whittier Boulevard, see a movie, or anything else you wanna do?" I told him I liked the letter a lot. So we're going to the movies tonight.

ROSALI. To the movies? It sounds serious. But be careful with those wandering hands.

ESTELA. He's not that kind of guy.

CARMEN. So what are you going to wear? Don't go dressing up like a scarecrow now.

ESTELA. I don't dress like that.

CARMEN. That's why you scare them away.

ESTELA. **Como es, Amá.** He likes me for me. Didn't you hear? He said I'm intelligent. He doesn't care how I dress.

CARMEN. Estela, let me make you a dress, **horitita te lo case.**

ESTELA. No. I can dress myself. And anyway, what are we doing sitting around. Lunch is over. Let's get to work. **¡A trabajar!** *(Lights fade old.)*

Scene Three

> AT RISE: *Lights fade in. The WOMEN are busy working in their designated working areas. PANCHA is by the racks attaching strings to hang the dresses.*

ANA. Estela, there are no more dresses to iron. What else should I do?

ESTELA. Ah…Pancha, can you show Ana what you are doing? *(ANA goes to the racks. ROSALI turns on the radio.)*

PANCHA. *(showing ANA).* **Así hazia.** This way, *(ANA quickly understands what she has to do and begins her work. The phone rings. ESTELA picks it up. On the radio we hear the following:)*

RADIO. *(voice-over).* It's 3:45 and another hot, beautiful day in L.A. This is KLOVE—Radín Arnor…Now back to our talk show, "Esperanza."

ESPERANZA. *(voice-over).* For those of you who just joined us today we are discussing abusive spouses. We have our last caller on the line. Caller, are you there?

CALLER. *(voice-over).* Hi, I'm not going to give you my name because my husband listens to this station. I wanted to know what I can do to…Well. I want to know how I can talk to my husband when he gets angry.

ESPERANZA. *(voice-over).* How long has he been abusive?

CALLER. *(voice-over).* Ah…Well, he wasn't like this when we got married…He was always sweet. So, I don't know what has happened to him. He tells me if I did whatever he asked he wouldn't have to hit me. But I do what he says and it's still not good enough. Last time he hit me because…

PANCHA. *(switches the dial on the radio).* Isn't there anything else?

CARMEN. **Pobre major,** I'm lucky **mi viejo** doesn't hit me.

ANA. Lucky? Why lucky? It should be expected that he doesn't. That woman should leave her husband. Women have the right to say "no."

PANCHA. You think it's that easy?

ANA. No, she's probably dependent on him financially, or the church tells her to endure, or she's doing it for the children.

PANCHA. You're so young. Did it ever occur to you that maybe she loves him?

ANA. I'm sure she does. But we can't allow ourselves to be abused anymore. We have to assert ourselves. We have to realize that we have rights! We have the right to control our bodies. The right to exercise our sexuality. And the right to take control of our destiny. But it all begins when we start saying…

(ANA quickly climbs on top of a sewing machine to continue preaching.)...
¡Ya basta! No more! We should learn how to say no! Come on, **Amá,** say it!
Say it!
CARMEN. What?
ANA. Say it! "No!"
CARMEN. Okay, I won't.
ANA. **Amá,** say "No!"
CARMEN. *(as in she won't).* No.
ANA. Good! Rosalí, say it.
ROSALI. *(casually).* **¿Pues por qué no?** No.
ANA. Pancha, say it. No! *(PANCHA stares at ANA, she won't say it.)*
ESTELA. **Ya, ya,** Norma Rae, get off and get back to work!
PANCHA. Why don't you run for office? **Tan pequeña** and she thinks and acts
like she knows everything.
ANA. I don't know everything, but I know a lot. I read a lot. But it just amazes
me to hear you talk the way you do. A women's liberation movement hap-
pened 20 years ago, and you act like it hasn't even happened.
PANCHA. **Mira,** all those **gringas** shouting about liberation hasn't done a thing
for me...And if you were married you would realize it. **Bueno,** and if you
know so much how come you're not in college?
ANA. Because I don't have the money. I have to wait a year to be eligible for
financial aid.
PANCHA. I always thought that if you were smart enough a college would give
you a scholarship. Maybe you should read some more and get one so you
don't have to be here making 67 dollars a week and hearing us talk the way
we do. *(A car honking is heard outside.)*
CARMEN. **Ya llegó mi viejo.** Ana, get ready. **Vámonos!**
ANA. No, **Amá,** you go. I'll take the bus...I want to finish this last pile.
CARMEN. You do? Ah, I know why you want to stay, **metiche. Bueno. Adiós.**
WOMEN. **Adiós.** *(CARMEN leaves. PANCHA collects her belongings. A car
honking is heard outside.)*
PANCHA. I'm leaving too.
ROSALI. Pancha, do you want a ride?
PANCHA. **Sí, sí.** *(They get ready to leave.)*
ROSALI. **Adiós,** Estela. Good luck on your date with your Tormento. Well, not
too good. I hope you won't need to go to confession tomorrow. *(ROSALI
and ESTELA giggle.)* **Hasta mañana.** *(They leave. Soon after ESTELA hangs
up the phone.)*
ANA. So who was that?
ESTELA. Maria...She called to wish me a happy birthday.
ANA. Isn't it this Friday?
ESTELA. Yes, but she couldn't wait to tell me that she's getting married in three
months. She wants me to make her wedding dress. *(They continue working.)*
Ana, before **el Tormento** gets here you have to leave.
ANA. Why?

ESTELA. Because I don't want you writing about it. I know what you do in the bathroom.

ANA. Come on, Estela, where else can I write? I come here and all it is, is "work, work, work" from you and **Amá.** I go home and then she still wants me to help her cook, and clean...

ESTELA. So what are you writing?

ANA. I'm keeping a journal so when I become "rich and famous" I can write my autobiography.

ESTELA. Ana, who do you think you are? "Rich and famous."

ANA. I'm not going to be stuck here forever.

ESTELA. And I am?

ANA. No...I didn't say that. **Amá y Apá,** always said that you wouldn't do anything with your life, but you're proving them wrong. It takes a lot of guts and courage to do what you're doing. And even if you're in a mess, you have your own business, at 24! I'm very proud of you.

ESTELA. *(a little embarrassed).* All right, Ana, you can stay.

ANA. So when is **el Tormento** picking you up?

ESTELA. In a few minutes. I won't even have a chance to freshen up. *(ESTELA goes to the sink and washes her face. She stares at herself in the mirror.)* Ana, do you have any makeup?

ANA. Not with me.

ESTELA. *(continues to stare at herself with an excited face).* I don't have anything to wear! *(ESTELA runs to look for clothes to wear. ANA goes to the bathroom and sits on the toilet and begins to write. Spotlight on ANA.)*

ANA. Another day and we're in deep...trouble...I keep having arguments with Pancha, and even though she doesn't like me, I feel sort of sorry for her. I wish I could tell her what to do, but she won't listen to me. Like the rest of the women, she won't take me seriously. They make fun of me...So why do I stay?...It's true. I stay. Because no matter how much my mother could try and force me to come, I could decide not to come back. But I do...Why? *(Fade out.)*

> *(Lights come on. ESTELA is holding the pink dress. She looks to the bathroom to see if ANA is watching. She then holds the dress to her body as if wearing it. She dances slowly with it, imagining herself dancing with el Tormento. Lights slowly fade.)*

Scene Four

> *AT RISE: Lights come on after a brief pause. On the calendar it is Tuesday, September 8, 1987. On the clock it is 7:10 a.m. Before the lights are fully on, ESTELA's crying is heard. The WOMEN are gathered around her.*

ANA. So what happened?!

ESTELA. He...He...

PANCHA. What did he do?

ESTELA. He...He...

ROSALI & ANA. What?!!

ESTELA. I don't want to talk about it! *(She pulls herself together.)* Let's forget about it and get started on the work…**Amá,** you said you were going to the bakery.

CARMEN. Ah, **sí, sí.**

ESTELA. Rosalí, how are you doing with the zippers?

ROSALI. I'm halfway done.

ESTELA. Ana, turn on the iron. There are a lot more dresses that need ironing. Pancha, are you almost done with the skirts for size 3/4?

PANCHA. No. I just started that lot a few minutes before I left yesterday.

CARMEN. Does anybody want anything from the bakery?

ESTELA. I want a juice…Ana, could you…? *(ESTELA decides to look in her purse instead. She takes out all of her pennies and gives them to CARMEN.)*

CARMEN. Estela, you can tell me. What could he have possibly done to get you this upset?

ESTELA. You're so stubborn, **Amá!** I said nothing happened. I'm just over-reacting.

CARMEN. Just remember, I'm your mother. If you can't trust your mother, who can you trust? *(The WOMEN agree with CARMEN, but ESTELA does not give in. CARMEN leaves. Quickly after, before ANA has a chance to lock the door, CARMEN runs back in and leans on the door to close it with her body. She is breathing heavily.)* It's out there again! Like a vulture!

PANCHA. What?

ALL. ¡La migra! *(They gasp. They all close the curtains and bolt the doors.)*

ROSALI. Was it going by slow or was it going by fast?

CARMEN. It was going slow like it was going to turn at the corner and circle around the block and come back!

ANA. You don't know that for sure!

CARMEN. Estela, it just occurred to me. Why don't you go home and work in the garage on our old sewing machine?

ESTELA. I could do that. But I can't. I don't trust you.

ROSALI. We'll work. Just go! **¡Rápido!**

ESTELA. And you'll work?

ALL. Yes!!

ESTELA. What should I take with me to work on?

ROSALI. Just go! I'll get my Jaíme to take you the work. Go!

ESTELA. Okay! *(ESTELA begins to leave. She opens the door.)* He's out there! *(ESTELA runs to the bathroom.)*

ANA. Who? The man in the van?

PANCHA. No. **¡El Tormento!**

ROSALI. Estela, come out of there! Go before they come. **¡Por favor!**

CARMEN. Estela, get out of there right now! **¡No seas mensa!** Men are not worth crying over. And they're certainly not worth you getting deported. *(CARMEN waits for ESTELA to come out.)* **Vas a verlo. ¡Entonces a la fuerza!** *(CARMEN pulls on the curtain and tries to drag ESTELA out. ESTELA wraps herself with the curtain and CARMEN is unable to get her out.)*

ESTELA. No! Leave me alone! I'm not coming out!

ANA. Estela, who's that **gringa** he's kissing? *(The curtain flies open and ESTELA races to the door.)*

ESTELA. Who?!! Where?!!

ANA. I lied. Now go home! *(ANA pushes ESTELA out the door and locks it. Beat.)*

ROSALI. *(looking out of the window).* I don't think they're coming.

PANCHA. Are you sure you saw it, **Doña** Carmen?

ANA. They would have been here by now. **¿Qué no?**

CARMEN. I guess so…I don't understand. *(They sigh in relief.)*

ESTELA. *(offstage, knocking on the door).* Ana, let me in.

(ESTELA knocks on the door and ANA finally lets her in.)

ESTELA. I'm going to stay.

CARMEN. All right. *(ESTELA closes the door, locks it. The WOMEN begin working; machines roar.)*

ANA. Shit! I wish we had a fan here. *(ANA turns on the radio.)*

ESTELA. I don't want the dresses getting dirty with the dust. *(Lights fade.)*

Scene Five

AT RISE: Lights come on. The WOMEN are busy working. ANA goes to the bathroom. She sits on the toilet and starts writing in her journal. Spotlight on ANA.

ANA. It feels just as bad as when I was doing the fries at McDonald's. Pouring frozen sticks of potatoes into boiling lard and the steam hitting my face for $3.35 an hour…This place stinks! I hate going to the store and having to climb over the winos, and ignore the catcalls of the sexist dope addicts and the smell of urine and marijuana on the street, and…I went to the store today and I saw an old friend. She's pregnant, again. She says she's happy and she doesn't care if she's on welfare. When she was still in high school she told me she knew I was going to do something with my life. I don't want her to know I work here.

(Lights come back on. The WOMEN shift in their chairs, uncomfortable with the heat in their buttocks. ROSALI fans herself and notices that CARMEN has an odd facial expression.)

ROSALI. **Doña** Carmen, why do you have that strange look on your face?

CARMEN. I reached over to get the next dress and I felt something moving inside. I think I'm pregnant.

PANCHA. Don't say that, **Doña** Carmen, or I'll lose faith in God. You're almost 50 and already have eight children. I'm barely 32 and can't have any.

CARMEN. Isn't that odd, I'm suppose to be an **abuelita** by now. **Pero no puede ser,** it can't be.

ESTELA. **Amá,** don't tell me you still have sex? At your age and in your physical condition?

ANA. **Cállense,** I heard something on the news about a raid. *(The WOMEN listen to the radio.)*

RADIO. *(voice-over).* KNXW News all the time…The time now is 2:35 p.m. Twenty illegal aliens were captured today at the Goodnight pillow factory…

PANCHA. That's only a few blocks away!

RADIO. *(voice-over).* The INS was given a tip by anonymous sources yesterday of the factory's illegal hiring of aliens. The owner was fined up to 2,000 dollars per alien… *(PANCHA, CARMEN, and ROSALI do the sign of the holy cross.)*

CARMEN. Estela, why don't you call the Glitz company and ask them, no, demand that they pay you for the past order of dresses. Even if they were late, they still have to pay us. You have to get the money. *(The radio is still on.)*

ESTELA. I don't want to be too pushy. They're the only company that has been willing to give us a contract.

CARMEN. Then do it for Pancha and Rosalí. You haven't paid them and **las pobrecitas** can't even buy groceries.

ROSALI. *(lying).* I'm all right, don't worry about me.

ANA. Well, I'm not. Estela, just call. *(ESTELA thinks about it, then she decides to do it.)*

ESTELA. Here I go. *(ANA turns off the radio. ESTELA dials the number on the phone and waits.)*

PANCHA. **¿Saben qué?** My neighbor who works at the Del Monte canning factory is missing. I have a feeling they deported her. I'm so scared that I'll be waiting for the bus one day and they'll take me.

CARMEN. But you're legal.

PANCHA. *(realizing).* Ayy, I keep forgetting.

ESTELA. Hello…Can I speak to Mrs. Glitz?…Hello, this is Estela. Estela Garcia…No, but we're almost finished…I know we agreed that you would pay me for the last two weeks this Friday, but I was wondering, maybe, if it isn't too much trouble, if I could get an advance check…today…I know…I know…You're right, Mrs. Glitz…Ah…But my workers…I know, but I've got a lawyer working on that…I'll get it to you by next week…No, I mean it this time. Next week…Okay, Mrs. Glitz…I'm sorry…Yes, I'll see you on Friday. *(ESTELA hangs up. Her face expresses worry and fear.)*

CARMEN. **¿Qué te dijo la vieja?**

PANCHA. What did she tell you?

ESTELA. She asked about my proof of employment papers again. Then she warned me that if **la migra** shuts us down, she won't pay us for all the work we've done.

CARMEN. **¡Mendiga vieja!**

ANA. Do you think she would really do that? *(CARMEN and ESTELA talk among themselves.)*

ESTELA. **Amá,** why is this happening to me? I'm going to get deported, aren't I, **Amá?**

CARMEN. **Mira,** supposing you do get deported, we'll get a coyote to smuggle you back in. Somehow we'll find the money.

ESTELA. But I would have let you and everybody down. I'll lose everything that I've worked for, the factory, and my self-respect. And I don't know if I can start again.

CARMEN. Estela, your **Apá** was thrown back to Mexico four times, but he kept coming back. If you did it once, you can do it again.

ESTELA. I hope so. *(ESTELA pulls herself together and continues working. She picks up a bundle of sewn skirts and looks at them. She discovers that they have been sewn wrong.)* Pancha, do you realize you sewed all of the size 3/4 skirts backwards?

PANCHA. I did? No, I didn't!

ESTELA. Look! This is the outside of the material and this is the inside. Have you been doing all the lots this way?

PANCHA. I think so.

ESTELA. ¡**Ay, no!** More repairs! Pancha, please do them again.

PANCHA. No! It's so hot. I don't even feel like working. How do you expect us to work with this heat?

ESTELA. Pancha, I'll help you take them apart.

ANA. Couldn't you open the door?

ESTELA. No!

PANCHA. I can't work like this.

ESTELA. We're going to have to. *(PANCHA grabs the skirt and begins to take them apart. ESTELA is looking at another lot and discovers the stained dresses that CARMEN hid.)* ¡**Amá!** What did I tell you about the **mole?!** *(ESTELA shoves a dress in CARMEN's face.)*

CARMEN. The stains are not so obvious. I was going to clean them, I swear. I didn't want you to see them and get worried.

ESTELA. It's going to be hell trying to take the stains out! *(ESTELA catches ANA accidently burning the tul.)* Not so close! You're burning the **tul!** Pay close attention to your work or don't do it. Have you been burning it on the other dresses too?! *(ESTELA quickly looks at the dresses on the racks and those that ANA has finished ironing.)*

ANA. I thought if I did it this way it would be okay and save us time. I can't stand the heat and the steam.

ESTELA. Can't any of you do anything right? Do I have to do everything myself so that these dresses get finished? *(PANCHA gets busy pulling on the two pieces of material on the skirt instead of cutting the sewn thread one stitch at a time.)* Pancha, don't pull on them or you'll tear them. I said I was going to help you do the repairs.

PANCHA. I want to get out of here and go home.

ESTELA. You have to finish this work.

PANCHA. Not in this heat!

ANA. Estela, please open the door!

ESTELA. For the last time, I won't!

PANCHA. Then I'll open it. *(PANCHA walks determinedly towards the door. ESTELA stands in her way.)* We're all burning in here. I'm getting dizzy.

ESTELA. I'm sorry it's so hot, but the van may be out there and I don't want them to see anything.

PANCHA. It's so selfish of you to keep the door closed when we are all burning!

ESTELA. I'm burning too!

PANCHA. But you're the one with the criminal record! It's not fair that we are all paying for your fault. We are all legal now!

ESTELA. Then go! Open the door, then leave.

PANCHA. All right! I'll leave, but with my work. *(PANCHA grabs the skirts, begins pulling on them, tearing the material.)* Let's see what else I've done. *(PANCHA continues tearing. ESTELA tries to stop her by holding PANCHA's hands. PANCHA and ESTELA begin to get physical, almost ready to strike each other. ROSALI quickly steps between them to prevent them from hitting each other.)*

CARMEN. Estela, ¡párale!

ROSALI. ¡Basta! ¡No se pelén! *(ROSALI faints and falls to the floor. ESTELA and PANCHA stop fighting.)*

CARMEN. Rosalí!

ANA. Rosalí, are you all right?

CARMEN. What could be wrong with her?

PANCHA. It's this **pinche** heat! It's your fault, Estela. Here you have us all locked up! See what happened?!

ESTELA *(shakes ROSALI, who does not respond).* Rosalí, please wake up!

PANCHA. Let's take her to the hospital!

CARMEN. ¡¿Pero que locura?! The hospital is three blocks away. We can't carry her, **la migra** is going to see us.

PANCHA. **Ayy sí, ¿entonces qué quiere?** You want her to die?

CARMEN. She's not going to die!

PANCHA. And how do you know?

CARMEN. Don't exaggerate! *(While PANCHA and CARMEN argue, ANA thinks quickly of what to do. She searches around the bathroom for something. She finds ESTELA's perfume and grabs some tissue. ANA uses it to wake up ROSALI. ROSALI becomes conscious and PANCHA and CARMEN finally stop arguing.)*

ROSALI. Ah...

PANCHA. Rosalí, you want to go to the hospital?

ROSALI. ¿Qué páso?

CARMEN. **M'ija,** you fainted.

ANA. Are you okay?

ROSALI. **Sí...Si...**I'm okay.

PANCHA. I'm gonna take you home.

ROSALI. I'll just rest a little...I'll feel better...

PANCHA. You can't continue working like this. I'll take you home. It's no bother, because I'm going home myself. *(CARMEN gets a glass of water and an aspirin.)*

CARMEN. **Pobrecita,** here, drink this.

ESTELA. Rosalí, I'm sorry.

PANCHA. *(helps ROSALI up).* Where's your bag? *(ROSALI points to it. PAN-CHA gets the bag.)* Let's go. *(PANCHA leaves with ROSALI without hesitation or saying good-bye. ESTELA fights the urge to cry.)*

ESTELA. *(to herself).* I'm sorry, Rosalí.

CARMEN. Don't blame yourself. Something like this was going to happen.

ANA. Isn't Rosalí the only one who knows how to set up the over-lock machine? *(ANA and CARMEN took at each other worried. ESTELA has an expression of hopelessness. Lights slowly fade out.)*

End of Act One

Act Two

Scene One

> AT RISE: CARMEN and ESTELA are the only ones present, working silently. On the clock it is 8:15 a.m. On the calendar it is Wednesday, September 9, 1987.

CARMEN. I don't think Pancha's coming back.

ESTELA. She's only an hour late. Maybe she went to visit Rosali at her house.

CARMEN. Pancha is never late. *Footsteps are heard outside. Then the code knock is heard. ESTELA smiles and goes to open the doors.)*

ESTELA. See, **Amá!** I knew she would come. *ESTELA rushes to open the door. ANA is at the door.)* Oh, it's just you.

> *(ANA quickly comes in carrying a brown paper bag with detergent which she puts on the table.)*

ANA. **¡Miren!** Come look out the window. There's this strange homeless person outside. *(They go look.)*

CARMEN. What's so strange about him?

ANA. I don't recognize him.

ESTELA. So?

ANA. I think he's just disguised. He doesn't look desperate enough.

CARMEN. I've never seen him before.

ANA. I think he's a spy?

ESTELA. A spy?

ANA. Look! There's Pancha!

ESTELA. God! Thank you! She's come back!

CARMEN. But look, he's talking to her and she's pointing this way! *(They drop to the floor. A few seconds later they go back to looking.)* I wonder what he's asking her?

ESTELA. I wonder what she's telling him?

ANA. **¡Aguas!** Here she comes.

(They scatter. ANA takes out the stain remover from the bag. CAR-MEN goes back to sewing. The code knock is heard and ESTELA opens the door. PANCHA comes in.)

ESTELA. Pancha, what did the bum ask you?

PANCHA. The bum? Ooo. He asked me where your Tormento lives.

ANA. I guess he wasn't a spy after all.

PANCHA. **¡N'ombre!** He's just another one of his **vago** friends.

CARMEN. **¡Bola de viejos cochinos!** No good drug addicts!

ESTELA. **Ya!** Stop talking about him!

CARMEN. Are you defending him? After what he did?

ANA. *(aside).* **Amá,** Estela finally told you?

CARMEN. No. I'm trying to get it out of her.

ESTELA. Forget it! I'll never tell you what happened on the date.

ANA. Okay, Estela. Be like that. I'll never tell you anything either. *(ESTELA doesn't budge. ANA and CARMEN give up.)*

CARMEN. Panchita, we were afraid you wouldn't come back.

PANCHA. Why?

CARMEN. Well, after what happened yesterday.

PANCHA. I have to come to work even if I don't want to…I went to visit Rosali this morning.

ANA. How is she doing?

PANCHA. She's doing better.

ESTELA. Is there any chance of her coming back this week?

PANCHA. **No se.** She looks pale. This heat will be bad for her. I'm surprised I didn't faint myself.

ESTELA. Maybe I will get a fan.

PANCHA. Estela, what do you want me to work on?

ESTELA. I don't know how we are going to manage without her. Pancha, please finish the zippers that Rosali was working on.

CARMEN. Estela, give me the manual for the over-lock machine. I'm going to try and set it up myself.

ESTELA. **Alli esta en el cajon.** We'll just have to go on without her. Ana, did you get the stain remover?

ANA. It's on the table. How many dresses need washing?

ESTELA. Twelve. I should put my mother to wash them, but since she'll be busy with the over-lock I guess I'll do them.

ANA. How many dresses have we finished?

ESTELA. They're on the racks. And there are a couple in that box that just need ironing.

ANA. *(looking at the racks).* That's all?

ESTELA. I found ten dresses with the tul burnt in them. Those were almost finished, but now the **tul** has to be replaced.

ANA. I guess I'll do that.

ESTELA. **Amá,** can you stay late today?

CARMEN. **Pues sí.**

ESTELA. Ana, will you stay late too?

ANA. Stay late?...Sure. (*ANA irons a dress carefully and slowly. ESTELA observes ANA for a few seconds.*)

ESTELA. Ana, can you iron faster? Just make them look decent. (*ANA frowns at her suggestion and looks to PANCHA who is attaching hanging strings on the dresses next to her.*)

ANA. (*to PANCHA*). It's not that I don't iron fast enough, it's that whenever I finish ironing a dress I stop for a minute to really look at it. I never realized just how much work, **puro lomo,** as my mother would say, went into making it. Then I imagine the dress at Bloomingdale's and I see a tall and skinny woman looking at it. She instantly gets it and with no second thoughts she says "charge it!" She doesn't think of the life of the dress before the rack, of the labor put into it. I shake the dress a little and try to forget it's not for me. I place a plastic bag over it then I put it on the rack and push it away. It happens to me with every dress.

PANCHA. What an imagination. So what are you gonna study when you go to college next year? Where are you going?

ANA. To New York University. I'm going to study writing.

CARMEN. **Asi es que** you better be quiet, don't tell her any chisme or one day you're gonna read about it.

PANCHA. And you think you'll make it?

ANA. I think so.

PANCHA. **Pos,** I do think you're a bit **loquita,** but if that's what you need. I think you'll make it.

ANA. **Gracias,** Pancha. (*PANCHA smiles at ANA seeing her differently for the first time. Meanwhile, CARMEN is frustrated with the over-lock machine.*)

CARMEN. ¡Ayy no! ¡No puedo! I try and I try and I can't! ¡Esta cochinada no sirve!

ESTELA. But what can we do? Who else could do it? Can you do it, Pancha?

PANCHA. I don't know anything about those new machines.

ESTELA. **Amá,** give me the manual. (*ESTELA grabs the manual and begins to work on the machine. Talking to the machine:*) Please, **maquinita.** If you behave I'll put on you all the oil you want. **Maquinita,** if you love me, help me.

CARMEN. (*touching her stomach*). Ana, come here, quick. Feel my stomach. (*ANA puts her hand over CARMEN's stomach.*) Can you feel the baby kicking?

ANA. No...**Amá,** are you sure you're pregnant?

CARMEN. I think so. **Aver,** Pancha, tell me if you feel anything.

PANCHA. I'm busy, **Doña** Carmen.

CARMEN. Just come quick, Panchita. Ana doesn't believe me. (*PANCHA gets up from her chair and goes over to CARMEN. She places her hand on CARMEN's stomach.*)

PANCHA. I don't feel anything. I think the heat is getting to you too.

CARMEN. **¿Cómo puede ser?** I can feel it! *(PANCHA nods her head and walks away fanning herself. She heads to the bathroom.)*

ANA. How many months should you be pregnant by now? I haven't noticed you getting any bigger.

CARMEN. I don't know. I've always been fat. I haven't noticed either.

ANA. Have you the symptoms?

CARMEN. Not all of them, but I've been pregnant enough times to know.

ANA. Are you going to keep it?

CARMEN. What do you mean?

ANA. You don't have to have it.

CARMEN. Ana, I don't want to talk about this.

> *(Spotlight on PANCHA. PANCHA stands on the toilet in front of the small window. She opens the window and bathes her face with the breeze. PANCHA begins to cry.)*

PANCHA. **Que bonito viento.** Wind, that's what I am. *(Touching her stomach.)* Empty, like an old rag... *(Praying.)* **Diosito,** why don't you make me a real woman? If I can't have children, why did you make me a woman? *(PANCHA wipes her tears.)*

> *(Lights come on.)*

ESTELA. *(talking to the machine).* **Maquinita,** I'm going to set you up even if it's the last thing I do in this country. *(She holds the manual and follows directions.)* All right. Five threads. They all start from their spools onto the holes, then straight down, into the loops. Then they turn, go in between more loops underneath, then they all go into their needles. Then the electricity comes on... *(She turns on the machine.)*...I insert a piece of material, step on the pedal and...Ta-da! A chain of interwoven threads! I did it!

CARMEN. You fixed it? **¿Pero cómo?**

ESTELA. I persisted and I did it!

CARMEN. **¡Mira que inteligente!**

ANA. That's great, Estela! Now we don't have to worry about it anymore. *(They hear footsteps outside. They instantly freeze and become silent. They look to each other then CARMEN, ANA, and PANCHA quickly go to their purses. Someone is heard outside, then letters are slipped in through the mail slot. The WOMEN relax.)* Just the mailman...

> *(The WOMEN suddenly realize that it probably means bad news for ESTELA. ESTELA picks up an envelope and reads it. No one asks what it says out of respect for her, but they all know it's another letter from the lawyer, ESTELA opens it and is about to read it when they hear footsteps outside. They grab their "Temporary Employment" cards from their purses. ESTELA hides behind CARMEN. Then the code knock is heard. The WOMEN rush to the door. ESTELA opens the door and ROSALI is behind the bar door.)*

EVERYONE. What are you doing here?!

ESTELA. Aren't you suppose to be resting?

ROSALI. I was in bed and I kept imagining Estela getting deported. So I had to come back. I know how badly you must need the over-lock machine.

ESTELA. I fixed it!

ROSALI. *(disappointed).* You did? Well, where are the zippers so I can get started now?

PANCHA. I finished all the zippers.

ROSALI. You did?

ESTELA. Rosalí, I'd rather you go back and get well.

ROSALI. No, Estela, I'm fine. I can help.

ESTELA. It's not worth it if we're fighting and getting sick because of this heat.

ROSALI. It wasn't just the heat…I hadn't eaten and that's why I fainted. I didn't want you to think it was your fault.

PANCHA. But why do you need to lose weight? **'Tas flaca.** *(ROSALI smiles, but doesn't believe PANCHA.)*

CARMEN. Have you eaten already, you still look pale?

ROSALI. No, I'm not hungry, **Doña** Carmen.

CARMEN. But that's what you have been saying and look what happened. Come on, eat something.

ROSALI. I am not hungry.

ANA. Rosalí, you can't see yourself the way we see you and that's why you think you're fat.

CARMEN. Rosalí, you need to eat something.

ROSALI. I'm not hungry!

CARMEN. You need to eat something! *(ROSALI looks at each of them and finally reveals the truth.)*

ROSALI. I'm not hungry because I've been living on diet pills.

CARMEN. So that's the secret diet? **Ayy,** Rosalí, don't you know those **cochinadas** are no good?

ANA. They're real bad for you because I read they're addictive.

ROSALI. I know. When I fainted I saw my body lying there, I thought I was going to die. I couldn't feel my body. And I just kept seeing Estela being deported. Estela. I want to come back to work. This is more important to me than being a size seven.

ESTELA. *(embraces ROSALI).* **Gracias**…Can you work late?

ROSALI. **Claro.**

ESTELA. And you too, Pancha?

PANCHA. **Pos bueno.**

CARMEN. **Entonces todas a trabajar!** *(The WOMEN go to their sewing stations. ESTELA takes out her notebook and dictates the work.)*

ESTELA. **Amá,** let Rosalí do the over-lock work, she's faster. I want you to do lots size two through six. Pancha, you do lots size seven through twelve. Ana, you know what to do. *(ESTELA takes control and the WOMEN are determined to finish. The machines roar like race cars taking off. Lights slowly fade.)*

Scene Two

> *AT RISE: Lights come on. It is 2:00 a.m., and street sounds are heard outside. ROSALI looks around and then stares at her stomach.*

ROSALI. Did you hear that?

ANA. No, what?

ROSALI. A stomach growling. Whose stomach was it?

ESTELA. I don't know, but I'm hungry.

ANA. Me too. **Amá,** is there any rice left?

ROSALI. Did you hear it again?

PANCHA. Rosali, it's your panza.

ROSALI. Yeah, it's me! I haven't heard my stomach growling in so long.

ESTELA. What's there to eat?

CARMEN. I might have something in my purse. Why don't we make something?

PANCHA. All this noise is driving me crazy. I'm going deaf. *(PANCHA turns on the radio. CARMEN gets up, looks around the table then in the refrigerator. All the WOMEN search in their purses for food.)*

CARMEN. **Aaaa,** I found something. Tortillas and…the **mole!**

ALL. Not the **mole!**

PANCHA. I've got something. *(PANCHA takes out a large amount of food from her purse. The WOMEN are surprised with every item she takes out: a box of fried chicken, a hamburger, a bag of chips, a bag of cookies, and a Diet Coke.)* I'm on a diet!

CARMEN. *(aside).* **Se ve.** *(On the radio a "cumbia" has just finished. Then a DISC JOCKEY with a very mellow voice comes on the air.)*

DISC JOCKEY *(voice-over).* It's 2:25 a.m. on an early Thursday morning…I'm falling asleep here to pay my bills. And if you're listening now, you probably are too. So this is for you night owls! The ones that do the night shifts no one wants to do! *(The song "Tequila" blasts on the radio. The WOMEN are so sleepy, they jump around to the music trying to awaken. They eat and shake at the same time. Lights slowly fade.)*

Scene Three

> *AT RISE: Lights come on. It is Thursday, September 10, 1987. On the clock it is 2 p.m. The WOMEN are wearing the same clothes as the day before. As usual, it is extremely hot.*

CARMEN. *(smelling her armpits).* Phueeehh! **¡Fuchi!** I stink. **Aquí huele a pura cuchupeta y pedo.** Phuehhh! Who farted?

ESTELA. **Amá,** it's probably you who did it. Like they say, the one who smells it first is the one who has it underneath her skirt.

ANA. **¡Que calor!** It feels like we're in hell!

PANCHA. How many more dresses to finish, Estela?

ESTELA. Fifteen.

ROSALI. Only fifteen?!

CARMEN. **Dios mio, ya mero acabamos.**

ESTELA. *(counting dresses on rack).* 184, 185, 186. No, we only need 14!

ANA. What a relief! We're almost finished. (*ANA decides to take off her blouse, leaving on her sweaty bra.*)

CARMEN. (*shocked at ANA's actions*). Ana, what are you doing?!

ANA. All this steam has me sweating like a pig.

CARMEN. We're sweating too, but we don't go taking our clothes off!

ANA. So why don't you? We're all women. We all have the same.

CARMEN. Not really. You have bigger **chichis.**

ANA. And you have a bigger **panza!**

CARMEN. That's because I'm pregnant!

ESTELA. You mean we're definitely going to have another baby brat to take care of?

ANA. **Amá,** do you really want to have it?

PANCHA. **Doña** Carmen, give it to me if you don't want it.

CARMEN. I can't just get rid of it, either way…But I don't want to have it.

PANCHA. But you're lucky, **Doña** Carmen.

CARMEN. No. It seems all I do is have children. One after another. I'm tired of this! I can't have this baby. I'll die. Last time I was pregnant the doctor said I almost didn't make it.

ANA. **Amá,** I didn't know that happened.

CARMEN. Every time your **Apá** touches me, the next day I'm pregnant. When he would leave me in Mexico to go to **el norte,** he would leave me pregnant so no man would look at me and desire me. I was very beautiful.

ANA. You still are, **Amá.**

CARMEN. I was always scared of him. And I let myself get fat after you were born hoping he would be disgusted by me and not touch me anymore.

ANA. Why didn't you just say "No"?

CARMEN. Because, **M'ija,** I was never taught how to say no.

PANCHA. (*comes forward and confesses*). It's easy, **Doña** Carmen. You tell him "No!" and you get out from the bed.

ANA. (*realizing what PANCHA is saying*). Pancha?

PANCHA. And then you take the blanket. (*ANA embraces PANCHA as the WOMEN laugh.*)

ANA. (*to the WOMEN*). Aren't you hot in those clothes? I feel sticky. I'm going to take off my pants. (*ANA takes off her pants. She is left wearing her bra and panties.*)

CARMEN. Ana, aren't you embarrassed?

ANA. Why? You already think I'm fat.

CARMEN. You know, Ana, you're not bad looking. If you lost 20 pounds you would be very beautiful.

ANA. Story of my life…Go ahead. Pick on me.

CARMEN. Why don't you lose weight? Last time you lost weight you were so thin and beatifuller.

ANA. I like myself. Why should I?

PANCHA. **Doña** Carmen, Ana is very pretty. She looks good the way she is.

ANA. Thank you, Pancha.

CARMEN. It's because she's young. At this age young girls should try to make themselves as attractive as possible.

ANA. Why? Why not always? You're overweight too.

CARMEN. But I'm already married.

ANA. Is that it? Make myself attractive so that I can catch a man?

ESTELA. *(sarcastically).* Ana, listen to them, learn now, "or you'll end up like Estela."

ANA. **Amá,** I do want to lose weight. But part of me doesn't because my weight says to everyone, "Fuck you!"

CARMEN. **¡Ave Maria Purissima!**

ANA. It says, "How dare you try to define me and tell me what I have to be and look like!" So I keep it on. I don't want to be a sex object.

ESTELA. Me neither.

CARMEN. **¡Otra!**

ROSALI. What's wrong with being a sex object? What's wrong with wanting to be thin and sexy?

ESTELA. Because I want to be taken seriously, to be considered a person...You know with Andrés, on our date...

CARMEN. **¡Aver cuentanos!** What happened on that infamous date?

ESTELA. On our date I got all fixed up...Then he showed up with jeans and a t-shirt and he smelled like he had been drinking...He wanted to take me to the drive-in and when I asked, "Why the drive-in?" He said because there he could kiss me and give me what I wanted...He said, "I don't care if you're fat. I like you even better; more to grab." That got me so angry! I thought he was interested in me because he was impressed that I owned this factory, my "intelligence," that I..."I'm smart"...When am I going to meet that man who will see the real me?

CARMEN. So that's what happened.

ROSALI. **Pues** if he has a brother, tell him about me. I think I'm going to die a virgin.

ANA. You're still a virgin?! Dang!

PANCHA. **¿Pero tu Jaime?** Nothing?

ROSALI. Nothing. I've felt fat ever since I can remember and I didn't want anybody to touch me until I got thin.

ANA. Is that why you were starving yourself?

ROSALI. That's part of it.

ESTELA. Rosalí, you're not fat.

ROSALI. Of course I am. Look at my **nalgas**...And my hips! **Paresen de elefante.**

ANA. No they don't!

ROSALI. I look like a cow.

CARMEN. You look like a cow? Where does that leave us?

PANCHA. Rosalí, you're so skinny in comparison to all of us.

ROSALI. No I'm not. Here, look at my fat hips. *(ROSALI pulls down her pants and shows them her hips.)*

ESTELA. That's nothing. **¡Mira!** *(ESTELA pulls down her pants and shows ROSALI her hips.)*

CARMEN. *(To ROSALI)*. At least you have a waist! *(CARMEN pulls down her skirt and shows ROSALI her stomach.)*

PANCHA. ¡**Uuuu!** That's nothing, **Doña** Carmen! *(PANCHA raises her skirt and shows them her stomach.)*

ROSALI. But you don't understand. I've got all these stretch marks on my arms... *(ROSALI opens her blouse and shows them the stretch marks close to her breasts.)*

ESTELA. They're small. I have stretch marks that run from my hips to my knees. *(ESTELA takes off her pants to show them.)*

CARMEN. Stretch marks?! Stretch marks!! You want to see stretch marks? *(CARMEN lifts her blouse and exposes her stretch marks and scars.)* Stretch marks!!! *(ANA sits back as she watches the WOMEN slowly undressing. They continue to compare body parts ad libbing. Finally they are all in their underwear and they stop to notice CARMEN's stretch marks.)*

ANA. **Amá,** what's that scar you have on your stomach?

CARMEN. This one? That was Estela.

ANA. It's such a big scar.

CARMEN. Estela was a big baby.

ESTELA. I gave you the most trouble, didn't I?

CARMEN. A-ha. But that's okay. I've heard Elizabeth Potaylor has one just like it.

PANCHA. *(suddenly realizing)*. Look how we are? What if somebody came in and saw us like this?

CARMEN. *(fanning her breasts)*. **Pero que bien se siente.** It feels so good to be rid of these clothes and let it all hang out.

ANA. **Pues sí.** Nobody is watching us. Who cares how we look.

ESTELA. So this is how we look without clothes?

CARMEN. Just as fat and beautiful... *(They all hug in a semicircle laughing triumphantly.)*

ANA. We can finally relax.

ESTELA. We're not finished yet.

ROSALI. Estela, all we need are 14 dresses.

PANCHA. Those we can finish tomorrow for sure.

CARMEN. So what are we going to do to celebrate?

ESTELA. To celebrate what? Finishing on time for the first time?

PANCHA. No. All of us, most of us, finally being legal.

CARMEN. It's true. And once you get the card you can do anything you want. **Tengo fe**...Estela, I've been thinking...You know what we could do? We could copy the patterns for these dresses, make the dresses ourselves, and have a fashion show. Maybe we could model them ourselves. *(The WOMEN laugh at the thought.)*

ANA. No, that's a great idea! Why don't we make them in larger sizes too?

PANCHA. **Está loquita,** but sometimes she makes sense. We could probably sell more if we made them in larger sizes.

ROSALI. You know what we could also do? Jaime could sell them in the flea market. If they sell, little by little we could grow…

ESTELA. *(jumping in).* And from there, if we make a lot of money, more money than what we're making now, maybe we can rent a place downtown on Broadway and start a boutique!!

ANA. But we'll need a name.

ROSALI. Well, why not just Estela Garcia?

ANA. I was thinking of something more French.

CARMEN. No. A French name would make it sound **chafas.** No, Estela Garcia sounds fine.

PANCHA. Estela, maybe you could go to school and study fashion design and design our dresses.

ESTELA. Yeah. I could do that. *(They all stop to imagine the possibilities.)*

CARMEN. So what are we doing to celebrate?

ESTELA. First let's finish, then we can talk about celebrating. *(They go back to work. CARMEN takes off her glasses as she fans her face.)*

CARMEN. **Que calor.** I'll be glad when all of this is over.

ANA. Estela, can we please open the door?

PANCHA. Open the door? **¿Pa qué?** So people that pass by can see us like this?

ROSALI. But it's so hot!

ANA. I don't think they're coming. Besides we're almost finished. *(The WOMEN look to ESTELA for a decision.)*

ESTELA. Okay…**Amá,** open the door. *(CARMEN goes to open the door. She turns back to ESTELA as if to make sure. CARMEN opens the door and fans herself with it. Beat. CARMEN holds the door wide open and walks outside. The WOMEN can't believe their eyes. A few seconds later CARMEN runs back in screaming.)*

CARMEN. Estela! It's out there! **¡La Migra!** They're coming!! *(CARMEN shuts the door. All the WOMEN immediately get dressed.)*

ESTELA. No! It's not fair! We were almost finished!! *(The WOMEN dig into their purses for their cards. ESTELA can only cry in desperation. She cannot find her clothes and has to head for the door in her slip. ROSALI and ANA peek through the curtains and quickly make a realization.)*

ROSALI. **Doña** Carmen, that's not **la migra!**

ANA. It's the police!

CARMEN. The police? *(She peeks through the curtain.)* **¡¿Cómo?!**

ANA. That's the guy I thought was a spy. He's an undercover cop!

ROSALI. Like in the movies.

ANA. It's a drug bust!

ESTELA. Where?

ROSALI. I think it's **el Tormento's** house. *(ESTELA moves for the door.)*

ANA. **¡Si, el Tormento!** They're taking him away. *(ESTELA and ANA jump up in excitement.)*

CARMEN. That's what he deserves! *(The police are heard driving away.)*

PANCHA. That's good they're taking him away in the van. **¡Bola de viejos cochinos!** *(The WOMEN laugh together. Then ANA stops laughing.)*

ANA. **Amá,** was that the same van you saw Monday?

CARMEN. *(nodding her head hesitantly).* I think so.

ANA. On Tuesday?

CARMEN. I think so.

ANA. On Wednesday?

CARMEN. *(sheepishly).* **Pos si.** *(She puts on her glasses.)*

ANA. **Amá,** that wasn't **la migra.** Everyone knows the vans are green!

CARMEN. I didn't.

ESTELA. How could you not know?

CARMEN. **Pos no se;** all those years of being undocumented I always imagined they were black.

PANCHA & ROSALI. **Ayy, Doña** Carmen!!!

CARMEN. **Phueehhh! Tanto pedo y para nada.**

ESTELA. Thank God! **¡Que susto!**

CARMEN. It's time to retire! *(They laugh in relief then they become silent.)*

ANA. Well, it's over...for now. *(Beat.)*

ESTELA. If you want to take the rest of the day off...We'll finish tomorrow.

PANCHA. We can go?

ESTELA. Yes. I know how tired you must be. Go ahead. I'll stay and continue working.

ROSALI. I can't wait to go home and take a shower.

CARMEN. **Si, por favor, bañate.** Tomorrow, I'm going to make a fresh batch of **mole.**

PANCHA. *(scared for her life).* **Doña** Carmen, why don't you make some rice? *(ANA, PANCHA, and ROSALI immediately run out.)*

CARMEN. *(muttering to them).* Ingrates! *(To ESTELA.)* Are you sure you won't need us anymore?

ESTELA. No. Now go! Before I change my mind. Don't you want to go outside? *(They gather their bags and quickly leave. ESTELA is left alone. Lights fade a little. She turns on the radio to a mellow jazz station. She goes around doing a final clean up, turning off lights and machines. She stops, recalling the five of them in their underwear, fantasizing about their own boutique. She grins to herself. She whispers.)* Large sizes? *(ESTELA shakes her head, dismissing the idea, but then stops and runs to a pile of stocked material. She eagerly searches and finds a roll of red fabric. ESTELA excitedly runs to a station and begins taking her measurements. As the lights slowly fade, we see ESTELA measuring herself with pride and pleasure, half laughing to herself, half defiantly...about to design and make her first dress. Lights slowly fade to black.)*

Scene Four

AT RISE: *Lights come on. There are no more dresses on the racks. It is Friday, on the clock it is 2:25 p.m. ANA and PANCHA are busy blowing up balloons. ROSALI is cleaning up. There is a birthday cake with a large candle of the number "25." A large sign reads: "Happy Birthday Estela." Footsteps are heard outside. ANA runs to turn off the electricity, the WOMEN hide... The door opens.*

WOMEN. Surprise!!!!! *(ROSALI takes a picture. CARMEN stands motionless holding a pot.)*

ANA. **Amá,** we thought you were...

ROSALI. **Doña** Carmen, what's wrong?

CARMEN. I just got back from the doctor.

PANCHA. What did she tell you?

ANA. **¿Amá?**

CARMEN. She says I'm not pregnant.

ANA. Then why are you sad?

CARMEN. She says, "it's only menopause." When you reach menopause it's over. You're no longer a woman. **Se te seca alli abajo.**

ANA. **Amá,** you are a real woman.

CARMEN. What I should be is a grandmother by now, but the way you and Estela are going, I won't be one for a long time...**¿Y** Estela?

ROSALI. She hasn't returned from delivering the dresses. She should be coming soon.

CARMEN. Here. *(Gives ROSALI the pot.)* I made rice.

(They hear footsteps outside. ANA turns off the lights. The door opens.)

WOMEN. Surprise!!! *(ROSALI takes another picture. Lights come on. ESTELA stands shocked in her new dress.)*

ESTELA. You remembered?

ROSALI. *(gives ESTELA a gift).* Happy twenty-fifth birthday, you old maid!

CARMEN. *(referring to her dress).* Estela, did you make it? **Que bonita te ves,** very nice. You see you're not ugly, you just didn't know how to dress.

ESTELA. *(hugs ROSALI).* I brought a gift for all of you. *(ESTELA goes outside and brings in a large fan.)*

PANCHA. Now the boss treats us pretty good.

ESTELA. Because now I have money.

CARMEN. Did Mrs. Glitz finally pay you?

ESTELA. Yes, she paid me, but she kept threatening me...I've written out all the checks. *(ESTELA pulls out the checks from her bag. She distributes them, the first check going to PANCHA.)*

PANCHA. *(looking at her check).* This is the biggest check I've ever gotten. *(ESTELA gives ROSALI her check.)*

ROSALI. Too bad I've already spent it on the **Americana** Express.

CARMEN. **¡Válgame!** I didn't realize how much money you owed me.

ANA *(looks at her check, disappointed).* Estela, come here. *(ANA and ESTELA talk among themselves.)* Estela, how come I only get this much?

ESTELA. I took out for taxes.

ANA. Taxes? But you're not reporting...

CARMEN. How much do you have left?

ESTELA. About six hundred. I'll send the lawyer some more money today. Maybe they won't take me to court.

PANCHA. But if they deport you and take everything, we won't be able to work towards the boutique.

ROSALI. We're also going to have to look for another job. *(The WOMEN stare at the floor.)*

ANA. Back to McDonald's. *(Beat.)*

PANCHA. Estela, I know my husband isn't going to like it, but here. *(PANCHA extends her check to ESTELA.)* Take it. Pay me back when you can.

ESTELA. Pancha, are you sure?

PANCHA. **No, pero,** take it before I change my mind.

ESTELA. **Muchas gracias**…*(They try hugging, but they find it difficult, it's awkward. To herself).* Let's see. How much more do I need? *(CARMEN stares at her check for a few more seconds and slowly says good-bye to it.)*

CARMEN. **Ten, ten.** Take mine too. What kind of mother would I be if I didn't give it back?

ESTELA *(hugs CARMEN).* **Que buena es!**

CARMEN. You see, **No que no te quiero?** It's because I love you that I make your life so miserable.

ESTELA. Don't love me so much. *(ROSALI thinks about it too.)*

ROSALI. I guess the **Americana** Express can wait…Here is my check too. *(ESTELA hugs ROSALI. Now they all look to ANA. ANA holds her check tightly.)*

ANA. No, not me…I'm going to buy a typewriter…I can't. *(The WOMEN don't say anything, but continue staring at ANA.)* I really need this typewriter. I have this essay I have to type up for a contest…All right…Take half of it. *(ESTELA semi-hugs ANA.)*

ESTELA. Excuse me for just a minute. I have to make a phone call. *(ESTELA picks up the phone and dials.)* Hello…May I speak to Mrs. Glitz? This is Estela Garcia. I'm just calling to thank you for keeping your word and finally paying us today. I also wanted to tell you that you are a mean, wicked, bitter, unsympathetic, greedy, rude, awful…

ANA. Capitalist!

ESTELA. Capitalist!…No! We quit…Yeah, well I'll see you in hell. *(The WOMEN are shocked, incredulous of her actions.)*

CARMEN. **¡Maldita!** What have you done?

PANCHA. You got us fired, didn't you?

ESTELA. No, we quit. *(ESTELA laughs excitedly.)*…Don't worry about the work. I got us a contract with Señor Vasquez!

EVERYONE. Señor Vasquez!!!

CARMEN. How did you convince him?

ESTELA. I just told him that we are the most hardworking women he could ever ask for. I know, I lied, but I got it.

EVERYONE. **¡Ayy!** *(All the WOMEN embrace excitedly. ROSALI brings out the birthday cake. They sing "Happy Birthday" not realizing that ROSALI is holding the cake backwards and it reads 52 instead of 25. They stop halfway through and turn it.)*

ESTELA. Fifty two?! *(They continue singing.)*

ROSALI. Ana, light up the candle so I can take a picture… *(ANA lights up the candle.)* Okay, Estela, blow out the candle. *(ESTELA stops to make a wish then blows it out. ROSALI takes a picture of her.)*

ANA. What did you wish for?

ESTELA. Maybe when you get back from New York you'll see. *(ANA and PANCHA give their gift to ESTELA.)*

ROSALI. Ana, here, take a picture of us to remember this week…*(ROSALI gives ANA the camera. The WOMEN gather for the photo.)*

ANA. Okay! Ready?…One…two…three! *(The WOMEN suddenly hold up their "Temporary Residence Cards.")*

WOMEN. Green!!! *(The WOMEN freeze in a pool of light. ANA steps out and turns to the audience. The WOMEN exit backstage. Spotlight on ANA.)*

ANA. I always took their work for granted, to be simple and unimportant. I was not proud to be working there at the beginning. I was only glad to know that because I was educated, I wasn't going to end up like them. I was going to be better than them. And I wanted to show them how much smarter and liberated I was. I was going to teach them about the women's liberation movement, about sexual liberation and all the things a so-called educated American woman knows. But in their subtle ways they taught me about resistance. About a battle no one was fighting for them except themselves. About the loneliness of being women in a country that looks down on us for being mothers and submissive wives. With their work that seems simple and unimportant, they are fighting…Perhaps the greatest thing I learned from them is that women are powerful, especially when working together…As for me, well, I settled for a secondhand typewriter and I wrote an essay on my experience and I was awarded a fellowship. So I went to New York and was a starving writer for some time before I went to New York University. When I came back the plans for making the boutique were no longer a dream, but a reality. *(ANA picks up a beautiful designer jacket and puts it on.)* Because I now wear original designs from Estela Garcia's boutique, "Real Women Have Curves."

> *(The lights come on and all the WOMEN enter the door wearing new evening gowns and accessories designed by ESTELA. The WOMEN parade down the theater aisles voguing in a fashion-show style. They take their bows, continue voguing, and slowly exit. Lights slowly fade out.)*

The End

Production Notes

Set

Many sewing machines can be seen to show that it is a sewing factory. On the floor are boxes, plastic bags, piles of trash, thread, loose material, etc. There is also a tailor's mannequin (size seven). Upstage, on the right, are two dress racks. On one is a pink evening dress that resembles a ballerina dress. On the right is an ironing board and steam iron. Close to it is a wooden table full of old fruit, dirty dishes, paper and plastic bags, and old lunches. Downstage is a toilet. Since it is part of the room, a shower curtain is used for privacy. Above the toilet is a mirror and a small window. Next to it is a sink. Upstage center, is the only door between two windows with the ugliest curtains. Above the door, on the wall, is a sign in red letters that says: ¡Se Prohibe Chismear! (Gossiping is Prohibited!) On the same wall is a large clock. On the left wall are fashion illustrations and magazine cut-ups of many slim models in the latest fashions. Close to the door is a large calendar with the picture of the **Virgen de Guadalupe.**

Costume List

Ana

3 t-shirts	1 pair shorts
1 pair tennis shoes	1 pair dressy black pants
1 pair black pumps	1 party blouse
1 backpack	1 designer jacket
1 bandanna	1 pair earrings
1 pair hoop earrings	1 plain bra
1 pair sweat pants	1 pair panties

Estela

1 dress	1 pair panties
1 pair pants	1 designer hat
2 blouses	1 red designer suit
1 skirt	1 pair designer earrings
1 pair flat shoes	1 pair black heels
1 plain bra	

Carmen

1 sweater	1 camisole
2 floral dresses	1 bra
1 party dress	1 girdle
1 pair pants	1 pair black pumps
1 blouse	1 designer evening gown
1 pair sandals	1 pair earrings

Pancha

1 sweater	1 designer bra
1 dress	1 pair panties
1 skirt	1 designer gown
2 blouses	1 pair black heels
1 party dress	1 pair earrings
1 nice camisole	

Rosali

1 colorful dress above the knee, tight	
2 mini-skirts	1 fancy bra with lace
2 colorful blouses	1 pair panties
1 pair hoop earrings	1 designer evening gown

1 party dress	1 pair heels
1 fancy bra with lace	1 pair earrings

Property List

Factory's Main Furniture & Props

2-3	sewing machines (industrial and home) with:
2-3	thread spools each
1	over-lock machine with:
3-5	thread spools
1	hem machine with:
2	thread spools
1	small refrigerator
1	container with drinking water
6	completed "factory-made" dresses
5	half-completed "factory-made" dresses
several	large size material scraps
several	small size material scraps
4-5	chairs: tacky floral kitchen and comfortable vinyl
3-4	wooden boxes for finished work
3	cardboard boxes
4	small personal plastic work boxes with:
several	machine foots and bobbins
1	plastic container of drinking water
1	measuring tape

Ana's Ironing Area

1	steam iron
1	ironing board
1	small ironing board on top of regular ironing board
2	dress forms
2	racks, one with:
1 pair	clipping scissors attached to racks by elastic cord
2	dress "samples"
1	plastic bagger
50	white plastic hangers

Estela's Work Area

1	dial phone
2	clipboards
1	spiral college bound notebook

Lunch Table Area

1	wooden lunch table
1	box tissues
1	radio with am/fm & cassette with 1 mono speaker
1	hot plate

1	small blue "Mexican style" pot for coffee
5	mugs: ceramic/plastic/"Mexican style" & plain
4	plates: various types
5	cups/glasses: promotional & colorful
4	wooden stools
1	coffee container
1	sugar container
several	spoons, forks & minor kitchen utensils

Bathroom Area

1	shower curtain
1	toilet
1	sink
1	small mirror
1	hair brush
1	bottle of perfume
1	deodorant
1	girdle
1	notebook & pen

Resting Area

1	comfortable bench or back seat of a van
3	blankets: Mexican & solid

On Walls

3-4	fashion illustrations
4	large collages of magazine "runway fashion" clippings
5	pattern cut-ups hanging
1	**"se prohibe chismear"** ("Gossiping Is Prohibited") sign
1	**virgen de guadalupe calendar**
2	plain/ugly curtains for windows
1	full body mirror
2	sets key rings with 3 keys on each

Environment/miscellaneous

1	mousetrap
4-5	rolls various colorful fabrics
1	roll red fabric
several	thread spools
1	pair large cutting scissors
1	bag with stale bread
several	size tags
several	wrapped piles of cut material for future work
1	extra-large bottle of aspirins
1	disco ball for finale

Carmen's Props

1	purse
5	1-dollar bills
1	colorful grocery plastic **"mandado"** bag
1	bag of corn tortillas
1	pair eyeglasses
1	pair reading glasses with chain
1	"Tupperware" container with **mole**
1	"special" pair of clipping scissors

Ana's Props

1	steno pad & pen
3	feminist & political books
1	backpack/gym bag
3	colorful "scroungies" for hair

Estela's Props

1	purse
5	1-dollar bills
1	clipboard
1	"special" pair of clipping scissors
1	spiral college bound notebook

Pancha's Props

1	purse
5	1-dollar bills
1	plain large **"mandado"** bag with:
1	fried chicken bucket
1	"Big Mac" in container
1	bag of chocolate-covered chocolate cookies
1	"Diet Coke"
1	"special" pair of clipping scissors

Rosali's Props

1	purse
5	1-dollar bills
1	"special" pair of clipping scissors
1	bottle of diet pills
1	American Express card (green)

Glossary / Spanish

A trabajar - To work it is
Abraza(r) - to hug
Abuelita - grandmother, granny
Adios - good-bye
Aguas - look out
Ahora si - okay, now

Alli esta en el cajon - It's there in the drawer
Amá - mama
¡Andenle! - Come on!
Apá - papa
Aqui huele a pura cuchupeta y a pedo - It smells like pussy and fart
Así es que - therefore/so
Asi hazlo - Do it this way
¡Ave Maria Purissima! - Oh holy Mary of God!
Aver - Let's see, to have
Aver cuentanos - Come on tell us
¡Aver dime, condenada! - Damn you, tell me!
¡Ayy! - Ahh!, Oh!
¡Ayy que buenote! - He's so fine
Bañate - take a shower
Barrio - neighborhood
Basta - enough
Besa(r) - to kiss
Blusas - blouses
Bola de viejos cochinos - bunch of dirty old men
Bueno - well, good
Buenos dias - good morning
Callense - be quiet
Chafas - tacky
Chicharron - pork rinds
Chichis - boobs, titties
Chisme - to gossip
Chismosa - gossip monger
Claro - of course
Cochinadas - junk
Como es - see how you are
¿Cómo estas? - How are you?
¿Como puede ser? - How can it be?
Corazón - heart
Coyote - someone who brings people across the border illegally for a price
Cumbia - Latin music from the Caribbean
¿de qué te apuras? - Why worry?
Desgraciada - ungrateful
Dios mio, ya mero acabamos - Oh, God, we're almost finished.
Diosito - God
Doña - a term of respect, literally meaning "old mother"; usually applied to the oldest woman present
¿Dónde los escondo? - Where shall I hide them?
¡Echame la culpa! - Blame me!
El Tormento - the heartthrob, or "crush"; or tormentor
Enojona - grouch

Entonces a la fuerza - then by force
¿Entonces que quiere? - Then what do you want?
¡Entonces todas a trabajar! - Then to work it is!
¡Esa perra! - That bitch!
Eso - that
¡Esta cochinada no sirve! - This piece of junk doesn't work!
Está loquita - she's a little crazy
Estamos odidas - We are screwed
Fresas - strawberries, snooty upper class people in Mexico
Gringa - non Latinas (Anglos)
Hasta mañana - until tomorrow
Hijole - short for son of a bitch
¡Hora si que estamos bien jodidas! - Now we're really messed up!
Horita te lo coso - I'll sew it for you right now
Hoye - listen
Huevona - lazy, good for nothing
La migra - US Immigration and Naturalization Service officials, border patrol
Las pobrecitas - the poor women
Listos para chupar - delicious enough to suck
Lonchera - the lunch mobile
Loquita - a little crazy
Maldita - goddamned woman
Maquinita - little sewing machine
¡Mendiga vieja! - Damn witch!
¡Mentirosa! - Liars!
Metiche - nosy
Mi viejo - my husband, my old man
M'ija - my daughter
Mira(r) - to look, Look!
Mira que inteligente - look how smart
Mira que paresco - see what I look like
¡Miren! - Look!
¡Miren cómo coquetea! - Look how she flirts!
Mole - a sauce made of chocolate and chili
Nada - nothing
Nalgas - buttocks
Ni lo mande dios - god forbid
No le da verguenza - she's not ashamed
No mas mira que paresco - Just look what I look like
No mas ven a ver - Just come take a look
¡No puedo! - I can't
No que no te quiero - And you say I don't love you
No se - I don't know
¡No se peleen! - don't fight
No seas mensa - don't be dumb

No seas terca - don't be stubborn
No te hagas de rogar - don't make us beg
No te va hacer daño - It won't do you any harm
N'ombre - no way
Nopal - cactus
¡Otra! - Another one!
¿Pa que? - For what?
Panza - stomach, belly
Panzonas - pregnant
Parele - stop it
Paresen de elefante - they look like they belong on an elephant
Patrona - boss
Pegame - hit me
Pero - but
¡Pero cómo? - But how?
Pero no puede ser - but it can't be
Pero que bien se siente - but it feels so good
Pero que loqura - what insanity
Pero tu - but you
Pinche - damn
¡Pinche rata! - Damn rat!
Pobre - poor
Pobre mujer - poor woman
Pobrecita - poor baby
Por favor - please
Por fin - finally
¿Pos cómo le hiciste? - Well, how did you do it?
Pos no nos queda otra - well we have no choice
Pos no se - Well, I don't know
¿Pos qué paso? - Well, what happened?
Pos yo ya no veo - I can't see a thing
Pues - Well
Pues por que no - well why not
Puro lomo - all back
Que bonita, te ves - How pretty you look
Que bonito - how pretty
Que bonito viento - what beautiful wind
¡Que buena es! - How good you are!
¡Que calor! - It's so hot!
¿Que hiciste? - What did you do?
¿Que le pico? - What bit you?
Que locura - What madness
Que metiches - how nosey
¿Que paso? - What happened?

¡Que susto! - What scare!

¿Que te dijo la vieja? - What did the old hag tell you?

Rapido - quickly

¿Saben qué? - You know what?

"Se prohibe chismear!" - "Gossiping is Prohibited!"

Se te seca alli abajo - it gets dried down there

Se ve - It shows

Señor - mister, Mr., Sir

Sí, ya se fue - Yes, he's already left.

Tambien - also

Tan pequeña - so young

Tanto pedo y para nada - all this fuss/worrying and for nothing

'Tas flaca - You're skinny

Ten - Take it

Tengo fe - I have faith

Tul - tul, a synthetic material

Vago - loser, lazy, good for nothing

Valgame - oh my

Vamonos - let's go

Vamos a estar como gallinas enjauladas - we're going to be like caged chickens

Vas a verlo - you'll see

Venganse - Come you all

¿Verá que sí? - Isn't it true?

Y los... - And the...

¿Y por qué no me habias dicho? - Why hadn't you told me?

¿Y tu? - And you?

Ya basta - enough already

Ya llego mi viejo - my husband is here

¡Ya ni la friegas! - You blew it

ESSAY

Luis Alberto Urrea

Luis Alberto Urrea was born in Tijuana, Mexico, to an Anglo mother and Mexican father, and is best known for his memoir, *Nobody's Son: Notes from an American Life* (1999), which earned him the National Book Award. The book was part of his *Border Trilogy*, preceded by *Across the Wire* (1993) and *By the Lake of Sleeping Children* (1996). He is also the author of a novel, *In Search of Snow* (1994); a collection of short stories, *Six Kinds of Sky* (2002); and a book of poetry, *Ghost Sickness* (1997). In 2004, he published a gripping account of illegal immigrants abandoned in the desert entitled *The Devil's Highway: A True Story*. He has received numerous accolades for his multi-genre writings and currently teaches at the University of Chicago.

Meet the Satánicos

Christmas was coming. Up north, the *gringos* had just celebrated their Thanksgiving. Tijuana, as always, was beginning to copy them, and many families here, too, had enjoyed "El Tenks-geevee." In Spanish, it is *el día de las gracias*, though what exactly Mexicans have to give thanks for on North America's Thanksgiving is not clear. Perhaps they're thanking God the Pilgrims landed in Massachusetts.

In *barrios* and *colonias*, orphanages and garbage dumps, hope stirred as the cold descended. In spite of the illness and the discomfort of late fall, they knew that the missionaries were preparing Christmas for them. Orphanages picked reluctant children to wrap themselves in sheets and blankets, to play Mary, Joseph, and the Wise Men in their yearly pageants. Invariably, a doll that had lost 75 percent of its hair played Jesus. And there always seemed to be a boy who had to crawl around on all fours playing the ass. The orphanage directors opened their doors to neighbors—thinking, somehow, that these Christmas plays would evangelize all the *barrio*, causing a mass exodus from Catholicism, a spiritual flocking to the Protestant banner.

The *colonia* was one of the new ones that caused so much controversy in Tijuana. It will remain nameless here. This was its first Christmas with Von and his crew. Created unofficially by *paracaidistas*, or "parachutists," the clever Mexican nick-name for squatters who descend on a piece of land from out of nowhere, it lay two hills over from the old dump area, and it was rumored to be under the control of a gangster who involved entire *barrios* in car thievery. Driving in, I was struck immediately by the rows of automotive husks lining the rough dirt street; in some places, stripped and burned-out cars were layered on top of each other. Certain arroyos were clogged with car bodies, many of them on their roofs. Yet this colorful so-called gangster took an interest in the missionaries of the area, and he looked out for their well-being. Often his largesse had to be politely deflected—one drug-treatment program in the area graciously rejected his repeated offers of new cars.

The *colonia*, being controversial, indeed not officially in existence, lacked any services whatsoever. Aside from the typical lack of water, there was no electricity. There was no bus service. There were no telephones, no streetlights, no doctor's offices, stores, schools. And there was certainly no police presence. The *barrio* was the Wild West. The missionary from the treatment center told me of his Saturday nights—he and the addicts in their plywood church and dorms, looking into the pitch-black canyons below them, watched the gunfire flash, listened to the yells and shouting. "Everything happens here on Saturday nights," he said. "Anything you can imagine. *Anything.*"

5   The vans rattled up the hill, cut left into a small clear area at the crest. Beyond lay the deep black of the unsettled out-skirts. The missionaries built a lit basketball court and a small clubhouse for the *barrio* kids. A gasoline generator made a racket. Kids flocked to the ball court and the clubhouse all through the fall. They had nothing else to do on the hill except sleep, listen to

radios, or sniff glue. None of them could afford drugs, and few of them could afford booze.

The local criminal element was a street gang called Los Satánicos. They gathered along the edge of the ball court, arrayed themselves along the retaining wall that kept the top of the hill from burying the youth center. They'd been sniffing glue and paint thinner.

Inside, foosball tables, video games. Scruffy children in various shades of adobe-brown competed noisily. Pastor Von provided them with about six elaborate ray guns, and they used them to shoot at flashing electrical targets. In a corner, a terrified head-banger in a Metallica T-shirt squatted on his haunches. His brown face was blotchy with panic, going an ugly ash-gray. Various *vatos* and *cholos* gathered around him. He had made the terminal mistake of punching the little brother of one of the Satánicos. They cornered him in the building. At one point, they sent in an expedition that clubbed him over the head with a hunk of cement. Efren, a *veterano* of these streets and one of Von's full-time employees, chased them out. "This is a Christian place," he told them. "Fight outside, not in here."

When spoken to, the head-banger did not respond. Once he got over the shock of the head blow, he stood up and assumed an air of nonchalance, pushing some smaller boys out of the way at the foosball table. His eyes darted to the door regularly; he was trapped and he knew it. Spies from the Satánicos filtered out the door to report on his condition.

Some of the recovering addicts from the treatment center watched the gang nervously. They had a strangely somber mien, quiet men with mournful eyes. "This is no good," one of them told me. "This situation is very bad. They're going to get him."

10   The Satánicos waited along the edge of the ball court. One boy sat on the retaining wall; a bearded boy was lying back between his legs. The top boy wrapped his legs around the bottom boy's abdomen and pulled him close. He rested his chin tenderly on his head, slipped his hands across his chest and belly. One of them had brought a pit bull. Another had a small black canister of Mace he compulsively pulled in and out of his pocket. They murmured their plans, laughing. The only girls hid at the far end of the gang—two thirteen- or fourteen-year-olds, with hard-sprayed *chola* hairdos rising in black splashes off their heads. A Satánico in a dusty black trench coat pulled a six-inch-long switch-blade from his pocket, flicked it open. They laughed. He cut the air. "How do you like it?" he said to his invisible victim. He stabbed. "Are you still alive?" he said. The Satánicos were excited. The ballplayers on the court ignored them: a drive to the basket, a hard shoulder block, a lay-up that clattered through the rim. The pit bull sat somberly, watching.

"They're going to cut him up," the addict told me. "They're going to make shredded meat—*machaca*."

Nobody could figure out how to get the Metallica boy out of the building. Perhaps, one of the missionaries suggested, we could divert the attention of the Satánicos for a minute, and the boy could jump out the back window.

Von said, "He's trapped in the building, eh?"

We nodded.

15 "Well," he said, "at least he'll be sure to stick around for the Bible study."

Then a curious thing happened. Four big old-timers, maybe nineteen or twenty years old, wandered into the alley outside the clubhouse. They all wore billed caps, and had long hair. Two of them had nut-brown scars on their faces, and their shoulders rocked as they walked. The Satánicos stowed the knife immediately, and they shuffled nervously. The four *veteranos* swaggered into the clubhouse and scanned the kids within. They gestured at the Metallica boy: come.

One of the addicts pulled me aside.

"They're his brothers," he said.

"An escort!"

20 "Yes. The Satánicos are bad, but these ones are *bad*. They came here to kill, not fight."

They appeared at the door of the clubhouse. They formed a rough diamond around the head-banger, a flying wedge. He grew cocky in their embrace, heavy-lidded and inscrutable. The Satánicos looked at their feet. One innocently busied himself with his pit bull.

The *veteranos* strolled along the top of the wall where the Satánicos sat; they walked up the slope, all four of them staring steadily at the gang, offering them a silent challenge. Nobody took them up on it. Nobody even looked. Eye contact would mean disaster. The only sound on the hill was the squeaking tennis shoes of the ballplayers rushing the net, the laughter of the children inside. The lead *veterano* snorted in derision, and the group vanished into the dark.

The Satánicos were suddenly revealed, in the pale light of the ball court, to be boys and girls, confused and chastened. The one with the knife was a skinny little geek with big ears and sticks for legs. The girls faded away, perhaps avoiding the Satánicos' wrath. The one boy holding the other nuzzled his ear, clutched him tight from behind. The one with the Mace suddenly scuttled along the edge of the court, threatening to Mace one of the players, but even this threat collapsed. These children were not helpless—they held up missionaries at gunpoint out in the street—but that night, their ferocity collapsed on them, just for an instant, and they seemed lost, unable to get it back.

BROADER HORIZONS: RESOURCES FOR WRITING AND CLASS DISCUSSION

Literary Critical Essay/Discussion Topics

1. The urban center has a long literary history of being both the center of modern decadence and the source of creative vitality. What is your relationship to an urban area nearest you? Compare that relationship with that of any of the characters in the chapter's stories. Discuss the similarities and differences.

2. Many of the characters depicted in the works are seeking some sort of escape from the many obstacles, traps, restrictions, etc., created by their urban environment. Choose

a character with similar situations and discuss how the urban landscape limits him or her, emotionally, socially, spiritually, or economically. How do the descriptions in the work reflect a character's inability to move, change, or grow?

3. Gangs, drugs, crime, and poverty are very real and complicated aspects of city life (as they are of rural life as well). Many of the works selected here avoid mentioning these negative influences. What other sides of urban life are presented in the works? Are there, for example, any benefits?

4. Many Latino characters grow up on the edges of a city, or within an urban world that is itself a border city, a landscape with two sides, two economies, two cultures. Choose a character and discuss the divided nature of the urban existence that character experiences. Is the physical division of the city relevant to the character's personality in any way?

5. As was true with the early High Modernist writing at the beginning of the twentieth century (see Chapter 1, "Latino Narrative"), many writers break up the perspective in a story, or divide the point of view so that no one viewpoint is ever given the ultimate authority over others. The story or poem remains told in multiple ways. Is there something about the city that makes modernist prose or poetry more fitting to a writer? Do people feel more fragmented in some way within urban landscapes? If so, why?

6. Choose two works from the selections above and discuss the issue of gender within the context of the urban world. Are the differences between male and female roles changed somehow in a city?

7. Urban models present different living situations for Latinos within a city. Examine how the design of a city impacts the writer's ideas or a character's life.

The Novel Connection

The Mean Streets

For years, New York City has been a source of artistic inspiration, so it is not surprising that it has also served as the subject of many works by Latinos, particularly Puerto Ricans. The connections between stateside Puerto Rican literature and the city of New York begin with the autobiographical sketches of Jesus Colon and Bernardo Vega, both of whom spoke of immigrating to the United States. Their writing, in a stylistically simple, straightforward prose, described life in New York in the 1920s through the 1950s. In 1967, Piri Thomas wrote his autobiography of making it through a life of crime (armed robbery, drugs, and prison) and his work, *Down These Mean Streets* (modeled after Claude Brown's *Manchild in a Promised Land*), instantly became one of the most famous works by a mainland Puerto Rican writer. Miguel Piñero followed with his powerful, award-winning drama *Short Eyes* (made into a film in which Piñero himself played a newly added part). The play portrayed the racial and cultural tensions of men in prison. Nuyorican poets like Pedro Pietri and Miguel Algarín spoke their words of defiance in powerful chants straight from the heart of the Lower East Side. Edwin Torres produced the novel *Carlito's Way* (1975), later made into a 1993 film. In the 1990s, the young Abraham Rodriguez Jr., first in a collection of stories, *The Boy Without a Flag* (1990), and then in a novel called *Spidertown* (1993), again told a story of a young man struggling to escape from drugs, crime, and poverty. The South Bronx is the site of his most recent novel, *The Buddha Book* (2001), as well. A short book by sixteen-year-old Gil Alicea called *The Air Down Here* (1995) continued this trend toward autobiography and the urban ghetto. Alba Ambert's *A Perfect Silence* (1995) claims the same South Bronx neighborhood for its setting. More recently, Ernesto Quiñonez, author of two novels, *Bodega Dreams* (2000) and *Chango's Fire* (2004) looks at the "yuppification" of Spanish Harlem and the issues of drugs, crime, and poverty in the Puerto Rican world. Puerto Rican women writers have also followed this autobiographical trend where memoir obviously overlaps with fiction. Judith Ortiz Cofer writes elegantly in *Silent Dancing* (1990) of life in "El Building" in Paterson, New Jersey (Paterson was also the subject of the famous poem with that city's name by William Carlos Williams, whose mother was from the island of Puerto Rico). Ortiz Cofer's autobiography mirrors her novel *The Line of the Sun*. One of the most well known mainland Puerto Rican writers today is Esmeralda Santiago, whose urban experiences stretch from the island to New York City and across genres from her autobiographies to her novels.

Barrios Beyond Manhattan

John Rechy's classic *City of Night* (1963) is perhaps the ultimate Latino urban novel spanning city after city in a neon tour of late night, underground gay culture of the 1960s. His later shorter work, *The Miraculous Day of Amalia Gómez* (1991) focuses on L.A. in equally brilliant detail. Jaime Manrique's *Latin Moon in Manhattan* (1992), which is about the world of Colombian nightlife in the boroughs of New York City, owes something to Rechy. Loida Maritza Perez's *Geographies of Home* (1999) chronicles a dysfunctional Dominican-American family in a fairly depressing Brooklyn. Daniel Chacón's first novel, *and the shadows took him* (2004), transplants a young barrio boy into a California suburb. Cuban-Americans in New York occupy the first two (and most important) novels by Oscar Hijuelos, *Our House in the Last World* (1983) and *The Mambo Kings Play Songs of Love* (1989).

In spite of the prevalence of New York as a setting in many Latino works, it is safe to say, however, that the city of Miami is as integral to the Cuban-American novel as the Spanish language influence is to all Latino literature. From the works of Roberto G. Fernández to Cristina Garcia to Virgil Suárez, almost all Cuban-American literature has some sort of connection to Miami. For exceptions, we can point to such works as Gustavo Pérez Firmat's novel *Anything but Love* (2000), a love story that stretches beyond the city. We can also note that Cubans in Los Angeles are the subject of Alex Abella's two detective novels, *The Killing of the Saints* (1991) and *Dead of Night* (1998), in which the practices of the syncretic religion Santería intertwine with crime and mystery. Beyond these two novels, in *The Great American* (1997), Abella tells the story of a U.S. Marine who travels to Batista's Cuba and winds up entrenched in the political revolution of Fidel Castro.

The Film Connection

In-depth Film Connection
Real Women Have Curves (2002)
Directed by Patricia Cardoso

While most of the modern-day films that have dealt with the urban Latino experience have traditionally focused on inner-city males and gang warfare, the film *Real Women Have Curves* (2002) steps outside of this very limited and stereotypical perspective. Directed by Patricia Cardoso, a native of Colombia, the film is based on the play (included in this chapter on pages xx–xx) of the same title and is also based on the life of the playwright and co-screenwriter, Josefina López.

Like the play, the movie focuses on the life of Ana, a young teenager who lives with her Mexican-American family in East L.A. and who is portrayed by Hollywood newcomer

America Ferrera. The setting is relatively similar to the East L.A. portrayed in other films in that at times it seems like there is no escape from the socioeconomic barriers placed on Ana's parents and her sister, Estela. However, unlike those films, *Real Women Have Curves* depicts the urban life of East L.A. as an inspiration to succeed rather than as a trap for a tragic downfall.

At the beginning of the film, Ana finds herself at a crossroads, where the demands of her parents, whose ideologies and beliefs are part of the old world, clash with her own personal ambitions. She follows her parents' desires, stays at home, and works alongside her mother at a small factory run by Estela. Meanwhile, her English teacher, played by George Lopez, persistently advises Ana to apply to college—an idea that her mother, especially, rejects. Yet after discovering the difficulties faced by her sister and her mother, and seeing that all their labor results in selling a dress for $18.00, which in turn will be sold by a retailer for $600.00, Ana begins to change her mind. Eventually, she applies and is accepted to Columbia University.

Of course, as the title implies, the central conflict extends much beyond the debate over whether Ana should continue her education. Ana's struggle with her mother, who constantly harasses her about being overweight, provides audiences with a look at the dynamics of a Latino family, while at the same time illustrating the types of pains that women, not just Mexican-American women, have to endure in modern-day society. Much like the other characters and poets in this chapter, Ana's life is complicated by living in a bicultural, urban environment. She perseveres in many respects, most importantly by having a strong sense of self-esteem and having full confidence that despite being overweight, she is beautiful. In this sense, her opinion of her Latina body helps serve as a metaphor for the strength that she sees in the Latina woman. She carries this message to the other women in the factory, who at first only see their extra pounds and cellulite but eventually see their bodies' own natural beauty. In a comical but poignant scene, Ana convinces them to strip off their clothes so that they can both show off their bodies and escape from the overbearing heat.

It is critical to note that although at the end of the film Ana winds up attending college and leaving her family in Los Angeles, she moves to another inner city—New York. The final scene in the movie shows a confident Ana walking through the Big Apple's streets, not escaping the urban world, but rather embracing it. The other authors in this chapter, also have an undeniable affinity for their urban worlds, for like Ana, they have an appreciation that has grown only through personal experience. This film helps amplify the love/hate relationship that writers such as Miguel Piñero, Luis J. Rodriguez, and Helena María Viramontes have with inner cities and all their problems—low-paying jobs, poor neighborhoods, and families that are not necessarily trying to escape their urban worlds, but rather are simply attempting to survive and make their lives better. After all, these cities offer a sort of comfort to these figures, providing them with the type of communal feeling that suburbia cannot offer. The women at the factory argue and gossip about each other, yet when it comes down to it, they support one another. Ana may leave her family, but that does not mean that she does not value the sense of family that her urban world offers.

Other Recommended Films:

Almost a Woman (2001)

American Me (1992)

Blood In, Blood Out (1993)

Distant Water (1991)

Mi Vida Loca (My Crazy Life) (1994)

Short Eyes (1977)

Washington Heights (2003)

West Side Story (1961)

Thematic Connection Listing

1. Stories of Urban Isolation

Fiction

Helena María Viramontes: "Neighbors"

Dagoberto Gilb: "Love in L.A."

Drama

Josefina López: *Real Women Have Curves*

2. New York City and the Urban Latino Voice

Fiction

Sergio Troncoso: "My Life in the City"

Poetry

Miguel Piñero: "La Bodega Sold Dreams"

"A Lower East Side Poem"

Jack Agüeros: "Psalm for Coquito"

Pedro Pietri: "Puerto Rican Obiturary"

Gloria Vando: "In the Dark Backward"

Julio Marzán: "Grand Central Station"

Victor Hernández Cruz: "Their Poem"

3. Traveling the Urban Tracks

Fiction

Sandra Cisneros: "Bread"

Junot Díaz: "Edison, New Jersey"

Poetry

Willie Perdomo: "Reflections of the Metro-North, Winter 1990"

Lorna Dee Cervantes: "Freeway 280"

"Beneath the Shadow of the Freeway"

Essay

Luis Alberto Urrea: "Meet the Satánicos"

7
The Fringe World

Outside Looking in, and Inside Looking Out

INTRODUCTION

Supposedly, some sort of fence lines the border between the United States and Mexico, but it has holes in it, and through these holes (or across the empty canals and dry river beds) people move back and forth, north *and* south, driven by personal and economic conditions. The border is actually porous, shifting with the movements of people working on both sides who maneuver between two worlds in order to improve their lives. Companies move their plants into the neighboring cities (outsourcing in search of cheaper labor), and in the wake of the North American Free Trade Agreement (NAFTA), global networks blur all the solid regional limits we used to see as rigid and certain. Cities like Los Angeles, Miami, and New York are constantly changing as centers of world culture. As the physical markers—a fence, a highway, a wire, or a railroad track—disappear, there arises the need to see these border areas as metaphors for the way people's lives depend on the mixing of cultures, the blending of lifestyles, and the inter-lingual, bilingual systems of communication. Some call this metaphorical area the borderlands, and the concept has led to an entire area of academic focus: Border Studies.

One thing is clear: between the "mainstream"—the "Pleasantville," suburban, middle-class, white American world—and the other side (el otro lado), there exist complex underground systems of life in which thousands of people, and many Latinos, network and operate. Invisible, underground, shadow, illegal, alien—all sorts of names exist for this marginal landscape and the "outsiders" who maneuver within it. What tends to be forgotten, however, is that outsiders are also insiders, that the pathways and connections run through the heart of the mainstream (beneath the surface sometimes, in clear view at others). All manner of social, economic, and cultural interdependencies exist, and no one can really hide entirely on one clear side or the other. As in Richard Wright's famous story, "The Man Who Went Underground," the parallel world beneath the visible is alive with importance and in constant interaction with the obvious, the recognized, and the mainstream. Foods and music tend to slip across boundaries faster than laws and attitudes, but everything is moving and Latino artists are always aware of the shifting, reinventing process that often fuels their writing, providing tensions for stories and empowering the language of their poems and plays.

Life on the Fringe

The selections in this chapter explore this marginal region where Latinos grapple with ambiguities. Conflicts and tensions arise from having to exist and live in the middle, perhaps not belonging entirely to either side of U.S. life. There are those who manipulate these liminal areas for their own good and others who wind up ostracized from both sides, becoming isolated outcasts. In many instances, U.S. culture pushes Latinos toward the fringes of an "American" mainstream culture. Some live beneath the mainstream like the heroes in the urban landscapes in Chapter 6, and others work the edges, surviving by learning the ropes of getting by in the alleyways and by manipulating the systems. Some rebel in quiet ways like "Barbosa" in the Vega Yunqué story. Still others celebrate the margins and rejoice in the multiple energies that result from being from both sides of the fence at once, double in importance and power, refusing to be channeled by the pressures of society's monocultural forces. Others, like Alma Ambert's heroine in "Rage is a Fallen Angel," never adjust and sideline themselves with some form of "cultural schizophrenia."

Outcasts and Rebels

Stories of outsiders and outcasts are obviously not new to world literature. In fact, some argue that the first fictional works derived from the pamphlets sold or distributed at executions so that people at public hangings could learn of the rogue hero's journey before they watched him die. From Moll Flanders to Tom Jones to William Faulkner's Joe Christmas or Richard Wright's Bigger Thomas, the outcast character is a staple of world literature. Stories about strange people who do not fit in are somehow infinitely more interesting than those about contented, well-rounded, "normal" people who are happy and successful.

The Latino outcast, particularly in economic terms, is an essential element of Latino literature. In a sense, all Latinos, as people of color, are outsiders, as are all those without the economic means to maintain the lives they want in a capitalist society. Stories of Latino rebels have a long and profound history from Sor Juana de la Cruz to Gregorio Cortez to Miguel Piñero. Through their stories, poems, plays, and essays, modern Latino writers often present the flaws in mainstream institutions of power.

Surviving in Gringolandia

The emphasis in this chapter is on those who cope (or do not) with life on the border, with the ambiguity of dual appreciation. How does the Latino fit within the dominant culture? Will a *casita* beneath the freeway be enough? Will a mural on the side of an L.A. building instill pride and value? Should the Latino "melt" into the system—or not? Will he or she be trapped or destroyed by it? How does one maintain one's own sense of Latin America in the midst of an overpowering explosion of consumer goods and "all things Gringo"? How far does one go from one's family and traditions? What is a Latino soldier supposed to feel when the reality of racism, prejudice, and class structure at home present real and practical obstacles to his or her obtaining the freedom for which he or she supposedly fights? When it comes to the literary view, how is one's language to be used or adjusted in the process of living within the "belly of the beast"?

Between Languages

Many of the works in this section openly celebrate the hybrid quality of the Latino voice. We find in various selections a willingness to play with the way two languages mesh and overlap. Writers of the borderlands juggle Spanish and English in a continuously lively process of melding allusions and reworking syntax, especially in their poetry.* A new language emerges in the spaces between Spanish and English, and Latinos sometimes live in an inter-lingual territory, a transitional space rich with energy and flavor where voices freely bounce between the two languages in a flurry of code-switching. All sorts of questions arise when readers pay attention to the language choices a writer makes. What types of feelings come in Spanish, which in English? Does one language point to the heart, the other to the head, one backwards in time, the other forward, and why? How does a word in one language reveal a character's identity better than its counterpart in the other? Is there an equivalent translation at all since the same word in Spanish carries different connotations and meanings to different Latino populations? What gets translated (or betrayed) and how does the writer do it exactly? These are the central questions in Latino literature raised in the following selections.

FICTION

Alba Ambert

Alba Ambert was born in San Juan, Puerto Rico, grew up in the South Bronx and now lives in England. She is a poet, an essayist, and a novelist (as well as psycholinguist). One of only a select number of female mainland Puerto Rican-American fiction writers, Ambert offers readers a sympathetic and insightful look into the

---

*See Chapter 2, "Latino Poetry."

psychological worlds of various Latina protagonists. She has published two novels, *A Perfect Silence* (1995) and *The Passion of Maria Magdalena Stein* (2004), and a collection of poems, *Alphabets of Seeds* (2004).

Rage Is a Fallen Angel

For Marina Catzaras

I

He said I had to be in here for two months.
At least.
I said, no way. And he said, or the public mental hospital.
I said, where do I sign?
5   I'm still fuming about it, but can't let my anger show.
Dr. Rhodes thinks I'm pliable. I suppose he was trained to believe everyone is. He gives me these silly tapes about unrealistic expectations and thinks that I listen to them. He thinks a lot of things that don't really exist.

All the lies I tell him, for example. But then maybe the lies do exist, once he believes in their existence.

Does something exist when it's only in someone's mind? Are lies not lies after all as long as someone believes them? Are lies lies if you think they're true? Maybe it's a matter of intent. Are lies not lies if there is no intention to lie?

The first time I remember lying, I hadn't even lied at all.

10   I was a little girl visiting an aunt in Ciales. One of my cousins and I returned from an afternoon walk to the river which was just behind the house. My aunt asked me about the walk and whether I had seen any freshwater shrimp. It turns out I hadn't. So I said, "No, *tia*," shaking my head vigorously, the way little girls like to do to show off their curls. In my case, I had new earrings on.

But just as I said this, and to my astonishment, my cousin said, "*Oh, sí, Mamá,*" and embellished her tale of unseen shrimp with florid adjectives and the wildest superlatives you can imagine. She was around twelve then and dreamed of becoming an actress. She was always practicing her art, as she called it. My aunt was furious because she thought the worst sin was to lie to a relative, and to lie to her, who was almost my mother, was certainly a serious transgression. She dragged me into her bedroom and forced me to kneel before a bloody Jesus on a wooden crucifix she had on the wall and beg for God's forgiveness. It was so humiliating, especially since my cousin kept peeking into the room and snickering through my entire ordeal.

Getting back to my lies to Dr. Rhodes, I suppose that the person who believes the lie is as important in this matter as the one who tells it.

What if I tell someone I went to Egypt and that person believes me? Does the lie both exist and not exist? Is it a lie in my mind, yet a reality in the other person's mind? When the person then goes on to tell someone else, you know so-and-so went to Egypt, does that constitute a truth? What if, having never been to Egypt, I become convinced that I did go? Is it true then? At least as far as I'm concerned?

Does it all boil down to (teleology,) then? It's not enough to describe something, nor to understand its cause and effect, we must also know its purpose. Or better said, the end that moves something. It's the only way to completely understand it. In other words, we must know why something is what it is, I know this sounds a bit Aristotelian, but I can't help having read all the books that I've read. It's the result of a liberal arts education. Sometimes it's a real burden.

15   I wind up entangled in an idea that spawns another idea and another and another until I can't remember where the hell I was going with it all. It's really disturbing.

But I have to write the ideas and what sparks them, so I can remember everything that I've learned. I'm not being arrogant by trotting out all the knowledge I've collected. It's just that I have to remember all that I'm forgetting. I must remember. I must.

The shocks don't help. They call it ECT. Electroconvulsive therapy. Everything's disguised in acronyms around here. Like the MMI, as though we couldn't figure out it was a test to determine whether we're paranoid or schizophrenic or both. It's all part of that secret language they have. And they assume we're too stupid to figure out their silly codes. Patients are supposed to be excluded from the professionals' clique this way. Oh well, this isn't the only place where language is used to exclude.

The rubber-sheeted bed is slick as ice. I start trembling every time they wheel the black machine to my bed side.

Which is often. Twice a day. Every day.

20   The big black box on a trolley. The tube of lubricating jelly. The mouth gag. It's hard not to stare at the knobs, the cords, the switches. The nurse plugs the machine in and the dials glow in the early-morning gloom. My stomach turns.

At first I begged them to give me a sedative to help me relax. They said it wasn't necessary.

This is how it goes.

Dr. Rhodes adjusts the settings on the black box and rubs jelly on my temples. He orders me to blow my nose, breathe deeply and open my mouth so he can fit the gag between my teeth. I clamp my mouth on the gag and shut my eyes. I feel something hard pressing against the sides of my head. I heard them once refer to these as electrodes. Dr. Rhodes holds the electrodes and orders the nurse to punch the button. I struggle and moan.

Go! he says and I feel a searing flash of pain. Then they do it again. And again.

25   And again.

I forget everything for a while. Then things come to me, things I haven't thought about in ages. This happens a lot when I can't sleep. Which is too bad because I like to sleep. That's when I feel no love or hate. But during those long stretches of insomnia, I become aware of my heart palpitations or worry about what to do with my arms and I can't sleep. Then an idea pops into my head and I keep thinking about it, worrying it in my mind, like a dog gnawing on a bone.

Like karma. I've been thinking about karma all the time. After sloshing it around in my mind for days, I realized that the concept of karma was generated by the privileged classes. To make sure the oppressed accepted their lot in life. That is, a life of exploitation by the very same privileged classes that thought up this karma business. And thus, secured their status. You can be sure it wasn't the poor working slaves who came up with it. What's in it for them, after all?

I really become agitated thinking about this. People rarely get what they deserve. Look at Hitler. All my life I had thought people were compensated for what they did. After all, I was already a teenager in the late sixties. If people were good, good would come to them. If they were cruel, vicious, mean, terrible people, they would pay for their acts. Like dying a slow agonizing death from pancreatic cancer.

Then I realized that this wasn't necessarily so, if you didn't believe in reincarnation. Which I don't.

30   Which made me think. I refuse to be born again. No way. I fought birth like mad the first time around (first, that is, if reincarnation doesn't exist, oh, please don't let it be). Anyhow, I was born buttocks first, cursing the world like a full-fledged Maori.

I was never meant to be, I think.

When the river spilled blood, I had been walking the path of the perfect place somewhere deep in my mother's darkness. Then I don't know what happened, but I got shoved out. And here I am, to make a long story short. Something I find congenitally incapable of doing.

"Here" is a psychiatric hospital in Hartford. Dr. Rhodes said I had to be in for two months. But I think I've been here longer than that. But I'm not sure. I forget things, so I'm really not sure about anything. Or something might be one way now, but who knows how it will be a moment from now?

I'm not insane, let me clarify that from the start. Not yet, that is. Even though I sometimes have to look at my photograph, the one I always keep in my gown pocket, to remember what I look like. They don't have mirrors here, you see.

35   Whether I wind up insane or not depends on how long I stay in this hospital. Mill said that good cannot engender evil and evil cannot engender good. This disputes Giordano Bruno's coincidences of contraries theory. (Lucretius's too.) Well, I might side with Mill on this one. As far as I'm concerned, this place is bad. No good can come of it. The longer I stay in here, the more likely it is I'll go mad. It's human nature. We adapt easily.

Dr. Rhodes says the shocks will help me deal with what happened to my baby. I've forgotten a lot of things, but I haven't forgotten my baby girl. When she died, suffocated in her own vomit, the world turned its back on me. I swallowed thorns that night. I became stone. I'll never forgive the world its love-lessness. Its cruelty.

In this place, I'm finally grasping the true meaning of silence. A concept that echoes in my mind like a nightmare. There's a place at my core where words don't exist. Where I discovered the multiple dimensions of pain. The core of desolation, loss and rage. It's what was left after my little girl died and my pain had no words. There's nothing worse than the inability to name your hurt. Will I ever be able to attach words to my loss?

That's when I rage. And I hate and I rave and I pound on the table and scream, no more, I won't take any more. And I cut myself with knives, and when they take away the knives, I cut myself with plastic forks, whatever there is to hurt myself more. And then they hide everything from me, but I find a plastic cup and I crush it in my hand like a freshly laid egg and there I find that in the mess, there is always an edge. That's all I need to open my flesh, to make blood flow from myself. To feel relief from the terrible rage.

Like Prince Hal in *Henry IV*, I ponder on ways to cope with rebellion. But if I run away from something, do I run toward something else at the same time? What I mean is, do I continue this pretense of pliability? I said Dr. Rhodes, like all shrinks I suppose, thinks people are pliable. I wonder if he thinks the same of himself? Does a psychiatrist consider that he is an exception? Sort of how religious fundamentalists think that only they enjoy the grace of a god.

40   It's so difficult for me to organize my hope.

As I said, Dr. Rhodes thinks I'm pliable, but I'm really not. I need desperately to rebel. Even if it's just to kill myself. Now I rebel in little ways, of course, so they don't certify me incompetent. Unless they've already done so. I don't trust this Dr. Rhodes. That's why I lie to him all the time. If I told him the truth, God only knows what he would do with it. Turn it around to hurt me, I suppose.

That's how they all are. Men, that is. Men who happen to be shrinks, especially. Can't trust them for a second. One minute they're talking to you in a soothing, almost motherly voice, and the next they're threatening to commit you to a mental institution. Just because a person's depressed after having lost everything there was to lose. And tries to commit suicide. Having no intention of hurting anyone. But herself. So what business is it of anyone's? It's not evil or anything as long as you don't hurt someone else.

Don't get me started on that one. Because what I hate to think about most of all is the nature of evil. I can really get stuck on it, like a scratched record. And can't seem to extricate myself.

Sometimes I don't tell the truth, but it's only because I don't know what the truth is. So I make it up. And it becomes real. So real I could taste it. Somehow I feel like the Egyptian god Ptah who by the mere act of thinking and speaking brought the world into existence.

45   That's why I'm a writer. Or was. To create my own world. To be my own god. (Heaven forbid I ever tell Dr. Rhodes this!)

I used to be a poet, then wrote screenplays.

Sort of like Anthony Burgess, who wrote music before writing novels. In an interview he once said that for years he was trying to write an opera about Sigmund Freud, but was having trouble with the libretto. I wonder if he ever finished it?

I was writing a script about a salsa queen's rise from the slums. I wonder if I ever finished it? Often, the most difficult thing for a writer is knowing when a work ends. One could spend a lifetime on a poem or a novel or a story or a script. What with all the revisions and everything. It's a miracle we ever finish anything.

What I said before about lying regarding a trip to Egypt isn't true. Though I may have given that impression. I did go to Egypt once. I remember being struck by the Egyptian word for bread, which is the same as the word for life. Eish. Sounds like a complaint.

50   I had the misfortune of visiting the Temple of Kom Ombo, that double temple of the crocodile-headed god Sebek and the falcon-headed god Horus. They were both actually one god, a god who was half good and half bad (reminding me of Bruno's coincidences of contraries theory).

With my propensity to dwell on this nature of evil business, I squandered the rest of the trip wondering whether evil lurks in me too. Maybe I shouldn't have sat on the clammy sarcophagus of the mummified crocodile, even though my feet were killing me. Maybe I entered the temple on its bad side. Maybe I sniffed too deeply of the ammonium chloride that is said to have been first made in Alexandria from the dung of camels, ammonia that could have easily wafted south to Aswan.

But I had terrible nightmares after that visit. Were they nightmares or visitations from ram-headed gods intoxicated with camel dung? How would I know?

Even lolling on the east side of the Nile in a felucca each sunset offered no solace. Even the smiling Egyptians.

Actually, the smiling Egyptians had little to smile about, which really got me going on the injustices of the world. Here you have people who believe that they live under a law of universal justice, and go about smiling as though it were true. As though the voluntary maiming of infants, so they can beg in the streets, or the bombing of mosques and tourists, or the hunger and constant dust and thirst of the implacable desert didn't exist.

55   Tutankhamen lies dead with crook and flail on his chest, that's what I always say when I have nothing better to say.

My first husband, Pepe, was Puerto Rican like me, but looked Egyptian. He was tall and dark and smiled a lot. Except that Pepe frittered away his time on this and that. I'm not entirely sure what he did. Maybe nothing. Well, what can you expect from a man you meet on the San Juan to Cataño ferry during off-hours.

He was the only person I'd ever met who called Mohammed Ali, Cassius Clay. He liked classical music, but didn't know much about it because when he was growing up, they only had Bach in his house. Then he read somewhere that the Japanese had discovered a cure for baldness: Mozart. But not all of Mozart. Only Concerto Number 3 for flute and harp and Piano Concerto Number 21. Pepe had an intense preoccupation with his physical appearance. Counted the number of hairs on his comb every morning and worried about his hair loss for the rest of the day. We listened to a lot of flute, harp and piano for a while. His hair never grew any thicker, though.

Pepe had some annoying habits that drove me up the wall. He straightened and twisted his arm to snap the elbow joint all the time. In the middle of the night I could hear his snapping elbow and felt murderous. That wasn't his most annoying habit, though. He liked to collect and file clippings from newspapers and magazines. I couldn't invite people over for dinner, because invariably Pepe would get into a discussion with someone, and when he wanted to make a point, he'd rush to his files to search for the relevant article that would prove his argument. Sometimes, hours would go by before he returned. By that time, the guests would jump out of their chairs and rush out the door, afraid of getting into another discussion with him and having to put up with another one of his searches.

Pepe was brought up in the city, but he liked to believe he was a country boy. Once, we were invited by some of his relatives to their *finca*[1] for a weekend. Our first morning was uneventful, except we stepped on some warm cow pies and had to rush to the river to clean up. Then on Sunday, Pepe's cousin made the mistake of saying she needed to slaughter a chicken for dinner. Pepe, in his usual self-assured manner, strutted up to her and volunteered to do the job. No sweat, he said, but not before instructing me to record it on his video camera. Sometimes he knew full well I hated to do. I have an ingrained fear of cameras. I think Balzac was right when he said that the self is peeled away like an onion every time a person is photographed.

60   Anyhow, I found myself under the blazing sun, holding the idiotic camcorder while Pepe shrieked directions. He grabbed a squawking guinea hen, jammed its head into his fist and wrung its neck while he yelled directorial instructions at me. "Get over here, you're too far! What're you doing? You stupid or something, can't you see the sun's behind you?"

When he flung the hen to the ground, it bounced back up, feathers ruffled, and scrambled off into the bushes. I was dutifully recording the hen's flight to freedom when Pepe snatched the camera out of my hands.

"That's enough," he growled, and stomped into the house.

I was so bored during that marriage that I read my way through all of Chekhov and discovered how ordinary heroes really are. My problem is that I expect ordinary people to act as heroes. But there are few heroes in the world, and it's hard for me to accept the ordinary, especially in myself. But even heroes have frailties, Chekhov says. Heroes are ordinary people who rise

---

[1]farm

to an occasion. That sounds pretty Chekhovian to me, but I think my second husband told me that.

I loved him very much. But I can't remember what happened to him. It's all a blur. The death of my baby girl. Slicing my wrists with a kitchen knife. I really wanted to say my hands off, but fainted when I saw all the blood.

65   Does death destroy love? I wonder.

Falling in love is different from loving, I've discovered.

An editor once said to me that I get lost in metaphors and literary allusions. She was right. I'm doing it right now. It's my way of hiding the pain of truth. I do it in therapy all the time. Dr. Rhodes never knows what I'm talking about. But he pretends to.

Here he comes. Dr. Rhodes, that is. His white robe flapping. Better hide the journal. Quick.

II

Last time I wrote, Dr. Rhodes had come to see me. His eyes were wide with excitement. Said I needed surgery. A hysterectomy. I stopped menstruating when they locked me up in here. Even though I'm still too young to be menopausal. I can't remember my age exactly, but the doctors have figured it out. The staff gynecologist thought I should have everything scooped out. It's a new kind of cancer prevention treatment, Dr. Rhodes said. Who did he think he was kidding? I wondered if they'd remove my testicles if I were a man. That's what's called an academic question, isn't it?

70   I wouldn't agree to sign the papers for the operation, and Dr. Rhodes started getting snippety with me. It's either surgery or an indefinite stay here, he said. Or the state mental institution. I said, where do I sign?

I couldn't write for a long time after the operation. I was so depressed.

The Mayans believed that when you cut down a tree, you must ask its forgiveness or else a star will fall out of the sky. I wonder what happens when a woman is eviscerated for no good reason. Will the sun fall out? Or the moon?

The walls seem to press against me. I draw the curtains, so I won't have to face the day and wonder about all the good things out there I might be missing. Complained of a migraine, so as not to arouse the suspicions of the hospital staff. They gave me a pill and left me alone.

I think about the mutilated women in Picasso's art and wonder why men need to mutilate us. Even symbolically. I wish Dr. Rhodes and the staff gynecologist had been harmless artists, instead of what they are.

75   The Ibans killed their enemies, then scooped out the brains through the nostrils. They tore off the cheek skin and ate it to ensure fearlessness. They decorated their sheaths and sword hilts with the shorn hair. Jaws were fastened, tongue cut off, head smoked over fire. They decorated the eye sockets with brightly colored studs and put wooden stoppers up the nostrils.

Are women the enemies of men?

Once, Dr. Rhodes accused me of having penis envy. Penis envy, my foot, I thought. Privilege envy is more like it. I didn't tell him that, of course. It would only prove his point.

After shock treatment today, I felt as though I were in a big black hole full of nothing. I was so afraid the hole would suck me into its nothingness. Now, I'm afraid to live and afraid to die, all at the same time. I wish I could scream.

I have no one to talk to in here. So I have conversations in my head. I ask questions and answer them, discuss problems with myself, presenting the pros and cons to every argument. When the nurses or the other patients talk to me, I'm too tired to talk. I do talk to Dr. Rhodes, if only to lie to him. Tell him I'm fine. Today he told me I needed more of everything they're giving me. How do I get out of here. I can't seem to escape.

80   For days, I've heard nothing but the howling and sobs of women. They've been giving us therapeutic injections every day. The world seems different now. Noisier.

I can recall things I had forgotten. Things that happened years ago are so clear in my mind. Too clear, like a blinding sun in the white desert. I'm writing everything I can remember. So if I forget, because of the shock treatment or the injections, it will be conserved somewhere. Then I can read it and know what I have learned in life, what I've lived through. I just wish I could remember what happened to Jaime and my little girl. I wish I could remember just that.

I do remember odd things, like Pepe and his guinea hen, like that school I worked in once, after Pepe and I got divorced.

I couldn't live on my poetry—it wasn't that good. And the screenplays were, as they say in the business, under consideration. I did substitute teaching in New Haven to make ends meet.

This was between husbands. Before my little girl was born. A perfect child. I remember how terrified I had been when I was pregnant. I had seen all those children in classes for the trainable mentally retarded and I was afraid for her.

85   I can recall climbing up that hill in New Haven and facing a rectangular brick structure. It was a clear spring day. The sky was a deep blue and filled with high billowy clouds that floated by effortlessly. The school had the bland architecture of urban schools with children's drawings taped on the windows in an attempt to cheer the gray, leftover-meat quality of its walls. With narrow, barred windows and a metallic entrance door, it looked like a jail or an insane asylum. Like here.

The children weren't allowed into the building until the bell rang at eight, so children and parents gathered around the school doors. A man was crying outside the gate because his little girl started school that day. I wondered what was so bad about that.

The assistant principal, Mrs. Hurley, a big woman with brown spots on her pale skin, had a bunch of keys clipped to the side of her leather belt. They jangled as she strode down the halls. After the necessary introductions, she escorted me to the classroom.

"You have a group of eight children," she explained while she glanced at her watch. She spoke as if the words were stuffed in her mouth.

"Eight to twelve years old and functioning at a very low level. They're toilet trained and can feed themselves, but that's about it. Can't teach them any more than that. You know, self-help skills. Some are Down's syndrome, others severely brain damaged. Just keep them calm and follow the regular teacher's lesson plan. Our teachers prepare a week's lesson plan just in case they're absent. If you follow it and keep the kids busy, you won't have any trouble. Understand?"

90 She had the teacher's mannerism of shaking the index finger at the person she addressed, while the rest of her hand made a fist. Teachers start doing this deliberately, but by the time they have taught for ten years or so it becomes a habit of which they are no longer aware. I could bet that Mrs. Hurley did it when talking to herself or on the phone.

"If you have any difficulty, here's the intercom." Mrs. Hurley took a few long steps to the wall. "Dial 3 and I'll pop in to help, if I have the time." She looked around the room, then glanced at me a bit skeptically.

"Better go down now, the bell's about to ring."

I studied the plan. It was neatly written with specific activities for each hour of the day. What the hell was gross motor coordination? I asked myself. And I thought this substitute teaching was going to be an easy way to make some money.

I was pulling teaching materials out of the classroom closets Mrs. Hurley had unlocked, when an aide brought in the children. All eight. They sat in their color-coded desks. Well, they recognized colors, I thought. That must be a hard thing to do. Or maybe it was the concept of color that was difficult to grasp. How would I know? Maybe they were all at the wrong desks.

95 Among the drooling, swaying children sat a child who looked entirely out of place. His desk had a green dot labeled Francisco. I checked the attendance sheet. Eight children on the rolls, eight children at their desks. No absences. On my only day here, wouldn't you know? When I called all the children's names, only Francisco, who had been scrutinizing me with big dark eyes, responded by raising his hand.

"Francisco," I said. He smiled and said nothing, but his eyes sparkled. "*Ven acá,*" Come here, I said in Spanish.

The boy walked up to my desk and I continued to speak to him in Spanish.

"What's your full name?" I asked him.

"Francisco Morales Rosario."

100 "I'm Miss González. I'm your teacher today because your teacher couldn't come to school. So, where do you live?"

"19 Sullivan Street."

"How old are you?"

"Ten."

"How long have you been in the United States?"

105 "A few months. We came from Puerto Rico. My father was here for a long time working before we came. And he had to save money to bring us."

"What's your mother's name?"

"Adela Rosario de Morales."

"Do you have any brothers and sisters?"

"Two brothers. I don't have any sisters."

110 "Do you speak any English?"

"Not yet, but I'm learning some things in school and on television."

This was my self-fashioned intelligence test. Based on my own judgment, this child was nothing but a normal ten year old.

I noticed the noise level in the room increase. Two kids were slapping each other in the face and one was rolling on the floor moaning. The swaying and drooling of the swayers and droolers was getting progressively worse and some of the droolers were making gurgling sounds deep in their throats, laughing and stamping their feet.

I put an arm around Francisco's shoulders and asked him to sit down.

115 "Okay, children, it's time to do some work. Everybody, sit at your desks, please."

I clapped a few times, since no one but Francisco was paying any attention to me.

Madre mía, I thought, this is going to be a long, long day.

When the aide took the children to the lunchroom, I picked up after them, the room was a mess by then, and went to the desk to search through the children's folders. Each folder had an educational plan and assessments done by psychologists, social workers and special education specialists. I pulled out Francisco's file. Just as I thought. His IQ test had been administered in English, a language the boy couldn't understand. Jesus, in this day and age, don't they know any better? I thought. His IQ was reported in the trainable mentally retarded range. I would be classified mentally retarded too, if someone gave me an IQ test in German. Couldn't the psychologist see the sparkle in the boy's eyes?

Clutching the file, I was halfway to the principal's office when I heard a terrible high-pitched scream coming from a closet.

120 "Don't mind her." Mrs. Hurley stood next to me at that moment. I had been so distracted with the scream, I didn't hear her keys jangling.

"It's the new girl. Started having tantrums the minute she stepped into the building. Can't understand English, so we can't reach her. Had to lock her up until she learns to behave herself."

"I can calm her down," I said quietly. "Put her in my class and I'll take care of her. At least for today."

"You think so?"

I nodded.

125 "Well, okay, but you have a handful without this behavior problem."

Mrs. Hurley pulled out one of her keys and unlocked the closet.

A little girl, who was no older than ten, cringed in the darkness. I spoke to her as gently as I could.

"Why are you so sad, *linda*?[2] I asked in Spanish.

The little girl looked up. Her face was tear-stained.

---

[2]beautiful

130   "Come on, I'll take you to my room, okay? There's a boy there, Francisco. You can talk to him, he's really nice."

She gave me her hand and we walked out of the closet.

"That's great!" Mrs. Hurley cried. "This child has been a real problem from the minute she got here."

"She doesn't speak English and can't understand why she's here. She's just frightened, that's all," I said.

"What does it matter? She's retarded, in English or Spanish or Chinese. That's why she's in this special school." Mrs. Hurley suddenly got defensive.

135   "Well, I'm just a substitute teacher."

"That's right, you're no expert."

"May I have a look at her file, just to see what her educational objectives are, and then I can maybe work with her a little this afternoon." I smiled my most innocent smile.

"Well, I don't know. Suppose there's no harm to be done by it."

Don't count on it, I thought.

140   When I looked at her file, I realized that Liliana had been tested by the same psychologist who tested Francisco, in English, of course. Someone was out there making sure all the Puerto Rican kids who filed past his desk were safely put away. This was one of the worst cases of child abuse I had encountered during my time as a substitute teacher.

I gave the other children some busywork to do with clay, and they slapped it delightedly on their tables and unstuck it to slap it down again. They would be entertained with this small chunk of clay for hours. Maybe. If I was lucky.

In the meantime, I sat in a corner with Francisco and Liliana. At first, Liliana had refused to enter the room when she saw the other children, but just as she screwed up her face to start crying again, I got Francisco to bring her in.

The next morning, I took out my credit card, which I kept hidden under my underwear for emergency use only, and took the shuttle to Washington, D.C. That's where I met Jaime, at the Department of Justice. I supposed, correctly, it turns out, that there would be someone in that office who had some notion of what justice was. Secretaries, assistants to this-and-that shunted me around for half the morning, until I finally alit at the Division of Civil Rights. And there he was, sitting behind piles of papers, cradling the telephone receiver with his shoulder while he took notes on a yellow legal pad.

To make this long story a bit shorter, Jaime and another Civil Rights lawyer took a statement from me as complainant, swooped into New Haven to investigate, confronted the school administrators with their evidence and they managed to get Francisco and Liliana retested, in Spanish, and placed in a regular bilingual program. Happy ending.

145   Amazing how I can recall this episode so vividly. So many stories woven into stories, spiraling in time to eternity.

But I still can't remember what happened to Jaime. He would visit me, if he were here. Wouldn't he? Maybe he's in Washington. The distance between us could be a problem. I can't ask Dr. Rhodes either because I pretend that I remember everything. Never know what he'll be up to next. These injections make me feel so strange and alienated from my own body. Some of my recollections are as crisp as an animated movie. Somehow they don't seem real. I'll tell Dr. Rhodes about this incident I remember so vividly. That should earn me a few points.

Points for what? This isn't a game. Or is it?

III

Dr. Rhodes, with his neck sticking out of his collar like a duck, came to my room to inform me of yet another increase in my injections. They keep us informed of these things, as though we had any choices. We don't and they know it. And we know it. The injections are the latest treatment for my problem, he said. In their code that means they're expreimental and he's using me as a subject. To test them out. It's easier to destroy than to construct.

I feel very strange. Afraid of things I can't name. Sometimes I can stare at the fold of a curtain for hours and find it the most fascinating thing in the entire universe.

150 After my shock treatment today, I had a flash. What I call one of my memory flashes. I'll recall something, but as though it were a dream, not as something I have experienced. It's like watching a film in which I'm the protagonist. And I stare at myself and in my initial confusion, I think I have somehow managed to leave my body and examine my entire life as it rolls in front of my eyes like a movie reel. But then, how can I see all of this, if I have abandoned my body and my eyes are now on the stranger I see playing my role in the dark theater? A terrible fear grips me at those times and it takes me hours of trembling and weeping to calm down.

This is what I remembered today. Jaime and I traveled to a tiny village in Naples once. It was quiet and quaint. One day I woke up at dawn and, while Jaime still slept, I took a walk through the dewy mist before my first espresso. I turned into a narrow cobblestone alley. The houses had red slate roofs and potted geraniums on the porches. It was a scene straight out of medieval times.

I stood at a corner and had an urge to look up when a middle-aged woman came out to the second-floor balcony of a house, her hair covering her chest all the way down to the waist. Dreamily, looking out into the distance, she brushed her long black hair and then swept it in a knot at the back of her head. That's when I realized she was bare-breasted. Big brown breasts, like country bread loaves, sparkled in the morning sun. I just stood there staring at her, wanting so badly to press my face against her breasts and take in that aroma of freshly baked bread. I almost cried. Then she stepped into the house and the spell was broken. I'll never forget her, despite the injections and the shocks and everything I've been through since then. Yet she doesn't even know that I exist.

This flash pitched me into the deepest of sorrows. I suddenly remembered what it feels like to be happy, to ache for something you want so badly you can taste it in the roof of your mouth, to stare unflinchingly at something beautiful, to want to live another day.

I had forgotten what it was like to hope.

155   I asked Dr. Rhodes today when I can go home.

He said not for a while.

I said, what does that mean?

He wouldn't answer me, which made me very angry.

I told him, in no uncertain terms, that my husband was a lawyer, and he couldn't keep me here against my will.

160   He said, what husband?

I said, Jaime.

He got up with that fake look of concern he likes to summon up every once in a while. He said, you're hallucinating again.

That's what he says when he catches me in a lie. Which really confused me, because I wasn't lying this time. I just wanted to get out of here. No more lies, no more anything to get around him.

Now, you know that you haven't been feeling well with this new treatment. That's all that's going on. Just go back to your room and rest. We'll talk about this later.

165   Then he patted my hand.

The sound of rain, hard and insistent, pounds in my head relentlessly. I can't sleep on this wet night. My heart is cold and damp, I can feel the outside of myself, a spectator of my own life. A nurse wanted to take the photograph I had in my pocket away from me, and I tore it up and flushed it down the toilet.

I don't know who I am anymore. What is me? The worms are back slithering out of my eyes. I have to keep rubbing my eyes and picking at them so I can write. I have to keep writing, I have to keep writing, keep writing. Writing. My brain is hemorrhaging. There's blood everywhere, but the worms lick it up. They're licking up my brain.

Oh, out there in the black rain, there's a rim of light. No, oh, no, it's fire! I can smell the flesh roasting. I have to get out of here, I have to get out. Out. Out of here.

Oh, no, no, no, there he comes, followed by a straggle of people. His white coat flapping, his neck craning out of his collar. A nurse holds up a hypodermic needle. Shush journal, be quiet. They'll all go away soon.

Daniel Cano

The author of two novels, Daniel Cano was a soldier in Vietnam in the mid-1960s. His first novel, *Pepe Rios* (1990), deals with the Mexican revolution and the second, *Shifting Loyalties* (1995), centers around the Vietnam War, but shifts back and forth in time to portray Latinos in the Korean War as well. He teaches English at Santa Monica College in Santa Monica, California.

Somewhere Outside Duc Pho

The night we heard that our good friend Jesse Peña was missing, we decided to get a search party together and check the bars in Duc Pho, an old city in Vietnam's central highlands. We were in the rear area for a short rest before beginning the next operation, and we knew that under stress, sometimes guys who reached the limit and could not go on another day ended up AWOL, lost in the delirium of booze and chaos. But our orders came through and we were restricted to base camp, forced to disband our posse.

Two days later a long line of double-propped Chinook helicopters with 105 howitzers and nets full of ammunition dangling beneath them choppered us into the mountains, about a half hour outside our base camp. They lifted us to the top of a mountain that was scattered with light vegetation. Below and all around us, the jungle landscape was immense. Mountain ranges stretched in every direction.

We began knocking down trees, clearing away brush, unloading tools, equipment, packs, and ammunition. On our bare shoulders we lugged 55-pound projectiles into the ammo dump…long lines of shirtless men, bodies shining with sweat. The sledgehammers clanged against metal stakes and echoed as the gun crews dug in their howitzers. We filled and stacked hundreds of sandbags, which formed long crooked walls, some semi-circular, others round or rectangular—all protecting the battery just like the walls of a castle. And above the shouting voices, the striking metal, and the popping smoke grenades roared the engines of the helicopters as they landed, dropped their cargo, and quickly lifted away.

Once the battery was settled in, I took up my position on the outpost. There were three of us. We dug a four-foot deep bunker for ourselves and stacked three rows of sandbags around the front and sides, protection from incoming rounds and something we didn't like to think about: human assaults on our position.

5   One night, after a week of wind and cold, a trip flare erupted, lighting up the jungle in front of us. We waited, then saw a shadow move across the perimeter. Instinctively we threw hand grenades and set off the claymores. Later, from another outpost, a machine gun burst into a steady stream of fire. The howitzers exploded, sending bright lights into the sky. I gripped my rifle tightly and watched the shadowy treeline as the flares descended and a cold silence filled the air. As always the flares burned out. Once the darkness hit, again the world rumbled around us.

An explosion sent a blast of light across our field of vision, the ground vibrated, my ears buzzed…and moments later, my left arm felt warm. I slid my fingers over the wet skin and touched a hole of punctured flesh, just below the shoulder. I told the others that I was wounded, and they got on the field telephone and called for a medic. The firing stopped. The jungle reverted back to an eerie blackness. Doc Langley, the battery medic, walked me back to our small infirmary and gave me some antibiotics, bandaged my left arm, and told me to get some sleep.

The next morning I was choppered to the field hospital at Pleiku. Doc Langley, who was also a good friend, went with me to take care of the paperwork and refill his supply of Darvon. The doctors sewed me up and I slept the whole day.

When I woke up, Doc Langley was sitting on my bunk. I caught most of his talk, even though I felt dizzy from the anesthetic. He told me that Jesse Peña had been spotted. Some men from the Tiger Force, a reconnaissance outfit, had been on a listening post in the jungle. They'd been observing a squad of Vietcong. As the enemy moved along the trail, there, right in the middle of the VC column, they saw Peña, or a chubby Mexican-looking guy in American fatigues. The Tigers claimed that Peña carried an M-16 and walked right along with the VC squad, not like he was a prisoner but like he was a part of them.

When Doc Langley left, I sat up in my bunk. There was no way I could believe that Peña was in the jungle with the VC. It was just too ridiculous, and I knew that none of our friends would believe it either. I started to think about Peña and the last time any of the guys or I had seen him.

10   Peña was part of a small group of friends. There were about ten of us when everybody showed up, but usually five or six regulars. Since most of us were assigned to different units of the 101st Airborne Division, we'd split up during the operations, but always get back together when we were in the rear area. Each night, we would meet at an isolated spot somewhere in the brigade area—behind a sandbag wall or trash dump—for what we called our sessions. We would drink beer, joke, and talk about hometowns and friends.

Peña, who could hold our attention for what seemed like hours, hadn't said much that last night he was with us. He'd been a bit removed, sitting slightly in the shadows, and he refused to drink any beer. Still, he had smiled a lot, as if nothing was wrong, and had eaten a couple of cans of peaches and just watched and listened. Someone had asked if he was all right, and he'd just answered, "Yeah, I'm O.K." While it was still early in the evening, he got up and said that he was tired—carrying the radio during the last operation had kicked his ass. He straightened his fingers into a mock salute, touched the tip of his cap, and said, "Time to go."

"So early? How come?" Little Rod had asked.

"I'm getting short...only three months. Gotta save all my energy so when I get back home, I'll have everything ready for you guys. Sabes?" said Jesse, his words confusing us.

"Come on, have a beer," Little Rod persisted.

15   "Can't, gotta keep my mind clear. Me voy."

Jesse turned, walked into the darkness of the brigade area, and that was the last we saw of him.

Jesse Peña was short, rotund, and always smiling, like one of those happy little Buddha statues. Although overweight, he was handsome. There was a childlike quality about him, a certain innocence and purity that made him immediately likeable. Two large dimples, one on each chubby cheek, brought a glow to his face.

After each operation, we'd look forward to our sessions, so we could hear more of his jokes and stories. His humor wasn't slapstick or silly, but intelligent, and always with a point or moral. Sometimes he'd reminisce about family and friends back home in Texas, like his cousin Bernie who was so much against the war that he had traveled down to Eagle's Pass, Texas, pretended to be a bracero, and was picked up by the U.S. immigration. According to Jesse, Bernie, who was American and fluent in English, spoke only Spanish to the INS agents. He was deported and went to live with relatives in Piedras Negras. All this, Peña said, just to beat the draft. In this way, Bernie could say that he hadn't dodged the draft; it was the U.S. that had rejected him.

His stories led to questions and analyses, and all of us participated, pulling out every piece of information and insight that we could. Peña always seemed to have the right answers, but he was never overly egotistical. Always he came across as sincere and gracious.

20   I envied his ability to switch from English to Spanish in mid-sentence. His words moved with a natural musical rhythm, a blend of talk-laugh, where even tragic stories took on an element of lightness. He didn't present himself as an intellectual. His speech had a sophistication that didn't come with schooling but with breeding. Someplace is his family's background of poverty, there must have been an honest appreciation of language.

And he loved his Texas. To hear him talk, one would think that San Antonio was San Francisco, New York, or Paris. In his mind, San Anto', as he called it, had culture and personality. When it came to music, no one could come close to the talents of Willie Nelson or Little Joe Y La Familia. Those of us from California didn't even know who they were. He'd play their music on his little tape recorder and we'd laugh and call him a goddamn cowboy, a redneck Mexican out of step with the times, and then we'd slip into arguing about our states and which was best, and how the city was better than the country...and on and on until we'd drained ourselves.

I placed my hands behind my head and looked at the wounded men around me. I didn't really see them, though, because I was thinking too much about Jesse Peña. It didn't make sense that he had suddenly shown up on his unit's duty roster as missing. Why would he go AWOL?

Three weeks later, the operation ended, the scab on my arm had hardened, and we were all back at our front area base camp. I wasn't the only one who'd heard the rumor. All of the guys knew about it. Big Rod, who was about six inches taller than Little Rod, knew some guys in the Tiger Force who confirmed the sighting.

Feeling superstitious about the whole thing, we decided to move the location of our next session. Two of the guys found an isolated spot near the edge of the brigade area. On one side it was separated from the rest of the brigade by a decaying sandbag wall about four feet high. Many of the bags were torn, but the heat and moisture of the tropical valley air had hardened the sand as if it were cement. Empty wooden ammo boxes, some broken and black with mildew, were scattered around the area. Twenty-five yards to our front was the jungle—not as thick as the field, but dense enough to hide someone or something. As the night moved in, the foliage darkened and the only protection from the wilderness beyond was a gun tower manned by two fellow paratroopers.

25 It didn't take long before the guys, and some interested new ones, started arriving. We discussed the possibilities that Jesse was either kidnapped or had deserted. Kidnap seemed impossible because our base camp was a fortress: guards securing the perimeter in gun towers, M.P.'s patrolling in gun Jeeps, units posting watches throughout the night; it just didn't seem possible. Besides, I argued, what interest would the VC have in a PFC radio operator from San Antonio, who only cared about getting home to his wife and child?

Alex Martínez, a surly Californian from the San Fernando Valley, stuck to the argument that Peña had just gone AWOL. "Old Peña split, man—just got tired of the shit. He's probably shacked up with some old lady downtown. Tiger Force probably saw some fat gook dressed in fatigues and thought it was him, man. He'll be back. Give him a few days."

We kicked the idea around. It wasn't absurd. We were reminded of Michael Oberson, a cook who had gone AWOL, changed his name, and lived with a Vietnamese waitress in Saigon for fourteen months. He'd gotten himself a job with an American insurance company and a nice apartment in the Chalon district. He finally turned himself in, and while he waited for his court martial, he was assigned to our unit. We remembered how he had laughed when he told us that the U.S. government subsidized a portion of the salaries of all the employees who worked for the insurance company. "So," he would say, "Uncle Sam was paying me to stay AWOL. How could I give it up?"

Danny Ríos argued that Jesse was too short. Nobody went AWOL with only three months left. It didn't make sense, any of it. Besides, he reminded us, Peña was so committed to his wife that he wouldn't even look at other women. Although he admitted he'd seen a change in Peña's personality over the past couple of months. Like everybody else, Danny took it as a mood swing. He shook his head, more confused than anything else.

Big Rod said that he suspected more. "I've been thinking, you know," Big Rod began. "Not too long ago Peña told me something was wrong…inside. I asked him like if it was his old lady or kid, but he said no, it wasn't like that. He said it was more of a feeling, like something that grabs at your stomach and twists and twists and doesn't let go. Not too much a pain, you know, more like a chunk of metal glued to your stomach, something that hangs and pulls until it feels like your insides are falling, and he said it wouldn't go away. Every day he woke up feeling like that."

30 After a few hours, many of the newer guys went back to their units. The night thickened and the five of us who were Peña's closest friends remained.

We sat in a circle. In the middle was a used C-ration can filled with lighted heat tablets that gave some relief from the darkness of the jungle—a darkness that loomed silently around us. Every once in a while, we heard the whispers of the perimeter guards who were positioned in the jungle…human alarms against a possible attack.

Little Rod, who was from Brownsville, Texas—"Right down in the corner of the goddamn country," he once told us—pulled out his Camels, slowly tapped the bottom of the pack, and placed a cigarette to his lips. He sat on an empty wood ammo crate and leaned back against the sandbag wall. After a long silence, Little Rod leaned over, stuck his cigarette into the heat tablet, and sucked on the tobacco until the tip swelled in an orange glow.

"I seen him start to change," said Little Rod, whose English was heavily accented. He wore his cap down low on his forehead so that the shadow from the brim buried his eyes.

"When Peña volunteered to carry the radio, I told him not to do it. He never saw much action—not until he started humping that radio. I saw how he kept laughing, real nervous, when he came to the sessions, but I saw that he was trying to hide it. I could tell, man, that he was scared, too, something in his eyes. He tried to not show it…but I seen it. I seen it."

35   "Sure he was scared, man," responded level-headed Danny Ríos, a Northern Californian who always tried to find a balance in every situation…a cause for every effect…a good reason for every tragedy. He wore his cap high on his head, like a star baseball player, so that his whole face was visible. He continued: "Peña didn't know what he was getting himself into. He said he wanted to see some action, said he was tired of filling sandbags and carrying ammo. Yep, he got his transfer all right, and I think he hated it out in the bush. That's Charlie's country. That's his backyard. You go messing around out there and you best be scared. Common sense, man…common sense."

Little Rod didn't turn to face Danny. He spoke, his back against the dirty sandbags and his voice came out of the darkness: a somber tone exploring, probing. "It ain't what I mean. Peña's a nice kinda guy, you know? He got his vieja and kid. Every time the priest comes out to the bush, Peña goes to communion. Something bad had to of happen to him. Maybe he learned that God ain't out there. Maybe he learned that God ain't here either. The first time he carried that radio was when his platoon went in to help out C Company. You remember, C Company got ambushed…bodies tore up into thousands of pieces. Peña smelt the burnt meat, bodies that belonged to his friends. He saw those dead, nasty eyes."

"So what are you saying?" argued Alex. "You believe it was Peña the Tiger Force saw out there, that Peña is out there fighting with the Cong, that death is going to make him run off with the gooks? It don't make sense, man, no sense at all."

Little Rod continued, "I remember one time his squad come in from the bush, must a been right after his transfer; he's carrying that radio. Remember, Ríos? You was there. We was set up someplace outside of Tuy Hoa.

"Rain come down in chorros. Everything was like a sponge. Peña come out of that jungle into our battery area…his eyes big…like two big ol' hard boiled eggs. That ain't a regular scared. He's soaked, dirty, smelly, and he's talkin' a hundred miles an hour. You had to slow him down. Hundred miles an hour, ese. That ain't regular scared. Something happen to Peña, man. I seen it. That ain't no shit; I seen it."

40   "Little Rod's right. Peña was panicked. His face was stretched, his skin white...cold, like a ghost." Danny Ríos confirmed Rod's words. "He talked like a machine gun and moved with quick jerks. I felt sorry for him. His lieutenant let him stay with us a couple of hours. We made him some hot chocolate and warmed him up. He just kept talking, man. He couldn't stop. Two hours later, when his squad moved out, Peña went. No questions asked, didn't complain, didn't fight it; just like the other guys in the squad. He walked back into the bush like a zombie, and that jungle, with rain still coming down, swallowed him right up. They said they had to find cover before dark. Little Rod's right. That wasn't no regular scared. Hell, made me thank God I was in the artillery. But it's just common sense, man. Put a dude in a situation like that and...hey."

         "Then it's still not logical. If he's scared," I asked, "why's he going to take off with the Cong? He wouldn't even know how to find them. And if he did, they'd probably shoot him first. Alex is right, man. It doesn't make sense."

         "Yup. Don't fucking sound like Peña to me," Alex said, the light shining against his square jaw and pitted skin. "He's probably in town right now, hung over and wanting to come back."

         Finally, Big Rod, who was like a brother to Peña, went through jump school with him, and had met his family while they were both on leave in San Antonio, spoke up, his voice more serious than I'd ever heard: "I think he went. I think he took off into that jungle and went with them. I don't know how he did it, why, or where he went, but he's out there looking for something...maybe looking for us...maybe looking for hisself. Remember his last words, 'I'll have everything ready for you guys.' He was trying to tell us something."

         The battery commanders from A and B batteries called each of us in to find out what they could. It was clear that they thought Jesse was AWOL and somewhere in Duc Pho. That's what most of the guys in the brigade thought, too. Jesse would come back, get court martialed, and that would be the end of it. But Jesse had never been in trouble before. He was the one who kept us out of trouble, making sure we'd get back to camp after a crazy day in town or calming us down after a run-in with an NCO or officer.

45   A month passed before a new rumor started. We were still operating somewhere outside of Duc Pho. A squad of grunts had made contact with a group of VC. They swore that a guy who looked like a Mexican, wearing GI camouflaged fatigues, had been walking point for the communists. It was no mistaken identity. One of the guys said he stared right into the pointman's eyes and that the Mexican just looked at him and smiled. Guns and grenades started going off, but Peña and his squad slipped back into the jungle.

         Everybody in the brigade was talking about it. The guys who saw Jesse swore that it was "a Mexican-American" they'd seen out there. "The guy looked me right in the eyes. He coulda' shot me if he wanted. I was froze shitless" were the words of one grunt. It was strange how the words flew and the story built, but then, after a short time, the story transformed itself into a legend.

The story of an American leading a Vietcong squad was not uncommon. Everyone had heard it one time or another during his tour. Usually, the American was blond, tall, and thin. No one who told the story had ever seen the guy. The story was always distanced by two or three narrators, and it was more of a fable or myth, our own type of antiwar protest, I guess. What made this thing about Jesse so different was that the guys reporting it claimed personally to have seen him. Still, not many guys really believed it, except Big Rod, Little Rod, and the grunts who said they'd seen Jesse.

"Things are so crazy 'round this place guys'll make up anything fer 'musement," said Josh Spenser, an Oklahoman, who added, "I just don't know, man. I just don't know."

Two weeks passed before the next sighting. "Saw Peña, man." The guys who were now reporting the sightings started using his name, as if they personally knew him. One evening, when we were in the front area base camp, Big Rod, Little Rod, Alex, and I walked across the brigade area to talk to one of the soldiers who said he'd seen Jesse.

50   At first he didn't believe we were Jesse's friends. The guy didn't trust anybody because, as he put it, guys were saying that he was making the whole thing up, but after we explained our relationship to Jesse, he began to talk.

"It's the shits, man. Captain tol' me he didn't want me spreadin' no rumors," his voice lowered, "but I saw 'em. Big as shit, I saw."

The guy's name was Conklin. He seemed wired, like he was high on speed, sincere...yet nervous. He told us his story like someone who had been trying to convince people that he'd seen a UFO. Conklin said that he and his squad were on an ambush. They had the whole thing set up by nightfall: claymores out, good cover, M-16s, grenades, and an M-60 at the ready. He said that it was quiet out there, no noise, no animal sounds, nothing. But, as he told it, the VC never showed.

Since there had been no contact, the choppers came out to pick them up the next morning. He described how he bent down low and made his way out to retrieve the claymores. He disconnected the cap, and squatting down low, started to wrap the wire around the curved, green device. As he wrapped, he kept his eyes on the trail, looking both ways and also checking the jungle to his front. And then he saw Peña. Just like that, Conklin said, using Jesse's last name.

"Peña," pronouncing it Peenya, "was down in the bush, a Thompson submachine gun pointed right at me. I was gonna reach for my rifle but he just nods, cool-like, slow...and I know he means for me to not go for it so's I jes' set there and stare at him, and all he does is stare back. I couldn't talk, man. I couldn't yell. It was like...like one of them night-mares where you feel suffocated and can't nobody help you. Then he moves back, real slowlike, still squatting, like gooks do, an' then I see two other gooks, one on each side of him. He stands up and the gooks stand up and they move backward into the brush, just like that, fuckin'-A, man, and he's gone."

55 "What's he look like?" asked Alex.

"Got on gook clothes, man. Pajamas—a black top and black bottoms, cut off just above the knees…light complexion, 'bout like you," he says pointing to Big Rod. "I guess he's close to 5′ 7″ or 8″, not too tall…probably 145 or 150 pounds."

"Peña's closer to 175, maybe 180," Alex tells Conklin.

"Not no more he ain't. Guy I saw wasn't no 180. And when he smiled, he made me feel O.K., you know. Even though I was scared and he could's blown a hole through me, still…made me feel like…O.K. Maybe had something to do with those dimples. Big mothers…one on each cheek."

Big Rod and I looked at each other.

60 "Kinda made him look like a kid. But he wasn't bullshitting, man. It wasn't no joke. If I'd a gone for my weapon, he'd a blowed my ass clean away. I can't figure it out, man. Gone, just like that…disappeared with those gooks right into the jungle. And nobody else seen it, only me."

Three months had passed since Jesse disappeared. His ETS date came and went. Maybe we expected a miracle, as if Jesse was going to walk into the base camp, say "hi," and tell us about his days with the VC as he packed his bags and prepared to catch a hop to Cam Ranh Bay where he'd DEROS home. But nothing. It was just another day; besides, by this time we were in Phan Rhang, our rear area base camp, and a long way from where Peña had last been seen.

That night, the night of Peña's ETS, we held a "session," more of a funeral, over by the training course, which was at the perimeter of the brigade area. Even some of the nonbelievers showed up.

We met in front of the mess hall, one of many in the brigade area. It was located on a hill at the east end of the base camp, where we could look out over the entire airborne complex.

The sun had descended and the work day completed. We could see GIs slowly walking the dirt roads, some going to the Enlisted Men's or Officers' Clubs, others to the USO, and still others strolling as if they were out for an evening in some country town. In an hour or so it would be dark and carefully rationed lights would bring a different life to the area. There would be drinking and card games, laughter and yells, tales about families and girlfriends, stories of heroics in the field with a few guys displaying the macabre trophies. Some guys would listen to records in their tents and wonder what their buddies back home were doing. At the USO, they'd be talking to the donut dollies, playing Monopoly, Scrabble, dominoes, and other games, while in their minds they'd be making love to the American women who sat at the opposite side of the gameboards.

65 We turned away and headed toward the obstacle course. A range of jungle-covered mountains formed the camp's eastern perimeter.

We followed a dirt trail down a hill and gathered in a clearing that was used for a map reading course. It was off-limits at night so we had to be quiet.

As the two Rods and I approached, we saw that Alex and Danny, with C-ration cans and heat tablets, had designed a church-like atmosphere. The small blue flames, much like candles, were spread out in a circle to our front, lifting the darkness so that our faces were barely recognizable. The jungle surrounded us with a heaviness that leaned more toward enigma than fear. After a short while, the shuffling of feet along the trail stopped, the whispering voices were silent, and about twenty of us sat on logs formed into a semi-circle.

Big Rod said that there would be no drinking, not yet, anyway. Doc Langley handed him a stack of joints. Big Rod passed them around and said to light up. Not everyone liked to smoke, but this night they all breathed in the stinging herb. It didn't take long for the weed to take effect. The jungle moved in closer. The trees came down over our heads like thick spider webs and the plants weighed against our backs. The joints moved around the circle until the air and smoke mingled into a kind of anesthetized gas.

Big Rod pulled a paper from his pocket, unfolded it, and began to read. It was from Margaret, Peña's wife. The army had told her that Jesse was listed as AWOL because it couldn't be determined when he officially had been lost. In her letter, which made Big Rod pause many times as he read, she wanted to know what happened to her husband. She trusted that Rod would tell her the truth since it seemed nobody else would. Was Jesse dead? That's what she really wanted to know.

70   "Please answer soon," were her last words. Rod wanted to know how he should respond, then, frustrated, he gave me the letter. He said that since I was the one with some college, I should answer.

Johnny Sabia, an infantryman from Sevilla, New Mexico, and a guy who didn't come around much, said that we shouldn't be moping but that we should be celebrating. "Write her," he said to me. "Tell her the truth. Her old man split. The dude's the only one with any balls. I don't know how, but this guy Peña understands that everything here means nothing. I've never met the guy, but I've been thinking about him and I've heard the stories. Everybody's talking about him. I heard that Peña lives in San Antonio, in some rat hole that he can't afford to buy because the bank won't lend him the money. I heard that in the summer when it hits a hundred, him and his neighbors fry like god-damn chickens because they can't afford air conditioning. So now they send him here to fight for his country! What a joke, man."

None of us ever talked about it. Peña never talked about it. Sabia was the first one who raised the issue. All we wanted to do was fight the war, get to the rear area, drink, joke, and never think about why we were here or what the truth was about our lives back home.

An argument started. Someone said that whatever we have it's better than what other people have. Even if we work in the fields in the states, it's better than working the fields in Mexico. An angry voice said, "Bullshit! We don't live in Mexico. We live in the U.S. Our parents worked to make the U.S. what it is; our fathers fought and died in WWII. We got rights just like anybody else."

Someone else wanted to know how come we get the worst duties. Whether it's pulling the shittiest hours on guard duty or going into dangerous situations, if there's a Chicano around, he's the one who gets it.

75   "Because we don't say shit, man. Whatever they want to push on us, we just take it. Like pendejos…we do whatever nobody else wants to do. We don't want to be crybabies. Well, maybe we should start crying."

"That's right," someone else said. "Gonzales got himself shot up because nobody else wanted to take their turn at the point. He walked the point for his squad almost every operation. What good did it do? He's dead now. Pobre Gonzales, man; talk about poor, he showed me a picture of his family who lived in someplace called Livingston, in Califas. His house looked like a damn chicken coop."

Then Alex stood up. He told how he was raised in the middle-class San Fernando Valley and remembered teachers who insulted him in front of his Anglo classmates, but only now, tonight, did he understand that it was because he was Mexican. Lamely, he said, "It never hit me. I just thought I was the only fuck-up in that school. There were a lot of white dudes who screwed up, but I don't ever remember the teachers jumping on them like they jumped on me."

Johnny Sabia talked some more, about tennis clubs built over fields where the townspeople of Sevilla had once grown corn and vegetables, about schoolhouses with holes in the roofs, streets still unpaved in 1967, primitive electrical systems for lighting. And he and others went on and on until they worked themselves into a fury.

Someone pulled out the beer. As the alcohol hit, the voices got louder and belligerent. Before long, the whiskey bottles started to make the rounds and nobody was talking about Peña any longer. Everyone talked about their friends back home, their girlfriends, or good places to find prostitutes in Phan Rhang. The session was over. Somebody kicked out the heat tabs, and the jungle, once again, distanced itself from us.

80   We marched over to the Enlisted Men's Club, toasted Jesse Peña several times, honoring him and wishing him well, and drank until they threw us out. Then we staggered along the roads, falling into ditches, staring at the stars splattered against the sky, and vomiting as we worked our way back to our units. We finally found our bunks and sank into a dizzying sleep.

The next morning when we woke up, most of us were hungover. We went through our usual routines, cleaning weapons and resupplying our units. A few days later, we flew out in C-130 transport planes to the next operation, somewhere outside of Chu Lai. There were a few rumors that Peña was still traveling with the VC, but no one would swear to the sightings. His memory became painful for those of us who knew him. When I left Vietnam, the new guys joining the Division heard about the Mexican who ran off to join the VC, and they kept the story alive, building on Peña's adventures. One squad reported that they saw his dead body after the ambush of a VC unit, but nobody believed that story either.

Leroy V. Quintana

Leroy Quintana was born in 1944 in Albuquerque, New Mexico. He has published six books of poetry including, *Interrogations* (1990), *The History of Home* (1993), *My Hair Turning Grey Among Strangers* (1996), and *The Great Whirl of Exile: Poems* (1999). His poetry is greatly influenced by his grandparents (who raised him), Mexican folklore, and his two years in Vietnam. He has been the recipient of the American Book Award twice for *Sangre* (1981) and *The History of Home* (1997), and his poetry has appeared in numerous anthologies. His latest book is a collection of short fiction entitled *La Promesa and Other Stories* (2002). He is professor of English at San Diego Mesa College.

The Man on Jesus Street—Dreaming

The one without a face, the one he shot after his recon squad had been hunted all day, the one he shot after the rain let up, the one without a face was always the last one, and always at dawn—as if his duty was to awaken him 365 days a year, year after year—after only a few minutes of sleep, exactly at 6:15.

The first one, a GI of about nineteen in jungle fatigues, with a shredded leg (the right one), was discovered at 8:15 by Donaldo Martínez (a distant cousin of María Martínez), the head custodian, as he was making his way up the stairs that led to the laundry room. Martínez called security and the emergency room, and the patient was promptly carted around the corner, where he was administered the last rites as the doctors worked on him for over four hours. He had lost a lot of blood on his journey up the hill to the VA hospital.

The admissions clerk had run a check on his dog tags and was totally dumbfounded when he called the chief attending physician, who was equally distressed when he reported to Alberto Martínez (a cousin of the honorable Raymundo Martínez), the head administrator: the young soldier was listed as KIA in Vietnam, near the Cambodian border, on a recon mission in 1967. He had, according to his records, bled to death during monsoon because the medevac had been unable to fly in. He had died three days short of his nineteenth birthday. His parents, in Peru, Indiana, had been contacted and had hung up angrily.

When the clerk wired them, confirming that their son was alive and recuperating at the VA hospital in San Miguel, New Mexico, they caught the first available flight. When Alberto Martínez called Washington, he was told that the VA was sending somebody, a top aide, immediately. Shortly afterward, the CIA, followed by the FBI, called to inform him they were sending a few people to "look into the matter."

5   Perhaps it was the summer rain that caused him to dream so heavily about JJ and his shredded leg. JJ had moaned all night, losing blood, a splinter of shrapnel in his eye (his left), moaning even while he bit down hard on his olive-green

kerchief. He was in unbearable pain. Pain nobody could ever ease or soothe or soften, unspeakable pain made worse with each passing minute, because the more he moved his eye the more it tore.

Perhaps it was the summer rain. From that day on, one thing was certain: JJ disappeared from his dreams. The others, however, persisted.

And always at dawn, always there was the one without a face, more reliable than any alarm clock.

The following night a VC came running at him, and he cut loose with a burst. The gook seemed to hang in midair for minutes as the rounds ripped through him, and then he hit the ground. Then another gook, and another, and another, faster than he could change magazines. And at the end of the long night, the one without a face was there to greet the new day.

There were twenty-three of them, all in black pajamas, with their inner tubes full of rice wrapped around them, some still clutching their AK-47s. Donaldo Martínez called Security immediately and then dialed the emergency room. One of the attending physicians refused to treat the VC, saying that this was a hospital for U.S. veterans only, not for gooks. Donaldo tracked down a cleaning woman in Oncology who was whisked in to translate. A VC with a gut wound, a man named Ngyuen, was demanding treatment, stating he was just as much a victim of American aggression as were the country's own veterans. He had ordered his men to lock and load and had held the security officers to a standoff. Nobody was getting out alive—not the nurses and certainly not the doctors—nobody. They had already survived a firefight with the Albuquerque Police Department's Asian Gang Unit that had been rushed in by chopper, and they had been informed that three SWAT teams had surrounded the building. A hostage negotiator had established phone contact.

10   The FBI and the CIA were trying to establish whether JJ was telling the truth. The attending physician had been ordered to administer by injection some of the medication provided by the CIA. The Pentagon had begun a complete review of JJ's recon missions in Nam: the dates, locations, and engagements with the enemy. Calls were made to Vietnam to investigate the possibility that JJ had been a prisoner and not KIA and to question Ho Chi Minh City as to whether it was sending sapper squads to the U.S. in order to intimidate Washington into normalizing relations. Agents were already pounding the streets, questioning everybody as they tried to trace the trail of blood left by JJ as far back as possible.

The next morning an entire village stormed into the VA hospital grounds, women clinging desperately to wailing infants, children—some with their clothes on fire—crying desperately for a lost mother, old mama sans searching for their grandchildren, venerable papa sans trying desperately to keep families together, a teenage girl clutching her fiancé's hand. The APD Asian Gang Unit was called in again: The villagers were herded together in the Oncology

Ward parking lot, where they remained until nightfall under heavy scrutiny, until the state National Guard was called in. Tents, cots, and cooking facilities were set up and medical attention provided. The cleaning woman from Oncology was happy to be putting in so much overtime, but more than that, she was overwhelmed when she recognized an aunt and several cousins she had presumed had died long ago when the Americans had destroyed their village.

The four tanks rumbled through the gates an hour and a half after the villagers. They had traveled up Martínez Street, not unnoticed but certainly unquestioned, thought to be part of a military training exercise. Nobody seemed to notice the leg tied to the first tank, the arms dangling from the second and the third, and the other leg being dragged along by the last. It wasn't until the following day, when a torso of a young VC, a woman, was discovered and reported to the Asian Gang Unit and then to the FBI, that it was linked to the tanks. And right behind the tanks were the GIs, twenty-five of them, their dicks hanging out, ecstatic with revenge, having not only raped their enemy but ordered the tanks to rev up and head north, south, east, and west.

Just how had he managed to get to the front door of the emergency room, not only blindfolded but with his hands tied behind his back and his dick still wired to the electric circuits of an old G-47 radio that had been given a full crank by the sergeant in charge of intelligence, making him scream secrets about his unit's strengths and movements to the American dogs?

There was, in addition to the one without a face, the infant. And also the brigade of NVA regulars that marched boldly through the gates of the hospital and surrounded the National Guard demanding freedom for the villagers. Henry Kissinger was called in for a quick briefing before catching a flight to Vietnam. The CIA was receiving computer printouts, constantly updated, detailing time, place, and unit for every VC, NVA, and GI in the VA compound, and the FBI had agents around the country searching for other GIs, former VCs, or NVAs who had served in any of these units.

15   The 101st Airborne was flown in and quickly surrounded the NVAs, claiming twenty-five KIAs and eleven wounded compared to only three KIAs and three wounded in the hour-long battle. The NVA wounded were interrogated—the info fed into the CIA's computer—and then treated.

More FBI agents were ordered in, combing their way down Martínez Street, finding splashes of blood, dried puddles as far down as The Emporium and then north on Eisenhower to La Golondrina bar, where some AK-47 rounds were located and where eyewitnesses pointed them west on Nixon.

Could it be the new medication the psychiatrist had prescribed? Perhaps he had taken it as directed. He couldn't honestly say. What he could tell the doctor was that he hadn't felt better since he had come home—not the cheap whiskey, not the drugs, the wife he had discarded, the children he had been incapable of caring for—nothing had been able to soothe his pain. Not even putting a gun to his head. Somehow, suddenly, they had disappeared: the woman who had been tied to the tanks; a hard-core VC they had captured and turned over for interrogation the morning after JJ had stepped on a booby trap; JJ had disappeared too, as had the VC that had come rushing at him night after night; the villagers with their clothes on fire, parents shouting desperately for lost children, old papa sans and mama sans barely able to keep up—they too were gone; the VC with his dick wired to a G-47, who refused to talk at first but once the interrogator cranked the handle had been willing to give up his mother—he, too, was gone.

Now, only the infant.

And the one whose face he had blown off, who, without fail, was there to greet the new day, every day.

20   Vietnam, of course, denied everything. Kissinger reminded them that he was not, most definitely not, going to play that Paris Peace Talks shit again. The Vietnamese presented him with documents proving that the entire battalion of NVAs under discussion had been wiped out in a skirmish near the Cambodian border. Kissinger warned them that the U.S. was not, most definitely not, going to be held responsible for any POWs that had been listed as KIAs twenty-four years prior to their arrival in the U.S. All Vietnamese personnel—NVAs, VC, villagers—would be flown back immediately. Not since Pancho Villa's raid had the U.S. been invaded. And any more hostile actions would result in a declaration of war. This was definitely, Kissinger stated in his most dignified and authoritative manner, not a step towards reconciliation, towards normalizing relations, towards business. A couple more years and the entire POW issue would be laid to rest, once and for all. But this? Just vat the fuck vas this?

He crawled slowly, slowly, hoping the VC would waste him before he got there. Slowly.

But no matter how slowly he crawled, he always found Bazooka.

Sometime during the night, they set up a bunker just outside the perimeter. At first light one of the machine gunners from the 101st spotted one of the gooks slinking back towards the bunker after turning the claymores around so they'd be set off in the direction of the Americans once the VC mounted their attack. The machine gunner opened fire, cutting the gook in half. The bunker returned fire, and three GIs went down.

Half an hour later, the 101st was still pinned down but the VC were running out of ammo. Suddenly, somebody threw a wailing infant on top of the bunker, and immediately the 101st ceased fire. The VC cut down another five GIs before the 101st opened fire again. But they were firing halfheartedly, trying to avoid hitting the infant. The officer in charge called for Bazooka, a nineteen-year-old who just happened to be from Mora, about 180 miles north of

San Miguel. Bazooka could knock the balls off a gnat at one hundred meters with a rocket launcher. When he arrived from the opposite end of the perimeter, Bazooka saw the infant and hesitated, hoping that the lieutenant would understand. The VC were expending the last of their ammo furiously, knowing full well they could not lose. They knew they were going to die; they knew the Americans had to finish them, but to finish them they had to kill the infant. The longer the Americans hesitated, the more of them got killed or wounded. They had to kill the infant, and in doing so they would live, but they would also sentence themselves to hell forever. The lieutenant ordered Bazooka to fire. Bazooka aimed. And blew the bunker to pieces.

25   Now only the man without a face remained. And today was the day that he went to see the psychiatrist to have his medication reviewed. The way things were going, in another week or so the one without a face would be gone, and then he would be allowed to die in peace.

On his way to the bus stop he noticed the two agents walking down Nixon Avenue and then turning left on Jesus Street towards his house. Weird, he thought. The law never went down there on foot.

Security seemed unusually tight at the hospital. He thought he saw Bazooka strapped to a gurney that was being wheeled to the emergency room—but in his camouflage fatigues like he was still in Nam? It had to be the medication. Lately he had sensed JJ and Bazooka around, not just the way you do in a dream but the way you can sense an ambush. There was no way of explaining it. Perhaps the doctor could.

"Feeling great, doctor," he said. They were all gone. All except for the one whose face he had blown off. Yeah, he could describe JJ, but what the hell for? The dude had bought the farm near the border, had bled to fuckin' death, and who gave a shit? Yeah, he remembered how. He had stepped on a goddamn booby trap and bled all the monsoonnight long, a splinter of steel in his eye. Yeah, the dreams of the bunker and Bazooka were gone, too.

But a funny thing. He swore he had seen Bazooka only a few minutes before, still wearing his jungle fatigues. Perhaps the doctor had an explanation for that, because he goddamn for sure didn't.

30   The villagers, too—gone. And the NVAs and the VC. The tanks. The young girl. Yes, he was doing well. And the one without a face, he asked, he too would go away?

He was certain he had seen JJ in one of the rooms (as certain as he had seen Bazooka), with what were certainly his parents weeping at his bedside.

But the doctor had rushed him into another office where he had been subdued, strapped to a gurney, and rushed into a room where they strapped him into a chair and immediately shot him full of a green medicine that made his heart seem both to slow down and speed up, though the period of rapid pounding seemed so much longer than the other, and pushed a piece of inner tube into his mouth for him to chomp on.

Abraham Rodríguez, Jr.

Abraham Rodríguez, Jr.'s first publication was hailed by critics as a major contribution to Latino/mainland Puerto Rican literature. Like Piri Thomas's work, Rodríguez's *The Boy Without a Flag* (1992) recounts the rancid world of inner city characters. The book was named a *New York Times* Notable Book of the Year. His novel *Spidertown* (1993) followed, and in 2001 he published *The Buddha Book*. He was born in 1961 in the South Bronx, dropped out of high school at sixteen, but went on to City College of New York.

The Boy Without A Flag

To Ms. Linda Falcón, wherever she is

Swirls of dust danced in the beams of sunlight that came through the tall windows, the buzz of voices resounding in the stuffy auditorium. Mr. Rios stood by our Miss Colon, hovering as if waiting to catch her if she fell. His pale mouse features looked solemnly dutiful. He was a versatile man, doubling as English teacher and gym coach. He was only there because of Miss Colon's legs. She was wearing her neon pink nylons. Our favorite.

We tossed suspicious looks at the two of them. Miss Colon would smirk at Edwin and me, saying, "Hey, face front," but Mr. Rios would glare. I think he knew that we knew what he was after. We knew, because on Fridays, during our free period when we'd get to play records and eat stale pretzel sticks, we would see her way in the back by the tall windows, sitting up on a radiator like a schoolgirl. There would be a strange pinkness on her high cheekbones, and there was Mr. Rios, sitting beside her, playing with her hand. Her face, so thin and girlish, would blush. From then on, her eyes, very close together like a cartoon rendition of a beaver's, would avoid us.

Miss Colon was hardly discreet about her affairs. Edwin had first tipped me off about her love life after one of his lunchtime jaunts through the empty hallways. He would chase girls and toss wet bathroom napkins into classrooms where kids in the lower grades sat, trapped. He claimed to have seen Miss Colon slip into a steward's closet with Mr. Rios and to have heard all manner of sounds through the thick wooden door, which was locked (he tried it). He had told half the class before the day was out, the boys sniggering behind grimy hands, the girls shocked because Miss Colon was married, so married that she even brought the poor unfortunate in one morning as a kind of show-and-tell guest. He was an untidy dark-skinned Puerto Rican type in a colorful dashiki. He carried a paper bag that smelled like glue. His eyes seemed sleepy, his Afro an uncombed Brillo pad. He talked about protest marches, the sixties, the importance of an education. Then he embarrassed Miss Colon greatly by disappearing into the coat closet and falling asleep there. The girls, remembering him, softened their attitude toward her indiscretions, defending her violently.

"Face it," one of them blurted out when Edwin began a new series of Miss Colon tales, "she married a bum and needs to find true love."

"She's a slut, and I'm gonna draw a comic book about her." Edwin said, hushing when she walked in through the door. That afternoon, he showed me the first sketches of what would later become a very popular comic book entitled "Slut At The Head Of The Class." Edwin could draw really well, but his stories were terrible, so I volunteered to do the writing. In no time at all, we had three issues circulating under desks and hidden in notebooks all over the school. Edwin secretly ran off close to a hundred copies on a copy machine in the main office after school. It always amazed me how copies of our comic kept popping up in the unlikeliest places. I saw them on radiators in the auditorium, on benches in the gym, tacked up on bulletin boards. There were even some in the teachers' lounge, which I spotted one day while running an errand for Miss Colon. Seeing it, however, in the hands of Miss Marti, the pig-faced assistant principal, nearly made me puke up my lunch. Good thing our names weren't on it.

5   It was a miracle no one snitched on us during the ensuing investigation, since only a blind fool couldn't see our involvement in the thing. No bloody purge followed, but there was enough fear in both of us to kill the desire to continue our publishing venture. Miss Marti, a woman with a battlefield face and constant odor of Chiclets, made a forceful threat about finding the culprits while holding up the second issue, the one with the hand-colored cover. No one moved. The auditorium grew silent. We meditated on the sound of a small plane flying by, its engines rattling the windows. I think we wished we were on it.

It was in the auditorium that the trouble first began. We had all settled into our seats, fidgeting like tiny burrowing animals, when there was a general call for quiet. Miss Marti, up on stage, had a stare that could make any squirming fool sweat. She was a gruff, nasty woman who never smiled without seeming sadistic.

Mr. Rios was at his spot beside Miss Colon, his hands clasped behind his back as if he needed to restrain them. He seemed to whisper to her. Soft, mushy things. Edwin would watch them from his seat beside me, giving me the details, his shiny face looking worried. He always seemed sweaty, his fingers kind of damp.

"I toldju, I saw um holdin hands," he said. "An now lookit him, he's whispering sweet shits inta huh ear."

He quieted down when he noticed Miss Marti's evil eye sweeping over us like a prison-camp searchlight. There was silence. In her best military bark, Miss Marti ordered everyone to stand. Two lone, pathetic kids, dragooned by some unseen force, slowly came down the center aisle, each bearing a huge flag on a thick wooden pole. All I could make out was that great star-spangled unfurling, twitching thing that I looked like it would fall as it approached over all those bored young heads. The Puerto Rican flag walked beside it, looking smaller and less confident. It clung to its pole.

10   "The Pledge," Miss Marti roared, putting her hand over the spot where her heart was rumored to be.

That's when I heard my father talking.

He was sitting on his bed, yelling about Chile, about what the CIA had done there. I was standing opposite him in my dingy Pro Keds. I knew about politics. I was eleven when I read William Shirer's book on Hitler. I was ready.

"All this country does is abuse Hispanic nations," my father said, turning a page of his *Post*, "tie them down, make them dependent. It says democracy with one hand while it protects and feeds fascist dictatorships with the other." His eyes blazed with a strange fire. I sat on the bed, on part of his *Post*, transfixed by his oratorical mastery. He had mentioned political things before, but not like this, not with such fiery conviction. I thought maybe it had to do with my reading Shirer. Maybe he had seen me reading that fat book and figured I was ready for real politics.

Using the knowledge I gained from the book, I defended the Americans. What fascism was he talking about, anyway? I knew we had stopped Hitler. That was a big deal, something to be proud of.

15   "Come out of fairy-tale land," he said scornfully. "Do you know what imperialism is?"

I didn't really, no.

"Well, why don't you read about that? Why don't you read about Juan Bosch and Allende, men who died fighting imperialism? They stood up against American big business. You should read about that instead of this crap about Hitler."

"But I like reading about Hitler," I said, feeling a little spurned. I didn't even mention that my fascination with Adolf led to my writing a biography of him, a book report one hundred and fifty pages long. It got an A-plus. Miss Colon stapled it to the bulletin board right outside the classroom, where it was promptly stolen.

"So, what makes you want to be a writer?" Miss Colon asked me quietly one day, when Edwin and I, always the helpful ones, volunteered to assist her in getting the classroom spiffed up for a Halloween party.

20   "I don't know. I guess my father," I replied, fiddling with plastic pumpkins self-consciously while images of my father began parading through my mind.

When I think back to my earliest image of my father, it is one of him sitting behind a huge rented typewriter, his fingers clacking away. He was a frustrated poet, radio announcer, and even stage actor. He had sent for diplomas from fly-by-night companies. He took acting lessons, went into broadcasting, even ended up on the ground floor of what is now Spanish radio, but his family talked him out of all of it. "You should find yourself real work, something substantial," they said, so he did. He dropped all those dreams that were never encouraged by anyone else and got a job at a Nedick's on Third Avenue. My pop the counterman.

Despite that, he kept writing. He recited his poetry into a huge reel-to-reel tape deck that he had, then he'd play it back and sit like a critic, brow furrowed, fingers stroking his lips. He would record strange sounds and play them back to me at outrageous speeds, until I believed that there were tiny people living inside the machine. I used to stand by him and watch him type, his black pompadour spilling over his forehead. There was energy pulsating all around him, and I wanted a part of it.

I was five years old when I first sat in his chair at the kitchen table and began pushing down keys, watching the letters magically appear on the page. I was entranced. My fascination with the typewriter began at that point. By the time I was ten, I was writing war stories, tales of pain and pathos culled from the piles of comic books I devoured. I wrote unreadable novels. With illustrations. My father wasn't impressed. I guess he was hard to impress. My terrific grades did not faze him, nor the fact that I was reading books as fat as milk crates. My unreadable novels piled up. I brought them to him at night to see if he would read them, but after a week of waiting I found them thrown in the bedroom closet, unread. I felt hurt and rejected, despite my mother's kind words. "He's just too busy to read them," she said to me one night when I mentioned it to her. He never brought them up, even when I quietly took them out of the closet one day or when he'd see me furiously hammering on one of his rented machines. I would tell him I wanted to be a writer, and he would smile sadly and pat my head, without a word.

"You have to find something serious to do with your life," he told me one night, after I had shown him my first play, eighty pages long. What was it I had read that got me into writing a play? Was it Arthur Miller? Oscar Wilde? I don't remember, but I recall my determination to write a truly marvelous play about combat because there didn't seem to be any around.

25   "This is fun as a hobby," my father said, "but you can't get serious about this." His demeanor spoke volumes, but I couldn't stop writing. Novels, I called them, starting a new one every three days. The world was a blank page waiting for my words to recreate it, while the real world remained cold and lonely. My schoolmates didn't understand any of it, and because of the fat books I carried around, I was held in some fear. After all, what kid in his right mind would read a book if it wasn't assigned? I was sick of kids coming up to me and saying, "Gaw, lookit tha fat book. Ya teacha make ya read tha?" (No, I'm just reading it.) The kids would look at me as if I had just crawled out of a sewer. "Ya crazy, man." My father seemed to share that opinion. Only my teachers understood and encouraged my reading, but my father seemed to want something else from me.

Now, he treated me like an idiot for not knowing what imperialism was. He berated my books and one night handed me a copy of a book about Albizu Campos, the Puerto Rican revolutionary. I read it through in two sittings.

"Some of it seems true," I said.

"Some of it?" my father asked incredulously. "After what they did to him, you can sit there and act like a Yankee flag-waver?"

I watched that Yankee flag making its way up to the stage over indifferent heads, my father's scowling face haunting me, his words resounding in my head.

30   "Let me tell you something," my father sneered. "In school, all they do is talk about George Washington, right? The first president? The father of democracy? Well, he had slaves. We had our own Washington, and ours had real teeth."

As Old Glory reached the stage, a general clatter ensued.

"We had our own revolution," my father said, "and the United States crushed it with the flick of a pinkie."

Miss Marti barked her royal command. Everyone rose up to salute the flag.

Except me. I didn't get up. I sat in my creaking seat, hands on my knees. A girl behind me tapped me on the back. "Come on, stupid, get up." There was a trace of concern in her voice. I didn't move.

35   Miss Colon appeared. She leaned over, shaking me gently. "Are you sick? Are you okay?" Her soft hair fell over my neck like a blanket.

"No," I replied.

"What's wrong?" she asked, her face growing stern. I was beginning to feel claustrophobic, what with everyone standing all around me, bodies like walls. My friend Edwin, hand on his heart, watched from the corner of his eye. He almost looked envious, as if he wished he had thought of it. Murmuring voices around me began reciting the Pledge while Mr. Rios appeared, commandingly grabbing me by the shoulder and pulling me out of my seat into the aisle. Miss Colon was beside him, looking a little apprehensive.

"What is wrong with you?" he asked angrily. "You know you're supposed to stand up for the Pledge! Are you religious?"

"No," I said.

40   "Then what?"

"I'm not saluting that flag," I said.

"What?"

"I said, I'm not saluting that flag."

"Why the...?" He calmed himself; a look of concern flashed over Miss Colon's face. "Why not?"

45   "Because I'm Puerto Rican. I ain't no American. And I'm not no Yankee flag-waver."

"You're supposed to salute the flag," he said angrily, shoving one of his fat fingers in my face. "You're not supposed to make up your own mind about it. You're supposed to do as you are told."

"I thought I was free," I said, looking at him and at Miss Colon.

"You are," Miss Colon said feebly. "That's why you should salute the flag."

"But shouldn't I do what I feel is right?"

50   "You should do what you are told!" Mr. Rios yelled into my face. "I'm not playing no games with you, mister. You hear that music? That's the anthem. Now you go stand over there and put your hand over your heart." He made as if to grab my hand, but I pulled away.

"No!" I said sharply. "I'm not saluting that crummy flag! And you can't make me, either. There's nothing you can do about it."

"Oh yeah?" Mr. Rios roared. "We'll see about that!"

"Have you gone crazy?" Miss Colon asked as he led me away by the arm, down the hallway, where I could still hear the strains of the anthem. He walked me briskly into the principal's office and stuck me in a corner.

"You stand there for the rest of the day and see how you feel about it," he said viciously. "Don't you even think of moving from that spot!"

55   I stood there for close to two hours or so. The principal came and went, not even saying hi or hey or anything, as if finding kids in the corners of his office was a common occurrence. I could hear him talking on the phone, scribbling on pads, talking to his secretary. At one point I heard Mr. Rios outside in the main office.

"Some smart-ass. I stuck him in the corner. Thinks he can pull that shit. The kid's got no respect, man. I should get the chance to teach him some."

"Children today have no respect," I heard Miss Marti's reptile voice say as she approached, heels clacking like gunshots. "It has to be forced upon them."

She was in the room. She didn't say a word to the principal, who was on the phone. She walked right over to me. I could hear my heart beating in my ears as her shadow fell over me. Godzilla over Tokyo.

"Well, have you learned your lesson yet?" she asked, turning me from the wall with a finger on my shoulder. I stared at her without replying. My face burned, red hot. I hated it.

60   "You think you're pretty important, don't you? Well, let me tell you, you're nothing. You're not worth a damn. You're just a snotty-nosed little kid with a lot of stupid ideas." Her eyes bored holes through me, searing my flesh. I felt as if I were going to cry. I fought the urge. Tears rolled down my face anyway. They made her smile, her chapped lips twisting upwards like the mouth of a lizard.

"See? You're a little baby. You don't know anything, but you'd better learn your place." She pointed a finger in my face. "You do as you're told if you don't want big trouble. Now go back to class."

Her eyes continued to stab at me. I looked past her and saw Edwin waiting by the office door for me. I walked past her, wiping at my face. I could feel her eyes on me still, even as we walked up the stairs to the classroom. It was close to three already, and the skies outside the grated windows were cloudy.

"Man," Edwin said to me as we reached our floor, "I think you're crazy."

The classroom was abuzz with activity when I got there, Kids were chattering, getting their windbreakers from the closet, slamming their chairs up on their desks, filled with the euphoria of soon-home. I walked quietly over to my desk and took out my books. The other kids looked at me as if I were a ghost.

65   I went through the motions like a robot. When we got downstairs to the door, Miss Colon, dismissing the class, pulled me aside, her face compassionate and warm. She squeezed my hand.

"Are you okay?"

I nodded.

"That was a really crazy stunt there. Where did you get such an idea?"

I started at her black flats. She was wearing tan panty hose and a black miniskirt. I saw Mr. Rios approaching with his class.

70   "I have to go," I said, and split, running into the frigid breezes and the silver sunshine.

At home, I lay on the floor of our living room, tapping my open notebook with the tip of my pen while the Beatles blared from my father's stereo. I felt humiliated and alone. Miss Marti's reptile face kept appearing in my notebook, her voice intoning, "Let me tell you, you're nothing." Yeah, right. Just what horrible hole did she crawl out of? Were those people really Puerto Ricans? Why should a Puerto Rican salute an American flag?

I put the question to my father, strolling into his bedroom, a tiny M-1 rifle that belonged to my G.I. Joe strapped to my thumb.

"Why?" he asked, loosening the reading glasses that were perched on his nose, his newspaper sprawled open on the bed before him, his cigarette streaming blue smoke. "Because we are owned, like cattle. And because nobody has any pride in their culture to stand up for it."

I pondered those words, feeling as if I were being encouraged, but I didn't dare tell him. I wanted to believe what I had done was a brave and noble thing, but somehow I feared his reaction. I never could impress him with my grades, or my writing. This flag thing would probably upset him. Maybe he, too, would think I was crazy, disrespectful, a "smart-ass" who didn't know his place. I feared that, feared my father saying to me, in a reptile voice, "Let me tell you, you're nothing."

75   I suited up my G.I. Joe for combat, slipping on his helmet, strapping on his field pack. I fixed the bayonet to his rifle, sticking it in his clutching hands so he seemed ready to fire. "A man's gotta do what a man's gotta do." Was that John Wayne? I don't know who it was, but I did what I had to do, still not telling my father. The following week, in the auditorium, I did it again. This time, everyone noticed. The whole place fell into a weird hush as Mr. Rios screamed at me.

I ended up in my corner again, this time getting a prolonged, pensive stare from the principal before I was made to stare at the wall for two more hours. My mind zoomed past my surroundings. In one strange vision, I saw my crony Edwin climbing up Miss Colon's curvy legs, giving me every detail of what he saw.

"Why?" Miss Colon asked frantically. "This time you don't leave until you tell me why." She was holding me by the arm, masses of kids flying by, happy blurs that faded into the sunlight outside the door.

"Because I'm Puerto Rican, not American," I blurted out in a weary torrent. "That makes sense, don't it?"

"So am I," she said, "but we're in America!" She smiled. "Don't you think you could make some kind of compromise?" She tilted her head to one side and said, "Aw, c'mon," in a little-girl whisper.

80 "What about standing up for what you believe in? Doesn't that matter? You used to talk to us about Kent State and protesting. You said those kids died because they believed in freedom, right? Well, I feel like them now. I wanna make a stand."

She sighed with evident aggravation. She caressed my hair. For a moment, I thought she was going to kiss me. She was going to say something, but just as her pretty lips parted, I caught Mr. Rios approaching.

"I don't wanna see him," I said, pulling away.

"No, wait," she said gently.

"He's gonna deck me," I said to her.

85 "No, he's not," Miss Colon said, as if challenging him, her eyes taking him in as he stood beside her.

"No, I'm not," he said. "Listen here. Miss Colon was talking to me about you, and I agree with her." He looked like a nervous little boy in front of the class, making his report. "You have a lot of guts. Still, there are rules here. I'm willing to make a deal with you. You go home and think about this. Tomorrow I'll come see you." I looked at him skeptically, and he added, "to talk."

"I'm not changing my mind," I said. Miss Colon exhaled painfully.

"If you don't, it's out of my hands." He frowned and looked at her. She shook her head, as if she were upset with him.

I re-read the book about Albizu. I didn't sleep a wink that night. I didn't tell my father a word, even though I almost burst from the effort. At night, alone in my bed, images attacked me. I saw Miss Marti and Mr. Rios debating Albizu Campos. I saw him in a wheelchair with a flag draped over his body like a holy robe. They would not do that to me. They were bound to break me the way Albizu was broken, not by young smiling American troops bearing chocolate bars, but by conniving, double-dealing, self-serving Puerto Rican landowners and their ilk, who dared say they were the future. They spoke of dignity and democracy while teaching Puerto Ricans how to cling to the great coat of that powerful northern neighbor. Puerto Rico, the shining star, the great lap dog of the Caribbean. I saw my father, the Nationalist hero, screaming from his podium, his great oration stirring everyone around him to acts of bravery. There was a shining arrogance in his eyes as he stared out over the sea of faces mouthing his name, a sparkling audacity that invited and incited. There didn't seem to be fear anywhere in him, only the urge to rush to the attack, with his arm band and revolutionary tunic. I stared up at him, transfixed. I stood by the podium, his personal adjutant, while his voice rang through the stadium. "We are not, nor will we ever be, Yankee flag-wavers!" The roar that followed drowned out the whole world.

90 The following day, I sat in my seat, ignoring Miss Colon as she neatly drew triangles on the board with the help of plastic stencils. She was using colored chalk, her favorite. Edwin, sitting beside me, was beaning girls with spitballs that he fired through his hollowed-out Bic pen. They didn't cry out. They simply enlisted the help of a girl named Gloria who sat a few desks behind him.

She very skillfully nailed him with a thick wad of gum. It stayed in his hair until Edwin finally went running to Miss Colon. She used her huge teacher's scissors. I couldn't stand it. They all seemed trapped in a world of trivial things, while I swam in a mire of oppression. I walked through lunch as if in a trance, a prisoner on death row waiting for the heavy steps of his executioners. I watched Edwin lick at his regulation cafeteria ice cream, sandwiched between two sheets of paper. I was once like him, laughing and joking, lining up for a stickball game in the yard without a care. Now it all seemed lost to me, as if my youth had been burned out of me by a book.

Shortly after lunch, Mr. Rios appeared. He talked to Miss Colon for a while by the door as the room filled with a bubbling murmur. Then, he motioned for me. I walked through the sudden silence as if in slow motion.

"Well," he said to me as I stood in the cool hallway, "have you thought about this?"

"Yeah," I said, once again seeing my father on the podium, his voice thundering.

"And?"

95 "I'm not saluting that flag."

Miss Colon fell against the door jamb as if exhausted. Exasperation passed over Mr. Rios rodent features.

"I thought you said you'd think about it," he thundered.

"I did. I decided I was right."

"*You* were right?" Mr. Rios was losing his patience. I stood calmly by the wall.

100 "I told you," Miss Colon whispered to him.

"Listen," he said, ignoring her, "have you heard of the story of the man who had no country?"

I stared at him.

"Well? Have you?"

"No," I answered sharply; his mouse eyes almost crossed with anger at my insolence. "Some stupid fairy tale ain't gonna change my mind anyway. You're treating me like I'm stupid, and I'm not."

105 "Stop acting like you're some mature adult! You're not. You're just a puny kid."

"Well, this puny kid still ain't gonna salute that flag."

"You were born here," Miss Colon interjected patiently, trying to calm us both down. "Don't you think you at least owe this country some respect? At least?"

"I had no choice about where I was born. And I was born poor."

"So what?" Mr. Rios screamed. "There are plenty of poor people who respect the flag. Look around you, dammit! You see any rich people here? I'm not rich either!" He tugged on my arm. "This country takes care of Puerto Rico, don't you see that? Don't you know anything about politics?"

110 "Do you know what imperialism is?"

The two of them stared at each other.

"I don't believe you," Mr. Rios murmured.

"Puerto Rico is a colony," I said, a direct quote of Albizu's. "Why I gotta respect that?"

Miss Colon stared at me with her black saucer eyes, a slight trace of a grin on her features. It encouraged me. In that one moment, I felt strong, suddenly aware of my territory and my knowledge of it. I no longer felt like a boy but some kind of soldier, my bayonet stained with the blood of my enemy. There was no doubt about it. Mr. Rios was the enemy, and I was beating him. The more he tried to treat me like a child, the more defiant I became, his arguments falling like twisted armor. He shut his eyes and pressed the bridge of his nose.

115   "You're out of my hands," he said.

Miss Colon gave me a sympathetic look before she vanished into the classroom again. Mr. Rios led me downstairs without another word. His face was completely red. I expected to be put in my corner again, but this time Mr. Rios sat me down in the leather chair facing the principal's desk. He stepped outside, and I could hear the familiar clack-clack that could only belong to Miss Marti's reptile legs. They were talking in whispers. I expected her to come in at any moment, but the principal walked in instead. He came in quietly, holding a folder in his hand. His soft brown eyes and beard made him look compassionate, rounded cheeks making him seem friendly. His desk plate solemnly stated: Mr. Sepulveda, PRINCIPAL. He fell into his seat rather unceremoniously, opened the folder, and crossed his hands over it.

"Well, well, well," he said softly, with a tight-lipped grin. "You've created quite a stir, young man." It sounded to me like movie dialogue.

"First of all, let me say I know about you. I have your record right here, and everything in it is very impressive. Good grades, good attitude, your teachers all have adored you. But I wonder if maybe this hasn't gone to your head? Because everything is going for you here, and you're throwing it all away."

He leaned back in his chair. "We have rules, all of us. There are rules even I must live by. People who don't obey them get disciplined. This will all go on your record, and a pretty good one you've had so far. Why ruin it? This'll follow you for life. You don't want to end up losing a good job opportunity in government or in the armed forces because as a child you indulged your imagination and refused to salute the flag? I know you can't see how childish it all is now, but you must see it, and because you're smarter than most, I'll put it to you in terms you can understand.

120   "To me, this is a simple case of rules and regulations. Someday, when you're older," he paused here, obviously amused by the sound of his own voice, "you can go to rallies and protest marches and express your rebellious tendencies. But right now, you are a minor, under this school's jurisdiction. That means you follow the rules, no matter what you think of them. You can join the Young Lords later."

I stared at him, overwhelmed by his huge desk, his pompous mannerisms and status. I would agree with everything, I felt, and then, the following week,

I would refuse once again. I would fight him then, even though he hadn't tried to humiliate me or insult my intelligence. I would continue to fight, until I...

"I spoke with your father," he said.

I started. "My father?" Vague images and hopes flared through my mind briefly.

"Yes. I talked to him at length. He agrees with me that you've gotten a little out of hand."

125   My blood reversed direction in my veins. I felt as if I were going to collapse. I gripped the armrests of my chair. There was no way this could be true, no way at all! My father was supposed to ride in like the cavalry, not abandon me to the enemy! I pressed my wet eyes with my fingers. It must be a lie.

"He blames himself for your behavior," the principal said. "He's already here," Mr. Rios said from the door, motioning my father inside. Seeing him wearing his black weather-beaten trench coat almost asphyxiated me. His eyes, red with concern, pulled at me painfully. He came over to me first while the principal rose slightly, as if greeting a head of state. There was a look of dread on my father's face as he looked at me. He seemed utterly lost.

"Mr. Sepulveda," he said, "I never thought a thing like this could happen. My wife and I try to bring him up right. We encourage him to read and write and everything. But you know, this is a shock."

"It's not that terrible, Mr. Rodriguez. You've done very well with him, he's an intelligent boy. He just needs to learn how important obedience is."

"Yes," my father said, turning to me, "yes, you have to obey the rules. You can't do this. It's wrong." He looked at me grimly, as if working on a math problem. One of his hands caressed my head.

130   There were more words, in Spanish now, but I didn't hear them. I felt like I was falling down a hole. My father, my creator, renouncing his creation, repentant. Not an ounce of him seemed prepared to stand up for me, to shield me from attack. My tears made all the faces around me melt.

"So you see," the principal said to me as I rose, my father clutching me to him, "if you ever do this again, you will be hurting your father as well as yourself."

I hated myself. I wiped at my face desperately, trying not to make a spectacle of myself. I was just a kid, a tiny kid. Who in the hell did I think I was? I'd have to wait until I was older, like my father, in order to have "convictions."

"I don't want to see you in here again, okay?" the principal said sternly. I nodded dumbly, my father's arm around me as he escorted me through the front office to the door that led to the hallway, where a multitude of children's voices echoed up and down its length like tolling bells.

"Are you crazy?" my father half-whispered to me in Spanish as we stood there. "Do you know how embarrassing this all is? I didn't think you were this stupid. Don't you know anything about dignity, about respect? How could you make a spectacle of yourself? Now you make us all look stupid."

135   He quieted down as Mr. Rios came over to take me back to class. My father gave me a squeeze and told me he'd see me at home. Then, I walked with a

somber Mr. Rios, who oddly wrapped an arm around me all the way back to the classroom.

"Here you go," he said softly as I entered the classroom, and everything fell quiet. I stepped in and walked to my seat without looking at anyone. My cheeks were still damp, my eyes red. I looked like I had been tortured. Edwin stared at me, then he pressed my hand under the table.

"I thought you were dead," he whispered.

Miss Colon threw me worried glances all through the remainder of the class. I wasn't paying attention. I took out my notebook, but my strength ebbed away. I just put my head on the desk and shut my eyes, reliving my father's betrayal. If what I did was so bad, why did I feel more ashamed of him than I did of myself? His words, once so rich and vibrant, now fell to the floor, leaves from a dead tree.

At the end of the class, Miss Colon ordered me to stay after school. She got Mr. Rios to take the class down along with his, and she stayed with me in the darkened room. She shut the door on all the exuberant hallway noise and sat down on Edwin's desk, beside me, her black pumps on his seat.

140   "Are you okay?" she asked softly, grasping my arm. I told her everything, especially about my father's betrayal. I thought he would be the cavalry, but he was just a coward.

"Tss. Don't be so hard on your father," she said. "He's only trying to do what's best for you."

"And how's this the best for me?" I asked, my voice growing hoarse with hurt.

"I know it's hard for you to understand, but he really was trying to take care of you."

I stared at the blackboard.

145   "He doesn't understand me," I said, wiping my eyes.

"You'll forget," she whispered.

"No, I won't. I'll remember every time I see that flag. I'll see it and think, 'My father doesn't understand me.'"

Miss Colon sighed deeply. Her fingers were warm on my head, stroking my hair. She gave me a kiss on the cheek. She walked me downstairs, pausing by the doorway. Scores of screaming, laughing kids brushed past us.

"If it's any consolation, I'm on your side," she said, squeezing my arm. I smiled at her, warmth spreading through me. "Go home and listen to the Beatles," she added with a grin.

150   I stepped out into the sunshine, came down the white stone steps, and stood on the sidewalk. I stared at the towering school building, white and perfect in the sun, indomitable. Across the street, the dingy row of tattered uneven tenements where I lived. I thought of my father. Her words made me feel sorry for him, but I felt sorrier for myself. I couldn't understand back then about a father's love and what a father might give to insure his son safe transit. He had already navigated treacherous waters and now couldn't have me rock the boat. I still had to learn that he had made peace with The Enemy, that The Enemy

was already in us. Like the flag I must salute, we were inseparable, yet his compromise made me feel ashamed and defeated. Then I knew I had to find my own peace, away from the bondage of obedience. I had to accept that flag, and my father, someone I would love forever, even if at times to my young, feeble mind he seemed a little imperfect.

Edgardo Vega Yunqué

Edgardo Vega Yunqué was born in Ponce, Puerto Rico, in 1936, and his family moved to New York City in 1949. He published his first three works of fiction under the name Ed Vega. His first book, *The Comeback* (1985), was a satirical parody of the typical Puerto Rican story of ghetto life popularized by the best-selling *Down These Mean Streets* by Piri Thomas. He followed this with the ingenious and humorous novel/story collection, *Mendoza's Dreams* (1987), from which the selection below comes, and a collection of stories, *Casualty Report* (1991). Long rumored to have other unpublished works, Vega Yunqué didn't publish anything else until 2003 when his long awaited "symphonic novel," *No Matter How Much You Promise to Cook or Pay the Rent You Blew It Cauze Bill Bailey Ain't Never Coming Home Again* finally arrived, quickly followed by *The Lamentable Journey of Omaha Bigelow* (2004). Vega Yunqué's work continuously pushes the boundaries of what one might think constitutes Latino literature, often with humor and stylistic experimentation. His latest novel is *Blood Fugues: A Novel* (2005).

The Barbosa Express

Several years ago, at the tail end of the big snowstorm. I was in Florindo's Bar on 110th Street and Lexington Avenue when Chu Chu Barbosa walked in cursing and threatening to join the FALN and bomb the hell out of somebody or other. Barbosa's name is *Jesús* but nobody likes being called Gee Zoos or Hay Siouxs, so it's convenient that the nickname for *Jesús* is Chu or Chuito because Barbosa was a motorman for the last seventeen years with the New York City Transit Authority.

Barbosa is your typical working class stiff, bitter on the outside but full of stubborn optimism on the inside. He has gone through the same kind of immigrant nonsense everyone else has to go through and has come out of it in great shape. In spite of ups and downs he has remained married to the same woman twenty-two years, has never found reason to be unfaithful to her, put one kid through college and has four more heading in the same direction. He owns a two-family home in Brooklyn and on weekends during the summer, he takes Bobby and Mike, his two sons, fishing on his outboard, "Mercedes," named after the children's mother.

Usually even tempered and singularly civic minded, he lists among his responsibilities his serving as treasurer of the "Roberto Clemente Little League of Brooklyn," vice-president of the "Sons of Cacimar Puerto Rican Day Parade Organizing Committee," Den Father for the Boy Scouts of America Troop

641, Secretary of the "Wilfredo Santiago American Legion Post 387" and member of the Courtelyou Street Block Association.

That night Barbosa was out of his mind with anger. At first I thought it was the weather. The snowstorm was wreaking havoc with the city and it seemed conceivable Barbosa was stranded in Manhattan and could not get back to his family in Brooklyn. Knocking the snow off his coat and stamping his feet. Barbosa walked up to the bar and ordered a boiler-maker. He downed the whiskey, chugalugged the beer and ordered another one. I was right next to him but he didn't recognize me until he had finished his second beer and ordered another. Halfway through his third beer he suddenly looked at me and shook his head as if there were no reason for trying anymore.

5   "This does it, Mendoza," he said, still shaking his head. "It makes no sense, man. The whole town is sinking."

"Yeah, the snow's pretty bad." I said, but it was as if I hadn't even spoken.

"The friggin capital of the world," he went on. "And it's going down the d-r-a-drain. I mean who am I kidding." I put on a uniform in the morning, step into my little moving phone booth and off I go. From Coney Island to 205th in B-r-o-Bronx. Fifteen years I've been on that run. I mean, you gotta be born to the job, Mendoza. And listen, I take pride in what I do. It isn't just a job with me. I still get my kicks outta pushing my ten car rig. Brooklyn. Manhattan and the Bronx. I run through those boroughs four times a shift, picking up passengers, letting them off. School kids going up to Bronx Science, people going to work in midtown Manhattan, in the summertime the crowds going up to Yankee Stadium. And that run from 125th Street to 59th Street and Columbus Circle when I let her out and race through that tunnel at sixty miles an hour. Did you know that was the longest run of my express train between stops?"

"No, I didn't," I said.

"It is," he said. "Sixty-six b-l-o-blocks."

10   "No kidding," I said, suddenly hopeful that Barbosa was pulling out of his dark mood. "That's amazing."

"You're damn right it's amazing," he replied, his face angry once more. "And I love it, but it's getting to me. How can they friggin do this? I mean it's their trains. Don't they know that, Mendoza? They don't have to shove it down my throat. But who the hell am I, right? I'm the little guy. Just put him in that moving closet and forget about him. Jeronimo Anonimo, that's me. I don't care what anybody thinks. For me it's like I'm pulling the Super Chief on a transcontinental run, or maybe the old Texas Hummingbird from Chicago to San Antonio along all that flat land, eighty, ninety miles an hour. I give 'em an honest day's work. It's cause I'm Pucrto Rican, man. It's nothing but discrimination."

I could certainly sympathize with Barbosa on that account. I had met severe discrimination in the publishing world and had been forced to write nothing but lies about the people. I was curious to find out what had taken place to make Barbosa so angry.

"I know how you feel, Chu Chu," I said.

"I mean you're a writer and it might sound strange, Mendoza. But I'm not a stupid man. I've read, so I know about words. When I'm in my rig going along the tracks and making my stops, it feels like I'm inside the veins of the city down in those tunnels. It's like my train is the blood and the people the food for this city. Sometimes there is a mugging of worse down there, but I say to myself, hell, so the system ate a stale *alcopurria* or some bad chittlins or maybe an old knish. Do you understand what I'm saying?"

15 "Of course I do," I said. "Subway travel as a metaphor of the lifeblood of the city."

"Right. It's the people, the little people that keep the city going. Not the big shots."

"Exactly."

"Then how can they do it? The trains belong to them."

"The grafitti's getting to you," I said, sympathetically.

20 "No, that's a pain in the ass but you get used to it. Those kids are harmless. I got a nephew that's into that whole thing. I wish the hell they'd find someplace else to do their thing, but they're nothing compared to the creeps that are running the system these days. Nothing but prejudice against our people. Mendoza."

I asked Barbosa exactly what had happened and he told me that nearly a thousand new cars had arrived. "They're beautiful," be said. "Not a spot on them. Stainless steel, colorful plastic seats and a big orange D in front of them for my line. Oh, and they also have this bell that signals that the doors are gonna close. Have you seen em yet?" I told him I had not since I avoid subway travel as much as possible, which he doesn't know nor would I tell him for fear of hurting his feelings. He then went on to tell me that even though he had seniority on other motormen, they didn't assign a new train to him.

"Why not?" I said.

"Discrimination," he said. " 'Cause I'm Puerto Rican. That's the only reason. Mendoza. Just plain discrimination. Even *morenos* with less time than me got new rigs and I got stuck with my old messed up train. I'm not saying black people are not entitled to a break. You know me. I ain't got a prejudiced bone in my body. Man, I even told them I'd be willing to take an evening trick just to handle one of the new trains, but they said no. I'm burnt up, Mendoza. I feel like blowing up the whole system is how I feel."

I immediately counseled Barbosa to calm down and not be hasty in his response. I said that there were legal avenues that he could explore. Perhaps he could file a grievance with his union, but he just kept shaking his head and pounding his fist into his hand, muttering and ordering one beer after the other. At the end of an hour he began laughing real loud and saying that he had the perfect solution to the problem. He patted me on the back and said goodbye.

25 Of course I worried about Chu Chu for three or four days because you couldn't find a nicer guy and I was worried that he would do something crazy.

Every time I stopped by Florindo's Bar I'd ask for him, but no one had seen him around. Once, one of the bartenders said he had seen him in Brooklyn and that he was still working for the Transit Authority. I asked if he had gotten a new train, but the bartender didn't know. I didn't hear from Barbosa or see him again for the next six months and then I wished I hadn't.

About a week before the Fourth of July I received a call from Barbosa. He was no longer angry. In fact he sounded euphoric. This made me immediately suspicious. Perhaps he had taken up drugs as a relief from his anger.

"How you doing, Mendoza?" he said. "How's the writing going?"

"It's going, but just barely," I said. "My caboose is dragging," I added, throwing in a little railroad humor.

He let loose a big roaring belly laugh and, speaking away from the telephone, told his wife, Mercedes, what I'd said. In the background I heard his wife say, "that's nice," and I could tell she wasn't too pleased with Barbosa's condition.

30 "Your caboose, huh?" he said. "Well, I got just the right maintenance for that. Something to get your engine going again and stoke up that boiler with fresh fuel."

"What did you have in mind?" I said, fighting my suspicion.

"A party, Mendoza. A Fourth of July party. We're gonna celebrate our independence."

This didn't sound too strange since Barbosa believed in the American Way of Life. He was a Puerto Rican, but he loved the United States and he wasn't ashamed to admit it. He didn't go around spouting island independence and reaping the fruits of the system. His philosophy was simple. His kids spoke English, were studying here and there were more opportunities for a career in the U.S. Whatever they wanted to do on the island was their business. "I don't pay no taxes there," he'd say. "I don't live there, I don't own property there, so why should I have anything to say about what goes on. Don't get me wrong. I love the island and nobody's ever gonna let me forget I'm from P.R., but it don't make no sense for me to be a phony about where I earn my rice and beans." I personally thought it was an irresponsible political stand, but I don't middle in how people think or feel, I simply report on what I see.

"What kind of party?" I said.

35 "That's a surprise, but it's gonna be a party to end all parties. Music. Food. Drink. Entertainment. Fire works. You name it, we're gonna have it."

"At your house in Brooklyn?"

"Naw, too small. Up in the Bronx. Ralph, my nephew, can come pick you up."

"I don't know," I said. "I got a backlog of stuff and I'm not too good at celebrating the independence of this country." I found myself saying, even though I like to keep politics out of my conversations. He knew that and sensed that I was simply trying to get out of it.

"Aw, com'on, Mendoza," he said. "It's gonna be great. I wouldn't be inviting you if I didn't think you'd enjoy it. I know how hard you work and what your feelings are about this whole American and Puerto Rican thing, okay? Trust me. You'll never forget this. You're gonna be proud of me. Everybody's coming. The whole clan. You never seen my family together. I don't mean just my wife and kids, but my eight brothers and five sisters and their husbands and wives and their kids and my aunts and uncles and my parents and grandparents. And Mercedes' side of the family which is not as big but they're great. You gotta come."

40   I couldn't help myself in asking the next question.

"Where are you holding this party, Yankee Stadium?"

"That's funny," he said, and again laughed so loud my ear hurt. "No, nothing like that. You gotta come. My niece, Zoraida, can't wait to meet you. She's a big fan of yours. She's doing her, what do you call it, to become a doctor, but not a doctor."

"Her PhD? Her doctorate."

"That's it. She's doing it on your books. She's just starting out, so she wants to talk to you and get to know you."

45   All of a sudden I felt flattered, even though most of what I've written doesn't amount to much. I felt myself swayed by the upcoming adulation, but I truly wish I hadn't participated in what took place between early evening on the Fourth of July and some time around four o'clock in the morning when all hell broke loose on the elevated tracks near Coney Island.

"Where is she studying?" I said.

"Some college in Michigan," Barbosa answered. "I don't know. You can ask her yourself. Ralph'll pick you up about 6:30 on July 4th, okay?"

"All right," I said, suddenly experiencing a strange feeling of foreboding about the entire matter. "But I can't stay long."

"Don't worry," Barbosa said. "Once you get up there and the party starts you can decide that."

50   "What does that mean?"

Barbosa laughed and said he'd see me on the Fourth.

So on the Fourth of July I got ready. I put on white pants, polished to my white shoes, got out one of my *guayaberas* and my panama hat and at 6:30 that afternoon Ralph Barbosa knocked on the door and down I went to one of my infrequent social activities.

I got into the car and off we went across the Willis Avenue Bridge into the Bronx. I asked him where we were going and he replied that his uncle had told him to keep it a surprise, but that it was up near Lehman College. I relaxed for a while, but still felt that feeling that something not quite right was about to take place. Some twenty minutes later we drove under the Woodlawn Avenue elevated line tracks and into the campus of Herbert H. Lehman College. Ralph parked the car, we got out and walked to a grassy area where a number of people were seated on blankets. Around them were boxes of food and drink, ice coolers, paper plates and cups, coffee urns and several other items that indicated we were to have a picnic.

I felt relaxed at once and as I was introduced to different members of the family I noticed that there were very few men. Out of the over 100 people gathered around several trees, most of them were women and children. I asked Ralph where I could find his uncle and I was informed that Barbosa was making final preparations. I was offered a beer, which I accepted gladly, was offered a beach chair, which I also accepted, and then was introduced to Zoraida Barbosa, the PhD student, a lovely, articulate young woman with a keen intellect and, unfortunately, a genuine interest in my work. So enraptured and flattered was I by her attention that more than an hour and a half passed. I then realized that the sun was going down and Barbosa still had not shown up. I once again began to worry.

55   Another half hour passed and now we were sitting in the dark and some of the younger children began to get restless. And then the word came that we were ready to move. "Move where?" I inquired. "It's all right, Mr. Mendoza," Zoraida said, taking my hand. "Just follow me." Such was her persuasiveness and her interest in me that I allowed her to take my hand and followed her as we crossed the grassy field. We walked for nearly a half mile until we were at the train yards. At that point I knew I was heading for a major catastrophe, but there did not seem to be any way of turning back.

I soon found out why the men had not been in attendance. I saw the plan clearly now. We were to descend into the train yards, a rather hazardous undertaking from the place where our crowd had stopped. The men, however, had constructed a staircase, complete with sturdy bannisters. This staircase went up over the wall and down some fifty feet into the floor of the train yard. I followed Zoraida and as we went I looked down on the nearly forty rails below, most of them with trains on them. This was the terminal of the Independent Subway System or IND as it is popularly known, a place where trains came to be cleaned and repaired or to lay up when they were not in use. Down we went and then guided by young men with flash-lights we walked along, seemingly dangerously close to the ever present third rails until we arrived at an enclosure where a train had been parked. I suspected this was where trains were washed.

Again, utilizing a makeshift staircase I followed Zoraida as we climbed up into a train. Although the light of the flashlights being employed by the young men was sufficient for us to find our way, it was impossible to see what I had walked into. I was directed to a place on the train and asked to sit down. Expecting to find a hard surface when I sat down. I was surprised to find myself sinking into a plush armchair. Moments later I recognized Barbosa's voice asking if everyone was on board. Word came back that everyone indeed had boarded the train. Then quite suddenly the motors in the car were activated. I heard doors close and lights came on. I found myself in a typical New York Puerto Rican living room, complete with sofas, armchairs with covers, little tables with figurines, lamps, linoleum on the floor and curtains in the windows. I thought I would have a heart attack and began to get up from my chair, but at that moment the train began moving slowly out and a loud cheer went up.

I turned to Zoraida sitting on the arm of my chair and she patted my shoulder and said I shouldn't worry. A few moments later we were moving at fairly rapid rate and then the music came on, at first faintly but then as the volume was adjusted it was quite clear: Salsa, I don't know who, Machito, Tito Puente, Charlie Palmieri. I didn't care. This was outrageous. Moments later Barbosa came into our car and smiling from ear to ear greeted me.

"How do you like it?" he said, after I explained to him that my heart was nearly at the point of quitting. "It's pretty good, right? My nephew, Ernest, he's an interior decorator, did the whole thing. Wait till you see the rest of it. It's not a new train but it'll do."

60   I wanted to tell him that I had seen enough, but was too much in shock to protest. With an escort of his two brothers who, to my great surprise, were members of the police department undercover detective squad, we went forward as the train began picking up speed. I asked who was driving and Barbosa informed me that he had another nephew who was a motorman on the IRT Seventh Avenue line and he was doing the driving. From the living room car we moved forward into the next car, which was a control center laid out with tables, maps and computers. I was introduced to another nephew, a computer whiz working on his PhD in electral engineering. Several young people were busily working away plotting and programming, all of it very efficient. The next car, the lead one, was laid out as an executive office with a switchboard connecting the other cars by phone. There also were several television sets and radios, all tuned to the major channels and radio station. "We're gonna monitor everything that happens," Barbosa said, and introduced me to yet another nephew, an executive from AT&T, dressed in a business suit, seated at a big desk with wood paneling on the walls around him. Off to the side a young woman was transcribing from dictaphone onto an IBM Selectric. My shock was indescribable.

We retraced our steps through the train until we came out of the living room car into the bar car. How they had managed to get a thirty foot oak bar with matching wall length mirror on the train is beyond me, but there it was, stools riveted into the floor. I was introduced all around to the men and women at the bar, all of them relatives of Barbosa and all of them grinning from car to car about this adventure.

"I hope you're doing the right thing." I said.

"Don't worry, Mendoza," he said. "Everything's under control."

The next car was a kitchen with six different stoves, four refrigerators, two meat lockers, cutting boards, kitchen cabinets. Here I was introduced to Monsieur Pierre Barbosa, the chef for the Lancaster Hotel, on leave especially for this occasion. Dressed in white and wearing a tall chef's hat, he greeted me warmly and invited me to taste one of his sauces. I did so and found it quite agreeable, if somewhat tart. "Too tart?" he said. I nodded and he spoke rapidly in French to one of his assistants, another Barbosa nephew who moved directly to the sauce with several condiments.

65   In the next car there was a nursery with cribs and beds for the children and a medical staff headed by Dr. Elizabeth Barbosa, a niece who was a pediatrician in Philadelphia. There were also bathrooms for ladies and gentlemen in the next car. Two cars were devoted to dining tables with linen and candlesticks, each with its own piano. The last car was the most magnificent and modern dance establishment I've ever seen. The floor gleamed and there were lights beneath it and on the ceiling colored lights were going on and off and young people were dancing. "Our disco," Barbosa said, proudly. "With D.J. Mike, my son." His oldest son waved and Barbosa laughed. "I hope you know what you're doing," I said. "But I have to hand it to you. How did you do it?"

"This is a family, Mendoza," Barbosa said. "We'd do anything for each other."

Ten subway cars decked out for partying were moving now through the Bronx, making stops but not letting anyone on, the Latin music blaring from loud speakers above four of the central cars. Every stop we made, people laughed and slapped their thighs and began dancing and very few people seemed angry that they couldn't board the train. All of them pointed at the train. I asked Barbosa why they were pointing and he explained that the train was painted. He described it but it wasn't until the following morning when the escapade came to an abrupt end that I truly was able to see what he was talking about. Each of the cars had been sprayed a different color: orange, red, yellow, pink, green, several blues, white (I think that was the nursery) and the disco which was black and even had a neon sign with the letters *El Son de Barbosa*. All along the cars in huge graffiti letters each car said *The Barbosa Express* and each one, rather than having the Transit Authority seal had BTA or Barbosa Transit Authority on it. All of them were decorated with beautiful graffiti "pieces," as I learned these expressions were called when I was introduced to Tac 121, the master "writer," as these young men and women are called. Tac 121 was in reality Victor Barbosa, another nephew, studying graphic design at Boston University.

The party began in full and we kept moving through Manhattan and then into Brooklyn and the elevated tracks. Everyone had eaten by now and it was then that all hell began to break loose. It was now close to midnight. At this point one of the dining rooms was cleared and converted into a launching pad for a tremendous fire works display. I was introduced to yet another nephew, Larry Barbosa, who was a mechanical engineer. He had managed to restructure the roof of the car so that it folded and opened, allowing his brother, Bill, a member of Special Forces during the Vietnam War and a demolitions expert, to set up shop and begin firing colored rockets from the car so that as we made a wide turn before coming into the Coney Island terminal I could see the sky being lit up as the train made its way. The music was blaring and the rockets were going off in different directions so that one could see the beaches and the water in the light from the explosions.

I was exhausted and fell asleep while Zoraida was explaining her project and asking me very intricate questions about my work, details which I had forgotten with the passage of time. Two hours or so must have passed when I woke up to a great deal of shouting. I got up and went to the control car where Barbosa, dressed in his motorman's uniform, and some of his relatives were listening to news of the hijacking of a train, the announcers insinuating that the thieves had gotten the idea from the film "The Taking of Pelham 123." One of the television stations was maintaining continuous coverage with interviews of high officials of the Transit Authority, the Mayor, pedestrians, the police and sundry experts, who put forth a number of theories on why the people had commandeered the train. They even interviewed an art professor, a specialist on the graffiti culture, who explained that the creation of art on the trains was an expression of youths' dissatisfaction with the rapid rate at which information was disseminated and how difficult it was to keep up with changing developments. "Using a mode of transportation to display their art," he said, "obviously keeps that art moving forward at all times and ahead of change."

70   In another corner a couple of young men and women were monitoring the communications from the Transit Authority.

"We gotta a clear channel, Uncle Chu Chu," said one of the girls. "They wanna talk to somebody."

Barbosa sat down and spoke to some high official. I was surprised when the official asked Barbosa to identify himself and Barbosa did so, giving his name and his badge number. When they asked him what was happening, he explained how the hijackers had come to his house and kidnapped him, took him down to the train yards and forced him to drive the train or they would kill him.

"What do they want?" said the official.

"They wanna a clear track from here to the Bronx," Barbosa said. "And they want no cops around, otherwise they're gonna shoot everybody. They grabbed some women and children on the way and they look like they mean business."

75   "Can you identify them?"

"The women and children?"

"No, the perpetrators."

"Are you crazy or what!" shouted Barbosa, winking at me and the rest of the members of the family around him, most of whom were holding their sides to keep from laughing. "Whatta you wanna do, get me killed, or what? There's a guy holding a gun to my head and you want me to identify him?"

"Okay, okay," said the official. "I understand. Just keep your cool and do as they say. The Mayor wants to avoid any bloodshed. Do as they say. Where are you now?"

80   "Kings Highway," Barbosa said.

I was amazed. The train had gone to Concy Island, backed up, turned around and had made another trip to the end of the Bronx and back to Brooklyn. I looked above and saw news and police helicopters, following the train as it moved.

"Okay, we'll clear the tracks and no police," said the official. "Over and out."

"Roger, over and out," said Barbosa, clicking off the radio. He raised his hand and his nephew, leaning out of the motorman's compartment, waved, ducked back in, let go with three powerful blasts from the train whistle and then we were moving down the tracks at top speed with the music playing and the rockets going off and people dancing in every car.

"We did it, Mendoza," Barbosa said. "Son of a gun! We d-i-d-did it."

85   I was so tired I didn't care. All I wanted to do was go home and go to sleep. I went back in to the living room car and sat down again. When I woke up we were up in the Bronx and Barbosa's relatives were streaming out of the cars, carrying all their boxes and coolers with them. There were no policemen around. Zoraida Barbosa helped me out of the train and minutes later we were in Ralph's car. A half hour later I was in my apartment.

The next day there were pictures of Barbosa dressed in his uniform on the front pages of all the newspapers. The official story as it turned out was that graffiti artists had worked on the old train over a period of three or four weeks and then had kidnapped Barbosa to drive the train. Why they chose him was never revealed, but he emerged as a hero.

Unofficially, several people at the Transit Authority were convinced that Barbosa had had something to do with the "train hijacking."

A month later I was in Florindo's Bar and in walked Barbosa, happy as a lark. He bought me a beer and informed me that shortly after the train incident they had assigned him a new train and that in a year or so he was retiring. I congratulated him and told him that his niece had written again and that her dissertation on my work was going quite well. One thing still bothered me and I needed to find out.

"It doesn't matter," I said. "But who thought up the whole thing?"

90   "I thought up the idea, but it was my nephew Kevin, my oldest brother Joaquin's kid, who worked out the strategy and brought in all the electronic gear to tap into the MTA circuits and communication lines. He works for the Pentagon."

"He does what?!" I said, looking around behind me to make sure no one was listening.

"The Pentagon in Washington," Barbosa repeated.

"You're kidding?" I said.

"Nope," Barbosa said. "You wanna another beer."

95   "I don't think so," I said, "I gotta be going."

"See you in the subway," said Barbosa and laughed.

I walked out into the late summer evening trying to understand what it all meant. By the time I reached my apartment I knew one thing for certain. I knew that the United States of America would have to pay for passing the Jones Act in 1917, giving the people automatic U.S. citizenship and allowing so many of them to enter their country.

As they say in the street: "What goes around, comes around."

POETRY

Julia Alvarez

See the biographical headnote of Alvarez on page 168.

Bilingual Sestina

Some things I have to say aren't getting said
in this snowy, blond, blue-eyed, gum-chewing English:
dawn's early light sifting through *persianas*[1] closed
the night before by dark-skinned girls whose words
5 evoke *cama, aposento, sueñas*[2] in *nombres*[3]
from that first world I can't translate from Spanish.

Gladys, Rosario, Altagracia—the sounds of Spanish
wash over me like warm island waters as I say
your soothing names: a child again learning the *nombres*
10 of things you point to in the world before English
turned *sol, sierra, cielo, luna* to vocabulary words—
sun, earth, sky, moon. Language closed

like the touch-sensitive *morívíví* whose leaves closed
when we kids poked them, astonished. Even Spanish
15 failed us back then when we saw how frail a word is
when faced with the thing it names. How saying
its name won't always summon up in Spanish or English
the full blown genie from the bottled *nombre.*

Gladys. I summon you back by saying your *nombre.*
20 Open up again the house of slatted windows closed
since childhood, where *palabras*[4] left behind for English
stand dusty and awkward in neglected Spanish.
Rosario, muse of *el patio*, sing in me and through me say
that world again, begin first with those first words

25 you put in my mouth as you pointed to the world—
not Adam, not God, but a country girl numbering
the stars, the blades of grass, warming the sun by saying,
Qué calor![5] us you opened up the morning closed
inside the night until you sang in Spanish.
30 *Estas son las mañanitas*, and listening in bed, no English

yet in my head to confuse me with translations, no English

---

[1]blinds
[2]bed, room, dreams
[3]names
[4]words
[5]What heat!

doubling the world with synonyms, no dizzying array of words
—the world was simple and intact in Spanish—
luna, sol, casa, luz, flor[6] as if the *nombres*
35   were the outer skin of things, as if words were so close
one left a mist of breath on things by saying

their names, an intimacy I now yearn for in English—
words so close to what I mean that I almost hear my Spanish
heart beating, heating inside what I say *en inglés*.

---

[6]moon, sun, house, light, flower

Naomi Ayala

Naomi Ayala was born in Puerto Rico and immigrated to the United States in the late 1970s. She has made her mark as a dedicated community activist. The author of *Wild Animals on the Moon: & Other Poems* (1997), Ayala also has been a teacher and worked with educators in Connecticut. Since 1997, she has consulted on school curriculum for national organizations in Washington, D.C.

A Coquí[1] in Nueva York

I am a loud mouth coquí
that broke out from the island
because the yanquis were
crowding the place, talking 'bout
5   chopping up trees in El Yunque — as if
paper products could feed
the eyes or fill the lungs — talking
'bout turning Loiza
into an open-air museum,
10   'bout eating broken English anthems
for breakfast at school
& how wonderful
& necessary it all was.
In the gallery
15   of their economic dreams
I sat by, shoving my song
deep into the fat briefcases
of their intentions
& sandwiched
20   between so much crap I knew
it would rot & make a stink

---

[1]a little frog indigenous to Puerto Rico

they'd have to tend to sometime.
All I wanted was to sing,
sing of my green onlyness.
25   I braved it to Nueva York with an attitude
I could sing where
I wanted what I wanted to.
I would invade the land of freedom with songs
that rotted into stinks
30   songs that drew people, made them move
toward the dance of action,
songs that composted
the garbage of nightmares
into fine, fine food.
35   I trained my song to live on air
years at a time, to leap

Sandra María Esteves

Sandra María Esteves was born on May 10, 1948, the daughter of a Puerto Rican father and a Dominican mother. Her parents separated before she was born, and she was raised by her mother and aunt in the South Bronx. In the 1970s, as a Nuyorican poet, she actively participated in civil rights campaigns, reading and performing her work on behalf of the efforts to gain the island of Puerto Rico its independence. Her collections include *Yerba Buena: Dibujos y Poems* (1981), *Tropical Rains: A Bilingual Downpour* (1984), and *Bluestown Mockingbird Mambo* (1990). Her poems celebrate the indigenous, African energies of her heritage, movingly detailing the urban and political struggles of working-class Latinos.

Here

I am two parts/a person
boricua/spic
past and present
alive and oppressed
5   given a cultural beauty
...and robbed of a cultural identity

I speak the alien tongue
in sweet boriqueño thoughts
know love mixed with pain
10   have tasted spit on ghetto stairways
...here, it must be changed
we must change it

I may never overcome
the theft of my isla heritage
15   dulce palmas de coco on Luquillo
sway in windy recesses I can only imagine
and remember how it was

But that reality now a dream
teaches me to see, and will
20   bring me back to me.

José B. Gonzalez

See the biographical headnote of Gonzalez on page 173.

Autobrownography of a New England Latino

In 1967, San Salvador, El Salvador fathered my brown,
And so I was born in the capital that salutes
The Pacific, the mother of so many brown rivers,
Lakes, ponds, that held hands with volcanic rocks
5   That tumbled brown, burned the soil brown, and
Browned the country in civil brown turmoil in the
1970s, when my family left to New England,
Where factories, my mother's sewing machine
And my father's spray paint machine were brown,
10   And I first attended John Winthrop Elementary School,
A school full of browns, a "separate but equal," type
Of brown that was not El Salvador brown but a
Desperate-to-move-out-of-the-projects brown,
And so my parents poured their wages into tuition
15   For a private middle school classroom where
I was the only brown, and I was taught to make my
Language a less subtle brown, so that by the time I
Attended New London High School, which had
Shades of Puerto Rican brown and tints of Latin
20   American brown, I had shed so much brown that I
Was accused of not being enough brown, but I figured
I knew the roots of my brown and felt comfortable
Enough with my brown, even if I was losing some
Of my Spanish brown, and I continued to lose
25   It too, not because I wanted to, but because
Most of the brown at the college I attended was
Republican brown, which was a different dialect
Of brown, and by the end of my four years, my

Spanish brown had faded so much that it became an
30 Anglicized Spanish brown, and I was awarded
The college's excellence in English award,
Which I was pretty sure had never been given
To a graduating brown, and when they said, "this
Year's recipient is, José B. Gonzalez Brown," I could
35 Have sworn I saw hundreds of people scrape
Their ears in an attempt to fix whatever was
Making them hear brown, and after graduating,
I figured I'd get a job teaching English, even if
I was brown, but at an interview for an English
40 Teaching position at a small boarding school, the
Headmaster's eyes told me that if I was serious about
Getting a job, I'd teach Spanish brown, because
There's such a shortage of Spanish browns,
To which I said, "thank you headmaster, but,
45 I, I, I'd just assume not teach Spanish brown,"
And when his office door responded with, "Thank you,
Mr. Brown, but unless you're willing to teach
Spanish brown, I won't have a job for you,
Mr. Brown," I changed my mind and did
50 What I had to, even if my first language was no
Longer Spanish brown, and I taught there until one
Brown day in the middle of the school year,
I just had to ask, "I know you hired me
For something else, but someday can I teach English
55 Here, even if I am brown?" And his desk looked
At me like, if you didn't want to teach
Spanish brown, maybe you shouldn't have
Been brown, which told me it was time for me
To leave that master and get my
60 Master's and I decided to attend what
Else? Brown University, which was
Ivy League brown, and you want to talk
About a different shade of brown? That
Was like a culture-shock brown, "Mamihelpme,
65 Thisisabadnovela, Ineverseenthisbefore," kind
Of brown, and there were so many educated,
Liberal browns, I thought that there had been some
Kind of going out of business clearance sale on
Diplomas for browns, not that the majority
70 Was brown, but I just wasn't too used to
Associating the college experience with
Browns, so even a little bit of brown
Was enough to make me think that colleges

Were turning somewhat brown, and while at Brown,
75 I student-taught at Providence's Hope
High School which had many browns, so I
Wanted very badly for my students to recognize
My brown and say if he's at Brown and he's brown,
There's hope for us young browns, but they just
80 Thought I was Brown University brown, not inner-
City brown, and students couldn't see themselves in my
Brown, and so unaccustomed were they to seeing
Any shade of brown in front of their class that they
Thought it was impossible that I could be raised
85 Brown, but I didn't let that get me too much down,
And when I graduated from Brown, I became a Brown
Brown, a brown squared, a Brown times brown, which
For some people, teachers even, only meant that I was
Ivy Brown because I am brown, which made me
90 Want to point to Brown graduates who were Brown
Because their parents or grandparents were Brown,
Making them legacy Browns, Browns cubed, and I
Continued my schooling at the University of Rhode
Island, and worked toward my Ph.D. because of,
95 Not in spite of being brown, and I studied literature
That was brown, because growing up, I had been
Assigned stories like "Young Goodman Brown," but
I had never been assigned a book by a brown author,
Which never made sense to me because I just knew
100 That in all the years that browns had been in the U.S.,
Even in the part that was brown before the U.S. became
The U.S., browns had to have something to say, even if
It wasn't about being brown, and while I worked on my
Brown dissertation, I taught English at Three Rivers
105 Community College, which had quite a few browns,
So many of whom juggled coursework with family
And jobs and being brown that it was tough for them
To one day say, "I have a college degree even though
I'm brown," which made me appreciate being educated
110 And being brown, and I became ABD, A Brown Doctor,
And probably became URI's first English Ph.D.
Brown, which isn't that big a deal because in higher
Education if you're brown you can lay claim
To being the first this and that as a brown, and
115 That's why when I tell people that I'm a professor
Of English, every once in a while someone says
Something like, "Dr. Brown, you must teach
A different type of English that has to have

Some kind of brown, maybe you teach second
120 Language Brown English or remedial brown
English, or development English for the brown,
Because after all you're brown."
But it matters none to me, master of my own
Brown destiny, because even on the coldest,
125 Snowiest day in Connecticut, even when it seems
I've been brownbeaten, I can still feel the power
Of my own brown, brown like a brown who
Beat the Board of Ed, brown like a brown trunk of
A brown tree that's been whacked and whacked and
130 Whacked and whacked until it's become nothing but
A strong, brown wooden frame that holds a brown
Diploma high up in the air, telling the world,
"I'm educated, and
I'm brown."

Caribbean Fresco in New England

No pure Caribbean tree grows
In my New England backyard
Full of hickories with Puritan bark.

Capes grow here, sowing
5   Colonials and Frost fences
        In Yankee farms never visited
        By palms of the tropics,
But subdivided by apples
And Thanksgiving veggies.

10 Museums of whales,
        Watered by fountains
        Of Gloucester watches,
Meet museums of witches,
        Filled with trials
15   Of Salem wizards,
            But no museums or wintry greenhouses
        Hold Caribbean frescoes.

        Still lives of mangoes and guavas,
Uneaten,
20   Unrecognized,
            Unsold,
            Sit at farmers' markets,
                Grown by hungry and nostalgic curators.

Tato Laviera

Tato Laviera was born in Santurce, Puerto Rico, in 1951, and moved to New York City in 1960. Poems from his three collections, *La Carreta Made a U-Turn* (1979), *Enclave* (1981), and *Mainstream Ethics* (1989), have been widely anthologized. He is involved in the arts world of New York, does frequent performance readings, and is especially renowned for bringing to Latino literature the sounds of urban music and the rhythms of the African/Latino oral speech patterns of El Barrio. He has been an influential force in the use of interlingual combinations of Spanish and English in poems.

AmeRícan

we gave birth to a new generation,
AmeRícan, broader than lost gold
never touched, hidden inside the
puerto rican mountains.

5 we gave birth to a new generation,
AmeRícan, it includes everything
imaginable you-name-it-we-got-it
society.

we gave birth to a new generation,
10 AmeRícan salutes all folklores,
european, indian, black, spanish,
and anything else compatible:

AmeRícan, singing to composer pedro flores' palm
trees high up in the universal sky!

15 AmeRícan, sweet soft spanish danzas gypsies
moving lyrics la española cascabelling
presence always singing at our side!

AmeRícan, beating jíbaro modern troubadours
crying guitars romantic continental
20 bolero love songs!

AmeRícan, across forth and across back
back across and forth back
forth across and back and forth
our trips are walking bridges!

25 it all dissolved into itself, the attempt
was truly made, the attempt was truly
absorbed, digested, we spit out
the poison, we spit out the malice,

we stand, affirmative in action,
30   to reproduce a broader answer to the
        marginality that gobbled us up abruptly!

AmeRícan, walking plena-rhythms in new york,
        strutting beautifully alert, alive,
        many turning eyes wondering,
35   admiring!

AmeRícan, defining myself my own way any way many
        ways Am e Rícan, with the big R and the
        accent on the í!

AmeRícan, like the soul gliding talk of gospel
40   boogie music!

AmeRícan, speaking new words in spanglish tenements,
        fast tongue moving street corner "que
        corta" talk being invented at the insistence
        of a smile!

45 AmeRícan, abounding inside so many ethnic english
        people, and out of humanity, we blend
        and mix all that is good!

AmeRícan, integrating in new york and defining our
        own destino, our own way of life,

50 AmeRícan, defining the new america, humane america,
        admired america, loved america, harmonious
        america, the world in peace, our energies
        collectively invested to find other civilizations,
        to touch God, further and further,
55   to dwell in the spirit of divinity!

AmeRícan, yes, for now, for i love this, my second
        land, and i dream to take the accent from
        the altercation, and be proud to call
        myself american, in the u.s. sense of the
60   word, AmeRícan, America!

Demetria Martínez

Demetria Martínez was born in Albuquerque, New Mexico, and has published
two collections of poetry, *Breathing Between the Lines* (1997) and *Turning*
(1987). Her novel, *Mother Tongue* (1994), won the Western States Book Award
for fiction. She writes about Hispanic and women's issues for the *National
Catholic Reporter* and has been active in political issues regarding the Mexi-
can/U.S. border, as is clear from the stance she takes in her latest collection of
poetry, *The Devil's Workshop* (2002).

Birthday

I was born in the Year of the Rat.
Black lung from the incense
Of burning American flags.
First poems penned by
5   The rocket's red glare.
Math was simpler:
58,000 soldiers
And then there were none.
I was born in the Year of the Rat.
10   Thirty-eight years, a life
Still at half-staff.

Pat Mora

See the biographical headnote of Mora on page 103.

Elena

My Spanish isn't enough.
I remember how I'd smile
listening to my little ones,
understanding every word they'd say,
5   their jokes, *their songs, their plots.*
       Vamos a pedirle dulces a mamá. Vamos.[1]
But that was in Mexico.
Now my children go to American high schools.
They speak English. At night they sit around
10   the kitchen table, laugh with one another.
I stand by the stove and feel dumb, alone.
I bought a book to learn English.
My husband frowned, drank more beer.
My oldest said, "*Mamá*, he doesn't want you
15   to be smarter than he is." I'm forty,
embarrassed at mispronouncing words,
embarrassed at the laughter of my children,
the grocer, the mailman. Sometimes I take
my English book and lock myself in the bathroom,
20   say the thick words softly,
for if I stop trying, I will be deaf
when my children need my help.

---

[1]Let's go ask Mom for some candy. Let's go.

Legal Alien

Bi-lingual, Bi-cultural,
able to slip from "How's life?"
to "*Me'stan volviendo loca,*"[1]
able to sit in a paneled office
5   drafting memos in smooth English,
able to order in fluent Spanish
at a Mexican restaurant,
American but hyphenated,
viewed by Anglos as perhaps exotic,
10   perhaps inferior, definitely different,
viewed by Mexicans as alien,
(their eyes say, "You may speak
Spanish but you're not like me")
an American to Mexicans
15   a Mexican to Americans
a handy token
sliding back and forth
between the fringes of both worlds
by smiling
20   by masking the discomfort
of being pre-judged
Bi-laterally.

Cherríe Moraga

The author of numerous books of plays, poems, and essays on gay Latina issues, Cherríe Moraga was born on September 25, 1952, in Los Angeles. The co-editor, along with Gloria Anzaldúa, of the classic anthology *This Bridge Called My Back: Writings by Radical Women of Color*, she is also well known for *Loving in the War Years: Lo que nunca paso por sus labios* (1983), a collection that includes both poetry and prose. She co-edited the immensely influential anthology, *Cuentos: Stories By Latinas* (1983), which in many ways opened the door to the entire field of Latina literature. Since then she has published a number of plays: *La extranjera* (1985), *Giving Up the Ghost: Teatro in 2 Acts* (1986), *Shadow of a Man* (1988), and *Heroes and Saints* (1989). Her most recent volume of plays, *Watsonville: Some Place Not Here* (2002), derives in part from interviews with the farm workers in California and was awarded the Fund for New American Plays Award from the Kennedy Center for the Performing Arts.

The Welder

I am a welder.
Not an alchemist.

---

[1]They're driving me crazy

I am interested in the blend
of common elements to make
5   a common thing.

No magic here.
Only the heat of my desire to fuse
what I already know
exists. Is possible.

10   We plead to each other,
we all come from the same rock
we all come from the same rock
ignoring the fact that we bend
at different temperatures
15   that each of us is malleable
up to a point.

Yes, fusion *is* possible
but only if things get hot enough—
all else is temporary adhesion,
20   patching up.

It is the intimacy of steel melting
into steel, the fire of our individual
passion to take hold of ourselves
that makes sculpture of our lives,
25   builds buildings.

And I am not talking about skyscrapers,
merely structures that can support us
without fear
of trembling.

30   For too long a time
the heat of my heavy hands
has been smoldering
in the pockets of other
people's business—
35   they need oxygen to make fire.

I am now
coming up for air.
Yes, I *am*
picking up the torch.

40   I am the welder.
I understand the capacity of heat
to change the shape of things.
I am suited to work

within the realm of sparks
45 out of control.

I am the welder.
I am taking the power
into my own hands.

Aurora Levins Morales and Rosario Morales

This mother and daughter team collaborated on the writing of the well-known book *Getting Home Alive* (1986). Aurora Levins Morales has subsequently written two collections of semi-nonfictional prose, *Medicine Stories* (1998) and *Remedios* (2001).

Ending Poem

I am what I am.
A child of the Americas.
A light-skinned mestiza of the Caribbean.
A child of many diaspora, born into this continent at a crossroads.
5 I am Puerto Rican. I am U.S. American.
I am New York Manhattan and the Bronx.
A mountain-born, country-bred, homegrown jíbara child,
up from the shtetl, a California Puerto Rican Jew.
A product of the New York ghettos I have never known.
10 *I am an immigrant*
and the daughter and granddaughter of immigrants.
We didn't know our forbears' names with a certainty.
They aren't written anywhere.
First names only, or mija, negra, ne, honey, sugar, dear.

15 I come from the dirt where the cane was grown.
My people didn't go to dinner parties. They weren't invited.
I am caribeña, island grown.
Spanish is in my flesh, ripples from my tongue, lodges in my hips,
the language of garlic and mangoes.
20 *Boricua. As Boricuas come from the Isle of Manhattan.*
I am of latinoamerica, rooted in the history of my continent.
I speak from that body. Just brown and pink and full of drums inside.

I am not African.
Africa waters the roots of my tree but I cannot return.

25 I am not Taína.
I am a late leaf of that ancient tree.
and my roots reach into the soil of two Americas.

Taíno is in me, but there is no way back.
I am not European, though I have dreamt of those cities.

30 Each plate is different.
wood, clay, papier mâché, metal, basketry, a leaf, a coconut shell.
Europe lives in me but I have no home there.

The table has a cloth woven by one, dyed by another,
embroidered by another still.
35 I am a child of many mothers.
They have kept it all going
All the civilizations erected on their backs.
All the dinner parties given with their labor.

We are new.
40 *They gave us life, kept us going.*
brought us to where we are.
Born at a crossroads.
Come, lay that dishcloth down. Eat, dear, eat.
History made us.
45 We will not eat ourselves up inside anymore.

And we are whole.

Achy Obejas

Achy Obejas was born in Havana, Cuba, and came to the United States as an exile
at the age of six. As a poet, fiction writer, and journalist, she has been published
in various anthologies and has won several awards, including the Studs Terkel
Award for journalism in 1996. She has written a novel, *Memory Mambo* (1996),
and a collection of short stories, *We Came All the Way from Cuba So You Could
Dress Like That* (1994).

Sugarcane

can't cut
cut the cane
azuca'[1] in chicago
dig it down to the
5 roots sprouting spray paint on the
walls on the hard cold
stone of the great gritty city
slums in chicago
with the mansions in the hole

---
[1]sugar

10 in the head of
the old rich left behind
from other times lopsided
gangster walls overgrown taken
over by the dark
15 and poor overgrown with no
sugarcane but you
can't can't cut
cut the water
bro'
20 from the flow and
you can't can't cut
cut the blood
lines from this island
train one by one throwing off
25 the chains siguaraya[2]
no no
no se pue'e cortar[3]
pan con ajo[4] quisqueya[5]
cuba y borinquen[6] no
30 se pue'en parar[7]

I saw it
saw black a-frica
down in the city
walking in chicago y
35 la cuba cuba
gritando en el solar[8]
I saw it
saw quisqueya
brown
40 uptown in the city
cryin' in chicago
y borinquen
bro'
sin un
45 chavo igual[9] but
you can't can't cut

---

[2]a type of plant
[3]can't be cut
[4]garlic bread
[5][refers to] Dominican
[6][refers to] Puerto Rican
[7]can't be stopped
[8]screaming in the ancestral home
[9]no one is alike

cut the water
bro'
from the flow and
50 you can't can't cut
cut the blood
lines from this island
train one by one throwing off
the chains siguaraya
55 no no
no se pue'e cortar
pan con ajo quisqueya
cuba y borinquen no
se pue'en parar[10]

60 ¡azuca'!

Alberto Ríos

See the biographical headnote of Ríos on page 149.

The Vietnam Wall

I
Have seen it
And I like it: The magic,
The way like cutting onions
5 It brings water out of nowhere.
Invisible from one side, a scar
Into the skin of the ground
From the other, a black winding
Appendix line.
10   A dig.
        An archaeologist can explain.
The walk is slow at first
Easy, a little black marble wall
Of a dollhouse,
15 A smoothness, a shine
The boys in the street want to give.
One name. And then more
Names, long lines, lines of names until
They are the shape of the U.N. building
20 Taller than I am: I have walked
Into a grave.
And everything I expect has been taken away, like that, quick:

---

[10]can't be stopped

> The names are not alphabetized.
> They are in the order of dying,
> 25   An alphabet of—somewhere—screaming.
> I start to walk out. I almost leave
> But stop to look up names of friends,
> My own name. There is somebody
> Severiano Ríos.
> 30   Little kids do not make the same noise
> Here, junior high school boys don't run
> Or hold each other in headlocks.
> No rules, something just persists
> Like pinching on St. Patrick's Day
> 35   Every year for no green.
>   No one knows why.
> Flowers are forced
> Into the cracks
> Between sections.
> 40   Men have cried
> At this wall.
> I have
> Seen them.

Carmen Tafolla

Carmen Tafolla was born in San Antonio, Texas. Her many publications include *Curandera* (1987), *Sonnets to Human Beings and Other Selected Works* (1995), and *Sonnets and Salsa* (2000). She has also written such children's books as *The Baby Coyote and the Old Woman/El coyotito y la viejita* (2000) and *The Dog Who Wanted To Be a Tiger* (1996). An early pioneer from the Chicano literary movement, Tafolla has held administrative and teaching posts in such schools as Texas Lutheran College and California State University. She has a Ph.D. in Bilingual Education and has performed one-woman shows all over the world.

Letter to Ti

—From Le Van Minh, 15 and Amerasian, after arriving in the U.S. from Viet Nam, having spent the last four years surviving being fed by and carried on the back of a friend called "Ti."

> It is strange being here
> like yellow fog wrapped softly around a dream.
> The wrapping paper comes undone
> and inside I see my face
> 5   reflected.
> Now, I do not try to look less American.
> I should try to look less Vietnamese.

But most times, I just rest,
and don't try anything at all.
10   The time to close one's eyes is good here
Except that I see you,
the stiff hairs on the back of your neck
laying flatter
with the sweat,
15   your hard breathing and your bony shoulders
body-friends to my riding body.
As much as I loved your eyes,
the back of your neck was just as dear to me,
the straining neck smiled just as much,
20   the light shone from around your ears
like the gentle friendship of your face
looking at me.
I knew your neck better than anyone.

Many carry me here.
25   There will be a chair too
in which I can carry myself.
I eat every meal.
I am in a bed at night.
People do not laugh at me
30   for my features,
my spine or legs.
I no longer make paper flowers.

I unwrap gifts from people I do not know.
The wrapping paper falls aside.
35   Sometimes I pick it up and fold it curve it
lay my cheek against it.
"Are you making flowers?" they ask me.
"No.
A neck.
40   The back of a neck,
Four years my home…
and still."

Gina Valdés

Gina Valdés was born in Los Angeles. Her works include *Comiendo Lumbre = Eating Fire* (1997); a work of translations, *Puentes Y Fronteras = Bridges and Borders* (1982, 1997); and the nearly forgotten but influential short story/novel *There Are No Madmen Here* (1981). She has taught language, literatures, and culture at San Diego State University and the University of California San Diego, among other universities. Valdés's work has been published in several collections in the United States, Mexico, and Europe.

Where You From?

Soy de aquí
y soy de allá[1]
from here
and from there
5   born in L.A.
del otro lado.
y de éste[2]
crecí[3] en L.A.
y en Ensenada
10   my mouth
still tastes
of naranjas[4]
con chile
soy del sur
15   y del norte[5]
crecí zurda[6]
y norteada
cruzando fron
teras[7] crossing
20   San Andreas
tartamuda
y mareada[8]
where you from?
soy de aquí
25   y soy de allá
I didn't build
this border
that halts me
the word fron
30   tera splits
on my tongue

---

[1] I am from here and from there
[2] from the other side and this one
[3] I grew up
[4] oranges
[5] I am from the south and north
[6] I grew up left-handed
[7] crossing frontiers
[8] stuttering and dizzy

Adeline Yllanes

Adeline Yllanes is a graduate of Central Connecticut State University and is an active participant in educational organizations for Latino students. She is a first-generation U.S. citizen born to parents of Peruvian descent. Her mother arrived in New York in 1980, a week before she was born. She was raised in Connecticut, far from her roots. She plans on continuing on to a Master's program in school counseling and writing a book about her extensive travels in Latin America.

Peruana Perdida[1]

Where are our heroes?
Our writers, famous singers, Peruvian role models on TV shows?
Blinded by brilliant works of Julia Alvarez, Esmeralda Santiago and
    Tessa Bridal
Latinas, recording their history beautifully, hardships they faced
5   Where are the records of the Peruvians placed?
Tell me I can't find it, I've been searching...
Weeded through pages of arroz con gandules, chuletas and sorullitos[2]
Music of Salsa, Merengue and Bachata...
slowly replacing the Huaynos[3] and Marinera[4] de los abuelos mios[5]
10 Searched in countless libraries...
hasta[6] el Internet
What irony, a search on Amazon.com "Peruvian-American Writers"...
a list of ten books, is all I get
The name Amazon that has a home in our pais[7]...
15 hiding us deeper in the fog, cutting us off from the raiz[8]
Strange, Peru is twenty times bigger than P.R, D.R and Cuba combined
So why is it so difficult to get a hold of what I'm trying to find?
Lost in a cultural abyss...
don't catch them in books I read, shows I see
20 Anybody notice, are they even missed?
Why isn't there literature shining in my face...
I know where you come from...
I'll show you *OUR* place!
Mystifying world, ancestral energy pours from thousand-year-old
    stones...

---

[1]A Lost Peruvian
[2]rice and beans, pork chops, and a Puerto Rican appetizer made of corn
[3]music of the Peruvian Andean people
[4]traditional Peruvian music influenced by Afro-Peruvians and Spaniards
[5]of my grandparents
[6]as far as
[7]country
[8]root

25   Machu Pichu, lost city, our culture zone
Exotic land, electrifying chatter of Quechua, official language of The
        Incan Empire...
sounds that light your soul and continue to inspire
Tierra poderosa[9], where the sky and the Andes collide
Where is that feeling of pride when you feel that no one is on your side?
30   Where is the little girl from Ica going to get her inspiration when she
        can't find it here?
Is she just meant to fade into the haze to forever disappear?
No, no I won't let it be!
Peruanos raise up, hold up your heads
Lift high your silver spoons of mazamorra morada[10]
35   Feel inspiration, our breathtaking views amazing deserts, lush jungles,
        spectacular sea
Costa, sierra, selva, eso es mi Perú[11]
Spit out your caramelos de chicha[12] open your eyes to our rich history
Don't dwell, corrupt politicians sinvergüenzas[13] who took what little
        we had and ran
Feel the energy radiating from Pachamama[14] our Mother Earth, take it
        and run
40   Use that power to tell the world, here we are, we are more than just
        llamas!
Soak up the force from Inti our Father Sun
Wipe your mouth of that chirimoya,[15] da una razon para crecer
        tus ramas[16]
Let us have a revolution, a revolution of words...
Peruanos write down your stories, chronicles of our ancestors fast,
45   before they fade... never to come back
Use the power of the written word to motivate your fellow paisanos[17]
Raise up, mis queridos Peruanos!

---

[9]Powerful land
[10]a dessert made from purple corn
[11]Coastline, mountains, jungle, that is my Peru
[12]candies made from purple corn
[13]shameless
[14]Earth Goddess, wife of Inti, the Sun god
[15]a fruit found mainly in Peru and Ecuador
[16]give a reason to grow your branches
[17]countrymen

DRAMA

José Rivera

José Rivera was born in 1955 in Puerto Rico and has authored *Marisol and Other Plays* (1997), *References to Salvador Dali Make Me Hot and Other Plays* (2003), and other dramatic works that have been performed throughout the U.S. He has earned such honors as the Obie Award (for *Marisol*) and a Whiting Foundation Writing Award, and has been the recipient of a Fulbright Arts Fellowship in Playwriting and grants from the National Endowment for the Arts. He has written for and has had his work produced for television and wrote the screenplay for *The Motorcycle Diaries* (2004). His writing owes something to the magical realism of García Márquez in its otherworldly qualities and the way he blends stark realities with the seemingly fantastic.

Cloud Tectonics

Characters

CELESTINA DEL SOL, in her twenties.
ANÍBAL DE LA LUNA, in his thirties.
NELSON DE LA LUNA, in his twenties.

Place and Time

The Prologue
Los Angeles. The present. Night.

The Play
Same. Later that night.

The Epilogue
Same. Forty years later.

Special thanks to Ivonne Coll
for the Spanish translation
of Celestina's speech.

Prologue

Los Angeles. Night. A bare stage with a floating bed, high in the air, tilted so the upstage headboard is slightly higher than the downstage footboard.

There is a freestanding glass wall downstage. Water drips down the side of the glass wall. It represents a city bus stop during a rainstorm. There are a pair of microphones on C-stands, downstage of the glass wall, a few feet apart.

The Prologue begins with bolero music: Los Panchos singing "Por El Amor De Una Mujer."[1]

---

[1]"For the Love of a Woman."

Celestina del Sol is standing at the bus stop. There's the sound of rain. Celestina is soaking wet. She carries a small shopping bag. She wears a thin maternity dress and she shivers. She looks exhausted, as if she's been wandering on foot for days. It's impossible to tell her actual age. It's impossible to tell if she's rich or poor. She's very, very pregnant.

As the bolero plays, Celestina holds her thumb out, hoping to catch a ride, but there doesn't seem to be any traffic in Los Angeles tonight. She reaches into a pocket, pulls out some saltine crackers and eats them hungrily, savoring each bite.

Car lights wash over Celestina. She sticks her thumb up higher. The lights cruise past her and disappear. Disappointed, Celestina eats another cracker.

We wait for the bolero to end or fade out. A moment's silence, then another car's headlights pass over Celestina. This time they stay on her. She holds her thumb up expectantly. The car's horn beckons her and she happily leaves the wall and goes to one of the microphones. The microphones are suddenly awash in red light.

Aníbal de la Luna enters and goes to the other microphone. Aníbal is a pleasant-looking man, thirties, dressed in an American Airlines ground crew uniform. Aníbal and Celestina perform the following scene into the microphones. At no time do they pantomime being in a car.

During the Prologue, Aníbal's house in the Echo Park section of Los Angeles is loaded in. This should take as long as the Prologue takes to perform.

CELESTINA: *(Shivering)*: Thank you so much for this.
ANÍBAL: Jesus, you're soaked. There's a jacket in the backseat.
CELESTINA: *(Putting on jacket)*: Thank you.

(Short beat.)

ANÍBAL: I can't believe anyone's out in that deluge. They're calling it the storm of the century.
CELESTINA: Where am I?
ANÍBAL: Los Angeles.
CELESTINA *(Troubled)*: Los Angeles?
ANÍBAL: Corner of Virgil and Santa Monica.
CELESTINA *(Means nothing to her)*: Oh.

(Celestina says no more. She just rubs her pregnant stomach and stares ahead. Her silence makes Aníbal a little nervous.)

ANÍBAL: Can you believe this rain for L.A.? *Coño!*[2] Raging floods on Fairfax...bodies floating down the L.A. River...LAX closed...if the Big One came right now, forget it, half this city would die. But that's L.A. for you: disasters just waiting to happen.

(Aníbal laughs. No response from Celestina.)

_____
[2]Damn!

I lived in New York. Lived in every borough except Staten Island. And Brooklyn. And Queens. And the thing is, New York kills its people one by one, you know? A gun here, a knife there, hand-to-hand combat at the ATM, little countable deaths. But this? This L.A. thing? We're talking *mass* death, *mass* destruction. One freak flood at the wrong time of year and hundreds die...the atmosphere sags from its own toxic heaviness and thousands perish...the Big One is finally born, eats a hundred thousand souls for *breakfast*. And I'm not even talking fire season!

(Celestina looks at Aníbal for the first time.)

CELESTINA: Why don't you go back to New York?
ANÍBAL: Are you kidding? I love it here. I have a house here. I have gorgeous fucking incredible-looking women falling outta the sky here! *Coño*, I've made a commitment to that!

(No response from Celestina. She eats a cracker quietly, her mind far away. Aníbal looks at her a long moment.)

You all right?
CELESTINA: The trucker that dropped me off kept touching my knees and I screamed.
ANÍBAL: How long were you out there?
CELESTINA: I don't know.
ANÍBAL: You don't know?
CELESTINA: I don't have a watch...I don't keep a watch...I don't keep "time".... "Time" and I don't hang out together!
ANÍBAL *(Not understanding)*: Oh. Where can I take you?
CELESTINA: I don't know.
ANÍBAL: Where were you hitching to?
CELESTINA: Nowhere. I'm not going anywhere. I don't know where I'm going, I'm sorry.
ANÍBAL: You're just out there hitching? In a hurricane? Pregnant? For fun?
CELESTINA: Are you going to ask me a lot of questions?
ANÍBAL: Why don't I take you to a hospital? Get someone to check out your baby.
CELESTINA: No! No! Don't do that! I don't want doctors asking me a lot of questions!
ANÍBAL: Maybe the police could...
CELESTINA: No police! Please! No police! I don't want to go to the police!
ANÍBAL: No friends or family in L.A.?
CELESTINA: No one. I have no one. You're the only one I have!
ANÍBAL *(Choosing to ignore that)*: Well, you're in my car, I gotta take you somewhere...
CELESTINA: Take me to this baby's father. I'm looking for this baby's father. His name is Rodrigo Cruz. Do you know him? He's a very handsome and dishonest man.

ANÍBAL: No, I don't think I...

CELESTINA: Nobody knows him. I ask everybody. That trucker took me to
every state looking for Rodrigo Cruz!

ANÍBAL: ...I'm sorry...

CELESTINA: I started my journey on Montauk Point: a room in a house, very
small, my Papi sailed boats for tourists, it was some distance back—but I—I
lost all track of "time"—I hate to use that word—"time"—but it's the only
word I have, isn't it?

ANÍBAL: *Coño*, I'm not following this...

CELESTINA: I can give you *details* of Rodrigo Cruz. He worked for Papi repair-
ing the boat. His eyes were ocean green. His back was wrinkled. But I can't
tell you *when* he was like that, okay? He might have *changed*, you see? I can't
tell you his *age*. Do you know how hard it is to find someone when you can't
tell anyone their age?

ANÍBAL: Well, it's not a problem I ever...

CELESTINA: All this traveling has been a blur! It's a huge country! I never
should have left my house in Montauk! I was safe in my house! Papi and
Mami had it all worked out for me! They took away all the clocks!

ANÍBAL *(Completely lost)*: The clocks?

CELESTINA: But I was sleeping when that gorgeous son of a bitch Rodrigo
Cruz came into my room! He knocked me up! He left! Now look at me! I'm
starving and lost and sick of these soggy FUCKING crackers...and I'm just
so tired of being *pregnant*!

ANÍBAL *(Worried)*: Take it easy...

CELESTINA: You can let me out right here, I'm sorry!

ANÍBAL: But we haven't moved. Light's still red.

CELESTINA: Please, I don't want to bother you anymore.

ANÍBAL: I don't want you sleeping outside. Not with a baby coming.

CELESTINA: I've done it before!

(The relentless rain slaps the car as Aníbal contemplates his options.)

ANÍBAL: *Coño*, okay, listen: if you promise me you're not an axe murderer...I
promise you *I'm* not an axe murderer too, okay? You can stay in my house
tonight, okay? Just tonight, okay? I'm right up here in Echo Park, okay?

CELESTINA: I can? I can't.

ANÍBAL: I promise not to touch your knees, okay?

(Celestina looks at Aníbal.)

CELESTINA: What's your name?

ANÍBAL: Oh I'm sorry. Aníbal de la Luna. Nice to meet you.

CELESTINA: I'm Celestina del Sol.

(She reaches out her hand. Aníbal and Celestina shake hands. She smiles.)

Okay. Let's go to your place.

(The light turns green. The lights go down on Aníbal and Celestina. The crew finishes assembling Aníbal's house. Aníbal and Celestina exit. The microphones are struck.)

The lights are dark in Aníbal's house, a modest pre-World War II wooden bungalow, working-class, not Hollywood.

The living room, kitchen and small eating area are basically one room full of sentimental family pictures and second- and thirdhand furniture. The door in the living room leads to the front porch. Another door leads to the bathroom. There are a couple of subtle plaster cracks in the walls from a recent earthquake.

Everything—sink, television, stereo, refrigerator, microwave, VCR, telephone, O'Keefe & Merrit stove, etc.—should be fully functional. There's a Sparkletts water dispenser in the kitchen: the bottle is empty.

The only light in the house comes from the glowing digital clocks on all the appliances. It's 8:05 P.M.

The glass wall has been incorporated into the house. Two ladders have been placed next to the floating bed to make it accessible to the living room.

We hear footsteps. The sound of keys unlocking the front door. The door opens. Suddenly all the digital clocks turn off and come back on blinking a new time: 12:00. It stays 12:00 for the rest of the scene.

Celestina and Aníbal enter from the porch. Both are dripping wet. Celestina now wears a thin suede jacket. Aníbal carries in a five-gallon bottle of Sparkletts water. With the door wide open we hear distant police, ambulance and fire truck sirens. Celestina closes the door and the sirens stop.

ANÍBAL: Watch your step.
CELESTINA: It's a pretty house.
ANÍBAL: It's a craftsman. Built in the forties.
CELESTINA: Is that old?
ANÍBAL: In L.A. it's the Middle Ages.
CELESTINA *(Not understanding)*: Oh.

> *(Aníbal puts the water bottle on the kitchen floor as Celestina takes off the wet jacket. They both take off their waterlogged shoes.)*

ANÍBAL: *(Re: her shoes)*: Just leave them anywhere.
CELESTINA *(Looking around, smiles)*: I'll never forget this as long as I live.
ANÍBAL: Let me turn up the heat. Get some light going here.

> *(Aníbal turns up the heat and turns on some lights. Aníbal looks over at Celestina—getting his first full view of her. She's much more pregnant, and much more beautiful, than he realized. She smiles warmly at him.)*

CELESTINA: You have the most beautiful house, Aníbal.
ANÍBAL: It's dry at least. More than I can say for you.

(Aníbal goes to the bathroom and comes back with a towel, which he tosses to Celestina. She dries her face, arms and feet.)

CELESTINA: You're the kindest, most beautiful man in the world! And this is the happiest night of my life!

ANÍBAL *(Smiles)*: Can I get you anything to drink?

CELESTINA *(Eager)*: Water. Please.

(Aníbal goes to the kitchen.)

ANÍBAL: So please make yourself at home. Sit. Relax.

(Aníbal puts the full Sparkletts bottle on the dispenser. He takes the empty bottle out to the porch: again, as he opens the door, we hear distant sirens, which stop when he closes the door.
  Too happy to sit still, Celestina starts exploring the house, checking out pictures on tables, books on bookshelves, etc.)

CELESTINA: Everything is so beautiful. Everything in order.

ANÍBAL: Debbie does that.

CELESTINA: My little room in Montauk had no order. It wasn't big, but it was my whole world. Things were everywhere, on top of everything: I'd sleep in my clothes, and eat in bed, and read detective novels, hardly ever sleep, dream wide-awake, make plans that were never fulfilled, watch storms coming in, laugh at the moon's neurotic phases, hear stars being scraped across the sky, dance, sing boleros, make love to myself over and over, live a whole life in one room!

(Celestina laughs as she holds herself and does a little dance around the room.)

ANÍBAL *(Giving her a look)*: You want a quesadilla?

CELESTINA: And my Mami and Papi worked so hard for me. They loved me so much. They thought I was cursed! They really did! They put everything in its proper place for me!

(Aníbal looks at Celestina a long moment, not sure what to make of all this.)

ANÍBAL: Your parents thought you were cursed?

CELESTINA: Yeah. They're dead. I'd love a quesadilla.

ANÍBAL: Wait.

CELESTINA: Papi used to cross himself when he looked at me. Mami wouldn't breast-feed me. They kept eighteen statues of Jesus Christ in my room!

ANÍBAL: Wait. Why did you live in one room...?

(Celestina looks at Aníbal, aware of his look. She laughs.)

CELESTINA: I'm not a lunatic. Hey. You're in no danger, stranger. It's just hard for me to tell a story. Straight.

ANÍBAL *(Worried about her baby)*: Just take it easy. For both of you.

CELESTINA *(Touching her stomach)*: This baby must think I'm a lunatic too!

ANÍBAL: But I don't—

CELESTINA: I wonder what this baby hears. Oh God! This baby must've heard me talking to that trucker, and all his dirty words! Ugly, filthy man!

> *(Celestina suddenly gets a fierce contraction that doubles her over. Aníbal goes to her and takes her hand.)*

ANÍBAL: Celestina, please…if you…if you sat down, I'd feel a lot better…

CELESTINA *(Pain)*: Why?

ANÍBAL: 'Cause if you get too agitated, you might…I mean, I don't want you having that baby all over my floor tonight…

CELESTINA: And your floor is so clean!

ANÍBAL: Yes…I mean, you're not, like, *coño, due* tonight, are you?

CELESTINA *(Pain subsiding)*: I don't know.

ANÍBAL: You don't know?

> *(The discomfort goes away and Celestina straightens up again. She smiles as if nothing happened.)*

CELESTINA: I don't think so.

ANÍBAL: Well, wait. How pregnant are you? Exactly.

CELESTINA *(Defensive)*: What do you mean?

ANÍBAL: How far along are you?

CELESTINA: I'm not really sure.

ANÍBAL: You're not *sure?*

CELESTINA: This is the warmest, most enchanting house I've ever…

ANÍBAL: Wait. Isn't knowing how pregnant you are…a little basic? Like knowing your age?

CELESTINA: Yes…yes it is…but you should never ask a woman's age, you might not like what you hear! *(Smiles at him)* Can I have my water?

> *(Aníbal looks at Celestina, then goes to the Sparkletts dispenser and pours Celestina a tall glass of water. He gives it to her.*
>
> *Celestina drinks the water very fast, almost choking on it, like she hasn't had water in a long time. Finished, she holds out her empty glass for more. As Aníbal takes Celestina's empty glass and goes back for a refill, Celestina finds a framed picture of a young woman on a table.)*

CELESTINA: So do you have a lot of "gorgeous fucking incredible-looking women" in your life, Aníbal?

> *(Aníbal hands Celestina the glass of water.)*

ANÍBAL *(Re: photograph)*: Well, no. Well, one. That one.

CELESTINA: She's beautiful.

ANÍBAL: That's Debbie.

(Celestina looks at the photograph a long time. Aníbal waits for her to say something.)

    She's at her office now. She sleeps there a lot. She works for Disney. She answers phones. She's gorgeous. She's Puerto Rican too but she changed her name from Epifania Niguayona Gonzalez to Debbie Shapiro. They still don't respect her. She thinks they do. But she's deluding herself. I can tell. I know guys. I know when a guy is thinking pussy and every guy she works with at Disney is thinking pussy. She thinks they're thinking brain cells. They're not going to make her an executive like she thinks. She's going to remain a receptionist until she turns thirty, then they're gonna fire her and get a younger, prettier, whiter-looking Latin girl to replace her.

CELESTINA: Will she mind my being here?

ANÍBAL: She'd hate it except you're pregnant. Deb doesn't believe in friendship between the sexes, she believes in sex between the sexes. Being pregnant makes you safe.

CELESTINA *(Surprised)*: I'm safe?

ANÍBAL: Guess so.

(Celestina puts the photograph down, finishes her glass of water and looks at Aníbal.)

CELESTINA: What do you believe? Sex or friendship?

ANÍBAL: I believe friendship between the sexes is not only possible, it's preferable. Makes everything cleaner. But then I don't work in the movie business. I load luggage at LAX. There's no sex in that job.

CELESTINA *(Shocked)*: None?

(Beat. Aníbal isn't sure how far he wants this conversation to go, but there's something about Celestina. He can't help but open up to her.)

ANÍBAL: The closest is…I look up at an airplane sometimes and it's full of people going to New York and sometimes I make eye contact with a woman at a window seat in first class. And she's looking down at me, daydreaming, maybe she's afraid of the flight, thinking this could be her last hour on earth, wondering if she's done enough, dared enough, eaten enough, and everyone around her seems dead already. And that fear of crashing is bringing all her latent sexual dreams up from their deep well, and she's getting all excited by her own images—and there *we* are, making split-second eye contact and suddenly that faceless male in her dream world has a pair of eyes…and they are vivid eyes, and they are Puerto Rican eyes, and they are my eyes, Celestina.

(A short silence. Celestina goes to Aníbal. She gets close to him—so close her huge belly gently touches his stomach. She looks into Aníbal's eyes. The intensity of this makes Aníbal a little nervous.)

What are you doing?

CELESTINA: Can I see?

ANÍBAL: Can you see? What? Can you what?

CELESTINA: Your vivid, Puerto Rican eyes, Aníbal, can I see them?

ANÍBAL *(Nervous)*: Why? No.

CELESTINA: Just because. Let me.

ANÍBAL: *Coño*, I brought you here on faith, now. That you're not a killer. Not a psycho. Not a hypnotizing, blood-drinking Scientologist…

(Celestina looks deep into Aníbal's eyes.)

CELESTINA: I think about sex all the time, though I've only had one lover in my life, only one time. Rodrigo Cruz. And I almost had two! That despicable trucker who kept touching my knees. But I ran away from him. I took my chances in the rain. But even he couldn't stop my endless daydreaming and nightdreaming about sex: about Rodrigo's wrinkled back, my legs wrapped around his face…this obsession of mine…this tidal wave that started sometime when I was younger, when I lived in that one room. When Papi bought me a bicycle to give me something else to think about besides my body, and one glorious day I was allowed to ride around and around the house, because my Papi wanted me to count numbers, count numbers, over and over; he said it would teach me about the nature of "time," and I tried and tried, I really did, but I didn't learn anything, I was just so grateful to be outside my little room for once! *(Beat)*

Then Papi hired Rodrigo to work on his boat "The Celestina." And I would stare at him from my window as he worked. He was beautiful. I wondered if I was in love. And he would look back at me and stare and his hair was so long and black. And I wondered is that what love looks like? And I don't know how many years passed…(I didn't know the word "years" then. I learned it on the road when the trucker taught me all kinds of words like "years" and "now" and "yesterday" and "minute" and "century")…and it must have been years…because years are longer than days (I learned this!)…and Rodrigo's hair was long and gray and he snuck into my room and did his dirty thing and left me…and my parents died in the other room and I went out to see because the house had grown so quiet and there they were in their little bed, holding hands, the green bedspread half covering their wrinkled bodies, they were naked and pale and covered in long gray hairs and very, very dead. That's the one time I stopped dreaming of sex when I called the police and told them Mami and Papi were dead, then I got dressed, and I lost all track of "time" and I got scared, and I ran out into the rain because I was sure they'd blame me and in my endless stay in my one room I didn't learn much, but I learned by reading detective novels that when somebody dies the police always come to take you away and kill you with a lightning chair. That's when I hit the road, pregnant, looking for Rodrigo Cruz, angry and excited because he was the only man I ever had sex with and I keep thinking about sex with Rodrigo and I love the word "sex" and if I could fuck fuck fuck all day I would!

(Aníbal impulsively, quickly, kisses Celestina. She gasps. Aníbal turns away.)

ANÍBAL: Let me start those quesadillas for you!

(Aníbal quickly turns on the griddle and busies himself in the kitchen.)

CELESTINA: I should leave.

(Celestina starts to go to the front door.)

ANÍBAL: I don't want you to leave.
CELESTINA: You don't think I'm strange?
ANÍBAL: I do think you're strange. But I don't want you to leave.
CELESTINA: But I don't know how long I've been here. I don't know if it's been too long! I should go!
ANÍBAL *(Re: the kiss)*: I'm sorry I did that! I never do that!
CELESTINA: Have I been here minutes? Days?! Shit! I knew this would happen!
ANÍBAL: A half hour at the most! Twenty minutes. Not days.
CELESTINA: Are you sure?

(Aníbal looks at his watch.)

ANÍBAL: My watch stopped.
CELESTINA *(Knew this would happen)*: I really have to go before Rodrigo turns into an unrecognizable old man and dies!

(Aníbal looks at all the digital clocks in the house—all are blinking 12:00.)

ANÍBAL: The clocks have stopped...

(Celestina goes to put on her shoes and the wet jacket.)

CELESTINA: I can't miss my chance to make that bastard do right by me!

(Celestina goes to the door, opens it. We hear sirens. Aníbal grabs Celestina's arm, physically stopping her from running out.)

ANÍBAL: Celestina, wait a second—
CELESTINA: *I can't wait a second; I don't know what you mean!*
ANÍBAL: You've been here only a few *minutes*. Just minutes. Tomorrow morning, when the sun comes up, it'll be only a few *hours*...

(Beat. She looks at him.)

CELESTINA: Hours? Is it a lot?
ANÍBAL: *Coño*...I think something has happened to you, Celestina, some kind of trauma, and you're not making any *sense*...
CELESTINA *(Offended)*: I have not lost my mind.
ANÍBAL: Please. Eat dinner. Sleep on the sofa bed. In the morning, we'll have a big breakfast and I'll give you some money. Drive you wherever you want, okay?

(Aníbal goes to the kitchen and comes back with another glass of water. He holds it out for Celestina. Still thirsty, Celestina comes back in and takes the glass of water.)

CELESTINA: Your beauty is overwhelming, Aníbal.

(Aníbal closes the door. The sirens stop. Celestina takes off her shoes and the jacket.

Keeping a watchful eye on Celestina as she drinks the water, Aníbal goes to the kitchen, opens the refrigerator and takes out packets of tortillas, cheese, salsa and guacamole. As Aníbal prepares dinner, he can't help but look at her in wonder.)

ANÍBAL: Who are you, Celestina?

(Celestina smiles at the inevitable question, then thinks a moment. She starts setting the table for dinner as Aníbal puts the tortillas and cheese on the hot griddle.)

CELESTINA: How do you know what "time" feels like, Aníbal?

(Aníbal looks at her a second.)

In your body? You feel it, don't you? Pushing at your heart muscles. Pricking the nerves in your brain. Turning some on, turning some off. Is that what "time" feels like? And where *is* "time"? Is the organ for "time" the heart? Is it the spinal chord, that silver waterfall of nerves and memories: is "time" in there? Is it the gonads? Does "time" have a sound? What bells, Aníbal, what vibrating string played by what virtuoso accompanies the passage of "time"? Is "time" blue? Does it taste like steak? Can you fuck it? Or is it just the invisible freight train that runs you over every single day…breaking you into smaller and smaller pieces…pieces so small they can't hold your soul to the earth anymore, and *that's* why you die? C'mon, Aníbal, help me out here!

ANÍBAL: We just know. Common sense tells us.

CELESTINA: Well, then…what if there are people born who don't have that sense? Don't have that inner clock telling them when a moment has passed, when another has started, how a day feels different from a year. What would you say to such people?

ANÍBAL: *Coño:* your imagination…

CELESTINA: And what if these people don't progress through space and "time" the same way you do? They don't age smoothly. They stay little far longer than they should. Or the rhythms of the day mean nothing. So they sleep for weeks at a "time." They stay awake all winter scaring the shit out of their parents! They can make love for two weeks straight without a break!

ANÍBAL: I don't know.

(Beat.)

CELESTINA: No. Of course not. How could you?

(Dinner is ready. The table is set. Celestina looks at the table appreciatively.)

I should wash my hands.

ANÍBAL *(Re: the bathroom)*: That way.

(Celestina starts to go off. Then she looks at Aníbal. She goes to him, kisses him on the cheek and embraces him. He holds her close.)

CELESTINA: Papi told me he was twenty-five when I was born. Before he died, we celebrated his seventy-ninth birthday. When the trucker picked me up outside of Montauk Point, I was pregnant and starting to show. When we crossed the frontier into Los Angeles, before he touched my knees, he put two candles on a little cake and said we were celebrating two years together. *(Beat)* So that's who I am: I'm a fifty-four-year-old woman, Aníbal, and I've been pregnant with this baby for two years.

(Celestina goes to the bathroom and closes the door. Aníbal is alone. Aníbal goes to the telephone in the living room. Picks it up. It's dead. Aníbal slams it down.)

ANÍBAL: Shit.

(Aníbal goes to the TV and turns it on. All he can get, channel after channel, is static. He turns on a radio. More static.

Aníbal goes back to the kitchen and hides all the knives. There's a knock at the door. Aníbal looks at the door, worried. A second knock. Aníbal goes to the door and opens it. Sirens.

Aníbal's younger brother, Sergeant Nelson de la Luna, is there. Nelson, twenty-five, is taller, broader than his older brother: he has a sweet baby face, short hair and a little mustache. Nelson wears an army-issue raincoat and army boots.)

Nelson?

NELSON *(Big smile)*: Brother!

(Nelson laughs and scoops up Aníbal in a big bear hug. The brothers kiss and pound each other's backs.)

ANÍBAL: Son of a bitch, Nelson, what the fuck are you doing here?!

NELSON: Surprise! Nice *house!*

(Nelson comes in, takes off his raincoat. Underneath he wears army-issue T-shirt, khakis, dog tags, etc. Aníbal still can't believe his brother's there. He closes the door. Sirens stop.)

ANÍBAL: Look at you. Fucking amazing. Are you alone?

NELSON: No, I got half the company out in the Grand National, asshole. Man look at you. You old.

ANÍBAL: Fuck you too. What an asshole; didn't even *call* me...

NELSON: Surprise, surprise, how much you pay for this dump?

ANÍBAL: What a dickhead! So what's up? I thought you were in Germany.

NELSON: Not anymore, bro. They shipped my ass to Fort Benning, Georgia, six months ago. Then they sent my ass out here for two days.

ANÍBAL: Are you in training for something? Getting ready to invade some hapless Third World country?

NELSON: "Hapless." What a homo. You got a beer?

(Nelson goes to the refrigerator and helps himself to a beer.)

ANÍBAL: Have a beer.

NELSON: I'm fucking out in Death Valley now. It's a fucking *lake*. I thought you lived in sunny Southern California, jerk-off.

ANÍBAL: It rains out here too, asswipe. *Coño*, it's great to see you, Nelson.

(They embrace exuberantly again, pound backs.)

NELSON: So yeah, got my ass shipped to Death Valley, I'm good to go, bro, desert training for the Middle East or some towel-head shithole with oil underneath it...fucking tanks all over the place, blow up anything stupid enough to get in our way—mostly stray sheep and coyotes—'cause we're *men*, Aníbal, not pussies like you: men, MEN!

ANÍBAL *(Laughs)*: Get outta my face with that shit.

NELSON: Yo, it beats jerkin' off all day like you, so this is your *house* finally, I gotta get me one of these, I guess loading luggage really pays, what: you helpin' smuggle drugs 'n' shit?

ANÍBAL *(Laughs)*: How long are you staying?

NELSON: Man, I'm hosed. I gotta be back in Death Valley oh-five-hundred tomorrow morning for a fucking dipshit meeting with my C.O. that's only supposed to last five *minutes*. So I can only hang 'bout an hour, 'cause the roads suck tonight.

ANÍBAL *(Disappointed)*: An hour? Nelson, I haven't seen you in six years.

NELSON: Time flies, motherfucker!

ANÍBAL: So why can't you call the guy—?

NELSON: No way. Gotta *be* there. They gotta *see* my ass in front of the C.O., in person. It's really fucking stupid.

ANÍBAL: The army's perfect for you.

NELSON *(Re: Aníbal)*: What a waste of a human being. Man, you get uglier and stupider all the time.

ANÍBAL: You're just pissed my mother loved me and she didn't love you.

(Nelson starts looking for the bathroom.)

NELSON: Aw shit, where's the head, man? All I've eaten is beef jerky and I gotta take a massive dump.

ANÍBAL: You're a poet, Nelson, you know that? A poet of our time.

NELSON: Yo, eat me!

ANÍBAL: There's somebody in the bathroom. A woman.

NELSON *(Surprised)*: You got a woman in your bathroom, Aníbal?

ANÍBAL: Her name is Celestina. I picked her up tonight.

NELSON *(Big smile)*: Brother! You're *not* a total waste!

> *(Nelson high-fives Aníbal.)*

ANÍBAL: No, she's pregnant, Nelson, and she's...I think...mentally disturbed or something...or she's living in a dream world, I don't know.

NELSON: Women.

ANÍBAL: She looks like she's twenty-five years old but she *says* she's fifty-four.

NELSON: That's fucking L.A., bro.

ANÍBAL: And she says she's been pregnant for two years.

NELSON: And you picked her up? *You're* not an asshole!

ANÍBAL: She was hitching. In this storm. I can't drive by somebody like that.

NELSON: A total fairy. What a liberal. Is she cute?

ANÍBAL: She's gorgeous.

NELSON: Oh well, that's cool. I could fuck an insane pregnant girl if she's gorgeous.

ANÍBAL: Don't be a pig, Nelson—

NELSON: What? I'll have that bitch howlin' at the moon!

ANÍBAL: She's not—

NELSON: Hey, I've been in a *tank* nine *weeks*, bro, I'm ready to seduce *goats*. Swear: my mother must've been exposed to radiation when you were born.

ANÍBAL *(Laughs)*: Fuck you through the head.

NELSON: *You're* the fucking poet of our time! Asshole! Liberal! I'mma fuckin' body slam you!

> *(Nelson lunges at Aníbal. Aníbal fights him off. They wrestle around the living room, knocking furniture around, laughing. Nelson catches Aníbal.*
>
> *Nelson lifts Aníbal over his head and prepares to body slam him.)*

ANÍBAL: Nelson—*DOOOOOOON'T*!!

> *(Celestina comes in. She's got a gun. She aims it at Nelson's head. Both men freeze.)*

NELSON: Oh shit.

ANÍBAL: Celestina...?

NELSON *(Already admiring her)*: Training and instinct tell me that's a gun.

CELESTINA: Put him down.

> *(Nelson quickly puts Aníbal down. Celestina continues pointing the gun at Nelson.)*

ANÍBAL: Celestina. Could you please put that away—it's fine...

CELESTINA: Who is he?

ANÍBAL: —this is my brother—Nelson—this is Nelson, it's okay...

(Celestina reluctantly puts the gun in a pocket. Both men are greatly relieved. Nelson laughs nervously.)

NELSON: Whoa. Fuckme. I love L.A.!

ANÍBAL: I didn't know you were armed, Celestina. *Christ.*

CELESTINA: I stole it from the trucker while he was sleeping.

NELSON: Whoa.

ANÍBAL *(Still shaken)*: Jesus.

CELESTINA: I'm sorry, Aníbal, I...

ANÍBAL: It's cool. It's just—*coño.* Heart attack.

CELESTINA: I wanted to protect you.

NELSON *(To Aníbal)*: She wanted to protect you, asshole!

ANÍBAL *(To Nelson)*: I'm not crazy about guns.

NELSON *(To Celestina)*: I am. *(Sotto to Aníbal)* She's gorgeous, man. Introduce.

ANÍBAL *(Wary)*: Fuck. Nelson, this is Celestina. Celestina, this is my little brother, Nelson.

(Celestina goes to shake Nelson's hand.)

CELESTINA *(To Nelson)*: Nice to meet you.

NELSON *(Big charming smile)*: So Celestina, what's *up*?!

ANÍBAL *(Sotto to Nelson)*: Nelson...slow...

NELSON *(Sotto to Aníbal)*: Step back or I'll body slam you...

ANÍBAL *(Sotto to Nelson; re: Celestina)*: ...*disturbed*...?

NELSON *(To Celestina)*: ...I'm married, okay? But. I'm separated from my wife. Bitch left me. Got drunk one night, said: "You know, Nelson, deep inside o' my heart, I just don't like you fucking little greasy Puerto Ricans!" I said, "Fuck you, 'ho" and threw a hand grenade at her.

CELESTINA *(Amused)*: You threw a hand grenade...?

ANÍBAL *(Horrified)*: You threw a hand grenade...?

NELSON *(Defensive)*: It didn't go off! We filed for divorce. That little baby got a father?

CELESTINA: I'm looking for him. His name is Rodrigo Cruz.

NELSON: You married to him?

CELESTINA: No but I'm going to make him!

NELSON: You love this man?

CELESTINA: I don't know.

NELSON: Well, if you don't find him, let me know. I love children. I understand children. You have beautiful eyes, Celestina.

CELESTINA: Thank you.

ANÍBAL: I may vomit.

NELSON: I can't stay too long, Celestina. I'm serving our country in the armed forces of the U.S. Protecting us from...uhm...not communists...uhm...illegal aliens, drug kingpins and Arabs. It's dangerous work. My life is on the line each and every day. But I'm good to go! And the thing is, I gotta be back in Death Valley tonight—*Death* Valley, so appropriate, huh?—I have very important meetings with high-ranking officers—then I go to Fort Benning, Georgia, Monday to finalize my divorce from my cracker wife. And then, in about two years, I'll be getting my discharge from the army. What I'm saying is...I won't be back this way for a while. But I'm gonna come back in two years and look you up, okay? And if you ain't found that baby's father, I just might ask you to marry me, 'cause no woman should raise her baby alone. You understand? This cool with you, Celestina? Can I ask you?

CELESTINA *(Not knowing what to say)*: Uhm. You can ask me.

NELSON: Yes! Good! Well, my work is done here. Bye.

(Nelson goes to his raincoat and starts putting it on.)

ANÍBAL: What do you mean? What are you doing?

NELSON: I gotta get back to Death Valley. Duty calls.

ANÍBAL: Right *now?*

NELSON *(Looking at his watch)*: No! My watch died! Fuckit. Yes. I gotta go. I'll take my dump on the road. I'm fucked I'm not there.

ANÍBAL: This is happening too fast—

NELSON: What's life? A fucking *blink*. Get used to it. And thanks for introducing me to the woman of my dreams, homeboy.

(Celestina smiles. Then she gets another pain in her belly.)

CELESTINA: Ohhhhhhhh.

(Nelson and Aníbal quickly go to Celestina.)

ANÍBAL AND NELSON: You okay??

CELESTINA *(Still in pain)*: It's okay. Thank you. *(Another jolt)* Why is my baby doing this? Why is he tapping my spine with his fingers? What code is that? What words?

(Nelson looks at her pregnant stomach.)

NELSON: May I?

(Celestina nods yes and Nelson kneels at her feet and rubs her belly. The pain slowly subsides. Celestina smiles with relief.)

CELESTINA: Thank you, Nelson.

(Nelson puts his head on her stomach, listening to the sounds inside.)

NELSON: Check it out. I can hear the ocean! Stars being scraped across the sky!

CELESTINA *(Delighted)*: You can?

NELSON: I hear a little body searching for the way out. Little bones. *(To her stomach)* Yo in there. I'mma wait for you, little man. Be the father of your dreams. You come outta this deep night you're in, *hijo de mi alma*, see my big-ass smile, you're gonna know what sunshine is! That cool? And you tell your beautiful mami to wait for me, okay *mijo*?

> *(Nelson kisses Celestina's stomach. Moved, Celestina gently kisses the top of Nelson's head.*
> *Nelson gets up. Nelson and Aníbal have a long embrace.)*

ANÍBAL: Six years, Nelson. Six fucking years.
NELSON: This is the happiest night of my life!

> *(Nelson opens the door. Sirens. He disappears into the rain. Aníbal goes to the door.)*

ANÍBAL: You'll never get to Death Valley in that rain...
NELSON *(Off)*: A *man* would!

> *(Aníbal watches Nelson driving away, his back to the audience. Aníbal sadly waves goodbye. Celestina looks at Aníbal. Aníbal closes the door, Sirens stop.*
> *Celestina is watching Aníbal, who is quiet a long moment, his mind far away.)*

CELESTINA: You okay?

> *(Beat. He tries to smile. He starts clearing up the kitchen table.)*

ANÍBAL: Are you really going to wait for him? Two years?
CELESTINA: I don't know what "two years" means, Aníbal.

> *(Aníbal rubs his tired eyes—then looks at his watch—then realizes it's not working.)*

ANÍBAL: I don't even know what time it is. It could be next week. I don't remember this morning. I don't remember kissing Debbie goodbye or working or eating or driving from LAX or finding a hitchhiker in the storm of the century. And was my fucking little *brother* really here? I can't believe he's a *man* already! Ten minutes ago, *I* was body slamming *him*!
CELESTINA: Why don't we eat?
ANÍBAL *(Trying to focus)*: Eat. Yeah. Eat.

> *(Aníbal and Celestina sit at the kitchen table. Celestina can hardly wait and immediately stuffs her mouth with food, eating with the passion of a starving person.)*

CELESTINA *(Mouth full)*: This is the best food!
ANÍBAL *(Concerned)*: Easy...Celestina...easy...

> *(Aníbal and Celestina continue their dinner. This should take it's natural time—despite the speed with which Celestina attacks her food—and should happen in silence.*

All the while Aníbal and Celestina may make periodic eye contact—smile—look away—sometimes Aníbal finds himself staring—sometimes Celestina does.

Suddenly the house is rocked by several claps of harsh thunder. The lightning outside lights up the house through the windows brighter than could possibly occur in nature.

Celestina looks at Aníbal.)

CELESTINA: *Me pregunto…me pregunto como será haberte amado en cada etapa de tu vida, Aníbal.*[3]

(Beat. He looks at her and she continues in Spanish.)

Amar al niñito que fuiste, y tomarte de la mano, y ayudarte a cruzar la calle, y besar tu barriguita gordita de bebé, y peinar tus greñitas de chiquillo. Y luego, mas adelante, amar al anciano en que te convertiste, y besar tus arrugas profundas, y suavizar tu pelo canoso, y deleitar tu sabio y cansado corazón, y mirar fijamente hacia adentro de esos ojos misteriosos, mas alla de las cataratas, y muy adentro de tí, bacia los verdes prados donde uno nunca envejece. ¿No te parecería lindo tener ese tipo de amor, Aníbal? ¿El amor de toda una vida?[4]

(Beat. Aníbal smiles nervously.)

ANÍBAL: What?
CELESTINA: What?
ANÍBAL: I didn't know you could speak Spanish.
CELESTINA *(Smiles): Solamente hablo Español cuando estoy enamorada.*[5]
ANÍBAL: What?

(Beat.)

CELESTINA: Don't you speak *any* Spanish?
ANÍBAL *(Sad)*: I don't.
CELESTINA: You don't?
ANÍBAL: I don't.
CELESTINA: Why not?
ANÍBAL: Sometimes…I don't know…you forget things…
CELESTINA: But how do you forget a *language?*
ANÍBAL: It happened, Celestina. It's not nice and I'm not proud of it, but it happened.

---

[3] I ask myself…I ask myself what it would be like to have loved you in every phase of your life.
[4] Love the child you were and take your hand, and help you cross the street, and kiss your fat baby belly, and comb your tangles. And then, love the elderly person that you become, and kiss your profound wrinkles, and soften your gray hair, and please your wise and tired heart, and gaze inside those mysterious eyes, beyond the waterfalls, and deep inside you, toward the green meadows where one never ages. Wouldn't it be beautiful to have this type of love, Aníbal? The love of a lifetime?
[5] I only speak Spanish when I'm in love.

CELESTINA: I'm sorry.

ANÍBAL: All I know is "*coño.*"

CELESTINA *(Laughs)*: Well, "*coño*"'s useful.

(Celestina laughs sadly. Aníbal laughs with her. He looks at her. She reaches out a hand. He takes it and holds it a moment.)

ANÍBAL *(Pulling away)*: I'll get the sofa bed ready for you.

(Beat.)

CELESTINA: Okay. I'll help you set up.

(During the following speech, Aníbal goes to the sofa bed, pulls it out. He goes to the closet and comes back with pillows, blankets and sheets. Together he and Celestina make the sofa bed. If necessary for timing, Aníbal could go through whatever bedtime ritual he needs: turning off lights, locking the door, turning on the security system, taking out the trash, etc.

Toward the end of the speech, while Aníbal is deeper in his memories, he stops looking at Celestina. Behind Aníbal, facing upstage, Celestina takes off her maternity dress and slips into a nightgown she keeps in her shopping bag. She lets her long hair down. She looks more unearthly, more angelic than ever.)

ANÍBAL: I made love with Debbie just last night. Or was it this morning? *(Beat)* I had to talk her into spending the night, instead of sleeping in her office again. It seems like a million years ago. *(Beat)* I know Debbie from high school in the Bronx. We went out. Then she went out of state for college and I couldn't afford college so I stayed behind and worked. She married her English professor and moved to Ohio. I wanted to kill myself. I spent the next five years getting into these other relationships. The first one, I was twenty-two. The woman I fell in love with was thirty-nine. We had a great time together. But I took her home to meet my parents and my father made a pass at her and it was over. Then I fell in love with a blonde. She was a real beauty. But she came from this fucked-up home and she had a drug problem and she drank too much and the night I told her I didn't love her anymore she tried to throw herself out of a moving car on the Belt Parkway. Then I fell in love with a series of lesbians. Every woman I liked turned out to be gay! Then one night, New Year's Eve, I'm living in the Lower East Side, the phone rings, it's Debbie. She left her husband. She left Ohio. She was staying at her sister's in Harlem. Would I like to get together. *(Beat)* I went to her place. I didn't know what to expect. She was staying in one of those worn-out tenements with the steam heat up too high and the steel radiators that clamored all night, and Willie Colón and laughing and partying and loud kissing coming at you from all the apartments all over us. People just exploding! Going nuts! I remember the smell of *tos—tos—*

CELESTINA: *Tostones!*

ANÍBAL: *Tostones!* And rice and beans and *lechón—lechón—*
CELESTINA: *Lechón asado!*
ANÍBAL: *Lechón asado!* You know: everything cooked with a lot of *man—*
CELESTINA: *Manteca!*
ANÍBAL: *Manteca!* And I held Debbie all night long. We didn't fuck. I kissed her a lot. We touched all over. But we didn't go to bed. We were starting over. I was figuring out this new body. She seemed richer. All the years we hadn't seen each other, miles she's traveled, all this married wisdom and experience she had that I didn't have. I felt like a *boy*, a child, in the arms of this mature *woman*. We decided that night to go to Los Angeles together and start over. Be in that one city where you can really remake yourself. Pan for gold in the L.A. River. She wanted to get rich on the movies. I wanted to get away from the racists who thought of me only as a spik. *(Beat)*
        As we were holding each other, touching each other, I started to remember something I thought I had forgotten. It was when I was a little boy. I don't even remember how old. We were living in Newark, New Jersey. We were visiting my cousins who lived in a big house in Patchogue, Long Island. My child's memory makes that house enormous, like a Victorian haunted house, but maybe it wasn't. They had thirteen kids. We used to watch *lucha libre*[6] together, professional wrestling, all the time. One time my cousin Ernesto got carried away watching Bruno San Martino on TV and he punched me in the stomach. Ernie liked to inflict pain. He had long, black curly hair and a thin black mustache, freckles, large, red lips, crooked teeth: he was the cousin that looked most like me. Another night, after a party, my cousin Cheo told me how he could feel his balls flapping around in his pants when he danced to American music. He balls went flap-flap-flap when he danced to rock 'n' roll. I liked Cheo. He never punched me like Ernesto did. Cheo taught me about exponents and square roots. He went to Vietnam. Everybody thought Ernesto would get into drug dealing. *(Beat)*
        One night I was on the second floor of my cousins' house. I remember walking past a dark bedroom: the door was open. I thought I heard a voice inside calling my name. I went in. My cousin Eva was there. She was older than Ernie or Cheo. Much older than me. I remember her standing by the window. I could see her face lit up by a streetlight—or was it the moon? I remember there was a heavy smell in the room. And I don't know how I eventually got there...but I ended up lying in bed with Eva. I was on my back, looking at the ceiling. Eva was kneeling next to me. Then Eva lifted her dress and she was straddling me and pressing her pelvis into me. I think she had her underwear on. I had my pants on and I didn't know why she was doing this to me, though I knew I had to do this because she was my older cousin, therefore she had authority. I remember her legs being smooth. I remember her face. She was looking out the window. I don't remember how long this lasted. I don't remember if anyone came in. I don't remember if anyone ever knew about this, though, later

---

[6]wrestling

on it seemed that everybody knew. I liked Eva on top of me. I remember her weight. I liked her weight. I don't remember if I got hard or not: I was only a little boy! I liked watching Eva's face, the way she looked out the window. How the light struck half her face. I wish I could remember her mouth! I think it was open. But I don't remember. Was there a smile? Did she bite her lower lip? Was she talking to me? Did she say something in Spanish? I remember her eyes. *(Beat)*

So I fell in love with Eva. She was all I thought about. And I think my mother suspected something and she was worried about us, though first cousins had married several times in my family. One night my mother and I were washing dishes together, side by side. And we had the only conversation about sex we were ever to have. Without looking at me, she said: "Aníbal, remember: there is some fruit you are not allowed to eat." And that's all she said. And I knew *exactly* what she meant. And it was all she had to say to me. *(Beat)*

I've never forgotten Eva. Even in Debbie's arms after five years of missing her and wanting her, I thought easily of Eva. It's like...the space around my body was permanently curved—or dented—by Eva's heaviness. I wonder if love sometimes does that to you. It alters the physics around you in some way: changing the speed of light and the shape of space and how you experience time.

CELESTINA: What do you think made you fall in love with those women?

ANÍBAL: Do you think I know?

(Aníbal turns around to look at Celestina, who has changed into her nightgown. She smiles at him. Beat.)

CELESTINA: Would you rub my feet?

ANÍBAL: What?

CELESTINA: Would you rub my feet? They're freezing.

(Beat.)

ANÍBAL: Uhm, sure.

(Beat. Celestina sits on the sofa bed and puts her bare feet up expectantly. Aníbal sits with her, her feet on his lap. He gently rubs her feet. She closes her eyes in bliss.)

CELESTINA: Hmmmmmm...yeah...

(Celestina seems to fall asleep, a look of peace and serenity on her face. Aníbal looks at her a moment and can't help but smile.)

ANÍBAL: *Buenas noches.*

(Aníbal starts to get up. Celestina opens her eyes.)

CELESTINA: Kiss my toes.

ANÍBAL: ...What?

CELESTINA: Just once?

ANÍBAL: Kiss your—what—?
CELESTINA: Please? Just once?

>   *(Beat.)*

ANÍBAL: Okay.

>   *(Aníbal kisses her toes one by one. She smiles with each little kiss, trying
>   not to giggle, eyes still closed.*
>   >   *Aníbal finishes and starts to leave.)*

CELESTINA: No you don't.
ANÍBAL: Now what?
CELESTINA: Higher.
ANÍBAL: ...Higher?
CELESTINA: Up the body.
ANÍBAL: Okay.

>   *(Aníbal kisses her knees. Celestina sighs deeply, stretching out.)*

CELESTINA: Little higher.

>   *(Aníbal kisses her thighs. Celestina whispers.)*

Up.

>   *(Aníbal kisses her enormous stomach.)*

More up.

>   *(Aníbal kisses her breasts.)*

Keep going.

>   *(Aníbal kisses her neck.)*

...Home, traveler. You're home!

>   *(Aníbal kisses Celestina lightly once on the lips. They hold each other a
>   long moment. We hear the sound of the rain beating against the house.
>   They don't look at each other as they talk.)*

ANÍBAL: I'm afraid.
CELESTINA: Don't be.
ANÍBAL: Not about bodies. I'm afraid we're going to be mixing my sad dreams
   with your wild ones.
CELESTINA *(Smiles)*: Maybe they'll have beautiful children, Aníbal.

>   *(Aníbal kisses her gently on the lips. She opens her mouth to him and
>   takes him in, kissing him back with all the passion in her body.)*

ANÍBAL: Celestina.

>   *(Celestina speaks to Aníbal as she holds him.)*

CELESTINA: I'm a stranger in my own body, Aníbal. A stranger to my own past. My memories don't make sense to me. I doubt everything. I don't even believe what people verify for me. I even wonder if my real name is Celestina del Sol! *(Beat)* Sometimes you're with somebody and you don't seem so strange to yourself anymore. Somehow, by luck or chemistry or divine intervention or insanity, you collide with another life, and there's an explosion followed by peace. For a second, a year, fifty years—whatever those things mean—you feel you've reached some kind of home. Sometimes there's no "time"—only an endless now that needs to be filled with life. To be rescued from habit and death. *(Beat)* C'mon.

ANÍBAL: Okay.

> *(Aníbal takes Celestina's hand and leads her to the ladders which go up to the floating bed.*
>
> *As they climb the ladders, the rest of the house seems to disappear and be replaced by vague twinkling stars and crescent moons and dark, silvery clouds.*
>
> *As they reach the bed, there's another knock at the door.*
>
> *The house instantly changes back to its normal state, like a spell broken. Aníbal looks at the door.)*

CELESTINA *(Sotto)*: Who's that?

ANÍBAL *(Sotto)*: Stay.

> *(Aníbal climbs down the ladder. Celestina stays up on the bed, partially hidden from view by the downstage footboard.*
>
> *Aníbal opens the door. Sirens. Aníbal is surprised by the sight of hundreds of Sparkletts water bottles covering the porch.*
>
> *Nelson is there. Nelson looks different. His hair is slightly longer. His mustache is gone. His army clothes have been replaced by blue jeans, sneakers and an old jean jacket. He walks with a cane.*
>
> *But that's not the only thing that's changed. Something child-like and happy has been taken away from Nelson. Though he mouths some of the same old lines, they lack his spirit.)*

Nelson?

NELSON *(Tired smile)*: Brother!

> *(Nelson scoops up Aníbal in a bear hug and pounds his back.)*

ANÍBAL *(Confused)*: What are you doing here?

> *(Nelson holds Aníbal for a long time. Aníbal has to pull away. Nelson won't let him.)*

NELSON: Look at you! You get older and uglier all the time!

ANÍBAL: Everything okay?

NELSON: Fucking just wanna hold you, man.

> *(Aníbal, worried, pulls away from Nelson.)*

ANÍBAL: What happened? Couldn't you get back to Death Valley? Are the freeways closed?

NELSON: Death *Valley?* What are you talking about? Everything's great. Hey,
I'm a free man! I can do whatever I want now!

ANÍBAL *(Noticing)*: Hey, what happened to you? Why's your face like that?

> *(Nelson comes into the living room, closing the door behind him. Sirens
> stop. Nelson looks around.)*

NELSON: Fuckme, the old place hasn't changed at all. Everything's just the way
I remember it!

ANÍBAL: Wait. Wait a minute. What happened to you? You look totally—why
are your clothes like that?

NELSON: Jesus, will you get over my *appearance?* What are you, *gay?* I'm lucky
to be *alive*, motherfucker. I need a beet.

> *(Nelson goes to the refrigerator to get a beer.)*

ANÍBAL *(Still confused)*: Have a beer.

NELSON: I was pissed at you, bro. I don't mind telling you. All my letters to
you came back, your phone's been disconnected, I thought, "That asshole
moved without telling me! He makes me drive cross-country—three fucking
days—and he's not there, I'mma kill him!"

ANÍBAL: You've been driving three days?

NELSON: Hello? From *Georgia?* Have you gone *stupid?* You have no *memory?*
What did I tell you two years ago? Soon's I get to Benning, get my discharge
and my divorce from Mein Kampf, I was comin' back here, find that girl, and
ask her to marry me.

> *(A short beat as Aníbal looks at Nelson.)*

ANÍBAL: Two years? Nelson are you drunk? That was only a few minutes ago
you left here and said that.

NELSON *(Laughs)*: You gotta get outta L.A., bro. Your *brain!*

ANÍBAL: A half hour—

NELSON: Maybe to *you!* Mr. Lalaland! You still got on the same boring clothes
you had that night! And wasn't it raining then?

ANÍBAL *(Nervous, worried)*: Cut the shit, Nelson...

NELSON: *You* cut the shit or I'll body slam you! Where's Celestina? You hiding
her? Did she have her baby? Does the baby know who I am? Does he ask
about me? I bet he loves me!

ANÍBAL *(Trying to focus)*: She...she uh...

NELSON: And you! You fuck! Why did all my letters come back? You think it
was fun being out in fucking Bosnia and not hearing from you all that fucking time!? Fuck you!

ANÍBAL: Bosnia?

NELSON: Yo, the *war?* The Battle of Mostar? Are you stoned or what? Don't
they get the news in L.A.? *(Nelson reaches into his raincoat and pulls up a*

handful of medals. He throws them across the room, one by one.) R-com with two oak-leaf clusters! Army Achievement Medal! Bronze Star with three oak-leaf clusters! Silver star with two oak-leaf clusters! Bosnia Liberation Medal!

(Nelson laughs and digs into another pocket and pulls out a dozen letters he wrote to Aníbal, all of which were returned to him. Aníbal looks with amazement at their postmarks.)

ANÍBAL: These letters are from Bosnia.

NELSON: Beautiful land. I met a pregnant girl, too. Man, I really wanted to marry her—broke my heart to leave her—but "no," I said, "I have the most beautiful girl named Celestina waiting for me in the States!"

(Aníbal, shaking, puts the letters down.)

ANÍBAL: How can one night be two years…Celestina…?

(Celestina sits up in the bed and climbs down the ladder to the living room during the following:)

NELSON: They had to fucking put me in a fucking army hospital 'cause I have a fucking nervous *breakdown*? I thought: I gotta live through this so I can see my bride and my child again! And I said this to myself, Aníbal, over and over, like a prayer, and you know *that was the only thing* that kept some fucking Serbian sniper bullet from finding the back of my head or some land mine from erasing my legs. The unbearable luck of her *name*!

(Celestina is in the living room. Nelson turns to face her. He can't believe what he sees.)

CELESTINA: Hi Nelson.

(A long pause as Nelson just takes her in and smiles.)

NELSON: Hey.

CELESTINA: How are you?

NELSON: That's really you.

CELESTINA: It's really me.

NELSON *(Answering her question)*: I'm a little tired. Ass hurts from driving three days from Georgia!

(Nelson starts to cry. Celestina goes to him.)

CELESTINA: Hey, hey, what is it?

NELSON: Nothing. It's nothing. No problem.

(Celestina wipes Nelson's eyes.)

CELESTINA: I heard what happened to you in the war. I'm really sorry.

NELSON: It's over. I lived. I'm gonna forget it as soon as I can.

CELESTINA *(Touching her stomach)*: I have a lot to tell you…as you can see…

NELSON: Oh yeah! Uh-huh! I can see a lot has happened in your life, Celestina!

ANÍBAL *(To Celestina)*: Do you know what's going on here?

CELESTINA *(Torn)*: Don't be afraid, Aníbal, please…

NELSON *(Not listening)*: But what's weird? I'm looking at you. It's like you never aged a day!

CELESTINA: That's because I haven't!

NELSON: And you're pregnant again. Just like that night!

CELESTINA: It's not—Nelson—that's what I have to tell you—and you know I'd only tell you the truth. You left Los Angeles. You went to war… but here, in this house, time didn't pass; it's still the same night; you left a little while ago. And this baby…it's Rodrigo's baby…do you understand that…?

NELSON *(Laughs)*: Fuck you!

CELESTINA: It's the truth!

NELSON: I can't believe you would lie to me!

CELESTINA: And Aníbal—two years have passed—whether you want to believe it or not!

ANÍBAL: How is that possible?

CELESTINA: It's me, Aníbal. I've infected you! I've changed the "time" around you—

ANÍBAL: But—who's been paying the light bill?! Who's been paying the rent?! Where's Debbie been?! What happened to my job?!

NELSON: What the fuck are you two trying to do to me?!

CELESTINA *(To both men)*: Things have *happened*…

NELSON *(Overlapping with Celestina)*: Look, I *know* that's Aníbal's baby! Okay?! I can see what happened!

CELESTINA: Nothing happened!

NELSON: You two fell in love! It's cool! And I guess we didn't make any promises to each other, huh Celestina?

CELESTINA: I'm sorry, Nelson…

NELSON: So I just want to see that little baby before I go! Where is he? Where's that little boy I talked to? Did something happen to him?!

CELESTINA: He hasn't been born!

NELSON *(Angry)*: Man, I don't need to hear this double-talk BULLSHIT any more! Fuck you both! I don't give a fuck if you two fell in love with each other! I was stupid to think you would wait for me! But you didn't! *You didn't wait for me, did you!?*

> *(Nelson makes a move toward Celestina. Aníbal tries to protect her. Nelson grabs Aníbal, lifts him up and body slams him into the floor.*
> *Celestina goes to Aníbal and holds him. Aníbal writhes in pain, speechless. Nelson is breathing hard, instantly sorry he hurt his brother.*
> *Silence.*
> *Nelson quietly cries.)*

ANÍBAL: *(In pain)*: Oh my God.

NELSON: I'm sorry, bro. I'm not myself. Something in myself got taken out
sometime as I was looking through the sights of the tank, lining up targets,
watching things blow up. Jesus shit! I got so much I gotta forget!

ANÍBAL: Jesus Christ, bro…

> *(Nelson goes to Aníbal, lifts him and puts him gently on the sofa bed.
> He holds Aníbal.)*

NELSON: I'm sorry, bro, you know I fucking love you, man! I'm a total asshole!
I shouldn't have come here! You got something good with your woman,
man, that's cool, that's great! I gotta step aside and let your happiness be,
man! Fuck me! I'm sorry! You're my fucking brother and I'm sorry!

ANÍBAL: Nelson…

> *(Nelson wipes his eyes and goes to the door. He opens it. Sirens. Nelson
> runs out into the night.)*

Nelson? Nelson!

> *(Aníbal gets up to follow Nelson.)*

CELESTINA: Aníbal—don't leave me alone!

> *(Aníbal goes to the door.)*

ANÍBAL: I gotta talk to him!

> *(Aníbal runs out into the night to chase down Nelson, closing the door
> behind him.*
>
> *Celestina is alone. She goes to the door and waits for Aníbal. She
> closes the door. She opens it again. She closes it again. She sits.*
>
> *In moments she has no idea how much time has passed since Aníbal
> left. For all she knows it could be days, weeks later. She's getting more and
> more nervous. Nervousness gives way to panic. She shakes. She looks around.*
>
> *Unable to bear the pain of waiting any longer, Celestina gets
> quickly dressed. She puts on her shoes and Aníbal's suede jacket. She goes
> to the door.*
>
> *Celestina runs out into the night, leaving the door open.*
>
> *The digital clocks stop blinking and a new time comes on: 8:06.*
>
> *Aníbal comes in. He's got his arm around Nelson, who is soaking
> wet and looks disheveled. Aníbal helps Nelson sit. Nelson sits with his face
> in his hands. Aníbal closes the door behind him. Sirens stop. Aníbal looks
> very shaken.)*

ANÍBAL *(To Nelson)*: …it's okay…it's okay, bro…you're home…

NELSON: Thanks, man.

ANÍBAL: Celestina! I found him! Bet you thought we'd never get back! Took all
night but I got him!

> *(No answer. Aníbal goes to the offstage bathroom.)*

Celestina?

(No response. Aníbal goes back to the living room.)

Celestina!

NELSON: Celestina!

ANÍBAL: Goddammit.

NELSON: Where is she?

ANÍBAL: Her shoes are gone…the jacket…all the clocks are going…she's taken off…*shit!*…stay here…*(He grabs a coat and runs out into the rain. From off-stage:)* Celestina!

The door closes with a slam. Nelson is left alone onstage. Lights start to go down on him.)

NELSON: Celestina.

(Lights to black. The sound of the rain stops. Nelson calls out in the dark, silent house.)

Celestina!

(Blackout.)

Epilogue

In the dark, the bolero from the Prologue starts again, though quieter, distorted if possible. Lights come up downstage.

During Celestina's speech, the crew comes on and disassembles the house. By the end of Celestina's speech, there should be nothing left of Aníbal's house in Echo Park.

The ladders next to the bed are removed and the bed is lowered to the stage. The glass wall is removed from the house and left freestanding, to the side. Water drips down the side of the glass wall, as in the Prologue. A microphone on a C-stand is placed down center.

It's forty years later.

Celestina enters and goes to the microphone. She's no longer pregnant. Her clothes are nicer than before. But otherwise she looks the same. She's pushing a stroller. She wears Aníbal's aged suede jacket. She's talking to the baby. She's in mid-conversation.

CELESTINA: Can you believe this rain for L.A.? *Coño! (Beat)* The last time I was here it was raining just like this, right before you were born, and Los Angeles has changed so much, *mijo.*[7] I can't get over it. The Big One was finally born—a monster with seven epicenters—releasing unimaginable waves of energy and killing many unprepared people—the six active oil fields on Pico exploded—glass came down from the towers in Downtown and Century City and Burbank like floating guillotines—there were fourteen million refugees—and Los Angeles died for a while. People went back to New York and the Midwest. There was a long sleep. *(Beat)*

[7]son

But people came back. They came back for the things they loved about L.A. the first time. They rebuilt the city. And the city was reborn—and now it's better than ever! Look, *mijo*, you see? That building over there? That's the White House. They moved it from Washington, D.C., and put it on Wilshire Boulevard. And there's the United Nations building and the World Trade Center. All of it is here in the new L.A. The new capital of the United States. The capital of world culture and trade. The capital of the Third World. Boy, they really fixed this place up, Aníbal! The largest subway system in the world is here, connecting everything from Catalina Island to the Angeles National Forest. The air is clean! It's chic to read! All the street signs are in Spanish! They integrated all the neighborhoods! There are no more poor sections! No more big earthquakes for another one hundred and fifty years! In L.A., that's forever!

> (*The house has been completely dismantled and removed from the stage. It looks like the opening of the play. The bolero ends or fades out.*
> *In the dark, Aníbal enters and lies on the bed.*
> *Celestina pushes the stroller to the bed.*
> *Lights on the bed go up. We can see clearly that Aníbal is an old man in his seventies. Aníbal lies in bed, reading a book.*
> *The light around the bed goes very dark, leaving the bed in limbo. The vague twinkling stars, crescent moons and dark, silvery clouds of the earlier scene could return: it should seem as if once again the bed were floating in space.*
> *Celestina goes to Aníbal's side and she looks at him a long moment.*)

CELESTINA (*Big smile*): Is that really you, Aníbal?
ANÍBAL (*Looking up from his book*): Huh?
CELESTINA: It's me, Aníbal! I'm back! I just got into L.A.! I didn't think I'd remember how to get to Echo Park—but that bus stop at Virgil and Santa Monica is still there—and your house is exactly the same—the earthquake didn't hurt it—I can't believe my luck!

> (*Aníbal looks at Celestina a long moment. He doesn't remember her.*)

ANÍBAL: Are you the new nurse?
CELESTINA: It's me. It's Celestina! I'm back!
ANÍBAL: You're not the new nurse? Who's going to give me a bath?
CELESTINA: ...I'm Celestina.
ANÍBAL: Who is Celestina?
CELESTINA: Aníbal, stop it.
ANÍBAL: Who are you?

> (*Beat.*)

CELESTINA: Celestina del Sol.

> (*Celestina waits for the name to click in Aníbal's memory. It doesn't. Aníbal holds out his hand.*)

ANÍBAL: I'm Aníbal de la Luna. Nice to meet you.

(Disappointed, Celestina shakes hands with Aníbal.)

CELESTINA: Nice to meet you.

ANÍBAL: Are you here for the house? It's a craftsman. Built in the last century. In the forties.

CELESTINA: Don't you remember me at all?

ANÍBAL: When did we meet?

CELESTINA: I think it was forty years ago, but I can't be sure.

ANÍBAL: Forty years! *Coño!* Memory doesn't go back that far!

CELESTINA: It's just like yesterday for me! You picked me up by the side of the road. I was pregnant. You took me to this house. We had quesadillas! You rubbed my feet!

ANÍBAL: I did?

CELESTINA: I remember every moment of that night! I never stopped thinking about you! And I meant to come back sooner, but I just lost track of the "time"!

ANÍBAL: It couldn't have been forty years ago. Eyesight isn't so hot—these damn cataracts, you know?—but—you're a kid. What're you, twenty-five? Twenty-six?

(Slight beat.)

CELESTINA: I'm not really sure.

(This response seems to jog something in Aníbal's memory, but he isn't sure what.)

ANÍBAL: Well, if you're here for the house, make yourself at home, look around—it's a craftsman!

CELESTINA: I know it's a fucking craftsman, Aníbal!

ANÍBAL *(Laughs; re: baby)*: And who's that little guy?

CELESTINA: My son. I think I was in labor with him for six months!

ANÍBAL: Again, please?

CELESTINA: Never mind!

ANÍBAL: How old is he?

CELESTINA: Do you think I know?

ANÍBAL: Why do I feel like I've had this conversation before?

CELESTINA: His name is Aníbal. Aníbal del Sol y la Luna. His father's dead. Rodrigo's body was pulled out of the L.A. River in the storm of the century.

ANÍBAL: *Coño!*

CELESTINA: It was the night that we met, Aníbal. Your brother was in the army. You had a girlfriend named Debbie.

ANÍBAL: Debbie? You're a week too late. We buried her last week in Anaheim. Disney did a fucking hell of a job burying my wife, let me tell you. Those people know how to throw a funeral! They are true merchants of death!

CELESTINA: So you married her, huh?

ANÍBAL: Had to. Knocked her up.

CELESTINA: And Nelson?

ANÍBAL: He's a war hero, you know. Lives up the street. Married a beautiful girl many years ago...a Bosnian. They have thirteen kids!

CELESTINA *(Smiles)*: Good.

(Aníbal stares at Celestina a long moment.)

ANÍBAL: You look...*coño*...you look so familiar. You look vaguely like...there was a young woman...on a night that seemed to last forever...she was... crazy...and very fat...

CELESTINA: I was pregnant!

ANÍBAL: ...but it was some forty years ago...before the Big One...before they moved the capital...something happened to me back then...I blacked out for a couple of years...nobody could explain it...I woke up and it was two years later! I had dreams in my coma that made no sense! *(Laughs)* But you know what? It was so long ago and so much has happened since then, so much life, so much dying, so many changes, it just gets buried under all the time between now and then, you know? It's like, somewhere in my mind is a ditch, a very dark and deep hole, and time keeps filling this hole with all the debris of my life, the *details*: every name, face, taste, sound: gone! Down the hole! Outta reach! *Coño!* What's the point of that, huh? Does that make any sense to you?

CELESTINA: No.

ANÍBAL: No. You're very beautiful, though. Kind. It would be nice to remember you. To have been in love with you.

CELESTINA: We were in love, Aníbal.

ANÍBAL: How do you know we were in love?

CELESTINA: We lived together for two years, didn't we?

ANÍBAL: We did?

CELESTINA: They were the happiest two years of my life.

ANÍBAL: You sure it was me?

(Beat. Celestina wipes her tears, then reaches out, touches his hand and kisses it.)

CELESTINA: I should probably let you get some sleep. It's been great seeing you again, Aníbal.

ANÍBAL: Yes.

CELESTINA: You take care of yourself, okay?

ANÍBAL: Thanks for dropping by. Listen, this house is a steal at this price! Great place to raise a family!

CELESTINA: I'll keep that in mind.

ANÍBAL: Yes. Good.

CELESTINA: Is there anything I can do for you before I go?

(Beat.)

ANÍBAL: Yes there is.

CELESTINA: What?

ANÍBAL: Would you rub my feet? They're freezing.

(Beat.)

CELESTINA *(Smiles)*: Okay.

> *(Celestina gets into bed with Aníbal. He puts his feet up on her lap. She rubs his feet gently. The feeling of her hands on his feet has an instant and electrifying effect on Aníbal. When he talks, he sounds like a young man again.)*

ANÍBAL: I searched Los Angeles for days and days after she left me. I went to that bus stop on the corner of Virgil and Santa Monica and waited there day and night. I called every hospital and went to every police station in L.A. County. *(Beat)* I imagined finding her. Living with her forever. I imagined long moments of silence between us when we didn't have anything to say. I imagined enduring the terror of a Los Angeles gone out of control because these quiet moments would be like iron wings and we'd be sheltered inside them. We wouldn't hear the noise of the earthquakes or the screams of a dying culture. But she never came back to me. I never saw her again. All I kept were memories of that extraordinary woman and a night that had that dream feeling to it, you know that feeling: there's a sound like suspended music, air that doesn't move, time that doesn't add to itself. It took me years but I finally understood that I had encountered a true mystery that night, that I had taken a living miracle into my house. That Celestina del Sol was from a world I would never understand. That sometimes Nature improvises. That Nature created a woman that lived outside the field of time and may never die. That someday everyone who ever knew her and remembered her would be gone. That she would live forever in that physical perfection like some kind of exiled and forgotten goddess. And that trying to understand such a life, and why love matters to it, why a god would need to be loved too, was like trying to understand the anatomy of the wind or the architecture of silence or cloud tectonics. *(He laughs)* Yeah. What better way to respond to a miracle than to fall in love with it?

> *(During the following, lights start to go down on the bed. The sound of the rain comes up.)*

And at one point in the evening, I heard the sound of Spanish, as love assumed the language my parents spoke the night I was conceived, the language I had forgotten...

> *(Celestina kisses Aníbal. She leaves the bed, takes the baby out of the stroller and starts walking to the bus stop with the baby in her arms.)*

Celestina said to me: "*Me pregunto como será haberte amado en cada etapa de tu vida, Aníbal...*"

(Aníbal continues the speech in Spanish, quietly, underneath Celestina's simultaneous, and louder, translation:)

CELESTINA *(To the baby)*: ...I wonder what it would be like to love you in every age of your life, Aníbal. To love the little boy you were, and hold your hand, and lead you across the street, and kiss your fat little baby stomach, and comb your little boy's hair. And then, later, to love the old man you've become, and kiss your deep wrinkles, and smooth out the gray hair, and delight your wise and tired heart, and stare into those mysterious eyes, past the cataracts, and deep into you, to the green landscapes where you never age. Wouldn't it be sweet to have that kind of love, Aníbal?

ANÍBAL: *"...El amor de toda una vida."*

(Celestina has reached the bus stop with the baby.)

CELESTINA: ...The love of a lifetime.

(Aníbal smiles sadly at the sweet memory. Then he forgets it again and goes back to his book as if nothing happened.
Lights slowly to black on the bed.
At the dark bus stop, Celestina holds her thumb up, hoping to catch a ride out of Los Angeles. She reaches into a pocket and pulls out saltine crackers. She gives one to the baby and eats the other.
Rain. Headlights. Blackout.)

ESSAY
Gloria Anzaldúa

Best known for her groundbreaking first book, *Borderlands/La Frontera: The New Mestiza* (1987), Anzaldúa also collaborated with Cherríe Moraga to edit the collection *This Bridge Called My Back: Writings by Radical Women of Color* (1983), which led in 2002 to a second similar effort entitled *This Bridge We Call Home: Radical Visions for Transformation*. Born in 1942 in South Texas, she wrote essays, stories, children's books, and poetry. Her writing often combines genres and mixes Spanish with English, confronting the tensions and alienation of the fringes of her Latina world. She died in May 2004.

La conciencia de la mestiza / Towards a New Consciousness

Por la mujer de mi raza hablará el espíritu.[1]

Jose Vascocelos, Mexican philosopher, envisaged *una raza mestiza, una mezcla de razas afines, una raza de color—la primera raza síntesis del globo.* He

---

[1]This is my own "take off" on Jose Vasconcelos' idea. Jose Vasconcelos, *La Raza Cósmica: Misión de la Razalbero-Americana* (México: Aguilar S.A. de Ediciones, 1961). [Anzaldúa's note]

called it a cosmic race, *la raza cósmica*, a fifth race embracing the four major races of the world.[2] Opposite to the theory of the pure Aryan, and to the policy of racial purity that white America practices, his theory is one of inclusivity. At the confluence of two or more genetic streams, with chromosomes constantly "crossing over," this mixture of races, rather than resulting in an inferior being, provides hybrid progeny, a mutable, more malleable species with a rich gene pool. From this racial, ideological, cultural and biological cross-pollinization, an "alien" consciousness is presently in the making—a new *mestiza* consciousness, *una conciencia de mujer*. It is a consciousness of the Borderlands.

Una lucha de fronteras / A Struggle of Borders

> Because I, a *mestiza*,
> continually walk out of one culture
> and into another,
> because I am in all cultures at the same time,
> *almaentre dos mundos, tres, cuatro,*
> *me zumba la cabeza con lo contradictorio,*
> *Estoy norteada por todas las voces que me hablan*
> *simultáneamente.*

The ambivalence from the clash of voices results in mental and emotional states of perplexity. Internal strife results in insecurity and indecisiveness. The mestiza's dual or multiple personality is plagued by psychic restlessness.

In a constant state of mental nepantilism, an Aztec word meaning torn between ways, *la mestiza* is a product of the transfer of the cultural and spiritual values of one group to another. Being tricultural, monolingual, bilingual, or multilingual, speaking a patois, and in a state of perpetual transition, the *mestiza* faces the dilemma of the mixed breed: which collectivity does the daughter of a darkskinned mother listen to?

El choque de un alma atrapado entre el mundo del espíritu y el mundo de la técnica a veces la deja entullada. Cradled in one culture, sandwiched between two cultures, straddling all three cultures and their value systems, *la mestiza* undergoes a struggle of flesh, a struggle of borders, an inner war. Like all people, we perceive the version of reality that our culture communicates. Like others having or living in more than one culture, we get multiple, often opposing messages. The coming together of two self-consistent but habitually incompatible frames of reference[3] causes *un choque*, a cultural collision.

5   Within us and within *la cultura chicana*, commonly held beliefs of the white culture attack commonly held beliefs of the Mexican culture, and both attack commonly held beliefs of the indigenous culture. Subconsciously, we see an

---

[2]Vasconcelos. [Anzaldúa's note]

[3]Arthur Koestler termed this "bisociation." Albert Rothenberg, *The Creative Process in Art, Science, and Other Fields* (Chicago, IL: University of Chicago Press, 1979), 12. [Anzaldúa's note]

attack on ourselves and our beliefs as a threat and we attempt to block with a counterstance.

But it is not enough to stand on the opposite river bank, shouting questions, challenging patriarchal, white conventions. A counterstance locks one into a duel of oppressor and oppressed; locked in mortal combat, like the cop and the criminal, both are reduced to a common denominator of violence. The counterstance refutes the dominant culture's views and beliefs, and, for this, it is proudly defiant. All reaction is limited by, and dependent on, what it is reacting against. Because the counterstance stems from a problem with authority—outer as well as inner—it's a step towards liberation from cultural domination. But it is not a way of life. At some point, on our way to a new consciousness, we will have to leave the opposite bank, the split between the two mortal combatants somehow healed so that we are on both shores at once and, at once, see through serpent and eagle eyes. Or perhaps we will decide to disengage from the dominant culture, write it off altogether as a lost cause, and cross the border into a wholly new and separate territory. Or we might go another route. The possibilities are numerous once we decide to act and not react.

A Tolerance For Ambiguity

These numerous possibilities leave *la mestiza* floundering in uncharted seas. In perceiving conflicting information and points of view, she is subjected to a swamping of her psychological borders. She has discovered that she can't hold concepts or ideas in rigid boundaries. The borders and walls that are supposed to keep the undesirable ideas out are entrenched habits and patterns of behavior; these habits and patterns are the enemy within. Rigidity means death. Only by remaining flexible is she able to stretch the psyche horizontally and vertically. *La mestiza* constantly has to shift out of habitual formations; from convergent thinking, analytical reasoning that tends to use rationality to move toward a single goal (a Western mode), to divergent thinking,[4] characterized by movement away from set patterns and goals and toward a more whole perspective, one that includes rather than excludes.

The new *mestiza* copes by developing a tolerance for contradictions, a tolerance for ambiguity. She learns to be an Indian in Mexican culture, to be Mexican from an Anglo point of view. She learns to juggle cultures. She has a plural personality, she operates in a pluralistic mode—nothing is thrust out, the good the bad and the ugly, nothing rejected, nothing abandoned. Not only does she sustain contradictions, she turns the ambivalence into something else.

She can be jarred out of ambivalence by an intense, and often painful, emotional event which inverts or resolves the ambivalence. I'm not sure exactly how. The work takes place underground—subconsciously. It is work that the soul performs. That focal point or fulcrum, that juncture where the mestiza stands, is where phenomena tend to collide. It is where the possibility of uniting all that

---

[4]In part, I derive my definitions for "convergent" and "divergent" thinking from Rothenberg, 12–13. [Anzaldúa's note]

is separate occurs. This assembly is not one where severed or separated pieces merely come together. Nor is it a balancing of opposing powers. In attempting to work out a synthesis, the self has added a third element which is greater than the sum of its severed parts. That third element is a new consciousness—a mestiza consciousness—and though it is a source of intense pain, its energy comes from continual creative motion that keeps breaking down the unitary aspect of each new paradigm.

10   *En unas pocas centurias*, the future will belong to the mestiza. Because the future depends on the breaking down of paradigms, it depends on the straddling of two or more cultures. By creating a new mythos—that is, a change in the way we perceive reality, the way we see ourselves, and the ways we behave—*la mestiza* creates a new consciousness.

The work of *mestiza* consciousness is to break down the subject-object duality that keeps her a prisoner and to show in the flesh and through the images in her work how duality is transcended. The answer to the problem between the white race and the colored, between males and females, lies in healing the split that originates in the very foundation of our lives, our culture, our languages, our thoughts. A massive uprooting of dualistic thinking in the individual and collective consciousness is the beginning of a long struggle, but one that could, in our best hopes, bring us to the end of rape, of violence, of war.

La encrucijada / The Crossroads

> A chicken is being sacrificed
> at a crossroads, a simple mound of earth
> a mud shrine for *Eshu*,
> *Yoruba* god of indeterminacy,
> who blesses her choice of path.
> She begins her journey.

Su cuerpo es una bocacalle. La mestiza has gone from being the sacrificial goat to becoming the officiating priestess at the crossroads.

As a *mestiza* I have no country, my homeland cast me out; yet all countries are mine because I am every woman's sister or potential lover. (As a lesbian I have no race, my own people disclaim me; but I am all races because there is the queer of me in all races.) I am cultureless because, as a feminist, I challenge the collective cultural/religious male-derived beliefs of Indo-Hispanics and Anglos; yet I am cultured because I am participating in the creation of yet another culture, a new story to explain the world and our participation in it, a new value system with images and symbols that connect us to each other and to the planet. *Soy un amasamiento*, I am an act of kneading, of uniting and joining that not only has produced both a creature of darkness and a creature of light, but also a creature that questions the definitions of light and dark and gives them new meanings.

We are the people who leap in the dark, we are the people on the knees of the gods. In our very flesh, (r)evolution works out the clash of cultures. It makes us crazy constantly, but if the center holds, we've made some kind of evolutionary step forward. *Nuestra alma el trabajo*, the opus, the great alchemical work; spiritual *mestizaje*, a "morphogenesis,"[5] an inevitable unfolding. We have become the quickening serpent movement.

15   Indigenous like corn, like corn, the *mestiza* is a product of crossbreeding, designed for preservation under a variety of conditions. Like an ear of corn—a female seed-bearing organ—the *mestiza* is tenacious, tightly wrapped in the husks of her culture. Like kernels she clings to the cob; with thick stalks and strong brace roots, she holds tight to the earth—she will survive the crossroads.

> *Lavando y remojando el maíz en agua de cal, despojando el pellejo, Moliendo, mixteando, amasando, haciendo tortillas de masa.*[6] She steeps the corn in lime, it swells, softens. With stone roller on *metate*, she grinds the corn, then grinds again. She kneads and moulds the dough, pats the round balls into *tortillas*.

> We are the porous rock in the stone *metate*
> squatting on the ground.
> We are the rolling pin, *el maíz y agua,*
> *la masa harina. Somos el amasijo.*
> *Somos lo molido en el metate.*
> We are the *comal* sizzling hot,
> the hot *tortilla*, the hungry mouth.
> We are the coarse rock.
> We are the grinding motion,
> the mixed potion, *somos el molcajete.*
> We are the pestle, the *comino, ajo, pimienta,*
> We are the *chile colorado,*
> the green shoot that cracks the rock.
> We will abide.

El camino de la mestiza / The Mestiza Way

Caught between the sudden contraction, the breath sucked in and the endless space, the brown woman stands still, looks at the sky. She decides to go down, digging her way along the roots of trees. Sifting through the bones, she shakes

---

[5]To borrow chemist Ilya Prigogine's theory of "dissipative structures." Prigogine discovered that substances interact not in predictable ways as it was taught in science, but in different and fluctuating ways to produce new and more complex structures, a kind of birth he called "morphogenesis," which created unpredictable innovations. Harold Gilliam, "Searching for a New World View," *This World* (January, 1981), 23. [Anzaldúa's note]

[6]*Tortillas de masa harina*: corn tortillas are of two types, the smooth uniform ones made in a tortilla press and usually bought at a tortilla factory or supermarket, and *gorditas*, made by mixing *masa* with lard or shortening or butter (my mother sometimes puts in bits of bacon or *chicharrones*). [Anzaldúa's note]

them to see if there is any marrow in them. Then, touching the dirt to her forehead, to her tongue, she takes a few bones, leaves the rest in their burial place.

She goes through her backpack, keeps her journal and address book, throws
away the muni-bart metromaps. The coins are heavy and they go next, then the
greenbacks flutter through the air. She keeps her knife, can opener and eyebrow
pencil. She puts bones, pieces of bark, *hierbas*, eagle feather, snakeskin, tape
recorder, the rattle and drum in her pack and she sets out to become the complete *tolteca*.

Her first step is to take inventory. *Despojando, desgranando, quitando paja.*
Just what did she inherit from her ancestors? This weight on her back—which
is the baggage from the Indian mother, which the baggage from the Spanish
father, which the baggage from the Anglo?

Pero es difícil differentiating between *lo heredado, lo adquirido, lo impuesto.*
She puts history through a sieve, winnows out the lies, looks at the forces that
we as a race, as women, have been a part of. *Luego bota lo que no vale, los
desmientos, los desencuentos, el embrutecimiento. Aguarda el juicio, hondo y
enraízado, de la gente antigua.* This step is a conscious rupture with all oppressive traditions of all cultures and religions. She communicates that rupture,
documents the struggle. She reinterprets history and, using new symbols, she
shapes new myths. She adopts new perspectives toward the darkskinned,
women and queers. She strengthens her tolerance (and intolerance) for ambiguity. She is willing to share, to make herself vulnerable to foreign ways of seeing and thinking. She surrenders all notions of safety, of the familiar.
Deconstruct, construct. She becomes a *nahual*, able to transform herself into
a tree, a coyote, into another person. She learns to transform the small "I" into
the total Self. *Se hace moldeadora de su alma. Según la concepción que tiene de
sí misma, así será.*

Que no se nos olvide los hombres

> "*Tú no sirves pa' nada*—
> you're good for nothing.
> *Eres pura vieja.*"

"You're nothing but a woman" means you are defective. Its opposite is to
be *un macho*. The modern meaning of the word "machismo," as well as the
concept, is actually an Anglo invention. For men like my father, being "macho"
meant being strong enough to protect and support my mother and us, yet
being able to show love. Today's macho has doubts about his ability to feed
and protect his family. His "machismo" is an adaptation to oppression and
poverty and low self-esteem. It is the result of hierarchical male dominance.
The Anglo, feeling inadequate and inferior and powerless, displaces or trans-
fers these feelings to the Chicano by shaming him. In the Gringo world, the
Chicano suffers from excessive humility and self-effacement, shame of self and
self-deprecation. Around Latinos he suffers from a sense of language inade-

quacy and its accompanying discomfort; with Native Americans he suffers from a racial amnesia which ignores our common blood, and from guilt because the Spanish part of him took their land and oppressed them. He has an excessive compensatory hubris when around Mexicans from the other side. It overlays a deep sense of racial shame.

20   The loss of a sense of dignity and respect in the macho breeds a false machismo which leads him to put down women and even to brutalize them. Coexisting with his sexist behavior is a love for the mother which takes precedence over that of all others. Devoted son, macho pig. To wash down the shame of his acts, of his very being, and to handle the brute in the mirror, he takes to the bottle, the snort, the needle, and the fist.

Though we "understand" the root causes of male hatred and fear, and the subsequent wounding of women, we do not excuse, we do not condone, and we will no longer put up with it. From the men of our race, we demand the admission/acknowledgment/disclosure/testimony that they wound us, violate us, are afraid of us and of our power. We need them to say they will begin to eliminate their hurtful put-down ways. But more than the words, we demand acts. We say to them: We will develop equal power with you and those who have shamed us.

It is imperative that mestizas support each other in changing the sexist elements in the Mexican-Indian culture. As long as woman is put down, the Indian and the Black in all of us is put down. The struggle of the mestiza is above all a feminist one. As long as *los hombres* think they have to *chingar mujeres* and each other to be men, as long as men are taught that they are superior and therefore culturally favored over *la mujer*, as long as to be a *vieja* is a thing of derision, there can be no real healing of our psyches. We're halfway there—we have such love of the Mother, the good mother. The first step is to unlearn the *puta/virgen* dichotomy and to see *Coatlapopeuh-Coatlicue* in the Mother, *Guadalupe*.

Tenderness, a sign of vulnerability, is so feared that it is showered on women with verbal abuse and blows. Men, even more than women, are fettered to gender roles. Women at least have had the guts to break out of bondage. Only gay men have had the courage to expose themselves to the woman inside them and to challenge the current masculinity. I've encountered a few scattered and isolated gentle straight men, the beginnings of a new breed, but they are confused, and entangled with sexist behaviors that they have not been able to eradicate. We need a new masculinity and the new man needs a movement.

Lumping the males who deviate from the general norm with man, the oppressor, is a gross injustice. *Asombra pensar que nos hemos quedado en ese pozo oscuro donde el mundo encierra a las lesbianas. Asombra pensar que hemos, como femenistas y lesbianas, cerrado nuestros corazónes a los hombres, a nuestros hermanos los jotos, desheredados y marginales como nosotros.* Being the supreme crossers of cultures, homosexuals have strong bonds with the queer white,

Black, Asian, Native American, Latino, and with the queer in Italy, Australia and the rest of the planet. We come from all colors, all classes, all races, all time periods. Our role is to link people with each other—the Blacks with Jews with Indians with Asians with whites with extraterrestrials. It is to transfer ideas and information from one culture to another. Colored homosexuals have more knowledge of other cultures; have always been at the forefront (although sometimes in the closet) of all liberation struggles in this country; have suffered more injustices and have survived them despite all odds. Chicanos need to acknowledge the political and artistic contributions of their queer. People, listen to what your *jotería* is saying.

25   The mestizo and the queer exist at this time and point on the evolutionary continuum for a purpose. We are a blending that proves that all blood is intricately woven together, and that we are spawned out of similar souls.

Somos una gente

> *Hay tantísimas fronteras*
> *que dividen a la gente,*
> *pero por cada frontera*
> *existe también un puente.*
> —Gina Valdés[7]

Divided Loyalties. Many women and men of color do not want to have any dealings with white people. It takes too much time and energy to explain to the downwardly mobile, white middle-class women that it's okay for us to want to own "possessions," never having had any nice furniture on our dirt floors or "luxuries" like washing machines. Many feel that whites should help their own people rid themselves of race hatred and fear first. I, for one, choose to use some of my energy to serve as mediator. I think we need to allow whites to be our allies. Through our literature, art, *corridos*, and folktales we must share our history with them so when they set up committees to help Big Mountain Navajos or the Chicano farmworkers or *los Nicaragüenses* they won't turn people away because of their racial fears and ignorances. They will come to see that they are not helping us but following our lead.

Individually, but also as a racial entity, we need to voice our needs. We need to say to white society: We need you to accept the fact that Chicanos are different, to acknowledge your rejection and negation of us. We need you to own the fact that you looked upon us as less than human, that you stole our lands, our personhood, our self-respect. We need you to make public restitution: to say that, to compensate for your own sense of defectiveness, you strive for power over us, you erase our history and our experience because it makes you feel guilty—you'd rather forget your brutish acts. To say you've split yourself

---

[7]Gina Valdés, *Puentes y Fronteras: Coplas Chicanas* (Los Angeles, CA: Castle Lithograph, 1982), 2. [Anzaldúa's note]

from minority groups, that you disown us, that your dual consciousness splits off parts of yourself, transferring the "negative" parts onto us. (Where there is persecution of minorities, there is shadow projection. Where there is violence and war, there is repression of shadow.) To say that you are afraid of us, that to put distance between us, you wear the mask of contempt. Admit that Mexico is your double, that she exists in the shadow of this country, that we are irrevocably tied to her. Gringo, accept the doppelganger in your psyche. By taking back your collective shadow the intracultural split will heal. And finally, tell us what you need from us.

By Your True Faces We Will Know You

I am visible—see this Indian face—yet I am invisible. I both blind them with my beak nose and am their blind spot. But I exist, we exist. They'd like to think I have melted in the pot. But I haven't, we haven't.

The dominant white culture is killing us slowly with its ignorance. By taking away our self-determination, it has made us weak and empty. As a people we have resisted and we have taken expedient positions, but we have never been allowed to develop unencumbered—we have never been allowed to be fully ourselves. The whites in power want us people of color to barricade ourselves behind our separate tribal walls so they can pick us off one at a time with their hidden weapons; so they can whitewash and distort history. Ignorance splits people, creates prejudices. A misinformed people is a subjugated people.

30 Before the Chicano and the undocumented worker and the Mexican from the other side can come together, before the Chicano can have unity with Native Americans and other groups, we need to know the history of their struggle and they need to know ours. Our mothers, our sisters and brothers, the guys who hang out on street corners, the children in the playgrounds, each of us must know our Indian lineage, our afro-*mestisaje*, our history of resistance.

To the immigrant *mexicano* and the recent arrivals we must teach our history. The 80 million *mexicanos* and the Latinos from Central and South America must know of our struggles. Each one of us must know basic facts about Nicaragua, Chile and the rest of Latin America. The Latinoist movement (Chicanos, Puerto Ricans, Cubans and other Spanish-speaking people working together to combat racial discrimination in the market place) is good but it is not enough. Other than a common culture we will have nothing to hold us together. We need to meet on a broader communal ground.

The struggle is inner: Chicano, *indio*, American Indian, *mojado, mexicano*, immigrant Latino, Anglo in power, working class Anglo, Black, Asian—our psyches resemble the border-towns and are populated by the same people. The struggle has always been inner, and is played out in the outer terrains. Awareness of our situation must come before inner changes, which in turn come before changes in society. Nothing happens in the "real" world unless it first happens in the images in our heads.

El día de la Chicana

> I will not be shamed again
> Nor will I shame myself.

I am possessed by a vision: that we Chicanas and Chicanos have taken back or uncovered our true faces, our dignity and self-respect. It's a validation vision.

Seeing the Chicana anew in light of her history. I seek an exoneration, a seeing through the fictions of white supremacy, a seeing of ourselves in our true guises and not as the false racial personality that has been given to us and that we have given to ourselves. I seek our woman's face, our true features, the positive and the negative seen clearly, free of the tainted biases of male dominance. I seek new images of identity, new beliefs about ourselves, our humanity and worth no longer in question.

Estamos viviendo en la noche de la Raza, un tiempo cuando el trabajo se hace a lo quieto, en el oscuro. El día cuando aceptamos tal y como somos y para en donde vamos y porque—ese día será el día de la Raza. Yo tengo el compromiso de expresar mi visión, mi sensibilidad, mi percepción de la revalidación de la gente mexicana, su mérito, estimación, honra, aprecio, y validez.

35   On December 2nd when my sun goes into my first house, I celebrate *el día de la Chicana y el Chicano*. On that day I clean my altars, light my *Coatlalopeuh* candle, burn sage and copal, take *el baño para espantar basura*, sweep my house. On that day I bare my soul, make myself vulnerable to friends and family by expressing my feelings. On that day I affirm who we are.

On that day I look inside our conflicts and our basic introverted racial temperament. I identify our needs, voice them. I acknowledge that the self and the race have been wounded. I recognize the need to take care of our personhood, of our racial self. On that day I gather the splintered and disowned parts of *la gente mexicana* and hold them in my arms. *Todas las partes de nosotros valen.*

On that day I say, "Yes, all you people wound us when you reject us. Rejection strips us of self-worth, our vulnerability exposes us to shame. It is our innate identity you find wanting. We are ashamed that we need your good opinion, that we need your acceptance. We can no longer camouflage our needs, can no longer let defenses and fences sprout around us. We can no longer withdraw. To rage and look upon you with contempt is to rage and be contemptuous of ourselves. We can no longer blame you, nor disown the white parts, the male parts, the pathological parts, the queer parts, the vulnerable parts. Here we are weaponless with open arms, with only our magic. Let's try it our way, the mestiza way, the Chicana way, the woman way."

On that day, I search for our essential dignity as a people, a people with a sense of purpose—to belong and contribute to something greater than our *pueblo.* On that day I seek to recover and reshape my spiritual identity. *¡Anímate! Raza, a celebrar el día de la Chicana.*

El retorno

All movements are accomplished in six stages,
and the seventh brings return.
—*I Ching*[8]

Tanto tiempo sin verte casa mía,
mi cuna, mi hondo nido de la huerta.
—*"Soledad"*[9]

I stand at the river, watch the curving, twisting serpent, a serpent nailed to the fence where the mouth of the Rio Grande empties into the Gulf.

40   I have come back. *Tanto dolor me costó el alejamiento.* I shade my eyes and look up. The bone beak of a hawk slowly circling over me, checking me out as potential carrion. In its wake a little bird flickering its wings, swimming sporadically like a fish. In the distance the expressway and the slough of traffic like an irritated sow. The sudden pull in my gut, *la tierra, los aguaceros.* My land, *el viento soplando la arena, el lagartijo debajo de un nopalito. Me acuerdo como era antes. Una región desértica de vasta llanuras, costeras de baja altura, de escasa lluvia, de chaparrales formados por mesquites y huizaches.* If I look real hard I can almost see the Spanish fathers who were called "the cavalry of Christ" enter this valley riding their burros, see the clash of cultures commence.

Tierra natal. This is home, the small towns in the Valley, *los pueblitos* with chicken pens and goats picketed to mesquite shrubs. *En las colonias* on the other side of the tracks, junk cars line the front yards of hot pink and lavender-trimmed houses—Chicano architecture we call it, self-consciously. I have missed the TV shows where hosts speak in half and half, and where awards are given in the category of Tex-Mex music. I have missed the Mexican cemeteries blooming with artificial flowers, the fields of aloe vera and red pepper, rows of sugar cane, of corn hanging on the stalks, the cloud of *polvareda* in the dirt roads behind a speeding pickup truck, *el sabor de tamales de rez y venado.* I have missed *la yegua colorada* gnawing the wooden gate of her stall, the smell of horse flesh from Carito's corrals. *He hecho menos las noches calientes sin aire, noches de linternas y lechuzas* making holes in the night.

I still feel the old despair when I look at the unpainted, dilapidated, scrap lumber houses consisting mostly of corrugated aluminum. Some of the poorest people in the U.S. live in the Lower Rio Grande Valley, an arid and semi-arid land of irrigated farming, intense sunlight and heat, citrus groves next to chaparral and cactus. I walk through the elementary school I attended so long

---

[8]Richard Wilhelm, *The I Ching or Book of Changes*, trans. Cary F. Baynes (Princeton, NJ: Princeton University Press, 1950), 98. [Anzaldúa's note]
[9]*"Soledad"* is sung by the group, Haciendo Punto en Otro Son. [Anzaldúa's note]

ago, that remained segregated until recently. I remember how the white teachers used to punish us for being Mexican.

How I love this tragic valley of South Texas, as Ricardo Sánchez calls it; this borderland between the Nueces and the Rio Grande. This land has survived possession and ill-use by five countries: Spain, Mexico, the Republic of Texas, the U.S., the Confederacy, and the U.S. again. It has survived Anglo-Mexican blood feuds, lynchings, burnings, rapes, pillage.

Today I see the Valley still struggling to survive. Whether it does or not, it will never be as I remember it. The borderlands depression that was set off by the 1982 peso devaluation in Mexico resulted in the closure of hundreds of Valley businesses. Many people lost their homes, cars, land. Prior to 1982, U.S. store owners thrived on retail sales to Mexicans who came across the border for groceries and clothes and appliances. While goods on the U.S. side have become 10, 100, 1000 times more expensive for Mexican buyers, goods on the Mexican side have become 10, 100, 1000 times cheaper for Americans. Because the Valley is heavily dependent on agriculture and Mexican retail trade, it has the highest unemployment rates along the entire border region; it is the Valley that has been hardest hit.[10]

45   "It's been a bad year for corn," my brother, Nune, says. As he talks, I remember my father scanning the sky for a rain that would end the drought, looking up into the sky, day after day, while the corn withered on its stalk. My father has been dead for 29 years, having worked himself to death. The life span of a Mexican farm laborer is 56—he lived to be 38. It shocks me that I am older than he. I, too, search the sky for rain. Like the ancients, I worship the rain god and the maize goddess, but unlike my father I have recovered their names. Now for rain (irrigation) one offers not a sacrifice of blood, but of money.

"Farming is in a bad way," my brother says. "Two to three thousand small and big farmers went bankrupt in this country last year. Six years ago the price of corn was $8.00 per hundred pounds," he goes on. "This year it is $3.90 per hundred pounds." And, I think to myself, after taking inflation into account, not planting anything puts you ahead.

I walk out to the back yard, stare at *los rosales de mamá*. She wants me to help her prune the rose bushes, dig out the carpet grass that is choking them. *Mamagrande Ramona también tenía rosales*. Here every Mexican grows flowers. If they don't have a piece of dirt, they use car tires, jars, cans, shoe boxes. Roses are the Mexican's favorite flower. I think, how symbolic—thorns and all.

Yes, the Chicano and Chicana have always taken care of growing things and the land. Again I see the four of us kids getting off the school bus, changing

---

[10]Out of the twenty-two border counties in the four border states, Hidalgo County (named for Father Hidalgo who was shot in 1810 after instigating Mexico's revolt against Spanish rule under the banner of *la Virgen de Guadalupe*) is the most poverty-stricken county in the nation as well as the largest home base (along with Imperial in California) for migrant farm-workers. It was here that I was born and raised. I am amazed that both it and I have survived. [Anzaldúa's note]

into our work clothes, walking into the field with Papí and Mamí, all six of us bending to the ground. Below our feet, under the earth lie the watermelon seeds. We cover them with paper plates, putting *terremotes* on top of the plates to keep them from being blown away by the wind. The paper plates keep the freeze away. Next day or the next, we remove the plates, bare the tiny green shoots to the elements. They survive and grow, give fruit hundreds of times the size of the seed. We water them and hoe them. We harvest them. The vines dry, rot, are plowed under. Growth, death, decay, birth. The soil prepared again and again, impregnated, worked on. A constant changing of forms, *renacimientos de la tierra madre.*

> This land was Mexican once
> was Indian always
> and is.
> And will be again.

BROADER HORIZONS: RESOURCES FOR WRITING AND CLASS DISCUSSION

Literary Critical Essay / Discussion Topics

1. One way of thinking about characters that live on the fringes or the margins of the mainstream culture is to diagram a series of concentric circles with the inner, smallest circle containing the mainstream culture and the outer circles representing the domain of the various peoples on the edges of that inner world. Applying such a diagram to a few of the works in this section, write an essay discussing the levels of marginalization of those characters you find interesting. How far out to the periphery do the characters exist and why? What sorts of conditions prevent characters from moving closer to the center? How do they feel about the pressures to move that way, or do they choose to rebel and consciously move themselves outward from the center?

2. Using the selections which focus on Latino soldiers, write an essay discussing some aspect of the Latino experience in the U.S. military that is brought up in one of the works. You might want to research such books as George Mariscal's *Aztlán and Vietnam.*

3. Many of the poems in this section focus on the writer's sense of alienation from his or her surrounding environment, of not belonging in some way, or even of being lost. Choose a few poems and identify the words that are used to connote this emotion. Analyze the appropriateness of each of these words and whether other words could be substituted to have a similar artistic effect.

4. The term "underground" is often used for a network (often illegal) that operates beneath the surface of the accepted customs and systems in a society. The institutions in control (legal, military, educational, religious, economic, etc.) rest on top and everything and everyone who does not or cannot conform is forced to operate below the surface. This is the idea behind metaphors like "to be paid under the table," "the underground railroad," or "a counter culture." Using a few of the stories from this section, analyze how the writers portray their characters in a way that fits this type of metaphorical description of the outsider.

5. As discussed in the introduction to this section of the book, "the border" is both a metaphor for the space between cultures—in this case, most often between U.S. mainstream and Latino life—as well as a physical barrier between this country and Latin America and the Caribbean. Using a few of the works in this section, write an essay that explores how the author portrays a border. Where do you think the author feels most comfortable and why? Does the work depict a movement across borders or a confrontation of some sort with a border as an obstacle? Or does the work somehow emphasize life in the middle, on the border (in a sort of contact zone)?

6. Many of the works in this section (and throughout the book as well) incorporate Spanish in the prose. Choose a series of poems and analyze how this is done. Some interesting questions to consider might be:

   a. What types of vocabulary words are in Spanish, and why is this important?

   b. How is the Spanish marked in a work? Is it emphasized, translated, italicized in any way, and what difference does this make?

   c. Why does the writer use Spanish or English at any given point?

   d. Does the language question dominate the poem in some way, or is it simply a stylistic device?

7. In some of these stories, the writer (or the characters in the works) suggests that one side of her culture and personality—the Latin American side, for example—is at odds with the U.S. mainstream in a political way. Consider the political side of a few selections here and discuss the issues raised.

The Novel Connection

Some of the most interesting writing in Latino fiction and certainly some of the most influential works of the last 15 years have been written by Latinas and center around a young girl coming of age in the United States. The following short novels (listed here in chronological order) could effectively supplement the stories included in this text.

Nicholasa Mohr, *Nilda* (1973)

Sandra Cisneros, *The House on Mango Street* (1985)

Estella Portillo Trambley, *Trini* (1986)

Roberta Fernández, *Intaglio* (1990)

Julia Alvarez, *How the Garcia Girls Lost Their Accents* (1991)

Esmeralda Santiago, *When I Was Puerto Rican* (1993)

Alba Ambert, *The Perfect Silence* (1995)

Diana López, *Sofia's Saints* (2002)

Carla Trujillo, *What Night Brings* (2002)

The Cisneros novel about young Esperanza growing up in South Chicago in many ways marks the beginning of modern U.S. Latina fiction. Its importance is indisputable. The novel's powerful mosaic of life in the barrio for young women became somewhat of an underground classic and inspires Latina writers to this day. Fernández's *Intaglio* is perhaps underrated and, like *The House on Mango Street*, reflects a narrative sophistication—combining the stories of several young women, several points of view—worthy of study. Julia Alvarez's first novel deals with the transitions of four young sisters from the Dominican Republic to the United States, from Spanish to English and from life under the dictator Trujillo to adolescent "freedom" stateside. Alba Ambert's novel about a young Puerto Rican girl struggling with poverty and oppression would be the closest thematically to Mohr's 1973 novel *Nilda*, and in fact, these two writers are central contributors to Puerto Rican Latina fiction. Along with Judith Ortiz Cofer (especially her moving and lyrical autobiographical work, *Silent Dancing*) and Esmeralda Santiago, these four women best represent the Latina side of Puerto Rican–American fiction. The most recent works in this list are both important contributions by Chicana writers, one dramatically portraying a young Chicana lesbian (by Trujillo) and the other a young Chicana's quest for independence (by López). *What Night Brings* is a dramatic story that is reminiscent of Cisneros's stories "Women Hollering Creek" and "One Holy Night." (The latter appears on page 67 of this anthology.) With its focus on the working class, Diana López's novel parallels the works of Dagoberto Gilb and Daniel Chacón.

The theme of the outsider can apply to hundreds of novels, but certainly the late Arturo Islas's classic *The Rain God* (1984) and its sequel *Migrant Souls* (1990) are essential books in portraying the theme of the non-macho male's isolation from Chicano tradition. Daniel Chacón's first novel, *and the shadows took him* (2004), a title alluding to Tomás Rivera's classic work, continues the theme of isolated young men and borderland identities. Jaime Manrique's *Latin Moon in Manhattan* (1992) portrays gay life in Queens and the underground New York worlds. John Rechy, though a great deal earlier, depicted the night world of gay Los Angeles in the now near classic *City of Night*. A recent novel by Francisco Stork called *The Way of the Jaguar* (2000) is the story of a death row inmate recollecting his disastrous route to execution. In a way that mirrors Eugene O'Neill's classic *The Iceman Cometh*, Dagoberto Gilb's first novel, *The Last Known Residence of Mickey Acuña* (1994), is about a group of destitute losers in a YMCA. For novels concerning the Latino at war, there is Daniel Cano's *Shifting Loyalties* (1995), about five Chicanos in Vietnam, as well as the latest works by Alfredo Véa and Edgardo Vega Yunqué. And then, perhaps the ultimate outsider, a man with no face, is the subject of the brilliant novel *Face* (1985) by Cecile Pineda.

Three writers can be mentioned as being essential in different ways to Latino literature: Roberto G. Fernández (Cuban-American), Edgardo Vega Yunqué (Stateside Puerto Rican), and Alfredo Véa (Chicano). What unites these three writers is not only the connections they make to Latino life on the edges of mainstream society, but also the fact that each of these writers—more so than many other Latino novelists—relies on humor. For our purposes, the most important work by Fernández is his first novel written in English, *Raining Backwards* (1988). Though relatively obscure, this work is stylistically innovative and often hilarious. It is a send off of all things Cuban-American and pokes fun at everything from the nostalgia of the non-transplantable exile in Miami to the soldiers of the Bay of Pigs. Vega Yunqué (who published under the name Ed Vega), in his classic novel *Mendoza's Dreams* (1985), is one of the funniest writers in the Puerto Rican literary sphere. The narrative complexity of this Chaucerian collection of interrelated stories goes far beyond most Latino fiction, just as Fernández, mimicking John Dos Passos, seems to use a different genre for each chapter of his wild story. The third writer in this list, Alfredo Véa, has now written three novels, each dealing with multiple, marginal characters: the disenfranchised in a small Southwestern town, the underclass in San Francisco's Mission district, and the Latino soldiers coping with the Vietnam War and its aftermath. Véa's multidimensional characters are always the marginal, the poor, the prostitutes, the murderers, and the multicultural hybrids, and his important novels are always filled with imagination, personality, and humor.

Film Connection

In-depth Film Connection
Piñero (2001)
Directed by Leon Ichaso

Few films have captured the true essence of "The Fringe World" the way that *Piñero* (2001) has as it portrays the life of the Nuyorican Poet and playwright Miguel Piñero. And few Latino films have been as misunderstood by critics as much as this work directed by Leon Ichaso. *Rolling Stone* called it "an annoyingly hyper biopic," while the *Village Voice* noted that the "movie is under the impression that Piñero's ethnic cachet somehow outweighs his status as literary pocket change." Indeed, these critics barely comprehended the significance of Piñero, never mind the purpose of Ichaso's directorial choices. Fortunately, enough critics appreciated how the film's careful editing, originality, and poetic approach to filmmaking were used to emphasize the Nuyorican poet's cultural hybridity, complexity, and an identity that defied categorization.

Benjamin Bratt, starring as Piñero, delivers a powerful performance, bringing to life the man who self-destructed before reaching his potential as an artist. Appropriately, the movie begins with Piñero proclaiming to a reporter that he started stealing when he was eight, then in a sudden juxtaposing shift, adding that, "when you think of Latin writers, you probably think of García Márquez, Neruda, or Cortázar, and magic realism, not here, not this. There are no floating butterflies around my head when I walk down Avenue B, you know. This is street reality. This is where we shout it out. *Tu sabes.*" Like the writers in this "The Fringe World" chapter, Piñero constantly struggled to affirm his identity as a Nuyorican Poet. Like Abraham Rodríguez, Jr.'s main character, he was in many ways "A Boy Without a Flag," or as poet Tato Laviera may have described him, "AmeRícan."

Many scenes in the movie are in black and white, reemphasizing the fact that beyond this paradigm exists a gray area that can make us uncomfortable. Ichaso does nothing to hide Piñero's drug addiction and dangerous lifestyle, but far from glamorizing a world of crime, the director depicts a figure whose work boldly approached taboo subjects such as sex abuse, pedophilia, homosexuality, and incest. His social consciousness, after all, is partly what placed Piñero in the fringes of American literature. He objects to the casting of Robert DeNiro and Ralph Macchio in Broadway's *Cuba and His Teddy Bear*, denouncing them as Italians who are being cast while a Latino boom is taking place. It is this awareness that leads him ultimately to his participation in the evolution of The Nuyorican Poets Café, establishing a tradition that still exists today.

The most pivotal scene in the movie takes place at a poetry reading, when Piñero returns to Puerto Rico, only to have his work rejected by the people he thought he represented. Like so many Latinos who have returned to their homelands only to find that they are seen as between two worlds, Piñero encounters a Puerto Rican audience that views him as an outsider. Just as the movie shifts between black and white and color, so too does Piñero's language alternate among English, Spanish, and Spanglish, much to the dismay of one audience member who refers to him as "a character that corrupts the language when you are calling yourselves Nuyoricans, as if it was a race." Hurt, but proud of his marginality, Piñero replies, "Even if I am half and half, any of those halves is more whole than all of you…I know what I am. I'm still the same Puerto Rican twenty-four hours a day."

Of course, what makes the scene so familiar to Latinos is that it shows that life on the fringes is not just a matter of Anglos outcasting Latino groups, but also of Latinos excluding each other from their own worlds. Hollywood has created an abundance of films about

Latinos in the streets who failed in one regard or other, but most of these, such as *American Me* (1992) and *Blood In, Blood Out* (1993), make heroes out of gangsters and thieves and oversimplify their struggles. *Piñero*'s reality is harsh, yet it more accurately represents the complexities of boundaries that individuals place on themselves and each other. A Puerto Rican in New York, as the film reminds us, may see himself as a Nuyorican, but that does not necessarily mean that others in New York, in the mainland United States, or in Puerto Rico will define him or her as such.

Other Recommended Films:

Amarte Duele (2002)

Black and White in Exile (1997)

Buena Vista Social Club (1999)

Calle 54 (2000)

Chicano: the History of the Mexican American Civil Rights Movement (1996)

Giant (1956)

I Am Joaquin (1969)

Maria Full of Grace (2004)

Palante, Siempre Palante! The Young Lords (1996)

Soldados: Chicanos in Vietnam (2003)

Stand and Deliver (1988)

Thematic Connection Listing

1. Voices of Outsiders

Fiction

Abraham Rodríguez, Jr.: "The Boy Without a Flag"

Alba Ambert: "Rage of a Fallen Angel"

Poetry

Tato Laviera: "AmeRícan"

Achy Obejas: "Sugarcane"

Drama

José Rivera: "Cloud Tectonics"

2. Outsiders at War: Latino Soldiers

Fiction

Daniel Cano: "Somewhere Outside Doc Pho"

Leroy V. Quintana: "The Man on Jesus Street—Dreaming"

Poetry

Demetria Martínez: "Birthday"

Carmen Tafolla: "Letter to Ti"

Alberto Ríos: "The Vietnam Wall"

3. Outsiders from Within: In the Belly of the Beast

Fiction

Edgardo Vega Yunqué: "The Barbosa Express"

8
Beyond Worlds

Beyond the Boom

INTRODUCTION

Latino literature is almost impossible to categorize in a complete way. Just when the reader assigns it to a particular genre or niche, a new work comes on the scene and the list of overall categories has to be expanded. While we can find certain general thematic elements in many works, no definable criteria could possibly cover the entire breadth of the literature. All we can genuinely say is that the field is in dramatic flux and growing exponentially.

The nature of Latino literature will continue to change as Latinos further explore the growing complexities of their evolving multiple identities. For example, as Latinos from the Caribbean migrate from one island to another and emigrate from the islands to the United States, the cultural, racial, sexual, and psychological crossovers will result in an ever-changing mixture in the Latino character; writers, as they always do, will track these multiple and complex factors in their own creative ways. Who can say with any precision what direction the artists will go? Surely, the themes for Latino writers will evolve from the complications inherent in the changing world of transnational Latino life. Such issues may include: the impact of tourism on the economics of the Spanish Caribbean islands, immigration laws for the U.S. borders, international trade arrangements between the Americas, intermarriages between Anglos and Latinos, the overall pace of Latino cultural influence on mainstream life in this country, or the general failures of the U.S. educational system in which too many Latinos are floundering. The number of topics we can expect to find in Latino literature is endless and ripe for literary exploration.

The works gathered in this chapter are those we feel break typical modes in some way, stylistically or thematically. Our intention here is to throw out all hint of categorization and compartmentalization in order to end the anthology with a suggestion of things to come and focus attention on writers who grapple with the changing cultural intricacies of today's Latino world.

Literary Trends Beyond the 1960s

Our focus on modern Latino writing in this anthology provides us with a way to detect certain general literary trends and gives us the basis for drawing some conclusions about the changes in literary work by Latinos over the last few decades. The clearest trend might be, as is the case with African-American literature, the rising popularity of works written by women, which is a shift from the late 1960s when figures such as Piri Thomas and Rudolfo Anaya dominated the Latino literary scene. Recently, the number of published Latina writers has surpassed the number of Latino authors. Stories of fathers and sons have given way to those of grandmothers, mothers, daughters, sisters, and mistresses. There also seems to be a move beyond the overtly politically conscious works of the late 1960s when writers like the Beat-inspired "Nuyorican" poets or the Chicano activists on the West Coast proclaimed their identity in powerful poems and ideological declarations. Spoken word poetry keeps the "Aloud Café" alive to some extent, but fictional narrative dominates the Latino literary harvest. What we see now are writers, no less political at times, but perhaps less autobiographical and grappling with a problematical and hybrid existence. There is at the same time an increasing attention paid to a celebration (or at least acceptance) of cultural influences that empower and sustain them. The influential words of such poems as Rodolfo "Corky" Gonzales's "I am Joaquin," which marked the beginning of the Chicano literary movement, have given way to the imagistic sketches in works by best-selling authors such as Julia Alvarez and Sandra Cisneros.

Reconstructing the Past

We have suggested in this anthology that a central tendency of Latino literature is for writers to look back into and through the traumas (personal and general) of Latino history and experience for the subject matter of their creative work. Thus, the literature itself progresses in two directions at once. On the one hand, writers struggle to invent new ways to express their contempory stories and ideas and on the other, they are in a constant battle to unearth and revisit the parts of their cultural heritage that have been made (for whatever reason) distant and obscure. They delve into historical facts and incidents in hopes of finding events to write about which speak to contemporary issues facing the Latino world. Puerto Rican writer Rosario Ferré, for instance, uses the political history of the island to ground her English novels. Cristina Garcia is moving backward into Cuba's complicated history with each successive novel. Yet Latino writers are also part of the larger literary world that forever demands the new and, like all writers, they are interested in forging ahead with the massive literary transformation of U.S. literature, placing their individual talent in the stream of this country's tradition of letters as we move into the multicultural twenty-first century.

Beyond the Horizon

At the heart of this literary transition are the constant questions related to race, gender, and class. Although they are hardly new subjects in Latino writing, these issues are more and more central to the literature, as writers of all backgrounds delve deeper into racial issues, sexual roles, and cultural traditions and find themselves increasingly interested in the intercultural and interracial obstacles common to a vast number of Latinos in this country. Writers search the Caribbean past for racial connections, and their fiction and poetry demonstrate a growing interest in exploring the dimensions of cultural rivalries between the various Latino groups.

Latino writers will surely publish more mysteries, detective novels, and romances, and they will delve into science fiction and fantasy as the readership expands. For sure, the range of characters inhabiting the fiction will grow in unforeseeable ways. At one point, all Latino protagonists seemed to live in East Harlem or Los Angeles or Santa Fe. We can expect future novels and poems depicting the illegal workers in Midwestern meatpacking plants (a Latino *The Jungle*, for example), but we should also anticipate the narratives of Latino judges in Colorado, soldiers from New Jersey, or retired Puerto Ricans in Florida. There may be stories and poems based on the lives of singers and musicians like Selena, Celia Cruz, or Tito Puente, just as there are now about Latin American artists like Frida Kahlo, Tina Mondotti, and Diego Rivera.

For a time, it looked like the postmodernist Latin American tradition would push the Latino writer toward the complexities of style found in writers such as Argentina's Julio Cortázar or Puerto Rico's Luis Rafael Sánchez or in the early stories of Rosario Ferré and the artful short works of Ana Lydia Vega. We saw such glimpses in Edgardo Vega Yunqué's *Mendoza's Dreams* (1987), in Ron Arias's classic *The Road to Tamazunchale* (1975) and in Roberto G. Fernandez's last two novels, *Raining Backwards* (1988) and *Holy Radishes!* (1995). Yet, with a few exceptions, such as Cisneros's experimental, genre-crossing latest work, *Caramelo* (2002), or the cleverly constructed, picaresque novel of John Rechy, *The Life and Adventures of Lyle Clemens* (2003), few postmodern novels have come round. Arias's latest book is a personal memoir called *Moving Target* (2002) about his own life and his father. Magical realism and metafictional game playing in Latino literature appear to be on the decline. Instead, the autobiographical mode holds firm, and the fiction is dominated by the multi-perspective, fragmented presentation of events found in books by writers like Cristina Garcia, Denise Chávez, or Julia Alvarez.

There is a sense that the Latino writer, perhaps more than most writers, now contemplates the past with an eye toward what is to come. In the end, what can be expected from Latino writers in the future is the unexpected itself.

FICTION

Jack Agüeros

See the biographical headnote of Agüeros on page 229.

Horologist

(By Appointment Only)

Wednesday

Without turning his head he felt a person approach and look into the window behind him. A male. Whether there was actually a physical clue like a small dimming of the light coming over his shoulder, or whether it was some slight motion reflected in one of the three magnifying lenses he wore attached to his working eyeglasses, he couldn't say, but he always knew when anyone was behind him, whenever anyone looked into the store window and whenever they moved away. His partner, Mr. Livrehomme, had arranged the store.

"This way, Mr. Vazquez," Livrehomme never called him by his first name Maximiliano or Max. Livrehomme didn't like that American instant familiarity where people who just met you called you Max and Joe as if they had known you forever—"This way, Mr. Vazquez, they can entertain themselves without coming in and actually standing over your shoulder. We'll put the workbench near the window. People always want to watch others at work. Especially at jobs they know nothing about and consider unusual and interesting. So they'll walk by, look in the window, and they won't bother you."

Greenwich Avenue in New York is one of the shopping streets of Greenwich Village, but mercifully they were down at the quieter end of it, near Eighth Avenue, where pedestrian flow tapers off substantially. Still, Vazquez could feel many people stopping and looking over his shoulder as he worked. At first it had been a great distraction. Every peeker made him stop and turn around. Then he and Livrehomme had installed a mirror and all he had to do was look up into the mirror to see who was watching him from the street.

That was when they opened the store here, workshop more than store, fifteen years ago. Now he never looked in the mirror, never turned around. Years ago, he realized that whenever he looked into the mirror it was because someone was approaching the window. It occurred to him that he was ahead of the mirror. And if he was ahead of the mirror in this way, could he be ahead of the mirror in other ways? If he could sense the people before seeing them in the mirror, perhaps he could sense other things as well. And he began guessing whether they were male or female, tall or short, fat or skinny, young or old, and then he would look in the mirror to confirm his guess. He had gotten so good at guessing that he rarely glanced at the mirror for confirmation.

5   Vazquez knew that the person watching him was a young man, medium stature, maybe his own height 5′9″ give or take a half inch. But his attention turned to his timer, which was about to go off, signalling him to remove a number of brass wheels he was soaking in an ammoniated soap solution. Village stores had been hit with a number of armed robberies in the recent past and as Vazquez removed his brass wheels and rinsed them in warm water washing off both the grime and the cleansing solution, he looked up in the mirror to see the face of the young man. Was it the face of a young robber, "casing the joint" as they used to say on the old radio programs? Well, if he looked around he would see that there wasn't anything really to rob. Not cash, and only a real expert would know anything about the many clocks or where to sell them.

Then again there was an article about a major clock robbery in the Bulletin just recently. Two in fact. Clock thefts from a house, and clock thefts from a dealer in California. And every time there was an auction at Southeby's and clock prices skyrocketed, that made things worrisome.

But it was always the unscrupulous who made things terrible. Not the thieves. The thieves only operated because the unscrupulous paid for stolen merchandise. They were the truly corrupt and the corrupters. No buyers of stolen property, no thieves.

And when the timer went off the young man walked away, away toward Eighth Avenue.

What do you call it when you always anticipate your timer by a few seconds? Mr. Livrehomme used to say in class that men and women who became horologists had a clock in them that sought out other clocks; a clock in them that could be heard in their own ears; that day or night they always knew the approximate time. "Why not the real time or the exact time?" some student would always ask. And Livrehomme would always reply, with an enigmatic smile on his lips, "Because there is no such thing, there is only approximate time, relative time." And he would go on to another subject.

Thursday

Vazquez was placing the mechanism for a long case clock up on the work-horse when he realized that something was happening across the street. The mirror was tilted so that he could see out about half way across the street on Greenwich, and then only at the pavement tar with its double yellow line. Through the window he saw a figure crossing the street and coming toward the store. The young man again.

10   Vazquez didn't want to be distracted. Mounting the case on the horse was a maneuver that required care. The clock work had to sit up well balanced so it wouldn't topple over, and level, so that the pendulum would swing properly. He looked for the wooden shims and the spirit level and worked the wood around under the brass plates until he was satisfied that he had a level clockwork in two directions. Next he had to attach the great weights to the chains, and finally hang the pendulum which was very beautiful.

This clock was a beautiful clock in a beautiful case. It was a historic clock, early American, 18th Century, perhaps pre-revolution, made in Pennsylvania. One of the earliest clocks completely made in the colonies. But the museum and its curators had too high an opinion of the piece and it was terribly over-estimated in dollar value as well.

Vazquez felt the mechanism was now well balanced, but the young man was not to be seen on either side of Greenwich Avenue.

The robberies were something to worry about. Hadn't he gotten a police circular warning about a stick-up team? But that circular talked about a young woman who would enter the store first, then a man would come in later. And they were after cash, they never took merchandise.

Friday

The Old Dutch Master's Club was located in midtown, near the Harvard Club. Its official name was the Lowlands Club, but only out of towners ever called it by that name. They wanted Vazquez to inspect a clock and offer an estimate for restoration. The Old Dutch Masters considered their clock an heirloom.

15 "An important clock," said the President of the club, "important in the history of our great city."

The clock was hung high on a wall in the club's main room, not far from a fireplace. They took it down clumsily, two kitchen employees teetering on chairs instead of using a stable ladder. Vazquez cautioned them to get adequate ladders before putting it back, and the club president looked irritated. Vazquez opened the clock, noticing the soot on one side of the case, and candle wax residue all over the case as he looked in. He opened the back, removed the pendulum, and flashed his penlight into the case. He didn't like what he saw. Heavy black incrustation everywhere. Oily brass plates. Thin, oily brass plates. Bad signs.

Vazquez asked the President when it had last been attended to, and when it had stopped.

"We had a member of the club who repaired clocks as a hobby, and he regularly oiled it and set it going," said the President who was bothered by this inspection. "It's truly a beautiful clock isn't it?"

Vazquez didn't agree, didn't comment at all, and then irritated the Dutch Masters more by telling them that he doubted if the clock was a very good timekeeper.

20 "How could you know that?" demanded the President of the club. "We haven't seen it working in about ten years."

"When I look inside I see certain clues. I get a first impression, but I'll give you a written statement of my findings and opinions, after a full examination."

"Do you say we shouldn't bother to fix it?" asked the President with an incredulous tone in his voice. "We had a horologist here before you who told us the clock was worth at least $30,000."

"Well," said Vazquez, taking a long time between his "well" and his next words, "have him restore it for you."

"You have higher recommendations," added another man, apparently a member of the committee on the clock.

25   The President looked flustered, and the other man asked sharply, "In your opinion, is the clock worth $30,000, if it's not a good timekeeper?"

Vazquez didn't like to think about the worth of clocks in dollar terms. "I don't appraise clocks, I don't buy or sell clocks. But if you respect the clock, or it has special meaning to you, then the clock is priceless, isn't it? And if we can get it to work at all..."

The committee of three men squirmed in their seats.

"You mean to tell us that it may not work at all?"

"It'll work. But you may have to set the time every two weeks."

30   "Twice a week! The appraiser told us it was a thirty day clock!"

"I said every two weeks. A hundred and fifty years ago when this clock was probably made..."

"You mean three hundred and fifty years ago," shot the President of the club. "That's what we were told."

The committee excused Vazquez, curtly thanking him for coming by. Vazquez went down to the main club room and looked at the clock again. It was a type of long case clock, nearly as long as a grandmother clock, but it had been designed to hang on a wall, rather than to stand freely. That suggested to Vazquez that it probably had been commissioned for a particular wall—perhaps a public building in a small town in Holland. It had good cabinetwork, the cabinet better than the clockwork. The face was uninteresting, with easy to read numbers and so-so hands. The innards he knew were European but not French. Although the works were of brass, they were very thin and didn't have the fine details of French clock-making like an oil sink. It probably had been made in some obscure workshop in Holland. And it was an example of low quality clock work, a mediocre work stuck in a much better quality cabinet. That happened and so did the opposite, very fine clockwork stuck in a so-so box.

Vazquez could guess who had given the appraisal. That was a job he never wanted. If the clock meant something in the history of the club, if it meant something to the members, a linkage with their past and the humble man who had brought the clock to America, why didn't that make it worth setting to go again? Why couldn't they be proud that at its age it could still be made to work at all?

35   He paused to look at it again from the door. It was hung too high on the wall, and looked awkward and out of proportion. Was it worth $300, let alone $30,000? Why did appraisers over-value, over-age?

It didn't matter to Vazquez, he would like to get it going. It deserved to be respected, to be restored, because if Vazquez understood one thing it was "sentimental value."

Saturday

The morning had been wonderfully quiet. He had opened the shop up at 10 p.m. as usual. It had been raining all morning and not one person had paused at the window, and before he knew it, it was 2:30 p.m. The phone rang sometime after that and it was the Old Dutch Master's Club.

"Max?"

"Mr. Vazquez speaking. Who is this, please?"

40 "This is Pete VanBramer, Max. We want you to fix the clock. We understand that you work with Livrehomme, and the committee wanted the assurance that it was so. Is it?"

"We have been partners for fifteen years and we discuss all the clocks together before we remove them from their cases. We keep a log of what we find, and what we do. We give you a copy for your files when we return your clock, and we keep one in our files."

"Good. And another thing, Max. We consider this a restoration. We don't want parts changed or fake things stuck in there. You know what I mean?"

"Mr. VanBramer, we do only restorations."

"Call me Pete, Max. We're not trying to hurt your feelings, but the committee has a right to make sure of these things. Now, how fast can we get the clock back?"

45 "Fast?"

"Yeah. Will it be a cupala weeks, or what?"

"Six to seven months more likely."

"What? Are you that backlogged? Well, look Max, we'll pay a little more for expediting, if you like."

"Mr. VanBramer, I believe your President said the clock hadn't been working for ten years. Six or seven months will pass relatively quickly. I'll be by to pick up the clock on Monday. Please arrange to have two good six foot ladders. Thank you and goodbye."

Monday

50 Livrehomme laughed. "I think you were easy on them. I can see from here you will have great difficulty with three of these pivots. You will have to bush them. The plates are so thin, if you don't bush them they'll be elliptical again in no time. And I wonder about the quality of the brass, not much copper in the plates. Look at the pivots: elliptical."

Livrehomme moved over so that Vazquez could get his head closer to the case. Vazquez swung two of the magnifying lenses into place in front of his eyeglasses and peeked into the case. "Yes. They're eggs. I don't think there are any broken teeth or wheels. By the way they said they didn't want any fake stuff."

They laughed together.

"What do you think they had in mind?" asked Livrehomme.

"I'm sure they hadn't the slightest idea. They think we take out good pieces and put cheap pieces back in, I guess."

55 "I didn't see any fragments on the floor of the case, did you?" asked Livrehomme.

Vazquez took his penlight and shined it into the case bottom. "Nothing down there but dust."

"A good cleaning and three new pivots, at least. The clock is filthy. You'll hope the arbors don't have flat sides. If they do, then you'll have real restoration questions. They look too thin to work on. Then you'll have to machine new parts."

"When they took the clock down so I could inspect it, I noticed different gradations of color on the wall. And the outline of the clock repeated. You could barely see it from up close. It's the old story, each time they wound it they moved it over just a bit. Over the years they took it way out of plumb, and I'm sure that's why the pivots are out of round. Everything pulling in this one direction."

"Sure. So their well meaning member took it down, obviously oiled it again and again, set it back up level, and it would work for a while. Until they slowly moved it again. Psst! Pivots out of round, arbors with flat sides. When will you start work on it?"

60 "Four weeks, at least. I just got the museum clock up on the horse on Thursday and I'm going to try and get it going tomorrow. By the way, I think the curator got us this job with the Old Dutch Masters. He told them this clock was worth $30,000 dollars."

"No. No curator gives appraisals now. It was our friend Hughard the dealer, and I'm sure they loved that figure."

"Yes, they did but they didn't like it when I told them it might not keep good time. I thought we wouldn't get the job."

"We are doing very good work on very good clocks. You didn't have to take this job."

"Something about the clock. I imagined an old immigrant Dutchman, running from the Germans, carrying his special clock to America. You know? You know Mr. Livrehomme?"

65 "Yes, I know, Mr. Vazquez, I know you make up good stories for all your clocks. You owe it to this man you never met, isn't that what you figure?"

"Sort of," answered Vazquez.

"Then you know what, Mr. Vazquez, there's a good chance that it might keep good time. Consider bushing all the pivots. There aren't that many wheels. And when you remount it on the wall, build in two level stop blocks so the clock can't be moved out of plumb."

And then they looked at the clock and didn't speak for awhile, like people who stare into a fireplace, gripped by the dance of the flames while their own thoughts fly.

"I've been thinking about talking to that woman who has the shop uptown. She's an old student of mine and she has a good apprentice. If we all came together we could have a real atelier. Reduce overhead and become even more picky." Livrehomme started laughing. "Seriously, there's now room in New York for a real old world atelier—I think maybe there is even room for us to manufacture some special clocks in limited editions. Three different clocks. Only ten of each. How would you like that? We could become really picky. This Dutch clock could be prepared by an apprentice while you and I could design clocks, supervise production, and especially control quality. I know a man who's an excellent cabinet maker."

70   "I'm not sure I'd like that. I like to take a clock apart down to the last pin and then put it all back together again. I hate production lines. I hate mass production. On the other hand I like the idea of being picky. Maybe we can have the owners fill out an application with a section for a statement, 'I want this clock repaired because...'" Then Vazquez laughed, and Livrehomme laughed more.

Tuesday

When Vazquez first became interested in clocks, he liked faces. Sometimes he also liked the cases. As he learned more about clocks, he came to love the inner works and to be very indifferent about face dials and cabinet work. Livrehomme had said at one of Vazquez's first classes, "You can form no opinion of a clock from the outside." Sometimes he would say it another way: "A clock is not the case."

Vazquez looked at it differently. When a man bothered to make a fine clock work, he was likely to put a handsome face on it, and to want it in a fine cabinet. But Livrehomme was right, a fine face and a fine cabinet could be the marks of a fine clock, but unscrupulous clock men made what are called "marriages" in the trade. He himself had found a fine french clock work in a very strange white metal cabinet. The clock looked as if it had been taken from some other cabinet and stuck into the metal one. Some dealers would have no compunction about passing such a marriage off as an original clock. Caveat emptor! A decent dealer would tell you it was suspected of being a marriage, and a good dealer would tell you it was probably a marriage and let you decide if you still wanted it. Some people collected "marriages," and didn't mind any price at all for one.

But this Pennsylvania clock was definitely very special. This clock had been made by one man, works and case. One gifted man from Pennsylvania with a vision and two skills. Clock and cabinet making. One man had been responsible for this fine work. Every detail of it conceived and executed by one demanding artisan. Maybe the museum is right, this Pennsylvania clock is worth $400,000.

"Now all I have to do is make it go," said Vazquez out loud. Then he bent down and gave the pendulum a little push. The clock tick-tocked, tick-tocked, and stopped.

75   Vazquez felt the young man staring through the window. The thought that maybe the young man knew the dollar value of the clock and wanted to steal it raced through his mind. But as Vazquez looked for a screwdriver to adjust the escapement, the man walked away from the window.

Good clocks always behaved in the same way. They would go for a little and then stop. Like a person resenting surgery, the clock needed to make a statement to its restorer. This moment, the moment of setting the beat always made him sad, because it was essentially the end of his work. He had grown accustomed to seeing the fine clock and its cabinet day after day and soon he would have to go to the museum to see his old friend. He was about to loosen a screw to adjust the crutch and pallets when the door bell rang. It gave him a start.

The young man presented a beautifully designed card in bright black raised thermofaxed letters that said:

GG Productions
Film & Video Studios
80   180 West Street
Tribeca, NY 10011

Gary Garcia
President

FAX: 1 - 212 - FILMDEO

85   There was a drawing of a piece of film reeling out from the screen of a television.

"What can I do for you, Mr. Garcia?"

"You can call me Gary, Mister...? Do you have a card?"

Vazquez searched in his pockets and found none. He went to his workbench and couldn't find one there either. Then he went to the desk and in the upper right hand drawer he found a whole stack of cards, took one from the middle.

Garcia looked at the card.

90   Horologist
(By Appointment Only)
Mr. Maximiliano Vazquez
NAWCC # 3757
(212) 243-2270

95   There was no drawing. Garcia read it out loud. "Horologist, by appointment only. Mr. Maximiliano Vazquez. It's perfect Max. I've come to see you because I'm going to make you famous."

"Goodbye Mr. Garcia. I'm very busy right now setting a clock."

"Look, I only need a few minutes of your time."

"I have no minutes for you. Good bye."

"Can I make an appointment? I'll call you. I'll call you tomorrow for an appointment. I'm sorry I interrupted you Max. I'll call you tomorrow. Sorry. Bye."

100   Vazquez locked the door, took his screwdriver and loosened a retaining screw. Then he shifted the pivot about 1/64th of an inch, which actually pulled

the pallets up just a bit on the escape wheel. Then he tightened the retaining screw, took the level and read all four sides of the horse, and gave the pendulum a shove. The clock tick-tocked, tick-tocked, but Vazquez did not like the sound. It wasn't robust, it wasn't balanced. He stopped the pendulum, and loosened the retaining screw again and again moved the pivot, but only a hair, and quickly tightened the screw, took the level all around again, shoved the pendulum. He listened with his ear close to the works. The sound was better. He looked at his wall clock and wrote the time down. It sounded right now. He felt it was going to go on.

Wednesday

The phone rang but he hesitated. Then he picked it up and was relieved to hear Mr. Livrehomme.

"Mr. Vazquez, a man in Sheepshead Bay in Brooklyn bought an old restaurant. In its heyday it was well known for its cheesecake and it had a big reputation as a sea food house. The man who owns it now found a clock in the attic and he wants me to go and look at it. Swears it's an antique."

"Are you?"

"He wouldn't take no for an answer. I told him I would have to charge him $500 for going out there. He said 'fine' without hesitating. What can I do?"

105   "Go see the clock. But forget about the cheesecake. It's probably been in the attic too."

"I'm taking a cab now, and I'll see you this afternoon."

Mr. Vazquez looked at the Pennsylvania clock and he looked at his wall clock. The Pennsylvania was now four minutes fast. He stopped the pendulum, turned the knurled screw four full times to the left, which lowered the pendulum's bob just a bit. He rolled the hands to the same time as his wall clock, and taking the level all around, nudged the pendulum. When he entered what he had done in the log, he began to look at his job tickets to see what clock was next, but the phone rang again.

"Mr. Vazquez speaking."

"Mr. Vazquez, this is Mr. Garcia. I would like to make an appointment with you. I know I started off on the wrong foot. And I want to correct it. May I take you to lunch? Pick a day."

110   "Mr. Garcia why don't you just tell me what you'd like over the phone."

"I want to make a one hour program about you as a horologist. I looked it up. I also now know what NAWCC stands for and that you are an old member. And I joined and I went to the library and looked at a copy of the Bulletin. But let me rewind. I'm trying to do a series of between 13 and 26 half hour programs that explore unusual occupations and minority people who not only work in those occupations, but are masters or experts in them. I have, just one example, a Puerto Rican who repairs antique radios, English, American, German or Italian. There isn't a radio that he can't repair. And when I say repair, I mean he can make the radio play. No matter what year it's from. So now. Fast forward. Each program goes like this. It's a mixture of history of the subject. Like clocks. Then it's your biography. How you got in. Then it takes a real look at restoring a clock. Whatever that is—I don't know yet. All the time we use a real classy background music. It's in there, down there, you hear it but not intrusive. A mellow voiced narrator. Sonorous voice. A wow voice. This costs you nothing. In fact. Rewind. I pay you for being on camera, I pay you for time lost while we do it, and you get a small residual right in the video. Now. Quick cut, Mr. Vazquez. This is not schlock video or amateur night. I bring you press clips, I bring you demo reels. I'm talking respect for craft. Creating interest in the history of clocks. Educating people. We do excellent photography. Mr. Vazquez. We are craftsmen like you. Dedicated to our craft. Only the super. Excellence, excellence, excellence. Let me take you to lunch. And I'll answer all your questions. Do you see…"

"Mr. Garcia, call me tomorrow about this time. I'll see if I have an open hour for you."

"Thank you very much Mr. Vazquez."

When Vazquez hung up the phone he looked out the window for a while and it occurred to him that Mr. Garcia had been carrying a still camera when he came into the shop, and that probably Mr. Garcia had been taking pictures of the store and maybe even of himself in it. From across the street. Outrageous!!!

115   The phone rang and Vazquez took it on the first ring.

"Hello!"

"Mr. Vazquez?"

"Yes."

"It's Mr. Livrehomme—what's the matter?"

120   "Oh, sorry Mr. Livrehomme. Some kid just put me in a bad mood. Wants to put me on television. Me on television, you in the cheesecake attic. It's our day for nuts."

"There are people in America who have so much money Mr. Vazquez, that they don't know what to do with it. I'm on my way with a Seth Thomas school clock that isn't even an antique. But he wants me to repair it and will give me $1,500 to do it. You figure it out."

"You told him you could get him one in mint condition for a third of that?"

"Yes. I told him. But he said, 'This one was in the attic here. It's different. It's in my family now.' What am I supposed to say after that? He reminded me of you."

Livrehomme laughed and Vazquez laughed more.

Thursday

125   "Max? This is Pete. Pete VanBramer. How's our clock doing?"

"Mr. VanBramer your clock is looking fine where it's mounted."

"How's the work going?"

"Mr. VanBramer, no work is going. I let the clock sit here for at least thirty days before anything happens. It has to get used to our shop. Sometimes old cases develop cracks in a new room, or old cracks badly repaired open up again."

"You mean you haven't done anything to it Max?"

130 "I inspected it more thoroughly than at your club. Mr. Livrehomme and I consulted on the clock, and I inspect the case every morning."

"You haven't done anything to it!"

"I'm getting to know your clock, and I finished my report and drawing."

"Listen Max, I don't want you to get to know my clock. I don't want any reports or drawings whatever they are. I want it repaired! I fought with my president to hire you. He hated you. I'm gonna look bad if this doesn't get done fast, do you understand? I wanna be the next president of the Dutch Masters. Max, this is important to me. Do you understand?"

"Mr. VanBramer…"

135 "Damn it Max, call me Pete! This 'Mr. VanBramer' is making me crazy!…Max? Max? Are you there? Max, say something!"

"Mr. VanBramer, I am here, but I don't know what to say. If you want I will bring the clock back immediately, and you can have someone else do the restoration."

"Max, Max, you want me kicked out of my club? They'll kill me if you bring that thing back! Max, I had a gut feeling you were the right guy for this job. How can you let me down like this?"

"Mr. VanBramer, I want to restore the clock, but it has to be done correctly."

"Correctly means you just let it sit there for a month?"

140 "Yes, Mr. VanBramer. It's one of our procedures. Plus every clock has to wait its turn."

There was a long silence, and Vazquez wished he could hang up.

"Look, Max, my president said all you clock guys were like old codgers even if you weren't old. What's the harm in moving our clock up on your agenda?"

"Wouldn't be fair to others, and it wouldn't be fair to you. We have to watch that case. We built a reputation because we do things right. No one complains about our restorations Mr. VanBramer. But if you want to take it elsewhere, that is your prerogative."

"I wanted it chiming before our election. People will hear it and say Pete VanBramer got it repaired. Max, you gotta do it. We'll pay you double. I'll match the fee out of my own pocket. Money's not a problem."

145 "You're right Mr. VanBramer. Money is not a problem. The problem is time. Get another restorer and call me. I'll cooperate fully with whoever you get. Goodbye!"

Friday

When Vazquez arrived the store smelled of coffee. Livrehomme had made a pot of espresso and wearing the lab coat he liked to wear while working on clocks, had the works of the Seth Thomas on his work table.

"I didn't know you were so eager to work on that Seth Thomas," said Vazquez sipping his straight black coffee.

"This is not eagerness. This is fear of the kind of man who is going to call me every day. You think VanBramer is bad? This man told me that he wants three weeks notice before the clock is ready so he can organize a homecoming and installation party. He's going to invite 1500 people. And next to the clock he's going to install a brass plaque that says, 'Seth Thomas, American School House Clock, circa 19 something.' He wants me to date it for him exactly."

"1500 people and an unveiling ceremony! And a sign as if it were a museum display. Isn't he embarrassed about the age? Is it dated in the case?"

150 "I didn't find the usual code. I'll look it up later in Tran Duy Ly's book, but I'm putting it between 1938 and 1942. It's in very good condition, but the winding spring is slipping on the arbor. By the way I forgot to tell you, the owner wanted me to put chimes in. I refused, thinking I had found a way out of servicing his clock, but after some grumbling he said forget the chimes but he insisted that I fix it. I told him I'd get him a really beautiful grandfather clock, for the entrance to the dining room for less money than he would pay me to repair the Seth Thomas, but he didn't like that idea. I'll give this a bath, work on the winding arbor. Maybe I reassemble it today. What about you?"

"The Pennsylvania is keeping good time on the horse. Today I'll put it back in the case and if it's still on time 30 days from now, it'll be ready to go back to the museum. I want to see it keep time until it's completely unwound. They'll be happy to get it a month from now. I'll be sad. But I can always pay four bucks and visit it at the Colonial Gallery of the museum."

"You forget that they gave you a complimentary membership. Then?"

"Then I have the collector's clock. The 19th Century French with the strange bell on top. It's so strange I like it. And there's the two from our friend Hughard the dealer. And don't forget I have to go up to that town up state to give an estimate on the street clock. If they accept the estimate—no, forget that. I have to figure out if I can restore it up there or if I have to figure out how to ship it down here, and whether they'll pay for that. I'll bet you I wind up going up there a couple of times."

"Why don't you hold off on Hughard. He has time. Get rid of the Old Dutch Masters."

155 "You think Hughard won't mind?"

"Give him a call. I'm sure he'll say it's OK."

"Then there's the kid who says he going to make me famous."

"What about him?"

"Nothing about him. Plenty about me. I don't want to be famous. I don't want to be on television."

160 "Mr. Vazquez, I think it would be good to have a program on clock restoration on television. Maybe people will get an appreciation of why we don't, can't, work fast fast fast. And the kinds of problems we come up against."

"Maybe you should do it."

"He wants a Puerto Rican."

"I know. I'm having lunch with him tomorrow."

"Where are you going?"

165 "He wanted to take me to a place owned by movie stars in Soho. I said I wanted pizza at John's on Bleecker Street."

"So enjoy your lunch, and keep an open mind. You don't have to decide tomorrow."

Saturday

Vazquez arrived at John's a little early. He had talked to Hughard yesterday and Hughard had agreed to wait for his clocks, so Vazquez had already taken the Dutch clock from its case, had inspected it carefully, made notes, and a drawing that he always made of the plates and wheels. By putting back pressure on the wheels he could see three arbors waddling in their pivots, instead of tightly and freely turning. And he could already clearly see one arbor with a flat side. That meant he had to get a new arbor made by his machinist, and perhaps also a new wheel cut. He anticipated VanBramer's voice echoing in his ear, "no fake stuff." But it was either a new arbor or a clock that would never keep time properly. So, let VanBramer decide on Monday.

Garcia was now late and Vazquez relished the thought that Garcia would never arrive, and if he missed this lunch, Vazquez need never speak to him again.

But Garcia arrived, twenty minutes late, dragging a luggage cart squatting under three boxes.

170 "Mr. Vazquez I had to come over here earlier this week to make special arrangements. Luckily, they don't have much of a lunch crowd on Saturdays, so they set aside this booth for us where I have outlets below. Don't these wooden booths remind you of church pews?"

"Best pizza in New York I think."

"Yeah, you're right, but is it a sin to sit on cushions?"

Vazquez smiled as Garcia began unpacking his three boxes and uncoiling a mass of cables.

"Do you want to order—this takes me a few minutes," said Garcia hauling a small color monitor onto the table.

175 "Pepperoni, mushrooms, anchovies," answered Vazquez detecting a grimace on Garcia's face at the word "anchovies."

"To drink?"

"A glass of wine, and if you don't mind, I would like a salad too."

"Go ahead, order two salads, I'm easy."

Garcia had removed a VCR from another box and from the third, a large number of video tapes. A worrisome number.

180 Garcia seemed to read his mind.

"Relax—you won't have to watch all these tapes. I have them cued. Piece here, piece there. That's video. Images popping."

One thing Vazquez liked about Garcia, he seemed to enjoy his profession. Just unboxing the equipment and hooking it up gave him pleasure and seemed to make him more excited.

As if again reading his mind, Garcia offered, "I know I'm slightly electric. When I walk by the image flutters. And the sound jumps. OK. I'm electric. But that's video. That's film. Movement. Action. Swift. Images. On Parade. I'm electric. So's the business. Bim Bam Boom."

And to the rhythm of his bim bam boom, Garcia had tossed in a cassette, turned on the VCR and the monitor, and hit the volume up button.

185 "Would you mind lowering…"

Garcia hit the volume down button without looking, the way a typist could hit the bracket keys without looking.

"This is a piece I did for a politician. Guy running for congress." Bim Bam Boom. Cassette stopped. Ejected. New one popped in. Play. "This is a piece I did in Spanish to get Latinos out to vote." Bim Bam Boom. "This is a piece I did which was poetic. It wasn't so good. But look at this image." Bim Bam Boom. "This is a piece I did for advertising. A stock brokerage house. Wanna look solid."

Vazquez suddenly found himself interested in all of them, disturbed that as he got caught up in one, he was watching another. He had seen people do that at home, madly clicking between channels. How could you decide what you were looking at if you only paused for 15 seconds?

"Why is everything so fast? Fifteen seconds, twenty seconds, gone. Wouldn't it be better to hold the picture and let me see it?"

190 "Not necessarily, Mr. Vazquez. You know what a microsecond is?"

"Mr. Garcia, I have worked on atomic clocks where nanoseconds were considered long measures."

"Oh. Sorry. You see the short images. You take them in. You know about subliminal?"

"I do."

"Then let me come in from a different angle. In video, long is boring; 45 seconds is ages. That's it."

195 "Mr. Garcia, would you mind if I watched something from beginning to end?"

"Not now. Here comes our salad. By the way you can call me Gary."

John's salad dressing had a distinctive vinegary side that Vazquez enjoyed, but John's never served you a glass of water. You always had to ask.

When the pizza arrived, Mr. Gary Garcia, President of GG Productions, wanted to know what half of the pizza had the "fish." Vazquez guessed that Garcia found even the word "anchovy" repellant. Vazquez ate with gusto asking the waiter for additional oregano, and reminding him that he had asked for water.

"I'm going to show you just under twelve minutes of tape about a minority man who is a specialist in jet engines and their failure. They fly him around the country testing engines and supervising their overhaul and maintenance. He says 'take it out' people take the engine off a plane. Knocking down three hundred thou a year at least. You remind me of him in this; he wanted breakfast. Anywhere he could get grits. And eggs."

200   Vazquez was trying to be open minded. He didn't like the bim bam boom, the hard slapping of cassettes and buttons. You were supposed to treat tools and equipment with care. He remembered the sergeant in the Air Force who brought a summary court-martial against an airman who had thrown a vacuum tube voltmeter onto a table.

    But what he watched seemed well done. A black man who had gone to college at night, studying engineering at City College in New York. In one part somebody asks him why he wears bow ties, and he answered, "because they don't dangle down into an engine when I bend down to look inside." It was funny and a nice touch. The picture looked clean, the music was very nice. And the man had been treated with a lot of dignity. It was a little jarring in places that cut between scenes.

    "Not bad," he said out loud to Garcia.

    "Not bad? I won awards for this piece." Garcia was obviously hurt, but he kept on talking. "Now I'm gonna do Latinos. Your face all over America. Inspiring kids. And old folks too."

    "A clock is not as dramatic as a jet."

205   "That's what Cordero said about radios. Not drama OK. Human interest. Man with talent. Specializing, in a nation of people who no longer know how to do anything themselves. A nation of men and women who push paper in faceless corporations. Men and women who are not sure what they have to do with what the company does. Then there is you. A man with a specialty. You do one thing from start to finish. With your hands. Know something. No executive bathroom and no desire for one. Eager to go to work in the morning. Unsung fame. Underground stars. That's what plays. Let me show you another. A whole commercial."

    The "whole commercial" wasn't sixty seconds long, but it was very effective raising questions of corruption against an incumbent who had been in office a very long time in New York.

    "Mr. Garcia I have to get back to work now, but I want to ask you two questions."

    "OK Mr. Vazquez, I guess you'll never call me Gary. Shoot."

    "Why don't you make one about yourself as a success in the film and video world?"

210   Garcia pursed his lips, and then said, "Nooooo. I wouldn't even know— naw, I don't like egovid. What's the other question?"

    "Did you take photos of me through the store window?"

    Garcia got visibly upset. "Mr. Vazquez, I never take pictures of anybody without their permission. I frequently carry a still camera, but I only take pictures of projects I'm working on."

    Vazquez started to dig into his pocket for money, and Garcia said, "Forget it. On me. Leave the tip if you want, but I want you to think about this—if the Latino men and women of America who are making it in interesting occupations don't cooperate with me how will the kids know that the world is full of interesting and fulfilling jobs? How? How will the people who are full of prejudices toward Latinos ever get to see us as decent and contributing citizens? How? Mr. Vazquez, I don't do this for money. I do it to meet my Puerto Rican burden. White man thought he had a burden. I think I got a burden. I can make money in commercials and other projects. But I gotta do this and people like you gotta help me. Otherwise, how do we change the image? How? Think about it Mr. Vazquez. We're making America great, so why are we hiding it? Think about it."

"I will, Mr. Garcia, I will. Goodbye."

215 "Mr. Vazquez, do I have to tell you that I'm in a rush? Time is everything to me."

"And I have nothing but time. Goodbye."

Monday

"Mr. VanBramer? This is Mr. Vazquez. I need to discuss a matter about your clock. Yes. I'm working on it. I have taken it completely apart. I have to have a new arbor and wheel cut for it Mr. VanBramer, or else the clock will never run right."

"Max, you do whatever you have to do to make that clock work and chime. When will you have it ready?"

"Mr. VanBramer, I'm trying to tell you that I have to fabricate a new arbor and wheel. I have to put a new piece into your old clock."

220 "Do it. When will you have it ready?"

"I don't know yet. When is your election?"

"Oh no you don't Max. I asked first."

"I really don't know yet. If the machinist is busy it might take two weeks to get the new wheel cut. Then six weeks after that."

"Well, don't talk to me anymore, call the machinist now and get busy. Two months is better than seven."

225 "Mr. VanBramer, I'm talking about having to make a whole new part for the clock. This is an important restoration question."

"Get it."

When VanBramer hung up, Vazquez started laughing and Livrehomme asked him why he was laughing.

"I guess I never learn. Mr. VanBramer doesn't give a damn what I do to his clock. Bottom line for him is to get it before the election. If it only works for two minutes after he is elected he wouldn't care. I thought he would object to making a new part. You know what I think Mr. Livrehomme? I think I could get a quartz movement with a chime, stick it in the case and bring it to VanBramer tomorrow, and he wouldn't even look in the case. He just wants to see it run."

Livrehomme had already reassembled the Seth Thomas and was parsimoniously applying minute quantities of clock oil to the tips of the escape wheel teeth. "We laugh at them, but look at how fast they have gotten us to work on their clocks. Meanwhile I'm embarrassed to take $1500 dollars from this man for this job."

230   "He forced you. He's crazy."

"Speaking of which, when are you making the video?"

"Mr. Livrehomme, I haven't decided yet. The kid makes good speeches. But I haven't been famous these many years, so what's the rush? By the way, who do you think should play me in the movie?"

Livrehomme laughed and Vazquez laughed.

Sandra Benítez

Sandra Benítez, born Sandy Ables in 1941, is the author of four novels: *A Place Where the Sea Remembers* (1993); *Bitter Grounds* (1997), which won an American Book Award; *The Weight of All Things* (2000); and *Night of the Radishes* (2004). The daughter of a Puerto Rican mother and a father from rural Missouri, she spent her childhood in Mexico and El Salvador. She began writing her novels at the age of 39. Her work often focuses on the political, emotional, and cultural tensions felt by bicultural, transnational Latinos of mixed backgrounds.

Fulgencio Llanos

El Fotógrafo (fotógrafo, n.m. photographer)

Fulgencio Llanos hurried around the corner just in time to see the bus pull away from the curb. He yelled out, but the bus did not stop. It rumbled off toward the highway, leaving behind a cloud of diesel fumes that set Fulgencio to coughing. "*¡Chinga!*" he exclaimed, hiking up the wooden tripod tucked under his arm. That was the last bus home.

Fulgencio set his tripod down on the sidewalk. He laid down the large, square valise that held his camera and the assortment of props that over the years he had diligently collected for his photo sittings.

In the valise, too, was the film he'd shot only yesterday of El Santo, the masked wrestler who was the toast of all Mexico. The photographs were sure to change Fulgencio's life. Next week, he planned a trip to Mexico City, where he would stride into the offices of *La Tribuna*, the newspaper known for carrying articles on the wrestler's matches and his exploits. "I have uncovered El Santo's identity," Fulgencio would announce, and for a stiff price and the certainty of celebrity, he would provide the newspaper with the photographs showing the wrestler frolicking in the surf at an out-of-the-way beach without the full face mask that was his signature.

Fulgencio pushed his gray felt hat back on his forehead. He looked down the road to see the bus turn onto the highway and disappear behind the side of the cantina at the end of the street. He spat on the sidewalk and took a handkerchief from his trouser pocket and mopped his face with it. He would have to find a ride. Santiago, the town that for now he called home, was nearly thirty kilometers away. It was almost six o'clock. He stuffed the handkerchief back into his pocket, nothing the way the sun spread its waning light over the dirt-packed street and up the smudged adobe wall of the cantina.

5   Fulgencio was weary and hungry. He was bent on reaching home and the bowl of soup and plateful of shrimp he customarily ordered in Lupe Bustos's *comedor*. From time to time, throughout the afternoon, his thoughts had turned to Lupe and how the sight of her strutting about her eating place was all he needed to feel revived.

Fulgencio gave the side of his valise a soft kick. He should have left doña Elvira Cantos's house a little earlier. But no, he had sat with the woman for what seemed like a thousand hours in the stuffy front room with the severe furniture, drinking the weak lemonade she offered, struggling to keep his eyes from settling on the dark stubble that sprouted from around her lips, telling her that though she was a woman of maturity, she was still a beauty and such beauty should, without a doubt, be captured by his camera. "You know the camera does not lie," he told her, and she raised a fat hand to her mouth and giggled behind it, rolling her eyes that were as small and moist as a pigeon's. "*Ay, Señor Llanos,*" she cooed, "*cómo exagera.*"[1] She poured him another glass of lemonade.

In the end, he drank three glasses, and despite the feat, she had still not agreed to sit for him. "Come back tomorrow and we'll discuss the matter further," she had said, grunting softly as she rose from her settee.

Out on the sidewalk, Fulgencio's bladder felt the weight of all that lemonade. I'm getting too old for this, he thought, determined to never set foot in the hag's house again. He was not yet fifty, and for more years than he cared to recall he had made his living roaming the Mexican countryside, photographing men, women and children, the events and possessions in their lives.

It was not easy to live his life: there was the constant travel, the heft and tug of his equipment as he went from town to town. And there was all that conversation to be made, all that nudging and cajoling. No, it was not an easy task he faced each day. It took hard work and subtle inducements to convince people that what they possessed, what they experienced, was deserving of a photograph. "Photographs," he was fond of saying, "photographs properly sized, properly framed, are precious and rightful additions to any home."

10   Of course, times had gone from bad to worse and money was scarce, and so his forms of persuasion had, by necessity, grown more and more inventive. It was draining to have to be so imaginative, so pleasant, when if truth be told, there were days when his heart was not in it. But that was all behind him. After his trip to the capital, his life would be changed. He thanked the stars that yesterday had placed him on the beach with his camera and his telescopic lens.

Fulgencio Llanos lifted his hat and scratched his head before patting the hat back in place again. He reached for his tripod and tucked it back under his arm. He yanked up his valise and started across the street. He would go into the cantina to relieve his bladder. Then a quick *cerveza*[2] before trudging to the highway to flag down a ride.

He was halfway through his Dos Equis when the gringo came in. The man was tall and, though somewhat slender, seemed to fill the room when he stepped through the door. The buzz of conversation that pervaded the

---

[1]how you exaggerate

[2]beer

cantina diminished when he came in, but the gringo seemed not to notice. He walked over to the bar and sat on the stool next to Fulgencio's.

"*Una Bohemia*," the gringo said to the bartender.

Fulgencio took a long swallow of beer. He kept a watch on the newcomer by means of the mirror hanging over the back of the bar. Others in the room soon lost interest. Not Fulgencio. Where there's gringo, there's usually a car, he thought. He envisioned himself riding in comfort all the way to Lupe Bustos's *comedor*. He pictured Lupe watching him step out of a long, sleek Cadillac. The bartender came up and set a Bohemia in front of the gringo.

Fulgencio examined the man reflected in the mirror. He wore a straw hat with a deep crease in its crown. A red bandanna was wrapped around its circumference. He looks like a cowboy, Fulgencio thought. Fulgencio knew gringo cowboys from the movies. They travel astride horses, but not this man. This one must own a Cadillac, parked just outside the door. Fulgencio tried to settle on the color of the car. Black, he thought. No, red. It would be red.

15 "Are you from here?" the gringo asked abruptly. He spoke the simple, direct Spanish of gringos who live just north of the border.

Fulgencio turned to the man. "Are you talking to me, Señor?"

"Yes, to you, but don't use *señor*. I am Jim, Jaime." He extended a hand.

Fulgencio took the man's hand. "*Soy Fulgencio.*"

The gringo was friendly, but this was not surprising—most gringos were friendly. What was surprising was the size of his hand, the power in his grip, and the fact that he wore his hair in a thick, blond ponytail that lay just under the back brim of his hat. Fulgencio wondered why he had not noticed this before. He turned back to his beer and took a gulp. Was that an earring gleaming in the gringo's earlobe? Fulgencio shook his head. He thought, The man is not a cowboy, he is a *heepee*. It had been some time since Fulgencio had seen one. He remembered, many years back, when hippies were a common sight in Mexico. There had been a movie popular then about a band of them traveling across the country in a dilapidated van. The red Cadillac parked in Fulgencio's mind underwent a sudden transformation.

20 "So, Fulgencio, are you from here?"

"No, Señor, I am from Santiago. It is down the road." Fulgencio hooked a thumb in the direction of home.

"I'm going to Santiago," the gringo said. "Actually to Manzanillo. That's not far from Santiago."

"No. It's not far." That *was* an earring the gringo was wearing. Fulgencio remembered that in the movie, the hippies had not owned a car. They had not owned much of anything. They'd sent their girls to stand at the edge of highways so that cars would stop for them. Fulgencio downed the last of his beer. This gringo probably doesn't own a car, he thought. He's probably being friendly to get a ride from me. Fulgencio felt tired again.

"You are a photographer?" the gringo said. "You have a tripod." He pointed to it leaning against the bar.

25   "*Sí. Soy fotógrafo*," Fulgencio said, adding nothing more. It was time to get going. He had wasted enough time talking to someone who did not own a car. If he was lucky, there was still enough daylight left to go out to the highway and flag down a ride.

"*¿Su cámara?*"

Fulgencio placed his foot on the valise resting on the floor next to the stool. "*Aquí.*"

"*¿Una Minolta? ¿Una Nikon?*"

Fulgencio shook his head. "*Una Speed Gráfica.*" He stepped down from the stool. "Well, Señor Jaime, I must be going. I have to find a ride. Soon it will be dark." There. The truth was out. He had no car. That was sure to put an end to all the friendliness.

30   The gringo said, "I have a car. You can ride with me."

"¡Ah!" Fulgencio exclaimed and smiled broadly. Well, well, he thought. "Do you have room for my equipment?"

The gringo nodded. "*Mi carro es muy grande.*"

They paid for their beers and Fulgencio picked up his things. The two went out to the street. Parked by the curb was an old Ford station wagon. It had high, wide wheel wells and a broad flaring hood. The sides of the car, and even the back, were covered with panels of creamy yellow wood. Inside, red-checkered curtains were drawn at the side windows.

The gringo walked over to the front passenger's door. "This is Woody," he grinned and gave the top of the car a little pat.

35   Fulgencio did not know what the name meant, but wishing to be polite, he raised a finger to the brim of his hat. "*Hola, Woodee,*" he said. It's not a Cadillac, he thought, but it has wheels and it will get me home.

The gringo unlocked the door and opened it wide. He reached a hand inside to unlock the back door and swung it open too. "Put your things in there," he said, motioning to the back.

Fulgencio poked his head inside.

The interior was something to behold. It too was covered with wooden panels. And the steering wheel was twice as large as that in most cars. Where the back seat should have been, a narrow mattress was stretched out. On the mattress were piles of clothing, a few pillows minus their cases and a bunched-up serape that was faded and frayed. Beside the mattress, occupying most of the remaining space, sat different-sized cartons spilling over with various objects. There were two nested mountains of straw hats, a boxful of sheathed machetes and stacks of undershirts imprinted with foreign words and colorful designs. There were piles of audiocassettes, small transistor radios and calculators no wider than one's palm. There were pottery platters and vases and jugs. A number of miniature mariachi bands—each group comprised of stuffed, dried frogs wearing fancy little sombreros and playing miniature instruments—sat in a corner of the car.

"*Ay, chihuahua,*" Fulgencio said under his breath. The gringo had a small *mercado* here. Fulgencio wondered how the man had amassed so much merchandise, but he would never pose such an indelicate question. Being in business himself, he knew it was a man's right to protect the secrets of his trade.

40 Fulgencio picked up his valise and stowed it halfway back on the mattress. He wedged his tripod between the case and the back of the front seat. In no time, he and the gringo were on the road heading for Santiago.

It was not yet dark and the traffic was light. Fulgencio Llanos sat back, his elbow jutting out the open window. He glanced over at the gringo. "Those mariachi bands in back…," Fulgencio said.

"*¿Sí?*"

"The frogs. Do you plan to sell them or are you collecting them?" Fulgencio threw in the last half of the question so as not to appear meddlesome. The truth was he could not imagine why a person would want to collect something as unsightly as dead frogs with hard bulging bellies and matchstick legs.

The gringo kept his eyes on the road. "Are you a buying man, or just a curious one?"

45 "I'm curious, I guess, because if you plan to sell the frogs, I have a proposition."

"And what is that?" This time the gringo turned his face to Fulgencio.

"I could photograph the frogs. I could set the bands up with interesting backdrops and photograph them. You could buy my photographs and then sell them yourself."

"You think so?"

"Yes, I really think so."

50 The gringo turned his gaze back up to the road again.

"So, what do you think?" Fulgencio said after giving the gringo a moment or two to mull it over. "I could set little palm trees behind the frog at the marimba. The two with guitars, I could set under a balcony as if they were serenading a señorita. I don't know if there are girl frogs, but I could put a wig on the one with the trumpet." He knew that there were no palm trees, no balcony, no wig among his props, but these were minor details that for now he could ignore.

"I don't think so," the gringo said after a moment.

"*¿No?*"

"*No, creo que no.*" The gringo gave a toothy smile.

55 Fulgencio shrugged and returned the smile. "*Muy bien.*" He was surprised at how readily he himself had backed down. But who could blame him. It was the end of the day and he was tired. Besides, after his trip to the capital next week, people would beg him for any kind of photograph.

Fulgencio turned his attention to the countryside rolling by. Now and then they passed a small roadside shrine that marked the place of a fatal accident. Though there were dangers present in these twisting roads, Fulgencio enjoyed traveling along them by car. He much preferred it to the bus. He pushed his hat back and leaned against the door, squinting into the wind. He liked the feel of the rushing air. He could smell the salty odor of the sea, the subtle fragrance of the lemon groves they passed. Fulgencio glanced over to the gringo who was lighting up a cigarette. Now the odor of tobacco mixed in with all the others.

"*¿Un cigarro?*" The gringo extended a pack of Delicados.

Fulgencio shook his head. "*No, gracias.*" He did not smoke cigarettes or any other kind of tobacco. He knew this was unusual for a man, but with him, that's the way it was. Lupe Bustos admired that about him. "I like to kiss your mouth, Fulgencio Llanos," she had whispered to him one night when they were lying across her bed. "You mouth tastes very good to me." Thinking of Lupe Bustos, of the sweet taste of *her* mouth, Fulgencio wished that he were driving. If he were behind the wheel, he would step more heavily on the gas pedal. He would cause the car to fly to Lupe Bustos's *comedor.*

A shift in the way the wind struck his face brought Fulgencio out of his reverie. The gringo was slowing down. They were halfway to Santiago, and the gringo was putting on the brakes. "*¿Qué pása?*" Fulgencio asked.

60   "That's the road to Playa de Oro," the gringo said. He pointed past Fulgencio to a road that lay just ahead and off to the right. A sign marking the road read PLAYA DE ORO—5 km. When the gringo reached the turnoff, he veered onto the road, the tires squealing in protest. Flung in the gringo's direction, Fulgencio placed a hand on the dashboard to steady himself. He could hear the merchandise slipping and sliding in the back. He glanced quickly behind him to check on his equipment. He could not see his tripod, but his valise looked undisturbed.

"Don't worry," the gringo said, pointing over his shoulder. "Everything is fine back there." He flicked the lighted stub of his cigarette out his opened window. "I want to see the beach," he said, nodding in the direction straight ahead.

"*Ah, la playa.*" Fulgencio managed a weak smile. What else could he do? He reminded himself that accepting a ride put him at the mercy of the driver's whims. Still, this side trip irked him. He had never been to this beach before, but from the sign back there, the drive to it and back should take ten or fifteen minutes. *Paciencia, Fulgencio, paciencia,*[3] he told himself. Laying eyes on Lupe Bustos would have to wait for now.

The road to Playa de Oro was cobblestoned and narrow. It curved sharply around dust-covered trees and dense vegetation. The going was slow because of the curves and because of the sudden washes in the road where cobblestones were missing. The gringo swung the car around the washes. He and Fulgencio bobbed up and down on the seats.

"The road is bad," the gringo said.

65   "*Sí, muy malo.*" Fulgencio visualized the beer he'd had at the cantina sloshing around inside him. He could hear the boxes in the back bouncing against each other. He threw an arm over the back of the seat, placing a protective hand on the top of his valise.

They had been on the road just a few minutes when night began to show itself. Darkness came down through the trees and settled over them. The gringo pulled a switch and light leaped from the car and penetrated the gloomy outline of the woods slipping past them.

---

[3]Patience, Fulgencio, patience

Fulgencio glanced over to see the gringo light up a second cigarette. The glow of the match cast a shadow over the curve of his cheek and up the side of his nose. Fulgencio looked quickly out the window again. Along the side of the road, the trees appeared huge and cerily distorted. A fear as misshapened as the trees came over him. Just who was this man, anyway? Since turning off the main road, he had hardly said a word. It was as if his friendliness had dissolved with the end of daylight. A terrible realization came to him. The gringo was out to rob him. Just as he must have robbed who knows how many shops of all that merchandise in back. It was the camera he wanted, Fulgencio was sure of it. He recalled how the gringo had asked about it. What a fool he'd been to tell him what he had. Fulgencio's mind raced to formulate a plan. He could open the door and jump from the car. He could do it, right now, the car was going slow enough. But if he did, he would have to leave his camera behind. The photographs of El Santo. He could never do that. He would wait until they reached the beach. He remembered the machetes in the back. If worst came to worst, he would reach for a machete.

From over the trees came the faraway sound of vesper bells and to Fulgencio, the tolling was like the voice of God calling out to him. He was not a churchgoing man, but he was a God-fearing one, and so he struck a bargain with the Lord. Señor, he thought, if You withdraw this danger, I will be a better man. He made a quick list of personal improvements. He would not take paper wreaths from road shrines to liven up his sittings. Because times were bad, he would decrease by a few hundred pesos his markup on the sizing and the framing. He would be more honest, less overly complimentary of the way that people looked, of their bleak possessions. He would do this even if it meant foregoing a few sales.

Fulgencio cut short his litany. Up ahead, the road widened and there was the sound of the surf. The air grew heavier, more humid. Leaving the road and trees behind, the car emerged under a dark canopy of sky. The gringo turned onto the beach. He pulled to a stop in the sand.

70   The headlights fanned out over a wild sea that crashed a slate-colored surf against the beach and the rocks clustered at one end of it. For a moment, the sight of the sea transported Fulgencio, but then he came quickly to his senses. He scanned the shoreline for signs of others, realizing in a rush that, just as the road had been deserted, so was the beach.

"The beach is good," the gringo said. He took a last pull from his cigarette and tossed it out the window.

Fulgencio was heartened by the gringo's voice, by the renewed friendliness in it, but he was wary just the same.

"What is that?" The gringo stuck his arm out the window and pointed.

Looking up the beach, Fulgencio saw what looked like a mountain rising from the sand.

75   "*Vamos*," the gringo said. He put the car in gear, and they went bumping off over the sand.

Fulgencio steadied himself against the back of the seat. Just what was that over there? As they drew near, he saw it was a building. A dark, abandoned building.

The gringo pulled up to it and stopped. He turned off the motor. "It looks like a hotel," he said.

The man was right. Caught in the glare of the headlights was the shell of an unfinished hotel. Empty door frames and window frames looked out across the beach. The gringo opened his door, lighting up the car's interior, and got out. A moment later, he returned and poked his head in the car. "Want to come?"

A movie Fulgencio'd once seen popped into his head. It was about a crazy gringo who took his family to a deserted hotel in the mountains. In the mountains, he went after his family with an ax. Fulgencio's scalp prickled at the remembrance of the man's face, of the insane look in his eyes, of the high-pitched way that he had laughed. Despite these thoughts, Fulgencio managed a friendly little wave. "*Andele,*" he said to the gringo. "I'll wait here." Until he could be sure of the man's next move, he would stay in the car with the machetes.

80   "*Bien.*" The gringo slammed the door shut and the inside of the car went dark again.

Fulgencio kept his eye on the gringo. The sheen of the headlights struck the gringo's back, throwing a giant shadow against the building. Soon both shadow and man disappeared through one of the yawning doorways.

Left behind, Fulgencio developed a fresh edge to his fear. His heart hammered in his chest. The gringo could be anywhere. He could be slipping out the other side of the building; he could be taking a wide path around the car. Right now he might be creeping up behind him. Lord, Fulgencio thought, please help me now, and to show the direness of his need, he reached into his heart and handed over to the Lord the one gift he was certain would extricate him from this danger. From this day forward, he pledged, I'll attend Mass every Sunday. He would sit in the front pew so the Lord could best see him. He would pronounce the Mass's responses in a sonorous voice and so give witness to the miracle of his deliverance.

Fulgencio scooted across the seat. He would start up the car. Yes! He would do it. He would drive off and leave the gringo at the beach. Fulgencio groped for the keys, feeling hastily up and down the steering column. There were no keys in the ignition. He leaned into the wheel, running his hand clumsily over the dashboard. No keys there. Fulgencio brought his fist down hard against the wheel. "*¡Chinga!*" He looked out the window. It was time to arm himself. He slid out from behind the steering wheel, turned, and reached back so that he lay halfway into the back of the station wagon.

He had a grip on the hilt of one of the machetes when the inside of the car lighted up. Fulgencio gasped as the gringo scrambled in. For an instant, it was as if Fulgencio's heart had stopped.

85   "*Mis machetes,*" the gringo said, his voice high and tremulous.

Fulgencio let go of the machete. He drew himself slowly back down on the seat.

"*¿Qué pasa aquí?*" the gringo said, a twitch pulling at the corner of his eye. His hat sat crookedly on the back of his head. His face appeared enormous and grotesque under the dome light.

"*Nada, Señor, nada.*" For proof, Fulgencio turned his hands up.

In a surprisingly quick move, the gringo reached across Fulgencio, pinning him for a moment against the back of the seat. The gringo tugged at the handle and thrust the door open. "*¡Fuera!*" he exclaimed.

90 The surf roared in Fulgencio's ears and he was stunned into immobility.

"I said get out. Get out now!"

One moment Fulgencio was in the car and now he lay half sprawled on the beach of Playa de Oro. He scrambled up, losing his footing for a moment in the loose sand. "But, Señor," he yelled, "you do not understand." He struggled to his feet again and was reaching for the door, when the car started up. Its wheels spun and its back end fishtailed before it pulled away.

"*¡Señor! ¡Señor!*" Fulgencio called, racing as fast as the sand allowed. He waved his arms wildly.

Ahead, the car cast two beams of milky light out toward the road and the trees lining it. Fulgencio trained his eyes on the light, a beacon, his heart pounding louder now than even the surf. "Wait," he yelled, running on a few more meters before he saw that catching up would be impossible.

95 The gringo's lights floated out over the beach and then over the road before they were swallowed up in the trees. *Madre de Dios.*[4] Fulgencio thought. He sank to his knees as the darkness fell over him.

Fulgencio Llanos looked up into the vastness stretching above him. A few stars twinkled now, and their cheeriness mocked him. Please Lord, he muttered, but he stopped there, for he could not think of the good in his life so that he might offer it up for bargaining. He dug his hands into the sand, feeling the cool moistness between his fingers and under him where he sat. He was alone. It was now only himself and the deafening sea. He had no camera. No equipment. No photographs of El Santo to turn his life in a new direction.

Standing, Fulgencio allowed his eyes to adjust to the darkness. The surf pounded around him as if he were trapped inside a drum. He looked out across the beach, to the road that led away from here. It would take an hour, he figured to reach the highway. He emptied his shoes of sand and started out, the awareness of what he lacked was a sharpness in his chest. He felt light without his possessions, unsubstantial and unimportant, as if he might float away without his valise to anchor him. He came to the place where the beach left off and the cobbled road began, and he emptied his shoes of sand again before continuing. It was darker on the road, and at each side of him the trees and brush offered large conspiring shadows.

He had walked perhaps a minute or two when he came around a bend. He stopped short.

Someone was crouched by the roadside.

100 "*¿Quién es?*"[5] he called, fearful it was the gringo waiting to spring on him. But no response came, and the object did not move when he clapped his hands on the chance it was some animal that had scurried out from the brush.

---

[4]Mother of God
[5]Who is it?

Fulgencio approached the object cautiously. When he neared it, he could not believe his eyes.

It was his valise.

He dropped down upon it, throwing his arms around it as if he'd found a lost child. He opened the valise, and in the light of the moon that just now showed itself, he saw the bulky outline of his camera. He groped around inside and felt the plates of film containing his bright new future. He gave a whoop and it was then he saw his tripod, lying in the road up ahead. Fulgencio closed his valise and hurried over to his tripod and scooped it up. He raised it high above his head and broke into a little dance. In spite of the cobbles in the road, he leaped and dipped and hollered and, after a moment, laid his tripod across his valise and sank down beside the two.

Fulgencio Llanos sat there for a time, his hand resting on all he needed to be somebody. He shook off the chill he felt at the thought of what might have been. He tried to make sense of his puzzling predicament. Why had the gringo dropped off his equipment? Hadn't the man wanted to rob him? Two images clicked in place in Fulgencio's mind: his own hand on the hilt of the machete and the look on the gringo's face when he'd returned to the car.

105 Fulgencio hung his head as understanding washed over him. What a crazy thing, Fulgencio thought. I feared the gringo and the gringo feared me. Tucking the tripod under an arm, he picked up his valise, its weight a comfort. He'd gone just a few paces when he stepped on his hat.

Fulgencio Llanos threw back his head and gave a laugh. "Hombre, Fulgencio," he said, "you've been a fool." He plucked up his hat and plopped it on his head, starting toward the highway again. He was hungry for a plate of shrimp and Lupe's salsa for dipping. On Sunday, he decided, he'd take Lupe on an outing. He would wait outside the church for her and then they would head for the beach. Taking her hand, they would run into the waves until the sea cradled them.

Yes, he thought, come Sunday, he would celebrate.

Lorraine M. López

Born in central New Mexico, Lorraine M. López is a teacher and scholar whose stories have been printed in various journals and anthologies. Her book *Soy la Avon Lady and Other Stories* was published by Curbstone Press in 2002 and won the Miguel Mármol Prize.

Soy la Avon Lady

It's already dark by the time David drives me home. I was going to take the Greyhound, but my brother was coming from Barstow to L.A. anyway to get some supplies for the horse motel. Normally, I can't stand being in the same city with David, let alone the cab of the same pickup. He's one of these guys thinks there's only one way to look at a thing, and he's the only one can see it that way, so you may as well forget it because if you're not him, you won't never understand. My brother wasn't always like this. Was the horse motel made him an ass. Everyone knows he was just a sawed-off volunteer fireman and fry-cook at the Denny's on the business route before he married that widow, la Betty Crocker, and got her to convert her dead husband's ranch into a horse motel. Now he's Mr. David Martinez, businessman extraordinaire, though, no matter how often he showers and changes his clothes, he always smells a little like his horse motel. I talk to him about it. I even try to get him to take a little Avon for this problem.

As soon as I get in the truck I rolls down my window to let in some desert air and I says, "You know, David, we carry some very effective men's colognes."

"That's the problem with this country," he starts in, pointing out a primered Chevy loaded to the gills with Mexicans.

"Now, I know you like the Skin-So-Soft for fishing."

5   "Keeps the mosquitos off." He nods. "Look at that. Can't even goddamn signal. Learn to drive, *mojados!*"[1] he shouts out the window.

"Yeah, well, we have some real good aftershave and soap, too."

"Listen," he says to me, sighing. "You're what? Forty-eight? I know I got a couple years on you, and I'm hitting fifty. But a good fifty, a solid fifty. I got my business, and I got my health. But you, look at you. All that makeup. I know you're my sister an' you're a chick. I seen your twat when mama used to give us a bath together. But I have to be honest here, you're big enough to play for the Forty-Niners. And you're running around like some overgrown campfire girl in drag for Godsake, selling cookies. Ain't no one uses Avon no more, except to keep mosquitos off. It's gutdamn irritating to hear you turn every conversation into a sales pitch. Whyn't you just settle down and stop bugging folks."

So that kind of puts me in a sour mood, even if it is coming from David, whose entire fortune and well-being comes from his settling down, marrying la Betty Crocker. Come to think of it, he's probably given me the best advice he knows. I only wish he could follow the second half of his own great advice because as soon as he made his little speech, he started in on the time Johnny Carson called him up at the horse motel.

"Now, I ain't sayin' I planned it thataway," says David, a grin cracking under his red beak of a nose. "Now, I'm not saying I arranged the call, but you gotta admit it was a pretty gutdamn strategic bit of public relations."

10   I just rolled my eyes, rubbing my fingers over the upsidedown "M" scarred on my forehead. David calls it my "W." His way of seeing things. Anyone else'd tell you, despite all the Avon fill and foundation, the powder and whisper blush, what I got is an inverted "M" up there, for my name, for Molly. Like some kind of cockeyed monogram. I trace the path of weals through one eyebrow and up toward my hairline, rising in the middle like a reverse widow's peak. Then I stare out the window at the neon-haloed car dealerships, K-marts, pizzerias, and dry cleaners blurring past along the highway. I have been back and forth

---

[1]wetbacks

between Barstow and L.A. at least a thousand times. There is no really scenic route, but you'd think that over time there would at least be a slightly less ugly way to go or that a person could get used to the boringness of it all.

The time Johnny Carson called David I happened to be watching the show. I was half-crocked from that wine you buy in a carton, I admit, but even I, stumbling in my negligee before the blue-gray haze of my black-and-white set, even I could see that old Johnny had just called my brother up to laugh at him. I have to jam a soup spoon between the wall and a critical place bulging out of the back of the set to get a good picture, and that night the spoon had popped out. So Johnny's smirking eyes boiled through a blizzard of static. Even so, those pebbly eyes clearly smirked, and I could even see Johnny bite back his lipless, lizard grin as he chatted on the phone with my brother.

"Johnny was pur-ty surprised to find out we have a horse motel in Barstow. Told him it was the only one in the state. Still is," David turned to nod at me in agreement with himself. "But, man, was he shocked about the elevator. 'State of the art' I says to him. 'State of the art.' "

Around that point in the famous conversation, I remember Johnny passing the phone to that big guy, the one who looks like a refrigerator wearing a suit and who laughs at everything Johnny says, that what's-his-name, on account of he, Johnny, that is, had to double over with spasms he made like he couldn't control.

"People need a horse motel, I 'splained to him," David goes on. "They's rodeos and horse shows and all kinds of reasons to take a horse somewhere overnight."

15 The thing is, though an idea like a horse motel sounds pure ridiculous to someone like Johnny Carson, who has like a castle in Malibu and makes jokes about how much alimony he has to shell out, and even to a person like me, who sells Avon between temporary secretarial jobs, plenty of people seem to truly feel the need for lodging their horses at my brother's motel.

"You know how much business shot up after that show aired?" David demands after he wound up the full retelling of his telephone conversation on the Tonight Show so many years ago.

I nod, closing my eyes and scrunching myself into a ball against the car door, so David might think I'm drifting off to sleep.

"How much, then?" he persists.

"A lot," I'm yawning by now.

20 "Gutdamn straight."

We pass a batch of black-and-white cows alongside the highway, grazing and staring without much curiosity at the passing cars.

"Hey, you remember when we first moved to Barstow? You were just a little thing, black as a bullfrog. Yammered your ugly little head off in Spanish. Scared those old folks in that diner. Remember? Musta thought they was being invaded."

"You're nuts. I never spoke Spanish."

"Don't tell me you don't remember. You were at least four or five. Coupla years later, I remember, we went back home for a visit on the train. Was on the train. You were staring out the window and pointing a dark little finger at a cow. You ast, 'Is thet a kay-ow?'" David does his best Southern drawl, which is purely pathetic. "I'll never forget. You were still as black as a bullfrog. An' I remember you had those floppy yellow shorts. A bullfrog in a pair of yellow shorts."

25   I let David laugh, enjoy his little make-believe story. Pulling my jacket over my shoulder, I let myself drift off. I must have slept the rest of the ride into the city because the next thing I remember is David shaking my shoulder and saying "end of the road." I thank him for the ride, and as usual he doesn't wait for me to fish my key out of my handbag or find my way to my apartment door before peeling off like some teenager playing chicken at a stoplight. And I live in a pretty rotten building, to be honest. If David was any kind of decent brother, he would have at least walked me to my door.

I have to step over all the usual wadded-up disposable diapers, fast-food wrappers and beer bottles, finally feeling my way along a mildewed mattress propped against the wall near my door. There's a cluster of Mexicans in undershirts, jabbering at each other and drinking cans of beer under the street lamp just across the way. Anyone might jump out with a switchblade and rob me of my Avon case, which was all I had of any value, as David, naturally, had forgotten to pay me for the bottles of Skin-So-Soft he ordered.

I make it to the door okay, but once inside I slam my hip on the telephone table, knocking the phone on the floor and scaring poor Fabian out of his little cat wits. "It's okay, Fabian, it's just me," I says in a calm voice because Fabian has pretty bad asthma, and stress can cause him to have an attack. I set my case on the floor and went to pet Fabian's thick gray fur. His breathing is already growing shallow and ragged. "Damn," I says, but quietly, and I drew him in my arms. He struggles and squeezes out of my grip, running around the house and hacking like he was trying to bring up a hair ball.

I pick the phone off the floor and dial real quick. The line rings twice, and then I hear a loud and gruff "Yah!"

"Uncle Enrique?"

30   "Yah!"

"It's me, Molly." Fabian, though heaving and retching, bounced from the couch to the coffee table like he's place-kicked by some unseen demon.

"He-e-e-ey, Mulligan! ¿Como estas?" Like a lot of old guys, my uncle never quite trusts telephone wires to carry his voice over any kind of distance, so he has to holler his head off into the mouthpiece.

"Uncle Rique, it's an emergency! Can you come over and take me to the hospital right now?" I have to hold the phone at least a foot from my head and shout back.

"Of course, *hita*, are you okay? Wanna ambulance?"

35   "NO! I just need a ride!"

"I'm coming right now!"

I don't mention it's Fabian that needs the hospital, and I know my uncle Enrique isn't the kind of uncle who presses too much for information, particularly personal information. He probably thinks I'm bleeding to death from a botched abortion, and if that's the case, he'd just as soon not know the particulars.

I catch up with Fabian in the bathroom where he's gagging over the plunger behind the toilet. I pull him out, wrap him in a bath towel and bring him to the kitchen, where I pour myself some handy carton chablis into a coffee cup. I stand there drinking the wine and cuddling Fabian while I wait the few minutes it takes my uncle to drive over. Fabian's plump body shudders as he gasps, struggling to breathe. This is the worst attack he has ever had, and I'm scared he's gonna die before Uncle Enrique gets here.

But still I could feel him fighting for air as I carried him to the door when I heard Uncle Enrique knocking. I'd turned on the outside light, and Uncle blinks on the threshold. I can tell when he makes out the towel-wrapped bundle in my arms because he quickly shifts his eyes away. "It's Fabian, Uncle Rique, he's having an asthma attack!" I push out the screen door.

40 "Fabian?"

"My cat! He's gonna die if we don't hurry." Saying the words makes my voice crack, and the tears leap out of my eyes.

"A cat? Is that what you got there? A durn cat?"

"It's Fabian. You remember Fabian?"

"I remember the movie star." My uncle scratches his chin, making a raspy sound with his fingernails. "Singer, too, wasn't he?"

45 "C'mon, please. Uncle, hurry. Where did you park?"

"Just out in front," he says, leading the way past the mattress. "Can't take no cat to the hospital, though. 'S not allowed, is it?"

"The animal hospital, Uncle. It's just down Glendale Boulevard near the freeway exit. Please, we have to hurry."

When we get to the car, Uncle Enrique chuckles a little.

"What?" I says, pretty pissed. "What's so funny?"

50 "Nothing," he shakes his head as he unlocks the door. "Here, *hita*, get in. You want me to hold that, that Fabian for you while you get the seatbelt?"

"I got it." It's tricky, but Fabian has gone even limper, and I'm able to set him on my knees while I click on the strap.

Uncle Enrique climbs in and starts the car, still laughing some. "I'm laughing at myself, *hita*. I'm laughing I got outa bed and got dressed like a fireman for a five-alarm fire to rush a cat to the hospital."

"What's funny about that?"

"C'mon, doncha cry. Mulligan. We're almost there." Uncle Enrique sighs, "I need to get myself re-married or something."

55 In the hospital, everything looks too bright. I feel like I should have my sunglasses on. Why do they keep places so bright? When I have to squint, my scar turns so white and the skin raises so much it looks like it's ready to spring off my forehead and run around the room. I can tell it spooks the girl at the counter. She kind of jumps back a little when she sees me, and her green eyes get bigger. (Uncle Enrique has dropped me off while he hunts for a parking

space. Even this late there's nowhere for him to park.) She seems to get over her surprise when she sees Fabian in my arms. "Yes?"

"My cat," I says, trying to hand her the bundle. "He has asthma, and he needs something. He had a bad attack." Since Fabian has gone limp in the car, I can't really tell if he's still breathing, and to be honest, I'm afraid to check.

"Have you been here before?"

"No, my usual vet is closed now. I just came here for the emergency hours."

"You'll have to fill out these forms, then." She hands me a clipboard.

60   "But Fabian needs to see the doctor now. This is an emergency," I says. "My cat might die while I'm filling in these papers!"

Just then a nice-looking Middle Eastern—maybe even Lebanese—man in a white coat steps into the waiting room from a door behind the counter.

"What is the matter here?" he asks in that choppy way foreigners have.

And I says that I think Fabian is going to die if he doesn't get help now and that I don't have time to fill forms.

"I will look at the cat," he says, reaching over to take Fabian. "You can fill out the paperwork while I examine your cat, Miss—"

65   "Martini," I says, smiling a little now and hoping there's no lipstick on my teeth, "Molly Martini."

"Okay, Miss Martini, I will be back momentarily."

My heart flutters a little when he said "momentarily," and he puts his dark eyes on mine. I feel sure he's Lebanese. My sister Gloria once dated Lebanese twins, both butchers, and I'd hoped she'd marry one and throw me the leftover. They were so darling in their matching bloodstained aprons. But Gloria decided she would rather dump them both and have a child out-of-wedlock with an anonymous Nordic type, who I never even met, let alone got to ask if he had a brother. But Gloria's like that; she can get anything. She was in the back seat when we had the accident. She didn't go through the windshield like me and Barbara and Grandma. And her skin is as white as the heart of a radish.

Uncle Enrique blinks his way into the glaring wait area, saying, "I had to park clear at that filling station near the freeway." He sits beside me and picked up a copy of *Cat Fancy* to thumb through. "Where's Fabian?" he asks.

"The doctor's looking at him. You got a pen, Uncle?"

70   He leans over to reach into his side pocket and pulls out his key chain with at least three million keys attached to it, a Swiss Army knife, a bottle opener, a teensy sewing kit and a little bitty pen and pencil set. He hands me a pen the size of a toothpick, saying, "Here you are, *hija*."

I take that itsy-tiny pen and start filling out the forms, while my uncle chews on his tongue and reads an article in *Cat Fancy*.

After a while, Uncle scratches his head. "Gotta story here," he says, "about a Siamese cat s'pose to beat up a grizzly bear to save the life of a *dog*. You believe that?"

I shrug and write something unreadable under "Current Employer." I didn't like to put Avon or "it varies" in case the doctor should look over my form.

"Says the cat jumped on the bear's head from a tree and scratched its eyes. Blinded him," Uncle continues. "I guess it could happen. But to save *a dog*?"

75   As I was signing the last sheet, the doctor appeared again. "Miss Martini," he says. "I am so terribly sorry."

"Martini?" asks my uncle, looking around though we're the only ones in the waiting room.

"This is my uncle," I says, not wanting to hear the doctor say anything else.

"Yes, it's good to meet you. I have some bad news I am afraid. Your cat has died. Of course, there will be no charge. I could do nothing to help him."

I remember how my mother threw herself on Grandma's casket when they were ready to lower it in the ground, and afterwards the aunts really criticized her for that because my mother is kind of an underachiever emotionally, so when she makes a display it's usually for show. Back then at the funeral, even I, in my turban of bandages which was coming unraveled and the gauze was falling in my face, even I could see my mother was making a show, and I felt so embarrassed I wished I could shrink up like a pine nut and roll into the earth right besides Grandma. But in the animal emergency hospital that night, I thought of my mother when I fell into that doctor's strong Lebanese arms, and I realized the truth about my mother's scene at the graveside: it was only part show.

80   "Miss Martini, please, please," says the doctor, patting my shoulder with one hand, but pushing me upright with the other.

"Name's not Martini," scoffs my uncle. He's often impatient with foreigners. "It's Mar*tinez*."

I have Uncle Enrique drop me at the VFW club. I'm way too depressed to go home and put up Fabian's little rolling toys, his catnip mouse and wash out his double-sided dish.

"Are you sure, *m'hija*? [2] It's pretty late."

"Yeah, I'm sure," I says, remembering I had no money. "How 'bout you come and have a drink with me?"

85   "No, no, no way," he says. "I gotta go to court tomorrow. Remember my friend Kiko? He gotta ticket. I said I would drive him."

"Isn't Kiko the one who rides a bicycle?" I says, recalling a fat guy in a Dodger cap, teetering on a Schwinn. "He doesn't even have a car. How'd he get a ticket?"

"Riding under the influence"

"Oh...You could still have one drink with me," I says.

"Oh, no. I better not." Uncle Enrique pulls along the curb in front of the VFW and leans again to reach in his back pocket. "You need some money, *hija*. I got a little extra." He hands me a twenty-dollar bill. "I'm real sorry about the cat, that Fabian," he says as I got out. "You take care of yourself, okay, Mulligan?"

90   "Hey, it's Molly! Molly Martini! We thought you was still in Barstow!" My best friend Charlene waddles over and climbs a barstool near the door to wrap her fat, freckled little arms around my neck.

"Hi, Shorty," I says, smiling a little, but sadly, so Charlene will know right off that I'm feeling down. I call her "Shorty" because she's a dwarf, a "little

---

[2] my girl

people," that's what she likes to be called, anyway, and not a dwarf or a midget. She's not just one of these shorter folks that everyone exaggerates about when they call her a dwarf. She really is under three feet tall. Her mother was a dwarf, an actress who had a part in the *Wizard of Oz*, and her father was a dwarf too, but I'm not sure what he does for a living. We met one time at a funeral for another dwarf we both happened to know and got to be friends at the bar afterwards.

"What's wrong, Miss Martini?" Charlene squeaks, seeing my sad smile.

"I lost my Fabian tonight," I says, starting to sob even before Willie, the bartender, can slide me my drink.

Well, you know, I cry a lot that night, and I have to say I drink a bit, too. I go through that twenty pretty fast, even though some people buy me drinks. Turns out it's our friend Fisher Boy's birthday, and his wife Millie, an ex-school photographer from Visalia, has a cake for him and a half a case of champagne. So you know I drink my share of that, and I eat a wedge of cake the size of Charlene's ox-blood prayerbook. I know they're the same size on accounta Charlene sets her prayerbook on the pool table alongside of my paper plate.

95 Fisher Boy has his own bottle of champagne, and he sits at the bar nursing on it like a baby. Has a bunch of friends with him, some guys I don't recognize. But old Fisher Boy won't talk to anyone 'til he's finished his drink. This heavy guy—bald on top, but with long hair, wearing a leather vest and no shirt underneath—lumbers up on the stage over past the shuffleboard table, his bootheels blasting like gunshots. He grabs the microphone, which wails in my ear painfully. Then he taps it some, causing a couple of thunder rolls. "I jes' wanna say," he mutters into the netted bulb of the mike, "we all of us here— all us veterans and friends of veterans in this club—come together to honor one of our own on his birthday. Now, don't matter if you fought in double-ewe, double-ewe one, two or three—"

I shoot a look at Charlene. I'm never good with numbers, but I'm pretty sure we'd only gotten to two with the wars. Charlene had her stubby index and middle fingers out, counting under her breath.

"Korea or Nam. Was in Nam myself, and I ain't proud of what I done. I raped. I pillaged. I even helped burn down some villages. And, in general, I ain't proud of those things, but I am proud to be a veteran of a foreign war and proud to be a member of this club and mostly proud to be a friend to this man we honor tonight on his birthday. Getcher ass up here, Fisher Boy! Willie, somebody, help him up the steps."

Fisher Boy steps up two of the stairs without help, then falls to his knees and crawls up the remaining two and over to the microphone. The rapist and pillager lifts Fisher Boy to his feet and pushes him toward the microphone stand, which Fisher Boy clings to as if it's a masthead on a ship tossed around in a storm.

"Hallo, everybody! I'm Fisher Boy, an' I'm a drunk!"

100 Everyone laughs, and some folks hoot back, "Hello, Fisher Boy!" It's like a reverse Alcoholics Anonymous meeting. Pretty funny, really, if you consider the circumstances.

"What I want to say is, first of all, I wanna thank my good friend, Lyle, for the innerduction—"

"Lowell," hisses the rapist and pillager.

"Huh?"

"Lowell. My name's Lowell."

105 "Oh, yeah, right. Well, anyway, thanks a lot. An' I wanna thank everyone for coming tonight, though you were probably coming here anyway and just found out it was my birthday a few minutes ago. What I got to say is, I'm seventy-eight years old, an' I'm a veteran a' World War Two. I don't think we got to Three yet, Lyle, but I ain't been payin' too much 'tention. I was a clerk typist in the army, an' I didn't get any opportunities to rape an' pillage too much, but I wisht they had invented white-out then because I ruint a whole lot of forms. Man, you shoulda heard the guys cuss when I screwed up their passes. Holy Moly! Anyway, point is, we're all here, and it's my birthday. So have some cake and have a drink!"

Fisher Boy hoists his champagne bottle and pours the dregs down his chin, darkening the front of the new t-shirt his wife has given him. The front of it says, HERE COMES FISHER BOY! and the back reads, THERE GOES FISHER BOY! I think it's pretty clever, almost as funny as the baseball cap someone else has given him with a fake ponytail attached to the back.

We all clap and sing "Happy Birthday," then "For He's a Jolly Good Fellow" and clap some more. While I'm beating my hands together for old Fisher Boy, Charlene dug a sharp little elbow in my rib cage. "Guess who just come in?" she hisses.

"Who?" I says, looking around.

"Suzy Q."

110 "Oh, no." Now, if I feel sad about losing Fabian, I feel almost worse when Charlene tells me my baby sister had just come into the VFW. Suzy Q is good or bad, hot or cold, dark or...only dark, actually. But, you get the picture. She's never in-between on anything, not ever.

When Suzy Q is good, she's at home, taking care of those three little half-Japanese children of hers, making a super-tasty supper for her husband Dean, and keeping that house so clean you could conduct major surgery on her bathroom floor, behind the toilet, even. But when, Suzy Q is bad, Lord, you sometimes have to scrape her off a gutter and throw her in the drunk tank at county for at least a week, if you can find her. Last time she was bad was around Christmas. She went missing for a week, and poor Dean had to hire a private investigator to find her in some by-the-hour hotel room with a skinhead junkie from Altoona, who was, Dean says, not sorry at all to cut her loose.

"Where is she?" I ask Charlene.

"Over to the back. That tall booth she likes."

"I guess I oughta go and talk to her." I says, real slowly, so's Charlene can interrupt and argue me out of it.

115 But she says, "I guess you oughta."

I make my way to the back of the bar, pulling off the party hat someone stuck on my head. You can't have a serious talk with someone like Suzy Q wearing a polka-dot cone spouting pink and green streamers over your hair.

Suzy Q favors a booth near the ladies room, one of the older ones that hasn't been reupholstered with scotch-guard like most of the others. The VFW used to be a decent kind of bar at one time, with wood floors, stained glass windows and real near-leather booths. But they covered the wood with parquet and sold the stained glass and only a few near leather-booths remain. People generally don't like to sit in them, though, because they tend to make your buttocks and backs of your legs sweat, and then you stick, so you make bathroom sounds as you peel yourself out of your seat.

But I doubt if my sister sweats all that much. She reminds me of a long cool glass of ice tea. Her clear copper skin chills your finger tips when you brush against it. And you can almost hear the ice cubes rattle when she walks. She even smells like a sprig of mint, a wedge of lemon. With her long brown legs, her wide eyes and Cleopatra-flat black hair, my baby sister could be a desirable woman if she wasn't so criminally insane when she was bad.

"Hullo, Suzy," I says, thinking how lovely she looked in a peppermint-striped shift—ice tea in a slender barber's cup.

120 "Amalia," she says, putting out her frosty fingers to delicately shake mine. "How good to see you." Suzy has the habit of whispering in a breathy way when she talks. You can barely hear her, and you can't help but hear every word at the same time. She has the kind of voice that I imagine would be just perfect for reading stories in the tabloids out loud. *Woman Gives Birth to Baby with Dog's Head*, would sound just right coming out of her mouth.

"Where's Dean?" I ask, noting the near-finished gin and tonic near her elbow. Poor Dean doesn't like Suzy Q to drink for all the obvious reasons.

"Dean?" Suzy Q repeats like it was a foreign word. "Dean? Dean?"

"Your husband, Dean Fujimori. Where is he? And the kids? How are the kids?"

"Bartender!" she roared right in my ear.

125 "Golly, Suzy, you about took my hearing out."

"Another, please," she says with a smile when Willie appeared at her elbow. Willie nods, giving me a nervous look. "Um, are you sure?"

"Perfectly sure," whispers Suzy, pulling a roll of twenties out of her handbag. "Just keep them coming, will you?"

Willie hesitates. "How long are you staying?"

130 "Not long," says Suzy. "Not very long at all."

"You aren't going to do the ladies room like last time, are you?"

"Don't be silly," Suzy laughs.

"'Cause they said they was gonna cancel my policy, that kind of thing happens again."

"I'm not staying long, Willie. I promise. Just bring me another, please."

135   Willie retreats in an undecided way, like he didn't get to say all he had to say, but he brought the drink in a few minutes anyway.

"So," says Suzy Q, staring at me from head to toe. "So, Amalia, how are you these days? My, you've grown a bit."

"Thyroid," I says. "And my metabolism's changing."

"I see."

"Heard you had some trouble around Christmas." I says, taking a chance.

140   "That!" she giggles. "That was not trouble. Nothing near trouble. I'll tell you what trouble is. Trouble is that people don't even know what trouble is and what trouble can do when it wants to, and that, my sister, is real trouble."

"Well, Dean was pretty upset."

"Dean?"

"Maybe you want to go home, Suzy, after your drink. Maybe I'll go with you. I haven't seen the kids for a long time."

"Listen, Amalia, do you remember when we were kids? Do you remember that skinny little tree Dad tried to get to grow in the front of the house? I keep thinking about that tree."

145   "What about it?" I remembered my father brought home what looked like a twig one day from the nursery and said we were going to have shade for the house in a couple of years. He propped that twig with a two-by-four, watered it, fertilized it and even built a short white wire fence around the base to keep dogs off. I can still see him, coming home from work in his rumpled overalls with his lunch-box and heading straight for the hose to feed his tree.

"That tree never had a chance, Amalia, the way we treated it."

"What do you mean?"

"You don't remember how we bent it and pulled the leaves, dancing around it like it was the Maypole. You don't remember that?"

"Maybe a little. But we didn't kill the tree. A tree like that can't survive in the desert."

150   "You were the worst one, Amalia, hanging on that tree and singing at the top of your lungs at anyone driving by. You remember that song you always sang."

"You're making this up, now." I was starting to get mad. Many of my conversations with my kid sister tend to go this way: she claims to remember something stupid or shameful I did when I was drunk or when I was a senseless kid, and I get all upset about it.

"I think it was from *West Side Story*," she persists, tapping her long red fingernails on the tabletop. "What was it? Oh, I know. It went like this, 'I wanna be Americana! I wanna be Americana!' You sang that all damn day long, every day one summer. Don't you remember? It was perfectly hideous! You would wear one of Mama's floppy skirts and pearls—I remember the pearls—and pin yellow yarn to your head to give yourself long blond hair. Then you'd scream 'I wanna be Americana!' at the top of your silly lungs at any car went by. God, I was six years younger than you, but I wanted to die from embarrassment. The whole neighborhood must have thought the natives were *very* restless that summer." Suzy laughs, lighting a cigarette.

"You know what. I do remember that summer. But it was you, Suzy Q, it was you sang that stupid song over and over and over and over and—"

"Don't be ridiculous." Suzy takes a huge swallow of her drink and a drag on her cigarette. "You were the one."

155   "Drop it, Suzy. Drop it, please." My eyes fill, blurring my long cool ice tea sister with her cigarette and her drink.

She snaps her fingers. "What does Uncle Enrique call you? What is that little nickname he gave you?"

"Mulligan."

"Just what does that mean? Mulligan?"

"I really don't know."

160   "Oh, I know, doesn't it mean 'do over'? Like in golf, when you make some horrid error. It's so bad, they call it a 'mulligan,' and you get the chance to try again."

"I'm not sure. I don't know golf."

"Good name," says Suzy, mashing out her cigarette.

"Suzy," I hear someone say. I glance up at Dean, standing by the booth and holding out his hand toward my sister. "Suzy, let's go home. I had to leave the kids alone to come here. Let's go home. It's late."

"How did you find me?" Suzy asks, half-rising from the booth, then sinking back down.

165   "Willie called me."

"You shit!" Suzy yells across the room. From where I sit, I can see Willie give a little shrug.

"Let's go home, Suzy. I'll make you a bath and light some candles. It will be so nice." Poor Dean keeps his hand out, so Suzy can grab it and steady herself to walk out. My brother-in-law is almost as large as a sumo wrestler, and I have no doubt he could have whipped Suzy out of the booth by her hair and tucked her—hissing and spitting like a cat—under one arm to carry out to the car. But Poor Dean favors a gentle approach with my sister—soft words, tender touches, candles and warm baths.

Suzy whispered some curse words, then she takes Poor Dean's hand and lifts herself noiselessly out of the booth. "I was ready to come home anyway," she says, looking at me. "It's so goddamn boring here."

Of course, I have to dance with the rapist and pillager after a few more drinks.

170   "I never danced with a raper and pillagist before," I admit as we hoof to some tune about Lubbock, Texas.

"Jes' call me Lowell," he says, smiling, and I notice he is either handsome in an ugly way or ugly in a handsome way. He had two full moons that stuck out on his chin, looked just like a stubbly baby's bottom and squinty green eyes hummocked in gooseflesh pouches. It sounds bad here, but if you blurred your eyes you might look at Lowell and think of Robert Mitchum. A bald Robert Mitchum with shoulder-length locks of dirty blond hair. You have to use your imagination some.

After a few more dances and a lot more drinks, I guess Lowell isn't so bad for a rapist and pillager. In between the dances, I tell him about Fabian, and he says he feels bad for me. He says he's done some time, and he can really appreciate a gal like me, then he winks. He offers to give me a lift home. So I tell him where I live, and I say good-bye to everyone: Charlene grabbed my elbow hard with her sharp little fingers as I'm on my way out. "Miss Martini," she says, "Miss Martini, you be careful. 'Sa full moon," she says. "Take care of yourself." Then she looked at Lowell and raised her eyebrows, rubbing her turned-up nose.

Turns out Lowell had a motorcycle. And, boy, am I glad I'm drunk because you can't get me on one of those things sober, I tell you. Lowell starts out a gentleman and lets me mash my big old hair under his greasy helmet, which is real good of him. Then I climb on behind Lowell, and the thing farts off down the street. Now, I don't drive. I never have, and I never want to, so I don't pay much attention to directions. I don't think it's too strange when Lowell gets on one freeway, then another. But along about the third freeway it seems like a lot of time has passed, and I know I don't live that far from the VFW.

With the rushing wind and the sounds of traffic—yes, there's traffic even in the middle of the night—it would be pretty useless to holler: "I think you're going the wrong way!" or "Where the hell are you taking me?" And anyone who's ever ridden the back of a motorcycle on a freeway knows there isn't any way of getting off or making the driver stop. So I just clutch at Lowell's lardy sides and thank God Above I'm loaded, or I would have been plenty scared.

175   It's one of those oily nights, when even the leaves of the oleander bushes along the freeway seem slick and slimy. A fish-smelling fog from San Pedro crawls over, clouds car windows and fuzzes the street lamps. Of course, I'm about dead blind anyway without my glasses. My mother is totally blind, and I expect I'll be there, too, one day. It runs in the family. But the fog muffling the moon and my eyes tearing up from the wind in my face makes it near impossible to see where I am. Just the sensation of moving downward, descending, makes me think we're headed toward the Valley.

I recognize the In-and-Out Burger at the off-ramp that leads to my cousin Elaine's house in Sylmar, where I always went for Thanksgiving and Christmas dinner. Awhile back, In-and-Out printed up a mess of bumper-stickers for advertising. Then some brilliant jokers had the idea to scratch out the "B" and "R" from "burger," and to this day you can spot all these cars with "IN-AND-OUT-URGE" pasted all over their back bumpers. Real hilarious.

I'm glad Lowell's getting off the freeway. Maybe he can drop me at Elaine's. I try to give people the benefit, you know. Maybe he's confused by my directions or too drunk to figure them out. He takes us to a little park not too far from Elaine's house. One of those small grassy jobs with the sandlot swingset near a baseball diamond and bleachers.

"My cousin Elaine lives near here," I says, climbing off the bike, my legs still atremble from the vibration of the engine. "You wanna take me to her house?"

"Let's take a walk," says Lowell. Then he grabs hold of my hand, leading me under the bleachers.

180 "What is that horrible stench?" I says because suddenly I smell the nastiest maggotty smell, like hundred-year-old banana skins layered with fertilizer, then soaked in soured milk.

Lowell just jerks a thumb at a nearby dumpster, and before I can say another word, he jumps all over me, and we both tumble in the dirt. Then he starts grunting and dry-humping my hip like a badly behaved hound. "Jesus," I says, "get off me, will you?"

His hands are all over me, squeezing my bra padding through my blouse, stroking my hips and reaching under my skirt. "Cuss me in Spanish," he moaned. "Cuss me in Spanish."

"What?" I says, pushing his hands away from my skirt.

"C'mon, baby. Cuss me in Spanish, bad boy," he says again.

185 "Will you get off me!" I holler. "I don't even speak Spanish! Get off before I yell 'rape'!"

One renegade hand shoots up my slip, and he froze.

"I mean it," I says, "I'll scream 'rape'!"

"My, God. What is this?" he asks, sitting up. "You *are* a chick! I thought—"

"What did you think?"

190 "At the bar, I thought they said.... You look...."

"What? Tell me?"

"No offense, but chicks ain't my thing."

"Just take me to my cousin's house, and we'll forget all about this," I says, smoothing my skirt, "or you can be looking at some pretty serious trouble."

Old Lowell doesn't say anything to that. He just stands up and brushes the dirt from his Levis and starts walking back to the bike. I get up, too, and follow after him, but it's hard to keep up because I'm wearing these lamé heels that kept sinking into the soft dirt, stalling me. "She just lives a few blocks from here. I can show you how to get there," I says. But I can tell by the hunch of his back and the blank look of the hairless cap of his head that Lowell isn't listening at all. And sure enough, he pulls that smelly helmet over his own head, climbs on the bike and sputters off without me.

195 "Shit," I says, "shit, shit, shit." Then I take off my heels, but not my pantyhose as there was a clammy feeling from the fog which leaked into the valley, and I start to walk, block by block, to Elaine's house. And I get lost and keep getting lost. The soles of my hose are shredded, only a few tough threads keep them from rolling up my ankles. I wander around looking for Elaine's place until the foothills glow like coals in the barbecue from the sun coming up. I tell you Sylmar is one hilly place, where I do not recommend tramping around in nearly bare feet. There's all these same-looking stucco houses made to look like Spanish-style adobe, some huge yards, horse property even, and at least twenty-five million loud barking dogs, snorting and throwing themselves into the chainlink as I pass by.

Somewhere I take a very wrong turn, then another and another. The ranch-style houses disappear, replaced by liquor stores, dry cleaners, Mexican markets and apartments like concrete blocks scrawled with graffiti. The signs, the bill-boards, the street names change from English to Spanish, and the few folks I see rushing out to work are short, dark and completely uninterested in me. I might be invisible as far as they're concerned. It's almost as if they hood their eyes against me. And I feel like I'm intruding in some foreign country, like I'm in the heart of Mexico or San Salvador or some place even more dangerous.

Then I get the idea that I've died, that Lowell has snuffed me by the dumpster, and it's my soul wandering unseen in these foreign streets. I always was slow to understand things in school. Maybe I have died and am just too shocked or too stupid to realize it. That's when I see a burnt-down gas station, which has a phone booth still standing at the edge of the charred lot, so I bolt across the street to see if it would work, and I hear the shriek of brakes and feel a whalloping thud against my thigh, which sends me sprawling to my knees. A lowered Chevy breathes hotly in my face. The driver blasts the horn like an afterthought, and I stand up, waving to show I'm fine.

"*Maricon!*"[3] the driver, a young man in a white uniform, screams at me before speeding away. That's when I know I'm not dead; I'm only in San Fernando or maybe in Pacoima. My hip hurts. There's probably a king-size bruise forming on it, but nothing's broken, and I check both ways before continuing across the street. The phone looks to be more or less unburnt, so I lift the receiver to hear the most wonderful sound you can hear when you're lost and you've finally found a phone booth—a dial tone. I reached into my handbag, fishing for my emergency quarter, which I found straightaway for once. I push it into the coin slot, but the dial tone persisted. Thirty-five cents, a little sticker under the coin slot reads, announcing the rate change. I only had the one quarter.

I have to call someone collect. Charlene and the others will be snoring it off—deaf, unconscious even until early afternoon. Elaine will have left for work by this time. There's only one person I can think to call collect this early, so I dial the number. The operator has me give my name after the recorded message asks whether charges will be accepted. Then I hear my uncle Enrique, his voice husky with sleep, but very clear, when he says, "No, no, no. thank you," and he hung up.

200   There are some things that are beyond crying about. Now I could cry and cry and cry when I lost Fabian. That's sad, but not too unbelievable. After all, he was an old cat, and he had the asthma pretty bad. Of course, I'll miss him, but I will get used to it. There are some things I will never get used to like being in a foreign country not twenty minutes from where I live, like almost being raped by a biker who mistakes me for a transvestite, like being hit by a car and then called *maricon*, like having the one person who never lets you down say finally and at last, "No, no, no, thank you," and mean, *no more, please, I don't want no more of you, Mulligan.*

I walk some more, but I don't know or care where I'm going. Then I notice this tiny old woman, wearing a dotted jersey dress and black high-top shoes

---

[3]"Faggot!"

like my grandmother used to wear, with the skinny black laces threading all the way up to her shins. She even has a rope of silver hair snake-coiled at the nape of her neck like Grandma's famous bun. Only thing is, her posture isn't too straight like Grandma's. Grandma used to walk around like she swallowed a broomstick, and it made her so straight she could barely bend. In fact, she used to unlace those high black shoes in the house, peel off her stockings and pick up fallen objects with her toes, rather than stoop for them. Remembering that feels like letting a warm breeze roll over me, a desert breeze fragrant with the smell of mesquite and piñon. So I follow that old woman, thinking she might lead me to a place that I would know where I was.

The aunts said I was her favorite grandchild. I used to pull a stool to the sink to try to help her with the dishes, but she would set me down, saying washing dishes wasn't work for me. She spoke only Spanish, and I don't know how I understood her, never speaking the language myself. Now I think we must have communicated through the bones. I remember brushing her long silver hair until it snapped and sparked with electricity, and I remember toying with the bottles and tubes on her dresser, rouging my cheeks with her compact and spritzing my neck with her atomizer of scent.

And in the car, we rode together in the front seat with Barbara, who liked to drive. We always rode together in the front, holding hands, Grandma and me. It made Gloria so mad, but Suzy Q was too young to care. Grandma liked to see who was out and about and make comments on everyone she saw. And that last day, a Sunday, we were coming from mass, she was the one to point to the station wagon bearing down on us like a cannonball, and she said, "¡Ai borracho!"[4] That's what she said, and I did know that word. I got gooseflesh remembering it while I followed that strange old woman in San Fernando or maybe in Pacoima.

I remember smiling, waiting for my grandma to make a joke about the drunken man, but instead there was screaming, then an explosion of glass and metal and a red veil poured over my face. The newspaper said my grandmother had died on impact, but there weren't any reporters there; they didn't know. I was there, and I crawled all the way out the wind-shield, pushing the veil out of my eyes. Everyone was quiet, as though under a sleeping spell like the kingdom in that fairy tale. Then I heard my grandmother's voice praying. Her vein-corded fingers groped, and I took her hand between my palms. I looked at her face, but I couldn't see her, or I don't remember. I did hear her, though. I heard what she said when I took her hand. "¿Quién es?" she whispered. "¿Quién es?"

205   Thinking about this, remembering all this, I've followed the old woman into a small fenced yard. She notices me when the springs of the gate squeak, slapping it shut behind me. She pinches at the sides of her skirt as though ready to shoo me away in case I came too close. I smile at her and turn my palms upward to show I mean no harm. I can't know what she thought staring at the wreckage of my make up, my dusty skirt and shoeless feet. "¿Quién es?" she calls out. "Who are joo?"

4"Oh, drunk!"

A hurricane of words seems to funnel into that tiny fenced yard, whirling and teasing about my head. They were in all languages, and I felt as if I knew them, each one. I can reach out and grab an armful and the Chinese, the Hindustani, the Dutch, the Swahili and the French will be mine and mine forever. If I wait and if I'm quiet, the Spanish will come, too. Then I can speak the language everyone says I know. I know if I wait and I'm quiet, the Spanish will come back to me.

The old woman has asked a very good question, and we both deserve an answer.

Jaime Manrique

Jaime Manrique was born in Colombia in 1949 and published several books in Spanish in the 1970s, including a best-selling novella. His first work written in English was *Latin Moon in Manhattan* (1992). He has a volume of poems, *My Night with Federico Garcia Lorca* (1995), and a second novel called *Twilight at the Equator* (1997). He is also a literary critic and editor of two books focusing on gay Latino writers, *Eminent Maricones* and *Besame Mucho: New Gay Latino Fiction*, both published in 1999.

The Documentary Artist

I met Sebastian when he enrolled in one of my film-directing classes at the university where I teach. Soon after the semester started, he distinguished himself from the other students because he was very vocal about his love of horror movies. Our special intimacy started one afternoon when he burst into my office, took a seat before I invited him to do so, and began telling me in excruciating detail about a movie called *The Evil Mommy*, which he had seen in one of those Forty-second Street theaters he frequented. "And at the end of the movie," he said, "as the boy is praying in the chapel to the statue of this bleeding Christ on the cross, Christ turns into the evil mommy and she jumps off the cross and removes the butcher knife stuck between her breasts and goes for the boy's neck. She chases the screaming boy all over the church, until she gets him." He paused, to check my reaction. "After she cuts off his head," he went on, almost with relish, "she places his head on the altar." As he narrated these events, the whites of Sebastian's eyes distended frighteningly, his fluttering hands drew arabesques in front of his face, and guttural, gross croaks erupted from the back of his throat.

I was both amused and unsettled by his wild, manic performance. Although I'm no great fan of B horror movies, I was impressed by his love of film. Also I appreciated the fact that he wasn't colorless or lethargic as were so many of my students; I found his drollness, and the aura of weirdness he cultivated, enchanting. Even so, right that minute I decided I would do my best to keep him at a distance. It wasn't so much that I was attracted to him (which is always dangerous for a teacher), but that I found his energy a bit unnerving.

Sebastian started showing up at least once a week during my office hours. He never made an appointment, and he seldom discussed his work with me. There's couch across from my chair but he always sat on the bench that abuts the door, as if he were afraid to come any closer. He'd talk about the new horror movies he'd seen, and sometimes he'd drop a casual invitation to see a movie together. It soon became clear to me that, because of his dirty clothes, disheveled hair, and loudness, and because of his love of the bizarre and gothic, he was a loner.

One day I was having a sandwich in the cafeteria when he came over and joined me.

5   "You've heard of Foucault?" he asked me.

"Sure. Why?"

"Well, last night I had a dream in which Foucault talked to me and told me to explore my secondary discourse. In the dream there was a door with a sign that said *Leather* and *Pain*. Foucault ordered me to open it. When I did, I heard a voice that told me to come and see you today."

I stopped munching my sandwich and sipped my coffee.

"This morning I had my nipple pierced," Sebastian continued, touching the spot on his T-shirt. "The guy who did it told me about a guy who pierced his dick, and then made two dicks out of his penis so he could double the pleasure."

10   My mouth fell open. I sat there speechless. Sebastian stood up. "See you in class," he said as he left the table.

I lost my appetite. I considered mentioning the conversation to the department chairman. Dealing with students' crushes was not new to me; in my time I, too, had had crushes on some of my teachers. I decided it was all harmless, and that as long as I kept at a distance and didn't encourage him, there was no reason to be alarmed. As I reviewed my own feelings, I told myself that I was not attracted to him, so I wasn't in danger of playing into his game.

Then Sebastian turned in his first movie, an absurdist zany farce shot in one room and in which he played all the roles and murdered all the characters in very gruesome ways. The boundless energy of this work excited me.

One afternoon, late that fall, he came to see me, looking upset. His father had had a heart attack, and Sebastian was going home to New Hampshire to see him in the hospital. I had already approved his proposal for his final project that semester, an adaptation of Kafka's *The Hunger Artist*. I reassured him that even if he had to be absent for a couple of weeks, it would not affect his final grade.

"Oh, that's nice," he said, lowering his head. "But, you know, I'm upset about going home because I'm gay."

15   "Have you come out to them?" I asked.

"Are you kidding?" His eyes filled with rage. "My parents would shit cookies if they knew."

"You never know," I said. "Parents can be very forgiving when it comes to their children."

"Not my parents," he snorted. Sebastian then told me his story. "When I was in my teens I took one of those I.Q. tests and it said I was a mathematical genius or something. That's how I ended up at M.I.T., at fifteen, with a full scholarship. You know, I was just kind of a loner. All I wanted was to make my parents happy. So I studied hard, and made straight A's, but I hated that shit and those people. My classmates and my teachers were as..." he paused, and there was anger and sadness in his voice. "They were as abstract and dry as those numbers and theories they pumped in my head. One day I thought, if I stay here, I'm going to be a basket case before I graduate. I had always wanted to make horror films. Movies are the only thing I care about. That's when I announced to my parents my decision to quit M.I.T. and to come to New York to pursue my studies in film directing."

His parents, as Sebastian put it, "freaked." They were blue-collar people who had pinned all their hopes on him and his brother, an engineer. There was a terrible row. Sebastian went to a friend's house, where he got drunk. That night, driving back home, he lost control of his car and crashed it against a tree. For forty-five days he was in a coma. When he came out of it, nothing could shake his decision to study filmmaking. He received a partial scholarship at the school where I teach, and he supported himself by doing catering jobs and working as an extra in movies. He told me about how brutal his father was to the entire family; about the man's bitterness. So now, a year after he had left M.I.T., going back home to see his father in the hospital was hard. Sebastian wasn't sure he should go, but he wanted to be there in case his father died.

20   When Sebastian didn't return to school in two weeks, I called his number in the city but got a machine. I left messages on a couple of occasions but got no reply. Next I called his parents. His mother informed me that his father was out of danger and that Sebastian had returned to New York. At the end of the semester I gave him an "incomplete."

In the summer I started a documentary of street life in New York. I spent a great deal of my time in the streets with my video camera, shooting whatever struck me as odd or representative of street life. In the fall, Sebastian did not show up and I thought about him less and less.

One gray, drizzly afternoon in November I had just finished shooting in the neighborhood of Washington Square Park. In the gathering darkness, the park was bustling with people getting out of work, students going to evening classes, and the new batch of junkies, who came out only after sunset.

I had shot footage of so many homeless people in the last few months that I wouldn't have paused to notice this man if it weren't for the fact that it was beginning to sprinkle harder and he was on his knees, with a cardboard sign that said HELP ME, I AM HUNGRY around his neck, his hands in prayer position, and his face—eyes shut—pointed toward the inhospitable sky. He was bearded, with long, ash-blond hair, and as emaciated and broken as one of Gauguin's Christs. I stopped to get my camera ready, and, as I moved closer, I saw that the man looked familiar—it was Sebastian.

I wouldn't call myself a very compassionate guy. I mean, I give money to beggars once in a while, depending on my mood, especially if they do not look like crackheads. But I'm not like some of my friends who work in soup kitchens or, in the winter, take sandwiches and blankets to the people sleeping in dark alleys or train stations.

25   Yet I couldn't ignore Sebastian, and not because he had been one of my students and I was fond of him, but because I was so sure of his talent.

I stood there, waiting for Sebastian to open his eyes. I was getting drenched, and it looked like he was lost in his thoughts, so I said, "Sebastian, it's me, Santiago, your film teacher."

He smiled, though now his teeth were brown and cracked. His eyes lit up, too—not with recognition but with the nirvana of dementia.

I took his grimy hand in both of mine and pressed it warmly even though I was repelled by his filth. At that moment I became aware of the cold rain, the passersby, the hubbub of the city traffic, the throng of the New York City dusk on fall evenings, when New Yorkers rush around in excitement, on their way to places, to bright futures and unreasonable hopes, to their loved ones and home. I locked my hands around his, as if to save him, as if to save myself from the thunderbolt of pain that had lodged in my chest.

"Hi, prof," Sebastian said finally.

30   "You have to get out of this rain or you'll get sick," I said, yanking at his hand, coaxing him to get off the sidewalk.

"OK, OK," he acquiesced apologetically as he got up.

Sebastian stood with shoulders hunched, his head leaning to one side, looking downward. There was a strange, utterly disconnected smile on his lips— the insane, stifled giggle of a child who's been caught doing something naughty; a boy who feels both sorry about and amused at his antics. The smile of someone who has a sense of humor, but doesn't believe he has a right to smile. Sebastian had become passive, broken, and frightened like a battered dog. Fear darted in his eyes.

"Would you like to come to my place for a cup of coffee?" I said.

"Thanks," he said, avoiding my eyes.

35   Gently, so as not to scare him, I removed the cardboard sign from around his neck. I hailed a cab. On my way home we were silent. I rolled down the window because Sebastian's stench was unbearable. A part of me wished I had given him a few bucks and gone on with my business.

Inside the apartment, I said, "You'd better get out of those wet clothes before you catch pneumonia." I asked him to undress in my bedroom, gave him a bathrobe, and told him to take a shower. He left his dirty clothes on the floor, and, while he was showering, I went through the pockets of his clothes, looking for a clue to his current condition.

There were a few coins in his pockets, some keys, and a glass pipe, the kind crackheads use to smoke in doorways. The pipe felt more repugnant than a rotting rodent in my hand; it was like an evil entity that threatened to destroy everything living and healthy. I dropped it on the bed and went to the kitchen, where I washed my hands with detergent and scalding water. I was aware that I was behaving irrationally, but I couldn't control myself. I returned to my bedroom, where I piled up his filthy rags, made a bundle, put them in a trash bag, and dumped them in the garbage.

Sebastian and I were almost the same height, although he was so wasted that he'd swim in my clothes. But at least he'd look clean, I thought, as I pulled out of my closet thermal underwear, socks, a pair of jeans, a flannel shirt, and an olive army jacket I hadn't worn in years. I wanted to get rid of his torn, smelly sneakers, but his shoe size was larger than mine. I laid out all these clothes on the bed and went to the kitchen to make coffee and sandwiches. When I finished, I collapsed on the living-room couch and turned on the TV.

Sebastian remained in my bedroom for a long time. Beginning to worry, I opened the door. He was sitting on my bed, wearing the clean clothes, and staring at his image in the full-length mirror of the closet. His beard and hair were still wet and unkempt, but he looked presentable.

40   "Nice shirt," he whispered, patting the flannel at his shoulder.

"It looks good on you," I said. Now that he was clean and dressed in clean clothes, with his blond hair and green eyes, he was a good-looking boy.

We sat around the table. Sebastian grabbed a sandwich and started eating slowly, taking small bites and chewing with difficulty, as if his gums hurt. I wanted to confront him about the crack, but I didn't know how to do it without alienating him. Sebastian ate, holding the sandwich close to his nose, staring at his lap all the time. He ate parsimoniously and he drank his coffee in little sips, making strange slurping noises, such as I imagined a thirsty animal would make.

When he finished eating, our eyes met. He stood up. "Thanks. I'm going, OK?"

"Where are you going?" I asked, getting frantic. "It's raining. Do your parents know how to reach you?"

45   "My parents don't care," he said without animosity.

"Sebastian, I'm sure they care. You're their child and they love you." I saw he was becoming upset, so I decided not to press the point. "You can sleep here tonight. The couch is very comfortable."

Staring at his sneakers, he shook his head. "That's cool. Thanks, anyway. I'll see you around." He took a couple of steps toward the door.

"Wait," I said and rushed to the bedroom for the jacket. I gave it to him, and an umbrella, too.

Sebastian placed the rest of his sandwich in a side pocket and put on the jacket. He grabbed the umbrella at both ends and studied it, as if he had forgotten what it was used for.

50   I scribbled both my home and office numbers on a piece of paper. "You can call me anytime you need me," I said, also handing him a $10 bill, which I gave him with some apprehension because I was almost sure he'd use it to buy crack. Sebastian took the number but returned the money.

"It's yours," I said. "Please take it."

"It's too much," he said, surprising me. "Just give me enough for coffee."

I fished for a bunch of coins in my pocket and gave them to him.

Hunching his shoulders and giving me his weird smile, Sebastian accepted them. Suddenly I knew what the smile reminded me of. It was Charlie Chaplin's smile as the tramp in *City Lights*. Sebastian opened the door and took the stairs instead of waiting for the elevator.

55   The following day, I went back to the corner where I had found him the day before, but Sebastian wasn't around. I started filming in that neighborhood exclusively. I became obsessed with finding Sebastian again. I had dreams in which I'd see him with dozens of other junkies tweaking in the murky alleys of New York. Sometimes I'd spot a young man begging who, from the distance, would look like Sebastian. This, I know, is what happens to people when their loved ones die.

That Christmas, I took to the streets again, ostensibly to shoot more footage, but secretly hoping to find Sebastian. It was around that time that the homeless stopped being for me anonymous human roaches of the urban squalor. Now they were people with features, with faces, with stories, with loved ones desperately looking for them, trying to save them. No longer moral lepers to be shunned, the young among them especially fascinated me. I wondered how many of them were intelligent, gifted, even geniuses who, because of crack or other drugs, or rejection, or hurt, or lack of love, had taken to the streets, choosing to drop out in the worst way.

The documentary and my search for Sebastian became one. This search took me to places I had never been before. I started to ride the subway late at night, filming the homeless who slept in the cars, seeking warmth, traveling all night long. Most of them were black, and many were young, and a great number of them seemed insane. I became adept at distinguishing the different shades of street people. The ones around Forty-second Street looked vicious, murderous, possessed by the virulent devils of the drugs. The ones who slept on the subways—or at Port Authority, Grand Central, and Penn Station—were poorer, did not deal in drugs or prostitution. Many of them were cripples, or retarded, and their eyes didn't flash the message KILLKILLKILLKILL. I began to hang out outside the city shelters where they passed the nights. I looked for Sebastian in those places, in the parks, along the waterfronts of Manhattan, under the bridges, anywhere these people congregate. Sebastian's smile—the smile he had given me as he left my apartment—hurt me like an ice pick slamming at my heart.

One Saturday afternoon late in April, I was on my way to see Blake, a guy I had met recently in a soup kitchen where I had started doing volunteer work. Since I was half an hour early and the evening was pleasant, the air warm and inviting, I went into Union Square Park to admire the flowers.

I was sitting on a bench facing east when Sebastian passed by me and sat on the next bench. Although it was too warm for it, he was still wearing the jacket I had given him in the winter. He was carrying a knapsack, and in one hand he held what looked like a can of beer wrapped in a paper bag. He kept his free hand on the knapsack as if to guard it from thieves; and with the other hand, he took sips from his beer, all the while staring at his rotting sneakers.

60   Seeing him wearing that jacket was very strange. It was as though he were wearing a part of me, as if he had borrowed one of my limbs. I debated whether to approach him, or just to get up and walk away. For the last couple of months—actually since I had met Blake—my obsession with finding Sebastian had lifted. I got up.

My heart began to beat so fast I was sure people could hear it. I breathed in deeply; I looked straight ahead at the tender new leaves dressing the trees, the beautifully arranged and colorful beds of flowers, the denuded sky, which wore a coat of enameled topaz, streaked with pink, and breathed in the air, which was unusually light, and then I walked up to where Sebastian sat.

Anxiously, I said, "Sebastian, how are you?" Without surprise, he looked up. I was relieved to see the mad grin was gone.

"Hi," he greeted me.

I sat next to him. His jacket was badly soiled, and a pungent, putrid smell emanated from him. His face was bruised, his lips chapped and inflamed, but he didn't seem withdrawn.

65   "Are you getting enough to eat? Do you have a place to sleep?" I asked.

"How're you doing?" he said evasively.

"I'm OK. I've been worried about you. I looked for you all winter." My voice trailed off; I was beginning to feel agitated.

"Thanks. But believe me, this is all I can handle right now," he said carefully, with frightening lucidity. "I'm not crazy. I know where to go for help if I want it. I want you to understand that I'm homeless because I chose to be homeless; I choose not to integrate," he said with vehemence. Forcefully, with seriousness, he added, "This is where I feel OK for now."

The lights of the buildings had begun to go on, like fireflies in the darkening sky. A chill ran through me. I reached in my pocket for a few bills and pressed them in his swollen, raw hands.

70   "I'm listed in the book. If you ever need me, call me, OK? I'll always be happy to hear from you."

"Thanks. I appreciate it."

I placed a hand on his shoulder and squeezed hard. I got up, turned around, and loped out of Union Square.

Several months went by, I won't say I forgot about Sebastian completely in the interval, but life intervened. I finished my documentary that summer. In the fall, it was shown by some public television stations to generally good reviews but low ratings.

One night, a month ago, I decided to go see a movie everybody was talking about. Because it was rather late, the theater was almost empty. A couple of young people on a date sat in the row in front of me, and there were other patrons scattered throughout the big house.

75   The movie, set in Brooklyn, was gloomy and arty, but the performers and the cinematography held my interest and I didn't feel like going back home yet, so I stayed. Toward the end of the movie there is a scene in which the main

character barges into a bar, riding his motorcycle. Except for the bartender and a sailor sitting at the counter, the bar is empty. The camera pans slowly from left to right, and there, wearing a sailor suit, is Sebastian. He slowly turns around and stares into the camera and consequently into the audience. The moment lasts two, maybe three seconds, and I was so surprised, I gasped. Seeing Sebastian unexpectedly rattled me so much I had trouble remaining in my seat until the movie ended.

I called Sebastian's parents early the next morning. This time, his mother answered. I introduced myself, and, to my surprise, she remembered me. I told her about what had happened the night before and how it made me realize I hadn't seen or heard from their son in quite some time.

"Actually, I'm very glad you called," she said softly, in a voice that was girlish but vibrant with emotions. "Sebastian passed away six weeks ago. We have one of his movie tapes that I thought of sending you since your encouragement meant so much to him."

Then she told me the details of Sebastian's death: he had been found on a bench in Central Park and had apparently died of pneumonia and acute anemia. Fortunately, he still carried some ID with him, so the police were able to track down his parents. In his knapsack, they had found a movie tape labeled *The Hunger Artist.*

I asked her if she had seen it.

80   "I tried to, but it was too painful," she sighed.

"I'd be honored to receive it; I assure you I'll always treasure it," I said.

We chatted for a short while and then, after I gave her my address, we said good-bye. A few days later, on my way to school, I found the tape in my mailbox. I carried it with me all day long, and decided to wait until I got home that night to watch it.

After dinner, I sat down to watch Sebastian's last film. On a piece of cardboard, scrawled in a childish, gothic calligraphy and in big characters, appeared THE HUNGER ARTIST BY SEBASTIAN X. INSPIRED BY THE STORY OF MR. FRANZ KAFKA.

The film opened with an extreme close-up of Sebastian. I realized he must have started shooting when he was still in school because he looked healthy, his complexion was good, and his eyes were limpid. Millimetrically, the camera studies his features: the right eye, the left one; pursed lips, followed by a wide-open smile that flashes two rows of teeth in good condition. Next we see Sebastian's ears, and, finally, in a characteristic Sebastian touch, the camera looks into his nostrils. One of the nostrils is full of snot. I stopped the film. I was shaking. I have films and tapes of relatives and friends who are dead, and when I look at them, I experience a deep ocean of bittersweetness. After they've been dead for a while, the feelings we have are stirring but resolved; there's no torment in them. However, seeing Sebastian's face on the screen staring at me, I experienced the feeling I've always had for old actors I love, passionately, even though they died before I was born. It was, for example, like the perfection of the love I'd felt for Leslie Howard in *Pygmalion,* although I didn't see that movie until I was grown up. I could not deny anymore that I had been in love with Sebastian; that I had stifled my passion for him because I knew I could never fulfill it. That's why I had denied the nature of my concern for him. I pressed the play button, and the film continued. Anything was better than what I was feeling.

85   Now the camera pulls back, and we see him sitting in a lotus position, wearing shorts. On the wall behind him, there is a sign that reads, THE ARTIST HAS GONE TWO HOURS WITHOUT EATING. WORLD RECORD! There is a cut to the audience. A woman with long green hair, lots of mascara, and purple eye shadow, her lips painted in a grotesque way, chews gum, blows it like a baseball player, and sips a Diet Coke. She nods approvingly all the time. The camera cuts to Sebastian staring at her impassively. Repeating this pattern, we see a man in a three-piece suit—an executive type watching the artist and taking notes. He's followed by a buxom blonde bedecked with huge costume jewelry; she is pecking at a large box of popcorn dripping with butter, and drinking a beer. She wears white silk gloves. We see at least half a dozen people, each one individually—Sebastian plays them all. This sequence ends with hands clapping. As the spectators exit the room, they leave money in a dirty ashtray. The gloved hand leaves a card that says, IF YOU EVER GET REALLY HUNGRY, CALL ME! This part of the film, shot in garish, neon colors, has, however, the feel of an early film; it is silent.

   The camera cuts to the face of Peter Jennings, who is doing the evening news. We cannot hear what he says. Cut again to Sebastian in a lotus position. Cut to the headline: ARTIST BREAKS HUNGER RECORD: 24 HOURS WITHOUT EATING.

   The next time we see the fasting artist, he's in the streets and the photography is in black and white. For soundtrack we hear sirens blaring, fire trucks screeching, buses idling, huge trucks braking, cars speeding, honking and crashing, cranes demolishing gigantic structures. This part of the film must have been shot when Sebastian was already homeless. He must have carried his camera in his knapsack, or he must have rented one, but it's clear that whatever money he collected panhandling, he used to complete the film. In this portion he uses a handheld camera to stress people to operate the camera for him. Sebastian's deterioration speeds up: his clothes become more soiled and tattered; his disguises at this point are less convincing—it must be nearly impossible for a starving person to impersonate someone else. His cheeks are sunken, his pupils shine like the eyes of a feral animal in the dark. The headlines read: 54 DAYS WITHOUT EATING...102 DAYS...111 DAYS. Instead of clapping hands, we see a single hand in motion; it makes a gesture as if it were shooing the artist away.

   Sebastian disappears from the film. We have footage of people in soup lines and the homeless scavenging in garbage cans. An interview with a homeless person ends the film. We don't see the face of the person conducting the interview, but the voice is Sebastian's. He reads passages from Kafka's story to a homeless woman and asks her to comment. She replies with a soundless laughter that exposes her diseased gums.

I pressed the rewind button and sat in my chair in a stupor. I felt shattered by the realization that what I don't know about what lies in my own heart is much greater than anything else I do know about it. I was so stunned and drained that I hardly had the energy to get up and walk to the VCR to remove the tape.

90   Later that night, still upset, I decided to go for a walk. It was one of those cold, blustery nights of late autumn, but its gloominess suited my mood. A glacial wind howled, skittering up and down the deserted streets of Gotham. I trudged around until the tip of my nose was an icicle. As I kept walking in a southerly direction, getting closer and closer to the southernmost point of the island, I was aware of the late hour and of how the "normal" citizens of New York were, for the most part, at home, warmed by their fires, seeking escape in a book or their TV sets, or finding solace in the arms of their loved one, or in the caresses of strangers.

I kept walking on and on, passing along the way the homeless who on a night like this chose to stay outside or couldn't find room in a shelter. As I passed them in the dark streets, I did so without my usual fear or repugnance. I kept pressing forward, into the narrowing alleys, going toward the phantasmagorical lament of the arctic wind sweeping over the Hudson, powerless over the mammoth steel structures of this city.

Ernesto Mestre-Reed

Ernesto Mestre-Reed is the author of the 1999 novel, *The Lazarus Rumba*. He was born in Guantánamo, Cuba, in 1964, and his family left the island for Spain in 1972. He graduated from Tulane University and now lives in Brooklyn, New York. His novel is stylistically innovative and, in the tradition of the famed Cuban novelist, G. Cabrera Infante, linguistically and experimentally humorous. His newest novel, *The Second Death of Única Aveyano* (2004), recounts the nostalgic dreams and memories of a terminally ill cancer patient in a Miami nursing home.

After Elián

She made up her mind on the morning that they took Elián away. She said the same thing many Cubans in Miami had said that balmy mid-spring Saturday, after watching countless replays on the special reports of the *puta*[1] marshal carrying the horrified boy away, "I can't live in this country anymore. *Yo me voy.*"[2] Leaving. All leaving this city they had invented, this *güajiro*[3] resort town that they had transformed into a sleek international metropolis in less time than it takes to build a cathedral. *Pero claro,* none of them had really meant it. Leaving? *¿A donde carajo?* Where could they go?

[1]bitch
[2]I'm leaving
[3]peasant

But Única Aveyano knew where to go. That Saturday evening she asked the head nurse, Lucas Duarte, to let her use the computer in the supervisor's office. She thought Lucas looked like Marlon Brando in *On the Waterfront*, young and ruggedly handsome, already a little balding, but not quite as pudgy. She often told him this (though she left out that middle part). When he thanked her, his voice was lispy and girlish, like Brando too. He had won her over almost from the day she had arrived with her husband, Modesto, after the first intense phase of the chemo, looking like a mad gypsy with a motley scarf wrapped around her head. Her daughter-in-law Miriam had decided it would be better if they had daylong professional care. That's how she put it, in a methodical, even voice that sounded as if she were reading directly from one of those dreadfully blithe pamphlets from the Leukemia & Lymphoma Society, or the American Cancer Society, or Jackson Hospital, which after her diagnosis appeared almost daily in all their festive birdlike colors, stuffed into the wrought-iron mailbox like a cluster of Christmas cards.

They arrived in the nursing home a few weeks before the celebration of the new millennium. When they were set up in their room, each with a bed (which was fine with Única; in the last weeks in Miriam's house, after she had come from the hospital, she had mastered the art of dozing in and out of her nights on the very edge of their bed), Lucas told her if there was ever anything she needed to ask, *sin pena ninguna*. And she did ask, for the thing she needed most then. There were four or five thin white hairs growing from her chin, and her husband would not pluck them anymore. Somehow, they had withstood the chemo. Could he do it? Could he pluck them, *por favor?*[4] Modesto let out a little noise, as if he had just dropped something small and fragile; but Lucas nodded and quickly returned with a pair of tweezers, and took her face in one hand, carefully, as if handling a newborn, and plucked her unsightly hairs. And from then on, he did it every third week.

On that night, after they had taken Elián away, Única assured Lucas it would only be a minute. She wanted to order some stuff on the Internet. She reminded him that she had her grandson's credit card, his AOL password. She whispered this in Lucas's ear, using her most practiced vanquished voice. Lucas was clearly of Patricio's type—what happens to all these men, she often wondered, that they forget about the joys of a woman?—so every time she mentioned her grandson's name, his face softened, lost all its boyish tension.

5   "*O sí, sí*, Patricio," he said, his ears reddening, his serpent green eyes cast away. And he let her into the supervisor's office, walking her to the wide mahogany desk and sitting her in front of the computer. He stood guard outside. It took Única less than half an hour to find what she wanted. The empty late-night hours that she had spent on her daughter-in-law's computer had paid off. She found it appropriate that the company that made the inflatable raft was called Caribe. Without a motor, it came to $289.95, plus shipping and handling. She charged it to her grandson's credit card. It would arrive at Miriam's house in eight to ten days, which was a little too soon, she thought,

---

[4]please

but at least it would give her time to plan, to tell Modesto (if she had to, if he ever talked to her again: his silence these days menacing and oversized as a butcher's knife). She would tell Miriam that it was Patricio's birthday present. She would ask her grandson to come visit them for his birthday, which was in May. She had already convinced Miriam to let them stay at her house again for a few days, like she had been promising for weeks now. Once there, it would be easy. Patricio rarely talked to his mother (though Patricio's silence was different from his grandfather's; he wore his silence like an athlete his medals, as something hard fought for, deserved), so he wouldn't call her before he left Key West and that would give them the time they needed. She thought all this out before she stepped out of the supervisor's office, and the only thing that bothered her about her ingenious plan was that she would have to lie outright to her grandson. She had never done that. She pulled out one of the forbidden cigarettes from the secret pocket in her robe and smoked half, till her dentures began to hurt (her palate felt like the soft rotted roof of a rain-soaked bohío, at any time ready to collapse from its own weight), and then she put it out on the silver ashtray and left it there. She leaned on the desk and on the walls and shuffled to the door. She knocked lightly and heard Lucas jangling his keys before he let her out.

"OK?" he said.

"OK."

"What were you ordering?"

"A birthday present, *para mi nieto*."[5] She took his forearm.

10   "What did you get him?"

She dismissed his question with a flick of her hand, "Something." She stumbled.

"Where is your new cane?"

"*¿Quién cojones sabe?*"[6]

"It's not funny." But he laughed, as he always did when she cursed in Spanish. Like so many young Cuban-Americans born in this country, Lucas didn't speak Spanish very well. So she spoke to him mostly in English, which she had forced herself to learn to speak in her old age, mostly by watching American movies that she had first seen during the early years of her marriage, when Modesto acted as if he were still courting her, surprising her with gifts that he would hide in their tiny apartment in Guantánamo and she would find only after he had left for work: in the mop bucket under the kitchen sink, potted violets whose tiny flowers were delicate and unfathomable as their new life; hanging by a meager thread from the lightbulb above her mother's fire-scarred four legged bathtub, a miniature gilded box of coconut truffles, succulent and lingering as grief; taped under the sewing machine that had been a wedding present (the only one) from Modesto's half-sister Rosana, an envelope with love notes written on pressed and dried magnolia leaves. Those first years, he

---

[5] for my grandson
[6] Who the heck knows?

courted his own wife as if he were not sure that the law of man meant anything as far as they were concerned, as if the tragedies that had immediately
preceded and followed the day of their wedding had rendered it void, annulled,
as if she were not yet, and could never be, his. On Friday nights, he took her
to *el teatro* on Calixto García to watch American movies. The badly dubbed
voices always reminded Ünica, as she watched the oblivious yanqui actors,
moving their lips and saying nothing, or screaming with their mouths shut, of
the possessed man in the Gospel of Luke. And when she watched these movies
again, so many years later, to learn English so she could talk to her own grandson, the actors having regained their voices (their very selves it seemed), it was
as if in the intervening years, the Lord had touched them and cast out all their
demons. She had learned to read English a long time ago, as a girl, with the
books her stepfather, Dr. Esmeraldo Gloria, snuck out of the library in the yanqui naval base for her to keep, only the best, as he said: the noble doomed language of Thomas Hardy and the voluminous excursions of Charles Dickens
and her favorite, the drunken prose of William Faulkner. But speaking English
was surprisingly more difficult than following the logic of the torrential sludgy
sentences of the Mississippian—all those silent letters hidden within syllables,
scarring pronunciations like a salty wind. But Ünica persisted, as she had done
with Faulkner, until she was better at it—speaking it, reading it, writing it—
than most native English speakers. At first, she had thought it was a shame that
so many young Cubans were losing their native language, but such things mattered less and less as time passed. She adapted; and now she spoke so much
English that some of her laziest thoughts—about the weather, about the movie
they had watched the previous night in the rec room, about her necessities—
appeared to her like clouds of mosquitoes in that menacing tongue.

15   She stopped and pulled out Patricio's credit card from her robe pocket. She
pointed to the little photograph on the corner.

"He's a good boy, *coño.*"

"Yes, and very handsome," Lucas said, which should have bothered her, but
it didn't. She nodded and looked into Lucas's startling green eyes and then
again at the little picture of Patricio, the swarthy complexion he had inherited
from his mother, the spiltink eyes set against the toothy bright smile that he
used to disarm others, and that he wore always, like a favorite wrinkled linen
shirt. "*Bueno, así es…*maybe…" but she couldn't finish her thought, so she
took Lucas's forearm again and let him lead her back to the rec room.

"My mouth hurts again."

"You shouldn't have smoked then."

20   She wasn't surprised that he smelled it on her. "I'd rather smoke cigars,"
she said, "but no one will get them for me."

He ignored this, as he always did her requests for the things that would kill
her, the only kind of request he would ever ignore. He led her to an examining room, put on some gloves and a mask and put his fingers under her chin
and examined the week-old wounds in her mouth. "Open." He stuck his finger in one side of her mouth and stretched it out gently. He peered in and she

could smell his citrusy breath through the mask. "You're lucky, you could have really hurt yourself."

"I left the butt in there," she said when he let go of her mouth. "Left it right on her ashtray." She nodded once, as if to make a point, but she knew Lucas hadn't been talking about the cigarette anymore.

"I know. I'll clean it up before morning."

"Poor boy."

25   Lucas didn't respond. She had heard him speaking to some of the other nurses about Elián, how he thought the boy belonged with his father. She wondered if Lucas had had a good father. Then she thought about her own son, who never had much of a chance to be a father.

"Poor boy," she said again, though Lucas couldn't know she wasn't talking about Elián this time.

He tapped her hand. "Anyway, they're due to fit you for new dentures next week, aren't they?"

"I won't need them."

"Please, señora Única, *no se ponga dramática*."[7] He addressed her in the formal mode. His Spanish was good when he tried. He took off his gloves and put out his hand. "Now, give me the cigarettes."

30   "No," she whispered, as if there were anyone else there to hide her contraband from.

"Give them." He wiggled his fingers. He had long feminine hands for such a well-built boy.

"*Ay niño, por favor,* what good is it not smoking now?" She wished she could pull away from him, leave this room, but she was afraid she would fall before she reached a wall. "Ya, ya, the price is paid. Anyway, if you take them…I can get more."

He reluctantly lowered his hand. It always worked, whenever Lucas challenged her, she summoned the specter of her illness.

"I want to see my husband," she said. He nodded consolingly.

35   Modesto was asleep on the couch in the rec room. His mouth was set in a pout, a dribble down one corner. His glasses had fallen off his nose and lay on his belly, strands of his neatly greased hair had come loose from the top of his head and hung over his forehead, and his long legs were splayed out in front of him like a pair of loyal sleeping hounds, but his hands were neatly folded over his chest (just like when he took his siestas). Lucas led her to the couch and politely asked one of the younger residents, a russetskinned woman from Alabama, to make room for Única. She took his glasses, folded the arms, and put them back on his belly.

No movie tonight. The television was tuned to the Cuban station, still blaring with news about Elián. A photograph, whose authenticity the newscaster questioned, had just been released. Elián in his father's arms. His famous smile. Única soon found herself translating the news bits for the woman from

---

[7]don't overreact

Alabama, as competently as she translated the old American movies for her husband. At first she agreed with the newscasters, the picture was certainly a fake. She knew what could be done with computers these days. But then she wondered if Elián wasn't the type of boy who could be happy anywhere, with his beautiful cousin, with his *comunista* father. There was an art to it—this living in happiness. One had to be born with it, she supposed, like an ear for music. And develop it, lest it wither.

"Too bad," she said to the woman from Alabama, "we won't see how he turns out."

The woman looked at Única over the rims of her glasses, her cloudy eyes puzzled, her lips wet and parted, as if she were waiting for a translation, though Única had spoken in perfect English.

Modesto stirred beside her, his hands unfolded and he grabbed her wrist frantically. She winced. Ever since the chemo, her bones felt as if they each had been dropped from a great height, shattered, and then hastily pieced together with the incompetence of a child gluing together a broken vase. Her kidneys were ailing, the doctors said, but there was hope, the cancer was taking a beating. They spoke of it like a wounded boxer. She imagined it otherwise. She imagined it leaking like a juicy rumor from the fatty part of her bones to every region of her unsuspecting body.

40   "*Estoy aquí. Aquí estoy.*" And she turned and translated for the woman from Alabama. "I am here. I am here for him." She shrugged and the woman smiled. Única pried her husband's fingers off her and made a note to trim his fingernails. If he ever let her near him again.

When he noticed how his hand had instinctively reached for her, Modesto quickly let go and grabbed his glasses. He pulled his heavy legs toward him, took out an old plastic comb from his pocket and passed it through his greased waxen hair, until it was all set back in place. He didn't ask her where she had been. It had been over a week since he had said *anything* to her. He grunted as the TV showed one more replay of the events of that morning and then cut to the smoky streets, erupting in riots. Everyone in the room seemed captivated and disgusted at the same time. Some eagerly looked for a glimpse of their grandkids at the riots, others cheered the rioters on, and one old man got up and poked the screen, pointing out someone he knew. Única wished they could watch a movie as they usually did on Saturday nights, but Lucas hadn't even bothered to rent a video, knowing the news about Elián would take precedence. Única had wanted to watch *Bringing Up Baby* again. She liked how Modesto laughed so long and hard when Cary Grant was forced to wear the lady's nightgown that she didn't need to translate any of the dialogue. She had heard that Cary Grant too had been like Lucas and her grandson, but at least he had been married, which is what they all should do, and keep their dirty little things on the side. *De todos modos,*[8] all men did it. O God she knew! Their dirty little things. That's how God made them. Of that she was thankful, that

---

[8]Anyway

God hadn't made her a man, as gawky and as jittery and as foolish as Cary Grant singing about love to the wrong baby, who could cleverly assemble his outsize dinosaur monster but not notice love when it was biting him in the cheeks. She looked up again at the endless reel of Elián being carried away, his boxer shorts slipping from his hips, his little hands like a frightened kitten's paws on the shoulders of the *puta* marshal, and she wondered what lucky girl would one day take his virginity from him, and how happy the young lovers would be that night, and how far away this night of terror would seem.

Única Aveyano had learned to go almost without sleep. She sometimes slipped her painkillers that she had hidden under her tongue into Modesto's daily dosage of pills so that he at least would get some sleep and not worry about her wandering the halls at night, pressed to the walls like a mouse. The other pills she took. Especially the little egg-shaped Marinols, which were supposed to combat nausea, but they made her tittery too, and daring. Later, they were to blame it on them, on the little egg-shaped pills, as if it had been the first time.

The nursing home was a six-story building, two blocks away from the fashionable beach. Storm shutters hung halfway down over the windows at all times like droopy eyelids, so very little light was ever let in. When the windows were left open, she could hear the music from the oceanfront cafes late into the night. Sometimes she asked a night nurse to bring her a chair, and she sat in the hallway, crouched by an open window, and listened to the sounds of life outside. She hadn't been to the beach in ages.

One night, a week before Elián had been taken away, she made up her mind to see the ocean as it is when the moon flirts with its restless surface. When Modesto fell asleep, she took her cane (which she rarely used) and made her way to the end of the hallway. She stood by a window, pretending to listen, and waited for the night nurse to forget her presence and then she lumbered into the stairwell. The two flights did not prove as painful as she imagined. She planted both feet firmly on each step before she proceeded to the next one, one hand on the railing, the other firmly on her cane, each step as precise and deliberate as a musical note. If this were all, she thought; her arthritic knee, her brittle bones. Before the chemo her cane had always stood in one corner of the bedroom that they used in Miriam's house, what had once been Patricio's room. When she made it up to the top floor, she was surprised to see the door to the roof ajar, a breeze passing through it. She had not been outside in weeks, since the last time she was in Jackson Hospital and the treatments had been temporarily stopped, and the night air sneaking into the stairwell felt as precious and as dangerous as something stolen. She wished she had woken Modesto and brought him up. He missed his long afternoon walks to the bodega, strolling patiently on the edge of the roads near Miriam's house. Única had accompanied him once and was surprised to see that most of the way to the bodega had no sidewalks. Nobody walks in this part of town, Modesto explained proudly, as if he were the last practitioner of an art long forgotten.

Sometimes Miriam came on weekends and took him out for a stroll on Ocean Drive, but the nurses forbade Única to go unless she used a wheelchair. They said she was still too weak from the treatment. A wheelchair! As if she were an invalid. ¿Y qué?[9] He always came back from his walks more depressed than when he left. He told her in two words he didn't like to be apart from her. Miriam had wanted him to stay in her house, and that's how he had responded, with the same two words, "No puedo."[10] It's true what they said about old age. He was turning into a boy again and he needed her as simply as a child needs its mother. Just to be there. Única gave a good push to the roof door and then climbed the last step and stood in the doorway, loving the way the gentle breeze teased the new naplike growth on her skull. She had not looked at herself in weeks, had hung a hand towel on the mirror over the bathroom sink (which Lucas kindly rehung every morning after Modesto was finished shaving), and now she wondered how much grayer her hair was; the doctors had said that it would probably grow in thicker but grayer, maybe even a little curlier. It was more difficult once she was out on the roof, having only the use of her cane. She wished she had worn something other than her slippers and her ratty night robe (but she wasn't sure if she still owned any shoes, and whatever old dresses hung in her closet always went unused). She had refused also, after the first phase of the chemo, when they were still living with their daughter-in-law, the use of those monstrous contraptions that they called walkers. She'd rather stay in bed all day, she told her daughter-in-law, rather have her bones in a sack.

45   "You don't listen to anyone," her daughter-in-law had told her the night after Thanksgiving, the day after they had found Elián floating on an inner tube. They had just eaten turkey sandwiches for dinner. "You never have. That's why it's better that you have daylong professional care. Them you'll have to listen to, coño. It is for your own good, mamá."

What use living in a country where family can say such things? How dare she call her mamá?

There were a couple of lawn chairs on the roof, a beach towel draped over one of them. Maybe the nurses came up here to sunbathe on their breaks. For a moment, looking at the chairs, Única lost her direction. Which way was the ocean? She shuffled on the sticky tar, leaning on the cane with both arms, to one edge of the roof and grabbed tight to the low concrete parapet. Below, there was only an alleyway and across an abandoned building, its windows shuttered with flimsy plywood. She found it odd that there were any buildings so near the ocean left to sit useless. In one of his rare talkative moments since they arrived here, Modesto had told her what a great job they had done with all the hotels on Ocean Drive, how they had restored them to their old art-deco splendor. Fifteen years before, when they had first moved to their little apartment on Meridian Street and Miami Beach wasn't as fashionable, the

---

[9]So what?
[10]I can't.

hotels were teeming with the old waiting on their porches, their ratty structures crumbling, the wood perforated with termite damage. She was very eager to see how much they had changed, but she did not let Modesto know. The breeze picked up and she heard the irascible rumbling of the ocean, as if it were expelling the elements of a chronic irritation. She stayed close to the parapet and moved toward the sound. When she saw the tall palms that lined Ocean Drive, their fronds swaying lazily as if they heard nothing of the troubled ocean, but only the music from the open-air cafes, she dropped her cane and grasped the edge of the parapet with both hands. She moved along faster, her back foot skittering up to the front one and then the front one sliding forward. The sea continued its rumbling and its constant perturbation inspired Ünica— this will to never let anything stay as it is. She dismissed the blood pulsing like an alarum on her swollen knee, the hundred needles of fire pricking at her bones, the suspicious feeling that her tongue could easily reach up and lick the seat of her brain. She made it to the corner and she felt the sea's presence before she could cast her eyes on it, its brackish breath assaulting her. She raised her chin.

"*Sí, sí*," she said, as if she were welcoming Modesto (as she never could anymore) in his still too-frequent attempted incursions into her ruined body, where he would end up doing everything himself, spilling his tepid come on her inner thighs, on her belly, on the fleshy hollow between her collar bones. (No child then.) She could not remember when she stopped loving him. But again, she wished he had come with her, though he would have certainly refused when she offered, called her *una loca,* as he often did these days. At seventy-eight, and though on plenty of preventive medication (twelve pills a day), he had never spent a night in a hospital, and now he was confined to a nursing home because of her. Yet, he had never had the strength to stand up to their daughter-in-law, had lost all vigor on the morning Ünica was given her diagnosis, had suffered all the doldrums and depression that the doctors had told her were her due. Ünica was glad, very glad that God hadn't made her a man. If it had been her, her the healthy one, oh the fight she would have put up.

She moved along the front parapet, keeping an eye on the dark sea. No moon tonight, but from the glow of the street lamps she could make out the white of the foam crashing on the sand like spilt sugar. A pair of men wearing only sandals and shorts strolled by holding hands. They too were listening to the embroiled sea. The bounty of that day's sun still stuck like sap to their burnt shoulders. Then a pack of wild pale boys ran by them, screaming obscenities, and for a moment the friends lost hold of each other, and for such virile young men seemed too easily parted, cowering—till the wild boys had passed, quickly and clamorously as an afternoon thunderstorm—and the friends found each other again and made their way toward the darkness of the shore before they held hands again. She thought about Patricio. She wondered if he ever held hands with his friends. Maybe that's why he had moved to Key West. It was safer there. They were less outnumbered.

50   If she leaned forward enough she would just stumble off the roof to the pavement below. Maybe the two friends would find her on the way back. Maybe the pack of wild boys. She let go of the parapet and found her body surprisingly light, as if she were floating in the warm sea. With her bent fingers she undid her robe, pulling it up to reach the lower buttons. She let it fall off her shoulders, and the sea air draped in around her, it whistled on the catheter above her breast. She had forgotten what a great joy it was to go without clothes. She could not unclasp her bra (the nurses always did that), so she pulled the straps over her arms and slid it down to her waist, twisting it around her till she found the clasp, but still she was not able to undo it, so she left it there and slid her hand under the band of her bloomers and let them drop, and she stepped out of her slippers and slid over, leaving the bundle of clothes aside like a shed skin. She felt feverish. As dangerous and as daring as the young friends holding hands. She laughed as if she were being tickled. She raised her hands in the air and called out to the friends, "*Aquí, aquí, mis vidas!*" But no one heard her, so she moved farther away from her pile of clothes. She wished she could get rid of her bra but it would not go down below her belly button, even though she was, like Miriam said, as thin as a lizard. It hung above her waist like garters, like a dancing girl, so she lifted her feet off the ground, one at a time, trying to keep rhythm to the song rising like a prayer from the street below. How she wished Modesto had come with her! She would relent. She would pretend to love him again. They would do it right here, *coño*, on the roof of the *maldita* nursing home. Why not? She would give in. He would hold her on the ledge of the parapet and fuck her and fuck her until both their bodies crumbled at last. He would fuck her and fuck her till they tumbled over together and they were no more.

Fuck.

She loved that word. It was one of the first English words she had learned to speak, though she rarely got to use it. For some reason the word always made her think of Faulkner, of poor Joe Christmas. She had used it a few times on her daughter-in-law and she was going to use it tonight if anyone tried to stop her.

"Fuck you," she mouthed it, pounding her fist into her palm in mock fury. "Fuck me."

Sometimes English to her was like one of those thin-headed shiny hammers used for precision nailing.

55   She kept dancing, her bare twisted feet barely lifting off the ground, the sea air like another's breath on the new soft hairs running up the inside of her legs, under her armpits. She would never shave them again. In Key West, she had once met a friend of Patricio, a short stout woman who let hair grow all over her body, except on her skull, which was buzzed like a soldier's. Única wondered how much she looked like this woman now, this woman she had then found loathsome, unnatural. Now, *comadre*. She kept on dancing and giggled provokingly, like someone who is holding back a great secret. And when she

laughed, she covered her dry rotted mouth, as if not to infect the guiltless night with all the ills that had befallen her.

Many songs rose from below, ballads whose words she could not quite hear but whose gist she understood by the baleful abandoned voice of the crooner, by the desperate plucking of chords—*así es la vida, señores y señoritas,*[11] only our wounds, our wounds, awaken us, make us compelling—and then the songs stopped and all she could hear were the sighs and the drunken broken laughter of those who had still not gone home, so she danced to the uneven beat of their noise. She had never in her long life been drunk, but this is what it must be like, the poisons transfigured into this windy riotous joy (she raised her empty hand in a toast)—and then the laughter stopped and all she could hear was the waking groans of the ocean, calling to her.

A light, soft and hushed as the steps of a lone ballerina, appeared in the frayed edges of the mantling sky; it should have comforted her, she knew, but she suddenly felt the excoriated folds of her innards, and she became frightened of the gentle light. She grabbed the parapet again and shuffled over to her cane. She took it and left the pile of clothes and made her way to the stairway. Pieces of stone dug at her soles, and just before she reached the doorway, she fell to her knees. The light grew, more suggestive now, as if others—more vigorous, more grounded dancers—had joined the lone airy ballerina. Única was on all fours, the siren pain at her bad knee and the hidden wounds within her and the proud young morning all denouncing her mad little excursion, so she crawled into the shadows of the stairwell, dragging along her cane. By the time she got up, both hands on the railing, dangerously close to the precipice of the stairway, the light fell on the roof like the waves of a thunderous symphony that had no use for dainty ballerinas. There was blood on her knees, which she touched with her fingers and spread on her breasts and on her cheeks. She slid along the wall with her hands, smearing it, and picked up her cane. She was as patient going down the stairway as she had been coming up, first the cane and then one foot and the other on each step and then the next step and the next one. She imagined the notes of Bach's *Goldberg Variations,* played in an impossibly slow tempo, each key struck one by one, as if the notes existed alone, independent of each other—Modesto had listened to it again and again on the night they had found out about their son. But the farther she got away from the garish morning light, the more she felt lost, forgetting which floor she was on (had she passed one doorway, two, three?) and the colder the concrete steps became, sending a chill up her legs, up her spine, till she was unsure of whether she was descending or climbing. She lost hold of her cane and heard it tumble eagerly away from her, as if it could be of better use elsewhere. And for a moment, she leaned forward and she thought she would follow it. But this passed. She turned and faced the wall and grabbed the railing with both hands and continued, sideways, unsure as a sleepy crab that has been dug out of its place, both feet on each step, passing her cane,

---

[11]That's life, ladies and gentlemen.

which she spitefully kicked aside twice (till it tumbled farther down the stairway). She passed doorways that looked out to empty hallways and kicked her cane along when she felt it graze against her feet, till she reached the bottom door and, ignoring the warning in bold red letters that this was only a fire exit and that an alarm would go off, she pushed it open and heard nothing of what had been warned and felt the morning's warmth again, and she thought she had just traveled in a loop back up to another roof. She picked up her cane and made her way out.

It was an alleyway, which she followed to its opening, not questioning how there could be streets up on a roof, as if a whole deserted city and its nearby beaches could naturally sit atop some great renovated art-deco building. She stayed close to the walls of the buildings, hiding in their shadows, her whole body turned away from the waking world, from the prying sun, as she plodded up the street toward the sound of the ocean. Someone called to her from a balcony, and then that someone called to her God, "*¿Dios mío, Dios mío, qué es esto? Una viejita sin nada.*"[12] She had to hurry, they would surely send someone after her (even though she was just what the woman in the balcony had called her, a little old woman with nothing), so she quickened her pace, pressed closer to the walls, as if she were blind now, ignoring the honks from cars and the bleary looks of those who like her had spent the night sleepless and were in various euphoric stages of undress. But when she made it to the corner of Collins Avenue, the wide street seemed as impassable as a rushing river. At the corner of the last building, she pressed her cheek to the wall and let her scorched feet rest in the thin strip of its shadow and looked out over the vast expanse, knowing how close the sea lay beyond it.

"*No puedo.*"[13] Then, "*Sí, coño, ¿cómo que no? Todo se puede.*"[14] So she went on—admonishing herself on what a fool she was and with the same breath calling on all the saints that she had not prayed to in ages not to abandon her in this quest, this way and that—till she whispered a quick plea to St. Lazarus of the Wounds and she found the courage to venture away from the wall, at first holding onto the frame of the wrought-iron fence that surrounded the building's front garden, at whose center sat a lone majestic almond tree, and then with only her cane as aid, both hands wrapped around it and the insufferable weight of her years bearing down on it. She did not make it far. Before she had reached the curb, she fell again, this time unable to break the fall with her arms so that her chin bounced on the pavement and she bit hard on her tongue and on her lips. The roof of her mouth rattled in its place and felt as if it had come loose and settled back in askew. She pushed her head up and then her torso till she was again on all fours like an animal. Bright drops trickled from her mouth and splattered on the sun-bleached sidewalk, giving a shocking splendor to the drab piece of cement. If she let go now, she could just let it happen here, on

---

[12]My God, My God, What is this? An old lady without anything.
[13]I can't.
[14]Yes, dammit, why not? Anything is possible.

this corner, in this sparkling hour before the morning truly came, before any-one save those who had not yet gone to bed were awake to bear witness. Her cane had bounced away from her and she could not see it anywhere. She could not recall where she had been heading, but something, the raw briny primeval odor perhaps, of nakedness, of a thing just killed and laid open, told her she could not be far. Here. Here. What better place? She crawled into the garden, under the shade of the almond tree, and pushed off her arms and sat back on her bottom, her useless legs folded in front of her. (She was going to a place where she would not need them.) Again, she smeared blood on her cheeks and on her breasts. More cars passed by now, but they wholly ignored her unless they were stopped at the light, and then she heard vulgarities about her droop-ing breasts, about her age, about her *tortillera's* haircut, about her shriveled sex, and they called her what Modesto would have called her, *loca, loca de remate*. No one stopped to inquire what she was doing at dawn, wearing her bra as a garter belt, seated and bare-assed, a trespasser in the garden. So why not here? Why not on this spot where no one would ask any questions? Here, here there would be no two-faced daughters-in-law, no *marica* nurses, no stone-hearted doctors to get in her way, to tell her of the need for patience, for fortitude, for faith, who talked as if these things were something one put on as easily as smearing blood on one's cheeks, on one's breasts.

60   It was funny, the way they talked to the condemned.

So on her little spot of private grass, she giggled and then laughed vehe-mently, but this time did not bother to cover her mouth. Her shoulders shook, her bloodstained breasts jiggled, her breath fouled the salty air, her peals filled the hushed morning, and now, when cars stopped at the light, the passengers would cast their eyes from her, and the driver would let the car dangerously inch up toward the intersection, away from her, and she was sure that none would ever be brave enough to approach her.

The boys were still dancing when they approached—the same wild dance that they had begun when they ambushed the friends who held hands the night before—dancing still, in a whirlpool, arms flailing, chanting their own song, as if casting a spell on the soberness of the new day, summoning back the out-landish night. There were five, six, seven of them, or more, she could not tell because by the time she noticed them, they had already surrounded her, some on their knees like supplicants, some rolling on the ground like fallen creatures, some hanging off the almond tree like monkeys, and some, she thought, hov-ering above her on their tiny wings, were whispering in her ear, blowing kisses on her neck and passing their soft hands over her bare scalp, and, except for their threadbare loose shorts were as naked as she was.

"*¿Qué pasa, Abuelita?*"[15] they whispered. "*¿Qué pasa?*"

One of them undid her bra and passed it to another, who wore it tied under his chin like a bonnet, and it was as if they had put on him a crown, for he forthwith became their leader. He tucked his long dark hair behind his ears

---

[15]What's happening, Grandma?

and straightened his milky lanky hairless frame. He barked orders simultaneously at those on the ground, those on their knees, those in the tree, those in
the air, his reptile eyes boring intently into them, as if their existence depended
on his seeing them, waving one hand around like a conductor, keeping one
finger of the other hand pointed directly at her, as if to signal, for those dumb
enough, or stoned enough, not to get it, who his orders were about, and then,
in a sugary voice that was half pitying, half mocking, he spoke to her:

65   "We're taking you, Abuelita. We're taking you where you were heading."
He reached down and touched the catheter above her breast, confused by it,
and then with his thumb he wiped some blood from her lips and traced a circle on his scrawny chest and smeared his tiny brown nipples. "*Vamos, vamos,*"
he yelled, turning from them and raising his bloodstained hand in the air, "take
her!"

She felt their hands under her armpits, grabbing at her waist, pushing up
on her rump. Others reached into her mouth and took her blood and smeared
it on their chests like the leader had done. Her arms flailed as she rose. "My
cane, *coño,*" she protested, "why can't you find my cane?"

The leader, who was already halfway across Collins Avenue, turned and
stared at her. Cars passed him, swerving wildly to one side or the other, as if
he were made of some substance that repelled all physical objects. He nodded
and moved back toward them, ignoring the screams and the horns blaring at
him. He returned to the garden. He surveyed its grounds and hopped up on
the almond tree, leaning one way and then the other, passing his hands over
the branches, till he found the right one and with one quick turn of his wrist
broke off a young branch, as easily as if he were cracking a chicken's neck. He
peeled off the leaves and branchlets and handed it to her. "Your cane,
Abuelita," he announced. And then he bowed before he was off again; and
with her new cane, the others surrounding her nakedness, pressed so close they
kept her from stumbling, she followed him, across Collins Avenue, across
Ocean Drive, toward the sea, and none dared stop them.

On the beach there was an early-morning jogger who would later tell those
in charge at the nursing home and the police investigators that he thought it
strange that a bald naked old woman was steadfastly making her way across the
wide stretch of sand toward the water, leaning on a long crooked staff, determined as a prophet crossing the desert toward Jerusalem, but that this was a
crazy town and that he had seen crazier things before, so he didn't stop her.
She seemed deranged, dangerous, caked in dirt, or blood. Maybe she was
homeless, going for her morning bath. Maybe she had just murdered someone. At any rate, he had been either not interested enough, or (more likely)
frightened too much to do anything but keep on jogging.

And there was no one else on the beach?

70   No, no one else, just the crazy old woman, and a pair of half-naked gay boys
sleeping on the sand, wrapped around each other.

"There was no one. You appeared on the beach by yourself. There were two
men sleeping there. They saw you go in the water and, like the jogger, they

thought you were *una loca, desnudita como el día así como estabas*,[16] going in for a morning swim."

"Ay Lucas, some people need to be blind. Those little wild angels came to get me, not them, that's why they couldn't see them. You can tell yourself that you saved me when others wouldn't. If it makes you feel better."

So she told Lucas all that happened just before he came and rescued her, all that had happened that the jogger and the two friends sleeping on the sand couldn't possibly tell him about.

Their numbers grew as they approached the water. Some she thought had surfaced from the foamy shore and were coming toward her. These were as naked as she was and thinner and darker than the others, and their skin glistened with droplets of broken light, like shimmering scales, and their hair was strung with seaweed, and their eyes spread wide on their heads, and their sex livid and heavy as ripe plums—these were all the other little ones, Única thought, who had had no band of dolphins to protect them, no mothers prescient enough to give them a bottle of fresh water, who had never made it across the treacherous straits and had grown older with the creatures of the sea—and they seemed ill at ease on the sandy earth, wobbling, their arms thrust out for balance, ungainly as newborn calves. They approached her, carrying handfuls of seashells that they tried to shove into the folds of her body to give it a drowning weight. The other boys joined them—joined her—in their nakedness. They slipped off their threadbare shorts and cast them in the air with a whoop. The boy who was their leader threw off his bra-bonnet and also cast it in the air, and when their shorts and her bra rained down, he was like them and they were all like her. Maybe that's when the others noticed them (if they noticed them at all), the friends who had been holding hands the night before, because they had been sleeping (on that detail the jogger had been right), wrapped around each other, the sand covering their lower halves up to their belly buttons, so that it seemed that they had been struggling up out of the earth and had perished just when they were almost there, had perished without letting go of each other. But at some point the two friends must have awakened (perhaps because of the whooping of the boys) because one of them raised his head and called out to her and that's when the wild boys left her. They seemed astonished that there was anyone else on the beach besides them and her. They crouched. They dropped their handfuls of seashells. They fell to the sand, grabbing at it as if it were a sheet. They looked up at the sky, at the sea, back out to the hotels on the street, their bright eyes wide and darting end to end. The ones that had come from the sea fell from their stagger and crawled on the ground back to the shore and disappeared into the foam. The others, once they had figured out where the voice came from, moved toward the half-buried friends and surrounded them in the same manner that they had surrounded her under the almond tree. Some dug under the sand and crawled beneath them, others lay beside them and tangled their long limbs with theirs and others yet tarried above them like days to come.

---

[16] a lunatic, naked as day, that's how you looked.

75   She could not tell for sure whether they meant to harm the friends (like the night before) or let them in on some great joy.

Única moved on without them. When she had made it deep enough into the water, with the aid of a rope that floated out to a faraway buoy, she let go of her almond branch. It was dragged back to the shore. The warm sea slapped off the blood from her breasts, from her cheeks, it gurgled in her catheter, it stung in her mouth, it lifted her and dropped her as casually as if she were a windblown scrap. She held on to the rope until her feet could no longer graze the bottom and when she let go, she felt little hands grabbing at her feet, at her thighs, kelplike arms wrapping furiously around her waist, tugging her outward, and it was as if a world of little fishlike saints had grabbed her and with all their diluvian cunning were whisking her to her glory.

Achy Obejas

See the biographical headnote of Obejas on page 373.

We Came All the Way From Cuba So You Could Dress Like This?

for Nena

I'm wearing a green sweater. It's made of some synthetic material, and it's mine. I've been wearing it for two days straight and have no plans to take it off right now.

I'm ten years old. I just got off the boat—or rather, the ship. The actual boat didn't make it: We got picked up halfway from Havana to Miami by a gigantic oil freighter to which they then tied our boat. That's how our boat got smashed to smithereens, its wooden planks breaking off like toothpicks against the ship's big metal hull. Everybody talks about American ingenuity, so I'm not sure why somebody didn't anticipate that would happen. But they didn't. So the boat that brought me and my parents most of the way from Cuba is now just part of the debris that'll wash up on tourist beaches all over the Caribbean.

As I speak, my parents are being interrogated by an official from the office of Immigration and Naturalization Services. It's all a formality because this is 1963, and no Cuban claiming political asylum actually gets turned away. We're evidence that the revolution has failed the middle class and that communism is bad. My parents—my father's an accountant and my mother's a social worker—are living, breathing examples of the suffering Cubans have endured under the tyranny of Fidel Castro.

The immigration officer, a fat Hungarian lady with sparkly hazel eyes and a perpetual smile, asks my parents why they came over, and my father, whose face is bright red from spending two days floating in a little boat on the Atlantic Ocean while secretly terrified, points to me—I'm sitting on a couch across the room, more bored than exhausted—and says, We came for her, so she could have a future.

5   The immigration officer speaks a halting Spanish, and with it she tells my parents about fleeing the Communists in Hungary. She says they took everything from her family, including a large country estate, with forty-four acres and two lakes, that's now being used as a vocational training center. Can you imagine that, she says. There's an official presidential portrait of John F. Kennedy behind her, which will need to be replaced in a week or so.

     I fold my arms in front of my chest and across the green sweater. Tonight the U.S. government will put us up in a noisy transient hotel. We'll be allowed to stay there at taxpayer expense for a couple of days until my godfather—who lives with his mistress somewhere in Miami—comes to get us.

     Leaning against the wall at the processing center, I notice a volunteer for Catholic Charities who approaches me with gifts: oatmeal cookies, a plastic doll with blond hair and a blue dress, and a rosary made of white plastic beads. She smiles and talks to me in incomprehensible English, speaking unnaturally loud.

     My mother, who's watching while sitting nervously next to my father as we're being processed, will later tell me she remembers this moment as something poignant and good.

     All I hold onto is the feel of the doll—cool and hard—and the fact that the Catholic volunteer is trying to get me to exchange my green sweater for a little gray flannel gym jacket with a hood and an American flag logo. I wrap myself up tighter in the sweater, which at this point still smells of salt and Cuban dirt and my grandmother's house, and the Catholic volunteer just squeezes my shoulder and leaves, thinking, I'm sure, that I've been traumatized by the trip across the choppy waters. My mother smiles weakly at me from across the room.

10   I'm still clutching the doll, a thing I'll never play with but which I'll carry with me all my life, from apartment to apartment, one move after the other. Eventually, her little blond nylon hairs will fall off and, thirty years later, after I'm diagnosed with cancer, she'll sit atop my dresser, scarred and bald like a chemo patient.

     Is life destiny or determination?

     For all the blond boyfriends I will have, there will be only two yellow-haired lovers. One doesn't really count—a boy in a military academy who subscribes to Republican politics like my parents, and who will try, relatively unsuccessfully, to penetrate me on a south Florida beach. I will squirm away from underneath him, not because his penis hurts me but because the stubble on his face burns my cheek.

     The other will be Martha, perceived by the whole lesbian community as a gold digger, but who will love me in spite of my poverty. She'll come to my one-room studio on Saturday mornings when her rich lover is still asleep and rip tee-shirts off my shoulders, brutally and honestly.

One Saturday we'll forget to set the alarm to get her back home in time, and Martha will have to dress in a hurry, the smoky smell of my sex all over her face and her own underwear tangled up in her pants leg. When she gets home, her rich lover will notice the weird bulge at her calf and throw her out, forcing Martha to acknowledge that without a primary relationship for contrast, we can't go on.

15   It's too dangerous, she'll say, tossing her blond hair away from her face.

Years later, I'll visit Martha, now living seaside in Provincetown with her new lover, a Kennedy cousin still in the closet who has a love of dogs, and freckles sprinkled all over her cheeks.

At the processing center, the Catholic volunteer has found a young Colombian woman to talk to me. I don't know her name, but she's pretty and brown, and she speaks Spanish. She tells me she's not Catholic but that she'd like to offer me Christian comfort anyway. She smells of violet water.

She pulls a Bible from her big purse and asks me, Do you know this, and I say, I'm Catholic, and she says that, well, she was once Catholic, too, but then she was saved and became something else. She says everything will change for me in the United States, as it did for her.

Then she tells me about coming here with her father and how he got sick and died, and she was forced to do all sorts of work, including what she calls sinful work, and how the sinful work taught her so much about life, and then how she got saved. She says there's still a problem, an impulse, which she has to suppress by reading the Bible. She looks at me as if I know what she's talking about.

20   Across the room, my parents are still talking to the fat Hungarian lady, my father's head bent over the table as he fills out form after form.

Then the Catholic volunteer comes back and asks the Colombian girl something in English, and the girl reaches across me, pats my lap, and starts reading from her Spanish-language Bible: Your breasts are like two fawns, twins of a gazelle that feed upon the lilies. Until the day breathes and the shadows flee, I will hie me to the mountain of myrrh and the hill of frankincense. You are all fair, my love; there is no flaw in you.

Here's what my father dreams I will be in the United States of America: A lawyer, then a judge, in a system of law that is both serious and just. Not that he actually believes in democracy—in fact, he's openly suspicious of the popular will—but he longs for the power and prestige such a career would bring, and which he can't achieve on his own now that we're here, so he projects it all on me. He sees me in courtrooms and lecture halls, at libraries and in elegant restaurants, the object of envy and awe.

My father does not envision me in domestic scenes. He does not imagine me as a wife or mother because to do so would be to imagine someone else closer to me than he is, and he cannot endure that. He will never regret not being a grandfather; it was never part of his plan.

Here's what my mother dreams I will be in the United States of America: The owner of many appliances and a rolling green lawn; mother of two mischievous children; the wife of a boyishly handsome North American man who drinks Pepsi for breakfast; a career woman with a well-paying position in local broadcasting.

25   My mother pictures me reading the news on TV at four and home at the dinner table by six. She does not propose that I will actually do the cooking, but rather that I'll oversee the undocumented Haitian woman my husband and I have hired for that purpose. She sees me as fulfilled, as she imagines she is.

All I ever think about are kisses, not the deep throaty kind but quick pecks all along my belly just before my lover and I dissolve into warm blankets and tangled sheets in a bed under an open window. I have no view of this scene from a distance, so I don't know if the window frames tall pine trees or tropical bushes permeated with skittering gray lizards.

It's hot and stuffy in the processing center, where I'm sitting under a light that buzzes and clicks. Everything smells of nicotine. I wipe the shine off my face with the sleeve of my sweater. Eventually, I take off the sweater and fold it over my arm.

My father, smoking cigarette after cigarette, mutters about communism and how the Dominican Republic is next and then, possibly, someplace in Central America.

My mother has disappeared to another floor in the building, where the Catholic volunteer insists that she look through boxes filled with clothes donated by generous North Americans. Later, my mother will tell us how the Catholic volunteer pointed to the little gray flannel gym jacket with the hood and the American flag logo, how she plucked a bow tie from a box, then a black synthetic teddy from another and laughed, embarrassed.

30   My mother will admit she was uncomfortable with the idea of sifting through the boxes, sinking arm-deep into other people's sweat and excretions, but not that she was afraid of offending the Catholic volunteer and that she held her breath, smiled, and fished out a shirt for my father and a light blue cotton dress for me, which we'll never wear.

My parents escaped from Cuba because they did not want me to grow up in a communist state. They are anti-communists, especially my father.

It's because of this that when Martin Luther King, Jr., dies in 1968 and North American cities go up in flames, my father will gloat. King was a Communist, he will say; he studied in Moscow, everybody knows that.

I'll roll my eyes and say nothing. My mother will ask him to please finish his *café con leche* and wipe the milk moustache from the top of his lip.

Later, the morning after Bobby Kennedy's brains are shot all over a California hotel kitchen, my father will greet the news of his death by walking into our kitchen wearing a "Nixon's the One" button.

35   There's no stopping him now, my father will say; I know, because I was involved with the counterrevolution, and I know he's the one who's going to save us, he's the one who came up with the Bay of Pigs—which would have

worked, all the experts agree, if he'd been elected instead of Kennedy, that coward.

My mother will vote for Richard Nixon in 1968, but in spite of his loud support my father will sit out the election, convinced there's no need to become a citizen of the United States (the usual prerequisite for voting) because Nixon will get us back to Cuba in no time, where my father's dormant citizenship will spring to life.

Later that summer, my father, who has resisted getting a television set (too cumbersome to be moved when we go back to Cuba, he will tell us), suddenly buys a huge Zenith color model to watch the Olympics broadcast from Mexico City.

I will sit on the floor, close enough to distinguish the different colored dots, while my father sits a few feet away in a LA-Z-BOY chair and roots for the Cuban boxers, especially Teófilo Stevenson. Every time Stevenson wins one—whether against North Americans or East Germans or whomever—my father will jump up and shout.

Later, when the Cuban flag waves at us during the medal ceremony, and the Cuban national anthem comes through the TV's tinny speakers, my father will stand up in Miami and cover his heart with his palm just like Fidel, watching on his own TV in Havana.

40   When I get older, I'll tell my father a rumor I heard that Stevenson, for all his heroics, practiced his best boxing moves on his wife, and my father will look at me like I'm crazy and say, Yeah, well, he's a Communist, what did you expect, huh?

In the processing center, my father is visited by a Cuban man with a large camera bag and a steno notebook into which he's constantly scribbling. The man has green Coke-bottle glasses and chews on a pungent Cuban cigar as he nods at everything my father says.

My mother, holding a brown paper bag filled with our new (used) clothes, sits next to me on the couch under the buzzing and clicking lights. She asks me about the Colombian girl, and I tell her she read me parts of the Bible, which makes my mother shudder.

The man with the Coke-bottle glasses and cigar tells my father he's from Santiago de Cuba in Oriente province, near Fidel's hometown, where he claims nobody ever supported the revolution because they knew the real Fidel. Then he tells my father he knew his father, which makes my father very nervous.

The whole northern coast of Havana harbor is mined, my father says to the Cuban man as if to distract him. There are *milicianos* all over the beaches, he goes on; it was a miracle we got out, but we had to do it—for her, and he points my way again.

45   Then the man with the Coke-bottle glasses and cigar jumps up and pulls a giant camera out of his bag, covering my mother and me with a sudden explosion of light.

In 1971, I'll come home for Thanksgiving from Indiana University where I have a scholarship to study optometry. It'll be the first time in months I'll be without an antiwar demonstration to go to, a consciousness-raising group to attend, or a Gay Liberation meeting to lead.

Alaba'o, I almost didn't recognize you, my mother will say, pulling on the fringes of my suede jacket, promising to mend the holes in my floor-sweeping bell-bottom jeans. My green sweater will be somewhere in the closet of my bedroom in their house.

We left Cuba so you could dress like this? my father will ask over my mother's shoulder.

And for the first and only time in my life, I'll say, Look, you didn't come for me, you came for you; you came because all your rich clients were leaving, and you were going to wind up a cashier in your father's hardware store if you didn't leave, okay?

50   My father, who works in a bank now, will gasp—*¿Qué qué?*—and step back a bit. And my mother will say, Please, don't talk to your father like that.

And I'll say, It's a free country, I can do anything I want, remember? Christ, he only left because Fidel beat him in that stupid swimming race when they were little.

And then my father will reach over my mother's thin shoulders, grab me by the red bandanna around my neck, and throw me to the floor, where he'll kick me over and over until all I remember is my mother's voice pleading, Please stop, please, please, please stop.

We leave the processing center with the fat Hungarian lady, who drives a large Ford station wagon. My father sits in the front with her, and my mother and I sit in the back, although there is plenty of room for both of us in the front as well. The fat Hungarian lady is taking us to our hotel, where our room will have a kitchenette and a view of an alley from which a tall black transvestite plies her night trade.

Eventually, I'm drawn by the lights of the city, not just the neon streaming by the car windows but also the white globes on the street lamps, and I scamper to the back where I can watch the lights by myself. I close my eyes tight, then open them, loving the tracers and star bursts on my private screen.

55   Up in front, the fat Hungarian lady and my father are discussing the United States' many betrayals, first of Eastern Europe after World War II, then of Cuba after the Bay of Pigs invasion.

My mother, whom I believe is as beautiful as any of the palm trees fluttering on the median strip as we drive by, leans her head against the car window, tired and bereft. She comes to when the fat Hungarian lady, in a fit of giggles, breaks from the road and into the parking lot of a supermarket so shrouded in light that I'm sure it's a flying saucer docked here in Miami.

We did this when we first came to America, the fat Hungarian lady says, leading us up to the supermarket. And it's something only people like us can appreciate.

My father bobs his head up and down and my mother follows, her feet scraping the ground as she drags me by the hand.

We walk through the front door and then a turnstile, and suddenly we are in the land of plenty—row upon row of cereal boxes, TV dinners, massive displays of fresh pineapple, crate after crate of oranges, shelves of insect repellent, and every kind of broom. The dairy section is jammed with cheese and chocolate milk.

60 There's a butcher shop in the back, and my father says, Oh my god, look, and points to a slab of bloody red ribs thick with meat. My god my god my god, he says, as if he's never seen such a thing, or as if we're on the verge of starvation.

Calm down, please, my mother says, but he's not listening, choking back tears and hanging off the fat Hungarian lady who's now walking him past the sausages and hot dogs, packaged bologna and chipped beef.

All around us people stare, but then my father says, We just arrived from Cuba, and there's so much here!

The fat Hungarian lady pats his shoulder and says to the gathering crowd, Yes, he came on a little boat with his whole family; look at his beautiful daughter who will now grow up well-fed and free.

I push up against my mother, who feels as smooth and thin as a palm leaf on Good Friday. My father beams at me, tears in his eyes. All the while, complete strangers congratulate him on his wisdom and courage, give him hugs and money, and welcome him to the United States.

65 There are things that can't be told.

Things like when we couldn't find an apartment, everyone's saying it was because landlords in Miami didn't rent to families with kids, but knowing, always, that it was more than that.

Things like my doing very poorly on an IQ test because I didn't speak English, and getting tossed into a special education track, where it took until high school before somebody realized I didn't belong there.

Things like a North American hairdresser's telling my mother she didn't do her kind of hair.

Like my father, finally realizing he wasn't going to go back to Cuba anytime soon, trying to hang himself with the light cord in the bathroom while my mother cleaned rooms at a nearby luxury hotel, but falling instead and breaking his arm.

70 Like accepting welfare checks, because there really was no other way.

Like knowing that giving money to exile groups often meant helping somebody buy a private yacht for Caribbean vacations, not for invading Cuba, but also knowing that refusing to donate only invited questions about our own patriotism.

And knowing that Nixon really wasn't the one, and wasn't doing anything, and wouldn't have done anything, even if he'd finished his second term, no matter what a good job the Cuban burglars might have done at the Watergate Hotel.

What if we'd stayed? What if we'd never left Cuba? What if we were there when the last of the counterrevolution was beaten, or when Mariel harbor leaked thousands of Cubans out of the island, or when the Pan-American Games came? What if we'd never left?

All my life, my father will say I would have been a young Communist, falling prey to the revolution's propaganda. According to him, I would have believed ice cream treats came from Fidel, that those hairless Russians were our friends; and that my duty as a revolutionary was to turn him in for his counterrevolutionary activities—which he will swear he'd never have given up if we'd stayed in Cuba.

75   My mother will shake her head but won't contradict him. She'll say the revolution uses people, and that I, too, would probably have been used, then betrayed, and that we'll never know, but maybe I would have wound up in jail whether I ever believed in the revolution or not, because I would have talked back to the wrong person, me and my big mouth.

I wonder, if we'd stayed then who, if anyone—if not Martha and the boy from the military academy—would have been my blond lovers, or any kind of lovers at all.

And what if we'd stayed, and there had been no revolution?

My parents will never say, as if somehow they know that their lives were meant to exist only in opposition.

I try to imagine who I would have been if Fidel had never come into Havana sitting triumphantly on top of that tank, but I can't. I can only think of variations of who I am, not who I might have been.

80   In college one day, I'll tell my mother on the phone that I want to go back to Cuba to see, to consider all these questions, and she'll pause, then say, What for? There's nothing there for you, we'll tell you whatever you need to know, don't you trust us?

Over my dead body, my father will say, listening in on the other line.

Years later, when I fly to Washington, D.C., and take a cab straight to the Cuban Interests Section to apply for a visa, a golden-skinned man with the dulled eyes of a bureaucrat will tell me that because I came to the U.S. too young to make the decision to leave for myself—that it was in fact my parents who made it for me—the Cuban government does not recognize my U.S. citizenship.

You need to renew your Cuban passport, he will say. Perhaps your parents have it, or a copy of your birth certificate, or maybe you have a relative or friend who could go through the records in Cuba for you.

I'll remember the passport among my mother's priceless papers, handwritten in blue ink, even the official parts. But when I ask my parents for it, my mother will say nothing, and my father will say, It's not here anymore, but in a bank box, where you'll never see it. Do you think I would let you betray us like that?

85   The boy from the military academy will say oh baby baby as he grinds his hips into me. And Martha and all the girls before and after her here in the United States will say ooohhh ooooohhhhh ooooooohhhhhhhh as my fingers explore inside them.

But the first time I make love with a Cuban, a politically controversial exile writer of some repute, she will say, *Aaaaaayyyyyyaaaaaaayyyyaaaaay* and lift me by my hair from between her legs, strings of saliva like sea foam between my mouth and her shiny curls. Then she'll drop me onto her mouth where our tongues will poke each other like wily porpoises.

In one swift movement, she'll flip me on my back, pillows falling every which way from the bed, and kiss every part of me, between my breasts and under my arms, and she'll suck my fingertips, and the inside of my elbows. And when she rests her head on my belly, her ear listening not to my heartbeat but to the fluttering of palm trees, she'll sit up, place one hand on my throat, the other on my sex, and kiss me there, under my rib cage, around my navel, where I am softest and palest.

The next morning, listening to her breathing in my arms, I will wonder how this could have happened, and if it would have happened at all if we'd stayed in Cuba. And if so, if it would have been furtive or free, with or without the revolution. And how—knowing now how cataclysmic life really is—I might hold on to her for a little while longer.

When my father dies of a heart attack in 1990 (it will happen while he's driving, yelling at somebody, and the car will just sail over to the sidewalk and stop dead at the curb, where he'll fall to the seat and his arms will somehow fold over his chest, his hands set in prayer), I will come home to Florida from Chicago, where I'll be working as a photographer for the *Tribune*. I won't be taking pictures of murder scenes or politicians then but rather rock stars and local performance artists.

90   I'll be living in Uptown, in a huge house with a dry darkroom in one of the bedrooms, now converted and sealed black, where I cut up negatives and create photomontages that are exhibited at the Whitney Biennial and hailed by the critics as filled with yearning and hope.

When my father dies, I will feel sadness and a wish that certain things had been said, but I will not want more time with him. I will worry about my mother, just like all the relatives who predict she will die of heartbreak within months (she has diabetes and her vision is failing). But she will instead outlive both him and me.

I'll get to Miami Beach, where they've lived in a little coach house off Collins Avenue since their retirement, and find cousins and aunts helping my mother go through insurance papers and bank records, my father's will, his photographs and mementos: his university degree, a faded list of things to take back to Cuba (including Christmas lights), a jaundiced clipping from *Diario de las Américas* about our arrival which quotes my father as saying that Havana harbor is mined, and a photo of my mother and me, wide-eyed and thin, sitting on the couch in the processing center.

My father's funeral will be simple but well-attended, closed casket at my request, but with a moment reserved for those who want a last look. My mother will stay in the room while the box is pried open (I'll be in the lobby smoking a cigarette, a habit I despised in my father but which I'll pick up at his funeral) and tell me later she stared at the cross above the casket, never registering my father's talcumed and perfumed body beneath it.

I couldn't leave, it wouldn't have looked right, she'll say. But thank god I'm going blind.

95   Then a minister who we do not know will come and read from the Bible and my mother will reach around my waist and hold onto me as we listen to him say, When all these things come upon you, the blessing and the curse...and you call them to mind among all the nations where the Lord your God has driven you, and return to the Lord your God, you and your children, and obey his voice...with all your heart and with all your soul; then the Lord your God will return your fortunes, and have compassion upon you, and he will gather you again from all the peoples where the Lord your God has scattered you.

There will be a storm during my father's burial, which means it will end quickly. My mother and several relatives will go back to her house, where a TV will blare from the bedroom filled with bored teenage cousins, the women will talk about how to make *picadillo* with low-fat ground turkey instead of the traditional beef and ham, and the men will sit outside in the yard, drinking beer or small cups of Cuban coffee, and talk about my father's love of Cuba, and how unfortunate it is that he died just as Eastern Europe is breaking free, and Fidel is surely about to fall.

Three days later, after taking my mother to the movies and the mall, church and the local Social Security office, I'll be standing at the front gate with my bags, yelling at the cab driver that I'm coming, when my mother will ask me to wait a minute and run back into the house, emerging minutes later with a box for me that won't fit in any of my bags.

A few things, she'll say, a few things that belong to you that I've been meaning to give you for years and now, well, they're yours.

I'll shake the box, which will emit only a muffled sound, and thank her for whatever it is, hug her and kiss her and tell her I'll call her as soon as I get home. She'll put her chicken bone arms around my neck, kiss the skin there all the way to my shoulders, and get choked up, which will break my heart.

100 Sleepy and tired in the cab to the airport, I'll lean my head against the window and stare out at the lanky palm trees, their brown and green leaves waving good-bye to me through the still coming drizzle. Everything will be damp, and I'll be hot and stuffy, listening to car horns detonating on every side of me. I'll close my eyes, stare at the blackness, and try to imagine something of yearning and hope, but I'll fall asleep instead, waking only when the driver tells

me we've arrived, and that he'll get my bags from the trunk, his hand out-stretched for the tip as if it were a condition for the return of my things.

When I get home to Uptown I'll forget all about my mother's box until one day many months later when my memory's fuzzy enough to let me be curious. I'll break it open to find grade school report cards, family pictures of the three of us in Cuba, a love letter to her from my father (in which he talks about want-ing to kiss the tender mole by her mouth), Xeroxes of my birth certificate, copies of our requests for political asylum, and my faded blue-ink Cuban passport (expi-ration date: June 1965), all wrapped up in my old green sweater.

When I call my mother—embarrassed about taking so long to unpack her box, overwhelmed by the treasures within it—her answering machine will pick up and, in a bilingual message, give out her beeper number in case of emergency.

A week after my father's death, my mother will buy a computer with a Braille keyboard and a speaker, start learning how to use it at the community center down the block, and be busy investing in mutual funds at a profit within six months.

But this is all a long way off, of course. Right now, we're in a small hotel room with a kitchenette that U.S. taxpayers have provided for us.

105 My mother, whose eyes are dark and sunken, sits at a little table eating one of the Royal Castle hamburgers the fat Hungarian lady bought for us. My father munches on another, napkins spread under his hands. Their heads are tilted toward the window which faces an alley. To the far south edge, it offers a view of Biscayne Boulevard and a magically colored thread of night traffic. The air is salty and familiar, the moon brilliant hanging in the sky.

I'm in bed, under sheets that feel heavy with humidity and the smell of clean-ing agents. The plastic doll the Catholic volunteer gave me sits on my pillow.

Then my father reaches across the table to my mother and says, We made it, we really made it.

And my mother runs her fingers through his hair and nods, and they both start crying, quietly but heartily, holding and stroking each other as if they are all they have.

And then there's a noise—a screech out in the alley followed by what sounds like a hyena's laughter—and my father leaps up and looks out the window, then starts laughing, too.

110 Oh my god, come here, look at this, he beckons to my mother, who jumps up and goes to him, positioning herself right under the crook of his arm. Can you believe that, he says.

Only in America, echoes my mother.

And as I lie here wondering about the spectacle outside the window and the new world that awaits us on this and every night of the rest of our lives, even I know we've already come a long way. What none of us can measure yet is how much of the voyage is already behind us.

Cecile Pineda

Cecile Pineda was born to a Mexican father and a French Swiss mother in Harlem, New York City, in 1942 and has lived in California since 1961. She is the author of five novels, including *The Love Queen of the Amazon* (1991), named Notable Book of the Year by the *New York Times; Frieze* (1986); and *Face* (1985), which was nominated for an American Book Award. From her lyrical and moving early novels to the parody and humor of *Love Queen*, Pineda's writing stretches the focus of traditional Latino fiction beyond the specifics of ethnic identity toward philosophical and metaphysical issues and ideas. In 2000, Pineda published two short novels, *Bardo 99* and *Redoubt*.

Notes for a Botched Suicide

"I SEEN A PICTURE IN THE PAPER ONCE. THIS WOMAN, SEE, THIS WOMAN IS FALLING. SHE IS FALLING PAST THIS HOTEL SIGN, SEE, SHE IS THROWING HERSELF OUT THIS HOTEL WINDOW."

1.

They say that for some brief moment on the way to the ground, a moment maybe too brief for anyone to know it—even the fallen—they say that the person flies, as weightless and graceful as a seabird. But the person doesn't know it, and almost no one ever sees it, and maybe the photojournalist who took the picture one morning outside the Genesee Hotel, maybe he didn't see it either. He was worrying about the focus because he knew if he got it right, it would make tomorrow's paper, and he'd have all the time in the world—all the time left to him anyway—to look at that woman coming down, turning into a pile of bricks as she slammed into the ground.

He wonders where he got her, where on the way down. Maybe just after she let go the sill, or maybe just on level with the sign, the sign that says Genesee Hotel, its letters big and clear and white, or maybe just silhouetted against the black frame of the recessed doorway. Or maybe as the first part of her touched the ground—a fingertip, perhaps, or a shoulder blade. He prods the Ilford paper in the acid bath, agitating the surface with his tongs. There she is, coming to life, a ghostly white. He can make out the letters clearly: G•E•N•E•S•E•E. He's got her as she's passing the Genesee Hotel! He studies the flash of her garment, the way it twists in the updraft, the way she flings one arm out ahead of her; the way her legs are cocked like scissor blades, severing the air.

She reminds him of the milk glass vase his mother used to have—the one he broke. She reminds him of the painting on glass in the window of the antique dealer downstairs. She reminds him of a rotogravure of some ballerina in swan feathers, a hinge gone stiff, all jack-knifed on herself. Someone his mother saw once at the Hippodrome.

He pulls the sopping paper from the cleansing bath. In the dark, he squeegees it, all but the bottom margin. He fumbles with the clothespins. He tacks it on the overhead line to dry. He waits for the last drop to find its way back into the pan. Plop. The room is quiet, dark, red. He studies the image. There it is:

2.

One time I went to Poland. Not really Poland. I went to Auschwitz. In Poland they have a word for it: smiercz. Everything is smiercz. In Polish it means death. The ground in Auschwitz is gray. You didn't know mud could be gray, but it's gray in Auschwitz. It comes from the gravel dust. They put it down after the rain, year after year, because when it rained in Auschwitz—in the heyday of Auschwitz—people sank in mud up to their ankles. Across the street, Birkenau was built by people up to their knees, half buried in the mud before the ovens took them.

You can go to the stalags if you like. If you like and have the stomach for it. The stalags are neatly numbered, 18 for the Yugoslavs, 19 for the Russians. Twenty four beds, four bunks to a bed. The Jews were different. They were all over the place, there were so many—and gypsies and priests, and homosexuals—they had to put numbers on their arms.

The stalags are a tourist attraction now. The walls are gray, the floors are gray. The ceilings are gray. The corridors are gray. In the glass cases are the exhibits. In one window there is a boxcar load of human hair. It is gray. You wonder how all that human hair could be gray. Were there no blondes, no brunettes, no redheads? Did the hair turn gray before it was cut to manufacture blankets for the bunks and shock absorbers for the tank gun emplacements? Or did it turn gray afterwards?

In another window you see baby clothes, little shoes with pearl button fasteners. Little lace bonnets, little vests and dresses, hand knitted some of them, by grandmothers. There are silver spoons, porringers, silver rattles. The case is bigger than a mansion living room.

In another case there is a display of prayer shawls. There are wool ones and synthetic ones. They are edged in dark blue stripes, the kind kafka talked about, and fringed at the edges. There are skull caps, there are the sable hats of Chassidim.

But in the suitcase window, everything is neatly numbered, labeled. You can read the addresses of all the cities in Europe. There are names from the 16th arrondissment. There are names from Kafka's home town. You can read the surnames of some of your best friends *share* if you want to spend some time. There are brown cardboard suitcases with straps. There are black trunks with rusting hoops. There are faded burgundy leather overnighters. There are dusty carpetbags. There are silver-clasped doctor bags. In Auschwitz smiercz is globalized. It doesn't need a passport.

3.

Sometimes I think about the Genesee Hotel. I imagine it sitting at the corner of a certain street. The neighborhood is never tony. Decay stalks the window frames, the doorways. There is flotsam clinging to the sewer drains. Sometimes the hotel sign is neon. Sometimes it's red or blue. Or yellow.

Sometimes it blinks on and off. Sometimes it pales beside the winking nipples of the neon gogo dancer gyrating next to it. And sometimes, when it's real hard times, the sign is black, a black box with letters cut out; inside light bulbs glow. The cutouts spell out G•E•N•E•S•E•E. They are not letters at all really, they are the ghosts of letters. Sometimes they are covered with milky white plastic. And sometimes, just before they flake or crack, the letters turn yellow, like the stale cigar smoke downstairs, or like your mother's dress shields gone brittle, stained with sweat, and the letters seem to stutter a little before the plastic gives up altogether. I never saw anyone change the light bulbs inside the box. But I guess they must need changing. They must burn out from time to time. But I never saw anyone replacing them.

4.

I didn't want to go to Tel Aviv. I didn't want to go—even before I got there. And when I got there, I knew for sure I didn't want to go. In Tel Aviv it looks exactly like Los Angeles. I have $200 for the whole trip. A plastic raincoat costs $85.00. My clothes are soaked, the color runs. Anyway, I wasn't exactly going there at all. I was going somewhere else. But I didn't want to get there, not just yet, so I went to Tel Aviv.

Someone met me at the airport with a Mercedes and a chauffeur. The chauffeur carried a gun under the seat. He was Iraqi with dark glancing eyes. He didn't really know how to use the gun, or even how to load it. Certainly not clean it. He liked to aim the gun, but only to show it to girls.

But getting out of Tel Aviv was another story. The plane left at eleven. But I had to get up at 4:00. It was still dark when we got to the airport. There were long lines of people with suitcases. The suitcases said Daytona Beach, Shaker Heights. There was airplane luggage, Samsonite luggage, Vuitton luggage. There were aluminum camera cases. There were handgrips, Kelty packs, overnighters, garment bags. There were women in snappy uniform hats scrutinizing passports. There were draped examining rooms past the first barrier. I had never been frisked before. They checked my breasts and inside my legs.

15 The cocky customs attendant rummages through my bag.

"Who were you staying with?"

"Where did you spend last night?"

"Who is your friend? Is he your lover? Is he Arab? Just a minute. I'll call the supervisor."

The supervisor hightails it over.

20 "What's this? Contraband?"

Why didn't I think of the stuff I'm carrying sooner. "Pills. I use them for sleep."

But I didn't need to worry. No one nods out in Israel. Getting bombed means different things in different places. She sticks my pills back in the side pocket. I hear them rattle against the plastic. I've been bopping around Israel for the past two weeks, running to escape their sound: Capharnaum, Galilee, Masada. Akko, Jaffa, Masada. The Dead Sea…

All the time I'm sitting in a white room watching a clock tick away white minutes. I'm not here at all. I'm somewhere else, a place I don't want to get to yet.

5.

Jerusalem. This is the street Jesus walked. What should I do? I don't even know the dosage. There's enough in that plastic bottle to choke a horse. What if there's too much? What if I cop out...? At the last minute....Father, father, let this cup pass from me. What should I do?

25 They say it works better if you use a plastic bag....Will I sit calmly next to her? Hold her hand? Wait? Wait for the Angel of Death to come, the Malach Ch'amovitz?

I find an Arab cabbie. "Take me to the tomb of Jehosephat," I tell him. "Wait for me."

I walk down the path. Old stones line the roadway. Inside garden walls ancient olive trees are twisting, their leaves shimmer silver as they have shimmered for a thousand years. The earth has been packed hard with centuries of human traffic. The path is white. It drops into the gully.

The tombs are carved into the rock. They're supposed to date back to the First Temple. The air is filled with light. There is a faint, paling winter sun. It turns the sweet grass emerald.

I sit on a stone dreaming. Where does the spirit go when the spirit flies? Does it fly into the sun? Is it forever suspended in the eternal night of space? Does it hum for a long time afterward? Can it see us? Does it hover still?

Three Arab boys herd a flock of sheep into the hollow. "Hey, hey, hey," they shout. The sheep trot briskly, their bells quicken the afternoon air.

30 The boys greet me as they pass. "Shalom," they say.
"Salam aleikum," I say. Peace be with you.
They laugh. "Aleikum salam."

6.

Sometimes I think of the Genessee Hotel. As you get to the top of the stairs, there is a door to the right. Its number is 18. The door has vertically set beveled panels. No one is staying there right now. It's an installation site. You can push the door open as the sign suggests.

Inside are suitcases. Nothing but suitcases. All kinds, all sizes, all shapes, all colors. You can't even read the labels, the names or the addresses, the serial numbers, the APO numbers because there's not enough light. The piles climb to the ceilings. They block light from the windows. And anyway the windows are all grimy. They haven't been washed in years.

35 The sign tells you the exhibit's called "In Transit." The suitcases are all ages, some from as far back as 1892, the year my godmother was born. They made sure to empty them before putting them here. You just look at them. There is nothing else to do with them. You can't take things from them. You can't open them—the room is too cluttered.

7.

My godmother's sitting on the commode. The day is bright, a fall day in New York. Bright sun. The afternoon light floods her room. I help her to stand up.

"Isn't it humiliating?" she asks. "Don't you think it's humiliating?" She pronounces it with a French accent, as if it had four syllables, not five. Hu.mil.YA.ting.

"Nonsense," I say. "What's humiliating about it? Everyone goes. It's proof you're still alive. Now imagine for a minute if you stopped going: it would be all over with you."

Sometimes we sit talking about death. It's our funniest conversation. We erect elaborate schemes to circumvent it. We dream up ways of cheating it, spying on it, mocking it, cheating it one way or another.

40   The social worker pays a visit.

"Mrs. Brown," she yells.

"She's not deaf," I say. "She can hear you very well. If you just listen to her, she makes herself very well understood."

But she has no time to listen. "Is she your mother?"

"No, my godmother."

45   Maybe that photographer, maybe he didn't see the woman flying after all. Maybe he didn't really see because already framed in his lens he thought he had a picture of a woman dying. A woman dying doesn't fly. Maybe she sinks in water—or an acid bath—but she doesn't fly.

Later she's back on the commode. "Of course, "she says, "when they look at me, everyone sees a spent old wreck."

"Try one more time," I urge her.

"Why don't I just die? I'm no good to anyone, I'm just a lot of trouble."

"Quit feeling sorry for yourself. You should be proud. Didn't you teach for nearly 70 years? Look at all the kids you helped. All that good energy you put in the world. Don't you think you're entitled to a little constipation now and then?"

50   She is laughing so hard, she hardly notices me helping her. She totters with the aid of her walker. She collapses in her chair.

"I think I need a banana," she says.

"One banana. Coming up."

8.

The heat in New York kills, especially in winter. I run. I fly. There's the commode that needs emptying, the bed to be changed. The groceries to be bought. The laundry to be washed. The thieves to be thwarted. Dinner to be cooked. Her to be washed, dressed, pushed in her wheelchair. Loved. There's 24 hours of it to be loved, reminded she is loved, not forgotten, not put away on a shelf to die.

"What will happen to me? Maybe we should put me in a home."

55   "Come on," I say, "that's just what we decided we wouldn't do. You don't belong in a home. You're too independent. A home would surely put an end to you."

"I'll die anyway…"

"Yes. But you could have fun dying."

She begins to laugh.

"Look at all these books you have…"

60 "I could read them if I still had eyes."

"Or I could read them to you. Or you could watch the tube."

"It's nothing but garbage."

"I thought you loved the game shows…"

"It's the look of unbridled greed that get's me—in the eyes of the contestants." She is giggling so hard she shakes the chair.

9.

65 It's been one day, two days. Three days since I'm here from Tel Aviv. She hasn't even asked for them. All through Jerusalem I puzzled (this is the street Christ walked) what should I do? I promised her.

"When the time comes," she says, "will you help me?"

I hold her hand. "Yes," I say, "Yes, I will help you. I will be there."

"It's very dangerous," she says, "you could go to jail."

"Everything is dangerous for you," I say. "Remember the time you got held up?"

70 She laughs. "Indeed I do."

She's on her way home with her bag of groceries, she tells me. Just what she can still manage to carry. And her change purse of course. She pauses to unlock the street door.

"I forgot my key," the young man says.

She smiles, "I'll let you in."

He holds her groceries for her while she fumbles for her key. She works it into the lock. The door swings open. He holds it for her, gives her back her groceries.

75 "This is a stickup," he says softly. "Give me all your money."

"This is all I have." She hands him her change purse.

"Don't be scared," he tells her. "I'm not going to hurt you."

"I know," she says.

10.

It's very dangerous. You could be arrested. On the plane at last I'm thinking about it. Very simple. If she asks for them, I will pass the pills to her. If she doesn't ask, I won't.

80 I am cleaning up in the kitchen. I hear her calling from the next room. I turn the water off.

"What did you say?"

"Did you bring it? The thing I asked you for?"

I walk into the room drying my hands. She is lying on the couch.

"Yes."

85 "How much?"

"Enough," I say.

11.

She lies in bed, waking. Sometimes I dream, she says. A smile comes over her. Impossible to describe. No words for it, a smile as vulnerable, as innocent as a child's. I dream of green. Green fields. Sunlight. It is summer. You can hear the insects. It's that quiet.

"What will Madame care to take for breakfast?"

"Madame would care to take a pee." She giggles and giggles. She sits on the edge of the bed, gasping with the effort. Her tiny feet in their white socks dangle over the edge. I set her knee warmers back in place. I help her stand.

90 "Oooo," she shrieks in terror. She is afraid of falling.

"I'm holding onto you."

She takes tiny little jerks of footsteps to set her body turning. At last she sits down. The smile returns. She is peeing, remembering the fields.

"I hope you won't think of me like this—just an old wreck, she says. I hope you'll remember me as I was."

12.

It's not every day I can bring up money. I have to watch myself very carefully, choose the time. When she started this final slide two years ago, she had savings. By this time next year she will reach what the bureaucrats in their philanthropic cubbyholes call "spenddown." (More like meltdown, only colder.)

95 I try to pick a time when she's not too tired. Or she will bring it up herself. My petite fille (she remembers the days as not so long ago when she minded me on her roof and I tried to run away), ma petite fille, we must do the accounts.

These days end badly. She sobs, she screams. I go into the bedroom and close the door. I come out much later, when she has had time to calm herself down.

"You work all your life. You save. And then you die a pauper."

"Come," I say to her gently as I can as I plump the pillows for her. "You don't know what pauper is. You're here. You have your place, your things around you."

"But when the money runs out, what will they do to me? I'll be out on the street like a bag lady."

100 "Bag lady! Don't be absurd. No one in his right mind would turn you loose in the street. You're too much of a menace."

Her look turns quizzical.

"Remember the time that guy grabbed your purse strap? Of course you were a mere child of sixty then, but you nearly creamed him all the same."

She begins to chortle.

"Decked him one, you did. He ran off howling."

105 She's laughing uncontrollably.

13.

She settles in the couch. Night is falling. I have trouble with the lamp pull. I spread a blanket over her knees.

"I used to have a recurring dream. I used to dream we were on vacation, myself and some of the other teachers. It was a beautiful resort. The lawns were manicured, the air was cooling, and the trees! We were having a good time. And then, when it was time to leave, everyone was there, paying her bill. But when it came my turn to pay, I had nothing. My purse was empty."

"I've made something special," I say, placing the tray on her lap.

"Mmmmmm. Shrimp!" Her voice purrs like a cat's She loves shrimp. I always try to make them for her on money days.

110 "Can we have the news?"

I swivel the set so she can see the TV from the couch. I turn the volume up. The newscasters blast away: New York transit system…New York welfare system…

She is talking to me as I try to eat. Impossible to hear her above the roar.

"I can't hear you when the set is on. You must decide: talk? or TV? We can't do both."

"Turn it off," she says, "it's garbage anyway…except for that program on Afghanistan…with all the nomads driving their sheep."

115 "And the Kalantar in his pick up, too old to make the trip." I get up from the table to turn off the set.

"You don't listen to the news?"

"Sometimes. But I'd much rather see those clansmen wrestling their sheep through the mountain passes. That's news to me."

"Of course," she says, "there's no comparison." She seems lost in thought. "Once I lived with people like, a whole year. One time, when I was maybe nine or ten. We moved to a small village. There was only one school. They were my classmates. And somehow they adopted me. After school, I used to go home with them. They loved me in a way we didn't know about. In my family, we children used to address our father as monsieur. I played games with them. They taught me to churn butter, to herd the cows. There was a way they had of driving them home at night when it got dark. They talked to them."

"How?"

120 She smiles remembering. "Quo, quo, ma belle. Quo. Then we moved."

"But quo…that's Latin!"

"Oh, yes. They probably called them like that from the Dark Ages, from before Christ probably."

"What happened to them?"

"Oh, none of them lived beyond fifty or so. They had tuberculosis, all of them. None of them survived."

125 I sit at her TV table, contemplating my empty glass, the crusted plate. The linen napkin still rests on my knees. I am crying softly, softly enough so she won't see.

14.

All over Masonic Street, the rain puddles, churning in the gutters, reaching for the high ground. We can hear it come licking down the hill, great brown tongues of it. It swells the intersection, creates cataracts. All the neighborhood dogs roll in it, scratching their backs. I dream somehow I am embedded in some bubble of air, of light. Going downstairs, diving into a subterranean garage. Having to swim. A test dive into the belly of some unnamed leviathan, but the approach is under water, and in its soft underbelly is an airlock. Eventually I give up, shut the door to the cellar stairs. And now some image of a crowd of appalled, appalling people, James Ensor's sinister clowns, grotesque. Waving. Whistling. Waiting for the Old Lady, so old, but in a curious way, she becomes younger, yet younger. A child at last, smaller, then smaller still. And at last, it is understood, the womb will grab her, pull her feet first into the darkness.

Benjamin Alire Sáenz

Benjamin Alire Sáenz was raised in the Southwest and writes of the borderlands of Texas and New Mexico. He has published a collection of short stories, *Flowers for the Broken* (1992); the novels *Carry Me Like Water* (1995), *The House of Forgetting* (1997), and *Sammy and Juliana in Hollywood* (2004); and three collections of poetry: *Calendar of Dust* (1991), winner of the American Book Award, *Dark and Perfect Angels* (1994), and *Elegies in Blue* (2002). Sáenz has also written children's books, holds a Ph.D. from Stanford University, and teaches at the University of Texas.

Obliterate the Night

I

Dearest Olivia,

Don't really know what to say about all this, except that it's a big mess. Everything's all wrong, always has been, maybe? I can't remember how it was in the beginning, except that I thought you were beautiful. Now that I think of it, I don't think you ever loved me. You know, I loved you a lot in the beginning— as much as I could love anyone. I don't think you married me for the right reasons—look, I don't know anything about us. I can't figure us out, and I'm not going to pretend I have all these deep insights into your psyche. Look, Olivia, I'm not good at playing analyst. You were wrong about me figuring things out— I'm not all that good at it—not when it comes to us, anyway.

You know, last night lying next to you was all I could take. There I was, trying to get to sleep—and your shape was there like a ghost. No, not like a ghost— more like a shadow. So dark, Olivia. Really, I wanted you to disappear. I wanted me to disappear. I almost got up right then and there. I almost woke you up. I almost said: Goodbye, Olivia, keep warm and well-fed. This sucker's walking. I didn't sleep all night.

So I've decided to move out. I can't explain it, nothing works between us anymore—not anything. It isn't true that I didn't want to get closer, but it's too damn hard. You stopped trying. OK, I stopped trying, too. We both did. What the hell difference does it make? The last two years have been the most terrible years of my life—worse than hell. I can't stand it anymore. Another second in this house and I'll explode. Just looking at our wedding picture makes me want to hit someone—maybe you. Maybe I want to hit me! Nothing was ever right. I couldn't resist that you were so beautiful. I didn't know it would be so terrible.

I've taken my clothes. I don't want anything else, except the painting my brother gave us—I've taken it. All the rest of the stuff, you can keep or get rid of. I don't think the whole process of divorce has to be messy. We've both known enough people that have been through all this. Let's split everything in half, lick our wounds, and keep on moving. It's important to keep on moving, Liv. It's a good formula to follow.

A letter isn't the best way to end anything. I know you think I'm a goddamned coward for not having the balls to say this to your face. All right, have it your way.

But I've never liked scenes the way you do. At first, you pretend everything's fine—and then you move in for the kill. I don't want to be around for that, Liv, I just can't handle it.

Look, do what you have to do. Olivia, I don't hate you—it's just that I can't stand being married to you anymore. You're as miserable as I am. Somebody has to play the heavy. I'm doing us both a favor.

Jonathan

Olivia read her husband's letter calmly. She stared at his perfect handwriting: it was all very clear—every single word. "I bet he got *A*'s in penmanship," she said. She placed the letter where she found it, back on the door of the refrigerator, and placed a watermelon magnet over the top of the right-hand corner. It hung there like an unread grocery list. She opened the refrigerator, took out a bottle of white wine her husband had uncorked the night before, and poured herself a glass. His favorite wine, she thought. She took off her blue shoes, stared at her feet through her blue nylons. *It's my feet*, she whispered, *I always had such ugly feet.* She took a sip from her husband's wine and thought a moment. She opened her briefcase and began to go through her papers. She took out her appointment book and shook her head. Damn, not tonight. She moved the phone from the counter and placed it in front of her on the table. *I'll make it ring like it's never rung before.* She pushed the phone buttons and waited for it to ring. She heard the familiar voice on the other end and spoke:

"Karen? I'm glad I caught you. This is Olivia."

"Livie—what's up, honey? I was expecting you to come by the office before you went home. You left some papers on top of your desk—you need me to drop them off on my way home?"

"Well, I'm not exactly calling about that—well, it does have something to do with those papers—well—look—something's come up. I need a favor." For an instant, she wished she had a cigarette. *I'll run out and buy some. Jonathan hated them.*

5   "Sure, Livie, be glad to help—if I can."

"Are you busy tonight?"

"Funny you should ask. I'm all dressed up—nowhere to go. Eldon canceled our date. You know, if this happens one more time, I'm going to dump that guy. He's either humping someone on the side, or even worse, he's in love with his job." She laughed. "You know, I used to think men were in love with their pricks, but now I think they're in love with being away from women. Why am I telling you all this?—just listen to me—as if you didn't have problems of your own. What was it you were saying?"

Olivia listened patiently, enjoying the chatter of her business partner. Karen was never all business—she didn't like living her life according to categories—Jonathan had never liked her. Olivia could get lost in her chatter for hours—her Texas drawl was like bathing in water. Every morning when she walked into the office, Karen said, "Honey, let's you and me have ourselves a talk—then we can get on with our work. Can't work without a little talk, now can we?"

"Livie, honey, you there?"

10   "Sorry, for a minute I forgot why I called. Look, I'm supposed to show a house tonight. Actually, they've already seen it once—they really want it. Can you show it for me? I think they just want to get the feel of the place and make sure they didn't miss any flaws—but the house is flawless. The foundation's been checked, no cracks after twenty-five years, and all kinds of old windows to let in the sun. It's perfect. That house is perfect—not like mine. We might even be able to close by the end of the week. Their credit checks out. That paperwork on top of my desk has all the info you'll need."

"Sure, honey, be glad to do it." She hesitated a moment. "Going out tonight with Jonathan?"

"I don't think Jonathan and I will be going out for a long time."

"Are you all right? You sound a little funny."

"Yeah, I'm fine. It's just that I have this headache—and—"

15   "I know that tone, Livie. Every time something serious happens, you get stoic. You put on this very tight tone, and your words come out sounding perfect—too perfect. Drop it, honey, I'm from Texas—I'm not impressed with good enunciation. I'm your friend, Livie. We go back a long ways, you and me."

"Jonathan's left."

"Jonathan's what?"

"He's left."

"What?"

20   "Don't make me say it again—and don't act so surprised. You know all about our wonderful marriage."

"Was there a scene?"

"No, there was a note."

"A note? A goddamned note?"

"Karen, you don't have to scream. It doesn't matter."

25   "What do you mean, it doesn't matter? Of course it matters. That spineless wonder! If I were you, I'd hop in my car and find him wherever he was hiding, skin him alive, and make a throw rug for my entry way."

Olivia burst out laughing, but there was something hollow in her laugh, and she could hear an echo in the room as if Jonathan had emptied out the house. "Is that what you do to your men back in Texas?"

"Back in Texas, men like to have their own way, and that's exactly why I'm not there anymore. But never mind Texas, Livie, and never mind men—it's you I'm thinking about. I'm coming to your house right this minute—you need to be with somebody. It's not good that you're there alone."

"No." Olivia bit her lip. "Karen, what I need is a bath and a good stiff drink. After that, I'm going to bed."

"I think I should stop by just in case."

30   "Karen, please. I just need some quiet time. Maybe tomorrow—tomorrow, let's have dinner."

Karen was silent a moment. "OK, honey, have it your way—but if you need anything, just call me. I don't care if it's two in the morning—just call. And if it's any consolation, Livie, he's not much of a loss. He was the dullest man I ever set my eyes on. He was nice to look at, I'll give him that, but even the television set was more interesting than that man. First time you met that man, you should've taken his picture, hung it up on your wall, and sent him on his way. Hell, Livie, they're all the same. Really, it's a shame we're not lesbians—"

"Karen!"

"What?"

"Why do you say things like that? You know you don't mean them. I never met a woman who likes men as much as you do."

35   "Oh, Livie, you got me all wrong. Oh, I do love men. I like sleeping with them—I like the shape of their bodies, the way they smell. But also like kicking them out in the morning. You don't see me getting married, do you?"

Olivia wanted to ask her if she felt like crying sometimes because everyone was so far away, but Karen was built different than she was. But she was wrong—they weren't all alike—not men, not women—everybody was different. She let Karen go on talking.

"—Listen to me carry on for filth. Look, Livie, I'll call you tonight when I get in. Don't worry about the deal—I can take care of it in my sleep. I'll call."

Olivia smiled to herself. "Thanks Karen, I don't know what I'd do without you. You're a real gem."

"We both are, honey."

40   She hung up the phone, picked up her husband's letter—her letter—off the refrigerator door, and walked into the bedroom. She placed the letter neatly at the foot of the bed, stepped back, eyed it to make sure it was in the center of the bed, and walked back over and moved it an inch to the right. She looked up and stared at the closet. He didn't even shut the closer door. She stared at the hangers where her husband's shirts had hung.

Jonathan, did I ever tell you I hated your taste in shirts? Blue and white and stripes, blue and white and stripes, and all of them with those button-down collars. Not once in eleven years did you ever buy an interesting shirt—not once. You even wore those goddamned shirts on Saturdays. I'm surprised you took them off your body when you made love. You know, Jonathan, the hangers look much better without your heavy shirts draped over them. They don't look bare, you know, they just look free.

She pulled at her blouse, ripping the buttons off—letting them fly across the room. She wadded up her blouse and threw it at the picture of her husband's parents, happy and white—the whitest people she'd ever known. "You have the most beautiful coloring I've ever seen," his mother had said the first time she'd met her, "Oh, I envy it."

Why didn't you take that goddamned picture?

She grabbed the photograph from the wall, opened the sliding door, and threw it into the back yard. It fell into the snow with a thud. She unzipped her skirt and let at fall to the floor. She tore off the rest of her clothing, piled her clothes in the middle of the room, and sat on top of them as she read her husband's letter to herself. She read it again and again, as if she were trying to memorize a poem.

II

45   She had given her baby a name: Celina. Her mother's name. When she was alone she spoke to her, told her everything about life, about her father, about her grandparents. She would speak to her in Spanish: "*Querida, que no sabes que te adoro? Tu papa era muy bueno y tu abuela era un alma de Dios.*"[1] Once she had been sitting in her office at home talking to Celina, and her husband had been watching her.

"Who are you talking to?" he had asked. It had been easy for her to lie to him—he did not speak that language.

"I was talking to my mother," she had told him, "her name was Celina."

"You never talk about her."

"No," she had answered, "but sometimes I like to speak to her. It makes me feel better."

50   He'd shrugged his shoulders. "Is that healthy?".

"Jonathan, it's cultural. Mexicans speak to the dead."

"It's awfully superstitious," he said, "I thought you said that you'd stopped being Catholic."

"No one ever stops being a Catholic," she wanted to say. "It's silly," she said, "all of us can be silly."

Jonathan smiled, shook his head, and walked out of the room.

III

55   Jonathan had wanted a baby. "The house is exactly like we want it. We have everything, Liv—don't you think it's time?" His voice was sure, friendly, analytical. He had added up the formula and had come out with the correct answer. Olivia, without even knowing it, had come to detest his reasoning. *Isn't it times?* I'm hungry = it's time to eat. The couch is worn out = let's go to the best furniture store in town and buy a new one. I need a new car = let's buy a Mercedes. We've been married six years, have built ourselves a new house, have fashioned ourselves into financial successes = let's have a baby. His logic was faultless. She sneered at his predictability. But hadn't she thought like him, too? Hadn't she?

She nodded. "Yes, I think it's time."

After two years of trying to have a baby (*it's not like making love*, she thought), there was no baby. Having sex did not add up to having babies. The different positions did not add up to anything. Jonathan urged her to go to her doctor.

---

[1]Dear, don't you know I adore you? Your dad was very good and your grandmother was a soul from God.

"Maybe something's wrong," he said. Olivia filled in the rest of the sentence: *with me*. Why does it have to be me? she thought. *Maybe it's you, Jonathan. You go to a doctor.*

"I'll go," she said. Maybe he was right. Maybe the abortion had done something to her body. Her doctor knew about her abortion, but she told her doctor again. "Could it have screwed up my body? My husband doesn't know—it wasn't his. I didn't even know him at the time."

60   "You think you should tell him?"

"Obviously not."

"Well, there's nothing physically wrong with you. You're in good shape, in perfect health. Perfect. There's nothing at all that would prevent you from having a baby. Sometimes, it just takes a little time. And then there's always your husband—there's two of you, you know? Why don't you tell your husband to have himself checked out? Some men are infertile—it's not always the woman." The doctor smiled. "They think it's always us, poor devils. It hurts their pride." She combed her hair back and smiled at Olivia.

Olivia laughed. "He comes from a long line of successful lawyers. It would kill him to think he was the end of the line."

"What about you?"

65   It's nice that she asks, Olivia thought. "Me, Doctor? Well, I come from a long line of farm workers. I don't think I'll mourn the end of that line."

Her doctor smiled, serious and warm. "Tell your husband to have himself checked out."

"Yes, I'll tell him." She went back to her office, and that night, when she went home, she did not tell him. She never told him. She said to him with that dark and calm look of hers, that look which was never calm but only looked calm, she told him with that look that hid: "I can't have—*can't have* children."

"Are they sure?" he asked. There was disappointment in his expression, but he did not say he was disappointed or sad, and he did not ask her if she was sad.

"They're sure." But she knew it was him. She like knowing it was him. That knowledge gave her something that resembled power, that resembled comfort. "In perfect health," she repeated to herself, "perfect."

70   Two years later, for whatever reason (they had ceased discussing their lives with each other), Jonathan had gone to his doctor for a checkup. While he was there, he decided to have some tests run. When his doctor gave him the results, he came home in a rage. "I went to the doctor the other day," he said, barely able to contain his anger. "Today, I went back and got the results for some tests. I can't have children. You lied to me—it was never you—you knew it was me all along—didn't you? Didn't you!" He was yelling, his beautiful face contorted, disfigured. "You've been laughing at me for the last two years—laughing your damn Mexican head off. You knew! You think it's funny, don't you! Goddamn you!" He moved a step closer to her.

"Don't come any closer," she said. Her voice stayed calm, not a hint of fear in it. She grabbed the phone. "I'll break this damn phone over your head. I'll make it ring like it's never rung before."

Jonathan slumped down on a chair.

"And don't ever refer to my head as being Mexican. True as it may be, Jonathan, I don't like the way you said it. I've never made references to your gringo mentality."

"Why should you? I thought my 'gringo mentality' was why you married me."

75 "I haven't a clue as to why I married you."

He said nothing. He was quiet for a long time. "You knew," he said.

"Yes," she nodded, "I knew. And I'll tell you something else, Jonathan, it wouldn't have mattered if you had found out two years ago or today—"

"Oh, yes, it would have mattered! My wife doesn't tell me the truth. Instead, I have to go to a doctor—a perfect stranger—to tell me the truth about my life."

"The truth about your life, Jonathan? No doctor can tell you the truth about your life." She took in a deep breath and looked at him. "All right, I should have told you. I should have told you. You think I've been laughing at you for the last two years? Ha! I haven't laughed for years. Two years ago or today—it doesn't matter—you would still have blamed me. When I told you it was me—and you thought it was me—did you comfort me? I knew, Jonathan, and I also knew you'd resent me for it. But Jonathan, let's get it straight—I don't give a damn if you're sterile or not. I know how you think: sterile = impotent. But that formula doesn't work. Sterile doesn't mean impotent—it just means you can't produce a baby—and I don't want one. Why do you think I didn't tell you? I didn't tell you because you'd have figured out a way to have one—if not to have one, to get one, to buy one. You'd have figured out a way. You're great about figuring things out. I don't want a baby, Jonathan! And if there's something wrong between me and you, don't blame it on your sperm count. And don't resent me for my fertility—it doesn't mean a damn thing—not to me."

80 "You knew," Jonathan repeated. The rest of the evening, they sat across from each other, no one moving, no one speaking.

IV

She sat in the bathtub, and reread the letter. She didn't know what the words said—no—she knew the meaning of each individual word, but she did not know how they added up. One letter = divorce. She laughed. *No, that's not it—that's not it at all. Come back here and fight, damn you! I have a few things to say before you leave. It's not that I want you to stay—it's just that I want you to*—she stopped and took a deep breath. The water was hot, and sweat ran down her face, her salt mixing with the water. "And your shape was there like a ghost," she muttered, "no, not like a ghost, but a shadow." She dipped the letter into the water. She watched the ink run the words together. *He wrote it with his favorite pen, the one his grandfather left him. Nice pen, but the ink runs, dear.* She held the letter at the top corner and clasped it with her thumb and forefinger. She dipped it into the water again and again as if she were washing a shirt—washing his shirts—washing the stripes out of all his shirts. Into the water, out of the water, into the water, out of the water. She let the letter dip in and out until every word was gone, until the letter began to dissolve. She wadded up the pulp in her hand, letting the excess water run down her arm. She tossed the wad into the toilet opposite her. Plunk, like the sound of a small pebble in a lake: that's all it was, she thought, just a tiny insignificant sound that had no meaning at all.

She fell back into the water and let go of her body. She closed her eyes and pretended she was floating in the warmest, calmest ocean in the world. Karen had told her that parts of the Indian Ocean were so warm that it felt like a heated pool. "Like a womb," she'd said. She imagined the blue all around her, blue beneath her, blue above her, nothing but blue as deep as her mother's eyes. But her mother's eyes weren't blue—why should blue remind me of her eyes? *Mama*, she whispered, *Mama, Mama...* She opened her eyes and looked up at the ceiling. She listened to the motions of her body in the water. It was warm here—the ceiling so white. (She loved the blankness of the ceiling; she could put anything up there she wanted; she could imagine anything, and put everything up there with her mind.) She looked at the white and put herself up there—on the white—up there along with her daughter. You never saw my face, Celina, but there you are—there—you and I—are. She dressed them both in white. She held the image up on the ceiling for as long as she could. Held it and held it and held it. "That's power," she whispered, "that's real power."

V

She rose from the bathtub and rubbed a towel against her skin. She rubbed hard until the towel felt like sandpaper; she rubbed until her skin felt like it might start bleeding. *Go ahead and bleed.* She wrapped an old robe around her thick frame and let her wet black hair fall free. She wanted to crawl out of her skin—it was her skin that was cold—it made others look at her as if she were nothing but skin. It was nothing more than a shell. But people buy books for their covers; people buy books for their titles; people buy books for their coffee tables, for their shelves. People did not buy books to read them. Jonathan had never read her—she was too hard to read. She was cold; she felt numb; she was lost; she refused to surrender herself to what she was holding in. Don't cry—you'll break—you'll never stop—don't cry. She breathed in and out slowly, in and out, until the tears were buried where they could not rise. She felt a calm. She walked from room to room and looked at her house as if it did not belong to her, as if she were in the market for a home and was browsing through a stranger's house.

God, why did I buy this house? Four bedrooms? Why in the hell did I want four bedrooms? I didn't even know what to do with one. In the back bedroom, she stood at the window and stared at the snow. It was almost spring. The snow was ugly this time of year—yellow and dirty—not white at all. In two or three weeks it would begin to melt and vanish. It was almost the color of pale, sick flesh, almost the color of her mother's skin before she died. She grabbed the curtains and pulled at them with all her strength. The curtain rod came tumbling down. See how easily they fall. All that money, and I could tear it down in a second. She took off her robe and wrapped herself in the curtains.

85   She walked into her office. Her husband had built and designed it for her—one of his many gifts. She had hated him for his gifts, but she had married him for the gifts he could give—of course she had. He was a lawyer and had "business interests" on the side: a handsome, successful W.A.S.P. who had a perfect body—he built it himself—built it day after day in a gym, but his body wasn't real. When she touched it, she almost expected it to feel like hard plastic. His body was built, but not from work, not like her father's solid body carved and molded from years of bending his back in the fields. Everything about Jonathan—everything he produced—seduced the eye. *I hate you, Jonathan, if you only knew how much I hate you. You hated everything I liked; you thought everyone who didn't think like you was pitiable, but you never hid those things, did you, Jon? From the second I met you, I knew exactly what kind of man you were. You never lied to me. You had no heart, but that's what I liked about you, Jonathan, but I hate you anyway. You weren't supposed to be real. Why are you real, Jonathan? You have no right to be.*

She sat down at her desk and remembered how important she felt the first time she sat in the chair. A leather chair and a desk that cost more than all the money she'd ever spent in four years of college. *It's what I wanted.* She opened the bottom drawer and took out the box in which she kept her diaries, old letters, and pictures. She stared at a picture of her mother and tried to remember what she smelled like. Bread, she smelled of bread. *Mama, what am I going to do?* She shuffled through the things in her box, looking for nothing in particular but hoping to find comfort. A record of the past ought to be comforting. *No, no, the past is no different than the present. Who'd said that?* Willie had said that. She found herself staring at a postcard of some Indian ruins in the desert, the only thing she'd kept to remind herself that he had been real. Early in their marriage, Jonathan had asked her why she kept that postcard. "Oh, it's just from a former boyfriend," she had said casually. Her heart had jumped, but she had learned to keep her voice steady through its moanings. "He was a nice guy—liked to write stories and poetry and play the guitar. I keep it around to remind myself that I was once young and stupid."

"Did he want to marry you?"

"Don't be silly, Jon," she'd laughed, "It was one of those relationships we all had when we were in college."

Jonathan had dropped the subject of the postcard, but she had always resented that he had found out about it. *Why did I resent it? He was my husband. Why shouldn't he know—why shouldn't he have known everything?*

90   The postcard didn't say anything important, but it was something she could touch, and it was real to her. It was real like a statue in a church that she could see and she could stare at, and it made her want to believe in God, and made her want to think that holy was real—that it was something more than the simple projections of the poor. The postcard was a nostalgic picture of a ruin, and

on the back, in very neat handwriting it said: "On my way west. Oh, Liv, you should see it. You could die under this sky and not mind at all. I think of you. I always think of you." He had not signed it, and she had never heard from him again. She was glad, glad because it would have been harder, taken longer to let go. But now she sat at her desk—a desk she'd fought hard to own, a desk where she sat and earned thousands and thousands of dollars—she sat at her desk and stared at an unsigned postcard that she'd received a week after her twenty-first birthday. Today, she could burn that desk and think nothing, feel nothing, but she could not burn that postcard.

Willie. William Michael Upthegrove. She smiled hearing herself whisper his name. They had been in a literature class together, and she remembered how he enjoyed interrupting the professor with questions too hard to answer. He was always asking questions, and yet he never felt like an interruption. It was not as if he were challenging the authority of the professor—she got the feeling his authority didn't matter a damn to Willie. He was just asking questions, honest questions, questions that mattered to him if to no one else. He was neither threatened nor threatening. She remembered the first day he ever spoke to her—

"You want to go for a cup of coffee? I know a great place—great coffee—and the art is kind of crazy. You might like it."

"I don't drink coffee," she'd said abruptly.

"You don't drink coffee? You know, it's something you have to try." He was sure—absolutely sure—that she was missing out on something essential and necessary.

95 "It's for adults," she'd said. And then she wanted to run away for admitting without any coaxing whatsoever that she felt she was just a little girl.

"And what are you?" he smiled, "You look pretty adult to me."

"I'm a nineteen-year-old college junior. Does that make me an adult?"

"Absolutely," he'd said. He was absolutely sure of it.

It was strange to her that he was so certain. So certain, and yet how was it that there was a lack of arrogance in his voice, in his tone, in his expression? He said it simply. "My name's Willie," he said, "Willie Upthegrove."

100 "Yes," she said, "I know. The professor is always calling your name. It's a funny name. And by the way, I don't think the professor likes you very much."

"I'm not in his class to be his friend. Besides, do you really figure he thinks about me very much? And yes, I do have a funny name, but it suits me. I come from a long line of funny names. What's yours?"

"Olivia Garcia."

"That's a funny name, too. You speak Spanish?"

"Yes, I speak Spanish. It's a good language—better than English." She had said it hoping he'd go away. She wanted to tell him that she didn't drink coffee with gringos, that she only went to school with them, that she wanted nothing to do with them—but it wasn't true, and she couldn't bring herself to tell him something that wasn't true. His eyes kept her from lying to him.

105 "So you want to have some coffee?"

She remembered how he smoked his cigarette, how he talked shyly, almost afraid of his own words, and yet there was something very right about the words he finally chose. He moved from shyness to animation, and she remembered how he moved his hands re-creating the entire scene in the air, and she would have liked to have been the air just then. And how he listened as if what she was saying was important. And yet, she felt he was not at all outgoing, no extrovert at all. He talked because he found it necessary, and when it was not necessary he said nothing. He was so incredibly present—the most present individual she had ever met. *Now* was everything to him; the future meant nothing at all, except that it would come, and he would be there to greet it.

Four weeks later they had gone to a movie, and afterwards they had gone to his studio apartment to have a cup of coffee. They never got to the coffee. It was an accident—she had not thought about having sex—not with him—it had not crossed her mind, and she was sure he was not preoccupied with thoughts of sex with her, and yet in one moment, they had both crossed a border, crossed that invisible line and entered into a country of touch where speech was useless, where speech was banished, a country where everything was seen through eyes that were closed.

She remembered taking off his glasses, how vulnerable he looked without them, and not even realizing that he was blind without them. He had looked at her with his eternally boyish smile, and she felt there was something sad about his smile, or perhaps it was the curious look of want that made his lips tremble. Was it want? Was it want? She had looked into his clear brown eyes and seen her reflection in them, but saw more than herself. For the first time in her life, she wanted to know what those eyes saw, what those eyes felt, what those eyes knew—they knew so much—she was certain—knew enough to know that the only way to live in the world was to stay calm, always calm, even in fear.

He was afraid, she could see that, but calm despite the feel of her skin. His palms broke out into a sweat as he touched her neck, and when she kissed him, she wanted to lock his body to hers and keep him locked in her until he died of hunger. Nobody had ever touched her with that mixture of innocence and aggression. She felt he wanted to swallow her whole, to destroy her, to hurt her, but she also felt he wanted to please her, to show her she could feel, to show her that touch was as real as anything else she'd ever known—as real as the loss of her mother, her father, as real as her ambitions to have a huge house that would be hers, a place. She remembered sometimes running to his tiny studio a few blocks away from the library and opening the door, watching him read a book, and whispering to him as her heart perspired like skin and thumped to cool itself off. Now, she would say, Now. The first time her husband had made love to her, she had wanted to cry with disappointment because his sweat did not smell or taste like Willie's.

110   He was not the best-looking man she'd ever met—not like Jonathan. Jonathan was molded in the image of a magazine. Willie was not in magazines. "What are you doing with a guy like Willie?" her roommate would ask. All her girlfriends asked her the same question. She knew what they were saying: Honey, you can do better—don't sell yourself short. According to the law of their world she should be dating her physical equal.

"Olivia," her roommate told her one night, "don't you know you're arresting? Jesus Christ! You should be dating the gods."

Olivia laughed, "Stop reading Greek myths." It was all she said in her defense. Willie *is* my physical equal, she wanted to say, but she told them nothing, and what did it matter, what were they to her? They all had real parents and real houses and went home for holidays. She cared nothing for their world. They could never know what she thought, could not even see that Willie was unbearably handsome. He was handsome in his modest way, and to them modesty was alien. Willie was a modest man, never even took off his shirt unless they were in bed. He was almost oblivious to what he looked like, was too busy thinking about the books he was reading and the world that was sad for him. He'd shake a newspaper at her and say, "We're killing ourselves with fossil fuels, Liv," and he'd launch into a speech and shake his head. No, Willie didn't give a damn about what he looked like. He didn't buy expensive clothes, could not afford them, and would not have bought them if he *could* afford them. She liked that he bought most of his clothes at a second-hand store. He had maybe five or six shirts—and a sweater all the time—the same sweatshirt, the same sweater, but he was always so clean. And one of his shirts was purple and his skin looked soft and white against the deep cotton fabric. He wasn't a pretty boy—but he was a boy. But he was a man, too.

There was something of the rebel in him, but unlike most rebels, he did not have the instincts of an exhibitionist. He was exasperatingly private, and most people mistook his quiet for arrogance. He had no patience with institutions— educational or religious. He knew they would not change, and knew, too, that they would not change him. And yet he was moved by her Catholicism, though it was foreign to his stark Protestant upbringing. Before meeting Willie, she had always detested what she felt was the naive niceness of Midwesterners who knew nothing of anyone who wasn't as white as they were. But Willie shattered her prejudice.

She pictured the first time she had undressed him—she had never undressed a man before she met Willie. He was wearing his purple shirt. She remembered his white skin, the whitest skin she'd ever touched, and how smooth he was when she rubbed her palms on his chest.

115   Olivia dropped the postcard she was clutching in her hand, and reached out to touch something in front of her. But there was nothing there.

She shook her head. She remembered when he had left that small city in the Midwest where they had gone to school. He had no plans. She had hated that about him.

"How can you have no plans, Willie?"

He shook his head. "I'm through with school, Liv."

"What are you going to do with a major in English?"

120   "What do you mean?" he asked. "Do I have to do something with it? You're talking like a capitalist."

She'd laughed. "I am a capitalist, Willie—a capitalist without any capital."

He'd smiled. "Well, we all are—we can't help it. But does an education equal a job—does it, Liv?"

"Oh, Willie, what are you going to do with your life?"

"Don't worry, Livie, I'm fine. Just relax about my life, OK? When you're rich, I'll write you for money."

125   He had wanted to marry her, though he had never asked her, but the unasked question was there the last six months they were together. She knew it was there on his tongue. She could taste it when she kissed him, but she never let him ask. He finished his career as a student and decided to head west.

"Why?" she asked him.

"Because I've never seen it, Liv, that's why."

She saw him, walking to his car before he left. He held her for a long time. He stared at her and repeated her name: "Liv, Liv, Liv. This is so sad, Liv. I'm so sad." He spoke clearly and simply, and she had said nothing in the face of his speech. All she remembered was the way he shook his head, and the heaviness in his eyes as she let his hand slip away. She pictured his hands even now. He was not a big man, but his hands were strong, the hands of a worker. She had dreamed of them many times, and now as she sat on her couch, she tried to remember them. She had written about them in her diary. When he left, she knew he would have stayed. She uttered it now: Stay. She laughed at herself. *He had stayed.*

VI

She found an entry in her journal. She read her messy handwriting:

> Last night, after Willie left, I sat on the back steps of my apartment house and stared at the trash cans. I'm pregnant, but I couldn't tell him— he would've stayed. I didn't want him to stay—I don't want to be poor with Willie, can't be poor with anybody. I sat there on the steps, and he was gone, but I talked to him about the baby, and after I told him I saw that he would marry me. But he was gone. He had that great sense of Midwestern decency. How is it, Willie, that you had the kind of heart that would always know to do the right thing? Willie didn't have casual relationships, not with anybody. All his friends—not that he had many—were serious friends. And they were all decent like him, all of them raised in small rural areas or on small farms, and all of them believing in the morality of work, and all of them with sensible, passionate minds.
>
> God, Willie, why did you have to be good? We're not all like that, Willie. Willie, you don't know what it's like to be born poor—not really— like me, Willie. Poor is not a good thing to be. Shit, Willie, how many times did I tell you that being born poor made me angry? You always nodded, and maybe I hated you because you did understand. But you never understood that my children were going to have everything, and I was going to give it to them. Mama died when I was fourteen, Willie. Fourteen and I already had the body of a woman, but I've never felt like one. I cooked for Dad, took care of him, he never spoke. I told you everything, Willie. That kitchen, those three rooms we lived in—they were chewing me up. School, Willie, that's what I lived for. You say things aren't important, Willie, that they're just things. But you didn't know, could never know what it was like to have nothing, but to watch a television that showed you everything. You don't know about that kind of shame. No, Willie, it's better for you to marry

someone like you, someone that's moral and decent, who believes in the pleasure of work. You love the land, Willie, but I'll always hate it. Do you know what the land did to my mother and my father, do you know? They worked it all their lives, following the picking seasons—taking me on that awful tour of America. They died with nothing. Mama died saying nothing, Willie, just looking at me. The year I entered college, my father died blessing God in Spanish. And when I buried him, I cursed both my parents for dying—and Willie, I cursed them in English. Willie, I told you these thing, and I don't even know what you heard.

Willie, it started raining after you left. I sat there, my hand still tingling from your touch. It started raining harder, and I had the urge to lie down on the wet grass, so I did. I rolled around in the green and felt like a little girl, the wonder of it, the wonder of everything. But the wonder wasn't good. It was awful. I wanted to be like the grass, wanted the rain to make me grow. I felt the baby inside me, and knew that I would never let it grow.

130   The entry went on and on for pages, but Olivia could not bear to read another word. She walked over to the fireplace, threw some logs into the empty space, and turned on the gas pipe to light it. So convenient to light a fire this way—no trouble at all. She took her journal, ripped out each page, one by one. Page by single page she threw it into the fire. She thought of jumping in after the pages, not to save them, but to burn with them.

She fought the memory that took her mind. That day, that day when she went to that man who said he was a doctor. It was an awful place, not a doctor's office. It was a closet, that's how she remembered it. She saw herself getting up early from her bed, showering, preparing herself. She dressed herself as if she were on going out on a date—a date with Willie. She stared at herself in the mirror—and she saw herself objectively. Pretty, really, she thought, really very pretty. "Stop it!" she yelled at herself, "Stop! Stop! Stop!" She banged the warm bricks next to the fireplace with her hand until it swelled. "Stop! Go away! Why do you have to remember?" As she banged, she heard Willie's voice saying that memories made us human. "Memories make us, Liv."

"Stop it!" she yelled, "stop it!" And suddenly the memory did stop. The fire burned calmly. The words she'd written in her journal were gone. It was a great and comforting silence. The same silence she had felt after her baby had been taken out.

She was crying now. She was crying and she knew she wouldn't stop, couldn't stop, didn't want to stop. She wanted to drown; it was good to drown in the water that came from within you, that unknown and unknowable ocean that she carried around from birth, the water where her daughter had lived—for a while—the water of her mother, the water of her father's sweat as he worked picking crops, that had made him look shiny and beautiful.

She banged her head on the wall, feeling nothing, again and again flinging herself against the walls of her house as if she wanted to make herself walk through them, make herself a shadow, a ghost, with no body, no flesh, no heart. But she could not make her flesh and bones disappear, and they thudded against the wall. And without knowing it, she wanted to break it, break it, break it, and fall broken and be broken, and be nothing but pieces. She banged herself, kept banging herself against that wall until she fell on the floor sobbing, sobbing, goddamn it, what happened, what's happening, don't know, Jonathan, shit, it was Willie, no, it was me, because I wanted a place and gave everything up to be safe and now am not safe because safe doesn't exist, safe. A place, there is no such thing. Not for me. Not for anyone. She lay silent on the floor for a long time and went to sleep wrapped in her curtains.

VII

135   She woke up and stared up the ceiling, the white ceiling, the white, white ceiling. She could put anything up there she wanted. She had picked the color herself. "I want the whole house white," she'd told Jonathan, "all white." She had painted it herself, had enjoyed erasing the dusty rose living room with three coats of white paint. Three coats, so the previous color would not show through. But she remembered the color, and she knew her paint job had been useless. The color was there again.

She felt a bump on her head. The logs in the fire were burning low now. She raised herself slowly off the floor, threw more logs on the fire, and turned off the light. She noticed she was naked, and felt cold—and yet something about her skin was good to her, and she wanted to shelter it, to protect it. She walked into her bedroom and saw her clothes piled in the middle of the room. She hung them on Jonathan's hangers. She slipped on a robe and tied her hair back. She remembered how her mother had tied back her hair and braided all her dark strands, and tied red and turquoise ribbons so that when she ran her braids looked like the tails of a kite. The smell of her mother entered the room. Bread, yes, that was it. Bread. She walked into the kitchen and found herself looking for yeast. No yeast in the house. She searched for her purse and suddenly she discovered she was in her car driving to the store. She walked down the aisle of the grocery store dressed only in her robe, and the lights all around were good. She found the yeast, found the flour, and paid for her goods at the counter. The woman at the counter asked her if she was all right. "Yes," she said, "I'm fine."

"You look a little beat up. Maybe you should call someone."

"I'm fine," she repeated.

"You know," she said, "my first husband used to—well, you know. Are you sure you're fine?"

140   "It's not like that," she said.

She put the yeast in warm water, added sugar. She stared at her hands. They were not like her mother's. Her mother's hands had been worn with work. Her hands were perfect—perfect and ugly from the way she had used them. "I can make them like yours, Mama—they were beautiful." She added flour and salt until the dough thickened. She kneaded it. The dough was warm and soft, and the muscles in her arms and hands hurt as she kneaded and kneaded. The tears ran down her face, and she felt clean. She thought of Jonathan and how she had never touched him, how she had never wanted to. She kneaded and kneaded and thought of Willie's white skin, and how she had felt like this dough when he had touched her—and how she had been too afraid to love him because she had wanted a firm place to live, and could not stay with him because she had been afraid that he, too, would die and leave her with no place to live. Jonathan had given her a place, but the place was hollow and empty—but it had not been his fault that she had painted everything in her life white. Now she was alone, but she had always been alone, and her hands in the dough made her feel strong. She had always felt like a little girl, but right then she didn't feel small at all, and she liked the feel of the tears on her face, warm and salty. Water, it was water, and she felt clean and she drank. And it was hers. She stared at her hands and noticed their deep brown color, and she thought it was a nice color to be. She was hungry and she was thirsty, and she wanted to eat and drink.

She placed the kneaded bread near the fireplace. She stared at the ashes. She poured herself a glass of red wine, and she liked the taste of it in her mouth. And she drank. She stared at the bread as it rose—little by little it rose. From the window, she could see that it was beginning to be light. She was sorry for everything, sorry for herself, sorry for Jonathan and for Willie, and for Celina her mother, and for Celina her daughter. She had carried them all within her, and they had become too heavy. What would it be like, she wondered, what would it be like not to carry them around? Would she look different? Would she feel different? Her heart was heavy as a stone, but it was solid and real, not a shadow. She stared out the window. The bread was almost ready to bake. She stared out the window and looked at the dawn, and waited—for the sun—to obliterate the night.

POETRY

Miguel Algarín

Miguel Algarín was born in Puerto Rico and moved to New York City in the 1950s. In the early 1970s, Algarín co-founded the Nuyorican Poets Café in New York's Lower East Side. Over the course of his long career, he has been a poet, translator, professor (at Rutgers University), editor, dramatist, radio host (at WBAI), and writer for television. He has contributed greatly to modern spoken-word Latino poetry and has helped maintain the Beat Generation aesthetic within the urban Latino community.

Body Bee Calling: From the 21st Century

XIII

A void
Avoid
A void is something to avoid,
it's hard to be at zero point
5   at the still point reflecting the whole
in that there isn't anything in nothing
just like a circle in all ways not flat

but rounder than a belly nine months
into that other eternal circle
10   around the biological/chemical time clock
measured accurately by Swiss-made
round-face father Timex,
avoid a void at the still point
where no thing becomes some thing
15   in that it is out of nothing that something comes,
avoid a void with a circumference,
it's a circle around the zero point
where a straight line that never goes round
begins a voyage that avoids a void
20   and heads towards a swell.

Ana Castillo

Ana Castillo is best known for her novels ranging from her 1986 epistolary work about two friends traveling from California into Mexico, *The Mixquiahuala Letters*, to her most recent work about a handicapped flamenco dancer, *Peel My Love Like an Onion* (1999). Perhaps her most famous book is the magical realist novel, *So Far From God* (1993). She has also written a collection of short stories, a book of essays on Xicanisma, *Massacre of the Dreamers* (1994), edited another collection of essays on the Virgin of Guadalupe, *Goddess of the Americas* (1996), and published a book of poems, *I Ask the Impossible: Poems* (2001). Combining political fire with humor and provocative feminism, Castillo is recognized as a major force in Latina literature.

Women Are Not Roses

Women have no
beginning
only continual
flows.

5   Though rivers flow
women are not
rivers.

Women are not
roses
10   they are not oceans
or stars.

i would like to tell
her this but
i think she
15   already knows.

Sandra María Esteves

See the biographical headnote of Esteves on page 362.

Puerto Rican Discovery #11

Samba Rumba Cha-Cha Be-Bop Hip-Hop

for Merian Soto and Pepetian

Feet jumping. Hips swaying
Arms swinging wide
She dances
Heating her body
5 Awakening her spirit
Drinking from the waters of her soul

Finding herself
Cancelling tears
Muddy and pain-filled
10 She dances
Mimicking birds
Whose flight is envied

Praying for rain
Blessing the harvest
15 Transforming herself to run free
She dances
Lifting her sorrow
Separating bondage
Breaking loose from a cluttered world

20 Healing wounds
Massaging sears
Absorbing light flowing into her
She dances
Feet on fire
25 Lighter than air
Swirling in the whirlpool wind within

Giving thanks to the moon
In homage to the stars
Flowers adorning her hair
30 She dances
Teaching her children
Sharing energy on her path
Empowered by the ancestors.

35 Dancing just to dance
Gaining momentum in movement
Saying what can only be experienced without words
Even when she's not dancing with her feet
She dances with her mind
Recharging the land
40 Regenerating wind
Planting syncopated seeds
In time/space motion.

Gringolandia

for Martín Espada

How I love to listen to north american intellectuals.
The way they utilize language, brutalize communication,
glibly flip speech from the tips of their flying longues,
spontaneous maneuverings
5 on the precise order of perfection.
Always knowing. Absolutely aware
of the exact format of correctness.
Never failing. Never mistaking
a lie for anything not resembling it.
10 Commanding the copywright of thought communication
with presumptuous ownership.
Definitively clear on the ingredients of the perfect poem,
the metamorphosis of the superlative metaphor,
the inharmonious insistence on
15 control-domination-instinctive-twitch.

How I love to listen.
Remind myself there is more to the world.
The whole of it.
The multinational ethnicity of it.
20 The many prismed expression of it.
The strength and struggle of it.
How I have learned to grow from it.
To love and praise myself from it.
To let the life force flow from it.
25 To be in tune as one to it.

Perceive the face of death whenever/wherever it stares at me.
Then establish the rhythm of counterbalance,
the offbeat note of discovery at the crossroads
30 where montuno[1] comes alive.

---

[1] a musical rhythm

Julio Marzán

See the biographical headnote of Marzán on page 237.

The Pure Preposition

Is the lonely night porter, the low-
Pay maintenance man,
Who keeps the toilet from flooding, the heat
In the boiler,

5 Down in the dingy basement of grammar. More
Brute force than matter, it is
Poetry's Caliban, nigger
Minus image or color,

Clean out of mind as the flatness we walk or
10 Hinges unfolding
The nothing of passage.
Tendon to the bone, yet esteemed below

An aristocracy of parts of speech, the reputed mus-
Cularity of metaphor;
15 Metaphor of some of us with each other, those
Least recorded

Unless they fist, punishing with
Their absence, or much too present, re-
Minding us our labor is a product of small parts:
20 With, by, for, in, on, against.

Aleida Rodríguez

See the biographical headnote of Rodríguez on page 107.

Plein Air

I'd like to explain
how difficult it is to work with words.
A painter sits down and lines up
little tubes of color cleansed of context.
5 The autistic tubes in a row
utter nary a sentence, don't waggle
with admonishment or squirm with shame.
There's no fear their tiny silver mouths
will whisper *fucking mustache* or *fat immigrant,*
10 *you never* or *I always* or *don't.*

No one has hissed cadmium yellow
in a fit of rage or spat chrome oxide green
while walking out the door.
Free from these radioactive insinuations,
15   the painter can open up the top of her head,
release the words blackening its ceiling
like trapped smoke and go to work
with the vocabulary of another planet.
Her materials are as forgiving as leaves,
20   which care not whether she says
detergent instead of *iconoclast*.
When she opens up the case,
the colors are all there exactly
as she left them, not dangling
25   between her and the checkout clerk.
They're pristine, untroubled,
idiot savants with an amnesiac's satin memory.
She doesn't have to autoclave
each one before she picks it up.
30   There should be such a box for writers,
filled with words brightly minted
but spared the smudge of circulation,
words denied to cruel, rapacious partners,
jealous coworkers, spin doctors, and ad copywriters.
35   Words one could pick up and squeeze
a little bit of on a palette, add
a splotch of medium and swirl
to just the right syrupy consistency.
Thus preserved, these words would sweep
40   the mind free of muddle, the sky of pollution,
and, virginal as illustrations in social studies books
before we understood the West was actually lost,
blue-creased mountains would loom, crisply visible,
their presence saying simply *winter*, saying *late afternoon*,
45   saying *here*.

Michele Serros

Michele Serros was born in Oxnard, California, in 1966. She is the author of *Chicana Falsa and Other Stories of Death, Identity and Oxnard* (1998) and *How to be a Chicana Role Model* (2000). A multitalented and emerging writer, her credits also include being a regular contributor to NPR, as well as writing for the television sitcom, *The George Lopez Show*. A popular spoken word poet, known for her humor, Serros has also produced a CD of her work.

Annie Says

My tia Annie told me:
"You could never be a writer,
let alone a poet.
What do you know?
I mean, what can you write about?

"You got a D on your last book report
you gotta be able to write English good,
use big words...
and you've never even been out of Oxnard.
Writers travel
all the time
New York, Paris, Rome...
Every place they make Oil of Olay.
That's where writers go,
that's where they live.
Your family doesn't have money to travel.
You never will.
And you don't even type.
Now, how you gonna be a writer?
Sure, some famous poets,
they say
wrote longhand
but that was long ago,
and they were men.
Men have it so easy,
worthless lazy dogs.
But you wouldn't know about that
'cause you've never been with one.
You've never
ate,
slept,
inhaled,
pure passionate love.
Writers are always in love,
like this *Harlequin* romance I'm reading.
Now, how are you gonna be a writer?
You don't even like boys yet.
You've never given your heart to a boy,
so he could take it,
hold it,
clench it,
wring it dry,

to toss away,
forgotten in the gutter.

45 "They make you cry,
hurt,
suffer.
Writers know stuff like that,
they heal their pain with words.
50 You don't know about pain,
anguish,
outrage,
protest.
Look on TV…
55 The Brown Berets,
they're marching.
The whole Chicano movement
passing you by and
you don't even know about that.
60 You weren't born in no barrio.
No tortilleria[1] down your street.
Bullets never whizzed
past your baby head.

"Chicana Without a Cause.

65 "No, mi'ja,
Nobody will ever buy your books,
so put your pencil down
and change the channel for me,
it's time for *As the World Turns.*"

Gary Soto

See the biographical headnote of Soto on page 108.

Chisme at Rivera's Studio

Siqueiros used a machine gun on Rivera's studio,
And Diego, I guess, ran his hands through his hair.
He didn't eat for two days.
He trudged his elephant weight around the patio
5 And waited for Frida,
Busy primping her eyebrow,
Busy wiggling her underwear into place,
Busy with a stiff brush and her bluish wounds,
Busy blowing smoke into the face of her clapping monkey.

---

[1]place that makes and sells tortillas.

10 And Rivera, I guess, tightened his belt.
He scolded Trotsky,
Poor guy who in the end crumpled under a knife,
Just as he was sitting down to lunch
Or was it a long letter to Russia?
15 Imagine this:
Rivera with his bad back,
Trotsky with his bleeding fountain pen,
These two greats, and now me, little piss ant,
Crawling through the studio in San Angel.

20 This was Mexico in the thirties,
With rain pelting the bellies of frolicking dogs,
With the president toasting dead colonels,
With Fords squashing the juicy life out of fruit stands.

This is me in the nineties,
25 Me and a buddy touching the walls
Where Frida leaned and said, Fuck off, America.
Maybe she laughed with smoke in both nostrils.
Maybe she touched her one eyebrow,
Maybe she went outside, cigarette lit,
30 And watched pine trees bleed the moon with their needles,
They were beautifully crazy as they howled
At each other from various beds.
I've never known anyone famous.
I've never known a singer
35 Or an actress with tears twisted into her handkerchief.
I've never known anyone on television,
Or even a barber humming "Dos Arbolitos."
I've only known my famous aunt,
Who could cha-cha-cha with a glass of water
40 On her head.

I'm wild crawling through Diego and Frida's studio.
Art happened here, and love, I guess.
I sneeze the dust of years, swallowing
My chewing gum when I look up at the sky light.
45 I drink water and crush my paper cup.
I remember the Spanish verb "to touch."
I touch the rope that keeps me
From the wheelchair where Frida sat,
A lasso of cigarette smoke in her hair,
50 Dead of light for thirty years.
The floor creaks. Voices carry to the second floor,
And I have nothing to carry home but two postcards.
I'm going to lean against the wall,
And rub fame and dirt into my peasant shoulders.

Tino Villanueva

Tino Villanueva was born in Texas in 1941 and has authored *Hay Otra Voz Poems* (1972), *Shaking Off the Dark* (1998), *Chronicle of My Worst Years/Crónica de mis años peores* (1994), and the book-length poem, *Scene from the Movie* Giant (1993), for which he won the American Book Award. Influenced by the voices of such a range of figures as Dylan Thomas and Jose Martí, Villanueva is considered one of the early poets of the Chicano movement. He holds a Ph.D. in Spanish from Boston University, where he currently teaches and is the Preceptor in Spanish Modern Foreign Languages and Literatures.

Variation on a Theme By William Carlos Williams

I have eaten
the *tamales*
that were on
the stove heating

5   and which
you were probably
having for dinner

Perdóname[1]
they were *riquisimos*[2]
10   so juicy
and so steaming hot

Scene from the Movie *Giant*

What I have from 1956 is one instant at the Holiday
Theater, where a small dimension of a film, as in
A dream, became the feature of the whole. It
Comes toward the end...the café scene, which
5   Reels off a slow spread of light, a stark desire

To see itself once more, though there is, at times,
No joy in old time movies. It begins with the
Jingling of bells and the plainer truth of it:
That the front door to a roadside café opens and
10   Shuts as the Benedicts (Rock Hudson and Elizabeth

Taylor), their daughter Luz, and daughter-in-law
Juana and grandson Jordy, pass through it not
Unobserved. Nothing sweeps up into an actual act
Of kindness into the eyes of Sarge, who owns this
15   Joint and has it out for dark-eyed Juana, weary

---

[1]Forgive me
[2]delicious

Of too much longing that comes with rejection.
Juana, from barely inside the door, and Sarge,
Stout and unpleased from behind his counter, clash
Eye-to-eye, as time stands like heat. Silence is
20   Everywhere, acquiring the name of hatred and Juana

Cannot bear the dread—the dark-jowl gaze of Sarge
Against her skin. Suddenly: bells go off again.
By the quiet effort of walking, three Mexican-
Types step in, whom Sarge refuses to serve...
25   Those gestures of his, those looks that could kill

A heart you carry in memory for years. A scene from
The past has caught me in the act of living: even
To myself I cannot say except with worried phrases
Upon a paper, how I withstood arrogance in a gruff
30   Voice coming with the deep-dyed colors of the screen;

How in the beginning I experienced almost nothing to
Say and now wonder if I can ever live enough to tell
The after tale. I remember this and I remember myself
Locked into a back-row seat—I am a thin, flickering,
35   Helpless light, local-looking, unthought of at fourteen.

At the Holocaust Museum: Washington D.C.

I—Before Our Eyes

We've had it told to us before;
we've seen annihilation, *Vernichtung*
at the movie house in town.
Videos reveal the same declensions of rage,
5   speech acts crowds shall act upon—
no principles governing reflection,
words shattering glass, building up the
circumstances of the fire,
the same conclusion mortality demands.

10   Now before our eyes: how darkly different
when a deep terrain of text persists with artifacts;
and photographs, each one a cell of time made real.
We turn, and make our way on cobblestones
pounded out from Mauthausen,
15   and through a freight car walk along once more,
fitting facts in place—
what led up to what; how a people lived
keeping at their tasks which came to be their lives
with the etched impression of their
20   history taking place,

until one day: were seized
and carted off in trains like perishable goods
squeezed into the mind-dark of enclosure,
breath coming hard.
25 Great god,
what geography of pain we are walking through.
What a season of convincing clouds that
hang like smoke, as when the soul,
unassailable,
30 has found release through manumission.
And what indecent will of those who
saw no cause to care, foreshadowing, therefore,
the concentric rush of time running out.

This is fact: the harsh articulation
35 of someone's life that, in the end,
will end too soon.

II—The Freight Car

We move on, affirming the proximity of everything,
eyes breaking open to the light: installations here,
photographs and objects there, the visual details of
40 time-kept dying. Suddenly: an intractable fragment
of truth—a freight car brought, finally, to a halt

on the same illicit logic of rails. No stench now;
human grime gone, washed away by water and soap
and the varnish of time. Still it affronts: the tight
45 seal of steel and wood, a prisonhouse suffocatingly
small, non-sequent, disconnected from the event.

If steel and scarred wood could recount their story
from memory, could beg forgiveness or bring back
the dead, then my hand might not flinch at their
50 touch as I enter, enter the past: One evening
a cantor was singing before a full congregation,

true worship known by heart. Peacefulness in
the infinite, and the lightness of candlelight
breathlessly still when: a muster of men from a
55 shadow realm broke forth, cutting off the prayer.
Cantor, families and friends by the thousands,

hundreds of thousands, were led to the station,
rabid soldiers barking out orders, firing pistols
in the air, dogs bringing up the right flank. So
60 many helpless immortals so far from their dwelling.

clutching their garments, huddled like the bundles
they carried, unable to run away from their names.
To think they leaned where I'm standing, squatted
or kneeled, dark-stricken, their children driven
65   to tantrums; or stood where they could against

steel-dug-into-wood, no heaven above them, no earth
below. Some in their places fell mute, were confused,
riddled with fright when the train screeched, jolted
forth, shimmied and swayed and pulled out. Others
70   kept faith, and for them the summit of sky remained

whole; still others felt death beginning to sink
into them—everyone drawing a breath: breath in,
breath out, holding their breath, sighing, inhaling-
exhaling full breaths, half-breaths, gasping with
75   all complexities of thirst. Long after Treblinka,

"Water," I hear them cry. "Water, air." I step
out, looking back as I move away with the crowd.
One freight car at a standstill, uncoupled from its
long concatenation of steel dissolved into this
80   artifact: the summation of all that advances no more.

III—The Photographs

To look
into devastated eyes is not enough; to touch
the photographs is not enough.
Even if their breath could reach me.
85   I could utter nothing among the ruins
written with light.
But someone such as I, a nobody in all of this,
has come to see (this much the heart allows):
what man has done to man, human acts of the profane,
90   and the defeated countryside.
Led to camps
by the uniform substance of hate,
one by one they held
still enough to be caught in the strict regulation
95   of natural or flat light. I read it in their eyes:
reluctance seeking its own landscape
with so much night to come. To myself I say:
this face, or that face had a name:
Joseph, Daniel, or *Hannah,*
100   but oh, you are a number—

sharp alchemy scored on skin.
I pray your soul remained intact until the end.

(Print after print: I am carried away by destruction
exhausted into fact, forgetting
105   the persecuted who escaped; who from the
edges of the battlefield were saved, here by a
timely neighbor, a benevolent baker; there by a
factory owner, a farmer, or by decent Catholic nuns
—reflexive acts of the unsung.)

110   Then there was Ejszyszki (A-shish-key), 1941:
a village of 4,000 that could not find the
doors to exodus—slaughtered in two days.
I touch the photographs of how it was
before it ended, in a great field of darkness...
115   and my body shrieks.
Five decades, and in another country,
I am too late as in a blazing nightmare
where I reach out,
but cannot save you, cannot save you.
120   *Sarah, Rachel, Benjamin*, in this light you have risen,
where the past is construed as present.
For all that is in me: Let the dead go on living,
let these words become human.

I am your memory now.

ESSAY

Judith Ortiz Cofer

See the biographical headnote of Ortiz Cofer on page 104.

The Story of My Body

Migration is the story of my body.

—Victor Hernandez Cruz

Skin

I was born a white girl in Puerto Rico but became a brown girl when I came
to live in the United States. My Puerto Rican relatives called me tall; at the American school, some of my rougher classmates called me Skinny Bones, and the
Shrimp because I was the smallest member of my classes all through grammar

school until high school, when the midget Gladys was given the honorary post of front row center for class pictures and scorekeeper, bench warmer, in P.E. I reached my full stature of five feet in sixth grade.

I started out life as a pretty baby and learned to be a pretty girl from a pretty mother. Then at ten years of age I suffered one of the worst cases of chicken pox I have ever heard of. My entire body, including the inside of my ears and in between my toes, was covered with pustules which in a fit of panic at my appearance I scratched off my face, leaving permanent scars. A cruel school nurse told me I would always have them—tiny cuts that looked as if a mad cat had plunged its claws deep into my skin. I grew my hair long and hid behind it for the first years of my adolescence. This was when I learned to be invisible.

Color

In the animal world it indicates danger: the most colorful creatures are often the most poisonous. Color is also a way to attract and seduce a mate. In the human world color triggers many more complex and often deadly reactions. As a Puerto Rican girl born of "white" parents, I spent the first years of my life hearing people refer to me as *blanca*, white. My mother insisted that I protect myself from the intense island sun because I was more prone to sunburn than some of my darker, *trigueño* playmates. People were always commenting within my hearing about how my black hair contrasted so nicely with my "pale" skin. I did not think of the color of my skin consciously except when I heard the adults talking about complexion. It seems to me that the subject is much more common in the conversation of mixed-race peoples than in mainstream United States society, where it is a touchy and sometimes even embarrassing topic to discuss, except in a political context. In Puerto Rico I heard many conversations about skin color. A pregnant woman could say, "I hope my baby doesn't turn out *prieto*" (slang for "dark" or "black") "like my husband's grandmother, although she was a good-looking *negra* in her time." I am a combination of both, being olive-skinned—lighter than my mother yet darker than my fair-skinned father. In America, I am a person of color, obviously a Latina. On the Island I have been called everything from a *paloma blanca*, after the song (by a black suitor), to *la gringa*.

My first experience of color prejudice occurred in a supermarket in Paterson, New Jersey. It was Christmastime, and I was eight or nine years old. There was a display of toys in the store where I went two or three times a day to buy things for my mother, who never made lists but sent for milk, cigarettes, a can of this or that, as she remembered from hour to hour. I enjoyed being trusted with money and walking half a city block to the new, modern grocery store. It was owned by three good-looking Italian brothers. I liked the younger one with the crew-cut blond hair. The two older ones watched me and the other Puerto Rican kids as if they thought we were going to steal something. The oldest one would sometimes even try to hurry me with my purchases, although part of my pleasure in these expeditions came from looking at everything in the well-stocked aisles. I was also teaching myself to read English by sounding out the labels in packages: L&M cigarettes, Borden's homogenized milk, Red Devil potted ham, Nestle's chocolate mix, Quaker oats, Bustelo coffee, Wonder bread, Colgate toothpaste, Ivory soap, and Goya (makers of products used in Puerto Rican dishes) everything—these are some of the brand names that taught me nouns. Several times this man had come up to me, wearing his blood-stained butcher's apron, and towering over me had asked in a harsh voice whether there was something he could help me find. On the way out I would glance at the younger brother who ran one of the registers and he would often smile and wink at me.

5   It was the mean brother who first referred to me as "colored." It was a few days before Christmas, and my parents had already told my brother and me that since we were in Los Estados now, we would get our presents on December 25 instead of Los Reyes, Three Kings Day, when gifts are exchanged in Puerto Rico. We were to give them a wish list that they would take to Santa Claus, who apparently lived in the Macy's store downtown—at least that's where we had caught a glimpse of him when we went shopping. Since my parents were timid about entering the fancy store, we did not approach the huge man in the red suit. I was not interested in sitting on a stranger's lap anyway. But I did covet Susie, the talking schoolteacher doll that was displayed in the center aisle of the Italian brothers' supermarket. She talked when you pulled a string on her back. Susie had a limited repertoire of three sentences: I think she could say: "Hello, I'm Susie Schoolteacher." "Two plus two is four," and one other thing I cannot remember. The day the older brother chased me away, I was reaching to touch Susie's blonde curls. I had been told many times, as most children have, not to touch anything in a store that I was not buying. But I had been looking at Susie for weeks. In my mind, she was my doll. After all, I had put her on my Christmas wish list. The moment is frozen in my mind as if there were a photograph of it on file. It was not a turning point, a disaster, or an earth-shaking revelation. It was simply the first time I considered—if naively—the meaning of skin color in human relations.

I reached to touch Susie's hair. It seems to me that I had to get on tiptoe, since the toys were stacked on a table and she sat like a princess on top of the fancy box she came in. Then I heard the booming "Hey, kid, what do you think you're doing!" spoken very loudly from the meat counter. I felt caught, although I knew I was not doing anything criminal. I remember not looking at the man, but standing there, feeling humiliated because I knew everyone in the store must have heard him yell at me. I felt him approach, and when I knew he was behind me, I turned around to face the bloody butcher's apron. His large chest was at my eye level. He blocked my way. I started to run out of the place, but even as I reached the door I heard him shout after me: "Don't come in here unless you gonna buy something. You PR kids put your dirty hands on stuff. You always look dirty. But maybe dirty brown is your natural color." I heard him laugh and someone else too in the back. Outside in the sunlight I looked at my hands. My nails needed a little cleaning as they always did, since I liked to paint with watercolors, but I took a bath every night. I thought the man was dirtier than I was in his stained apron. He was also always sweaty—it showed in big yellow circles under his shirt-sleeves. I sat on the front steps of the apartment building where we lived and looked closely at my hands, which showed the only skin I could see, since it was bitter cold and I was wearing my quilted play coat, dungarees, and a knitted navy cap of my father's. I was not pink like my friend Charlene and her sister Kathy, who had blue eyes and light brown hair. My skin is the color of the coffee my grandmother made, which was half milk, *leche con café* rather than *café con leche*. My mother is the opposite mix. She has a lot of café in her color. I could not understand how my skin looked like dirt to the supermarket man.

I went in and washed my hands thoroughly with soap and hot water, and borrowing my mother's nail file, I cleaned the crusted watercolors from underneath my nails. I was pleased with the results. My skin was the same color as before, but I knew I was clean. Clean enough to run my fingers through Susie's fine gold hair when she came home to me.

Size

My mother is barely four feet eleven inches in height, which is average for women in her family. When I grew to five feet by age twelve, she was amazed and began to use the word tall to describe me, as in "Since you are tall, this dress will look good on you." As with the color of my skin, I didn't consciously think about my height or size until other people made an issue of it. It is around the preadolescent years that in America the games children play for fun become fierce competitions where everyone is out to "prove" they are better than others. It was in the playground and sports fields that my size-related problems began. No matter how familiar the story is, every child who is the last chosen for a team knows the torment of waiting to be called up. At the Paterson, New Jersey, public schools that I attended, the volleyball or softball game was the metaphor for the battlefield of life to the inner city kids—the black kids versus the Puerto Rican kids, the whites versus the blacks versus the Puerto Rican kids; and I was 4F, skinny, short, bespectacled, and apparently impervious to the blood thirst that drove many of my classmates to play ball as if their lives depended on it. Perhaps they did. I would rather be reading a book than sweating, grunting, and running the risk of pain and injury. I simply did not see the point in competitive sports. My main form of exercise then was walking to the library, many city blocks away from my barrio.

Still, I wanted to be wanted. I wanted to be chosen for the teams. Physical education was compulsory, a class where you were actually given a grade. On my mainly all A report card, the C for compassion I always received from the P.E. teachers shamed me the same as a bad grade in a real class. Invariably, my father would say: "How can you make a low grade for *playing games?*" He did not understand. Even if I had managed to make a hit (it never happened) or get the ball over that ridiculously high net, I already had a reputation as a "shrimp," a hopeless nonathlete. It was an area where the girls who didn't like me for one reason or another—mainly because I did better than they on academic subjects—could lord it over me; the playing field was the place where even the smallest girl could make me feel powerless and inferior. I instinctively understood the politics even then; how the *not* choosing me until the teacher forced one of the team captains to call my name was a coup of sorts—there, you little show-off, tomorrow you can beat us in spelling and geography, but this afternoon you are the loser. Or perhaps those were only my own bitter thoughts as I sat or stood in the sidelines while the big girls were grabbed like fish and I, the little brown tadpole, was ignored until Teacher looked over in my general direction and shouted, "Call Ortiz," or, worse, "Somebody's *got* to take her."

10   No wonder I read Wonder Woman comics and had Legion of Super Heroes daydreams. Although I wanted to think of myself as "intellectual," my body was demanding that I notice it. I saw the little swelling around my once-flat nipples, the fine hairs growing in secret places; but my knees were still bigger than my thighs, and I always wore long- or half-sleeve blouses to hide my bony upper arms. I wanted flesh on my bones—a thick layer of it. I saw a new product advertised on TV. Wate-On. They showed skinny men and women before and after taking the stuff, and it was a transformation like the ninety-seven-pound-weakling-turned-into-Charles-Atlas ads that I saw on the back covers of my comic books. The Wate-On was very expensive. I tried to explain my need for it in Spanish to my mother, but it didn't translate very well, even to my ears—and she said with a tone of finality, eat more of my good food and you'll get fat—anybody can get fat. Right. Except me. I was going to have to join a circus someday as Skinny Bones, the woman without flesh.

Wonder Woman was stacked. She had a cleavage framed by the spread wings of a golden eagle and a muscular body that has become fashionable with women only recently. But since I wanted a body that would serve me in P.E., hers was my ideal. The breasts were an indulgence I allowed myself. Perhaps the daydreams of bigger girls were more glamorous, since our ambitions are filtered through our needs, but I wanted first a powerful body. I daydreamed of leaping up above the gray landscape of the city to where the sky was clear and blue, and in anger and self-pity, I fantasized about scooping my enemies up by their hair from the playing fields and dumping them on a barren asteroid. I would put the P.E. teachers each on their own rock in space too, where they would be the loneliest people in the universe, since I knew they had no "inner resources," no imagination, and in outer space, there would be no air for them to fill their deflated volleyballs with. In my mind all P.E. teachers have blended into one large spiky-haired woman with a whistle on a string around her neck and a volleyball under one arm. My Wonder Woman fantasies of revenge were a source of comfort to me in my early career as a shrimp.

I was saved from more years of P.E. torment by the fact that in my sophomore year of high school I transferred to a school where the midget, Gladys, was the focal point of interest for the people who must rank according to size. Because her height was considered a handicap, there was an unspoken rule about mentioning size around Gladys, but of course, there was no need to say anything. Gladys knew her place: front row center in class photographs. I gladly moved to the left or to the right of her, as far as I could without leaving the picture completely.

Looks

Many photographs were taken of me as a baby by my mother to send to my father, who was stationed overseas during the first two years of my life. With the army in Panama when I was born, he later traveled often on tours of duty with the navy. I was a healthy, pretty baby. Recently, I read that people are drawn to big-eyed round-faced creatures, like puppies, kittens, and certain other mammals and marsupials, koalas, for example, and, of course, infants. I was all eyes, since my head and body, even as I grew older, remained thin and small-boned. As a young child I got a lot of attention from my relatives and many other people we met in our barrio. My mother's beauty may have had something to do with how much attention we got from strangers in stores and on the street. I can imagine it. In the pictures I have seen of us together, she is a stunning young woman by Latino standards: long, curly black hair, and round curves in a compact frame. From her I learned how to move, smile, and talk like an attractive woman. I remember going into a bodega for our groceries and being given candy by the proprietor as a reward for being *bonita*, pretty.

I can see in the photographs, and I also remember, that I was dressed in the pretty clothes, the stiff, frilly dresses, with layers of crinolines underneath, the glossy patent leather shoes, and, on special occasions, the skull-hugging little hats and the white gloves that were popular in the late fifties and early sixties. My mother was proud of my looks, although I was a bit too thin. She could dress me up like a doll and take me by the hand to visit relatives, or go to the Spanish mass at the Catholic church, and show me off. How was I to know that she and the others who called me "pretty" were representatives of an aesthetic that would not apply when I went out into the mainstream world of school?

15   In my Paterson, New Jersey, public schools there were still quite a few white children, although the demographics of the city were changing rapidly. The original waves of Italian and Irish immigrants, silk-mill workers, and laborers in the cloth industries had been "assimilated." Their children were now the middle-class parents of my peers. Many of them moved their children to the Catholic schools that proliferated enough to have leagues of basketball teams. The names I recall hearing still ring in my ears: Don Bosco High versus St. Mary's High, St. Joseph's versus St. John's. Later I too would be transferred to the safer environment of a Catholic school. But I started school at Public School Number 11. I came there from Puerto Rico, thinking myself a pretty girl, and found that the hierarchy for popularity was as follows: pretty white girl, pretty Jewish girl, pretty Puerto Rican girl, pretty black girl. Drop the last two categories; teachers were too busy to have more than one favorite per class, and it was simply understood that if there was a big part in the school play, or any competition where the main qualification was "present-ability" (such as escorting a school visitor to or from the principal's office), the classroom's public address speaker would be requesting the pretty and/or nice-looking white boy or girl. By the time I was in the sixth grade, I was sometimes called

by the principal to represent my class because I dressed neatly (I knew this from a progress report sent to my mother, which I translated for her) and because all the "presentable" white girls had moved to the Catholic schools (I later surmised this part). But I was still not one of the popular girls with the boys. I remember one incident where I stepped out into the playground in my baggy gym shorts and one Puerto Rican boy said to the other: "What do you think?" The other one answered: "Her face is OK, but look at the toothpick legs." The next best thing to a compliment I got was when my favorite male teacher, while handing out the class pictures, commented that with my long neck and delicate features I resembled the movie star Audrey Hepburn. But the Puerto Rican boys had learned to respond to a fuller figure: long necks and a perfect little nose were not what they looked for in a girl. That is when I decided I was a "brain." I did not settle into the role easily. I was nearly devastated by what the chicken pox episode had done to my self-image. But I looked into the mirror less often after I was told that I would always have scars on my face, and I hid behind my long black hair and my books.

After the problems at the public school got to the point where even non-confrontational little me got beaten up several times, my parents enrolled me at St. Joseph's High School. I was then a minority of one among the Italian and Irish kids. But I found several good friends there—other girls who took their studies seriously. We did our homework together and talked about the Jackies. The Jackies were two popular girls, one blonde and the other red-haired, who had women's bodies. Their curves showed even in the blue jumper uniforms with straps that we all wore. The blonde Jackie would often let one of the straps fall off her shoulder, and although she, like all of us, wore a white blouse underneath, all the boys stared at her arm. My friends and I talked about this and practiced letting our straps fall off our shoulders. But it wasn't the same without breasts or hips.

My final two and a half years of high school were spent in Augusta, Georgia, where my parents moved our family in search of a more peaceful environment. There we became part of a little community of our army-connected relatives and friends. School was yet another matter. I was enrolled in a huge school of nearly two thousand students that had just that year been forced to integrate. There were two black girls and there was me. I did extremely well academically. As to my social life, it was, for the most part, uneventful—yet it is in my memory blighted by one incident. In my junior year, I became wildly infatuated with a pretty white boy. I'll call him Ted. Oh, he was pretty: yellow hair that fell over his forehead, a smile to die for—and he was a great dancer. I watched him at Teen Town, the youth center at the base where all the military brats gathered on Saturday nights. My father had retired from the navy, and we had all our base privileges—one other reason we had moved to Augusta. Ted looked like an angel to me. I worked on him for a year before he asked me out. This meant maneuvering to be within the periphery of his vision at every possible occasion. I took the long way to my classes in school just to pass by his locker, I went to football games, which I detested, and I danced (I too was a good dancer) in front of him at Teen Town—this took some fancy footwork, since it involved subtly moving my partner toward the right spot on the dance floor. When Ted finally approached me, "A Million to One" was playing on the jukebox, and when he took me into his arms, the odds suddenly turned in my favor. He asked me to go to a school dance the following Saturday. I said yes, breathlessly. I said yes, but there were obstacles to surmount at home. My father did not allow me to date casually. I was allowed to go to major events like a prom or a concert with a boy who had been properly screened. There was such a boy in my life, a neighbor who wanted to be a Baptist missionary and was practicing his anthropological skills on my family. If I was desperate to go somewhere and needed a date, I'd resort to Gary. This is the type of religious nut that Gary was: when the school bus did not show up one day, he put his hands over his face and prayed to Christ to get us a way to get to school. Within ten minutes a mother in a station wagon, on her way to town, stopped to ask why we weren't in school. Gary informed her that the Lord had sent her just in time to find us a way to get there in time for roll call. He assumed that I was impressed. Gary was even good-looking in a bland sort of way, but he kissed me with his lips tightly pressed together. I think Gary probably ended up marrying a native woman from wherever he may have gone to preach the Gospel according to Paul. She probably believes that all white men pray to God for transportation and kiss with their mouths closed. But it was Ted's mouth, his whole beautiful self, that concerned me in those days. I knew my father would say no to our date, but I planned to run away from home if necessary. I told my mother how important this date was. I cajoled and pleaded with her from Sunday to Wednesday. She listened to my arguments and must have heard the note of desperation in my voice. She said very gently to me: "You better be ready for disappointment." I did not ask what she meant. I did not want her fears for me to taint my happiness. I asked her to tell my father about my date. Thursday at breakfast my father looked at me across the table with his eyebrows together. My mother looked at him with her mouth set in a straight line. I looked down at my bowl of cereal. Nobody said anything. Friday I tried on every dress in my closet. Ted would be picking me up at six on Saturday: dinner and then the sock hop at school. Friday night I was in my room doing my nails or something else in preparation for Saturday (I know I groomed myself nonstop all week) when the telephone rang. I ran to get it. It was Ted. His voice sounded funny when he said my name, so funny that I felt compelled to ask: "Is something wrong?" Ted blurted it all out without a preamble. His father had asked who he was going out with. Ted had told him my name. "Ortiz? That's Spanish, isn't it?" the father had asked. Ted had told him yes, then shown him my picture in the yearbook. Ted's father had shaken his head. No. Ted would not be taking me out. Ted's father had known Puerto Ricans in the army. He had lived in New York City while studying architecture and had seen how the spics lived. Like rats. Ted repeated his father's words to me as if I should understand *his* predicament when I heard why he was breaking our date. I don't remember what I said before hanging up. I do recall the darkness of my room that sleepless night and the heaviness of my blanket in which I wrapped myself like a shroud. And I remember my parents' respect for my pain and their gentleness toward me that weekend. My mother did not say "I warned you," and I was grateful for her understanding silence.

In college, I suddenly became an "exotic" woman to the men who had survived the popularity wars in high school, who were now practicing to be worldly: they had to act liberal in their politics, in their lifestyles, and in the women they went out with. I dated heavily for a while, then married young. I had discovered that I needed stability more than social life. I had brains for sure and some talent in writing. These facts were a constant in my life. My skin color, my size, and my appearance were variables—things that were judged according to my current self-image, the aesthetic values of the times, the places I was in, and the people I met. My studies, later my writing, the respect of people who saw me as an individual person they cared about, these were the criteria for my sense of self-worth that I would concentrate on in my adult life.

BROADER HORIZONS: RESOURCES FOR WRITING AND CLASS DISCUSSION.

Literary Critical Essay/Discussion Topics

1. Find two short stories from the selections in this chapter that are told from a first person point of view. Discuss the similarities or differences in the narrators' voices or personae. Examine the language of each narrator. What stylistic choices do you think the writers have made to communicate a sense of the narrator's personality and attitudes? You can do the same exercise using any two narrative poems.

2. Several of the selections in this section allude directly to other writers from the Pan-American literary canon such as William Carlos Williams, Pablo Neruda, Gabriel García Márquez, or Langston Hughes. Are there any literary influences that you think are at work in the readings, and can you argue that these connections are worthy of notice? Check other sources to determine whether the writers themselves mention influences, and write an essay suggesting the connections between Latino literature and past masters.

3. Choose one immediate family relationship (father/son, mother/daughter, father/daughter, etc.) from any poem or story and discuss what you think the writer is suggesting about familial relationships in Latino cultures and in general? Is there anything that is particularly Latino about these suggestions?

4. Several of the stories and poems in this section are unconventional in that they might be fantastic in some sense, might bend the rules of traditional fiction, or simply might seem strange, confusing, or even shocking. Find a selection you want to explore in more depth and describe the qualities you find to be different, intriguing, or unusual. Discuss the effect these qualities have on you as a reader.

5. Analyze any poem in this section for variations of rhyme and rhythm and the sounds of words—the music of the poem. How does the music of the language contribute to the poem's content?

The Novel Connection

Who can say what sorts of Latino novels will arrive in the coming years? One can only scan the existing trends and speculate, assuming at the beginning that the field is so vast, so complicated, and so full of potential that we can only expect to be surprised.

On the one hand, a growing number of writers are publishing works aimed at Latino youth, and demographic studies clearly show that publishers have financial reasons to remain interested in such a population. A quick look at the shelves of books in the young adult sections of bookstores makes it clear where publishers have decided the markets exist. But novels for the adult reader (as opposed to stories, poems, and drama) are always the bread and butter for publishers of fiction and who knows from where the next Latino best-seller will come?

One interesting trend is that more and more books are being published immediately in paperback by the mainstream presses. Aside from cost issues, these works are much more rapidly available for the classroom and consequently get into the hands of new readers—those not accustomed to buying the latest first edition, hardback novel. While small presses have used such a system for years (Arté Publico Press, Bilingual Press, and Curbstone Press, to note three major contributors), the success of a book like Ernesto Quiñonez's *Bodega Dreams* (2000) perhaps helped larger presses continue the practice. Abraham Rodriguez Jr.'s *The Buddha Book* (2001) followed, as did important new novels like Luis Manuel Martinez's *Drift* (2003) and the latest work by Cuban-American Ernesto Mestre-Reed, *The Second Death of Unica Aveyano* (2004).

The purpose of this last chapter is to suggest ways that Latino writers are engaged in a changing, vibrant process of imaginative creation that encompasses much more than what some would think the typical subject matter for Latino works. While perhaps we can sometimes group a collection of novels in some meaningful way, there are just as many works that slip beyond categories. There are, for example, a number of Latino novels that depict the conflicts of Central America, particularly during the civil wars and political turmoil of the 1980s in Nicaragua, El Salvador, and Guatemala: Graciela Limon's *In Search of Bernabé* (1993), Francisco Goldman's first novel, *The Long Night of the White Chickens* (1992), Demetria Martínez's *Mother Tongue* (1994), and two more recent works, Rick Rivera's *Stars Always Shine* (2001) and Héctor Tobar's *The Tattooed Soldier* (1998). Many Chicano/a writers take their characters across the U.S. borders into parts of Mexico. Sandra Benítez's *Bitter Grounds* (1997) and Ana Castillo's first work, *The Mixquiahuala Letters* (1986), come to mind. The novels of Montserrat Fontes bring readers inside the times of the Mexican Revolution (*Dreams of the Centaur*, 1996) and into the lives of Mexicans and Chicanos south of the Texas border (*First Confession*, 1991). Still other writers travel farther south into the histories and traditions of Latin America and the Caribbean.

In this last group, the novel *The Tree of Red Stars* (1997) by Tessa Bridal is a gripping account of the Uruguayan political climate of the late 1960s and early 1970s when much of the southern cone of South America underwent a gruesome period of militarization. Julia Alvarez reaches into the political history of dictator Rafael Leónidas Trujillo Molina in her well-known novel *In the Time of the Butterflies* (1994) about the Mirabal sisters in the Dominican Republic. Nelly Rosario's first novel, *The Song of the Water Saints* (2002), meanders through the crucial events of that country's twentieth-century political history, stopping briefly for various U.S. military occupations of the island and Trujillo's 1937 massacre of Haitians along the banks of the Dajabón river. Rosario Ferré's last three novels written in English, *The House on the Lagoon* (1995), *Eccentric Neighborhoods* (1998), and *Flight of the Swan* (2002), take readers into the families, histories, and class conflicts of twentieth-century Puerto Rico. Contrasting Ferré's novels with Rosario's work would highlight the difference between class systems in the Spanish Caribbean, as one author derives her perspective from her family's ties to the elite of Puerto Rico and the other writes of the underclass in the barrios of the Dominican Republic.

Even farther from the U.S. Latino landscape, Cecile Pineda's 1992 parody of magic realism, *The Love Queen of the Amazon* (1992), places her heroine in a brothel in rural Peru, but the novel could have been set in any number of locations as the purpose of her work has more to do with satire and humor than with presenting a realistic depiction of South America. Pineda's first novel, *Face* (1985), takes place in the favelas of Brazil, and her second, *Frieze* (1986), in Java, Indonesia. Her latest two novels, *Bardo99* (2000) and *Redoubt* (2000), stretch readers even further into post-modernist worlds more comparable to Kafka and Coetzee than to any other Latino writer.

The three important novels by Alfredo Véa, *Gods Go Begging* (1999), *La Maravilla* (1993), and *The Silver Cloud Café* (1996), represent a new type of Latino novel in which character identity is not always clearly tied to distinctive Latino cultural backgrounds. Véa's protagonists have mixtures of cultural connections: They are combinations of Filipino, Chicano, Asian, African, and Native American even as they share such things as lack of money and marginalization by mainstream society. In a sense, these novels resemble Caribbean-based, post-colonial fiction, in which many writers are often intent on displaying the radiance of mixed racial and cultural heritage. Given the globalization of U.S. society and the merging of peoples throughout the world, it seems fairly obvious that future Latino novelists will continue to write more and more about people with mixed backgrounds. Publishers' interest in single Latino populations (i.e., Chicanos, Nuyoricans, Dominican Americans) will give way to stories of people with networks of relationships, loyalties, and traditions spreading over ever increasing spheres. We see some of this in the most recent effort by Edgardo Vega Yunqué, a long book with the longest title in Latino fiction: *No Matter How Much You Promise to Cook or Pay the Rent You Blew It Cauze Bill Bailey Ain't Never Coming Home Again: A Symphonic Novel* (2003). Formerly publishing under the name Ed Vega, Vega Yunqué now concentrates on a huge collage of characters woven together in one of the world centers for cultural complexity: New York City.

Some Latino novels, either in subject matter or in stylistic innovation, bend traditional patterns from the onset. We have mentioned some of these in Chapter 1 in our discussion of Latino fiction. We could add the humorous, telenovela-style work of Louie García Robinson's *The Devil, Delfina Varela and the Used Chevy* (1993), which satirizes San Francisco's Mission District, or the equally funny novel of Cuban Miami, the parody by Roberto G. Fernandez—*Holy Radishes!* (1995). More recently, H.G. Carrillo's inventive novel, *Loosing my espanish* (2004) follows a collection of Cuban Americans in Chicago.

Even as readers of the present anthology begin to look outward toward the wide range of imaginative novels by Latino writers, a whole new crop of titles will be coming into play. Few areas in American fiction seem more dynamic and exciting. As with the modernist creativity of the early part of this century, readers should prepare themselves for an explosion of imaginative fiction that might, in the poet, Gina Valdés's words, "Latinize" the "American" novel.

The Film Connection

In-depth Film Connection
The Puerto Rican Mambo (Not a Musical) (1992)
Directed by Ben Model

Few films in the history of Latino cinema have dared to be as politically incorrect and have made as much fun of their own stereotypes as *The Puerto Rican Mambo (Not a Musical)* (1992), starring comedian Luis Caballero. A provocative predecessor to John Leguizamo, who ironically has a secondary role in the film, Caballero himself is a true representative of "The World Beyond." A short, dark actor, with atypical Hollywood looks, he made small appearances in such films as *Piñero* (2002), in which he played a heroin user, and never had a breakthrough movie. When the film first opened, both Caballero and *The Puerto Rican Mambo* were hailed by numerous critics, even earning Gene Siskel and Roger Ebert's patented seal of approval: "two thumbs up." Caballero immediately drew comparisons to Woody Allen, and the film was shown in numerous film festivals, including Cannes, and even at the Smithsonian Institute. *The New York Times* proclaimed, "It is unlikely that the Puerto Rican experience has been portrayed with more sardonic humor." Yet despite the critical acclaim, both the movie and the lead actor remained relatively obscure, even until his untimely death in 2005.

The Puerto Rican Mambo challenges many conventions, not only through its content, but through its untraditional style. It is and has the feel of a low-budget film as it wavers between Caballero's stand up routine, which gives the impression that he is improvising, and brief sketches where characters poke fun at real-life situations. Watching this film, at times one is not sure whether to laugh or cry, as Caballero touches upon so many tragicomic incidents that are all too familiar to Latinos*. He sarcastically and boldly points to the lack of success of Puerto Ricans in the United States, yet he does not hesitate to point fingers. Criticizing Anglos in a much more direct way than in what we have seen in feature films, Caballero ingeniously uses comedy to present situations that are so pathetic that one cannot help but chuckle. Although connected by theme, the skits do not follow a linear or chronological order. At one moment, the screen shows Caballero facing the camera, describing life in inner-city New York. The next moment, it displays Caballero alongside Leguizamo, playing the role of a naïve farmer in Puerto Rico speaking to government officials about the benefits of moving to the United States.

Likewise, the literary selections in this chapter have a distinct flavor that distinguishes them from so many American literary pieces. The authors draw upon that difference to make their works that much more powerful. They challenge us to consider the ramifications of being members of Latino groups. How, after all, do we dress after we arrive from Cuba, as Achy Obejas might ask. Using English, Spanglish, and Spanish, these works dare us to think about tomorrow, and they give us a sampling of what that tomorrow might hold for the future of Latino literature.

The parallels between this film's star, Caballero, and the authors in "Beyond Worlds" do not end with their unique approaches to creating art. Much can be said about the fame that many of these writers have been denied. For example, Sandra Maria Esteves, a self-proclaimed Puerto Rican-Dominican-Boriqueña-Quisqueyana-Taino-African, has published five books of poetry and has won numerous awards, yet within American literature in general, she remains a relatively obscure figure. Tino Villanueva won an American Book Award for his book, *Scene from the Movie* Giant, yet outside of Chicano studies, his name rarely appears in print. One could go on and on about each author's exclusion from the American literary canon. However, the point not to be missed is that Latino writers often bend the rules of conventional writing, not just by virtue of being Latino, but by writing works that defy the expectations that audiences may have of Latino writing. Through its own innovation, *The Puerto Rican Mambo* reminds us, as Julia Alvarez might say, that Latinos, too sing, America.

Other Recommended Films:

A Day Without a Mexican (2004)

Born in East L.A. (1987)

---

*Viewers might need reminding that *The Puerto Rican Mambo* is a comedy since few have seen race or ethnicity presented with such dark humor.

Culture Clash's *Bowl of Beings* (1991)

Crazy/Beautiful (2001)

Frida (2002)

Girlfight (2000)

I Like It Like That (1994)

In the Time of the Butterflies (2001)

Mambo Mouth (1991)

Thematic Connection Listing

1. Story of the Ultimate Beyond

Fiction

Cecile Pineda: "Notes for a Botched Suicide"

2. Stories in All Directions

Fiction

Jack Agüeros: "Horologist"

Ernesto Mestre-Read: "After Elián"

Benjamin Alire Sáenz: "Obliterate the Night"

Lorraine M. López, "Soy la Avon Lady"

Jamie Manrique: "The Documentary Artist"

Achy Obejas: "We Came All the Way from Cuba So You Could Dress Like This?"

Sandra Benítez: "Fulgencio Llanos: El Fotógrafo"

3. Poems in All Directions

Poetry

Miguel Algarín: "BODY BEE CALLING: FROM THE 21ST CENTURY"

Julio Marzán: "Emergency"

"The Pure Preposition"

Tino Villanueva: "Variation on a Theme by William Carlos Williams"

"At the Holocaust Museum: Washington D.C."

"Scene from the Movie *Giant*"

Michele Serros: "Annie Says"

Sandra María Esteves: "Puerto Rican Discovery #11: Samba Rumba Cha-Cha Be-Bop Hip-Hop"

"Gringolandia"

Gary Soto: "*Chisme* at Rivera's Studio"

Aleida Rodriguez: "Plein Air"

Ana Castillo: "Women Are Not Roses"

4. Latino Identity and Beyond

Essay

Judith Ortiz Cofer: "The Story of My Body"

Credits

Benítez, Sandra. Sandra Benítez, "Fulgencio Llanos" from *A Place Where the Sea Remembers.* Copyright © 1993 by Sandra Benítez. Reprinted with the permission of Coffee House Press, Minneapolis, Minnesota, USA, www.coffeehousepress.com.

Burciaga, Jose Antonio. "Pachucos and the Taxi Cab Brigade" from *Spilling The Beans: Lotería Chicana* by Jose Antonio Burciaga. Published by Joshua Odell Editions, 1995. Reprinted by permission of Cecilia Burciaga.

Cano, Daniel. "Somewhere Outside Duc Pho," copyright © 1992 by Daniel Cano. Used by permission of the author.

Cantú, Norma. "Se me enhina el cuerpo al oír tu cuento..." by Norma Cantú. Originally published in *New Chicano/Chicana Writing*, edited by Charles M. Tatum, published by The University of Arizona Press, 1992. Reprinted by permission of the author.

Castillo, Ana. "Women Are Not Roses" from *My Father Was a Toltec and Selected Poems.* Copyright © 1984 and 1995 by Ana Castillo. Published in paperback by Vintage Anchor. Originally published in *Women Are Not Roses* by Arte Público Press in 1984. Reprinted by permission of Susan Bergholz Literary Services, New York. All rights reserved.

Cervantes, Lorna Dee. "Beneath the Shadow of the Freeway" by Lorna Dee Cervantes. Originally published in the *Latin American Literary Review*, Vol. 5, no. 10, Spring-Summer 1977. Reprinted by permission of the publisher, Latin American Literary Review.

———. "Freeway 280" by Lorna Dee Cervantes. Originally published in the *Latin American Literary Review*, Vol. 5, no. 10, Spring-Summer 1977. Reprinted by permission of the publisher, Latin American Literary Review.

Chacón, Daniel. "The Biggest City in the World" by Daniel Chacón is reprinted with permission from the publisher of *Chicano Chicanery* (Houston: Arte Público Press—University of Houston, 2000).

Cisneros, Sandra. "Bread" from *Woman Hollering Creek.* Copyright © 1991 by Sandra Cisneros. Published by Vintage Books, a division of Random House, Inc. and originally in hardcover by Random House, Inc. Reprinted by permission of Susan Bergholz Literary Services, New York. All rights reserved.

———. "One Holy Night" from *Woman Hollering Creek.* Copyright © 1991 by Sandra Cisneros. Published by Vintage Books, a division of Random House, Inc. and originally in hardcover by Random House, Inc. Reprinted by permission of Susan Bergholz Literary Services, New York. All rights reserved.

Cruz, Victor Hernández. "African Things" by Victor Hernández Cruz. Copyright © 1973 by Victor Hernández Cruz. Reprinted by permission of the author.

———. "Their Poem" from *Snaps; Poems* by Victor Hernández Cruz. Copyright © 1969 by Victor Hernández Cruz. Reprinted by permission of the author.

de Anda, Diane. "Abuelos" by Diane de Anda. Copyright © 1994 by Diane de Anda. "Abuelos" originally appeared in Vol. 9 of *Saguaro.* Reprinted by permission of the author.

Díaz, Junot. "Edison, New Jersey," from *Drown* by Junot Díaz. Copyright © 1996 by Junot Díaz. Used by permission of Riverhead Books, an imprint of Penguin Group (USA) Inc.

Espada, Martín. "Jorge the Church Janitor Finally Quits" and "Federico's Ghost" from *Rebellion Is the Circle of a Lover's Hands* by Martín Espada (Curbstone Press, 1990). Reprinted with permission of Curbstone Press. Distributed by Consortium.

———. "Who Burns for the Perfection of Paper," from *City of Coughing and Dead Radiators* by Martin Espada. Copyright © 1993 by Martin Espada. Used by permission of W. W. Norton & Company, Inc.

Piñero, Miguel. "A Lower East Side Poem" by Miguel Piñero is reprinted with permission from the publisher of *La Bodega Sold Dreams* (Houston: Arte Público Press—University of Houston, 1980).

———. "La Bodega Sold Dreams" by Miguel Piñero is reprinted with permission from the publisher of *La Bodega Sold Dreams* (Houston: Arte Público Press—University of Houston, 1980).

Quintana, Leroy V. "The Man on Jesus Street—Dreaming." From *La Promesa and Other Stories*, by Leroy V. Quintana. Copyright © 2002 by the University of Oklahoma Press. Reprinted by permission of the publisher. All rights reserved.

Ríos, Alberto. "The Vietnam Wall" by Alberto Ríos. Reprinted by permission of the author.

———. "The Child" is reprinted from *The Iguana Killer: Twelve Stories of the Heart*, copyright © 1984 by Alberto Rios, and reprinted with the permission of Confluence Press.

Rivera, José. "Cloud Tectonics" from *Marisol and Other Plays* by José Rivera. Copyright © 1997 by José Rivera. Published by Theatre Communications Group. Used by permission of Theatre Communications Group.

Rodríguez, Abraham Jr. "The Boy Without a Flag." Abraham Rodríguez Jr., "The Boy Without a Flag" in *The Boy Without a Flag* (Minneapolis: Milkweed Editions, 1992). Copyright © 1992 by Abraham Rodríguez Jr. Reprinted with permission from Milkweed Editions.

Rodríguez, Aleida. "The First Woman" is from *Garden of Exile* by Aleida Rodríguez, published by Sarabande Books, Inc. Copyright © 1999 by Aleida Rodríguez. Reprinted by permission of Sarabande Books and the author.

———. "Plein Air" is from *Garden of Exile* by Aleida Rodríguez, published by Sarabande Books, Inc. Copyright © 1999 by Aleida Rodríguez. Reprinted by permission of Sarabande Books and the author.

Rodríguez, Luis. "Hungry" from *Trochemoche* by Luis Rodríguez (Curbstone Press, 1998). Reprinted with the permission of Curbstone Press.

Rodriguez, Richard. "Go North, Young Man" by Richard Rodriguez. Copyright © 1995 by Richard Rodriguez. Originally appeared in *Mother Jones* magazine July/August 1995. Reprinted by permission of Georges Borchardt, Inc., on behalf of the author.

Sáenz, Benjamín Alire. "Obliterate the Night" from *Flowers for the Broken* by Benjamín Alire Sáenz. Copyright © 1992 by Benjamín Alire Sáenz. Reprinted by permission of the Patricia Moosbrugger Literary Agency.

Serros, Michele. "Annie Says" from *Chicana Falsa and Other Stories of Death, Identity and Oxnard* by Michele Serros. Copyright © 1993 by Michele Serros. Reprinted by permission of the author.

Soto, Gary. "*Chisme* at Rivera's Studio" from *New and Selected Poems* by Gary Soto. Copyright © 1995 by Gary Soto. Used with permission of Chronicle Books LLC, San Francisco (visit ChronicleBooks.com).

———. "The Elements of San Joaquin" from *New and Selected Poems* by Gary Soto. Copyright © 1995 by Gary Soto. Used with permission of Chronicle Books LLC, San Francisco (visit ChronicleBooks.com).

———. "History" from *New and Selected Poems* by Gary Soto. Copyright © 1995 by Gary Soto. Used with permission of Chronicle Books LLC, San Francisco (visit ChronicleBooks.com).

———. "Mexicans Begin Jogging" from *New and Selected Poems* by Gary Soto. Copyright © 1995 by Gary Soto. Used with permission of Chronicle Books LLC, San Francisco (visit ChronicleBooks.com).

Index